Life Styles

_ʃ C_

LIFE STYLES
Diversity in
American Society

A 15042 963162

Edited by

Saul D. Feldman
Case Western Reserve University

HN
59
F45
WEST

Gerald W. Thielbar
University of Wisconsin

LITTLE, BROWN AND COMPANY
Boston

COPYRIGHT © 1972, BY LITTLE, BROWN AND COMPANY (INC.)

ALL RIGHTS RESERVED. NO PART OF THIS BOOK MAY BE REPRODUCED IN ANY FORM OR BY ANY ELECTRONIC OR MECHANICAL MEANS INCLUDING INFORMATION STORAGE AND RETRIEVAL SYSTEMS WITHOUT PERMISSION IN WRITING FROM THE PUBLISHER, EXCEPT BY A REVIEWER WHO MAY QUOTE BRIEF PASSAGES IN A REVIEW.

LIBRARY OF CONGRESS CATALOG CARD NUMBER 76-166968

THIRD PRINTING

Published Simultaneously in Canada by
Little, Brown & Company (Canada) Limited

PRINTED IN THE UNITED STATES OF AMERICA

This book is dedicated
to the memory of
Giuseppe Verdi (1813-1901)

Acknowledgments

We would like to acknowledge the contributions of those who assisted in the creation of this book. Katherine Lloyd, David Riesman, and Patricia Thielbar suggested inclusion of some of the key articles. Alex Inkeles provided us with many helpful editorial comments. Lynn Buller, Charles McCaghy and James Skipper, James Spradley, and Evan Stark contributed original papers. Irwin Rinder provided us with an updated version of his article. Debbie Bowman, Richard Harris, and Richard Scheffer aided us in many of the technical and editorial problems that we faced. Clerical assistance was provided by Janet Kruger. Al Browne, Milton Johnson, and Marian Weil of Little, Brown guided the production of this book.

Saul D. Feldman
Gerald W. Thielbar

Berkeley, California

Contents

Life Styles

IS THERE AN AMERICAN LIFE STYLE?

This book—about beauty queens, rich people, homosexuals, tramps, Indians, Southern Californians, and other assorted Americans—examines the great diversity of life styles within American society. Max Weber, who contributed the word "charisma" to the sociological vocabulary, also coined the term "life style." Such terms, once they have been popularized, mean different things to different people. Thus we want to make clear our use of the term life style.

1. Life style is a group phenomenon. *A person's life style is not a unique or individual pattern of behavior; it is influenced by his participation in various social groups and by his relationships with significant others. We can predict a person's life style with reasonable accuracy from certain social and demographic characteristics. For example, the life style of a teen-ager is different from that of a sexagenarian. The life style of a hairdresser differs from that of a college professor. And the life style of a man who is concerned with his reputation in the community is different from that of a man who has rejected the values of society.*

2. Life style pervades many aspects of life. *Knowing how an individual behaves in one area of his life may allow us to predict how he will act in other areas. For example, people who prefer oil and vinegar on salads are more likely to attend a ballet than are those who prefer commercial French dressing. People whose self-rated political leanings are "left" or liberal will more likely attend an art film than conservative or middle-of-the-road individuals. A journalist has noted, "When people tell me what they think about disarmament, I have a pretty good idea what they are likely to think about school integration."* *

3. Life style implies a central life interest. *In American society, many things may be of central interest to a person: work, ethnic heritage, politics, lineage, children, avocational pursuits, and others. A distinct life style is evident when a single activity or interest pervades a person's other interests and unrelated activities—a drug addict is an extreme example. Avid baseball fans, television enthusiasts, and professional San Franciscans also provide examples of life styles based on a central life interest. Some people are interested in astrology; if this interest is central, it too may color their lives. They may wear signs of the zodiac, prefer to interact with and marry only those of certain birth signs, and make crucial decisions according to the position of the planets. Central life interests are not always a matter of choice. A black person may prefer to order his life around his job rather than his race, but others may define him as black rather than by his occupation. Thus his situation demands that race become a central life interest.* †

4. Life styles differ according to sociologically relevant variables. *The first writings about life styles* ‡ *took the view that different ways of life within a society are stratified. Karl Marx* § *felt that the sole determinant of a person's life style is his position in a system of production. People who control the means of production also control the means of consumption. Thus, according to Marx, life style is an economic matter. Max Weber observed that all people at a given economic level need not share a common life style, but those with a similar degree of prestige generally do. "Status honor is normally expressed by the fact that above all else a specific style of life can be expected from all those who wish to belong to the circle."* ‖ *In the United States, there is not a single circle, but many circles. Life*

---

*Calvin Trillin, "G. T. Miller's Plan," *New Yorker,* **46** (August 29, 1970), p. 54.
†See, e.g., Everett C. Hughes, "Dilemmas and Contradictions of Status," *American Journal of Sociology,* **50**, pp. 353–359.
‡Max Weber, "Class, Status, and Party," in Hans H. Gerth and C. Wright Mills (eds. and trans.), *From Max Weber* (New York: Oxford Univ. Press, 1946), pp. 180–195; Thorstein Veblen, *Theory of the Leisure Class* (New York: Macmillan, 1899).
§Karl Marx, *Capital* (New York: Modern Library, 1906).
‖Weber, *op. cit.,* p. 187.

styles in America vary according to age, sex, ethnicity, religion, region, and more.

The United States thus could be viewed as a conglomeration of more than 200,000,000 people who have little in common. Another view would be that this nation is polarized along ethnic, religious, age, sex, or economic lines; while a third view might regard all citizens of this nation simply as Americans, sharing a more or less similar life style.

To the world outside the United States, our diversity may be a parochial issue of interest only to Americans, who make up less than 6 percent of the world's population. Many American blacks, proud of their race and acutely conscious of life style differences between blacks and whites, are surprised to discover when they visit Africa that they are not viewed as fellow blacks but simply as Americans. To a New Yorker, there may seem to be a crucial distinction between Brooklynites and Manhattanites, or, to a Minnesotan, between Minneapolitans and St. Paulites. But a European sees little or no difference between a New Yorker and a Midwesterner—they are all Americans. From the perspective of the outsider, there is a recognizable American character type based on a common life style.

The common experiences of Americans include the products and the mass media that they consume and the manner in which these are presented to them for consumption. With the rise of mass marketing (especially franchising), an American can have tacos in Duluth, chow mein in Dallas, and Coney Island hot dogs in San Diego. The franchised taco is the same in Albuquerque and Duluth; thus food becomes uniformly bland. Diversity in packaging creates the myth of great diversity in America, while the contents of these packages indicate its great uniformity.*

The theme in American mass merchandising is uniformity, quantity, and mediocrity. Some say that these traits typify American character and American values. In air-conditioned suburban shopping malls from coast to coast are found "hippie boutiques" selling mass-produced psychedelic posters, plastic love beads, and peace-symbol dresses, necklaces, and roach clips. The mass market is not a recent development in the United States; neither is criticism of it. Speculation about the effects of mass marketing on American society has been a popular theme of journalists, social critics, and social scientists.†

---

*Adrian Delfino, writing for United Airlines' *Mainliner,* has commented on the Hawaiian luau encountered by tourists on the manicured lawns of some Hawaiian hotels: "While the color is all there and the aroma is all there, the native foods have been intentionally debased to spare the digestive tracts of the uninitiated." Adrian G. Delfino, "Culinary Traditions of Hawaii," *Mainliner,* **14** (September, 1970), p. 26.

† See, e.g., David Riesman and Howard Roseborough, "Careers and Consumer Behavior," in Lincoln H. Clark (ed.), *Consumer Behavior,* Vol. II: *The Life Cycle and Consumer Behavior* (New York: New York Univ. Press, 1955), pp. 1–8; Don Martindale, "Manipulation of Taste and Values," in *American Society* (Princeton, N.J.: Van Nostrand, 1960), pp. 18–40.

Calvin Trillin, a free-lance writer who writes regularly for The New Yorker *on the current American scene, describes buying and selling in one county in Pennsylvania. In Lower Bucks County, there is a lot of what may best be described as typically American.*

Trillin's description of commerce in suburban Philadelphia could as easily have been written about Los Angeles County in California or Cook County in Illinois. Three-scoop ice-cream cones, discount stores, and "the world's largest" car dealers are a familiar part of American life.

Lower Bucks County, Pa. . . . Buying and Selling Along Route 1

CALVIN TRILLIN

I WAS A PIG AT GREENWOOD DAIRIES

An ice-cream cone at the Greenwood Dairies has half a pound of ice cream on it—making it so topheavy that it is ordinarily presented to the customer upside down, resting on a piece of waxed paper. That's the single-dip cone. The double-dip cone has an even pound, or about a quart of ice cream—the same amount that Greenwood serves in a locally famous sundae called a Pig's Dinner. A Pig's Dinner has four scoops of ice cream resting on a bed of sliced bananas, covered with a choice of topping, and served in an eight-inch plastic trough. The customer also gets a yellow button that says "I Was a Pig at Green-

From *The New Yorker* (November 15, 1969), pp. 169–175. Reprinted by permission; copyright 1969 by The New Yorker Magazine, Inc.

wood Dairies." The buttons are a particularly popular item.

In the thirties, when Paul Sauerbry, a former 4-H champion from Oelwein, Iowa, came to Lower Bucks County, the area between Philadelphia and Trenton, it was almost as rural as Iowa—despite the impression Sauerbry had received at a Washington 4-H convention that "lots more was going on in the East than in Iowa, and where things are going on there must be money." Sauerbry bought Greenwood Dairies, a small, two-route milk business, and moved it to Route 1, then the main route up the East Coast and the only direct road between Philadelphia and New York. There was plenty of milk available from farmers right across the highway—at least until the early fifties, when all of that farmland became Levittown, Pennsylvania, a community of seventeen thousand houses. Even before Levittown, Sauerbry had steadily expanded his operation. He now has a fleet of green-and-white trucks that deliver ten to twelve thousand quarts of milk a day. The store that he began in the early forties to sell his own ice cream now looks more like a restaurant than a store and does a few hundred thousand dollars' worth of business a year in bulk ice cream, ice-cream cones, Pig's Dinners, light lunches, a small line of groceries, souvenirs, and stuffed animals.

Sauerbry still thinks of himself as a dairyman. The store has a modest sign, decorated with a sundae not much larger than the ones served inside. The store accounts for less than a third of Greenwood's annual sales—although, as the *Milk Plant Monthly* has pointed out in an admiring article on Sauerbry, it brings in not only money but prospective customers for milk delivery. Sauerbry and his son, who also works in the business, are proud that their ice cream is made of freshly condensed milk rather than dried milk, that the mint chocolate chip has the same kind of authentic chocolate found in a chocolate bar, and that the vanilla is made with real vanilla beans. But they realize that the size of the portions is what brings many people into the store.

Sauerbry is also aware that a lot of people can't finish the portions, causing a certain amount of waste. The trash bin in front of the dairy always contains a number of half-eaten half-pound ice-cream cones. Sauerbry has thought of cutting down portions rather than steadily raising prices; in fact, the Pig's Dinner used to have five scoops of ice cream rather than four.

But he doesn't think his customers will stand for further reductions. The most common complaint at Greenwood is not that helpings are too big but that the customer did not receive his fair share. Sometimes people return a sundae complaining of niggardliness, and the Sauerbrys have to put the sundae on the scale to demonstrate that it does indeed weigh a pound. The Sauerbrys do not seem to be the kind of people who might spend a lot of time musing on why a dairy that makes its vanilla from real vanilla beans finds it necessary

to sell it by serving more than most people can eat—and throwing in a pig button. "When we started dipping cones, in them days there were quite a few dairy stores," Sauerbry says. "We all gave big portions." If the younger Sauerbry is asked why Greenwood Dairies customers are so fond of large portions, he just shrugs and says, "Everybody wants quantity."

WORKING OUT A DEAL

The merchandising method of Reedman's, the world's largest car dealer, seems to be based on the theory that a lot of Americans have bought so many new cars that they consider themselves experts at the art. Respecting the fact that a man of experience will have gone beyond loyalty to any one make of car, Reedman salesmen are equally helpful about selling him a new Chevrolet or a new Plymouth or a new almost anything else; Reedman's has fourteen new-car franchises. Reedman salesmen will reassure a customer that the small Plymouth station wagon and the small Dodge station wagon, both of which Reedman's handles, are virtually the same car—the slight difference in headlights and the different names being merely a way to make one car do for two different dealers. Good hard shop-talk is expected among experts. Included in the Reedman display of the Plymouth Duster and the American Motors' Hornet is the competing car not handled by Reedman's, the Ford Maverick—its roof decorated with a sign drawing attention to the relative puniness of its wheelbase, its trunk open to reveal a sign that says "The Exposed Gas Tank Is in the Trunk Floor." Since the customer will be sophisticated enough to know precisely what he wants in a car—whether, for example, he can do without air-conditioning but must have vinyl bucket seats—Reedman's has an inventory of some five thousand cars, and a computer that will instantly find out if a particular model is available and will then type out a precise description of it before the customer's eyes. An enormous selection being a great advantage in dealing with expert car purchasers, some people in the trade say that Reedman's sells so many cars because it has so many to sell—a merchandising adaptation of Mies van der Rohe's "Less is More" dictum that comes out "More is More."

The Reedman newspaper advertisement invites customers to a hundred-and-fifty-acre, one-stop car center that has a ten-million-dollar selection of cars —and then, adding the note of exclusivity that is considered necessary in advertising even the world's largest, it says, "Private Sale Now Going On." The premises on which the private sale is held look like the average citizen's vision of the supply depot at Cam Ranh Bay. Behind a series of showrooms on Route 1, just down the road from the Greenwood Dairies, the five thousand cars are lined up on acres and acres of asphalt—the neat rows interrupted by occasional watchtowers and the entire area surrounded by a heavy, iron, electronically monitored fence. On a busy Saturday, attendants direct streams of traffic in and out of the customers' parking lot. Hostesses with the dress and manner of airline stewardesses circulate in the showrooms offering to call a salesman for anybody who feels the need of one. Muzak, which reaches the most remote line of hardtops, is interrupted every two or three bars by calls for salesmen.

The opportunity to perfect a veteran car buyer's style is so great at Reedman's—the opportunity to shrug off a computer's offer of a Dodge Coronet with fourteen extras, to exchange jargon about engines and wheelbases, to take a new model for a few spins around the Reedman test track and make some observations to the family about how she handles on the curves—that some people seem to make Saturday at Reedman's a kind of outing. A lot of them, of course, find themselves buying a car, with vinyl bucket seats *and* air-conditioning. The route back to the customers' parking lot leads through a small building where the customer is greeted by a man even more helpful than the hostesses. "How'd you make out, sir?" the man asks. "What kind of car were you looking at? What was your trade-in? Who was your salesman? Of course you want to think about it, but why wait?" There is no reason for an experienced car buyer to concern himself with the fact that his most recent experience was so recent that he has yet to pay for the car he has; the first sign on the Reedman lot begins, "If you still have payments on your present car, truck, etc., we will pay off the balance and work out a deal."

Although selling at Reedman's is based on working out a deal rather than on glamour or showmanship, a car dealer cannot afford to create an atmosphere of pure, unglamorous functionalism. If anyone is going to be totally practical, why should he spend his money on an overlarge, gas-eating, nonfunctional, instantly depreciating new car? Although the Chevrolet section of the Reedman showrooms is crowded with as many models as can be crammed in, the décor includes huge crystal chandeliers and wallpaper of raised-velvet fleur-de-lis patterns on ersatz gold leaf. On one wall of the showroom, a picture display of Reedman service facilities describes one of the three waiting rooms available for service customers as having "fifteen stereophonic speakers mounted in the acoustical ceiling," as well as "embossed vinyl covered walls, plus carpeting, velvet draperies, a crystal chandelier and living-room type furniture." Any car buyer of experience recognizes that as a description of something that, with the addition of some heavy-duty whitewall tires, could provide great transportation until next year's models come out.

DON'T SIT DOWN

Only a few small, arrow-shaped signs lead customers a mile or so off Route 1, near Reedman's, to the farm outlet of Styer's Orchards. Styer's advertises in a local shopping paper, but Walter Styer believes that, basically, satisfied customers bring business and dissatisfied customers keep it away. "It's important never to have anybody griping on you," he says. Styer's will usually replace a jug of spoiled apple cider even if the customer himself let it spoil by leaving it unrefrigerated—as if it contained preservatives, like the processed cider that Styer cannot mention without a slight grimace. Walter Styer is a small, almost bald man in his seventies. His family came to Lower Bucks County in 1910 to start a tree-nursery business, which gradually changed into a fruit business. In the forties, people in the area used to come down the narrow lane to the Styers' farmhouse to buy apples, and eventually the Styers started using the barn as a store and the neighbors started coming in to help with the selling. After the building of Levittown and the open-

ing of a United States Steel plant in Fairless Hills, the Styers finally opened a store out on the road. Styer says the business has now grown to the point of having an overhead of three hundred and fifty thousand dollars a year.

Styer believes in salesmanship. "I used to sell at the Farmer's Market in Trenton, and we almost took over that market," he has said. "It got so the other farmers didn't like us. For one thing, I never sat down. I was always ready to help the customer. Some of the farmers would turn over a box and sit down and just stare at people, but I would always get people talking—ask them what kind of apples they liked, or something like that. Once, I was selling strawberries at fifteen cents a box, and next to me a fellow was selling the identical strawberries at two boxes for a quarter. Pretty soon, I sold all my strawberries, and he hadn't sold any. And he asked me why. I looked at his strawberries and I said, "First of all, look how you've got them arranged. The stems are sticking up. People don't eat stems. Rearrange them with the stems down. Then you ought to get paid for your time for doing that, so charge fifteen cents a box like I did.' Then I stayed to watch, and I told him, 'Don't sit down.' Pretty soon, he sold all his strawberries."

The Styers are not in the position of having to think up sales pitches to justify changes made in this year's model by somebody they don't even know. Almost everything sold at the farm outlet is from their own farm. A lot of the salesmanship is merely a matter of presenting well what they are confident is good merchandise. The store is immaculate. All of the apples are washed and displayed in neat rows of clean half-bushel baskets. There is always a bin of free apples near the door. The apple pies and pumpkin pies are baked in stainless-steel ovens before the customers' eyes. The walls are decorated with Indian corn. There are a few standard signs for Pennsylvania apples ("Nature's Toothbrush"), but most of the signs are done in crayon—giving them a nice, neat homemade look, as if they had been commissioned to the best drawer in the sixth grade.

Styer is proud of the store, although he laments the failure of most of the clerks to lead customers into conversation. "You *got* to be a salesman," he says. When Styer greeted an out-of-town visitor at the farmhouse recently, he had just returned from a business meeting (the family has other interests in Lower Bucks County, including some of the real estate on Route 1), and he looked like a banker who had been home only long enough to take his jacket off. Before taking his visitor to see the store, he excused himself for a few minutes and returned wearing an old pair of corduroy pants and a dark cardigan sweater very much like one Paul Sauerbry wears around the dairy. "That's a farm outlet, and people don't want to see a business executive out there," he said. "You got to look the part."

MOSTLY SELL

The Two Guys Discount Department Store in the Levittown Country Club Shopping Center, across Route 1 from Reedman's, is small by the standards of Two Guys stores but large by the standards of, say, football fields. It is a hundred and five thousand square feet, and, like all Two Guys stores, it is what

people in the Two Guys chain call "mostly sell"—that is, most of its space is space in which customers actually buy merchandise. In a Two Guys store, the stockrooms and the sales space are virtually identical; one step in the supply process is saved by having customers help themselves from merchandise that is brought in by Two Guys trucks from a central warehouse and stored right on the selling floor. The Two Guys store in Levittown has a kind of warehouse look—one huge room containing massive stacks of every type of merchandise, with the merchandise on the lower part of some stacks still in packing cartons. In the toy department, the customer sees not just one or two Talk 'n' Do Choo-Choos but twenty Talk 'n' Do Choo-Choos. In the hardware department, a dozen or so examples of each type of hammer extend from racks on the wall. The art department has three-dimensional "Last Supper's" fifteen deep. In Boutique Shoes, one shelf includes thirty-five identical pairs of black pumps.

Displaying merchandise in mass contributes to the efficiency of the Two Guys central-warehouse operation, and it also makes people buy more. Since the advent of the supermarket, retailers have known that seeing, say, twenty cartons of avocado-colored Tahiti tumblers in a mass creates an impulse to buy some avocado-colored Tahiti tumblers. A lot of shoppers who might pass up a display demonstrating the virtues of a hair dryer find a six-foot stack of hair dryers irresistible. Two Guys had even discovered that if all the red coats are hung together rather than scattered among the other coats on the rack, they sell faster. More is More.

COME FLY WITH US

Jim Flannery's Constellation Lounge is a Constellation. It originally belonged to Cubana Airlines. Flannery bought it two years ago from an airline based in Delaware and had it placed over his restaurant, on Route 1, not far down the road from Two Guys. Motorists approaching from the south come around a curve just before Flannery's and find the Constellation suddenly in front of them—coming in low over the Esso station, as if some desperate T.W.A. pilot who had been on a holding pattern over La Guardia since before the jets came in finally decided to land on Route 1.

Except for having a Constellation on top of it, Jim Flannery's looks like a lot of suburban restaurants—a windowless building with the owner's name written on the side in plastic script. It has leatherette booths as well as tables, a menu specializing in steaks and seafood, a bar, and a piano player who was once with Arthur Godfrey. The walls are lined with the paintings of local artists—many of the local artists in this case being Levittown housewives who specialize in still-lifes and matadors and sad-faced clowns. The Constellation provides a second bar, entered from the main restaurant by a stairway decorated with a mural called "A History of Flight."

Flannery says that a lot of men whose wives have been reluctant to take their first flight bring them to the Constellation Lounge as a kind of transition step. The waitresses have found that the reaction of most people to being in a lounge that is also an airplane is to make a joke about hijacking. As part of his effort to give a feeling of actual flight, Flannery covered the windows with color transparencies of aerial views of places like Miami and New York, and some customers complain about not being able to see the actual view out the window—although the actual view happens to be a section of Route 1 lined with four or five filling stations, a furniture store, a Kiddie City discount toy store, a used-car lot, and an enterprise called the Skyline Diner and Carwash. Flannery, who considers the Constellation a "functional sign," serves drinks in the kind of throwaway glasses used in airplanes and uses "Come Fly with Us" as his motto for billboards and radio ads and napkins. He gives away souvenir pins and tie clasps that are in the shape of Constellations but do not mention the name of the restaurant. "It's subtle," he says. "Very subtle."

On a week night recently, the downstairs bar was crowded—a jolly group was singing "Happy Birthday" to somebody named Arthur—but there were few diners, and the Constellation Lounge looked like a ghost ship. Flannery said business had been slow all week. He thought it might have had something to do with the President's asking people not to spend so much. "Have you seen those TV ads they're running where the guy keeps buying things and pretty soon he turns into a pig?" he asked a guest. Flannery shook his head in wonderment over the ways of government, and said, "A few years ago they were encouraging people to buy."

Buying and selling along Route 1, as described by Trillin, may be an accurate portrait of the public American. But is there any reason to believe that Americans behave any differently in the privacy of their own living rooms? Behavior in public may be too superficial a basis on which to judge Americans' life style. American life style, rather than being merely a product of the mass market, may be importantly influenced by other forces. For example, America's pervasive Protestant Ethic, the frontier, institutionalized slavery and a tradition of racism, physical isolation of the nation, characteristics of American immigrants, a heritage of Anglo-Saxon institutions, and other historical factors may have been important forces in shaping American life style. The two following essays take contrasting views with regard to the historical forces that influence current American life style.

The American People

DON MARTINDALE

By origin the American people are Europeans with significant non-European components, formed into a new unity by distinctive collective experiences. The American people have established the oldest and most conservative democracy, the most radical technology, and the most exclusively middle-class society of the contemporary nationalities. Though composed of more heterogeneous ethnic groups than any other contemporary nation, the American people have been homogeneously integrated by four major events: the frontier, immigration, the rise of mass society, and a unique pattern of national crises. On the foundation of these collective experiences the

From Don Martindale, *Community, Character and Civilization* (Glencoe, Ill.: Free Press, 1963), pp. 291–360. Reprinted by permission; copyright 1963 by The Free Press of Glencoe, a division of The Macmillan Co.

structure of a distinctive American civilization is arising.

Practices appearing in the collective experiences of a people belong to all who adopt them, for they reflect cultural, not biological, continuities. All Americans, not simply the biological descendants of the pioneers, share the heritage of the frontier, even though their parents arrived only a generation ago. Similarly, the one-time powerful everyday ethic born in early American Protestant circles is a common heritage of all Americans, and at times is more strictly observed among second-generation American Catholics or Jews than among the actual descendants of the early Protestants. This diffusion of the experience of some to the whole is no different, to choose a famous historical example, from the manner in which the Exodus from Egypt under Moses by one section of the people became a common symbol for the entire ancient Jewish nation. The great distinctive experiences of a people in first instance only affect a segment, but when they send out waves from this center they become bonds of unity in the whole.

The Frontier Experience

The frontier experience of Americans codetermined (1) its class structure, (2) its sectionalism, (3) the character of its agriculture, (4) the form of its industrial revolution, (5) the nature of its religion, and (6) the distinctiveness of its popular culture.

Social Class and the American Frontier

Quite different social structures have emerged in the northern and southern hemispheres of the New World, for in the latter, colonization was pressed by military adventurers and peasants from Portugal and Spain, while in the former, colonization was accomplished by middle-class townsmen from northern Europe, particularly from England. Originally the voyage across the Atlantic was long, expensive, and hazardous. The primary motive for undertaking it among north Europeans was the opportunity for wealth from New World resources. When individuals (rather than politically sponsored military adventurers) came, they represented persons who could afford the trip (which ruled out the peasants) and who were motivated by the prospect of commercial profits (which largely ruled out the aristocrats). At times commercial companies organized to exploit New World resources and in need of labor to do so presented the opportunity of immigration to poor persons, many of whom were seeking to avoid religious or political persecution. The fate of colonial North America lay primarily in the hands of well-to-do, middle-class entrepreneurs from northern Europe. In the New World they established a social structure in which the middle classes served as a norm for all later development.

After America became a state, its frontiersmen were recruited from middle-class groups along the seaboard in much the same manner that colonial America had derived from middle-class north Europeans. The poorest elements of the seaboard were left behind, for capital was required to make penetration of the frontier effective. The richest elements also stayed behind, for they had more to gain by remaining in the East, from which vantage point they supplied capital and manufactured items needed on the frontier. Successive waves of middle-class recruits opened the frontiers: the Old Northwest (Midwest), the Southwest, the Far West (spurred on by the discovery of gold), the Oregon Territory, and finally, the Northwest.

The formation of the American territory and of an Indian policy were byproducts of the frontier. Again, as one frontier after another was pierced, the spearhead of expansion was supplied by the middle classes. Jefferson, who was personally oriented toward the frontier, took the lead in consummating the Louisiana Purchase (1803), which doubled the territory of the Union by adding to it one million square miles. Similar middle-class pressures were urging an often reluctant government to the acquisition of Florida from Spain (1819), the annexation of Texas (1845), the acquisition of California (1848), the Gadsden Purchase (1853), and the settlement of the Oregon territory (1848). The aggregate territory of the United States at present is 3,628,130 square miles.

Each frontier brought new conflicts with the Indians, from the days of the Pequot War (1637) led by John Endicott to the final submission, through superior numbers and technology, of the Indians who resisted both the frontier advance and federal reservation policies. The last great Indian wars were the Cheyenne–Arapaho War (1861–1862), the Red River War (1874), the Sioux Wars (1865–1867), the Apache War (1871–1887), and the Ghost Dance Uprising (1890). Indian troubles of the Old Northwest led President Monroe to sponsor (in 1825) the policy of transferring eastern Indians to trans-Mississippi regions. This reservation policy got under way with the transfer of the Cherokees to a strip of land in Kansas and Oklahoma.

The Frontier and Sectionalism

A somewhat different organization of middle-class colonial enterprise occurred in the northern and southern colonies, laying the foundations for its first regional sectionalism. In the North, where commercial companies, in part for climatic and geographic reasons, did not enjoy commercial success, the companies were succeeded by the colonists, who then took social and economic affairs into their own hands and formed self-governing village communities.

In the South, the large-scale plantation producing for European export proved profitable. However, it was faced with the perennial problem of a labor shortage. Since he had no tradition of disciplined agricultural work, the male American Indian proved to be an unreliable labor source. Indentured servants also proved to be unsatisfactory, for their ship passage was costly and once they arrived in the New World they set about to become independent farmers as rapidly as possible. Negro slavery,

first introduced by Portuguese traders, solved the labor problems of the plantations, only to spawn a devastating series of other social and economic problems later, some of which the country wrestles with to this day.

In the expansion of groups of Americans into areas outside the original sphere of colonial settlement, the social forms of the northern colonies with their small, self-sufficient village communities resting on free labor and those of the large agrarian plantations resting on slave labor came into conflict. As the slave population increased from 697,000 (1780) to nearly 4,000,000 (1860), sectional tensions mounted. In the first clash of northern and southern institutions in the Old Northwest, institutional arrangements of the northern colonies won and supplied the social and political forms by means of which the frontier was organized and formed into new states. The Basic Land Ordinance (1786), modeled after the New England village, provided for the rectangular survey of territorial lands and the division of them into townships six miles square with 36 lots of 640 acres each, one of which was set aside for support of a public school. The Northwest Ordinance (1787) provided for the division of the western domain into states and for a procedure by which they could enter the Union on terms of equality with the original members. These ordinances served as a basis for incorporating new territories, such as the statehood of Alaska and Hawaii, into the Union.

The Frontier and Agriculture

The class derivation of colonist and frontiersman and the unique conditions of the hemisphere sent American agriculture on a course distinct from that of Europe. American agriculture fused Old World crops and farming techniques with those of the American Indians. New World crops destined to become of world importance included corn, tobacco, white potatoes, and sweet potatoes. Some twenty-seven other crops were also taken over from the Indians.

In colonial times agriculture in Europe was largely in the hands of peasants engaged in subsistence farming for home consumption. The New World colonist and frontiersman were townsmen by vocation; rural husbandmen were so only by necessity. They applied a townsman's standards to their rural activities, and moved from the land into the evolving businesses and industries of the frontier towns as soon as possible. From the beginning, the New World rural husbandman was a farmer selling his agricultural products for a profit and in turn purchasing manufactured articles he himself could not make.

The southern planter was as different from the medieval lord as the northern farmer was from the European peasant. He was not an hereditary aristocrat living from the income of his estates but an entrepreneur or rural businessman. He produced for the market, particularly the overseas market. Thus from colonial days the South has been a low tariff area. The labor on his plantation was performed by slaves, not by peasants. The southern plantation was not a medieval estate, but a form of agrarian capitalism.

Meanwhile, the abundance of new land lured the young men into the West. However, if one went into debt for the capital to establish a farm or estate, the tie between agrarian activity and the market tightened, for one now had to sell enough produce to pay one's debts. In the course of western expansion, American farmers became a perennial debtor group at odds with their fellow businessman, the eastern capitalists. Since the farmers needed access to markets, which they were unable to provide out of their own resources, they petitioned the state and federal governments for aid in developing roads, turnpikes, canals, and railroads.

Frontier farmers also sought government assistance in securing better settlement conditions (resulting in the Homestead Act of 1862), and for assistance in securing higher education for their children (resulting in the Morrill Act of 1862 granting each loyal state thirty thousand acres of land for each senator and representative with which to provide for one agricultural college, and sixty-nine land grant colleges were established). The market orientation of the farmer was an important component in the formation of the Department of Agriculture in 1862 and its continuous expansion. Attempts to control their markets and the political conditions bearing on them provided the impetus for the formation of the great farm organizations: The Grange (1867), the Farmers' Alliance (1880), the Farmers' Union (1902), and the American Farm Bureau Federation (1915).

The Frontier and the Industrial Revolution

The frontier shaped participation in the industrial revolution. From the earliest colonial days it was so costly to import manufactured items from Europe that only the southern planters could afford them. The northern colonists immediately entered into the production of things they needed. Raw materials were cheap, human labor was expensive, markets were expanding. America became the home of labor-saving inventions. America's industrial innovations are illustrated by the automatic milling sequence of Oliver Evans (1783), who employed a conveyor belt and other labor-saving devices in flour milling and loading, by the "dis-assembly lines" introduced by the hog butchers of Chicago, and by the assembly lines of the early Ford factories, which supplied the model for those of American industry at large.

In the wake of the frontier, supplied by its wealth of raw materials and answering to its needs, a great series of commercial and industrial cities came into being. The five major cities of the United States—New York, Chicago, Philadelphia, Los Angeles, and Detroit—vary from two million to eight million in population, and in size from 127 square miles (Philadelphia) to 458 square miles (Los Angeles). On the northeast seaboard there are areas with a density of population of more than three thousand persons per square mile.

The Frontier and Religion

The middle-class north Europeans who dominated the American colonial population were predominantly Protestant. In their isolated village communities they were free to work out their religious destinies. At times they formed intense little theocracies such as John Cotton's (1584–1652) Boston. In reaction to the religious bigotry generated by such theocracies, they formed new communities in which religious toleration was practiced, such as Thomas Hooker's

(1586–1647) Hartford and Roger Williams' (1603–1683) and Anne Hutchinson's Narragansett Bay (1613–1662). On the frontier, religions developed local, intense, self-sufficient forms. Religious fragmentation on a local scale has characterized America to the present.

In the face of religious splintering, the only possibility of collective action avoiding explosive sect differences was political neutralization of religion by the separation of Church and State. This, too, has characterized American religion from colonial days and throughout the years.

Finally, in shifting responsibility for religion into the hands of a local community, the frontier brought about periods of religious dilution alternating with intense revivalism. In predominantly Protestant America the leading Protestant groups became the frontier sects—the Baptist and Methodist. These, too, have been a focal point for waves of evangelicalism. These have periodically shaken America from the days of George Whitefield (1715–1770), the associate of the Methodist Wesleys who, more than anyone else, preached the first great evangelical movement, the Great Awakening of 1739, to the later religious crusades including those of Billy Sunday following World War I and Billy Graham after World War II.

The Frontier and Popular Culture

From the days of Cooper's Leatherstocking through the tall tales of Paul Bunyan and his Blue Ox to the latest TV horse operas, the frontier experience has directly and indirectly through literary elaboration entered the forms of popular culture. Many actual frontiersmen have gradually acquired a semi-mythical status as folk heroes: Daniel Boone, Kit Carson, Jim Bridger, and Buffalo Bill are typical. Folk heroes, legendary tales, and a store of popular lore remain as a residue of the frontier.

IMMIGRATION

As a shaping influence on the American people, immigration is comparable to the frontier. Such observers as Margaret Mead and Geoffrey Gorer have even taken a third-generation psychology to be America's most distinctive feature. Immigration has (1) helped fix the character of the American economy, (2) helped determine the character of its labor, (3) added distinctive properties to its religion, (4) established the American language, and (5) added lustrous names to its pantheon of fame.

The Volume and Periods of American Immigration

Into the vast land opened by the frontiersman surged the populations of the Old World. In 1610 there were 210 persons from Europe in North America; by 1790 there were 3,929,214. By 1950 the American population was over 151,000,000, and by 1990 there will be an estimated 230,000,000 to 272,000,000 people in the United States. Historically, the American population was largely formed through immigration, though it has been increasingly self-recruited (by birth) in the twentieth century. From 1820, when the first statistics on immigration were drawn up by the United States Census, more than 40,000,000 persons have immigrated. Of these more than 34,000,000 came from Europe, more than 5,000,000 from the Americas, more than 1,000,000 from Asia, and a few

hundred thousand from Africa, Australia, New Zealand, and the Pacific Islands. (This does not include the millions of Africans brought over as slaves.) Throughout its history America has faced a continuous problem of absorbing varied immigrant groups.

American immigration may be differentiated into four periods: (1) the colonial, ending with the Revolutionary War, (2) the period from the Revolutionary War to the Civil War, (3) the period from the Civil War to World War I, and (4) the period from World War I to the present.

Immigration and America's Socioeconomic Requirements

Colonial immigration (1610–1790) occurred in response to New World opportunities for commercial exploitation. The great storehouse of New World raw materials was ready for persons with capital to venture and entrepreneurial skills. The predominant immigrant was an upper-middle-class North European. Although occasional groups did not fit this pattern, such as the German-Swiss peasant Mennonites (1683) led by Daniel Pastorius (1651–1720) who formed into hermetically sealed ethnic communities in a manner which later was to occur frequently, the great majority of immigrants were so similar in socioeconomic background that they mingled freely. In 1790 more than 60 percent of the population was English and the remaining groups were of closely related stock: 8 percent Scotch, 9 percent Irish, 8 percent German, and so forth.

From the Revolution to the Civil War the economic requirements surrounding immigration changed. There was no longer so great a need for entrepreneurial types, for America was beginning to supply them out of her own resources. There was, however, a strong demand for skilled laborers in the emerging American industries. Moreover, since the pioneer was leaving the farm and taking up the commercial and industrial pursuits of the towns, a vacuum was being created on the land. America had a need for better and more stable farmers.

Immigrants were needed from socioeconomic classes somewhat lower than those required in the colonial period: artisans, skilled workers, and well-to-do farmers. The cost of immigration still had to be borne by the immigrant; hence this operated as a screen, for though transportation was more rapid and less costly than it had been in the colonial period, it was still beyond the means of the very poor. While revolutionary ferment in Europe, such as existed in 1830 and 1848, brought some highly educated and wealthy professional and businessmen to America, and while some disasters, like the Irish potato famine, bought some very poor peasants to American shores, the bulk of the migration prior to the Civil War consisted of lower-middle-class tradesmen, artisans, skilled workers, and well-to-do farmers. The first large contingents of well-to-do German, Irish, and Scandinavian peasants came to the New World at this time and formed the core of the most stable farm groups of the United States.

From the time of the Civil War to World War I, American industry left the household and the artisan's shop for the great factories. The need for skilled workers declined. For the first time America began to dip deeply into the vast labor pool represented by the poor peasant masses of eastern and southern Europe. Since these could not pay their own passage, they were recruited by agents sent out by land companies interested in sales, railroads and steamship companies interested in fares, and budding industries interested in workers. Masses of immigrants had their fares paid in return for contracts to work out their debts in the new mass industries. On the West Coast a similar importation of coolie labor from China and Japan was under way.

This type of immigration accelerated early in the twentieth century. Twice as many Austrians, Italians, and Russians, for example, came to America between 1901 and 1910 as had come in the entire period from 1820 to 1900. From Europe as a whole, half as many immigrants came in the first decade of the twentieth century as had come in all previous history.

Traditional middle-class America soon began to respond in alarm to what, from its perspective, it could only view as an invasion of barbarians. Sporadic rejection of the new immigration began with the Chinese Exclusion Act of 1882. In 1903 the inspection of immigrants was instituted. The Bureau of Immigration was established in 1906. Literacy tests and various bans on types of immigrants deemed undesirable were introduced between 1917 and 1920. Finally the first quota law on immigrants was passed in 1921. Thereafter immigration control was dominated by the concept of reducing the number of immigrants from any group to a fixed percentage of numbers of that group present in the country at some previous date. The quota law was revised in 1924, and again in the McCarran–Walter Act of 1952.

Immigration and the Labor Movement

Economic requirements steered the New World immigration from its inception, leading from the beginning to a linkage of ethnic group and occupation: the English and Scotch businessman, the Dutch trader, the French chef, the Welsh miner, the German musician, the German and Scandinavian farmer, the Irish railroad worker and politician, the Italian road worker, the Polish steel worker, the Japanese abalone fisherman and market gardener.

As one ethnic group followed another, tensions often developed between them when they were forced into competition for the same jobs. Other tensions developed between employers and workers, intensified by unscrupulous employers who played one ethnic group against another. These conflicts rose to fever pitch with the rise of large-scale industry after the Civil War, when the older skilled laborers were facing displacement by the new unskilled workers.

When the middle-class derivation of the traditional American laborer is taken into account, the failure of enduring union activity to appear in the pre-Civil War period becomes comprehensible. The traditional American laborer was an individualist who dreamed of someday setting up a business of his own—rather than of forming into unions for collective action on the assumption that his laboring status was permanent and that his only recourse toward bettering his lot was through collective action. However, when these traditional, conservatively inclined, skilled laborers found their level of living menaced by mass importations of unskilled workers, they responded by organizing the first enduring national labor unions of America. Between 1864 and 1873 twenty-six major unions formed, with a membership of more than 300,000. The first semi-successful national union, the Knights of Labor, was organized in 1871; it declined after the Haymarket Massacre of 1886. More enduring was the American Federation of Labor (AF of L), organized in 1914 with a backbone of skilled laborers. The AF of L, in accord with the middle-class inclinations of its members, shunned radical movements and avoided political involvement.

Sporadically the new unskilled workers were swept into union activity. These organizations, however, often undertook radical political or revolutionary activities. Their fate is typified by the revolutionary Industrial Workers of the World (IWW), which survived only from 1905 to 1918, when its leaders were jailed as subversives. American labor came fully into its own only after 1933, when organized labor largely divided into two great camps: the AF of L and the powerful group led by the Committee for Industrial Organization (CIO), formed in 1938 by leaders expelled from the AF of L.

Thus American labor acquired its first stable national forms when its point of gravity was located in conservative craft groups threatened by the unskilled immigrants. All politically radical or revolutionary labor groups, such as the IWW, were short-lived. However, in the course of time and accompanying the stabilization of mass industry, the descendants of the same immigrants against whom the conservative unions had been formed quietly moved into position in the great unions, where today they form the bulk of organized labor in America. By the time these new groups had become integrated into organized labor, their psychology had also become middle-class in orientation.

Immigration and Religion in America

As the *milieu* in which immigration occurred changed, new kinds of immigrants began arriving in numbers. In place of the north European Protestant townsman, there came the south European Roman Catholic peasant. Among the Jews a similar change was evident: in place of the sophisticated, secularized Spanish Jews who composed the first Jewish immigration and the educated professional German Jews who formed the second, there came the intensely religious, culturally backward Russian Jews. As masses of such aliens with their strange language, customs, and religion moved into predominantly middle-class Protestant America, they were often met with intense prejudice, usually from nearby ethnic groups. The German Jews, for example, were of all groups most immediately threatened with a loss of status when the Russian Jews appeared on the scene. German immigrants spearheaded resistance to the Irish; the Irish sharpened the lances of prejudice against the Italians and Poles. Time has modified or eliminated all of these forms of prejudice.

Two religious principles developed under frontier conditions came into play to ease ethnic tensions: particularism and the separation of Church and State. The acceptance of religious particularism left every ethnic group free to form withdrawn communities around its own church. In the heart of the cities, church-centered ethnic ghettos formed by the hundreds. A variety of other specialized institutions developed around their churches: labor unions, foreign language presses, parochial schools, nationalistic societies, burial societies, insurance associations. The principle of separation of Church and State then came into play, permitting these formations to develop without official interference.

Within the ghetto it was possible for the alien to pursue a semi-protected life apart: to speak his native language, eat his national food, participate in specialized cultural activities, and perhaps send his children to a parochial school. This could continue until institutions of the wider world, such as the factory and public school, gradually dissolved the walls of his subcommunity and began to absorb its members. The thousands of ethnic communities served as decompression chambers in which the transition from ethnically alien status could be accomplished by stages. Furthermore, the withdrawn ethnic communities sealed off the worst of the potential tensions between American religious groups. Ironically, closely related sects and ethnic communities, made accessible to one another by their very similarity, often despised one another wholeheartedly, while major religious differences serenely coexisted. And when evangelical movements shook the sects of the wider society, they usually stirred the adherents of the ethnic religions as well.

The American Language

The form of American immigration played a significant role in establishing English as a national language without the slightest need for political pressure.

The language of the first inhabitants of a region has considerable advantage over its later-arriving rivals. When the Normans conquered England, they imposed French on the English nation from the top, but the language of the Anglo-Saxons carried out a cultural reconquest of the Normans. People coming to a new area are usually compelled to adopt the place designations of the inhabitants. In the United States one often encounters a basic layer of Indian place names, on which is imposed a stratum of French names, above which flows the current English. Place names often represent a cryptic history of the cultural tides which washed over a region.

English moved without contest to unquestioned dominance over colonial speech, and then, as the language of the first predominant American group, to become the speech of the country. The original non-English immigrations were small, usually less than one percent of the existing population in any given year. Non-English immigrants usually took up the language of the majority as fast as possible. Without the slightest need for external pressure, by the third generation, the language of the non-English immigrant had vanished without a trace. Although as larger groups of immigrants arrived, American English was often enriched by the incorporation of many terms from the various non-English groups, by this time it was too strongly entrenched to be shaken.

The only exception to the dominance of a region by the English language is found in the Spanish-speaking Southwest. There, Spanish was the resident language over which English swept as an incoming tide. Among the states, only New Mexico is bilingual and many of its citizens still speak only Spanish. There are also a few language islands: some Indians retain their native languages, and French is spoken in parts of Louisiana. Otherwise, non-English languages are used only in parochial schools.

The ethnic ghettos in which the immigrants usually assembled promoted the smooth transition to English. For a time, in the confines of the ethnic ghetto, the alien could depend on his national language. From this vantage point, when he was ready, the immigrant learned English as easily and naturally as he learned to practice the everyday ethic which early Protestantism bestowed on the nation—as cultural equipment essential for success in the wider society.

Immigrant Contributions to the American Pantheon of Fame

The varied immigrations have placed at America's disposal highly diversified cultural resources and offered the possibility for each ethnic group to find the niche where it could make its best contribution to the whole. The French have played a unique role in molding American etiquette and elaborating its most refined cuisine. The Germans have made contributions to the development of its agriculture and its musical tastes. The Irish have contributed a genius for organization. The Japanese developed its West Coast fishing and market gardening. These are mere illustrations of an endlessly varied drama.

Each immigrant group has also supplied candidates for the American pantheon of famous persons. Some ten percent of the entries in the *Dictionary of American Biography* are wholly or partly of French descent, including the Deweys, La Follettes, and Du Ponts. The Du Ponts are not only one of America's top industrial families, but they have produced famous soldiers, naval officers, and diplomats. Prominent Americans of German stock include politicians like Robert F. Wagner, artists like Emil Ludwig, scientists like Albert Einstein, industrialists like Henry G. Kaiser, inventors like Steinmetz, and scholars like H. L. Mencken. Again, these are mere illustrations, for every ethnic group has made its contributions to America's hall of fame.

THE RISE OF MASS SOCIETY

While the frontier and immigration were great shared experiences of the American people, they bore within themselves a powerful impetus toward particularism and the atomization of society into tiny hermetically sealed independent groups. Every frontier community developed its own peculiar solution to its local problems, and every ethnic group intensified its linguistic, institutional, and historical peculiarities. By themselves the frontier and immigration experiences terminated in thousands of specialized local communities which differed endlessly in detail.

The Homogenization of Taste

At the very time when the frontier and immigration were particularizing the American people, the Industrial Revolution was reversing the process. The Industrial Revolution was one of the most significant offspring of the Old World that migrated to the American frontier. In contrast to its parental forms in England, the New England version

of the Industrial Revolution did not have to contend with the vested customs of a traditional society.

In the Old World the products of the mechanically powered machine industry were forced to appeal to the tastes of a people adjusted to the refinements of ancient traditions of craftsmanship. In the New World the machine product was presented to tastes modified by the makeshift necessities of frontier and immigration. The New World buyer was more inclined to accept a standardized machine-made item, so long as it was better or cheaper than his make-do home product, than the European immersed in the traditions of craftsmanship which had been evolving toward perfection since the Middle Ages. In the New World the Industrial Revolution offered to the American people a crude, practical, and cheap product during the period when the struggle with the frontier and with immigration prevented them from supplying qualitatively superior items out of their own resources. While the frontier and immigration were tending to crystallize the customs of the American people into infinitely varied local forms, the Industrial Revolution, like a giant cement mixer, was homogenizing their tastes.

The Destruction and Reconstruction of the Mass Society

A shortage of labor and an eagerness to substitute machine for hand labor, a vast reservoir of cheap raw materials, and expanding markets provided the conditions in which the North American branch of the Industrial Revolution could experiment with its potentials and gradually achieve its own unique perfections. To the present day the crafted quality product is characteristic of European industry; the reliable standardized item is characteristic of American industry. To the industry of the world, America bestowed the assembly line and interchangeable parts.

A vast liquidation of traditional culture was necessary for machine productivity to realize its potentials. Production was transferred from the home and the small artisan's shop to the great industrial plant. Women and children who had operated the home industries moved to the factory and returned home as equals of the men. The patriarchal family became a thing of the past. Small industries collapsed under competition with the machine product. The old middle classes of independent small businessmen, artisans, and professionals melted away, and a new tide of white-collar workers in giant industrial and commercial bureaucracies replaced them. To acquire the new skills and knowledge of the industrial society, pressure for professional education developed. To transform consumption into the forms needed by giant industry, a new army of experts appeared.

Thus, accompanying the destruction of traditional ways of life was a reconstruction of life to fit it to the needs of a mass world: production was consolidated in giant concerns; labor was organized; the arts of advertising which mobilized taste and adjusted it to the standardized product were consolidated in the hands of advertising shock troops. Great bureaucracies of business and government appeared; white-collar persons, the salaried employees, and bureaucratically organized professionals replaced the old self-employed professionals and small businessmen; and a development of higher and professional education was carried out.

THE EFFECT ON THE LEVEL OF LIVING

In the United States mass production and distribution have lifted income and consumption to the highest in the world. The *per capita* income in the United States is twice as high as that of its nearest rival, Great Britain; it is three times higher than that of France; it is seven times higher than that of the rest of the world. Three-fourths of the world's automobiles are owned by people of the United States. In the United States in 1950, one passenger automobile was registered for every four persons, as compared to one for every twenty-one in Great Britain, one for twenty-six in France, and one for one hundred and ninety in Italy. With 6 percent of the world's population and 7 percent of its land area, America produces and consumes more than one-third of the total goods and services of the world. It produces nearly one-half of the world's factory goods.

On Being
an American

H. L. MENCKEN

Apparently there are those who begin to find it disagreeable—nay, impossible. Their anguish fills the Liberal weeklies, and every ship that puts out from New York carries a groaning cargo of them, bound for Paris, London, Munich, Rome and way points—anywhere to escape the great curses and atrocities that make life intolerable for them at home. Let me say at once that I find little to cavil at in their basic complaints. In more than one direction, indeed, I probably go a great deal further than even the Young Intellectuals. It is, for example, one of my firmest and most sacred beliefs, reached after an inquiry extending over a score of years and supported by incessant prayer and meditation, that the government of the United States, in both its legislative arm and its executive arm, is ignorant, incompetent, corrupt, and disgusting—and from this judgment I except no more than twenty living lawmakers and no more than twenty executioners of their laws. It is a belief no less piously cherished that the administration of justice in the Republic is stupid, dishonest, and against all reason and equity—and from this judgment I except no more than thirty judges, including two upon the bench of the

From H. L. Mencken, *Prejudices: Third Series* (New York: Knopf, 1922). Reprinted by permission of Alfred A. Knopf, Inc.; copyright 1922 and renewed 1950 by H. L. Mencken.

Supreme Court of the United States. It is another that the foreign policy of the United States—its habitual manner of dealing with other nations, whether friend or foe—is hypocritical, disingenuous, knavish, and dishonorable—and from this judgment I consent to no exceptions whatever, either recent or long past. And it is my fourth (and, to avoid too depressing a bill, final) conviction that the American people, taking one with another, constitute the most timorous, sniveling, poltroonish, ignominious mob of serfs and goose-steppers ever gathered under one flag in Christendom since the end of the Middle Ages, and that they grow more timorous, more sniveling, more poltroonish, more ignominious every day.

So far I go with the fugitive Young Intellectuals—and into the Bad Lands beyond. Such, in brief, are the cardinal articles of my political faith, held passionately since my admission to citizenship and now growing stronger and stronger as I gradually disintegrate into my component carbon, oxygen, hydrogen, phosphorus, calcium, sodium, nitrogen and iron. This is what I believe and preach, *in nomine Domini,* Amen. Yet I remain on the dock, wrapped in the flag, when the Young Intellectuals set sail. Yet here I stand, unshaken and undespairing, a loyal and devoted Americano, even a chauvinist, paying taxes without complaint, obeying all laws that are physiologically obeyable, accepting all the searching duties and responsibilities of citizenship unprotestingly, investing the sparse usufructs of my miserable toil in the obligations of the nation, avoiding all commerce with men sworn to overthrow the government, contributing my mite toward the glory of the national arts and sciences, enriching and embellishing the native language, spurning all lures (and even all invitations) to get out and stay out—here am I, a bachelor of easy means, forty-two years old, unhampered by debts or issue, able to go wherever I please and to stay as long as I please— here am I, contentedly and even smugly basking beneath the Stars and Stripes, a better citizen, I daresay, and certainly a less murmurous and exigent one, than thousands who put the Hon. Warren Gamaliel Harding beside Friedrich Barbarossa and Charlemagne, and hold the Supreme Court to be directly inspired by the Holy Spirit, and belong ardently to every Rotary Club, Ku Klux Klan, and Anti-Saloon League, and choke with emotion when the band plays "The Star-Spangled Banner," and believe with the faith of little children that one of Our Boys, taken at random, could dispose in a fair fight of ten Englishmen, twenty Germans, thirty Frogs, forty Wops, fifty Japs, or a hundred Bolsheviki.

Well, then, why am I still here? Why am I so complacent (perhaps even to the point of offensiveness), so free from bile, so little fretting and indignant, so curiously happy? Why did I answer only with a few academic "Hear, Hears" when Henry James, Ezra Pound, Harold Stearns and the *emigrés* of Greenwich Village issued their successive calls to the corn-fed *intelligentsia* to flee the shambles, escape to fairer lands, throw off the curse forever? The answer, of course, is to be sought in the nature of happiness, which tempts to metaphysics. But let me keep upon the ground. To me, at least (and I can only follow my own nose) happiness presents itself in an aspect that is tripartite. To be happy (reducing the thing to its elementals) I must be:

1. Well-fed, unhounded by sordid cares, at ease in Zion.
2. Full of a comfortable feeling of superiority to the masses of my fellowmen.
3. Delicately and unceasingly amused according to my taste.

It is my contention that, if this definition be accepted, there is no country on the face of the earth wherein a man roughly constituted as I am—a man of my general weaknesses, vanities, appetites, prejudices, and aversions—can be so happy, or even one-half so happy, as he can be in these free and independent states. Going further, I lay down the proposition that it is a sheer physical impossibility for such a man to live in These States and *not* be happy—that it is as impossible to him as it would be to a schoolboy to weep over the burning down of his school-house. If he says that he isn't happy here, then he either lies or is insane. Here the business of getting a living, particularly since the war brought the loot of all Europe to the national strong-box, is enormously easier than it is in any other Christian land—so easy, in fact, that an educated and forehanded man who fails at it must actually make deliberate efforts to that end. Here the general average of intelligence, of knowledge, of competence, of integrity, of self-respect, of honor is so low that any man who knows his trade, does not fear ghosts, has read fifty good books, and practices the common decencies stands out as brilliantly as a wart on a bald head, and is thrown willy-nilly into a meager and exclusive aristocracy. And here, more than anywhere else that

I know of or have heard of, the daily panorama of human existence, of private and communal folly—the unending procession of governmental extortions and chicaneries, of commercial brigandages and throat-slittings, of theological buffooneries, of aesthetic ribaldries, of legal swindles and harlotries, of miscellaneous rogueries, villainies, imbecilities, grotesqueries, and extravagances—is so inordinately gross and preposterous, so perfectly brought up to the highest conceivable amperage, so steadily enriched with an almost fabulous daring and originality, that only the man who was born with a petrified diaphragm can fail to laugh himself to sleep every night, and to awake every morning with all the eager, unflagging expectation of a Sunday-school superintendent touring the Paris peep-shows.

A certain sough of rhetoric may be here. Perhaps I yield to words as a chautauqua lecturer yields to them, belaboring and fermenting the hinds with his Message from the New Jerusalem. But fundamentally I am quite as sincere as he is. For example, in the matter of attaining to ease in Zion, of getting a fair share of the national swag, now piled so mountainously high. It seems to me, sunk in my Egyptian night, that the man who fails to do this in the United States to-day is a man who is somehow stupid—maybe not on the surface, but certainly deep down. Either he is one who cripples himself unduly, say by setting up a family before he can care for it, or by making a bad bargain for the sale of his wares, or by concerning himself too much about the affairs of other men; or he is one who endeavors fatuously to sell something that no normal American wants. Whenever I hear a professor of philosophy complain that his wife has eloped with some moving-picture actor or bootlegger who can at least feed and clothe her, my natural sympathy for the man is greatly corrupted by contempt for his lack of sense. Would it be regarded as sane and laudable for a man to travel the Soudan trying to sell fountain-pens, or Greenland offering to teach double-entry bookkeeping or counterpoint? Coming closer, would the judicious pity or laugh at a man who opened a shop for the sale of incunabula in Little Rock, Ark., or who demanded a living in McKeesport, Pa., on the ground that he could read Sumerian? In precisely the same way it seems to me to be nonsensical for a man to offer generally some commodity that only a few rare and dubious Americans want, and then weep and beat his breast because he is not patronized. One seeking to make a living in a country must pay due regard to the needs and tastes of that country. Here in the United States we have no jobs for grand dukes, and none for *Wirkliche Geheimräte,* and none for palace eunuchs, and none for masters of the buck-hounds, and none (any more) for brewery *Todsaufer*—and very few for oboe-players, metaphysicians, astrophysicists, assyriologists, water-colorists, stylites and epic poets. There was a time when the *Todsaufer* served a public need and got an adequate reward, but it is no more. There may come a time when the composer of string quartettes is paid as much as a railway conductor, but it is not yet. Then why practice such trades—that is, as trades? The man of independent means may venture into them prudently; when he does so, he is seldom molested; it may even be argued that he performs a public service by adopting them. But the man who has a living to make is simply silly if he goes into them; he is like a soldier going over the top with a coffin strapped to his back. Let him abandon such puerile vanities, and take to the uplift instead, as, indeed, thousands of other victims of the industrial system have already done. Let him bear in mind that, whatever its neglect of the humanities and their monks, the Republic has never got half enough bond salesmen, quack doctors, ward leaders, phrenologists, Methodist evangelists, circus clowns, magicians, soldiers, farmers, popular song writers, moonshine distillers, forgers of gin labels, mine guards, detectives, spies, snoopers, and *agents provocateurs*. The rules are set by Omnipotence; the discreet man observes them. Observing them, he is safe beneath the starry bed-tick, in fair weather or foul. The *boobus Americanus* is a bird that knows no closed season—and if he won't come down to Texas oil stock, or one-night cancer cures, or building lots in Swampshurst, he will always come down to Inspiration and Optimism, whether political, theological, pedagogical, literary, or economic.

·   ·   ·

All of which may be boiled down to this: that the United States is essentially a commonwealth of third-rate men—that distinction is easy here because the general level of culture, of information, of taste and judgment, of ordinary competence is so low. No sane man, employing an American plumber to repair a leaky drain, would expect him to do it at the first trial, and in precisely the same way no sane man, observing an American Secretary of State in negotia-

tion with Englishmen and Japs, would expect him to come off better than second best. Third-rate men, of course, exist in all countries, but it is only here that they are in full control of the state, and with it of all the national standards. The land was peopled, not by the hardy adventurers of legend, but simply by incompetents who could not get on at home, and the lavishness of nature that they found here, the vast ease with which they could get livings, confirmed and augmented their native incompetence. No American colonist, even in the worst days of the Indian wars, ever had to face such hardships as ground down the peasants of Central Europe during the Hundred Years War, nor even such hardships as oppressed the English lower classes during the century before the Reform Bill of 1832. In most of the colonies, indeed, he seldom saw any Indians at all: the one thing that made life difficult for him was his congenital dunderheadedness. The winning of the West, so rhetorically celebrated in American romance, cost the lives of fewer men than the single battle of Tannenberg, and the victory was much easier and surer. The immigrants who have come in since those early days have been, if anything, of even lower grade than their forerunners. The old notion that the United States is peopled by the offspring of brave, idealistic and liberty loving minorities, who revolted against injustice, bigotry and mediaevalism at home—this notion is fast succumbing to the alarmed study that has been given of late to the immigration of recent years. The truth is that the majority of Anglo-Saxon immigrants before the Revolution, have been, not the superior men of their native lands, but the botched and unfit: Irishmen starving to death in Ireland, Germans unable to weather the *Sturm und Drang* of the post-Napoleonic reorganization, Italians weed-grown on exhausted soil, Scandinavians run to all bone and no brain, Jews too incompetent to swindle even the barbarous peasants of Russia, Poland and Roumania. Here and there among the immigrants, of course, there may be a bravo, or even a superman—e.g., the ancestors of Volstead, Ponzi, Jack Dempsey, Schwab, Daugherty, Debs, Pershing—but the average newcomer is, and always has been, simply a poor fish.

Nor is there much soundness in the common assumption, so beloved of professional idealists and wind-machines, that the people of America constitute "the youngest of the great peoples." The phrase turns up endlessly; the average newspaper editorial writer would be hamstrung if the Postoffice suddenly interdicted it, as it interdicted "the right to rebel" during the war. What gives it a certain specious plausibility is the fact that the American Republic, compared to a few other existing governments, is relatively young. But the American Republic is not necessarily identical with the American people; they might overturn it tomorrow and set up a monarchy, and still remain the same people. The truth is that, as a distinct nation, they go back fully three hundred years, and that even their government is older than that of most other nations, e.g., France, Italy, Germany, Russia. Moreover, it is absurd to say that there is anything properly describable as youthfulness in the American outlook. It is not that of young men, but that of old men. All the characteristics of senescence are in it: a great distrust of ideas,

an habitual timorousness, a harsh fidelity to a few fixed beliefs, a touch of mysticism. The average American is a prude and a Methodist under his skin, and the fact is never more evident than when he is trying to disprove it. His vices are not those of a healthy boy, but those of an ancient paralytic escaped from the *Greisenheim.* If you would penetrate to the causes thereof, simply go down to Ellis Island and look at the next shipload of immigrants. You will not find the spring of youth in their step; you will find the shuffling of exhausted men. From such exhausted men the American stock has sprung. It was easier for them to survive here than it was where they came from, but that ease, though it made them feel stronger, did not actually strengthen them. It left them what they were when they came: weary peasants, eager only for the comfortable security of a pig in a sty. Out of that eagerness has issued many of the noblest manifestations of American *Kultur:* the national hatred of war, the pervasive suspicion of the aims and intents of all other nations, the short way with heretics and disturbers of the peace, the unshakable belief in devils, the implacable hostility to every novel idea and point of view.

All these ways of thinking are the marks of the peasant—more, of the peasant long ground into the mud of his wallow, and determined at last to stay there—the peasant who has definitely renounced any lewd desire he may have ever had to gape at the stars. The habits of mind of this dull, sempiternal *fellah*—the oldest man in Christendom—are, with a few modifications, the habits of mind of the American people. The peasant has a great practical cunning, but he is unable to see any further than the next farm. He likes money and knows how to amass property, but his cultural development is but little above that of the domestic animals. He is intensely and cocksurely moral, but his morality and his self-interest are crudely identical. He is emotional and easy to scare, but his imagination cannot grasp an abstraction. He is a violent nationalist and patriot, but he admires rogues in office and always beats the tax-collector if he can. He has immovable opinions about all the great affairs of state, but nine-tenths of them are sheer imbecilities. He is violently jealous of what he conceives to be his rights, but brutally disregardful of the other fellow's. He is religious, but his religion is wholly devoid of beauty and dignity. This man, whether city or country bred, is the normal Americano—the 100 percent Methodist, Odd Fellow, Ku Kluxer, and Know Nothing. He exists in all countries, but here alone he rules—here alone his anthropoid fears and rages are accepted gravely as logical ideas, and dissent from them is punished as a sort of public offense. Around every one of his principal delusions—of the sacredness of democracy, of the feasibility of sumptuary law, of the incurable sinfulness of all other peoples, of the menace of ideas, of the corruption lying in all the arts— there is thrown a barrier of taboos, and woe to the anarchist who seeks to break it down!

The multiplication of such taboos is obviously not characteristic of a culture that is moving from a lower plane to a higher—that is, of a culture still in the full glow of its youth. It is a sign, rather, of a culture that is slipping downhill— one that is reverting to the most primitive standards and ways of thought. The taboo, indeed, is the trade-mark of the savage, and wherever it exists it is a relentless and effective enemy of civilized enlightenment. The savage is the most meticulously moral of men; there is scarcely an act of his daily life that is not conditioned by unyielding prohibitions and obligations, most of them logically unintelligible. The mobman, a savage set amid civilization, cherishes a code of the same draconian kind. He believes firmly that right and wrong are immovable things—that they have an actual and unchangeable existence, and that any challenge of them, by word or act, is a crime against society. And with the concept of wrongness, of course, he always confuses the concept of mere differentness—to him the two are indistinguishable. Anything strange is to be combatted; it is of the Devil. The mobman cannot grasp ideas in their native nakedness. They must be dramatized and personalized for him, and provided with either white wings or forked tails. All discussion of them, to interest him, must take the form of a pursuit and scotching of demons. He cannot think of a heresy without thinking of a heretic to be caught, condemned, and burned. . . .

The average American of the Anglo-Saxon majority, in truth, is simply a second-rate Englishman, and so it is no wonder that he is spontaneously servile, despite all his democratic denial of superiorities, to what he conceives to be first-rate Englishmen. He corresponds, roughly, to an English Nonconformist of the better-fed variety, and he shows all the familiar characters of the breed. He is truculent and cocksure, and yet he knows how to take off his hat when a bishop of the Establishment passes.

He is hot against the dukes, and yet the notice of a concrete duke is a singing in his heart. It seems to me that this inferior Anglo-Saxon is losing his old dominance in the United States—that is, biologically. But he will keep his cultural primacy for a long, long while, in spite of the overwhelming inrush of men of other races, if only because those newcomers are even more clearly inferior than he is. Nine-tenths of the Italians, for example, who have come to these shores in late years have brought no more of the essential culture of Italy with them than so many horned cattle would have brought. If they become civilized at all, settling here, it is the civilization of the Anglo-Saxon majority that they acquire, which is to say, the civilization of the English second table. So with the Germans, the Scandinavians, and even the Jews and Irish. The Germans, taking one with another, are on the cultural level of green-grocers. I have come into contact with a great many of them since 1914, some of them of considerable wealth and even of fashionable pretensions. In the whole lot I can think of but a score or two who could name offhand the principal works of Thomas Mann, Otto Julius Merbaum, Ludwig Thoma or Hugo von Hofmannsthal. They know much more about Mutt and Jeff than they know about Goethe. The Scandinavians are even worse. The majority of them are mental clods, and they are sucked into the Knights of Pythias, the chautauqua and the Methodist Church almost as soon as they land; it is by no means a mean accident that the national Prohibition Enforcement Act bears the name of a man theoretically of the blood of Gustavus Vasa, Svend of the Forked Beard, and Eric the Red. The Irish in the United States are scarcely touched by the revival of Irish culture, despite their melodramatic concern with Irish politics. During the war they supplied diligent and dependable agents to the Anglo-Saxon White Terror, and at all times they are very susceptible to political and social bribery. As for the Jews, they change their names to Burton, Thompson and Cecil in order to qualify as true Americans, and when they are accepted and rewarded in the national coin they renounce Moses altogether and get themselves baptized in St. Bartholomew's Church. . . .

. . . The changes in the American character since the Civil War, due partly to the wearing out of the old Anglo-Saxon stock, inferior to begin with, and partly to the infusion of the worst elements of other stocks, have surely not made for the fostering of the military virtues. The old cool head is gone, and the old dogged way with difficulties. The typical American of today has lost all the love of liberty that his forefathers had, and all their distrust of emotion, and pride in self-reliance. He is led no longer by Davy Crocketts; he is led by cheer leaders, press agents, word-mongers, uplifters. I do not believe that such a faint-hearted and inflammatory fellow, shoved into a war demanding every resource of courage, ingenuity and pertinacity, would give a good account of himself. He is fit for lynching-bees and heretic-hunts, but he is not fit for tight corners and desperate odds.

Nevertheless, his docility and pusillanimity may be overestimated, and sometimes I think that they *are* overestimated by his present masters. They assume that there is absolutely no limit to his capacity for being put on and knocked about—that he will submit to any invasion of his freedom and dignity, however outrageous, so long as it is depicted in melodious terms. He permitted the late war to be "sold" to him by the methods of the grind-shop auctioneer. He submitted to conscription without any of the resistance shown by his brother democrats of Canada and Australia. He got no further than academic protests against the brutal usage he had to face in the army. He came home and found Prohibition foisted on him, and contented himself with a few feeble objurgations. He is a pliant slave of capitalism, and ever ready to help it put down fellow-slaves who venture to revolt. But this very weakness, this very credulity and poverty of spirit, on some easily conceivable tomorrow, may convert him into a rebel of a peculiarly insane kind, and so beset the Republic from within with difficulties quite as formidable as those which threaten to afflict it from without. What Mr. James N. Wood calls the corsair of democracy—that is, the professional mobmaster, the merchant of delusions, the pumper-up of popular fears and rages—is still content to work for capitalism, and capitalism knows how to reward him to his taste. He is the eloquent statesman, the patriotic editor, the fount of inspiration, the prancing milch-cow of optimism. He becomes public leader, Governor, Senator, President. He is Billy Sunday, Cyrus K. Curtis, Dr. Frank Crane, Charles E. Hughes, Taft, Wilson, Cal Coolidge, General Wood, Harding. His, perhaps, is the best of trades under democracy—but it has its temptations! Let us try to picture a master corsair, thoroughly adept at pulling the mob

nose, who suddenly bethought himself of that Pepin the Short who found himself mayor of the palace and made himself King of the Franks. There were lightnings along that horizon in the days of Roosevelt; there were thunder growls when Bryan emerged from the Nebraska steppes. On some great day of fate, as yet unrevealed by the gods, such a professor of the central democratic science may throw off his employers and set up a business for himself. When that day comes there will be plenty of excuse for black type on the front pages of the newspapers.

I incline to think that military disaster will give him his inspiration and his opportunity—that he will take the form, so dear to democracies, of a man on horseback. The chances are bad today simply because the mob is relatively comfortable—because capitalism has been able to give it relative ease and plenty of food in return for its docility. Genuine poverty is very rare in the United States, and actual hardship is almost unknown. There are times when the proletariat is short of phonograph records, silk shirts and movie tickets, but there are very few times when it is short of nourishment. Even during the most severe business depression, with hundreds of thousands out of work, most of these apparent sufferers, if they are willing, are able to get livings outside their trades. The cities may be choked with idle men, but the country is nearly always short of labor. And if all other resources fail, there are always public agencies to feed the hungry: capitalism is careful to keep them from despair. No American knows what it means to live as millions of Europeans lived during the war and have lived, in some places, since:

with the loaves of the baker reduced to half size and no meat at all in the meat-shop. But the time may come and it may not be far off. A national military disaster would disorganize all industry in the United States, already sufficiently wasteful and chaotic, and introduce the American people, for the first time in their history, to genuine want—and capital would be unable to relieve them. The day of such disaster will bring the savior foreordained. The slaves will follow him, their eyes fixed ecstatically upon the newest New Jerusalem. Men bred to respond automatically to shibboleths will respond to this worst and most insane one. Bolshevism, said General Foch, is a disease of defeated nations.

But do not misunderstand me: I predict no revolution in the grand manner, no melodramatic collapse of capitalism, no repetition of what has gone on in Russia. The American proletarian is not brave and romantic enough for that; to do him simple justice, he is not silly enough. Capitalism, in the long run, will win the United States, if only for the reason that every American hopes to be a capitalist before he dies. Its roots go down to the deepest, darkest levels of the national soil; in all its characters, and particularly in its antipathy to the dreams of man, it is thoroughly American. Today it seems to be immovably secure, given continued peace and plenty, and not all the demagogues in the land, consecrating themselves desperately to the one holy purpose, could shake it. Only a cataclysm will ever do that. But is a cataclysm conceivable? Isn't the United States the richest nation ever heard of in history, and isn't it a fact that modern wars are won by money? It is not a fact. Wars are won

today, as in Napoleon's day, by the largest battalions, and the largest battalions, in the next great struggle, may not be on the side of the Republic. The usurious profits it wrung from the last war are as tempting as negotiable securities hung on the wash-line, as pre-Prohibition Scotch stored in open cellars. Its knavish ways with friends and foes alike have left it only foes. It is plunging ill-equipped into a competition for a living in the world that will be to the death. And the late Disarmament Conference left it almost ham-strung. Before the conference it had the Pacific in its grip, and with the Pacific in its grip it might have parleyed for a fair half of the Atlantic. But when the Japs and the English had finished their operations upon the Feather Duster, Popinjay Lodge, Master-Mind Root, Vacuum Underwood, young Teddy Roosevelt and the rest of their so-willing dupes there was apparent a baleful change. The Republic is extremely insecure today on both fronts, and it will be more insecure tomorrow. And it has no friends.

However, as I say, I do not fear for capitalism. It will weather the storm, and no doubt it will be the stronger for it afterward. The inferior man hates it, but there is too much envy mixed with his hatred, in the land of the theoretically free, for him to want to destroy it utterly, or even to wound it incurably. He struggles against it now, but always wistfully, always with a sneaking respect. On the day of Armageddon he may attempt a more violent onslaught. But in the long run he will be beaten. In the long run the corsairs will sell him out, and hand him over to his enemy. Perhaps—who knows?—the combat may raise that enemy to genuine strength and dignity. Out of it may come the superman.

All the while I have been forgetting the third of my reasons for remaining so faithful a citizen of the Federation, despite all the lascivious inducements from expatriates to follow them beyond the seas, and all the surly suggestions from patriots that I succumb. It is the reason which grows out of my mediaeval but unashamed taste for the bizarre and indelicate, my congenital weakness for comedy of the grosser varieties. The United States, to my eye, is incomparably the greatest show on earth.

Rather than attempting to investigate the life style of a nation, many social scientists have conceptualized personality traits that people share through their membership in a national community as "national character." Because national character has been a popular concept among social scientists, much that has been written about a nationally shared life style has been regarded simply as an expression of national character. This mode of thought implies that national character is some essence within Americans that serves to explain their behavior. The term life style, *we believe, more clearly denotes a unified pattern of behavior and is less likely to be accepted as a simplistic explanation of behavior than is "national character." David Riesman, sociologist and social critic, has been one of the most prolific writers about American national character. His discussion of the sociological variables affecting national character should also be seen as affecting what may be peculiarly "American" about life style in the United States.*

Some Questions About the Study of American Character in the Twentieth Century

DAVID RIESMAN

The importance attached to studies of national character has fluctuated with intellectual fashions and also in terms of the requirements of applied work. It is a field inevitably "contaminated" by lay stereotypes about groups and nations—and by the scientific effort to get away from these, if not to deny their relevance completely. Easy assumptions of the fixity of national character contradict the evidence of human plasticity provided by studies of acculturation, and the history of societies such as the English or Swedish reminds us that peoples now well known for stability and law-abidingness were in the eighteenth century a valiantly disorderly people.[1] The confluence of psychoanalytic and anthropological perspectives on nonliterate peoples such as the Dobuans or the Alorese encouraged the attempt to link everything in a given society to everything else, so that even dissidence could

be made part of the cultural character, and mythology, child-rearing, lovemaking, and war-making could all be embraced. But when, during and after the Second World War, holistic analyses were attempted of enemies, allies, and ourselves, the difficulties soon became apparent. In ethnocentric and partisan hands, such approaches could become contaminated by chauvinistic propaganda, and scholars began to question whether a modern highly differentiated society could be treated as if it were an isolated tribe on an island. Cross-cultural work on "Westernization" and modernization presented the question whether nations were the appropriate boundaries for comparing group or social character. And empirical questions began to be raised as to the concept of character itself: How was it to be distinguished from values, from behavior, and from specific traits? Clarification of such issues as these aimed to make work in this area less impressionistic while retaining its interdisciplinary flavor.[2] It is little wonder that, as their own methodological finesse increased, and as psychoanalysis began to lose its *avant-garde* quality, anthropologists were in-

From *The Annals* of the American Academy of Political and Social Science, **370** (March, 1967), pp. 36–47. Reprinted by permission of the author and the American Academy of Political and Social Science.

[1] See, for example, Geoffrey Gorer, *Exploring English Character* (New York: Criterion Books, 1955).

[2] The most important critique is that of Alex Inkeles and Daniel J. Levinson, "National Character: The Study of Modal Personality and Sociocultural Systems," in Gardner Lindzey (ed.), *Handbook of Social Psychology*, Vol. II (Cambridge, Mass.: Addison-Wesley, 1954), pp. 977–1020. Cf. also A. R. Lindesmith and Anselm Strauss, "A Critique of Culture-Personality Writings," *American Sociological Review*, Vol. 15 (1950), pp. 587–600. A bibliography both of studies of American character and of criticisms appears in Michael McGiffert, "Selected Writings on American National Character," in *The Character of Americans: A Book of Readings* (Homewood, Ill.: Dorsey Press, 1964), pp. 361–377.

clined to turn to less holistic topics.

Yet something would be lost if the area of inquiry signified by "national character" were abandoned because of the criticisms which our scientific superegos can bring against its more ambiguous uses. As the influence of Erik H. Erikson's work suggests, the psychoanalytic impetus has not exhausted its utility and is now being extended to the understanding of new and developing countries.[3]

Despite such reassurances, work on American national character has always seemed to me at best fragmentary and footloose. With its mixture of ethnic groups, regional differences, and other overlapping stratifications, search for *the* American character is bound to include too much or leave out too much. I am in no position to answer the questions as to definition and method raised by the Inkeles-Levinson essay. Instead, I shall once again be unsystematic, at best suggestive, through raising questions about variations by sex, by social class, by age group, and by generation that must be taken account of if one is to talk about contemporary American character.[4] As Inkeles and Levinson

point out, a fractionated society may not possess a modal character covering any substantial segment of the population; correspondingly, we shall be talking about a construct or fiction—American national character—which has not been conclusively demonstrated to exist.

THE "NEED" FOR GROUP OR NATIONAL CHARACTER

The fact that the great majority of Americans can respond to the same signals and share similar attitudes and values does not demonstrate that the underlying dynamics of character structure are similarly shared. Uniformity of behavior does not in principle require uniformity of socialization and internalization. Perhaps, in a society governed by natural stringencies (such as scarce water supply, discussed by Karl A. Wittfogel in *Oriental Despotism*), there can be little leeway for idiosyncratic impulse, and the group cannot take a chance that an individual can respond intelligently and without characterological precoding to what is immanently demanded. But why cannot our own affluent society relinquish its "despotism" over character, as Norman O. Brown and Herbert Marcuse have, in effect, argued might be possible? I do not myself assume that there exists a basic human nature, potentially benign, which needs only to be liberated. But the, perhaps characteristic, fear of being fenced in may lead many Americans to overemphasize the despotism of socialization and to understate our need for a common language, internalized in our

[3]Cf. Erik H. Erikson, *Childhood and Society* (1st ed., New York: W. W. Norton, 1950; 2nd ed., 1963). See also the essay on Mexican national character by Michael Maccoby in this issue of *The Annals,* reflecting, among other intellectual currents, the work of Erich Fromm on the concept of social character. Cf. also Yehudi A. Cohen, *Social Structure and Personality: A Casebook* (New York: Holt, Rinehart & Winston, 1961), for illustrations of the directions in which contemporary scholars are working.

[4]For an earlier attempt see David Riesman, "The Study of National Character: Some Observations on the American Case," *Harvard Library Bulletin,* Vol. 13 (1959), pp. 520–524; reprinted in *Abundance*

for What? and Other Essays (Garden City, N.Y.: Doubleday, 1964).

character structure, which allows us to communicate, to express ourselves to others, and to be creative in culturally recognizable terms. The very emphasis on individualism is only possible in a society which trains its members for self-reliance and builds this ability and its appreciation into character structure.[5] Erich Fromm sees the social character as arising, even in a complex and differentiated society, from the social imperative that individuals drive themselves to respond to the tasks of that society as if they wanted to do or could not help doing what in fact they had to do.[6]

FIXATION VERSUS FLEXIBILITY

In some earlier psychoanalytic studies, national character was thought to be formed in the very earliest months and years of childhood. Thus, bottle feeding was sometimes claimed to be creating a mechanically minded or impersonally oriented American character. At best such linkages are marginal: a mother could convey warmth in spite of the bottle and frigidity in spite of the breast. Moreover, such work assumed that the norms of the middle class had hegemony throughout the country, whereas it soon became clear that there were very great differences in terms both

of class and ethnicity.[7] Furthermore, while early childhood training may orient some American children toward achievement and toward adaptation, partial resocialization as they pass through stages and enter new settings is an evident capacity of millions of Americans. Paradoxically, while psychoanalysis has tended to emphasize the overwhelming importance of the early childhood years, it has been taken up by Americans seeking redemption from those years as by the people of no other nation: the United States is a second-chance country for character as well as for fortune.

WHAT IS AMERICAN ABOUT AMERICA?

This apparent fluidity is one of the aspects of American society that strikes many visitors. Their reactions would seem to be one approach to the question of American distinctiveness—although again one cannot infer *characterological* distinctiveness from behavior as such. Thus, non-American critics have often commented on apparent uniformity of motive and outlook premised on the similarity of suburbs, superhighways, and supermarkets. We can perhaps get farther if we ask what immigrants rather than visitors experience when they try

[5]Cf. Clifford Geertz, "The Impact of the Concept of Culture on the Concept of Man," in John R. Platt (ed.), *New Views of the Nature of Man* (Chicago: Univ. of Chicago Press, 1965), pp. 93–118.
[6]Cf. Erich Fromm, "Individual and Social Origins of Neurosis," *American Sociological Review,* IX (1944), p. 380; reprinted in Clyde Kluckhohn and Henry Murray (eds.), *Personality and Nature, Society and Culture* (New York: Knopf, 1948); also Erich Fromm, *Psychoanalysis and Religion* (New Haven: Yale Univ. Press, 1950).

[7]Cf. Urie Bronfenbrenner, "Socialization and Social Class Through Time and Space," in E. E. Maccoby, T. M. Newcomb, and E. L. Hartley (eds.), *Readings in Social Psychology* (3rd ed.; New York: Holt, Rinehart & Winston, 1958). However, the interesting study by Daniel Miller and G. E. Swanson, *The Changing American Parent* (New York: Wiley, 1958), while suggesting that parental origin and occupation does influence the childhood training and presumptive destiny of the young, also suggests that the differences within a single American city are not very great.

to come to terms with American life. Margaret Mead has argued that, in effect, all Americans are virtual immigrants, deferring to their more "American" offspring and anxious lest they not be American enough.[8] Obviously, not all immigrant groups have faced similar pressures or responded to them in the same way. The Nisei encountered middle-class Americans in such a way as to permit retention of some basic Japanese values beneath an apparent conformity, while the encounters, for example, of Southern-born Negroes with Northern whites (in a way, like the earlier encounters of Polish immigrants) were often more catastrophic.[9] However, what is specifically American, if anything, may be more evident in the experience of those Americans who not only travel abroad, but try to immerse themselves in an alien culture. For example, seeking to prepare Foreign Service officers for overseas confrontations, the anthropologist, Edward Hall, at the Foreign Service Institute, asked them such questions as: "How long is just a minute?" alerting them to the potentially disagreeable consequences of imposing American time-expectations on, say, Syria or Peru.[10] More striking still has

been the overseas experience of young college-educated Americans in the Peace Corps and like ventures who have regarded themselves as almost "un-American" in their rejection of material greed, of vulgar ethnocentrism, and, in general, of many of the tastes, pursuits, and styles of the middle-brow middle-aged Americans. In the training programs where I have encountered them, for example, many Volunteers have assumed that they could readily adapt to work with host-country nationals if the latter were sufficiently underprivileged, since what was "really" human would unite them underneath the sham societal forms. Their real culture shock came at their discovery of how "American" they were in spite of themselves, being imbued with egalitarianism, activism (or at least nonfatalism), candor, and impatience.[11]

The orientation toward achievement of these young Americans, which, in some cases, they discovered only overseas, does not, of course, mark them as distinctively American but as a member of one of the cultures that have undergone modernization. And even their specifically egalitarian outlook is also found in some parts of Canada, Australia, and New Zealand, although in each case with shadings of difference which have been only marginally explored.[12] Thus, I

[8] Margaret Mead, *And Keep Your Powder Dry: An Anthropologist Looks at America* (New York: William Morrow, 1943).

[9] On the Japanese-Americans, see the brilliant account by William Caudill, "Japanese-American Personality and Acculturation," *Genetic Psychology Monographs*, Vol. 45 (1952), pp. 3–102; on Negro-Americans, see, for example, Abram Kardiner and Lionel Ovesey, *The Mark of Oppression: Explorations in the Personality of the American Negro* (Gloucester, Mass.: Smith, Peter, 1951).

[10] Cf. Edward T. Hall, *The Silent Language* (Garden City, N.Y.: Doubleday, 1959), and *The Hidden Dimension* (Garden City, N.Y.: Doubleday, 1966).

[11] The first Director of the Peace Corps program in the Philippines has described just such experience as a way of delineating American character. Cf. Lawrence H. Fuchs, *"Those Peculiar Americans": The Peace Corps and American National Character* (New York: Meredith, 1967). Cf. also Robert B. Textor (ed.), *Cultural Frontiers of the Peace Corps* (Cambridge, Mass.: M.I.T. Press, 1966).

[12] Cf. Seymour Martin Lipset, *The First New Nation* (New York: Basic Books, 1964); David Mc-

think it likely that comparison of the overseas experience of English-speaking Canadians and Protestant Americans would show some considerable differences when faced, for example, with a hierarchical and authoritarian society in Asia or Latin America.

NATIONAL CHARACTER FOR MEN AND WOMEN

In all these comparisons, whether we emphasize differences or similarities depends on what we are interested in. We can speak of national character as the dominant mode or filter of experience and then see the two sexes and social class or ethnic groupings as variations; or, depending on the particular problem that interests us, we can work the other way around and see the differences among groups as primary and their way of experiencing or interpreting the national culture as principally determined rather than determining.

One important difference, for instance, between Americans and Australians lies in the expectations placed on the two sexes. American women are given a somewhat greater opportunity for expressiveness, and yet from infancy on, men are supposed to exercise more authority and take up more room.[13] In

Spanish America the term *machismo* designates efforts of a man to appear manly in the approved ways, often caricaturing himself in the process. We have no comparable term in the United States, but we have somewhat comparable behavior. Boys must disentangle themselves in childhood and adolescence both from their mothers and from female authorities of the elementary school, sometimes defying all adult-imposed restraints and rejecting school itself as a place for girls and sissies.[14] In contrast, while American women strike visitors as extremely independent and even domineering, they are, nevertheless, expected to be more receptive and somewhat more compliant than men.[15] But the different behavior of the two sexes is not conclusive evidence of characterological difference, for behavior is at best obliquely linked with character structure, and the social definitions of sex role are not invariably internalized. Furthermore, as is evident, the differences between men and women, like others discussed in this essay, are overlapping: one can find women who behave assertively and men who behave compliantly; hence, these modal distinctions

Clelland, *The Achieving Society* (New York: Van Nostrand, 1963). David P. Ausubel, *The Fern and the Tiki* (New York: Holt, Rinehart & Winston, 1965), describes New Zealand national character from the vantage point of an American psychologist on a Fulbright year; his reactions say a good deal about some very important differences between New Zealand egalitarianism and that of the United States.

[13]The historian David M. Potter has amusingly argued that most writing on American national character deals only with males. Cf. David M.

Potter, "American Women and the American Character," *Stetson University Bulletin,* Vol. 62 (January 1962), p. 122.

[14]Cf., for a recent discussion, Jackson Toby, "Violence and the Masculine Ideal: Some Qualitative Data," in *The Annals,* Vol. 364 (March 1966), pp. 19–27, and references there given. Cf. Michael Maccoby, *The Game Attitude,* Ph.D. dissertation, Department of Social Relations, Harvard University, 1960, for discussion of sex differences vis-à-vis school, and the consequences for cognitive and emotional development.

[15]Cf. articles by Erik Erikson, David McClelland, and Alice Rossi in Robert J. Lifton (ed.), *The Woman in America* (Boston: Houghton Mifflin, 1965).

between groups are not decisive for particular individuals. Yet it seems reasonable to suppose that national character shapes the interpretation individuals give to the sexual polarities. Sex in the United States, like other statuses, often seems as much achieved as ascribed, so that neither men nor women can assume that their sex role is biologically given but rather that it must be "proved" in conduct and feeling against the torments of inner anxiety and outer peer-group judgment.

ETHNIC AND SOCIAL-CLASS DIFFERENCES

One reason why American girls even in the upper class are anxious about their femininity is that aristocratic status gives little or no protection against democratic norms. In Asian countries where the greater majority of women have been kept in quasi-feudal bondage, upper-class women may have considerably greater freedom—to serve in the government, for example—than American women. Membership in the elite matters more than belonging to the less-prized sex. However, the degree to which boys in the United States must assert their masculinity varies by social class.[16] Correspondingly, at the very bottom of society one can find matriarchs as family heads without whom everything would go to pieces and on whom the men are extremely dependent.[17]

As has often been noted, efforts to apply European systems of social-class stratification to the American scene have led to considerable distortion, since ethnicity has, in effect, taken the place of class. Lloyd Warner and others have pointed to parallel hierarchies among the different ethnic groups, at least in our Eastern Seaboard cities.[18] Religion interacts with ethnicity, so that to be an Irish or German Protestant may make for quicker assimilation to national upper-middle-class norms than might be the case for Catholics.[19] These differences are, in turn, of variable weight depending on the size of the group in a particular community; in other words, on whether it is able to create a fairly encompassing environment for its members. Region makes a difference, too; thus, an Italian in Rhode Island may hail from a Sicilian village while an Italian in San Francisco came from Providence or Brooklyn along with everybody else and as early as almost everybody else.

There are a great many more poor whites in the United States than poor Negroes, although, because of their greater visibility and concentration, the

where peasants—including Southern Negroes—have come into transitional urban settings into which the "national" character intrudes with very uneven force.

[18]For discussion of the tenacity of ethnic–religious heritage, cf. Nathan Glazer and Daniel Patrick Moynihan, *Beyond The Melting Pot: The Negroes, Puerto Ricans, Jews, Italians, and Irish of New York City* (Cambridge, Mass.: M.I.T. Press, 1963).
[19]Cf. Gerhart Lenski, *The Religious Factor* (Garden City, N.Y.: Doubleday, 1961). Lenski's conclusions have been challenged by more recent writers like Father Andrew Greeley, and Catholic–Protestant differences are certainly becoming attenuated in many parts of the country.

[16]Cf., for example, the article by Jackson Toby cited in footnote 14 above; also Lee Rainwater, *And the Poor Get Children* (Chicago: Quadrangle Books, 1960); Lewis Yablonsky, *The Violent Gang* (New York: Free Press, 1962).
[17]Cf. Michael Maccoby, "On Mexican National Character." Arguably, a "culture of poverty" exists

latter come more and more to be taken as the modal poor. They live neither on an Indian reservation nor in the self-seclusion of the Amish or the Hutterites. It remains an arguable question to what extent Negro culture is that of poverty, of the rural South, or of African survivals.[20]

The persistence of class and ethnic variations reflects differential patterns of socialization in the family and even in the peer groups of childhood. It is not that childhood training is designed to prepare boys and girls for their later roles at home, in the labor force, or in civic society generally. Indeed, the home is ordinarily managed without any specific relation to the occupational or marital prospects of the children. In the upper- and upper-middle-class home, the young person acquires the qualities and motivations that will later be useful in professional roles depending on the pursuit of advanced education. Even so, the home does not turn out a "product" that is going to be marketable several decades later, but a more or less self-reliant

learner who will respond to changing labor-force pressures and inducements.[21] Parents and their surrogates act as filters for the social atmosphere: for the expectations, responses to authority, handling of anxiety and other contagious psychic qualities which channel and organize character structure. In large measure the home directs children away from home and early provides them with direct access, through their peers, through school, and through the mass media, to moods and imperatives which may not be in harmony with the parental ones.

The Role of the Mass Media

Since Americans are freed from many ascribed bonds, as Tocqueville and many later observers have pointed out, they are correspondingly in search of guidance and support beyond the orbit of family and clan. The ever more massive media play a role in that guidance which in spite of many investigations seems to me not well understood, for most studies have concentrated on campaigns, whether for a brand of cars or for a particular party candidate. It is the longer-run impact of the media that seems to me of far greater import for character and conduct. The media help to tutor us in how to be American: to be cheerful rather than sullen and forlorn; slender rather than fat; peppy rather than inert; aspiring rather than resigned; hedonistic and gregarious

---

[20]Cf. Stanley M. Elkins, *Slavery: A Problem in American Institutional and Intellectual Life* (Chicago: Univ. of Chicago Press, 1959; paper ed., New York: Grosset & Dunlap, 1963). Even when Negroes react most aggressively against American middle-class values, as with the Black Muslims, their reaction inevitably takes some characteristic American form, as in the development of a kind of Protestant ethic among these black nationalists. A clearly separate working-class culture, such as that which Richard Hoggart celebrated for England, would seem to exist in the United States largely in ethnic variants which increasingly share middle-class aspirations if not middle-class modes of achieving these. But, again: this does not determine the question of national character, for the large-scale psychoanalytically oriented work that would be necessary to examine class variations does not exist.

[21]Cf. Basil Bernstein, "Social Class and Linguistic Development," in A. H. Halsey, Jean Flood, and C. Arnold Anderson (eds.), *Education, Economy and Society* (New York: Free Press, 1964); although Bernstein deals with English children, his findings would seem applicable also to the American scene.

rather than pinched, postponing, or withdrawn. In the term "media" I include not only the images of movie and television screen and of advertising, but also the manner in which the more mobile Americans carry themselves, the way they publicly greet each other, and the way they design houses, cars, and public places.[22]

The media, in combination with our egalitarianism and our dating system, have made us something of a physiological democracy in which we look at looks rather than at less readily visible indices of birth, breeding, and connection. This may be an aspect of our racism and also (often unconscious) prejudice against the obese, the short, the too tall, and those lacking in appropriate poise.[23]

To be sure, there are class as well as mass media, and minorities such as the one referred to in footnote 23 can keep up a considerable osmotic pressure against the dominant channels. Yet even in those mountain or Southern states where the national networks have a hard time penetrating, and where fundamentalist religion and politics predominate, *Life, Look, Time, Newsweek,* and *U.S. News and World Report* all circulate, along with popular music and conventionally pretty girls—and of course the awareness that elsewhere things are different and that the young people may be lured away. While exposure to specific content is spotty, so that millions do not know the name of their own Senator, they will hardly escape knowing who Elizabeth Taylor is, what a bikini is, or that teeth—and people—should be white and clean.

POCKETS OF RESISTANCE

These messages, of course, are not confined within the national boundaries, but spill over our borders to influence young people on an almost world-wide basis (as part of an international subculture of youth) and with varying impact upon nations and subgroups proceeding, with whatever resistances, toward modernization. Within the United States also, the impact is uneven. Notice has already been taken of the young people who express in their dress and manner their resentment of the all-American way. Their outlook calls to mind the alliance characteristic of hierarchial societies between upper-class insouciance and lower-class resentment or vandalism, as against middle-class achievement-oriented norms. But a more politically relevant and culturally widespread form of resistance exists among the elderly, who so often feel themselves to be displaced persons of contemporary America. Raised in an era when saving was admired, when Prohibition was preached if not practiced, and when inhibition appeared associated with ascent, the elderly find themselves in a society where the mass media deride such attitudes as old-fashioned and

[22]Marshall McLuhan goes too far in saying that "the medium is the message," thus denying the long-run impact of content, although not denying that exposure to the electronic media as such involves profound shifts in outlook. Cf. Marshall McLuhan, *Understanding Media* (New York: McGraw-Hill, 1964).

[23]The preoccupation with "looks" has made it possible for a small minority of young Americans to express their rejection and defiance of middle-brow values by wearing scruffy beards, or unkempt hair and clothes, and some have the sullen or vacant expressions of those who, as a result of age, race, or other conditions of servitude, cannot convey their full Americanism in their appearance.

square. Feelings of generational displacement are no novelty: we have already referred to Margaret Mead's *And Keep Your Powder Dry,* arguing that parents and grandparents have been perennially less "American" than their better-schooled offspring. The rejected are seldom able to unite on a program vis-à-vis an America that seems to be moving too far and too fast away from them; instead, whether in turning down the fluoridation of water or voting against an issue of school bonds, they express resentment through symbolic gestures of negation.[24]

Yet, here again, we cannot extrapolate character structure simply from actions and ideologies. If we are interested in national character, we want to see the extent to which those Americans who resist the prevailing national styles characterologically resemble those who purvey or adopt them. Possibly, many resisters can be compared to those "negative changers" in small-group experiments who, in the very act of resisting influences from outside, are guided by those same influences to "do the opposite."[25] However, if our concern is with the dynamics of American politics, it may be more important to discriminate within American character in terms of such variables as authoritarianism.

[24]Cf. the brilliant discussion in chapter 7 of Joseph R. Gusfield's *Symbolic Crusade* (Urbana: Univ. of Illinois Press, 1962) of the significance of such crusades as a way of stating who belongs to America and to whom America belongs.

[25]Compare, for example, the discussion by Elaine Graham Sofer, "Inner-Direction, Other-Direction, and Autonomy," in Seymour Martin Lipset and Leo Lowenthal (eds.), *Culture and Social Character: The Work of David Riesman Reviewed* (New York: Free Press, 1961), pp. 316–348.

NATIONAL CHARACTER AND NATIONAL INSTITUTIONS

One of the "mass media" which plays an increasing part in drawing young Americans away from local attachments is the college, soon to be attended by a majority of the relevant age-grades. Through higher education, Americans are prepared to enter the orbit of national employers, including the nation itself, and to move without grave discomfort from their parishes of origin to any part of the country. They are also prepared to enter specific occupational subcultures so that homogenization and differentiation proceed simultaneously. As child-rearing becomes more permissive and as higher education becomes more widespread, it can be argued that authoritarianism tends to decline and that tolerance becomes not only a desired ideal but, in effect, a character trait. With growing affluence, well-endowed young Americans can afford to behave less competitively toward others and to become less authoritarian vis-à-vis their own impulses. As argued in *The Lonely Crowd,* Americans need no longer learn to be as thrifty as heretofore, when Keynesian methods of fiscal and wider economic management transfer these once necessary personal attributes to the political economy as a whole. Habits of work once drilled into individual character can now be built, as it were, into machines, including organizational machines, with the qualification that the supervisory work force still must respond to the older imperatives.[26] These structural changes also

[26]Indeed, as Nathan Glazer reminds me, the authors of *The Lonely Crowd* overestimated the degree to which the compulsion to work—what Veblen called

affect the patterns of conspicuous consumption. The landscape is littered with the baronial castles of nineteenth-century and early twentieth-century magnates, which now, it would appear, have become funeral homes, or Catholic colleges for women, or conference centers—perhaps eventually parking lots. This development cannot be explained simply because of the difficulty of finding servants or keeping up the taxes on such estates. In a less overtly rivalrous world, the trophies of success seem meaningless and even inhuman and, in any case, out of place.[27]

Institutions rather than individuals are now taking over the function of making show for us. In corporate affairs this leads to lavish office buildings, to the new double standard in which a man can live his life lushly on his expense account while his wife is at home eating leftovers on her nonaccount. Moreover, as people are pulled away from their local and traditional attachments, they often become even more firmly attached to the nation itself as the symbolic corporation; and to whatever extent we may share a national character or set of characters, it is hard to escape our

national "parish" cut off by wealth, bellicosity, and historic experience from the greater part of the planet.[28]

A CHANGING AMERICAN CHARACTER?

Comparative studies across cultures would seem to offer the best possibilites to bring out systematically such determinants of social character as stage of industrialization, of urbanization and affluence, of exposure to mass media, and of social mobility. For example, Lipset's comparisons of American, Canadian, and Australian patterns of values may, as suggested above, help clarify the salience of egalitarianism in the United States.[29] *The Lonely Crowd,* focused as it was on the United States alone, did not attempt to deal with national character as such, but to suggest hypotheses about changes in upper-middle-class social character in the twentieth century. Such a limited inquiry could not conceivably resolve the often agitated question as to whether Americans at present are more flexible—or more compliant or more conformist—than in an earlier day. Lipset has cogently argued that Americans have always seemed "other-directed" to foreign observers, such as Alexis de Tocqueville and Harriet Mar-

---

the instinct of workmanship—could be moderated in America with growing affluence. The expectations Americans now have for social and educational services require much more diligence and craftsmanship than many Americans are now prepared to provide. Cf. Robert S. Weiss and David Riesman, "Work and Automation: Problems and Prospects," in Robert K. Merton and Robert A. Nisbet (eds.), *Contemporary Social Problems* (2nd ed.; New York: Harcourt, Brace and World, 1966), pp. 553–618.

[27]Nothing that is said here is meant to suggest that there are radical discontinuities here and that one cannot find precursors. Veblen noticed that among the very rich a "rustic" life of careful underconsumption was beginning even in the Gilded Age.

[28]In a penetrating essay, C. Vann Woodward argues that the South is in certain crucial respects "un-American": it has been poor; it has lost a war; it has a stronger sense of tragedy and defeat. Cf. "The Search for Southern Identity," *Virginia Quarterly Review,* 34:3 (Summer 1958), pp. 321–338; cf. also David Riesman, "National Purpose," reprinted in *Abundance for What? and Other Essays, op. cit.,* pp. 19–27.

[29]Cf. Lipset, *The First New Nation, op. cit.;* and for general comparative discussion, cf. Alex Inkeles, "Industrial Man," *American Journal of Sociology* (1960), pp. 1–30.

tineau; while Talcott Parsons has maintained that Americans have from the beginning been performance-oriented, not addicted to consummatory pleasures, and in that sense always "inner-directed."[30]

This discussion, like other work in American studies, has not avoided issues raised by popular nostalgia for a supposedly more self-reliant past, nor the wish to fend off characteristic anti-American criticisms concerning slavish conformity. Recent historical work makes it somewhat more difficult to cling to the notion that earlier generations of Americans were aggressively independent of social constraint. Thus, Scott Miyakawa argues in *Protestants and Pioneers* that, in the groups which undertook western settlement, tight conventions, monitored by the churches, circumscribed all behavior very strictly—even the ebullient Americans who appear so dramatically in the pages of Daniel Boorstin's history were also surrounded, even on the move westward, by collective restraint.[31]

Here again, it must be repeated that behavior and proclaimed values give only inferential clues as to character structure, either in individuals or in social groups. We can neither interview the dead nor give them projective tests, although we can interpret projectively the memorials of all sorts that they have left behind. And since some people are

[30]Cf. their essays in Lipset and Lowenthal (eds.), *op. cit.*

[31]Cf. C. Scott Miyakawa, *Protestants and Pioneers: Individualism and Conformity on the American Frontier* (Chicago: Univ. of Chicago Press, 1964); Daniel Boorstin, *The Americans,* Vol. 2: *The National Experience* (New York: Random House, 1965).

likely to leave a heavier sediment or deposit of this sort than others, if we are talking about modal character as our definition of national character (or, more precisely, a set of modal characters), we must be as careful as with the living that the voiceless are not crowded out of history—arguably, our effort to include them will seem to some observers as distinctly "American." For if one is comparing American character or values with those of other countries, undoubtedly Americans have enjoyed more equality with each other from the very beginning. Institutions such as established churches, chaperonage, and a tight kinship system could not easily maintain themselves in a setting where the young males could always light out for the Territory. To visitors from abroad, Americans have always appeared egalitarian, competitive, striving, and optimistic, although a few observers have also noticed the counterparts of these qualities in characteristic narcissism concerning minor status differences, in flights from competition and striving, and in underlying notes of tragedy and even hysteria in our literature, our evangelical revivals, and in some of our deviant strains of political prophecy. Whether in such matters one emphasizes change or continuity depends upon the nature of the question one is posing.

In *The Lonely Crowd,* my coworkers and I advanced a modest hypothesis: that for those social strata for whom adequate subsistence was no longer an issue, fundamental goals were changing, so that what was sought was less pelf and power than resonance with relevant others. These others were seen not as material to be opportunistically exploited but as sources of direction in taste and feeling. We argued that such a change reflected the decline of self-evident goals in a complex society where people were no longer sure of what they wanted out of life and had many choices open. We contended also that, as the fortresses of family and class became less convincing, people were becoming responsive to wider circles of others, both directly and vicariously through the mass media. We saw these changes as a matter of degree, of emphasis, in the metropolitan upper middle class, certainly not as a drastic institutional or characterological drift which has overtaken America as a whole. Were we writing such a book today, it seems likely that other changes would seem salient, other comparisons than with our own past more compelling.

NATIONAL CHARACTER: POLITICS AND FOREIGN POLICY

Indeed, national character is obviously only one of a variety of pressures on national conduct, while, in turn, national conduct, through the complex gear chains of socialization, may eventually alter national character. For whatever the modal character structure (or structures) of the people may be, any large-scale society always contains individuals capable of the most grandiose aims or the most sadistic and brutal means who, in given historical circumstances, can be mobilized—at least within certain limits—to exploit the weaknesses and harness the strengths of the great majority. Effective men may nevertheless be idiosyncratic; they may set purposes, provide models, create *faits accomplis* for the nation and hence for

themselves. It is dangerous to overgeneralize about the national character and to underestimate the variety of "types" in the United States who can affect the national destiny.

Recently, a Harvard undergraduate sought to examine in terms of national character the response of Americans to President Kennedy's decision to put a man on the moon.[32] He argued that American competitiveness made such a decision seem natural to many who projected onto the "race" with the Soviet Union attitudes engendered in less global rivalries. Yet to frame the issues in just this way and also as a challenge to American purpose and venturesomeness required a certain style of leadership and perhaps one that followed on the Eisenhower period of relative Presidential inaction. In the light of the decision, it is interesting to reread the proceedings of a conference where it was debated whether or not there is an American national style, especially in foreign policy.[33] A number of the participants have since had a hand in shaping and interpreting foreign policy; their comments show them to be activists, nationalists, discriminatingly anti-Communist, and eager for the country to be moving and not to appear sluggish. President Eisenhower's non-activist way was not represented among the assertive conferees but was, perhaps, a backhanded stimulus to a kind of nationalism that, in some respects, harked back to

[32]Albert Schneider, "The American Response to the Kennedy Moon Program as an Index of National Character," unpub. ms., 1966.
[33]See Elting Morison (ed.), *The American Style: Essays in Value and Performance* (New York: Harper, 1958).

Theodore Roosevelt.[34]

Yet, as already suggested, political action initiated by a small minority of elite and even visionary Americans may have consequences for the character structure of large populations by shaping the conditions under which these latter may develop. Hence, given the slate of character types to be found in our society, and the strains and pressures on these types from history and from their interaction with each other, it would seem that many different kinds of national conduct could be evoked. Much that actually occurs seems to be a kind of Brownian motion of all these inner dynamisms. The possibilities for future development are therefore wide, though not unlimited. Reflecting on these matters, I am impressed with how very little we know concerning the social character types prevalent in any large-scale society, and hence concerning what these limits are.

[34]Of course, not all the participants were activists of the sort suggested here. George Kennan was not, nor the present writer.

LIFE STYLE
VARIATIONS

This section can be considered as an alternative viewpoint to that expressed in Part 1, where it is intimated that Americans share a common life style, and this suggested commonality led some to say that there is an American character type. In this part, however, we look for differences rather than similarities. In one sense, both views are correct. A paradox appears because the United States is characterized at the same time by both great uniformity and great diversity. Diversity of life style generally has been inferred from the investigation of aspects of everyday life.* Specific behavior patterns are often studied without regard to how they are related to life style.† For example, the survey researcher might investigate the relationship between political party preference and religion without trying to ascertain the central life interests of individuals. Or observational studies might be conducted of a situation—for example, life within schools,

---

*For examples of the study of everyday life, see Erving Goffman, *Presentation of Self in Everyday Life* (Garden City, N.Y.: Doubleday, 1958); *Interaction Ritual: Essays in Face-to-Face Behavior* (Chicago: Aldine, 1967); Harold Garfinkel, *Studies in Ethnomethodology* (Englewood Cliffs, N.J.: Prentice-Hall, 1967); and Alfred Schutz, *Collected Papers, I: The Problem of Social Reality* (The Hague: Martinus, Nijhoff, 1962).

†This is not a condemnation of studies that narrowly focus on a specific pattern of behavior and attempt to identify specific causes; however, the way a specific pattern of behavior is integrated into a way of life is itself an important problem.

hospitals, or prisons—ignoring the relationship of behavior to influences outside the particular setting.*

Merely to know that both executives and skilled workers engage in leisure-time activities is not to understand their behavior. More important is how their leisure activities relate to their central life interests. Recreation for an executive may mean a temporary escape from work (so that he can function better when he returns to the office) or may serve as an informal setting for business contacts. For a skilled worker, recreation may serve as a family-centered activity. Thus leisure activities for executives may be integrated with their central life interest of career and for skilled workers with their central interest of family.†

Thus, to identify life styles, it is not enough to study isolated behavior of everyday life—e. g., card playing or telephoning.‡ These activities must be placed into a larger social context. Patterns of leisure and communication, superstition, death and mourning, dancing, marriage ceremonies, and family life are all aspects of daily activity. Anthropologists turn to these behavior patterns when they want to learn about a society. Unlike studies of isolated aspects of daily life, the anthropologist's ethnographic studies deal with many aspects of daily life, attempting to uncover a theme that explains how these many mundane behavior patterns are interrelated.§

As we have pointed out, descriptions of some segment of American society may too readily be taken as capturing the essence of American life style or character. Thus to Don Martindale American character is embodied in white Anglo-Saxon Protestants and their New England ancestors; to Calvin Trillin and David Riesman, American life style is best exemplified by middle-American, middle-majority consumption patterns; and to H. L. Mencken it is best characterized in the "Boobus Americanus," incompetent offspring of incompetent immigrants.

In the United States, forms of behavior such as dancing are subject to homogenization through the mass media. Thus Latin-American dances may bear little resemblance to their Latin-American roots. Popular dances, choreographed for television variety shows, become standardized or ste-

---

*For a discussion of the consequence of such narrow focus, see Virginia Olesen and Elvi Whittaker, *The Silent Dialogue* (San Francisco: Jossey-Bass, 1968), pp. 2–13.
†See, e. g., "The Working Man: Do Marketing Men Know Him?," *Printer's Ink,* **277** (December 1, 1961), pp. 48–49.
‡ Irving Crespi, "The Social Significance of Card Playing as a Leisure Time Activity," *American Sociological Review,* **21** (1956), pp. 717–721; Donald W. Ball, "Toward a Sociology of Telephones and Telephoners," in Marcello Truzzi (ed.), *Sociology and Everyday Life* (Englewood Cliffs, N.J.: Prentice-Hall, 1967), pp. 59–75.
§See, e. g., Elmer R. Service, *Profiles in Ethnology* (New York: Harper, 1963; H. G. Barnett, *Becoming a Palauan* (New York: Holt, 1960); C. W. M. Hart and Arnold R. Pilling, *The Tiwi of North Australia* (New York: Holt, 1960); Roger C. Owen, James Deetz, and Anthony Fisher, *The North American Indians: A Source-Book* (New York: Macmillan, 1967).

reotyped. *Their mass-media version often is less blatantly sexual, and the spirit of improvisation is stifled. We do not know the limits of mass media in exerting a homogenizing influence on American life, but there are indications that the influence is increasing.* *On the other hand, we have not yet seen the demise of ethnic groups, although this outcome has frequently been predicted.† Economic differentials persist in the United States, and the gap between rich and poor, compared with other industrial nations, is extreme.‡*

In the following article, Schatzman and Strauss report the results of an investigation of communication patterns that differ in intelligibility, grammar, and vocabulary between middle-class and lower-middle-class respondents. Differences in thinking and perceiving appear to be well established and are likely to be resistant to change. These authors present evidence that leads to questioning whether exposure to the mass media constitutes sufficient opportunity for absorbing middle-class culture, except in its more superficial aspects.

*Marshall McLuhan and Quentin Forie, *Understanding Media* (New York: McGraw-Hill, 1964) and *The Medium Is the Massage* (New York: McGraw-Hill, 1967); Alex Edelstein (ed.), *Perspectives in Mass Communication* (Copenhagen: Einar Harcks, Forlag, 1966).

† For a good discussion of the persistence of ethnic diversity, see Nathan Glazer and Daniel P. Moynihan, *Beyond the Melting Pot* (Cambridge, Mass.: M.I.T. Press, 1963); Herbert Gans, *The Urban Villagers* (New York: Free Press, 1962).

‡ Herman Miller, *Income Distribution in the United States* (Washington, D.C.: U.S. Dept. of Commerce, 1966); Gabriel Kolko, *Wealth and Power in America* (New York: Praeger, 1962).

Social Class and Modes of Communication[1]

LEONARD SCHATZMAN AND
ANSELM STRAUSS

Common assumptions suggest that there may be important differences in the thought and communication of social classes. Men live in an environment which is mediated through symbols. By naming, identifying, and classifying, the world's objects and events are perceived and handled. Order is imposed through conceptual organization, and this organization embodies not just anybody's rules but the grammatical, logical, and communicative canons of groups. Communication proceeds in terms of social requirements for comprehension, and so does "inner conversation" or thought. Both reasoning and speech meet requirements of criticism, judgment, appreciation, and control. Communication across group boundaries runs the danger—aside from sheer language difficulties—of being blocked by differential rules for the ordering of speech and thought.[2]

If these assumptions are correct, it follows that there should be observable differences in communication according to social class and that these differences should not be merely matters of degree of preciseness, elaboration, vocabulary, and literary style. It follows also that the modes of thought should be revealed by modes of speaking.

Our data are the interview protocols gathered from participants in a disaster. The documents, transcribed from tape, contain a wealth of local speech. Respondents had been given a relatively free hand in reporting their experiences, and the interviews averaged twenty-nine pages. These seemed admirably suited to a study of differences between social classes in modes of communication and in the organization of perception and thought. We used them also to explore the hypothesis that substantial intra-class differences in the organization of stories and accounts existed; hence low-class respondents might fail to satisfy the interviewer's canons of communication.

Approximately 340 interviews were available, representing random sampling of several communities ravaged by a tornado. Cases were selected by extreme position on educational and income continuums. Interviewees were designated as "lower" if education did not go beyond grammar school and if the annual family

From *American Journal of Sociology,* **60** (1955), pp. 329–338. Reprinted by permission of the American Journal of Sociology, University of Chicago Press.

[1]The writers are greatly indebted to the National Opinion Research Center in Chicago, which allowed them to use data gathered during a study of responses to disaster. The disaster occurred as the result of a tornado which swept through several small Arkansas towns and adjacent rural areas.

[2]Cf. E. Cassirer, *An Essay on Man* (New Haven, 1944); S. Langer, *Philosophy in a New Key* (New York, 1948); A. R. Lindesmith and A. L. Strauss, *Social Psychology* (New York, 1949), pp. 237–252; G. Mead, *Mind, Self, and Society* (Chicago, 1934); C. W. Mills, "Language, Logic, and Culture," *American Sociological Review,* IV (1939), 670–680.

income was less than two thousand dollars. The "upper" group consisted of persons with one or more years of college education and annual incomes in excess of four thousand dollars. These extremes were purposely chosen for maximum socioeconomic contrast and because it seemed probable that nothing beyond formal or ritual communication would occur between these groups.

Cases were further limited by the following criteria: age (twenty-one to sixty-five years), race (white only), residence (native of Arkansas and more than three years in the community), proximity (either in the disaster area or close by), good cooperation in interview (as rated by interviewer), and less than eight probes per page (to avoid a rigid question-answer style with consequent structuring of interview by the interviewer's questions). The use of these criteria yielded ten upper-group cases, which were then matched randomly with ten from the lower group.[3]

DIFFERENCES BETWEEN CLASSES

Differences between the lower and upper groups were striking; and, once the nature of the difference was grasped, it was astonishing how quickly a charac-

[3] Each document was scrutinized by both authors, and comprehensive notes were taken to help establish categories descriptive of the communicative style and devices of each respondent. From these notes, profiles of respondents were constructed. From the notes and case profiles, there emerged the separate profiles for lower and upper groups that will be described. We had expected to code the documents to bring out the degree of overlap between groups, but it turned out that there was literally no overlap; nevertheless, each reader coded separately as he went along. Agreement upon coding scores between readers was virtually perfect.

teristic organization of communication could be detected and described from a reading of even a few paragraphs of an interview. The difference is not simply the failure or success—of lower and upper groups, respectively—in communicating clearly and in sufficient detail for the interviewer's purposes. Nor does the difference merely involve correctness or elaborateness of grammar or use of a more precise or colorful vocabulary. The difference is a considerable disparity in (a) the number and kinds of perspectives utilized in communication; (b) the ability to take the listener's role; (c) the handling of classifications; and (d) the frameworks and stylistic devices which order and implement the communication.

PERSPECTIVE OR CENTERING

By perspective or centering is meant the standpoint from which a description is made.[4] Perspectives may vary in number and scope. The flexibility with which one shifts from perspective to perspective during communication may vary also.

Lower class. Almost without exception, any description offered by a lower-class respondent is a description as seen through his *own* eyes; he offers his own perceptions and images directly to the listener. His best performance is a straight, direct narrative of events as he saw and experienced them. He often locates himself clearly in time and place

[4] Cf. J. Piaget, *The Psychology of Intelligence* (London, 1950). See also a suggestive treatment of inadequate thinking analyzed in terms of centering in Max Wertheimer, *Productive Thinking* (New York, 1945), pp. 135–147.

and indicates by various connective devices a rough progression of events in relation to his activities. But the developmental progression is only in relation to himself. Other persons and their acts come into his narrative more or less as he encountered them. In the clearest interviews other actors are given specific spatial and temporal location, and sometimes the relationships among them or between them and himself are clearly designated.

The speaker's images vary considerably in clarity but are always his own. Although he may occasionally repeat the stories of other persons, he does not tell the story as though he were the other person reconstructing events and feelings. He may describe another person's act and the motive for it, with regard to himself, but this is the extent of his role-taking—he does not assume the role of another toward still others, except occasionally in an implicit fasion: "Some people was helping other people who was hurt." This limitation is especially pronounced when the behavior of more than two or three persons is being described and related. Here the description becomes confused: At best the speaker reports some reactions, but no clear picture of interaction emerges. The interaction either is not noticed or is implicitly present in the communication ("We run over there to see about them, and they was alright"). Even with careful probing the situation is not clarified much further. The most unintelligible speakers thoroughly confound the interviewer, who tries to follow images, acts, persons, and events which seem to come out of nowhere and disappear without warning.

Middle Class. The middle class can equal the best performance of the lower class in communicating and elaborating a direct description. However, description is not confined to so narrow a perspective. It may be given from any of several standpoints: for instance, another person, a class of persons, an organization, an organizational role, even the whole town. The middle-class speaker may describe the behavior of others, including classes of others, from their standpoints rather than from his, and he may include sequences of acts as others saw them. Even descriptions of the speaker's own behavior often are portrayed from other points of view.

Correspondence of Imagery Between Speaker and Listener

Individuals vary in their ability to see the necessity for mediating linguistically between their own imagery and that of their listeners. The speaker must know the limits within which he may assume a correspondence of imagery. When the context of the item under discussion is in physical view of both, or is shared because of similarity of past experience, or is implicitly present by virtue of a history of former interaction, the problem of context is largely solved.[5] But when the context is neither so provided nor offered by the speaker, the listener is confronted with knotty problems of interpretation. In the accounts of the most unintelligible respondents we found dream-like sets of images with few connective, qualifying, explanatory, or

[5]For a good discussion of this see B. Malinowski, "The Problem of Meaning in Primitive Language," in *Magic, Science and Religion and Other Essays* (Boston, 1948), pp. 228–276.

other context-providing d---   —   -s,
the interviewer was har
make sense of the accoun
forced to probe at every turn le.
speaker figuratively run away with the
situation. The respondents were willing
and often eager to tell their stories, but
intention to communicate does not
always bring about clear communication. The latter involves, among other
requirements, an ability to hear one's
words as others hear them.

Lower class. Lower-class persons
displayed a relative insensitivity to disparities in perspective. At best, the respondent corrected himself on the exact
time at which he performed an act, or
became aware that his listener was not
present at the scene and so located objects and events for him. On occasion
he reached a state of other-conscious-
ness: "You can't imagine if you wasn't
there what it was like." However, his
assumption of a correspondence in imagery is notable. There is much surnam-
ing of persons without genuine identification, and often terms like "we" and
"they" are used without clear referents.
The speaker seldom anticipates responses to his communication and seems
to feel little need to explain particular
features of his account. He seldom qualifies an utterance, presumably because
he takes for granted that his perceptions
represent reality and are shared by all
who were present. Since he is apt to take
so much for granted, his narrative lacks
depth and richness and contains almost
no qualifications and few genuine illustrations. The hearer very often is confronted with a descriptive fragment that
supposedly represents a more complete
story. The speaker may then add phrases
like "and stuff like that" or "and every-

thing." Such phrasing is not genuine
summation but a substitute for detail
and abstraction. Summary statements
are virtually absent, since they signify
that speakers are sensitive to the needs
of listeners. Certain phrases that appear
to be summaries—such as "That's all I
know" and "That's the way it was"—
merely indicate that the speaker's
knowledge is exhausted. Other sum-
mary-like phraseologies, like "It was
pitiful," appear to be asides, reflective
of self-feeling or emotion rather than
résumés of preceding detail.

Middle class. The middle-class respondent also makes certain assumptions about the correspondence of the
other's images with his own. Nevertheless, in contrast with the lower group,
he recognizes much more fully that imagery may be diverse and that context
must be provided. Hence he uses many
devices to supply context and to clarify
meaning. He qualifies, summarizes, and
sets the stage with rich introductory
material, expands themes, frequently
illustrates, anticipates disbelief, meticulously locates and identifies places and
persons—all with great complexity of
detail. He depends less on saying "You
know"; he insists upon explaining if he
realizes that a point lacks plausibility
or force. Hence he rarely fails to locate
an image, or series of images, in time
or place. Frequent use of qualification
is especially noteworthy. This indicates
not only multiple centering but a very
great sensitivity to listeners, actual and
potential—including the speaker himself.

In short, the middle-class respondent
has what might be called "communication control," at least in such a
semiformal situation as the interview.
Figuratively, he stands between his own

images and the hearer and says, "Let me introduce you to what I saw and know." It is as though he were directing a movie, having at his command several cameras focused at different perspectives, shooting and carefully controlling the effect. By contrast, the lower-class respondent seems himself more like a single camera which unreels the scene to the audience. In the very telling of his story he is more apt to lose himself in his imagery. The middle-class person—by virtue, we would presume, of his greater sensitivity to his listener—stands more outside his experience. He does not so much tell you what he saw as fashion a story about what he saw. The story may be accurate in varying degrees, although, insofar as it is an organized account, it has both the virtues and the defects of organization. The comparative accuracies of middle- and lower-class accounts are not relevant here; the greater objectivity of the former merely reflects greater distance between narrator and event.[6]

In organizing his account, the middle-class respondent displays parallel consciousness of the other and himself. He can stop midstream, take another direction, and, in general, exert great control over the course of his communication. The lower-class respondent seems to have much less foresight, appearing to control only how much he will say to the interviewer, or whether he will say it at all, although presumably he must have some stylistic controls not readily observable by a middle-class reader.

[6]Our discussion of objectivity and of mediation between self and image in communication is reminiscent of some of the literature on child, schizophrenic, and aphasic thought.

CLASSIFICATIONS AND CLASSIFICATORY RELATIONS

Lower class. Respondents make reference mainly to the acts and persons of particular people, often designating them by proper or family names. This makes for fairly clear denotation and description, but only as long as the account is confined to the experiences of specific individuals. There comes a point when the interviewer wishes to obtain information about classes of persons and entire organizations as well as how they impinged upon the respondent, and here the lower-class respondent becomes relatively or even wholly inarticulate. At worst he cannot talk about categories of people or acts because, apparently, he does not think readily in terms of classes. Questions about organizations, such as the Red Cross, are converted into concrete terms, and he talks about the Red Cross "helping people" and "people helping other people" with no more than the crudest awareness of how organizational activities interlock. At most the respondent categorizes only in a rudimentary fashion: "Some people were running; other people were looking in the houses." The interviewer receives a sketchy and impressionistic picture. Some idea is conveyed of the confusion that followed upon the tornado, but the organizing of description is very poor. The respondent may mention classes in contrasting juxtaposition (rich and poor, hurt and not-hurt), or list groups of easily perceived, contrasting actions, but he does not otherwise spell out relations between these classes. Neither does he describe a scene systematically in terms of classes that are explicitly or clearly related, a performance which would involve a shifting of viewpoint.

It is apparent that the speakers think mainly in particularistic or concrete terms. Certainly classificatory thought must exist among many or all of the respondents; but, in communicating to the interviewer, class terms are rudimentary or absent and class relations implicit: relationships are not spelled out or are left vague. Genuine illustrations are almost totally lacking, either because these require classifications or because we—as middle-class observers—do not recognize that certain details are meant to imply classes.

Middle class. Middle-class speech is richly interlarded with classificatory terms, especially when the narrator is talking about what he saw rather than about himself. Typically, when he describes what other persons are doing, he classifies actions and persons and more often than not explicitly relates class to class. Often his descriptions are artistically organized around what various categories of persons were doing or experiencing. When an illustration is offered, it is clear that the speaker means it to stand for a general category. Relief and other civic organizations are conceived as sets or classes of coordinated roles and actions; some persons couch their whole account of the disaster events in organizational terms, hardly deigning to give proper names or personal accounts. In short, concrete imagery in middle-class communication is dwarfed or overshadowed by the prevalence and richness of conceptual terminology. Organization of speech around classifications comes readily, and undoubtedly the speaker is barely conscious of it. It is part and parcel of his formal and informal education. This is

not to claim that middle-class persons always think with and use classificatory terms, for doubtless this is not true. Indeed, it may be that the interview exacts from them highly conceptualized descriptions. Nonetheless, we conclude that, in general, the thought and speech of middle-class persons is less concrete than that of the lower group.

ORGANIZING FRAMEWORKS AND STYLISTIC DEVICES

One of the requirements of communication is that utterances be organized. The principle of organization need not be stated explicitly by the speaker or recognized by the listener. Organizing frames can be of various sorts. Thus an ordering of the respondents' description is often set by the interviewer's question, or the speaker may set his own framework ("There is one thing you should know about this"). The frame can be established jointly by both interviewer and respondent, as when the former asks an open-ended question within whose very broad limits the respondent orders his description in ways that strike him as appropriate or interesting. The respondent, indeed, may organize his account much as though he were telling a special kind of story or drama, using the interviewer's questions as hardly more than general cues to what is required. The great number of events, incidents, and images which must be conveyed to the listener may be handled haphazardly, neatly, dramatically, or sequentially; but, if they are to be communicated at all, they must be ordered somehow. Stylistic devices accompany and implement these organizing frames, and the lower and upper groups use them in somewhat different ways.

Lower class. The interviewer's opening question, "Tell me your story of the tornado," invites the respondent to play an active role in organizing his account; and this he sometimes does. However, with the exception of one person who gave a headlong personal narrative, the respondents did not give long, well-organized, or tightly knit pictures of what happened to them during and after the tornado. This kind of general depiction either did not occur to them or did not strike them as appropriate.

The frames utilized are more segmental or limited in scope than those used by the middle class. They appear to be of several kinds and their centering is personal. One is the personal narrative, with events, acts, images, persons, and places receiving sequential ordering. Stylistic devices further this kind of organization: for instance, crude temporal connectives like "then," "and," and "so" and the reporting of images or events as they are recollected or as they appear in the narrative progression. Asides may specify relationships of kinship or the individuals' location in space. But, unless the line of narrative is compelling to the speaker, he is likely to wander off into detail about a particular incident, where the incident in turn then provides a framework for mentioning further events. Likewise, when a question from the interviewer breaks into the narrative, it may set the stage for an answer composed of a number of images or an incident. Often one incident becomes the trigger for another, and, although some logical or temporal connection between them may exist for the speaker, this can scarcely be perceived by the interviewer. Hence the respon-

dent is likely to move out of frames quickly. The great danger of probes and requests for elaboration is that the speaker will get far away from the lifeline of his narrative—and frequently far away from the interviewer's question. As recompense the interviewer may garner useful and unexpectedly rich information from the digressions, although often he needs to probe this material further to bring it into context. General questions are especially likely to divert the speaker, since they suggest only loose frames; or he may answer in general, diffuse, or blurred terms which assume either that the listener was there too or that he will put meaningful content into the words. If a question is asked that concerns abstract classes or is "above" the respondent—a query, say, about relief organizations—then very general answers or concrete listing of images or triggering of images are especially noticeable. When the interviewer probes in an effort to get some elaboration of an occurrence or expansion of an idea, he commonly meets with little more than repetition or with a kind of "buckshot" listing of images or incidents which is supposed to fill out the desired picture. The lack of much genuine elaboration is probably related to the inability to report from multiple perspectives.

One requirement of the interview is that it yield a fairly comprehensive account of the respondent's actions and perceptions. With the lower-class respondent the interviewer, as a rule, must work very hard at building a comprehensive frame directly into the interview. This he does by forcing many subframes upon the respondent. He asks many questions about exact time sequence, placement and identification of persons, expansion of detail, and the like. Especially must he ask pointed questions about the relations of various personages appearing in the account. Left to his own devices, the respondent may give a fairly straightforward narrative or competently reconstruct incidents that seem only partially connected with each other or with his narrative. But the respondent seldom voluntarily gives both linear and cross-sectional pictures.

The devices used to implement communication are rather difficult to isolate, perhaps because we are middle class ourselves. Among the devices most readily observable are the use of crude chronological notations (e.g., "then, . . . and then"), the juxtaposing or direct contrasting of classes (e.g., rich and poor), and the serial locating of events. But the elaborate devices that characterize middle-class interviews are strikingly absent.

Middle class. Without exception, middle-class respondents imposed overall frames of their own upon the entire interview. Although very sensitive generally to the needs of the interviewer, they made the account their own. This is evidenced sometimes from the very outset; many respondents give a lengthy picture in answer to the interviewer's invitation, "Tell me your story." The organizing frame may yield a fluid narrative that engulfs self and others in dense detail; it may give a relatively static but rich picture of a community in distress; or, by dramatic and stage-setting devices, it may show a complicated web of relationships in dramatic motion. The entire town may be taken as the frame of reference and its story portrayed in time and space.

Besides the master-frame, the mid-dle-class respondent utilizes many subsidiary frames. Like the lower-class person, he may take off from a question. But, in doing so—especially where the question gives latitude by its generality or abstractness—he is likely to give an answer organized around a subframe which orders his selection and arrangement of items. He may even shift from one image to another, but rarely are these left unrelated to the question which initially provoked them. He is much more likely also to elaborate than to repeat or merely to give a scattered series of percepts.

One prerequisite for the elaboration of a theme is an ability to depart from it while yet holding it in mind. Because he incorporates multiple perspectives, the respondent can add long asides, discuss the parallel acts of other persons in relation to himself, make varied comparisons for the enrichment of detail and comprehension—and then can return to the original point and proceed from there. Often he does this after first preparing his listener for the departure and concludes the circuit with a summary statement or a transitional phrase like "well—anyhow" that marks the end of the digression.

The stylistic devices utilized by any respondent are many and varied. But each speaker uses some devices more frequently than others, since certain ones are more or less appropriate to given frames. There is no point in spelling out the whole range of devices; they are of the sort used in any clear detailed narrative and effective exposition. If the respondent is pressed to the limit of his ability in explaining a complex point or describing a complicated scene, he calls into play resources that are of immensely high order. Sometimes a seemingly simple device will turn out on closer inspection to demand a sophisticated handling of communication—for instance, the frequent and orderly asides that break into exposition or narrative and serve with great economy to add pertinent detail.

INTRACLASS DIFFERENCES

Middle class. Although all middle-class accounts were informative, there were considerable differences of construction among them. The frames utilized by any respondent are multiple, but respondents tend to use either a frame emphasizing sequence, human drama, and personal incident or one stressing interlocking classes of civic acts. Each orientation is implemented by somewhat different stylistic techniques. There are of course different ways of narrating; thus one can dwell more upon conditions for activity than upon the acts themselves. Similarly, accounts focused upon town organization vary in such matters as the scope of description and the degree of emphasis upon temporal sequence. Both frameworks are interchangeable, and their use is a function either of the speaker's habitual orientation or of his definition of the interview situation rather than of his ability to use one or the other mode.

Lower class. Lower-class persons can best be distinguished in terms of ability to meet the minimum requirements of the interview. Some literally cannot tell a straight story or describe a simple incident coherently. At the other extreme we find an adequate self-focused narrative, with considerable detail tightly tied to sequential action,

including retrospective observation about the narrator's facts as he develops them. Midway between these extremes are the people who can tell portions of narrative but are easily distracted: either an image suggests some other image, or the interviewer asks a question focusing interest and concentration elsewhere than upon the narrative or he calls for some expansion of detail. Then the interviewer must remind the speaker of the break in narrative. The interviewer constantly must be on the *qui vive* to keep the story going and to fill in gaps.

In the best accounts, also, competent description is handled by linking a variety of perceptions to the narrative. Images then appear to the listener to be in context and thus are fairly comprehensible. At the other extreme, images and incidents are free-floating. Probing improved the quality of this sort of interview but slightly. More frequently, the interviewer was confronted with fragments of the narrative and its related imagery. Then he had to piece together the general lineaments of the story by a barrage of probes: "Who?" "When?" "Where?" Even then the reader of these interviews will come across stray images and be hard pressed to fit them into the context. Competence in recounting narrative generally is accompanied by competence in making understandable departures from the narrative itself, and, lacking both skills, some lower-class respondents gave quite baffling and unintelligible reports. The best accounts are moderately clear, although subject to all the limitations already discussed.

DISCUSSION

Only if the situation in which the

respondent spoke is carefully taken into account will we be on safe ground in interpreting class differences. Consider, first, the probable meaning of the interview for the middle-class respondents. Although the interviewer is a stranger, an outsider, he is a well-spoken, educated person. He is seeking information on behalf of some organization, hence his questioning not only has sanction but sets the stage for both a certain freedom of speech and an obligation to give fairly full information. The respondent may never before have been interviewed by a research organization, but he has often talked lengthily, fairly freely, and responsibly to organizational representatives. At the very least he has had some experience in talking to educated strangers. We may also suppose that the middle-class style of living often compels him to be very careful not to be misunderstood. So he becomes relatively sensitive to communication *per se* and to communication with others who may not exactly share his viewpoints or frames of reference.

Communication with such an audience requires alertness, no less to the meanings of one's own speech than to the possible intent of the other's. Role-taking may be inaccurate, often, but it is markedly active. Assessing and anticipating reactions to what he has said or is about to say, the individual develops flexible and ingenious ways of correcting, qualifying, making more plausible, explaining, rephrasing—in short, he assumes multiple perspectives and communicates in terms of them. A variety of perspectives implies a variety of ways of ordering or framing detail. Moreover, he is able to classify and to relate classes explicitly, which is but another way of saying that he is educated to assume

multiple perspectives of rather wide scope.

It would certainly be too much to claim that middle-class persons always react so sensitively. Communication is often routinized, and much of it transpires between and among those who know each other so well or share so much in common that they need not be subtle. Nor is sensitive role-taking called forth in so-called "expressive behavior," as when hurling invective or yelling during a ball game. With the proviso that much middle-class speech is uttered under such conditions, it seems safe enough to say that people of this stratum can, if required, handle the more complex and consciously organized discourse. In addition to skill and perspicacity, this kind of discourse requires a person who can subtly keep a listener at a distance while yet keeping him in some degree informed.

Consider now, even at risk of overstating the case, how the interview appears to the lower group. The interviewer is of higher social class than the respondent, so that the interview is a "conversation between the classes." It is entirely probable that more effort and ability are demanded by cross-class conversation of this sort than between middle-class respondent and middle-class interviewer.[7] It is not surprising that the interviewer is often baffled and that the respondent frequently misinterprets what is wanted. But misunderstanding and misinterpretation are only part of the story.

[7] Somewhat like this is the I.Q. testing session which involves a middle-class test (and tester) and a lower-class subject. The many and subtle difficulties in this situation are analyzed by Allison Davis in *Social Class Influences Upon Learning* (Cambridge, Mass., 1951).

Cross-class communication, while not rare, probably is fairly formalized or routinized. The communicants know the ritual steps by heart, and can assume much in the way of supporting context for phrase and gesture. The lower-class person in these Arkansas towns infrequently meets a middle-class person in a situation anything like the interview. Here he must talk at great length to a stranger about personal experiences, as well as recall for his listener a tremendous number of details. Presumably he is accustomed to talking about such matters and in such detail only to listeners with whom he shares a great deal of experience and symbolism, so that he need not be very self-conscious about communicative technique. He can, as a rule, safely assume that words, phrases, and gestures are assigned approximately similar meanings by his listeners. But this is not so in the interview or, indeed, in any situation where class converses with class in nontraditional modes.

There still remains the question of whether the descriptions of perceptions and experiences given by the lower-class respondent are merely inadequate or whether this is the way he truly saw and experienced. Does his speech accurately reflect customary "concrete" modes of thought and perception, or is it that he perceives in abstract and classificatory terms, and from multiple perspectives, but is unable to convey his perceptions?[8] Unless one assumes that, when talking in familiar vein to familiar audiences, speech and gesture incorporate multiple perspectives, which is, as we have already indicated, improbable,

one concludes that speech does in some sense reflect thought. The reader is perhaps best left at this point to draw his own conclusions, although we shall press upon him certain additional evidence and interpretation arising from examination of the interviews.

In any situation calling for a description of human activities it is necessary to utilize motivational terminology, either explicitly or implicitly, in the very namings of acts.[9] In the speech of those who recognize few disparities of imagery between themselves and their listeners, explicit motivational terms are sparse. The frequent use among the lower class of the expression "of course" followed by something like "They went up to see about their folks" implies that it is almost needless to say what "they" did, much less to give the reason for the act. The motive ("to see about") is implicit and terminal, requiring neither elaboration nor explanation. Where motives are explicit ("They was needin' help, so we went on up there"), they are often gratuitous and could just as well have been omitted. All this is related to preceding discussions of single centering and assumed correspondence of imagery. To the speaker it was quite clear why people did what they did. There was no need to question or to elaborate on the grounds for acts. Under probing the respondent did very little better: he used

---

[8]"The lower class is even more concrete in its outlook than the lower-middle class. For example,

a question . . . where chewing gum is usually purchased will be answered by an upper-middle person: 'At a cashier's counter or in a grocery store.' By the lower-middle: 'At the National or the corner drugstore.' By the lower class: 'From Tony' " ("Marketing Chewing Gum in New England: A Research Study" [Chicago: Social Research, Inc., 1950]).

[9]Cf. K. Burke, *Grammar of Motives* (New York, 1945).

motivational terms but within a quite narrow range. The terms he used ordinarily reflected kinship obligations, concern for property, humanitarian ("help") sentiments, and action from motives of curiosity ("We went down to see"). Such a phrase as "I suppose I went to her house because I wanted reassurance" would rarely occur.

Middle-class persons exhibit familiarity with a host of distinct "reasons" for performing particular acts. Their richness in thinking allows activities to be defined and described in a great variety of ways. Here, indeed, is an instrument for breaking down diffuse images ("They was runnin' all over") into classes of acts and events. The middle-class person is able to do this, for one thing, because he possesses an abstract motivational terminology. Then, too, the fine and subtle distinctions for rationalizing behavior require devices for insuring that they will be grasped by the hearer. In a real sense the need to explain behavior can be linked with the need to communicate well—to give a rational account as well as to be objective. Hence, there is a constant flow of qualifying and generalizing terms linked with motivational phraseology ("I don't know why, but it could be he felt there was no alternative . . .").

It is not surprising to find the middle class as familiar with elements of social structure as with individual behavior. Assuredly, this familiarity rests not only upon contact with institutions but upon the capacity to perceive and talk about abstract classes of acts. The lower-class person, on the other hand, appears to have only rudimentary notions of organizational structure—at least of relief and emergency agencies. Extended contact with representatives of them, no doubt, would familiarize him not only with organizations but with thinking in organizational, or abstract, terms. The propensity of the lower class to state concretely the activities of relief organizations corroborates the observation of Warner that the lowest strata have little knowledge or "feel" for the social structures of their communities.[10] It also suggests the difficulty of conveying to them relatively abstract information through formal media of communication.

It may be that rural townspeople of the lower class are not typical of the national or urban low strata. This raises the question—vital to urban sociology but to which currently there is no adequate answer—of whether pockets of rural-minded folk cannot live encapsulated in the city[11] and, indeed, whether lower-class persons have much opportunity to absorb middle-class culture without themselves beginning the route upward, those remaining behind remaining less urban.[12]

---

[10]W. L. Warner, *American Life: Dream and Reality* (Chicago: Univ. of Chicago Press, 1953), pp. 193–194.

[11]David Riesman, "Urbanity and the Urban Personality," in *Proceedings of the Fourth Annual Symposium, The Human Development Bulletin* (Chicago: Univ. of Chicago, 1953), p. 37.

[12]William Henry, of the University of Chicago, has conveyed his impression to us that urban lower-class and middle-class people perform on Thematic Apperception Tests much as our Arkansas respondents did in the interview.

We have also examined interviews about disasters in Brighton, N.Y., a middle-class suburb of Rochester, and Elizabeth, N.J., an urban community near New York City. There are no observable differences between the middle-class respondents of these areas and those of Arkansas. Four interviews with Elizabeth lower-class respondents paralleled the modes of the Arkansas lower class. A fifth exhibited considerable middle-class characteristics.

The suggestion by Schatzman and Strauss that upward mobility may be the only means of absorbing middle-class culture expresses a pervasive assumption. Upward emulation was regarded by one sociological theorist as a dominant social pattern.* Although an individual's aspiration to improve his life style by emulating those thought to be his social superiors may not be universal, it is the most sought-after means of life style change. Upward emulation is marketed and forms the basis for a distinct industry. The encyclopedia industry, for example, capitalizes on desires for upward emulation. What may be purchased is an embourgeoisement consisting of symbols without substance. The following essay by Lynn Buller, a college undergraduate, is based on her experience selling encyclopedias.

*Thorstein Veblen, *Theory of the Leisure Class* (New York: Macmillan, 1899).

The Encyclopedia Game

LYNN M. BULLER

Many people want to make a fast buck, and college students are no exception. They aspire to the high standard of living that comes to those with college degrees. Moreover, their few marketable skills and need for seasonal employment may heighten their receptivity to schemes that promise fast money. During the month of May, when college students most tenaciously seek summer jobs, the classified sections of newspapers are filled with provocative want-ads offering quick and easy money in the promotional field. Encyclopedia companies advertise positions for "advertising representatives" which promise time for boating and water-skiing, travel within

This article was prepared especially for this book.

a five-state area, and a salary of $150 or more per week. With this kind of appeal and few available alternatives, it is not difficult to explain why each summer hordes of students across the country turn to selling encyclopedias. It was such an advertisement that resulted in my spending an entire summer participating in what turned out to be a complex manipulative racket and a fascinating subculture.

RECRUITMENT, INDOCTRINATION, PERSONNEL

Upon answering by telephone a provocative advertisement much like the one described above, I was told the employment supervisor was not in but that his "assistant," to whom I was speaking, would help me. He "just happened" to have an appointment available Saturday at one o'clock, and asked if I could come in then for a personal interview. When I asked the nature of the job, he explained that it would take several hours to explain the job and that he had seven other phones to answer. I had already been conned.

On Saturday, there were twenty other people at my "personal interview," and I later discovered the office had only two telephone lines. The absent "employment supervisor" did not exist, which made it possible for any employee answering the phone to set up job interviews.

A man resembling W. C. Fields—fifty-five-ish, complete with dime-store socks and cheap initial cufflinks—whisked into the room, the inevitable cigarette dangling from his busy mouth. He told us we were permitted to leave during the presentation if we objected to any part of the program or felt we wouldn't like the job; all he asked was that we display enough courtesy to stay until one of the three breaks he would give us. First we saw a film featuring a gentleman wearing a maroon smoking jacket seated in his private library, his soft hand resting fondly upon a leather globe. The musty aura of Classic Education pervaded the room. We were shown scholarship winners from previous summers receiving their thousand-dollar checks, and travelogue stills of the foreign city where all the successful salesmen would vacation late that summer.

Then the salary was explained to us. We were to receive a base salary of $115 for three weeks, which would be increased to $154 the fourth week. For this amount we were required to "place" two sets of encyclopedias each week with families who promised to "value and appreciate" the books, although we were allowed two fruitless weeks without being fired. For each ten sets above our quota of two per week we were to receive a $500 bonus. Fantastic, we thought.

Following the movie and the salary talk we were given the opportunity to leave, with Oil Can Harry standing in front of the class, daring us to scrape our folding chairs and crawl over six pairs of feet in the quivering silence. His beady eyes accused us, one by one, of disbelief.

No one left, and our mesmerizer demonstrated the material we would be offering in the "promotional combination offer," complete with commitment questions which were directed at us. He was, in fact, trying to convince us to accept the books. We agreed that the material was truly beautiful and would "place" itself. He said all we had to do was show the material to three interested couples each night and one of them would surely accept the books. It sounded like a whiz. Leading us to anticipate giving three demonstrations nightly made us think we'd be chatting with lots of interested, supportive people and knocking on comparatively few doors.

This was far from the truth. (A corporation higher-up confirmed later in an interview that prospective employees are purposely led to believe that they will place more sets than it is likely they will.) He didn't tell us that there would be nights when everyone in a salesman's territory with school-age children was attending high school graduation, or nights when the wind came up and the rain came down hard, and the field manager sat out the storm in a local bar, not deigning to rescue his rain-soaked crew a minute before the appointed hour. Or that we'd be dodging police all summer and, even more difficult, trying to keep frustration and depression, those white-eyed dogs, from constantly nipping at our heels. Although I didn't believe the job would be as easy as it sounded, I liked the idea of being an advertising representative for a large corporation and living in my own apartment for the summer, instead of going back home to fry hamburgers.

After the pitch we were called into the district manager's office in pairs and asked if we wanted the job. I didn't know whether I'd like it or not, but for $154 a week it seemed an irrelevant point. The girl in the office with me, however, insisted that she couldn't assess something until she'd tried it. I never saw her again. I remember the Weasel asking me some closing question akin to "Do you take this company as your personal Savior and promise to uphold it with your prayers, your presence, your gifts, and your future," and I remember the guilty twinge of my mouth as I answered yes. He looked like a congenital con-man to me, but if he was capable of asking silly questions like that, maybe he was stupider than I thought. There was a chance I could beat him at his own game. I got the job.

Later that week, at the end of the training period (unpaid), we were given a test in which we were asked the names of several corporation higher-ups, five reasons why we believed in the company, and whether, "given the choice," we would rather be paid the salary or a straight commission of $83 each for the first ten placements, $92 for each order thereafter, and a free set of encyclopedias as soon as we'd sold twenty sets. Though the employees could nominally choose between the pay plans, I knew of no one who was on the salary plan more than two weeks, either because he

quit before that time or because he changed pay plans. The test was a means by which the field managers selected their crews. Anyone who had designated the salary plan was not cheerfully chosen by the field managers, for they had no motivational whip to use on the salary boys.

A small but irritating part of our salaries went to pay for the savings banks we gave to our "placement families" in which to daily save their dimes. Another small portion went into a bail fund to aid salesmen run afoul of local Green River ordinances (prohibiting unlicensed solicitors). The field managers (staff sergeants for one to five advertising representatives) were given no car expense, although they did get a substantial override (kickback) on any orders written out of their cars. In fact, everyone up the management line of the sales division received a percentage of the profit. No employees were salaried; consequently, everyone in management rode the salesmen ("advertising representatives") for orders, and rode them all the time. The salesmen paid for their own motel and food expenses while traveling and for demonstration materials, and had no money deducted for taxes or Social Security.

After I'd worked with the company some time, I realized that almost anyone was hired. It was also practically impossible to be fired (mainly because for tax purposes we were considered individual contractors). One man, I heard, was welcomed back "like a long-lost brother" after serving five years in the pen for grand larceny. One girl was said to be an ex-call girl; at any rate, she was a cocktail waitress on weekends. Two seminary students were also hired, plus an honors graduate with a fellowship in psychology at a top university.

SALESMEN

According to my observations, the typical experienced bookman has been married twice, has three children, and is occupationally unskilled, although his intelligence is well into the second standard deviation. As a youth, he had high aspirations which were deflected by circumstance or frustration; he aspires to professional status. Most often he grew up on a farm; converted to city-dwelling, he regards small-town residents as cornball and sometimes feels revengeful toward farmers. His style is flamboyant and unsophisticated; his sexual attitudes are adolescent.

Even though nearly all the men in my office had frequent extra-, post-, or premarital sexual relations, they talked about their conquests in the same way ninth-graders are said to brag in the locker room. Any virgin was "open game"; and other salesmen heard about every aspect of the hunt. Some salesmen always had a girlfriend. One female seemed to fulfill their need about as well as another, and they followed a sequential pattern of courtship-monogamy. Other men tried to manipulate several salesgirls at once. One in particular was such a lady-killer that he talked the psychology graduate out of her fellowship so she could follow him to sell books and live with him in Sioux Falls, South Dakota. Meanwhile he courted the cocktail waitress, and later spontaneously married her. Several months later his wife departed with his car and color television. Lately, I hear, he's been dodging authorities regarding a charge of statutory rape. This man is 23 years old; he was the president of his high school graduating class, and has experienced two unsuccessful marriages. He is an extreme case. Another extreme case is a man who carried his pajamas, a clock-radio, and a fifth of whiskey in his briefcase to be prepared for any available sexual conquest.

Not all the men were disloyal to their wives—several were very happily married. But when one considers that all were away from their families at least twelve hours a day, from noon to midnight, and that most of their wives worked from eight to five, it's easily understandable that their marriages were characteristically less-than-ideal.

Of course, the female employees were hardly prudish. Several of them had strange habits too. One girl hitchhiked home seven miles through a woods each night after work. She'd been "raped" twice since Christmas. Strangely enough, although she claimed to hate men because of their disloyal and lustful natures, she seduced any available male. After she climbed into bed with me one morning, however, we decided she was most likely a lesbian.

It was not unusual for a crew of males and females to share one motel room, either. This probably was quite a wholesome arrangement, considering the potential audience. But it was hardly the thing to write home to mother.

The book business attracts men of similar life style. Most of the salesmen with my company drove big, bright-colored cars with factory air-conditioning: Pontiac convertibles, Chryslers, Buicks. One salesman drove a Jaguar and sold realty on the side. Their clothes were frequently flashy, but never cheap.

They treated themselves to three-dollar lunches and good clothes because the money came in easily, if they worked. (Not working was referred to as "leaking off.") The fact that they were paid commissions instead of a salary encouraged free spending. Purchases were priced in order-units: a salesman considered that his rent was two orders a month, food another one, a new coat was one order, and a pinky ring cost a half.

Alan Lippett[1] writes that diamond pinky rings signified success among the salesmen with whom he worked. In my company, no one wore pinky rings. My cohorts apparently aspired to conspicuous consumption of higher class indication than did the other company's salesmen. This statement is supported by my observations within Alan's former company, where I noticed that salesmen drove late-model Fords and Chevrolets and Ramblers with home-installed stereo systems, although they too, frequented the best restaurants and bars. I think they were less likely to know they were selling books, although my company did a pretty good job of keeping the truth from us. Maybe they were just dumber.

In my company, sales representatives and field managers (called "F.M."s) were very chummy. We called each other by first names from the start. We knew each other's past and present states of mind and affairs, as well as the number of orders each had written for the week. The other company's representatives seemed reluctant to divulge the circumstances of their private lives to each other, and offered no references to their

business success or unsuccess. There was apparently less sexual fraternization than in my company, too. Of course, I observed them during the winter when there were fewer opportunities for the kind of hanky-panky which went on within my company while we were traveling in the summer.

Motel owners were not always enthusiastic about letting rooms to encyclopedia salesmen, because of their reputation for sneaking off without paying. I never knew salesmen who did this. I did know of a young crew who had a water fight in their cabin one night and sopped the furnishings so thoroughly they couldn't sleep there. They left the motel, after paying, by telling the proprietor that one fellow's father had got his leg caught in a cornpicker and they had to rush to another city to see him. That the informing telephone call would have had to come across the motel switchboard, if the family even knew where their son was staying, must never have occurred to the innkeeper.

One salesman's many subpoenas on charges of damage to motels and hotels became a joke among the salesmen. Whenever this salesman came off a road trip, his friends would go over to his house to have a few beers, see the subpoenas he'd accumulated, and hear the story behind each one. This particular salesman was a legend in his own time. One night, the story goes, he and a buddy bought a watermelon. Because they didn't have a knife in their hotel room, the big brute smashed the melon down upon the sink to break it open. He also broke the lavatory off the wall and was accordingly sued for several thousand dollars after twelve inches of water filled the whole motel. On a bet,

[1]Alan Lippett, "There's One Born Every Minute," *Seattle Magazine,* 5 (June, 1968), pp. 25–30.

this same fellow cut a square of deer meat from an animal they'd struck with a car and ate it raw, impaled on his jack knife, and chased it down with straight whiskey. He was also known to drink whiskey for breakfast—tumblersful.

REVELATIONS

It took me almost six weeks to figure out that I wasn't really an advertising representative for the company; I was a book peddler. The "Promotional Combination Offer" was a gimmick clean through. Although people allegedly got the books for writing the company a letter of endorsement, and paying only for the services which kept the set up-to-date, they actually paid for everything they received. Their letters of endorsement were used only, if ever, to parlay new promotional participants.

It was claimed by the management that the product was far superior to any other encyclopedia. This encyclopedia had "just been completely rewritten and, indeed, was not on regular sale yet." It was new in the sense that a new edition is printed each year, and it was actually true that the set had been completely rewritten, even though the new version had been on regular sale since 1962. The "new edition" ploy was helpful in several ways. Whenever a prospective buyer voiced a complaint against this brand of encyclopedia, the salesman could answer assuringly, "That was our *old* set." The completely revised edition was also the basis of the promotional pitch. Placement families were supposedly pre-testing this new publication which was "not yet on the general market," and writing letters of endorsement

to be used to persuade their neighbors to buy the encyclopedias when they were finally released "for general consumption." Actually, the promotional families are the most general market to which the product is released. Families can obtain the books only through direct sales methods. The sales pitches are informally synthesized by innovative salesmen and lower management personnel. Yet somehow, these bubble-gum and bobby-pin methods sell $450 million worth of books each year.[2]

It was claimed that we were giving the people something they really needed, even if they were sometimes too stupid to realize their need. After all, it was not like we were peddling cyanide pellets disguised as diet pills. If purchasers used the books, they were sure to become better people. Representatives might even have looked upon themselves as missionaries bringing enlightenment to the backwoods. Pouring on the book pitch like cod-liver oil, confident that it was all "for their own good," employees could gloat in good conscience all the way to the bank.

Through talking with many people, especially those in small towns, we came to see ourselves as serving another positive social function—that of relieving people's boredom. Several times, I'm sure, people bought books from me because they were hopelessly bored, and I'd come from afar to entertain them for an hour. They were simply grateful.

The salespeople's true purpose was supposedly withheld from new employees; however, the varying levels of operational awareness within the district's

[2]Eric Geller, "Selling Encyclopedias," *New Republic* (August 24, 1968), p. 10.

personnel made it nearly impossible to keep the pose intact. Because my field manager confirmed that I wasn't giving books away, I was in a good position to watch other employees' reactions to what they thought they were doing for the company.

It is my theory that three classes of people were hired: "fishes," "sneakers," and "con-men." The fishes actually believe they are advertising representatives and they stay with the company not only for the money, but because they believe in education and in the product. (These people become very defensive of their jobs to outsiders and bristle at the mention of any other encyclopedia.) The sneakers figure the sales pitch isn't all on the up-and-up, but for the money they aren't going to bother with details. If they realized the extent of their deception, the sneakers probably would be forced by their disquieted consciences to quit. They need the rah-rah of product emotionalism to keep their minds from wandering where it might not be economically advisable. The con-men will do anything for the money offered. Even though the con-men don't always know precisely how they are misleading the public, they are fully aware that the public is being misled. Consequently, the fishes and the sneakers are protected from the truth by the con-men, who build up fine rationalizations to keep everyone enthusiastic and productive. Strangely enough, management is not composed primarily of con-men. It is easier for these people, too, to believe they are doing something worthwhile for mankind than to try to live with a conscience of conflict; some have become almost fish-like themselves.

Promotion in the encyclopedia game

is quick and not difficult. If a representative has sold ten orders, holds the business attitudes of either the sneaker or the con-man, and owns a car, he'll soon become a field manager. When he's more senior than most employees (which may mean he's been with the company one year) and has won a sales contest or two, he's likely to be offered an office of his own within the district. This offer is largely a doggie bone tossed out to make eager young men come into the office two hours earlier, without salary, to train recruits, or to run from office to office within the district to help train recruits. The most strenuous aspect of the trainer's job is keeping curious neophytes from discovering what they'll really be doing. By and by someone who heads one of the offices will quit or go to another district or be proselytized by another company and the trainer will get an office of his own. Whoopee. He can now be at work by 9:30 every morning (which means at least a twelve-hour day) to interview, hire, train, and pick his own crews, a task which leaves him too tired to go out and write personal orders in the evening. Any money he earns will be in the form of commissions, overrides on the orders written by his crew, or trainer's fees on recruits he's trained, so it is imperative that his crew be in the field every evening, primed to write orders, and that he himself be knocking on numerous doors, lest he go broke on car, lunch, and bar expenses.

District managers, regional managers, and regional vice-presidents are all paid healthy percentages of the volume of business in their jurisdiction. It must be said that they work hard, goading their inferiors to better performance through sales contests, summer vacation contests, and short-term prize agreements. But their wages are almost ridiculously ample. Regional and district managers are paid in five figures; vice presidents get six, plus lots of time to parlay their earnings. Ironically, education is in no way the primary consideration for promotions within the encyclopedia business. Enthusiasm, endurance, and the ability to hold one's own are the main prerequisites of a management job. One regional vice-president was a dentist. He had no business training whatsoever—no knowledge of marketing, business law, or management. He is probably in the position he now holds because he is one of the few people in the business with a college degree, although he wouldn't have been considered for the job if he hadn't been phenomenally successful as a sales representative.

MOOCHES

In American society there exist people classified by encyclopedia salesmen as "mooches." Mooches can be generally defined as people who like to buy the product; they see the encyclopedia salesman as the bearer of a rare and desirable gift. Mooches are people whose incomes and occupational levels exceed their educational attainments; persons whose income is in the middle-middle range but whose education doesn't exceed high school, or may not even attain that level. Without education, mooches cannot have professional status, although they might make as much money as a professional; consequently, mooches try to assume professionalism by accruing what they think are indications of professional status. A conspicuously dis-

played set of encyclopedias tells the mooch's friends that he can afford to consume conspicuously, that he values a highly normative product over creature comforts, and that he provides for the long-range benefit of his protectorate. The mooch associates all these characteristics with professional persons. For him, then, encyclopedias function as easily interpreted professional-status indicators.

Mooches are vulnerable in two ways to a book pitch—because books themselves are status symbols, and because books are considered the tools of professionalism (if not for the parents, then for their children). Being uneducated, mooches cannot differentiate between being wise and being knowledgeable. Even if they memorized all twenty-four full-color volumes, they wouldn't have an Oxford education. But such is the dream mooches are made of.

It doesn't take a new salesman long to spot a mooch, because he's constantly schooled by his seniors to look for specific criteria and readily develops the intuitive knack of mooch-hunting. Mooches show status incongruity in all their material possessions, and are more easily described than defined. Tools in a station wagon typify the moochiness of an artisan, who brings home good money but has no professional status because he works with his hands. Brick houses are not moochy, as opposed to clapboard houses with paint peeling from the siding, because brick houses are too substantial. Someone who buys a small, well-built brick house will not easily be sold on the quick idealistic emotionalism of an encyclopedia pitch; he's too careful an investor.

A mooch is someone who: drives a red

Mustang and lives in a small yellow frame house with hurricane fencing around it; leaves rained-on kids' books in the front yard; has all the neighborhood kids' trikes in his driveway plus a portable barbecue; buys a huge turquoise contemporary couch and burns a cigarette hole in it; lives in a maroon house in the midst of white houses; furnishes the living room with lots of big, gaudy ashtrays which match the drapes; buys a series of science books for his children but sits on a slip-covered couch; lives in a $15,000 stucco house in the midst of new $40,000 houses; has a swing set; drives a Cougar, Camaro, or other hot, flashy American car (foreign car owners are usually not moochy, being more economical and probably better educated); works as a mechanic and whose wife drives a bus for Head Start; has too much furniture in his living room, especially if it's formica-topped and includes a color TV set and console stereo; hangs plaster birds on his wall or has plastic flowers in the living room; has a shrine in his bedroom (these people will believe anything); or has a new rocking chair or a piano with sheet music standing on it. While novices are expected to knock on every door, experienced salesmen simply drive around "smelling out" mooches.

SELLING TECHNIQUES

After three days of training and observing experienced salesmen for two evenings, we novices were dropped into the "field" to finagle on our own. Propagandized and at least half-believing, we were ready to sell encyclopedias for profit, for the good of mankind, or for both. We didn't knock on every door, though we were supposed to. The general age and status of people in a neighborhood proved to be the key to potential sales, and we sought this information in order to economize our effort. Spotting a house inhabited by an older couple we'd knock on the door, greet the woman, appearing as friendly and innocuous as possible, and ask, "Say, is it the green house or the pink house next door that has the children in it?" and ramble on bewilderedly. We usually found out not only about the pink house, but about children's ages and husbands' employments all up and down the block. Another information-gathering tactic was to ask for a glass of water, or use of the bathroom. (It is surprising how many people will admit a stranger to their bathrooms; a family that will let you use their bathroom will tell you nearly anything you want to know.) By these means, we could meet potential customers with some preparation, and we learned which families in the neighborhood needed our services.

Many opening lines were used for getting inside the door. The tactic recommended by my company was composed of a friendly hello, an announcement of one's name as though it were well-known and ought to be recognized, and a request for the spouse of the salesperson's gender by saying, "Stopped out to see your wife (husband)." (Since many of the salesmen were pimple-faced eighteen-year-olds, their briefcases dropped conspicuously beside the front stoop, this tactic wasn't always successful.) The salesman explains that he's doing some work in the area and asks if he may step in and ask the people a couple of questions. Although it is forbidden for him to describe his work by using the words "survey," "market research," "advertising work," "promotional work," "school district," or any phrase which might indicate that the salesman is involved in one of the above types of work, it is intended for people to believe just that.

Once the salesman announces himself to the spouse of similar gender, he maneuvers the couple together and begins to deliver the spiel called "the Qualifier." This five-minute explanation of the promotional program is the most important tool of the trade. During the Qualifier, the salesman either wins or loses the people's interest and confidence, while taxing their emotions and reasoning to the point of submission. He can also assess the couple's interests, means of income, and special vulnerabilities, and utilize these assessments during the material demonstration. Most of the assessment is accomplished nonverbally by observing the family's material acquisitions, looking especially for signs of moochiness. Whenever possible he angages them in seemingly idle chatter.

After the Qualifier, the salesman brings his bottomless bag of educational goodies into the house and asks the couple to sit side by side facing him across the kitchen table or coffee table, where they can see his materials simultaneously. Saleswomen demonstrate the materials on a high table or on the living room floor from a kneeling position, in order to keep all eyes on the printed matter.

First, the size and binding of the set are displayed by means of a "stretcher," which is simply a foldable, two-dimensional replica of the book-backs with spacing between each volume, which makes the stretcher a third longer than the actual set of encyclopedias. The salesperson stresses that the lettering is stamped in "24-carat gold," sure mooch-bait. Then the couple is shown the Prospectus, a sample volume which contains nearly all the color pictures in the whole set, and generally highlights the encyclopedia. The "Pros" (rhymes with "loss") is broken down into sections which appeal to different age groups, including pre-schoolers, although the encyclopedia is written on at least junior-high reading level. Testimonials are numerous and flashy. The Pros of another company includes a full-page color picture of Pope Paul VI autographing their encyclopedia. Such audacity could only be tolerated by a true-blue mooch! Sports, hobbies, and practical skills are stressed, besides the academic appeal of this "particularly excellent recording of the sum knowledge of mankind."

During the demonstration of the Prospectus, the innovative salesman utilizes the earlier observations. If before entering the house he noticed a motorboat in the garage, he will show the couple a few boating pictures as he flips through the Pros; if they have an obvious interest in fine dogs, or their child has won a prize at a local science fair, he will pitch his demonstration to that particular interest. People often believe the salesman mentions their particular interest because it is part of his regular pre-placement demonstration. This makes them feel their hobby is considered especially worthy of stress by the company and, transferring the impression, they feel important themselves. Of course, the salesman means for the couple to perceive his craftiness in this way. Hopefully it will make them feel so important that they readily believe their letter of endorsement will be an asset to the company, and consequently agree to "participate in the program." In other words, buy the books.

After signing the duplicate contract, in which the merchandise is described as a "combination offer" and the promotional program and required letter of endorsement are not mentioned, the couple has bought all 24 color volumes of the encyclopedia, 10 supplemental yearbooks, 100 reference service coupons (all of which they most certainly will not use), a dictionary, a bookcase, and 10 volumes of children's books, all at regular retail price. Their one-page, handwritten letter of endorsement received within ninety days of delivery will probably never be used. But the salesman's technique was effective because he kept "talking the letter" and making the people feel they were truly privileged to be one of a few chosen families in the area. The usual parting line was, "Well, John and Mary, it's been fun getting to know you, and I'm very glad to be able to accept you as one of our advertising families here in the area. I'd like to feel free, if I'm in the vicinity again sometime, to stop in for a cup of coffee with you. May I do that?" Of course, the couple assure the salesman that he is always welcome and the salesman is assured by their submission to his self-invitation that they won't suspiciously cancel the order.

INDIVIDUAL SALES TACTICS

Several guises are successful aids to book peddling. Some representatives use a hard-sell approach, misquoting any

source which occurs to them to convince the victim-family that their children will be grammar school dropouts if their parents haven't the foresight or love to provide their children with this complete home reference library. One often-used line goes like this: "You know, John and Mary, we all love our children"—this said by 18-year-old, single college students— "but there are so few things we can give them. One is our good name, and the other is a good education. If I died tomorrow and could leave my child $100,000, he could spend it and be poor within six months. But if I give him my good name and a better-than-average education, no one can take from him the potential to earn five times the money I could have left him." From there on, if the parents refuse to take the books, the salesman makes them feel they've cheated their child out of half a million bucks. This kind of salesman often has difficulty giving a pitch when an observer (potential salesman) accompanies him because, even though observers are strictly told not to say a word during the pitch, some novices burst out laughing when the diabolical haze becomes thick. The con-man types spontaneously make up religious affiliations, relatives, and common acquaintances to try to win the family's confidence. They are quite successful if they can find enough people to intimidate, so they seek out mooches, potential fascists, and people without enough courage to shove them out the door.

Sometimes the salesmen appear downright threatening. There is no doubt in my mind that encyclopedia contracts have been signed just to get the salesman out of the house and, hopefully, out of town. One bookman of my acquaintance is particularly successful in Montana and North Dakota, where he drives right out into a farmer's field, urges him off his tractor, slaps him on the back and offers the fellow a beer from the cooler in his trunk, then drives the man back to the farmhouse to talk with the wife about their views of education. This salesman looks like the original Hell's Angel, is usually half-soused, and doesn't brush his teeth for days. When he flails his timberlike arms in the air and yells, "Ah, you're stupid! Your wife's stupid! Ya want the kids ta be stupid? Sign the fucking card," they sign. For some odd reason his orders are verified the next morning, too.

Another approach, often used by students, is the innocent-little-girl approach. This type of saleswoman appears at the door looking like a runaway teenager needing directions or a glass of water, and is invited into nearly every home whose door she knocks upon. Once inside, she gives the Qualifier in an explanatory yet wide-eyed way, and if accosted with suspicion, jokes, "You know it can't be a trick—I couldn't sell anything if I tried." She never polishes her pitch but follows a routinized pattern, knocking on every door, looking sweet, showing the material, and collecting a reasonable check at the end of the week.

Wives often regret admitting college coeds into their living rooms to kneel on the floor in front of their husbands. For this reason it is expedient for female employees to wear wedding bands and explain that their husbands are in the business also, or serving in the armed services. Husbands are not usually hard to fool; wives, unthreatened by a young woman they think to be married, are reminded of their own early marriages

and are usually quite friendly, asking particulars which give them an excuse to relate their own wedding stories. Sometimes male and female representatives sell books together, posing as man and wife. Frequently this arrangement represents an actual mobile living arrangement, and works quite well if both salespeople are good actors and the age gap is not extreme.

An approach which is consistently successful when pitching married college students is the authoritative approach. This stance seems quite professional; it is very low-key, shows almost no enthusiasm for the product and, by so doing, assumes that the students are already aware of its great intrinsic value. College students are considerably more enthusiastic than most older couples about subscribing to the reference service, which purports to write term papers. This factor contributes to a low-key approach. One salesman pitches to no one but married college students and had developed the search for these couples into a technique which the FBI would be well-advised to emulate. He can spot an outside second-story staircase from a half-block away, and distinguish at the same distance if it's being rented to college students or pensioners. The authoritative approach complements the advertising representative pose advised by the company. Within the pitch it is emphasized that the representative has been asked to place the set only with families he or she deems worthy—reverse psychology at its money-making best.

Some salesmen stress the personal relationship between themselves and their customers while addressing the couple as they do all customers. This is the promiscuously personal approach. Foreign students have been particularly successful utilizing this technique. They appear friendly, casual, and informative, and people almost invariably invite them in to chat, if not to look at books. One foreign summer representative spent Thanksgiving at the home of a family to whom he'd sold a set of books, and hadn't previously known. They loved him! Several representatives worked on Sundays and holidays, and would walk right into the midst of a family's Fourth of July picnic to sell them the educational deal of a lifetime while patriotism, the Good Life, and the American Way were still primary in their minds.

The representative's manner of dress doesn't seem to affect his selling success, except that his dress should reinforce whatever poses he presents. One company's top salesman often went into the field dressed in shorts and a paint-spattered sweatshirt. He appeared at people's doors looking like the man next door wanting to borrow some paint to finish painting his boat, and often sold five sets of books over a weekend.

Although encyclopedias are almost always books of fine quality and an asset to any family receiving them, the shame of most encyclopedia companies is that they do not grant their customers the conscious privilege of buying books when, in fact, they are. They also do not allow their employees the knowledge that they are selling books when, in fact, they are. As long as the industry provides its customers with professional status indicators, and its employees with good wages and something to believe in, this colorful subculture will probably thrive among us, remindful evidence that the race goes not to the diligent, but to the crafty. And when it comes to crafty persuasion, encyclopedia salesmen could give the patent medicine hawkers of the Old West a sure run for the money.

According to Buller, the "mooch" is one who attains the symbol but not the substance of "high culture." There are some, however, who possess both, while still others have neither. Russell Lynes suggests that society is stratified not upon traditional sociological variables such as power, privilege, or prestige, but upon the relationship to high culture. Thus he labels as "highbrows" those who possess the symbols and substance of high culture. "Middlebrows," in his terminology, possess the symbols but not the substance, while "lowbrows" care about neither the symbols nor the substance. To a highbrow, culture forms the central life style interest, whereas to the lowbrow, culture would not be the basis of an upward emulation in life style. Although Lynes probably overstates the case when he argues about culture as the new stratifying variable, his argument is as relevant today as when it was originally stated in 1948. Simon and Gagnon's description of variations in marital sex patterns (see table following Lynes' article) is based on Lynes' four classes.

Highbrow, Lowbrow, Middlebrow

RUSSELL LYNES

My wife's grandmother, the wife of a distinguished lawyer, once declined to dine with the Cartiers of jewelry fame because they were, as she put it, "in trade." Life for grandmother was relatively simple where social distinctions were concerned, but while there are still a few people who think and act much as she did, the passage of time has eliminated a great deal of that particular kind of snobbishness from American society. We are replacing it with another kind. The old structure of the upper class, the middle class, and the lower class is on the wane. It isn't wealth or family that makes prestige these days. It's high thinking.

Our heroes now are not the Carnegies or the Morgans but the intellectuals—the atomic scientists, the cultural historians, the writers, the commentators, the thinkers of global thoughts who, we assume for lack of another faith, know better than anyone else how we should cope with what we call with new resonance our national destiny. What we want are oracles, and the best substitutes we can find are the intellectuals. Einstein makes headlines as Milliken never did. Toynbee's popularity is to be reckoned with as Spengler's never was. Even Calvert whiskey has selected as Men of Distinction more artists, architects, writers, and commentators than it has industrialists or financiers. What we are headed for is a sort of social structure in which the highbrows are the elite,

From *Harper's*, **145** (February, 1949), pp. 175–180. Reprinted by permission of the author; copyright © 1949 by Harper's Magazine, Inc.

the middlebrows are the bourgeoisie, and the lowbrows are *hoi polloi*.

For the time being this is perhaps largely an urban phenomenon, and the true middlebrow may readily be mistaken in the small community for a genuine highbrow, but the pattern is emerging with increasing clarity, and the new distinctions do not seem to be based either on money or on breeding. Some lowbrows are as rich as Billy Rose, and as flamboyant, some as poor as Rosie O'Grady, and as modest. Some middlebrows run industries; some run the women's auxiliary of the Second Baptist Church. Some highbrows eat caviar with their Proust; some eat hamburger when they can afford it. It is true that most highbrows are in the ill-paid professions, notably the academic, and that most middlebrows are at least reasonably well off. Only the lowbrows can be found in about equal percentages at all financial levels. There may be a time, of course, when the highbrows will be paid in accordance with their own estimate of their worth, but that is not likely to happen in any form of society in which creature comforts are in greater demand than intellectual uplift. Like poets they will have to be content mostly with prestige. The middlebrows are influential today, but neither the highbrows nor the lowbrows like them; and if we ever have intellectual totalitarianism, it may well be the lowbrows and the highbrows who will run things, and the middlebrows who will be exiled in boxcars to a collecting point probably in the vicinity of Independence, Missouri.

While this social shift is still in its early stages, and the dividing lines are still indistinct and the species not yet frozen, let us assume a rather lofty position, examine the principal categories, with their subdivisions and splinter groups, and see where we ourselves are likely to fetch up in the new order.

Highbrow

The highbrows come first. Edgar Wallace, who was certainly not a highbrow himself, was asked by a newspaper reporter in Hollywood some years ago to define one. "What is a highbrow?" he said. "A highbrow is a man who has found something more interesting than women."

Presumably at some time in every man's life there are things he finds more interesting than women; alcohol, for example, or the World Series. Mr. Wallace has only partially defined the highbrow. Brander Matthews came closer when he said that "a highbrow is a person educated beyond his intelligence," and A. P. Herbert came closest of all when he wrote that "a highbrow is the kind of person who looks at a sausage and thinks of Picasso."

It is this association of culture with every aspect of daily life, from the design of his razor to the shape of the bottle that holds his sleeping pills, that distinguishes the highbrow from the middlebrow or the lowbrow. Spiritually and intellectually the highbrow inhabits a precinct well up the slopes of Parnassus, and his view of the cultural scene is from above. His vision pinpoints certain lakes and quarries upon which his special affections are concentrated—a perturbed lake called Rilke or a deserted quarry called Kierkegaard—but he believes that he sees them, as he sees the functional design of his razor, always in relation to the broader cultural scene. There is a certain air of omniscience about the highbrow, though that air is in many cases the thin variety encountered on the tops of high mountains from which the view is extensive but the details are lost.

You cannot tell a man that he is a lowbrow any more than you can tell a woman that her clothes are in bad taste, but a highbrow does not mind being called a highbrow. He has worked hard, read widely, traveled far, and listened attentively in order to satisfy his curiosity and establish his squatters' rights in this little corner of intellectualism, and he does not care who knows it. And this is true of both kinds of highbrow—the *militant,* or *crusader,* type and the *passive,* or *dilettante,* type. These types in general live happily together; the militant highbrow carries the torch of culture, the passive highbrow reads by its light.

The carrier of the torch makes a profession of being a highbrow and lives by his calling. He is most frequently found in university and college towns, a member of the liberal-arts faculty, teaching languages (ancient or modern), the fine arts, or literature. His spare time is often devoted to editing a magazine which is read mainly by other highbrows, ambitious undergraduates, and the editors of middlebrow publications in search of talent. When he writes for the magazine himself (or for another "little" magazine) it is usually criticism or criticism *of* criticism. He leaves the writing of fiction and poetry to others more bent on creation than on what has

been created, for the highbrow is primarily a critic and not an artist—a taster, not a cook. He is often more interested in where the arts have been, and where they are going, than in the objects themselves. He is devoted to the proposition that the arts must be pigeonholed, and that their trends should be plotted, or as W. H. Auden puts it—

> Our intellectual marines,
> Landing in Little Magazines,
> Capture a trend.

This gravitation of the highbrows to the universities is fairly recent. In the twenties, when the little magazines were devoted to publishing experimental writing rather than criticism of exhumed experimental writing, the highbrows flocked to Paris, New York, and Chicago. The *transatlantic review, transition,* and the *Little Review,* of the lower-case era of literature, were all published in Paris; *BROOM* was published in New York; *Poetry* was (and still is) published in Chicago. The principal little magazines now, with the exception of *Partisan Review,* a New York product but written mostly by academics, are published in the colleges— the *Kenyon Review,* the *Sewanee Review,* the *Virginia Quarterly,* and so on—and their flavor reflects this. But this does not mean that highbrows do not prefer the centers in which cultural activities are the most varied and active, and these are still London, Paris, New York, and more recently Rome. Especially in the fine arts, the highbrow has a chance to make a living in the metropolis where museums are centered and where art is bought and sold as well as created. This is also true of commercial publishing, in which many highbrows find suitable, if not congenial, refuge.

But no matter where they may make their homes, all highbrows live in a world which they believe is inhabited almost entirely by Philistines—those who through viciousness or smugness or the worship of materialism gnaw away at the foundations of culture. And the highbrow sees as his real enemy the middlebrow, whom he regards as a pretentious and frivolous man or woman who uses culture to satisfy social or business ambitions; who, to quote Clement Greenberg in *Partisan Review,* is busy "devaluating the precious, infecting the healthy, corrupting the honest, and stultifying the wise."

It takes a man who feels strongly to use such harsh words, but the militant highbrow has no patience with his enemies. He is a serious man who will not tolerate frivolity where the arts are concerned. It is part of his function as a highbrow to protect the arts from the culture-mongers, and he spits venom at those he suspects of selling the Muses short.

The fact that nowadays everyone has access to culture through schools and colleges, through the press, radio, and museums, disturbs him deeply; for it tends to blur the distinctions between those who are serious and those who are frivolous. "Culturally what we have," writes William Phillips in *Horizon,* "is a democratic free-for-all in which every individual, being as good as every other one, has the right to question any form of intellectual authority." To this Mr. Greenberg adds, "It becomes increasingly difficult to tell who is serious and who not."

The highbrow does not like to be confused, nor does he like to have his authority questioned, except by other highbrows of whose seriousness he is certain. The result is precisely what you would expect: the highbrows believe in, and would establish, an intellectual elite, "a fluid body of intellectuals . . . whose accepted role in society is to perpetuate traditional ideas and values and to create new ones." Such an elite would like to see the middlebrow eliminated, for it regards him as the undesirable element in our, and anybody else's, culture.

"It must be obvious to anyone that the volume and social weight of middlebrow culture," Mr. Greenberg writes, "borne along as it has been by the great recent increase in the American middle class, have multiplied at least tenfold in the past three decades. This culture presents a more serious threat to the genuine article than the old-time pulp dime novel, Tin Pan Alley, *Schund* variety ever has or will. Unlike the latter, which has its social limits clearly marked out for it, middlebrow culture attacks distinctions as such and insinuates itself everywhere. . . . Insidiousness is of its essence, and in recent years its avenues of penetration have become infinitely more difficult to detect and block."

By no means all highbrows are so intolerant or so desperate as this, or so ambitious for authority. Many of them, the passive ones, are merely consumers totally indifferent to the middlebrows or supercilious about them. Others without a great deal of hope but in ardent good faith expend themselves in endeavor to widen the circle of those who can enjoy the arts in their purest forms. Many museums, colleges, and publishing houses are at least partly staffed by highbrows who exert a more than half-hearted effort to make the arts exciting and important to the public. But they are aware that most of their labors are wasted. In his heart of hearts nearly every highbrow believes with Ortega y Gasset that "the average citizen [is] a creature incapable of receiving the sacrament of art, blind and deaf to pure beauty." When, for example, the Metropolitan Museum planned to expand its facilities a few years ago, an art dealer who can clearly be classified as a highbrow remarked: "All this means is less art for more people."

There are also many highbrows who are not concerned in the least with the arts or with literature, and who do not fret themselves about the upstart state of middlebrow culture. These are the specialized highbrows who toil in the remote corners of science and history, of philology and mathematics. They are concerned with their investigations of fruit-flies or Elizabethan taxation or whatever it may be, and they do not talk about them, as the dilettante always talks of the arts, to the first person they can latch onto at a cocktail party. When not in their laboratories or the library, they are often as not thoroughly middlebrow in their attitudes and tastes.

The real highbrow's way of life is as intellectualized as his way of thinking, and as carefully plotted. He is likely to be either extremely self-conscious about his physical surroundings and creature comforts or else sublimely, and rather ostentatiously, indifferent to them. If he

affects the former attitude, he will within the limits of his income surround himself with works of art. If he cannot afford paintings he buys drawings. Color reproductions, except as casual reminders tucked in the frame of a mirror or thrown down on a table, are beneath him. The facsimile is no substitute in his mind for the genuine, and he would rather have a slight sketch by a master, Braque or Picasso or even Jackson Pollack, than a fully-realized canvas by an artist he considers not quite first-rate. Drawings by his friends he hangs in the bathroom. His furniture, if it is modern, consists of identifiable pieces by Aalto, or Breuer, or Mies van der Rohe, or Eames; it does not come from department stores. If he finds modern unsympathetic, he will tend to use Biedermaier or the more "entertaining" varieties of Victorian, which he collects piece by piece with an eye to the slightly eccentric. If he has antiques, you may be sure they are not maple; the cult of "early American" is offensive to him.

The food that he serves will be planned with the greatest care, either very simple (a perfect French omelette made with sweet butter) or elaborate recipes from *Wine and Food* magazine published in London and edited by André Simon. If he cannot afford a pound of butter with every guinea fowl, he will in all probability resort to the casserole, and peasant cookery with the sparer parts of animals and birds seasoned meticulously with herbs that he gets from a little importer in the wholesale district. His wine is more likely to be a "perfectly adequate little red wine" for eighty-nine cents a half-gallon than an imported French vintage. (Anybody with good advice can buy French wines, but the discovery of a good domestic bottle shows perception and educated taste.) He wouldn't dream of washing his salad bowl. His collection of phonograph records is likely to bulk large at the ends and sag in the middle—a predominance of Bach-and-before at one end and Stravinsky, Schönberg, Bartok, and New Orleans jazz at the other. The nineteenth century is represented, perhaps, by Beethoven quartets and late sonatas, and some French "art songs" recorded by Maggie Teyte. His radio, if he has one, is turned on rarely; he wouldn't have a television set in the house.

The highbrow who disregards his creature comforts does it with a will. He lives with whatever furniture happens to come his way in a disorganized conglomeration of Victorian, department store, and Mexican bits and pieces. He takes care of his books in that he knows where each one is no matter in what disorder they may appear. Every other detail of domestic life he leaves to his wife, of whose taste he is largely unaware, and he eats what she gives him without comment. If he is a bachelor, he eats in a cafeteria or drugstore or diner and sometimes spills soup on the open pages of his book. He is oblivious to the man who sits down opposite him, and if Edgar Wallace is right, to the woman who shares his table. He is not a man without passions, but they have their place. Dress is a matter of indifference to him.

The highbrows about whom I have been writing are mainly consumers and not creators—editors, critics, and dilettantes. The creative artists who are generally considered highbrows—such men

as T. S. Eliot, E. M. Forster, Picasso, and Stravinsky—seem to me to fall in another category, that of the professional man who, while he may be concerned with communicating with a limited (and perhaps largely highbrow) audience, is primarily a doer and not a done-by. When Eliot or Forster or Picasso or Stravinsky sits down at his work-table, I do not know whether he says to himself, "I am going to create Art," but I very much doubt if that is what is in his mind. He is concerned rather with the communication of ideas within the frame of a poem, a novel, a painting, or a ballet suite, and if it turns out to be art (which many think it frequently does), that is to him a by-product of creation, an extra dividend of craftsmanship, intelligence, and sensibility. But when this happens he is taken up by the highbrow consumer and made much of. In fact he may become, whether he likes it or not, a vested interest, and his reputation will be every bit as carefully guarded by the highbrows as a hundred shares of Standard Oil of New Jersey by the middlebrows. He will be sold—at a par decided upon by the highbrows—to the middlebrows, who are natural gamblers in the commodities of culture.

In a sense it is this determination of par that is the particular contribution of the highbrow. Others may quarrel with his evaluations, but the fact remains that unless there were a relatively small group of self-appointed intellectuals who took it upon themselves to ransack the studios of artists, devour the manuscripts of promising writers, and listen at the keyholes of young composers, many talented men and women might pass unnoticed and our culture be the poorer. Their noncommercial attitude toward discovery of talent is useful, though they have an obsession with the evils of the monetary temptations with which America strews the artist's path. They stand as a wavering bulwark against the enticements of Hollywood and the advertising agencies, and they are saddened by the writers and painters who have set out to be serious men, as Hemingway did, and then become popular by being taken up by the middlebrows. They even go so far as to say that a story published in *Partisan Review* is a better story than if it were published in the *New Yorker* or *Harper's Bazaar,* for the reason that "what we have is at once a general raising and lowering of the level, for with the blurring of distinctions new writing tends to become more and more serious and intellectual and less and less bold and extreme. . . ."

This attitude, which is the attitude of the purist, is valuable. The ground in which the arts grow stays fertile only when it is fought over by both artists and consumers, and the phalanx of highbrows in the field, a somewhat impenetrable square of warriors, can be counted on to keep the fray alive.

LOWBROW

The highbrow's friend is the lowbrow. The highbrow enjoys and respects the lowbrow's art—jazz for instance—which he is likely to call a spontaneous expression of folk culture. The lowbrow is not interested, as the middlebrow is, in preempting any of the highbrow's func-

tion or in any way threatening to blur the lines between the serious and the frivolous. In fact he is almost completely oblivious of the highbrow unless he happens to be taken up by him—as many jazz musicians, primitive painters, and ballad writers have been—and then he is likely to be flattered, a little suspicious, and somewhat amused. A creative lowbrow like the jazz musician is a prominent citizen in his own world, and the fact that he is taken up by the highbrows has very little effect on his social standing therein. He is tolerant of the highbrow, whom he regards as somewhat odd and out-of-place in a world in which people do things and enjoy them without analyzing why or worrying about their cultural implications.

The lowbrow doesn't give a hang about art *qua* art. He knows what he likes, and he doesn't care why he likes it—which implies that all children are lowbrows. The word "beautiful," which has long since ceased to mean anything to the highbrow, is a perfectly good word to the lowbrow. Beautiful blues, beautiful sunsets, beautiful women, all things that do something to a man inside without passing through the mind, associations without allusions, illusions without implications. The arts created by the lowbrow are made in the expression of immediate pleasure or grief, like most forms of jazz; or of usefulness, like the manufacturing of a tool or a piece of machinery or even a bridge across the Hudson. The form, to use a highbrow phrase, follows the function. When the lowbrow arts follow this formula (which they don't always do), then the highbrow finds much in them to admire, and he calls it the *vernacular.* When, however, the lowbrow arts get mixed up with middlebrow ideas of culture, then the highbrow turns away in disgust. Look, for example, at what happened to the circus, a traditional form of lowbrow art. They got in Norman Bel Geddes to fancy it up, and now its special flavor of authenticity is gone—all wrapped up in pink middlebrow sequins. This is not to say that the lowbrow doesn't like it just as much as he ever did. It is the highbrow who is pained.

Part of the highbrow's admiration for the lowbrow stems from the lowbrow's indifference to art. This makes it possible for the highbrow to blame whatever he doesn't like about lowbrow taste on the middlebrow. If the lowbrow reads the comics, the highbrow understands; he is frequently a connoisseur of the comics himself. But if he likes grade-B double features, the highbrow blames that on the corrupting influence of the middlebrow moneybags of Hollywood. If he participates in give-away quiz programs, it is because the radio pollsters have decided that the average mental age of the listening audience is thirteen, and that radio is venal for taking advantage of the adolescent.

The lowbrow consumer, whether he is an engineer of bridges or a bus driver, wants to be comfortable and to enjoy himself without having to worry about whether he has good taste or not. It doesn't make any difference to him that a chair is a bad Grand Rapids copy of an eighteenth-century *fauteuil* as long as he's happy when he sits down in it. He doesn't care whether the movies are art, or the radio improving, so long as he has fun while he is giving them his attention and getting a fair return of

pleasure from his investment. It wouldn't occur to him to tell a novelist what kind of book he should write, or a movie director what kind of movie to make. If he doesn't like a book he ignores it; if he doesn't like a movie he says so, whether it is a "Blondie" show or "Henry V." If he likes jive or square-dancing, he doesn't worry about whether they are fashionable or not. If other people like the ballet, that's all right with him, so long as he doesn't have to go himself. In general the lowbrow attitude toward the arts is live and let live. Lowbrows are not Philistines. One has to know enough about the arts to argue about them with highbrows to be a Philistine.

UPPER MIDDLEBROW

The popular press, and also much of the unpopular press, is run by the middlebrows, and it is against them that the highbrow inveighs.

"The true battle," Virginia Woolf wrote in an unmailed letter to the *New Statesman*, ". . . lies not between highbrow and lowbrow, but between highbrows and lowbrows joined together in blood brotherhood against the bloodless and pernicious pest who comes between."

The pests divide themselves into two groups: the Upper Middlebrows and the Lower Middlebrows. It is the upper middlebrows who are the principal purveyors of highbrow ideas and the lower middlebrows who are the principal consumers of what the upper middlebrows pass along to them.

Many publishers, for example, are upper middlebrows—as are most educators, museum directors, movie producers, art dealers, lecturers, and the editors of most magazines which combine national circulation with an adult vocabulary. These are the men and women who devote themselves professionally to the dissemination of ideas and cultural artifacts and, not in the least incidentally, make a living along the way. They are the cultural do-gooders, and they see their mission clearly and pursue it with determination. Some of them are disappointed highbrows; some of them try to work both sides of the street; nearly all of them straddle the fence between highbrow and middlebrow and enjoy their equivocal position.

The conscientious publisher, for instance, believes in the importance of literature and the dignity of publishing as a profession. He spends a large part of his time on books that will not yield him a decent return on his investment. He searches out writers of promise; he pores over the "little" magazines (or pays other people to); he leafs through hundreds and hundreds of pages of manuscript. He advises writers, encourages them, coaxes them to do their best work; he even advances them money. But he is not able to be a publisher at all (unless he is willing to put his personal fortune at the disposal of financially naive muses) if he does not publish to make money. In order to publish slender volumes of poetry he must also publish fat volumes of historical romance, and in order to encourage the first novel of a promising young writer he must sell tens of thousands of copies of a book by an old hand who grinds out one best seller a year. He must take the measure of popular taste and cater

to it at the same time that he tries to create a taste for new talent. If he is a successful publisher he makes money, lives comfortably, patronizes the other arts, serves on museum boards and committees for the Prevention of This and the Preservation of That, contributes to the symphony, and occasionally buys pictures by contemporary painters.

The highbrow suspects that the publisher does not pace his book-lined office contriving ways to serve the muses and that these same muses have to wait their turn in line until the balance sheet has been served. He believes that the publisher is really happy only when he can sell a couple of hundred thousand copies of a novel about a hussy with a horsewhip or a book on how to look forty when forty-five. To the highbrow he is a tool to be cultivated and used, but not to be trusted.

The museum director is in much the same position, caught between the muses and the masses. If he doesn't make a constant effort to swell the door-count, his middlebrow trustees want to know why he isn't serving the community; if he does, the highbrows want to know why he is pandering to popular taste and not minding his main business—the service of scholarship and the support of artists currently certified to be "serious." Educators are in the same position, bound to be concerned with mass education often at the expense of the potential scholar, and editors of all magazines except those supported by private angels or cultural institutions know that they must not only enlighten but entertain if they are to have enough readers to pay the bills. To the highbrow this can lead to nothing but compromise and mediocrity.

The upper-middlebrow consumer takes his culture seriously, as seriously as his job allows, for he is gainfully employed. In his leisure hours he reads Toynbee or Sartre or Osbert Sitwell's serialized memoirs. He goes to museum openings and to the theater and he keeps up on the foreign films. He buys pictures, sometimes old masters if he can afford them, sometimes contemporary works. He has a few etchings and lithographs, and he is not above an occasional color reproduction of a Van Gogh or a Cézanne. Writers and painters are his friends and dine at his house; if, however, his own son were to express an interest in being an artist, he would be dismayed ("so few artists ever really pull it off")— though he would keep a stiff upper lip and hope the boy would learn better before it was too late. His house is tastefully decorated, sometimes in the very latest mode, a model of the modern architect's dream of functionalism, in which case he can discourse on the theory of the open plan and the derivations of the international style with the zest and uncertain vocabulary of a convert. If his house is "traditional" in character, he will not put up with Grand Rapids copies of old pieces; he will have authentic ones, and will settle for Victorian if he cannot afford Empire. He, or his wife, will ransack second-hand shops for entertaining bibelots and lamps or a piece of Brussels carpet for the bedroom. He never refers to curtains as "drapes." He talks about television as potentially a new art form, and he listens to the Saturday afternoon opera broadcasts. His library contains a few of the more respectable current best sellers which he reads out of "curiosity" rather than interest. (Membership in any sort of book club he considers beneath him.) There are a few shelves of first editions, some of them autographed by friends who have dined at his house, some of them things (like a presentation copy of *Jurgen*) that he "just happened to pick up," and a sampling of American and British poets. There is also a shelf of paper-bound French novels—most of them by nineteenth-century writers. The magazines on his table span the areas from *Time* and the *New Yorker* to *Harper's* and the *Atlantic,* with an occasional copy of the *Yale* and *Partisan Reviews,* and the *Art News.*

From this it can be seen that he supports the highbrows—buys some of the books they recommend and an occasional picture they have looked upon with favor—and contributes to organized efforts to promote the arts both by serving on boards and shelling out money. In general he is modest about expressing his opinion on cultural matters in the presence of highbrows but takes a slightly lordly tone when he is talking to other middlebrows. If he discovers a "little" painter or poet, the chances are excellent that the man has already been discovered and promoted by a highbrow or by an upper-middlebrow entrepreneur (art dealer or publisher). Once in a while he will take a flyer on an unknown artist, and hang his picture inconspicuously in the bedroom. He takes his function as a patron of the arts seriously, but he does it for the pleasure it gives him to be part of the cultural scene. If he does it for "money, fame, power, or prestige," as Virginia Woolf says he does, these motives are so obscured by a general sense of well-being and well-meaning that he would be shocked and surprised to be accused of venality.

LOWER MIDDLEBROW

If the upper middlebrow is unsure of his own tastes, but firm in his belief that taste is extremely important, the lower middlebrow is his counterpart. The lower middlebrow ardently believes that he knows what he likes, and yet his taste is constantly susceptible to the pressures that put him in knickerbockers one year and rust-colored slacks the next. Actually he is unsure about almost everything, especially about what he likes. This may explain his pronouncements on taste, which he considers an effete and questionable virtue, and his resentment of the arts; but it may also explain his strength.

When America and Americans are characterized by foreigners and highbrows, the middlebrows are likely to emerge as the dominant group in our society—a dreadful mass of insensible back-slappers, given to sentimentality as a prime virtue, the willing victims of slogans and the whims of the bosses, both political and economic. The picture painted by middlebrow exploiters of the middlebrow, such as the advertisers of nationally advertised brands, is strikingly similar to that painted by the highbrow; their attitudes and motives are quite different (the highbrow paints with a snarl, the advertiser with a gleam), but they both make the middlebrow out to be much the same kind of creature. The villain of the highbrow and the hero of the advertisers is en-

visaged as "the typical American family"—happy little women, happy little children, all spotless or sticky in the jam pot, framed against dimity curtains in the windows or decalcomania flowers on the cupboard doors. Lower-middlebrowism is a world pictured without tragedy, a world of new two-door sedans, and Bendix washers, and reproductions of hunting prints over the living-room mantel. It is a world in which the ingenuity and patience of the housewife are equaled only by the fidelity of her husband and his love of home, pipe, and radio. It is a world that smells of soap. But it is a world of ambition as well, the constant striving for a better way of life—better furniture, bigger refrigerators, more books in the bookcase, more evenings at the movies. To the advertisers this is Americanism; to the highbrows this is the dead weight around the neck of progress, the gag in the mouth of art.

The lower middlebrows are not like this, of course, and unlike the highbrows and the upper middlebrows, whose numbers are tiny by comparison, they are hard to pin down. They live everywhere, rubbing elbows with lowbrows in apartment houses like vast beehives, in row houses all alike from the outside except for the planting, in large houses at the ends of gravel driveways, in big cities, in medium cities and suburbs, and in small towns, from Boston to San Francisco, from Seattle to Jacksonville. They are the members of the book clubs who read difficult books along with racy and innocuous ones that are sent along by Messrs. Fadiman, Canby, Beecroft *et al.* They are the course-takers who swell the enrollments of adult education classes in everything from "The Technique of the Short Story" to "Child Care." They are the people who go to hear the lecturers that swarm out from New York lecture bureaus with tales of travel on the Dark Continent and panaceas for saving the world from a fate worse than capitalism. They eat in tea shoppes and hold barbecues in their backyards. They are hell-bent on improving their minds as well as their fortunes. They decorate their homes under the careful guidance of *Good Housekeeping* and the *Ladies' Home Journal,* or, if they are well off, of *House and Garden,* and are subject to fads in furniture so long as these don't depart too radically from the traditional and the safe, from the copy of Colonial and the reproduction of Sheraton. In matters of taste, the lower-middlebrow world is largely dominated by women. They select the furniture, buy the fabrics, pick out the wallpapers, the pictures, the books, the china. Except in the selection of his personal apparel and the car, it is almost *infra dig* for a man to have taste; it is not considered quite manly for the male to express opinions about things which come under the category of "artistic."

Nonetheless, as a member of the school board or the hospital board he decides which design shall be accepted when a new building goes up. The lower middlebrows are the organizers of the community fund, the members of the legislature, the park commissioners. They pay their taxes and they demand services in return. There are millions of them, conscientious stabilizers of society, slow to change, slow to panic. But they are not as predictable as either the highbrows or the bosses, political or economic, think they are. They can be led, they can be seduced, but they cannot be pushed around.

Highbrow, lowbrow, upper middlebrow, and lower middlebrow—the lines between them are sometimes indistinct, as the lines between upper class, lower class, and middle class have always been in our traditionally fluid society. But gradually they are finding their own levels and confining themselves more and more to the company of their own kind. You will not find a highbrow willingly attending a Simon & Schuster cocktail party any more than you will find an upper middlebrow at a Rotary Club luncheon or an Elks' picnic.

The highbrows would like, of course, to eliminate the middlebrows and devise a society that would approximate an intellectual feudal system in which the lowbrows do the work and create folk arts, and the highbrows do the thinking and create fine arts. All middlebrows, presumably, would have their radios taken away, be suspended from society until they had agreed to give up their subscriptions to the Book-of-the-Month, turned their color reproductions over to a Commission for the Dissolution of Middlebrow Taste, and renounced their affiliation with all educational and other cultural institutions whatsoever. They would be taxed for the support of all writers, artists, musicians, critics, and critics-of-criticism whose production could be certified "serious"—said writers, artists, musicians, and critics to be selected by representatives of qualified magazines with circulations of not more than five thousand copies. Middlebrows, both upper and lower, who persisted in "devaluating the precious, infecting the healthy, corrupting the honest, and stultifying the wise" would be disposed of forthwith.

But the highbrows haven't a chance; things have gone too far. Everybody but the genuine lowbrow (who is more wooed than wedded by the highbrow) is jockeying for position in the new cultural class order. *Life* magazine, sensing the trend, has been catching us up on the past of Western Civilization in sixteen-page, four-color capsules. *Mademoiselle* walks off with the first prizes in the annual short-story contests. The Pepsi-Cola Company stages the most elaborate and highest-paying art competition in the country. Even *Partisan Review,* backed by a new angel, runs full-page ads in the *New York Times* Book Review. The Book-of-the-Month Club ships out a couple of hundred thousand copies of Toynbee's *A Study of History* as "dividends."

If life for grandmother, who wouldn't dine with the Cartiers, was simple in its social distinctions, life is becoming equally simple for us. The rungs of the ladder may be different, it may even be a different ladder, but it's onward and upward just the same. You may not be known by which fork you use for the fish these days, but you will be known by which key you use for your *Finnegans Wake.*

Sex, Marriage, and Social Class

WILLIAM SIMON AND JOHN GAGNON

	Highbrow	Upper Middlebrow
How Girl Meets Boy	He was an usher at her best friend's wedding	At college, in the psychology lab
The Proposal	In his room during the Harvard-Princeton game	In the back seat of a Volkswagen
The Wedding	In her living room, by a federal judge	College chapel (nondenominational)
The Honeymoon	Mediterranean	Bahamas
Marriage Manual	*Kama Sutra*	*Sexual Efficiency in Marriage,* volumes I and II
Sex Novels She Reads	Jane Austen	*Lady Chatterley's Lover*
Sleeping Arrangements	Double bed	King-size bed or twin beds with one headboard
Sleeping Attire	He: nothing. She: nothing	He: red turtleneck nightshirt. She: gown with matching peignoir
Background Music	Ravi Shankar or the Beatles	Wagner
Turn-Ons	Pot	Champagne and oysters
The Schedule	Spontaneously, on an average of 2.5 weekly (that means 2 times one week and 3 times another)	Twice a week and when the kids go to the Sunday matinee
Number of Children	1 each by a previous marriage, or as many as God provides	2.4
Anniversary Celebrations	A weekend in Dublin	He gives her a new dishwasher. She gives him a power lawn mower
Quarrels	"I don't care what your analyst says"	"I don't care if he is your brother"
If the Marriage Needs Help	He consults her analyst. She consults his	They go (a) to a marriage counselor; (b) to the minister
The Affair	"But I assumed you knew"	"It was basically a problem in communication"
Sex Education	"Ask Doctor Grauber, dear, when you see him tomorrow"	"Well, you see, Daddy has something called a . . . etc. And Daddy and Mommy love each other very much"
Vacations	Europe in May. She takes the children to the Cape. He commutes	Europe in July. Family camping in Yosemite
Financial Arrangements	Separate trust funds	Joint checking account
Who Raises the Children	English nanny, boarding school, and Dr. Grauber	Mommy and Daddy, Cub Scouts, and Dr. Freud

From William Simon and John Gagnon, "How Fashionable Is Your Sex Life?," *McCall's,* **94** (October 1969), pp. 58–59. Reprinted by permission of the authors and *McCall's.*

Lower Middlebrow	Lowbrow
In the office, by the water cooler	On the block
After three drinks in an apartment he borrowed	In her home one night when Mom and Dad were at the movies
City Hall	Neighborhood church
Any Hilton hotel	Disneyland
Van de Velde	None
Myra Breckinridge and any novel by Harold Robbins	*Valley of the Dolls*
Twin beds with matching night tables	Double bed
He: pajamas. She: pajamas	He: underwear. She: nightgown
Sound track of *Dr. Zhivago*	Jackie Gleason and the Silver Strings
Manhattans and whisky sours	Beer
Twice a week and when the kids go to Sunday school	Twice on Saturday night
3	As many as God provides
Corsage and dinner out	Whitman Sampler and dinner at Howard Johnson's
"What do you think I'm made of?"	"Drop dead!"
He: to his successful brother. She: to her best friend	He: to the bartender. She: to her mother
"It was bigger than both of us"	"Some things no woman should have to put up with"
"Well, you see, Daddy puts the seed in Mommy's tummy, etc., etc."	"We got you at the hospital"
He hunts or fishes. She visits Mother with the children	They visit Brother Charlie in Des Moines
She budgets	He gets weekly allowance
Mom and Dad, the Little League, and Dr. Spock	Mom, the gang, Ann Landers, and good luck

Political ideology is also a component of life style: for some it is their central life interest, while others are apolitical. Political ideologies generally are predictable from other aspects of life style. The American ideology of equal opportunity may be thought of as an important element of a shared American life style. This ideology affirms that individuals are free to choose their way of life, restricted only by their own limits of ability and initiative. From the "diversity perspective" comes the prediction that the rich are different from the poor; the rich are likely to believe that everyone in the United States has opportunity, while the poor feel that opportunity is denied them. In the following article by Rytina, Form, and Pease, belief in the American ideology of equal opportunity is investigated.

Income and Stratification Ideology: Beliefs about the American Opportunity Structure[1]

JOAN HUBER RYTINA,
WILLIAM H. FORM, AND
JOHN PEASE

IDEOLOGY AND STRATIFICATION

Social stratification may be defined as the generational persistence of unequal distribution of valued rewards in a society. An ideology is a set of emotionally held beliefs and myths that account for social reality. The ideology of a stratification system explains and vindicates the distribution of rewards in an actual society or in a society believed to be possible,[2] and contains both normative and existential statements about the way things ought to be and the way things really are.[3] Thus, in American society a man who works hard ought to get ahead, does get ahead, and in getting ahead proves he has worked hard. By definition, then, a dominant stratification ideology justifies the distribution of power and rewards in the society. Transmitted by the communication and educational channels, this ideology becomes the "public ideology" which most social scientists study.

The integrative function of an ideology is high when all strata of the society support its tenets and concur in its mode

From *American Journal of Sociology* (1970), pp. 703–716. Reprinted by permission of the American Journal of Sociology, University of Chicago Press.
[1] This project was supported by grant no. 91-24-66-45 from the U.S. Department of Labor, Office of Manpower Policy, Evaluation and Research, pursuant to the provisions of the Manpower Development and Training Act of 1962. We are grateful for the department's support.

[2] We do not follow Mannheim's distinction of ideology as a myth of an ongoing system and utopia as a myth of a system believed to be possible (Mannheim, 1954).
[3] For the elaboration of concepts of normative and existential elements in ideology, see Form and Rytina (1969).

of application.[4] Ideologies lose this integrative character when people in various strata either reject the goals implicit in the ideology or believe that its tenets have little or no validity; that is, when they feel that the institutions of a society are failing to implement desired societal goals.

The major assumption of this study is that all strata in the United States generally accept the normative tenets of the American ideology of equality of opportunity, the description of how things ought to be. But we expected some reservation, especially among lower strata, in accepting the idea that American institutions are effective in implementing the opportunity norms. Probably most adults in literate societies tend to test their life situations against the existing ideology. Since the symmetry between normative and existential tenets of an ideology is generally higher for upper strata, they are less inclined to test the validity of its existential tenets. The reverse situation probably is true for lower strata. In closely integrated social systems, the differences among the strata may be small, especially if the stratification ideology is buttressed by religious beliefs, as in the Indian caste system. In such cases one may indeed speak of a "theodicy of stratification," or the need to justify the suffering resulting from the inequality which God has ordained (Weber, 1946, pp. 275–277). In urban-

secular societies, strata will probably vary in the degree that they test the validity of an ideology's existential tenets.

Most sociologists probably assume there is wide support for the normative aspects of the ideology of equal opportunity (Smelser, 1967, p. 8; Lipset, 1963, p. 101), but current unrest among some segments of American society indicates that belief in some aspects may be more problematical (Miller and Rein, 1966). Clearly, most studies have tested adherence to the ideology as it is expressed in general, ideal, or normative terms. It is relatively easy to obtain a consensus with regard to vague statements on how a system ought to and does operate.[5] Such statements, especially as presented in most public opinion studies, do not concretize the tenets of an ideology. The acid test of a system which offers money as its main reward, especially from the point of view of people in lower strata, is whether a person who is poor has the same opportunities as a person who has more money. The problem for this research was to devise a technique which permitted people to respond to both (*a*) general statements about how the American opportunity system operates and (*b*) specific statements of how the system operates for persons in different economic strata.

RESEARCH DESIGN

Two major hypotheses guided this research: (1) all income strata will tend

---

[4]The idea that an ideology plays a societal integrative function and the idea that an ideology serves to consolidate the power of an elite parallel two conceptions of the function of a stratification system: as a societal integrator (Parsons, 1953) and as a political formula of the elite (Mosca, 1966, p. 240).

[5]Ossowski (1963, pp. 110–113) has pointed out that on a high level of generality the normative structure of the American and Soviet stratification systems are very similar.

to agree more with highly generalized statements than with situationally specific statements about the operation of the American opportunity system, but (2) lower strata will show less agreement than higher strata with both types of statements. This hypothesis was based on the proposition that for most people income is the most salient stratification variable.

The major areas of ideology explored were:

1. The existence of an open opportunity structure in the United States, the equality of chances for upward and downward occupational mobility, and the relative opportunity for mobility in the United States and in Europe. These areas focus on beliefs concerning the relative openness of the economic institution.
2. The relative accessibility of educational resources to all strata as the vehicle for mobility.
3. The impartial functioning of the political and legal systems.
4. Personal or social responsibility for economic status or rank. We hypothesized that those with higher incomes support tenets of personal responsibility for a person's economic status, while the poor place greater reliance on social structural explanations, which would follow from the belief that, for the poor, the economic, educational, political, and legal institutions fail to operate in accord with democratic norms of equality of opportunity.

Annual family income was used as the major independent variable in this study for two reasons:

First, one of our research aims was to discover how poor people perceive the structure of economic opportunity; for poor people, the most salient reward of the stratification system is probably income. If income is combined with incommensurate variables, such as occupation or education, the synthetic scale that results "will be concerned with social consciousness rather than objective position" (Ossowski, 1963, p. 56). However adapted to a particular environment, there is no a priori way of knowing whether the components of the scale have equal salience for all strata.[6] Annual family income, however, cannot be equated with class situation as Weber defined it (Weber, 1946, p. 181), nor is monetary income a completely adequate indicator of the economic position of a person (Miller and Rein, 1966, p. 433); nevertheless, although the income data obtained for this study are inexact,[7] they are sufficient to classify a respondent as rich, middle income, or poor.

The second reason for using income as the major variable is that we wanted to discover whether the rich support the tenets in the stratification ideology differently than other strata. Because they are a small part of the population and, consequently, of samples, most studies include the rich in a stratum with persons whose income is only a few thousand dollars above median family income. Yet the opinions of the rich may have disproportionate influence because

---

[6]Ossowski (1963, p. 55) says that a synthetic scale is the result of the predilections of the evaluating individual because "in different social classes the particular criteria of class affiliation carry a different weight."

[7]For example, we obtained information only on the incomes of the household head and/or spouse, not for other dependents. Nor did we attempt to obtain information on income-in-kind.

they contribute great financial support to political parties.[8] Such an assumption enables one to interpret the finding of McClosky et al. (1960, p. 416) that, on social welfare measures, Republican followers tend to have much the same opinions as Democratic followers, while Republican leaders are far more conservative. A reasonable assumption is that the leaders reflect the views of those who support them financially, namely, the rich.

Finally, our problem was to construct interview items which would elicit adherence to general and situational tenets in the ideology of opportunity. Because statements derived from the dominant ideology tend to sound like clichés, they probably represent "what everybody knows," and, consequently, most respondents would tend to agree with them. Such general statements are often not meaningfully nullifiable. For example, the statement, "Ambitious boys can generally get ahead," does not specify whether "getting ahead" means rising a few points on the NORC scale or crossing a major occupational boundary (e.g., from clerical to professional). In order to obtain a more meaningful response, we elaborated a technique developed by Prothro and Grigg (1960) and Westie (1965), who presented highly generalized normative statements followed by specific ones of application. An example of a general statement is, "Minorities

should be free to criticize the majority," while a specific statement is, "If a person wants to make a speech against churches and religion in this city, he should be permitted to."

In using this technique, we first presented to respondents a highly generalized statement on opportunity derived from the dominant ideology; later in the interview we presented a statement similar in logical content but specifically linking opportunity and income. All statements were worded in "either-or" form because some investigators have suggested that lower-class people tend to agree with any positive statement regardless of substantive content (Campbell et al., 1960, pp. 510–515; Christie and Jahoda, 1954).

Respondents were heads of households or their spouses who, in December 1966–January 1967, lived in the area included in *Polk's City Directory* (1965) for Muskegon, Michigan, an industrial community whose Standard Metropolitan Statistical Area population in 1960 was 149,943. For the larger study of which this report is a part, a systematic sample (N = 186) was drawn. Because such samples typically include few respondents at income extremes, we drew supplementary samples of rich and poor.[9] The small number of rich in the systematic sample did not justify running statistical tests of significance for income strata. "Rich" was defined as annual family income of $25,000 or more which, in the 1959 Census, was the top 1 percent of the income distribution. "Poor" was defined in terms of a scale

---

[8]Heard (1962, pp. 46–48) says that "it has long been realized that the bulk of the income received by formally organized *national-level* campaign groups from individual contributors has arrived in sums of $500 or more. . . . Only people of means can make even a $100 contribution. Consequently, the forces of wealth dominate the political life of the nation."

[9]Any definition of poverty is arbitrary. For definitions similar to the one used, see Keyserling (1964), Orshansky (1965), and Miller (1965).

adjusted for the number of dependents; for example, a respondent was poor if his annual family income was less than $3,500 for four persons.

The analytic sample (N = 354) upon which this paper is based consisted of the systematic sample and the supplementary samples of rich and poor. By strata of income and race, the analytic sample included 37 poor Negroes, 70 poor whites, 48 middle-income Negroes, 152 middle-income whites, and 47 rich whites. The per capita income for the Negro poor was $671; for the white poor, $907; for middle-income Negroes, $1,591; for middle-income whites, $2,310; for rich whites, over $6,000. The sex division in each stratum was almost even. Education was associated with income: three-fifths of the respondents with 0–7 years of education were poor, and three-fifths of the college graduates were rich. We shall report Negro responses separately because there is ample evidence that Negro and white experiences with the opportunity structure differ greatly. All findings must be regarded with great caution because of the small sample.

FINDINGS

Background findings show that about three-fourths of the respondents in all income strata liked Muskegon as a place to live and work. Respondents were also asked to identify themselves as middle, lower, working, or upper class.[10] A little more than half identified with the work-

[10]The question was adapted from Centers (1949). For a discussion of the consequences of using a forced choice or free choice question to ascertain class identification, see Gross (1949).

ing class, and a little less than half with the middle class. In a series of questions designed to tap interest in making money, Negroes and poor whites showed the highest interest, and larger proportions of them reported having fewer economic opportunities than "other people." These and other data point to the importance of money to lower-income strata and their feelings of economic deprivation. These feelings are also reflected in their attitudes toward economic opportunity.

Beliefs in the Tenets of Economic Opportunity

Three tenets of the ideology of economic opportunity were explored: the importance of working hard for "getting ahead," the relevance of father's occupation to getting ahead, and whether occupational mobility is easier in the United States than in European countries. According to the main hypothesis, we expected more agreement with the general statements than with the specific statements, but we also expected respondents with higher incomes to show greater agreement to ideological tenets, however stated.

A general statement on economic opportunity was adopted from Campbell et al. (1954, p. 221):

> *Some people say there's not much opportunity in America today—that the average man doesn't have much chance to really get ahead. Others say there's plenty of opportunity and anyone who works hard can go as far as he wants. How do you feel?*

From this statement we derived an income-linked specification:

Do you think that a boy whose father is poor and a boy whose father is rich have the same opportunity to make the same amount of money if they work equally hard, or do you think that the boy whose father is rich has a better chance of earning a lot more money?

In response to the general statement, over eight-tenths of the white respondents and less than six-tenths of the Negroes thought that America is a land of equal opportunity (see Table 1). But in response to the income-linked statement, almost three-fifths of the rich, a half of middle-income and poor whites, and less than one-fifth of the Negroes thought that rich and poor boys had equal opportunity (see Table 1).

Since sociologists commonly use occupation of father rather than family income as the base point for studies of occupational mobility, we decided to ask respondents about the relationship of father's occupation to mobility. Situational questions reflected significant mobility, that is, crossing a major occupational stratum boundary.

The first question pertained to upward occupational mobility:

Who do you think are more likely to become business executives and professional men: the sons of big business executives and professional men, or the sons of factory workers and small businessmen?

TABLE 1

BELIEFS ON CHANCES TO GET AHEAD AND TO GO TO COLLEGE
BY INCOME AND RACE (PERCENTAGES)

Income and Race	Plenty of Opportunity (General) (a)	Rich and Poor Have Equal Opportunity (Income-Linked) (b)	Equal Opportunity for College (General) (c)	Poor as Likely to Be in College (Income-Linked) (d)
Poor:				
Negro	56	11	22	11
White	90	47	57	38
Middle:				
Negro	58	21	41	28
White	80	49	75	37
Rich:				
White	93	57	96	43
Total, analytic sample:				
%	78	42	64	34
(N)	(342)	(351)	(348)	(344)
Total, systematic sample:*				
%	76	41	69	38
(N)	(177)	(184)	(184)	(181)

*For race, col. (a)—χ^2 = 4.35, df = 1, $p < .05$; col. (b)—χ^2 = 4.03, df = 1, $p < .05$; col. (c)—χ^2 = 4.91, df = 1, $p < .05$.

The second situational question pertained to downward occupational mobility:

> *Who do you think are more likely to become factory workers and small businessmen: the sons of factory workers and small businessmen, or the sons of big businessmen and professionals?*

The questions must have appeared almost fatuous to the respondents, because nine-tenths or more of all income groups felt that occupational inheritance was more likely than upward or downward occupational mobility (see Table 2). Although none of the poor Negroes thought that sons of fathers in lower occupational strata had more chances for upward mobility than other

sons, almost one-fifth of them thought that sons of executives had more chances for downward mobility than sons of fathers in lower strata. Perhaps there is some comfort in the thought that, if one's own sons are not likely to rise, the sons of men in prestigious occupations may fall. We may well ask, if the question used in the interview situation seemed fatuous, do similar general or normative statements of the ideology repeated in everyday life also appear fatuous? Surely people must test public ideologies against their daily life experiences.

Popular patriotic orators often proclaim that opportunity is greater in America than in European countries.

TABLE 2
BELIEFS CONCERNING GENERATIONAL MOBILITY AND OPPORTUNITY STRUCTURE
IN AMERICA COMPARED WITH EUROPE, BY INCOME AND RACE
(PERCENTAGE WHO AGREE)

Income and Race	Blue-Collar Son More Likely to Become Executive (a)	Executive Son More Likely to Become Blue-Collar (b)	Opportunity Better in America (c)
Poor:			
Negro	0	19	16
White	11	6	9
Middle:			
Negro	4	4	7
White	8	3	19
Rich:			
White	9	0	30
Total, analytic sample:			
%	7	5	16
(N)	(344)	(347)	(351)
Total, systematic sample:*			
%	6	2	15
(N)	(178)	(180)	(184)

*For middle income and poor, col. (c)—χ^2 = 4.95, df = 1, $p < .05$.

Lipset and Rogoff have presented evidence casting doubt on the validity of such proclamations, but they nevertheless assumed that the belief was "traditional and universal" in the United States (Lipset and Rogoff, 1954; Lipset and Bendix, 1959). On the assumption that this belief is most supportive to the strata which have "made it," we predicted that the rich would be most likely to believe it and the poor least likely. Using situated class referents, we asked the respondents:

Do you believe that ambitious sons of lower-class fathers are able to rise into the middle class in most European countries like Germany, France, and England, or do you think that such ambitious boys can rise only in the United States?

Unfortunately, the statement used did not call for a judgment of relative mobility rates, although some respondents (mainly, 19 percent of the rich and 32 percent of college graduates) gave a free response, indicating that mobility was possible in Europe but easier in the United States. About one-sixth of the total sample responded that mobility was possible only in the United States, or that it was easier, but three-tenths of the rich and four-tenths of the college graduates endorsed the "myth" (see Table 2). The responses obtained to this question cast some doubt on the universal acceptance of the idea that the United States has a more open opportunity structure than Europe.

In conclusion, the responses to the three statements on economic opportunity indicate considerable range and certainly no unanimity in support of the public ideology. Moreover, when family income and father's occupation are specifically mentioned in ideological statements, the degree of support for them is greatly reduced. Yet the rich consistently see greater equality of opportunity than the poor, except in the occupational structure, where the bulk of the respondents, rich and poor, white and Negro, see the general tendency of occupational inheritance. Even when the opportunity structure of the United States is compared with that of Europe, there is a general consensus that little or no difference exists.

Operation of Educational, Governmental, and Legal Institutions

A basic tenet of the ideology of opportunity is that educational resources needed for occupational mobility are equally available to all. Similarly, the government, the law, and the courts are supposedly blind to conditions of birth. General and situated questions involving education, government, and the law were devised to tap how different economic strata evaluated their functioning.

The general statement on education concerned the chance to go to college:

Do you feel that all young people of high ability have fairly equal opportunity to go to college, or do you feel that a large percentage of young people do not have much opportunity to go to college?

The income-specific corollary was:

Do you think that most young people in college come from families who can give them financial help or do you think that young people whose parents are poor are just as likely to be in college as anyone else?

The pattern of responses to the general question was similar to that dealing with economic opportunity, that is, greater support by the higher income strata and the whites. However, the range of responses among the strata was much greater, from one-fifth support by poor Negroes to total support among the rich (see Table 1). For the income-linked statement, there was a uniform decrease in support by all income groups, about one-half the proportions agreeing with the general statements. Responses to both types of statements show a much smaller degree of confidence in equal access to education in the United States than the literature suggests (Cremin, 1951; Coleman, 1968; Williams, 1967).

Education is primarily governmentally sponsored in the United States. Does this relative lack of confidence in the ability of the educational institution to function equitably hold for government itself? A basic tenet of democratic ideology is that the imperfections in the system are reparable—that the system is self-adjusting in response to inequities because voters are able to demand and generally get what they think the system should supply. The market analogy is clear. People who are trained to believe in political pluralism feel that all income strata should have equal influence on the operations of government and other social institutions. To explore adherence to this tenet, we prepared the following general statement on the opportunity to obtain political equality through participation in the electoral process:

Some people think that voting is a vital part of the governmental process in this country, while others think it really doesn't make much difference who gets

elected because the same people go on running things anyway. What do you think?

The income-linked specification:

Some people say that, regardless of who gets elected, people who are rich get their way most of the time, while others say that people who are poor have just as much influence in government as people who are rich. What do you think?

Almost nine-tenths of all the respondents thought that voting was vital, the rich most of all and the poor Negroes least of all (see Table 3). Agreement with the specific statement shifted dramatically downward, with only three-tenths supporting it. The lower the income strata, the less the belief that wealth played no role in influencing governmental policies. Poor whites were the exception, for their rate of support was the same as middle-income whites. Similar findings appeared for different educational levels. However, the range of differences among the educational strata was smaller than for the income strata, and this again points to the "softening effect" of the educational variable.

Equality before the law was the last institutional tenet of American ideology we examined. The general statement was:

A number of people believe that in America everyone gets equal and fair treatment from the law, while others believe that the police and courts are basically unfair in the administration of justice. What do you think?

The income-linked corollary:

Do you think that, if he breaks the law, a rich man is just as likely to end up in jail as a poor man, or do you think it's a lot easier for a rich man to stay out of jail?

A clear majority of the white respondents, irrespective of income, agreed to the general statement, but only a minority of the poor and middle-income Negroes agreed (see Table 3). In the income-linked corollary, the data clearly reveal that all income strata do not support the tenet of a fair legal system, for only one-fifth or less of the respondents in all strata felt that the courts operated equitably. When responses to the general and situated questions dealing with the legislative branch of government are compared with those dealing with the courts, there seems to

be considerably less confidence in the operation of the judicial branch of government.

Why Are the Rich, Rich and the Poor, Poor?

What makes some people rich and others poor? The implications of this question are political. The traditional ideology is specific. Wealth is the result of hard work, ability, motivation, and other favorable personal attributes. Wealth is earned and deserved. Poverty is the result of laziness, stupidity, and other unfavorable personal attributes, and it too is earned and deserved. People in a society get what they deserve, and

TABLE 3

BELIEFS ABOUT LEGAL AND POLITICAL EQUALITY, BY INCOME AND RACE
(PERCENTAGE WHO PERCEIVE EQUALITY)

Income and Race	Voting Influences Government (a)	Rich and Poor Influence Government Equally (b)	Law and Courts Are Fair (c)	Jail Equally Likely for Rich or Poor (d)
Poor:				
Negro	76	3	46	8
White	88	30	75	23
Middle:				
Negro	89	15	27	20
White	89	30	59	20
Rich:				
White	94	55	75	22
Total, analytic sample:				
%	88	29	58	20
(N)	(303)	(345)	(340)	(343)
Total, systematic sample:*				
%	91	35	60	21
(N)	(182)	(172)	(177)	(178)

*For middle income and poor, col. (b)–χ^2 = 4.34, df = 1, $p < .05$; col. (c)–χ^2 = 4.41, df – 1, $p = .05$. For race, col. (c)–χ^2 = 12.84, df = 1, $p < .01$.

the social structure is just. Since justice prevails, changes in the social structure are rarely needed. In testing support for these beliefs, we expected that those who have the most of what there is to get would be most likely to define the system as just. We therefore expected that the higher the income, the greater the tendency to assign personal factors as causes of wealth or poverty; and the lower the income, the greater the tendency to assign social structural factors as causal.

Respondents were first asked two open-ended questions, why are rich people rich, and why are poor people poor?[11] The answers were coded as pointing to personal attributes, to social structure, or to a combination of these. Only the responses which were solely in terms of personal attributes are presented in the tables. The rich are much more convinced than others that wealth is a result of favorable personal attributes;

[11]A number of respondents wanted to know the definition of "rich." Very few raised questions about the definition of "poor." Respondents were told that "rich" and "poor" meant whatever they meant to the respondent in the context of the Muskegon area.

TABLE 4

PERSONAL ATTRIBUTES AS A CAUSE OF INCOME BY INCOME AND RACE (IN PERCENTAGES)

Income and Race	Wealth (a)	Poverty (b)	Being on Relief Last Six Years (c)	Poor Don't Work as Hard (d)	Poor Don't Want to Get Ahead (e)
Poor:					
Negro	17	17	28	3	0
White	34	30	46	13	19
Middle:					
Negro	29	19	45	4	6
White	35	42	59	30	29
Rich:					
White	72	62	78	39	46
Total, analytic sample:					
%	37	36	54	21	23
(N)	(350)	(341)	(347)	(343)	(347)
Total, systematic sample:*					
%	31	40	57	25	25
(N)	(183)	(177)	(185)	(186)	(180)

NOTE—In the wealth column, the percentages represent those who saw favorable traits as a "cause" of wealth; in the poverty columns, unfavorable traits as a "cause" of poverty. The residual categories for the wealth column would include respondents who indicated both personal and structural responses as causal, and those who saw only structural factors as causal.

*For race, Col. (b)–χ^2 = 10.29, df = 2, $p < .01$; col. (c)–χ^2 = 9.63, df = 2, $p < .01$; col. (d)–χ^2 = 4.85, df = 1, $p < .05$; col. (e)–χ^2 = 7.6, df = 1, $p < .01$.

72 percent of the rich and 17 percent of the poor Negroes felt this way (see Table 4). As one rich white man said, "Inheritance is the exception today. If you have to generalize, it's the self-discipline to accumulate capital and later to use that capital effectively and intelligently to make income and wealth." An opposite point of view was held by a poor Negro: "The rich stole, beat, and took. The poor didn't start stealing in time, and what they stole, it didn't value nothing, and they were caught with that."

The rich are also much more convinced than the poor that poverty is the result of unfavorable personal attributes. Six-tenths of the rich and 17 percent of the poor Negroes supported this idea (see Table 4). The same general pattern of responses to the two questions was found when the data were analyzed by the educational level of the respondents. Support for the ideology increased directly with educational level, but the differences between educational extremes were smaller than for the top and bottom income strata.

The explanation for being on relief was similar. Only about 5 percent of the total sample thought that people were on relief during the Great Depression because of personal attributes. But four-fifths of the rich and three-fifths of the middle-income whites thought that relief status in the past six years was the result of personal characteristics, while less than half of those in other strata thought so (see Table 4). One rich man reported, "People on relief just don't want to work. I'm biased. I run a plant where we try to hire men and they just won't stay." Another rich man said, "It's an easy way to receive their allotments. It's just too easy. Like

ADC and that kind of stuff. To me, it's just criminal." In contrast, a poor Negro woman reported, "I've been on for six years or more and it's because I can't make enough on a job to take care of my six kids."

Hard work and motivation to get ahead are also basic tenets in the ideology of opportunity. Respondents were first asked:

Naturally, everyone can think of exceptions, but on the whole, would you say that poor people work just as hard as rich people, or do you think that poor people generally don't work as hard as rich people?

Although only one-fifth of the total sample felt that the poor do not work as hard, two-fifths of the rich but almost no Negro respondents thought so (see Table 4).

Respondents were then asked about the attitudes of poor people toward getting ahead:

Do you think that poor people want to get ahead just as much as everyone else or do you think that basically poor people don't care too much about getting ahead? Please try not to think of individual exceptions you know of, but rather in terms of the group in general.

About one-fourth of the respondents thought that the poor did not want to get ahead, and the response variation was like that of the previous question (see Table 4).

CONCLUSIONS

Empirical studies of ideologies are only primitively developed in the social sciences, and we hope that this research provides some suggestions about how to proceed further in this study. Obviously, national studies are sorely needed in this area, for any community study necessarily has limited generalizability. However, our hypotheses seem to be verified in the community studied. There is far from universal acceptance of the tenets of the American ideology of opportunity, even when those tenets are enunciated in the most general and vague terms. There is even less acceptance of statements in which economic inequality is made the test for accepting a tenet on equality of opportunity. The shift downward in degree of support of a tenet from its general statement to concrete specification is not a surprising finding. This phenomenon has been observed in research whenever situations are specified (Centers, 1949; Prothro and Grigg, 1960; Jones, 1941). Our data confirm the hypothesis that the support of an ideology is strongest among those who profit most from the system which the ideology explains and defends, the rich in this case. In addition, the data reveal that people from various economic strata differ in their evaluation of the effectiveness of different institutions to implement the ideology of opportunity. Such differences are also found between Negroes and whites.

We may reasonably assume that ideologies are most firmly held when they are accepted as given and not concretely tested in life situations; yet scientific analysis of ideologies cannot proceed without ascertaining how firmly the public supports them when they are enunciated in both normative and existential terms. Apparently social scientists do not know what everyone else seems to know, that people test the validity of public ideologies concretely in everyday life. We are inclined to conclude from our data that there is less "false class-consciousness" than most social scientists assume. The best audience of an ideology is the audience which profits most from its repetition. Others may not really be listening, or not listening well.

It is important for social scientists to study how firmly various segments of the community adhere to various ideological tenets, for data from such studies should provide information needed to predict the formation and activation of social movements. Clearly, such data should be gathered periodically, so that historical trends in the degree of support for old ideologies and the emergence of new ideologies can be discerned. Participation in social movements occurs when large proportions of the people in certain strata believe that institutions are not functioning to meet societal norms. They then feel that the norms must be changed or support for them must be withdrawn. In both cases, the universality of collective representations is reduced. Our data show that some people are facing a second American dilemma by questioning how they can support the ideology of opportunity in the face of massive intergenerational poverty. The dilemma is being resolved differently by people who are located differently in the social structure. We have focused on the income variable in this study, but obviously other indicators of social location are important and need to be studied. Research on ideology must become the study of the layman's sociology of the society in which he lives. Only when sociologists have this picture clearly, can they elaborate a theory on the ideology of stratification.

REFERENCES

Campbell, Angus, Gerald Gurin, and Warren E. Miller. *The Voter Decides*. Evanston, Ill.: Row, Peterson, 1954.

Campbell, Angus, Phillip E. Converse, Warren E. Miller, and Donald E. Stokes. *The American Voter*. New York: Wiley, 1960.

Centers, Richard. *The Psychology of Social Classes*. Princeton, N.J.: Princeton Univ. Press, 1949.

Christie, Richard, and Marie Jahoda (eds.). *Studies in the Scope and Method of "The Authoritarian Personality."* Glencoe, Ill.: Free Press, 1954.

Coleman, James S. "The Concept of Equality of Educational Opportunity." *Harvard Educational Review*, **38** (Winter 1968): 7–22.

Cremin, Lawrence. *The American Common School: An Historical Conception*. Teachers' College Studies in Education. New York: Bureau of Publications, Columbia Univ., 1951.

Form, William H., and Joan Rytina. "Income and Ideological Beliefs on the Distribution of Power in the United States." *American Sociological Review*, **34** (February 1969): 19–31.

Gross, Llewellyn. "The Use of Class Concepts in Sociological Research." *American Journal of Sociology*, **54** (March 1949): 409–421.

Heard, Alexander. *The Costs of Democracy*. Garden City, N.Y.: Doubleday, 1962.

Jones, Alfred Winslow. *Life, Liberty and Property*. Philadelphia: Lippincott, 1941.

Keyserling, Leon H. *Progress or Poverty*. Washington, D.C.: Conference on Economic Progress, 1964.

Lipset, Seymour M. *The First New Nation*. New York: Basic Books, 1963.

Lipset, Seymour M., and Natalie Rogoff. "Class and Opportunity in Europe and the United States." *Commentary*, **18** (December, 1954): 562–568.

Lipset, Seymour M., and Reinhard Bendix. *Social Mobility in Industrial Society*.

Berkeley: Univ. of California Press, 1959.

McClosky, Herbert, Paul J. Hoffman, and Rosemary O'Hara. "Issue Conflict and Consensus among Party Leaders and Followers." *American Political Science Review*, **54** (June 1960): 416.

Mannheim, Karl. *Ideology and Utopia: An Introduction to the Sociology of Knowledge*. New York: Harcourt, Brace, 1954.

Miller, Herman P. "Changes in the Number and Composition of the Poor." In *Poverty in America*, Margaret Gordon (ed.). San Francisco: Chandler, 1965.

Miller, S. M., and Martin Rein. "Poverty, Inequality and Policy." In *Social Problems: A Modern Approach*, Howard S. Becker (ed.). New York: Wiley, 1966.

Mosca, Gaetano. *The Ruling Class*. (Ed. Arthur Livingston, trans. Hannah D. Kahn.) New York: McGraw-Hill, 1966.

Orshansky, Mollie. "Counting the Poor: Another Look at the Poverty Profile." *Social Security Bulletin*, **28** (January, 1965): 3–29.

Ossowski, Stanislaw. *Class Structure in the Social Consciousness*. (Trans. Sheila Patterson.) New York: Free Press, 1963.

Parsons, Talcott. "A Revised Analytical Approach to the Theory of Social Stratification." In *Class, Status and Power: A Reader in Social Stratification*, Reinhard Bendix and Seymour M. Lipset (eds.). Glencoe, Ill.: Free Press, 1953.

Prothro, James W., and Charles M. Grigg. "Fundamental Principles of Democracy: Bases of Agreement and Disagreement." *Journal of Politics*, **22** (May 1960): 276–294.

Smelser, Neil J. (ed.). *Sociology*. New York: Wiley, 1967.

Weber, Max. *From Max Weber: Essays in Sociology*. (Ed. and trans. H. H. Gerth and C. Wright Mills.) New York: Oxford Univ. Press, 1946.

Westie, Frank. "The American Dilemma: An Empirical Test." *American Sociological Review*, **30** (August 1965): 527–538.

Williams, Robin M., Jr. *American Society*. New York: Knopf, 1967.

Much like the abstract statements found in national-character studies, the abstract statement of the American Creed was found to be a generally accepted belief. Much like the life style variations covered previously in this section, beliefs about the American opportunity structure were found to vary according to such important variables as income level. Once again we are confronted with the paradox of diversity and similarity. When we examine life style in relation to specific variables such as income, ethnicity, sex, age, and region, however, it is possible to speak meaningfully about the extent to which life styles are shared and the degree to which they vary. The remainder of this book examines life styles according to sociologically important variables that serve to order our knowledge about life styles in America.

"UPPER-CLASS" LIFE STYLES

Social inequality occurs in all societies. Sociologists generally refer to unequal categories of people as social classes; *moreover, they generally recognize that people in different social classes differ in life style. The relationships between social inequality and life style variation are generally so clear and widely recognized that many sociologists have come to the conclusion that* all *life style variation can be explained in terms of social inequality. Although this conclusion is an overstatement, it is nevertheless true that many of the behavioral patterns we regard as components of life style vary according to inequality in income, education, and occupational standing.*

Social class has traditionally been considered the most potent variable in explaining life style differences, and studies in sociology are regarded as lacking if they disregard it. Practically every aspect of life from sexual behavior* to pronunciation† has been demonstrated to be class-related. Currently there is debate regarding what social classes are. Some feel

*Alfred C. Kinsey, Wardell B. Pomeroy, and Clyde E. Martin, *Sexual Behavior in the Human Male* (Philadelphia: Saunders, 1948).

†William Labov, "Phonological Correlates of Social Stratification," *American Anthropologist,* **66** (December, 1964—part 2), pp. 164–176.

that they are easily recognized and distinct entities; others believe that class boundaries are arbitrary and misleading.† Thus, when we use the term* social class, *we do so cautiously.*

Market researchers are interested, for practical reasons, in delineating social classes. Frequently they get a sense of the market—that is, they identify what kinds of people will buy a product—by categorizing interviewees into social classes. Their categories may be crude—such as upper, upper middle, middle, and lower—but they prove to be useful even though they are no more than a convenient fiction. Researchers make decisions about the category into which a respondent should be placed on the basis of available indicators. For example, the interviewer may make a judgment about the neighborhood or the house of his respondent, or he may make an assessment of the furnishings in a living room if he enters the house. Other indicators from which the researcher makes an inference about social class may be the occupation or educational level of the respondent. Sometimes these factors are combined in a standardized index.‡

Taken singly or in some combination, these crude indicators distinguish life styles that are stratified or varied according to social class. The people discussed in this section on upper-class life styles are dissimilar to those discussed in Parts 4 and 5 on middle- and lower-class life styles. Rarely are people participants in the social circles of more than one of these strata. Thus, although there may not be distinct classes, there are distinct life styles.

*In attempts to characterize upper-class life styles, a distinction frequently is made between the upper-upper and the lower-upper class. The distinction separates those with old, inherited wealth and family background from the nouveau riche.§ The lower-upper-class person may have more power and more wealth than a person who is upper-upper class, but he lacks the name and family background necessary for membership in "the American elite."‖ Although the distinction is meaningless to most people, it may identify the central life interest of upper-class life style—lineage. To Kahl it is "graceful living,"¶ to Baltzell, "the club."** In the following article by MacNamara, lineage, graceful living, and the club are shown to be closely interrelated.*

* W. Lloyd Warner et al., *Social Class in America* (New York: Harper, 1960).

† Dennis H. Wrong, "Social Inequality Without Stratification," *Canadian Review of Sociology and Anthropology,* 1 (1964), pp. 5–16. For a more complete discussion of this issue, see Gerald W. Thielbar and Saul D. Feldman (eds.), *Issues in Social Inequality* (Boston: Little, Brown, 1972).

‡ For a discussion of measuring social class, see Thielbar and Feldman, *op. cit.;* and Thomas Lasswell, *Class and Stratum* (Boston: Houghton Mifflin, 1965).

§ W. Lloyd Warner, *Social Life of a Modern Community* (New Haven: Yale Univ. Press, 1941), p. 88; Joseph Kahl, *The American Class Structure* (New York: Holt, 1957), pp. 187–193.

‖ E. Digby Baltzell, *The Protestant Establishment* (New York: Vintage, 1966).

¶ Kahl, *op. cit.,* p. 187.

** Baltzell, *ibid.,* p. 353, *passim.*

Social Register, Philadelphia 1969

CHARLES H. MACNAMARA

Assiduous observers of the Soviet hierarchy constantly study photographs of state functions. By noting relative positions of high-ranking personages, they are able to gauge who is moving to the center of power and who is on the way to managing cement factories in Kazakhstan.

For the study of society in Philadelphia there are similar techniques. There are those newspaper anachronisms, the society pages. One may note there the rise of young matrons by the company they keep in photos of charitable committees. At formal dress functions young protégés cling limpet-like to starchy elders of repute. And in the columns of type, alliances among first families are detailed in reports of engagement and marriage, followed at respectable intervals by announcement of heirs to the crossed bloodline.

To gain a little perspective for these minute stirrings in the pond of local society, however, there is nothing like the *Philadelphia Social Register*. The 1969 edition (its discreet black and orange binding looking like a course catalog for Princeton) has already been resting for several months on telephone tables and escritoires from Delancey Place to Paoli and beyond. It is by care-

From *Philadelphia Magazine*, **66** (March, 1969), pp. 66ff. Reprinted by permission of Philadelphia Magazine.

ful gleaning of the *Social Register* that one is able to glimpse something of the flaky structure of Philadelphia's upper crust. It is not to be studied as photos of the Kremlin crowd, to discover the latest clue on who is close to the center occupied by the Biddles, Ingersolls, Morrises, Cadwaladers, Robertses and Wisters. For several generations it has been obvious that this space has been occupied by Scotts, Smiths, Cassatts, Lippincotts, Woods, Peppers, Pews, Disstons and the like. And since Wilmington is included in the *Philadelphia Social Register,* several hundred du Ponts, a sui generis family, must be reckoned with.

Beyond the solid nucleus of old-timers, observation becomes a fascinating parlor sport. Society may be dying as a directional force, but its members are spawning at a handsome rate. The first issue of the local *Register* in 1890 contained 135 families. By 1940 the count was 5,150. A calculated estimate of the current issue is that there are 7,400 households and approximately 20,000 individuals. (Young children are not listed.)

For the past year there were 350 marriages solemnized against only 200 deaths. To restructure Ripley's famous speculation on marching Chinese in "Believe It Or Not," one has the feeling that if everyone in the current *Social Register* were lined up two abreast on the tracks of the Main Line in Paoli and began marching in stately grace to the beat of Meyer Davis's orchestra playing "Pomp and Circumstance," they would reproduce at such a rate that they and their heirs would file through 30th Street Station for eternity.*

*"Main Line" refers to the main line of the com-

Although it can be held comfortably in one hand, the *Social Register* is by no means a pamphlet. For 573 pages it celebrates the virtues of blood and distinction. A typical listing goes something like this: family name and Christian name of male, maiden name of wife in parenthesis, enumeration of approved clubs in cryptic abbreviation, college with year of graduation, phone number and address, listing of other adults in household, listing of juniors in household (males 14 to 20; misses 12 to 17).

For example: "Lippincott Mr & Mrs R Schuyler (Jones—Elizabeth W Hanger) Ph Cr. Fw. Myf. Pc. Ac. Ncd. Pa '39; Juniors Misses E Hadley & Edith B Jones; Phone No CH 8-000. . . ."

This listing indicates that Mr. R. Schuyler Lippincott graduated from the University of Pennsylvania in 1939 and is now a member of the prestigious Philadelphia Club, Corinthian Yacht, the Military Order of Foreign Wars, Society of Mayflower Descendants, and Philadelphia Cricket. Mrs. Lippincott is a member of Acorn, considered the ultra women's club in Philadelphia. The two juniors listed are from Mrs. Lippincott's previous marriage to Mr. Jones. The phone number (altered here) and address (which we skipped) indicate that the family resides in Chestnut Hill, a perfectly acceptable neighborhood for a *Social Register* family.

Despite the length of the *Social Register,* it is an exclusive listing. Keeping people *out* is half the fun. The easiest way to get into the *Social Register* is to be born into it. This way there is no

social climbing and no subsequent guilt feelings.

The second method of entering is by marriage. The typical Philadelphia arrangement is for fresh money to marry old blood. The offspring of such marriages thereby combine the best of both worlds. This is as close to mixed marriage as society cares to contemplate.

The trickiest method of entering the elite is by application to the Social Register Association, publisher of the Philadelphia directory and 11 companion volumes for other cities. According to a Philadelphia social consultant (one who aids the elite in planning parties), "The *Social Register* is administered by a secret board in New York City, and anyone here who gives information is also kept under wraps." Those in the *Social Register* have the privilege of recommending new names for listing, and the quality of the recommender frequently droppeth as a gentle rain on the recommendee.

Gentility and status are the primary qualifications for listing—plus the backing of those who are already listed. Five or six endorsers of the application are sufficient, if they are the right ones. Time is relative. When Stuart Saunders moved to Philadelphia as chairman of the city's most social business institution, the Pennsylvania Railroad, everyone tripped over each other's patent leather pumps to get him into the *Social Register* and the best clubs in the area. The average social climber, however, may have to wait a decade or so before being rewarded. Some never make the grade.

Kicking people out can be great sport. There is no black-bordered card announcing the event, no braid stripped

muter route of the Pennsylvania Railroad, which goes through "elite" communities such as Paoli, Haverford, and Bryn Mawr, ending in Philadelphia at the 30th Street Station. [Eds.]

from a uniform to the slow roll of drums in Rittenhouse Square. One is simply not in the next edition of the *Register*. One is not surprised by this absence, because one has already noted a falling off of invitations to social affairs.

In truth, however, there are more voluntary delistings than purges. This can come about simply by neglecting to provide the information necessary for listing, particularly after a change in address or marital status.

Divorce, once considered a scandalous breach of the social ethic, is no longer reason for anything other than a change in listing. Nor, for that matter, are dipsomania, kleptomania, homosexuality or participation in sex orgies causes for exile—so long as these eccentricities are not indulged in a proletarian manner. Shoplifting at Bonwit's, for example, displays a sense of social form. Doing the same thing at Woolworth's exhibits a deplorable lack of class. Wife swapping in Levittown is separated by more than just a few miles from the high society cavortings of yore on Hound Dog Hill.

For public sins, exclusion may be the penalty. As with entrance, much depends on family. Members of peripheral families may be snuffed out with as little ceremony as guttering candles. A member of a family closer to the center of things may be allotted *two* messy scandals before the name disappears. It can be heartbreaking to older members of the family. Youth, of course, is rebellious in all strata today. One never knows when the child of a *Social Register* family will do something wild and crazy like joining the Communist Party, dating a Negro, or marrying a Jew.

Speaking of Jews, they are as likely to be found in the *Social Register* as

rabbis officiating at the Church of the Holy Trinity. . . . After all, since they are excluded from most of the social clubs enumerated in the *Social Register,* it is only logical that they be excluded from society and from the book.

• • •

Whatever the occupation, coupon clipper or life insurance salesman (both are in the directory), it is a man's clubs that mark his station in society. These are recorded in the *Social Register* in a sometimes baffling (to outsiders) shorthand. Altogether there are 48 men's and women's clubs considered worthy of listing, from Ac (for Acorn) to Y (for Yale Club). Some are based on historical orientation, such as Ds (Descendants of Signers of the Declaration of Independence) and Sar (Sons of the American Revolution).

Others are social-suburban, such as Sg (Sunnybrook Golf) and Rh (Rose Tree Fox Hunt). Still others are social-city, the men's clubs such as Ph (Philadelphia Club) and R (Rittenhouse). A few are exclusive men's cooking clubs, Ssk (State in Schuylkill) and Rb (The Rabbit). For the political-business set there is the Republicans-only Union League. And for those with literary leanings there is the democratic Franklin Inn.

The club that has been most exclusive from its founding in the 18th century is the State in Schuylkill. Membership is limited to 40, vacancies being filled from apprentices, who have usually seen the shad broach the Delaware at least 50 springs before attaining full membership. So exclusive is the group that few Philadelphians, out of society's inner circle, would be able to identify a single member. And even when the names are known they will hardly jolt the response of memory.

.   .   .

While the clubs listed in the *Social Register* have remained the same for a generation, the colleges have not. When Digby Baltzell examined various *Social Registers* for his study *Philadelphia Gentlemen,* he noted that in 1940 the upper class in each directory favored the Big Three (Harvard, Yale, and Princeton). In addition the upper class of each city had a local school that it favored, the Philadelphia choice being the University of Pennsylvania. These four local schools still dominate the local *SR*. The circle is widening, however.

For years the choices beyond these four schools seemed to be limited to the East, roughly from Bowdoin in the north to the University of Virginia in the south. But today the thirst of the upper class for education is so great that its sons and daughters are attending schools unknown to the *SR* listings of a generation ago. At Main Line teas, matrons these days are proudly spreading the word that grandson J. Jared the Fourth has been accepted at New Mexico, Miami, U. of Alaska, Colorado State, Santa Fe, or what have you. . . .

More static are the addresses of the elite listed in the *Register.* Their ghettos are shady, their homes from sound to magnificent. The presence of a single rat in the vicinity prompts a discreet call to an exterminator with an unmarked panel truck.

Chestnut Hill and center city are the only acceptable areas to live inside Philadelphia. The repetition of addresses in the suburbs seldom deviates from the expected—Devon, Berwyn, Penllyn, Wayne, Bryn Mawr, Villanova, Rosemont, Spring House, Paoli, Wawa, Uniontown. As is evident from the *Social Register,* the upper class feels stultified by street addresses. They may be necessary in Chestnut Hill, but in the outlying districts a list of properties echoes manorial names of the English squirearchy. There are Heathcote Farm and Fairthorne, Journey's Ended and Rebel Fox Farm, Pheasant Run and Spring Meadow Farm.

The most famous names are probably the Biddles' Andalusia and George Widener's Erdenheim Farm, a name known to horse players completely ignorant of the family's heartbreaking struggle to enter society at the turn of the century. For reasons known only to its editors, the names of estates appear in quotation marks in *SR*. At least the upper class has avoided that pitfall of the exurban bourgeoisie—picking out a cutesy or punny name for their 18th-century farmhouse-cum-plumbing and surrounding three acres of rabbit burrows.

Some families would not be caught with a street address if it could possibly be avoided. Perhaps an extreme example is that of the Woods family of Wawa. Various branches of the Woods may be addressed at Blossom Hill, Blossom Hill Cabin (even the elite subdivide), Tree Tops, Logtown Farm, and Hurricane Hollow (presumably located in the declivity between Blossom Hill and Forge Hill). All of this in Wawa, a Delaware County community that hardly matches the Ponderosa ranch in size.

As for location, it is not the suburban addresses that impress the reader of the *Social Register*. It is that Philadelphia society, as listed in the *SR*, is international in character. The listings begin with Mr. and Mrs. John Abbate in Perugia, Italy, and end with Mr. and Mrs. Alexandre Zvegintzov in Paris. There are in fact very few pages in the directory that do not contain an alien address. It is not just a du Pont plantation in South Carolina or a Dixon ranch in Wyoming. There are people living in New York City, Connecticut, Washington, Palm Beach, Rio de Janeiro, Dar es Salaam (Tanzania), and Ras Tanura (Saudi Arabia), who are considered and consider themselves members of Philadelphia society.

The mass of Philadelphians and suburbanites, the 4.5 million who are not listed in the *Social Register,* undoubtedly have very little concept of that world behind the closed doors of the clubs and nestled in the quiet confines of Berwyn and Paoli. How much relevance does the *Social Register* crowd have for society—not that introverted society, but for the society that forms the totality of our relationships? Does this self-perpetuating upper class actu-

ally provide motivating leadership? In *Philadelphia Gentlemen,* Baltzell matched the upper class of the 1940 *Social Register* with the listings in the 1940 *Who's Who,* which he accepted as a directory of the active elite leadership. Of the elite in *Who's Who* living in this area, he found that 29% were also listed in *SR.*

A partial check of the current *Who's Who* and the *Social Register* indicates that society is providing a diminishing role in leadership. In *Who's Who* there are 146 area residents with last names beginning with B. Only 30 of these are also listed in the *Social Register* (including Catherine Drinker Bowen, listed in *SR* as Mrs. T. McKean Downs). This is only 20%—a drop of nine points in a single generation. Such figures can have only one meaning to the investment bankers of social observation: family stock has been in decline as a factor in the market and shows little chance for rejuvenation. Management has refused to diversify or make significant merger with steadily rising, newer issues. Drop society from investment portfolios.

It is not by accident that one thinks of Philadelphia and Boston in connection with upper-class life style. Not all American cities have their own social registers—they are found in New York, Philadelphia, Boston, Washington, Chicago, Baltimore, St. Louis, San Francisco, Pittsburgh, Cincinnati, Buffalo, and Cleveland. These older American cities have sufficient history and sufficiently old families to warrant a social register. Individuals listed in these volumes may lack social power and great wealth, but they recognize one another as part of an old elite—an American aristocracy. Like many elite groups, they have their own institutions, from clubs to popular causes (often local orchestras or art museums), and their own educational institutions. Current social registrants lack the wealth and influence that their forebears once had, and are no longer automatically admitted to elite educational institutions.

In the following article, Gene Hawes notes that almost all the older male members of the New York social register went to one of three schools —Yale, Harvard, or Princeton. Their sons, however, are not limiting their education to these institutions, although most still attend eastern schools. Their daughters are more likely to attend elite women's colleges or junior colleges rather than universities.

America's Upper-Class Colleges

GENE R. HAWES

Social class, like sex and religion, is something that no truly tactful person discusses in ordinary conversation. To bring it up except as a joke is a breach of egalitarian manners. But privately, it matters a great deal to many Americans.

Whether admitted or not, it is a subject of particular concern to many persons connected with America's colleges. Administrators who are responsible for their college's finances must maintain ties with circles of wealth and influence to insure its continued sustenance. Alumni, who are asked to support their college, to befriend its recent graduates, and to send their children back to Alma Mater, are understandably interested in its social prestige as well as its academic reputation. Students, who unavoidably exchange subtle condescensions in meeting friends, relatives, and potential employers, become increasingly aware of the status ascribed to their college. And

From *Columbia College Today* (Fall, 1963), pp. 30–36. Reprinted by permission of Columbia College Today and the author.

parents, who seek the "right college" for their children, often act on impressions of social as well as academic rectitude, a fact that has created the largest admissions jams at the small number of colleges thought to be most desirable.

In view of such special connections between colleges and social standing, we might well ask what kind of relation exists between the colleges and America's highest social class. Do students from upper-class homes go to many colleges or tend to converge on a few? Has their choice of colleges changed over the years? Is it shifting now? Is the attitude of the colleges changing toward them?

First, let us define "upper class." This cannot be done in any absolute sense because American society is exceptionally fluid and diverse. In both popular and scholarly convention, though, the American upper class consists of the families of long-established social prominence and great inherited wealth. Its members are descendants of highly successful individuals of at least one, but usually two or more, generations past. Since their wealth has been gained and maintained chiefly by business enterprise, America's upper class is largely a business aristocracy. Most of the families in this class follow a distinctive style of life, attending the same schools, living in the same areas in or near large cities, frequenting the same resorts, marrying among themselves, and manifesting a kind of group solidarity.

The best index to the upper class, though by no means an exhaustive one, is the *Social Register*. Published annually since 1888, the *Register* has 12 current editions that list the families deemed highest in social standing in as many major urban regions of America. The *Register* reflects certain ethnic biases—for instance, relatively few of the most prominent Jewish families are included—but its biases follow those of the upper class itself. It also suffers from some mistaken judgments and important omissions. Still, its heavy use as a standard reference by the upper class itself testifies to its general reliability as an index of upper-class status. It should not be confused with *Who's Who in America,* which is a much larger index that includes those persons who have made significant individual achievements.

A study of the *Social Register* discloses that the alumni listed in it have enrolled at three colleges in particular: Harvard, Yale, and Princeton. Leading families in the different cities have different preferences within this trinity: New Yorkers prefer Yale, then Harvard and Princeton (as Table 1 indicates); Bostonians prefer Harvard, then Yale and Princeton; and Philadelphians (according to E. Digby Baltzell's *Philadelphia Gentlemen: The Making of a National Upper Class*) prefer Harvard, then Princeton and Yale. But virtually every metropolitan edition shows a concentration at these three institutions. The three are undeniably America's most popular undergraduate institutions for men of the upper class.

Other colleges that have regularly attracted socially prominent young men from many parts of the nation during the last half century are Amherst, Brown, Columbia, Cornell, Dartmouth, M.I.T., Pennsylvania, Stanford, Virginia, and Williams, and the military academies at Annapolis and West Point. Another dozen colleges or so have also had a modest representation of upper-class students, but of a more regional character.

Although there has been a heavy concentration at three colleges, scrutiny of the various editions of the *Register* discloses that there is a strikingly wide dispersion of upper-class men at more than 100 other colleges. As a tabulation of the *New York Social Register* suggests (see, for example, Table 1), almost two-thirds of America's socially prominent have attended only three colleges, but more than one-third have attended a variety of other colleges. The high concentration may surprise many Americans, but the wide dispersion would positively amaze, say, the British, whose upper class almost to a man has attended only Oxford and Cambridge.

Hence, America does have upper-class colleges—three identified with the upper class to a marked extent and about a dozen to a moderate extent—but the nation also has many other colleges that frequently have had a handful of socially prominent young men among their students.

One other fact emerges from a study of the *Social Register*. Two universities stand out far beyond the rest among those preferred by the upper class for graduate and professional study: Harvard and Columbia (see Table 1, bottom). The fact takes on an obvious special interest in the light of Columbia's past, as we shall see.

This list of colleges with upper-class affiliations has not been an entirely stable one during the past century. There have been noteworthy shifts in upper-class representation, many of which were the results of two great changes in upper-class allegiances. The first change, which can be traced by a perusal of earlier editions of the *Social Register,* and the letters, diaries, and other writings of upper-class family members, took place between the end of the Civil War and World War I.

Before the Civil War, a venerable college could be found in almost every Eastern state: the Universities of Georgia, North Carolina, South Carolina, and Virginia; William and Mary, also in Virginia; Pennsylvania in that state, Princeton in New Jersey, Columbia in New York, Yale in Connecticut, Brown in Rhode Island, Harvard in Massachu-

TABLE 1

COLLEGES ATTENDED BY MEN LISTED IN
THE 1963 *Social Register,*
NEW YORK EDITION*

College	No. of Men	College	No. of Men
Yale	2234	Oxford (England)	22
Harvard	1746	Wisconsin	22
Princeton	1422	Stevens Institute	21
Williams	325	Cambridge (England)	20
Columbia	311	Hobart	18
Virginia	160	Duke	17
Cornell	144	Rutgers	16
Dartmouth	115	Washington & Lee	15
Amherst	94	Haverford	13
M.I.T.	85	Middlebury	13
Trinity	82	St. Lawrence	13
Pennsylvania	79	Chicago	12
Brown	76	Davidson	12
Annapolis	75	Fordham	12
West Point	53	Vanderbilt	10
N.Y.U.	41	Vermont	10
California (Berkeley)	36		
Georgetown	35	LEADING GRADUATE AND PROFESSIONAL SCHOOLS ATTENDED BY MEN IN THE NEW YORK *Social Register,* 1963**	
Colgate	34		
North Carolina	33		
Hamilton	32		
Wesleyan	31	University	No. of Men
Stanford	29		
Union	28	Harvard	478
Johns Hopkins	24	Columbia	475
Michigan	24	Yale	92
Bowdoin	23		
Lehigh	23		

*Colleges attended by less than 10 men are omitted.
**Universities attended by less than 50 men are omitted.

setts, the University of Vermont, Dartmouth in New Hampshire, and Bowdoin in Maine. The affluent and powerful families of those states generally sent their sons to the old colleges nearby. Traveling far away to college was not only difficult but pointless, for very few students who were not from "the best families" went to college in those years. True, some families sent their sons, for reasons of health, discipline, or religion, away to such rural seats as Union College in upstate New York and Williams or Amherst in Western Massachusetts. But, for the most part, upper-class loyalties were attached to the colleges of their regions before the Civil War.

After the Civil War, the biggest American businesses became national in scope as great industrial and financial combines were organized. Many of the large old family fortunes multiplied enormously; many new ones were created. The American upper class became a national one, and the old local aristocracies formed many new ties with each other, in business at first and shortly after in social life. It needed a Register, and one was forthcoming. The new national upper class warily recognized new members, centered its work and its homes more and more on New York, grew well accustomed to travel by rail, and started sending its sons away to college.

It was in this era of immense business growth that some 15 colleges, but especially Harvard, Yale, and Princeton, increasingly became the colleges of the national upper class then in formation. Growing concentrations of both the old and the new rich at these three colleges enjoyed campus days marked by big-time football, rowing regattas, fraterni-

ties and clubs, riots, and good parties. University clubs were even built in New York so that college ties could continue in gentlemanly quarters after graduation.

This change can be aptly illustrated from Columbia's past. On the eve of the Civil War, George Templeton Strong, Class of 1838, could still call Columbia College "a day school for the sons of New York's leading families." But after the 1880's, and especially after the turn of the century, young New Yorkers began to go out of town in greater numbers.

The Fish family serves as a good example. The prominent New Yorker Nicholas Fish was a friend of Alexander Hamilton, Columbia Class of 1778, and was chairman of Columbia College's trustees. His son, Hamilton Fish, Class of 1827, was also chairman of the trustees, both before and after his distinguished service as Secretary of State in the otherwise lackluster Grant administration. Hamilton Fish's three sons were Columbia men of the Classes of 1867, 1869, and 1871. (Typically for that era, the youngest, Stuyvesant, captained Columbia's first football team and built the Illinois Central Railroad into a large system as its president.) However, Hamilton Fish III went to Harvard, where he became a football hero before graduating in 1910.

By 1914, Frederick Paul Keppel '98, Dean of Columbia College from 1910 to 1917, could write, "While doubtless the old New York stock will always be represented, Columbia is not likely ever again to be a fashionable college *per se,*" that is, a college patronized largely by upper-class sons.

Why did a large portion of Columbia

College's upper-class following go else-where? Why, when it was located in the center of American upper-class social life, did Columbia not become one of the new group of fashionable colleges?

One factor was that New York continued as a great immigration center. This brought a kind of student to Columbia College with whom upper-class gentlemen could not be at ease. These immigrant sons were predominantly Jewish, Irish, and Italian. Aggressive, and lacking knowledge or appreciation of America's genteel college traditions, they seemed not only deficient in money, manners, and cultural interests but excessively prone to taking academic work seriously. An example in the 1880's was one penniless lad from Hungary who spoke broken English, Michael Idvorsky Pupin '83. He went on to become the great inventor, author, and Columbia professor for whom the present Pupin Hall is named. The presence of these immigrant classmates at Columbia prompted some young socialites to consider seeking their education among more agreeable companions at colleges that were less ready to admit talented youngsters without consideration of their background.

Perhaps the most important factor in the decrease in the College's upper-class following, however, is suggested by the quip of some nameless observer, "While Eliot was building houses at Harvard, Butler was building schools at Columbia." It was precisely through the period of rapid change in the composition, outlook, and collegiate ties of the upper class that Columbia strained every resource to transform itself from an old classical college into a great modern university. In doing so, it broke its tan-gible and traditional links with the past, and did not provide the facilities and atmosphere then expected in college by young men of social position and wealth.

From its original home in lower Manhattan, Columbia had moved in 1857 to a cramped and improvised campus at 49th Street and Madison Avenue. While there, it built no residence halls or playing fields, but instead founded unfamiliar schools like Mines, Law, and Political Science, and even at one point called the venerable old College merely the School of Arts. In 1897, after Manhattan's runaway commercial growth had again engulfed its campus, Columbia moved to semi-rural Morningside Heights. On Morningside, the University officials built some grand structures, but there were still no residence halls or playing fields—nor even a Columbia College classroom building—in the early years. The changes in physical form and collegiate spirit that resulted were striking, and they shocked and alienated many of the old Columbia families.

By the end of World War I, Columbia had realized its goal. It was the largest and perhaps the greatest American university. But many of the sons from upper-class homes, who at that time preferred fun and congeniality to intellectual development, were not attracted by the increased seriousness at Morningside and Columbia's departure from tradition.

President Nicholas Murray Butler, who so successfully continued the work of his predecessors, Presidents Barnard and Low, in transforming the old college into a renowned university, ironically never reconciled himself to the loss of the boys from many leading families. According to Frank Bowles '28, Columbia admissions director from 1934 to 1948, Dr. Butler asked him repeatedly in the 1930's to try to get more of these boys back into the habit of attending Columbia.

But the time was not ripe for all but a handful of upper-class families whose sons continued to become Columbia men. Years before, Dean Keppel had more accurately seen the social consequences of Columbia's academic pioneering during America's gilded age. The future of Columbia College, he wrote, lay with young men "who are willing to ask frankly the question as to what one pays for the luxury of country-club existence, who have no desire to prepare themselves for a career of being amused, and who wish to begin to test their capacity with rivals of like mind, not in professional or graduate school, but in college."

The drift of the upper class from the old regional colleges to Harvard, Yale, and Princeton continued through the 1920's and 1930's, reaching its peak per-

TABLE 2
COLLEGES BEING ATTENDED BY SONS
LISTED IN THE 1963 *Social Register,*
NEW YORK EDITION*

College	No. of Men	College	No. of Men
Yale	171	California (Berkeley)	4
Harvard	123	Duke	4
Princeton	76	Lake Forest	4
Pennsylvania	44	Annapolis	3
Trinity	22	Bowdoin	3
Middlebury	20	Citadel	3
Virginia	19	Clarkson	3
Stanford	15	Colorado	3
Williams	13	Denver	3
Hobart	12	Lawrence	3
North Carolina	12	Northwestern	3
Boston U.	11	St. Lawrence	3
Dartmouth	10	Union	3
Columbia	9	Wesleyan	3
Brown	8	Denison	2
Colby	8	Dickinson	2
Cornell	7	Kenyon	2
Rollins	7	Lafayette	2
Amherst	6	M.I.T.	2
Rutgers	6	Michigan	2
Georgetown	5	New Hampshire	2
Hamilton	5	Oberlin	2
Lehigh	5	Vanderbilt	2
Syracuse	5	Wisconsin	2
Washington & Lee	5		
Arizona	4	*Colleges being attended by one son are omitted.	

haps just before World War II. Through these years, in continuation of a trend that had begun after the Civil War, scions of the upper class were joined in college by more than equal numbers of young men from the middle class, and even some numbers of the lower-class sons who possessed great skill in athletics.

After World War II, the second great change in upper-class allegiance began. All respected colleges found themselves inundated with admissions applications from returning veterans in addition to the normal crop of secondary school graduates. At the most sought-after colleges, three and four times as many academically qualified applicants as they could accommodate appeared. Suddenly, faculty admissions committees had to decide upon priorities. Who gets admitted—the extremely gifted son of a mechanic in Missouri with his G.I. Bill benefits, or the gentlemanly C student from a prominent family and a noted prep school? The choice lay between

TABLE 3
COLLEGES BEING ATTENDED BY
DAUGHTERS LISTED IN THE
1963 *Social Register,*
NEW YORK EDITION*

College	No. of Daughters	College	No. of Daughters
Smith	48	Goucher	4
Vassar	37	Manhattanville	4
Radcliffe	32	North Carolina	4
Wellesley	31	Rollins	4
Wheaton	30	Skidmore	4
Bryn Mawr	28	Syracuse	4
Sarah Lawrence	25	Centenary Jr.	3
Bradford Jr.	22	Colby	3
Bennett Jr.	19	Marymount	3
Briarcliff Jr.	18	Pembroke	3
Hollins	17	Arizona	2
Connecticut College	13	Boston U.	2
Mt. Holyoke	13	Lake Erie	2
Wells	10	Lake Forest	2
Barnard	6	Knox	2
Colorado	6	Middlebury	2
Colby Jr.	6	Mills	2
Sweet Briar	6	Northwestern	2
Endicott Jr.	5	R.I. School of Design	2
Finch Jr.	5	Scripps	2
Pine Manor Jr.	5	Sorbonne	2
Stanford	5	Vermont	2
Wheelock	5	Wm. Smith	2
Bennington	4		
Garland Jr.	4		

*Colleges attended by one daughter are omitted.

professed commitment to develop intellect and long and rich associations with the upper class.

Intellect won, though not easily or decisively, even today. Gradually, painfully, the upper-class colleges severed as amicably as possible their links with the least qualified members of the prominent families. And as the number of talented applicants has continued to mount, the average academic ability of the students at the leading social colleges has climbed to a point within the top 10 percent intellectually among all college students in the nation.

Upper-class applicants who could not meet the academic demands have had to go elsewhere to college. And, some of those applicants who could meet them *preferred* to go elsewhere. Wilbur J. Bender, Harvard's former admissions chief, recently noted:

> *There is no evidence that poverty and genius go together or that the rich are necessarily stupid. There is a real possibility, however, that an academically elite college would lose its appeal for the ablest boys from upper-income families who might prefer a college with a different kind of atmosphere.*

A perceptive observer, it might be noted, could well have made a similar observation about Columbia College a few generations ago.

This development has not led Harvard, Yale, and Princeton to experience any marked decrease in attendance by upper-class sons, although there have been important changes in the academic atmosphere at each of these schools, especially Harvard. Upper-class undergraduates at these colleges can still associate with each other by being ac-

cepted into Harvard's Porcellian, A.D., Fly, and Spee, the upper-class clubs; or into Yale's Fence Club, D.K.E., Zeta Psi, and St. Anthony Hall; or into such eating clubs at Princeton as Ivy, Cap and Gown, Cottage, Colonial, and Tiger Inn.

Two noteworthy social consequences have resulted from the aggregate admissions decisions of the most socially desirable colleges. One is a new dispersion of upper-class sons (as indicated in Table 2). As a very rough measure of the increased dispersion, the *New York Social Register* discloses that less than 45 per cent of the socially prominent boys now in college are concentrated at Harvard, Yale, and Princeton, while more than 55 per cent are dispersed among the 40 colleges listed in Table 2, and another 30 or 40 colleges not listed there. It seems warranted to conclude that, whereas nearly two-thirds of all upper-class sons attended three particular colleges during the first half of this century, less than one-half do so at present. (A similar dispersion seems to be taking place among the upper-class daughters [see Table 3].) The dispersion of upper-class sons and daughters is generating a new set of socially desirable colleges that has some of the flavor of the old upper-class institutions but less of their academic rigor.

The other, and far more important, consequence is the one that the admissions competition has had on the upper class itself. It could not be said of any period up through the 1940's that most young members of the upper class had to pursue rigorous intellectual training before they could take responsible stations in life. However, this is all too true today. It seems just as well, in view of the world in which they come to their power.

America's upper-class colleges would have found it difficult to pursue the course they have taken since the late 1940's unless great needs existed within our advanced industrial society for more leaders equipped with distinguished intellectual training. Such needs do exist, and most upper-class colleges are responding to the vital requirements of national life—now beset by urgent demands from within and determined threats from without. But they are not pioneering to meet them as Columbia did so dramatically decades ago.

In part because of these needs, a new kind of American upper class is slowly being forged. Large-scale organizations, government taxation, and explosive growth in the development and application of knowledge are working to reduce the potency of enormous hereditary wealth and power. As Stimson Bullitt suggests in an excellent chapter on "Class Patterns" in *To Be A Politician,* "money's close connection with power, education, and refinement has ceased." The new upper class that is forming is one of socially valuable talent and learning, not unlike Thomas Jefferson's prophesied "natural aristocracy of talents and virtues." It is assuming much of the power but not necessarily the great wealth—and certainly not the leisure—of the old upper class.

The colleges with upper-class affiliations, with the spectacular increase in the amounts of their scholarship aid and levels of academic standards, are helping to produce this new aristocracy of the able. They are compounding it of the best of the old upper class and the most talented of the lower and middle classes.

And several of the more conscientious of the prep schools are beginning to follow suit. Ogden Miller, headmaster of The Gunnery and a Yale man, recently said, "Forget about the rich and well-born. We must put education into the hands of the just plain able, whether or not their parents have money or connections."

In contributing to this new kind of upper class, the foremost American upper-class colleges are displaying a new style of learning. It stems primarily from the large, high-quality universities that dominate American higher education today. At most of the colleges attended by upper-class sons, undergraduate education is still committed to the liberal arts tradition—frequently patterned after Columbia College's famous general education program. As in Columbia College, however, the undergraduate program is more and more inspired by the advanced scholarly disciplines for which the universities exist. Less and less are studies in the leading upper-class colleges suffused by the old dominant spirit of sportive and leisured cultivation.

For Columbia men, the new style is old stuff. In the 1870's, young Nicholas Murray Butler '82 first became excited about Columbia because of the College's championship crews; but already in the 1920's, young Jacques Barzun '27, whose family had moved to the United States from France, came to the College because "to Europeans, Columbia appeared to be the finest intellectual institution in America."

Through the first half of this century not many sons of socially prominent families chose as young Barzun did, though a large proportion of them did choose Columbia for their *graduate* education after four years of less serious college life elsewhere. Columbia, which stood in the forefront of those colleges for the new upper class—ones whose demands for students of high academic talent took priority over social, religious, or racial background—unwittingly alienated much, though by no means all, of its following among the old upper class. In essence, Columbia sacrificed continuity with a proud past to realize a still more important future. That sacrifice—a costly one financially—was only a partial one, it should be noted, and there are an increasing number of indications that it may have been a temporary one.

The new alignment of "haves" and "have-nots" according to highly developed talents rather than accumulated wealth and social position may have fundamental consequences for American democracy. Already we hear outcries against the growing "meritocracy." However, to run our complex economy, to prevent nuclear disaster, to extend freedom, and to try to make life more humane and beautiful in our increasingly bureaucratic and mechanized world, we require leaders of the very highest intellect, imagination, sensibility, and wisdom. To help develop them is more than ever the urgent task of our leading colleges.

"MIDDLE-CLASS" LIFE STYLES

Americans have demonstrated a propensity to label themselves as middle class when offered in opinion surveys the choice of upper, middle, or lower. Even when "working class" is added to the alternatives, many still prefer to see themselves as middle class.* This preference may be interpreted as a denial of class differences or an affirmation that the United States is a middle-class society in which class differences should have no part. Most Americans are neither rich nor poor, but somewhere in the middle. The middle class is the largest class and is becoming larger as a result of the expansion in the proportion of middle-class occupations that require technical skill or advanced education.

Because the term middle class *may be applied to so many people whose life styles are quite diverse, it may be useful to distinguish categories within the middle class—for example, "upper-middle class," "middle-middle class," and "lower-middle class."*

What is upper-middle class? "The snobs. They're people with money. They look down on those that don't have as much as they do. They feel that money makes them better people, that anyone that has less than they

---

*Richard Centers, *The Psychology of Social Classes* (Princeton, N.J.: Princeton Univ. Press, 1949); Raymond J. Murphy and Richard T. Morris, "Occupational Situs, Subjective Class Identification and Political Affiliation," *American Sociological Review,* **26** (1961), pp. 383–392.

do is beneath them," said P.H., a clerical job-seeker, in response to the question of the day in the San Francisco Chronicle,* *"What is your idea of the upper-middle class?" C. W., another job-seeker, said, "Upper-middle class implies wealth. Professional people. Usually means the silent majority. Upper-middle class politically would mean the conservatives. But that's not always the case." Finally, W. E., a radio interviewer, stated: "The term upper-middle class should be discarded. It's outmoded today. Upper-middle class is someone who makes about three hundred dollars a week and lives beyond his means and is buying everything on time." Respondents did not agree on what it is to be upper-middle class, nor on who upper-middle-class people are. But they do imply that to be upper-middle class is to have a particular life style.*

"Career" has been identified as the central life interest of the upper-middle class.† But career patterns differ and so do their related life styles. The college professor or physician differs from the corporation executive or business owner. In the following article, Calvin Trillin portrays the Junior Chamber of Commerce version of upper-middle class. Scientists, engineers, and professors, who are much more "highbrow" than Jaycees, are frequently taken as the upper-middle class. There is, however, no single life style that can be characterized as upper-middle class.

*December 4, 1969.
†Joseph Kahl also makes this generalization in *The American Class Structure* (New York: Holt, 1957), p. 193.

Phoenix . . . Practice, Practice, Practice

CALVIN TRILLIN

A campaign for the presidency of the United States Jaycees, a service club for men between the ages of twenty-one and thirty-five, ordinarily costs fifteen thousand dollars. It's a bargain. There is probably no way to come closer to the

From *The New Yorker* (July 13, 1968), pp. 88ff. Reprinted by permission; copyright 1968 by The New Yorker Magazine, Inc.

feeling of being nominated for the Presidency of the United States except to be nominated for the Presidency of the United States—and the only Jaycees that has ever happened to are Barry Goldwater and Richard M. Nixon. If there are more Nixon posters displayed at the Republican convention in Miami than there were A. Bruce Coble posters at the Jaycee convention I have just attended in Phoenix, it will only mean that Miami, for some reason, offers more flat surfaces. In Phoenix, a presidential candidate like Roger R. Jenkins, a badge-and-trophy dealer from Seattle, could take it for granted that wherever he went he would be accompanied by a squad of aides who wore neat business suits, talked intently into walkie-talkies, and stood out among the Oklahoma Jaycee Indian costumes and the Mississippi Jaycee Confederate uniforms and the Indiana Jaycee basketball-referee shirts like Secret Service agents at a college reunion. Campaign workers in the headquarters suite of the candidate from Michigan answered the phone with "Smith for president," and everyone knew they were talking about Wendell E. Smith, a division zone manager for a grocery firm.

At the annual conventions of the Jaycees (formerly called the Junior Chamber of Commerce but never officially connected to the senior chamber), demonstrators are dependable and uniformly enthusiastic. During the week of a convention, demonstrations wind through the hotels every evening on schedule, and after the candidate's name is finally placed in nomination he can be assured of a demonstration lasting the full twenty minutes allotted by convention regulations. In Phoenix, each candidate was wheeled through the convention hall on a kind of mobile speaker's platform—one hand on his wife's shoulder, one hand waving to the cheering thousands—followed by hundreds of supporters blowing whistles, beating drums, waving placards, and chanting a slogan like "We Back Mack" or "Align with Glines." During the polling of the delegations, if a state leader walked to a floor microphone and said something like "Mr. Chairman, the great state of Missouri, home of the world-champion St. Louis Cardinals, is proud to cast its seventy-five votes for that great little razorback from Arkansas, the next president of the United States Jaycees—MACK KOONCE!," Mack Koonce,

an insurance man from Pine Bluff, Arkansas, could rest assured that every single member of every single delegation supporting him would stand up, wave a Mack Koonce placard, and make as much noise as possible.

All this is carried on with the knowledge that the winning candidate will give up his ordinary business for a year and move to the Jaycee White House, a ranch-style presidential residence in Tulsa, Oklahoma. His wife goes with him, of course; Jaycees sometimes refer to her as the First Lady. According to Jaycees, whoever does reach the Tulsa White House has "a lot of doors open for him" in the business world, and, according to the approved Jaycee history, a book entitled *Young Men Can Change the World,* he becomes the most lionized young man in the country. ("He's an honored guest at the Indianapolis 500, the Phoenix Rodeo, and the Apple Blossom Festival in Virginia, to name just a few events he attends with bells on.") But "the experience of leading three hundred thousand young men" is usually mentioned by Jaycees as the most important plum of the presidency. In a chapter on the presidency, called "How to Make a Halfback Cry," the Jaycee history says, "If the Jaycee movement as a whole is a great college of practical experience, as many have described it, the intensive experience gained by the one top leader in the movement must be a valuable postgraduate course indeed."

At a time when there are warnings that the world is being taken over by the young, some people may find it comforting that so many thirty-three- and thirty-four-year-old men are still just practicing. Although Jaycee chapters are noted for running an unremitting stream of projects—holding Safe Driving Road-e-os, sponsoring beauty pageants, leading get-out-the-vote drives, building playgrounds—Jaycees consider a project less important for its own ends than for the opportunity it provides to amass experience and leadership training. The Jaycee presidential election seems to be an example of experience in pure form, since there are no issues. The impression made by the candidates themselves is considered only a minor factor, and the outcome is decided largely not by the demonstrating delegates but by a group of Jaycees known to all as "the politicians." A presidential candidate is almost always one of ten vice-presidents, and he automatically receives the support of those states he has been assigned to look after during his vice-presidency; other states are attracted by the politicians with reminders of past voting support and hints of future voting support. Jaycees appear to enjoy the political process for itself, no matter who the candidates are. It is a matter of some pride among them that the balloting in Phoenix lasted all night. Once a candidate withdrew, the delegates from states supporting him would merely switch placards and jump up with undiminished enthusiasm at every mention of their new favorite.

Jaycees believe officially in God and the free-enterprise system. Support for both is pledged in the Jaycee Creed. *Young Men Can Change the World* has a description that might be taken as the Jaycee ideal of a young man operating in a free-enterprise economy: "Tall, handsome, with a pleasing personality and a quiet but driving ambition, Tom worked his way up the ladder." The commercial-exhibit area at the convention included several ground-floor offers for young men interested in a free-enterprise opportunity. As I watched a lady demonstrate how Swipe could clean almost anything, I was approached by a man about selling some Swipe myself. "You see, I sign you up and then I get a cut of what you sell, and then you sign people up and you get a cut of what they sell," he said. "That's free enterprise." In large cities, where Jaycee chapters have often not been as strong as they are in small towns, the Jaycees are just beginning to become involved in some ghetto projects, and a former president who addressed a convention meeting on urban problems explained that the key was to give those who live in the ghetto a chance to become "dynamic free enterprisers." The only time the welcoming speech by the mayor of Phoenix was interrupted by applause was when he said that property taxes had not been raised in Phoenix for eighteen years.

Jaycees also believe in a kind of constituency of young people. A Jaycee president once testified against the Medicare bill on the ground that Jaycees "and others like us must immediately begin payments to finance the cost of medical care for those over sixty-five currently receiving Social Security benefits who have not contributed a cent toward these medical costs." The Jaycees have always been a young man's crowd. When a member passes the age of thirty-five, he automatically becomes what Jaycees call "an exhausted rooster." Even professional staff members are not permitted to stay on in that condition. The most successful Jaycee public-relations project is its annual recognition of Ten Outstanding Young Men—an honor that in one year of uncharacteristically bad handicapping was awarded both to Douglas R. Stringfellow, the Utah congressman who later admitted to having invented most of his war record, and to Billie Sol Estes. Jaycees call everybody under thirty-five by his first name—a custom that, combined with their respect for the prerogatives of office, led them to refer to their national president in Phoenix speeches as President Jim.

In or out of presidential campaigns, Jaycees concentrate hard on youthful enthusiasm. On the first day of the convention, Paul J. Meyer—the president of Success Motivation Institute, Inc., of Waco, Texas, a Jaycee consultant, and a man introduced as the Master Motivator—lectured a Key Men luncheon on the value of enthusiasm. "Maybe the enthusiasts aren't the most cultured people in the world," Meyer told the Jaycees, "but they're the only ones who make history." It was like lecturing to a group of life-insurance salesmen on the need for planning against unforeseen disasters. In their own public speaking—encouraged by a project called Speak-Up—Jaycees tend to inject enough enthusiasm to transform a speech into what used to be called a declamation. Both Speak-Up speakers and presidential candidates lean toward the inspirational—why a citizen shouldn't let the other fellow do it, or how one Jaycee "became on fire that he, Lewis Timberlake, could make Stamford, Texas, a better place in which to live." Jaycee speakers are apt to use a phrase like "the hallowed halls of our nation's capital" even when referring to the place where programs shouldn't

come from. The national winner of the Speak-Up competition gave his speech at a general meeting of the convention. He told the history of the United States, speaking in the first person, as if he had personally seen it from the beginning. It was the first time I had ever heard anybody sound angry when discussing the behavior of the British during the period of the American Revolution. "They taxed our tea!" he shouted.

Jaycees seem to treasure an image of themselves as rowdy conventioners —being young, they are supposed to have more staying power than the Shriners or the American Legion—but at the end of the convention one of the Phoenix Jaycees in charge of local arrangements said that both the police department and the night-club owners had overestimated the impact that several thousand Jaycees would have on the city. One factor, he explained, was that there were seven candidates for the presidency, an unusually large number, and Jaycees from the candidates' assigned states had spent a lot of time demonstrating, when they could have been in night clubs. Many Jaycees were accompanied by their wives (Jaycettes), wearing feminine versions of the appropriate state costumes, and some brought their children. The traditional convention debauchery seemed to be represented mostly by the dancing of two or three indefatigable go-go girls, who appeared, in one bikini or another, at convention social events in the evening and at the booth of Mr. Lucky's night club, among the free-enterprise opportunities and real-estate offers of the commercial exhibits, from nine to five. At an event called the State Parties—two nights of more or less potluck dinners, with booths featuring the specialties of various states—a huge line formed for cherry pie being handed out by Michigan while at the next booth Tennessee Jaycees, dressed in coonskin hat and buckskin-style suits, were having trouble finding takers for free Jack Daniel's bourbon.

At Jaycee conventions, distinctions among the states are maintained with considerable enthusiasm. The annual convention parade is called the Parade of States, and states compete, mostly through membership figures, for their positions in the line of march. (This year, a state might have been better off finishing low enough in the competition to be left out completely. National Jaycee leaders disregarded the suggestion of the locals that parades in Phoenix during the summer should be held in the evening, if at all—the evening has always been reserved for state caucuses, President Jim later explained—and about a hundred and fifty paraders were overcome by the heat.) Jaycees can find something distinctive about any state, and a visitor may lose track of the fact that the delegates in referee shirts and the delegates in Indian costumes probably live in cities that are physically and culturally almost exactly alike. The Nebraska delegates wore white sailor uniforms, signifying the legendary Nebraska Navy. The Jaycees from Georgia had vests with a symbolic peach on the back, those from Oregon had shirts featuring pictures of lumberjacks, Kansans wore yellow vests with a sunflower design, and the delegates and wives from Idaho wore dun-colored outfits that succeeded in making some of them look like potatoes. Almost every state west of Ohio seemed to have some Western

element in its costume. In Phoenix, where it is common for adults to own cowboy outfits, it was sometimes the presidential candidates in business suits rather than the delegates in cowboy shirts who looked out of place. One night, I passed two young men who were wearing Western hats, boots, gun belts, and tight Western-style shirts; I looked at their patches to see if they were Jaycees from Montana or Nevada or Michigan, and discovered that they were deputy sheriffs of Maricopa County, Arizona.

At the State Parties, Florida delegates, dressed in orange blazers, served orange juice, the Hawaiians served pineapple juice, and Kentucky colonels served mint juleps. At the New Mexico booth, small shots of tequila were given away, and New Mexico Jaycees, wearing tasselled Mexican hats, helpfully poured salt on the back of each guest's hand so that he could drink in the authentic manner. Texas cowboys ladled out pinto beans and rattlesnake meat, and Wyoming cowboys gave away beef jerky. On the first night of the State Parties, immense crowds lined up for provisions like Illinois hot dogs and Wisconsin cheese. The hall became so hot that a number of people took what food they could get and went out on the lawn, where the temperature was one hundred and nine. The heat seemed to have little effect on the enthusiasm of the guests or the hosts at the Georgia booth, which featured Jesse Jewell's Portion Controlled Pre-Cooked Chicken Drumettes (wrapped in Delta Airline napkins), hard-boiled eggs from the Georgia Egg Commission, Coca-Cola, and, on two platforms behind the serving line, a rock band and a go-go dancer. A large crowd gathered in front of the booth to watch the go-go girl, and when the demand for chicken was finally satisfied, the Georgia servers gathered around the platform to stare up at her while clapping to the music. One Jaycee stood on a chair behind the dancer flicking water from a wet cloth in her direction to mitigate the heat. Jaycees in referee shirts blew whistles and Michigan Jaycees sounded auto horns. Arkansas delegates in red berets and several varieties of Jaycee cowboys came up to take pictures. At around eight o'clock, the closing time for the State Parties, the band began to play "Dixie," and a half-dozen Georgia Jaycees climbed up on the platform with the go-go girl to wave Georgia flags. Finally, one of them started throwing Jesse Jewell's Portion Controlled Pre-Cooked Chicken Drumettes to the crowd.

Local chapters also compete at Jaycee conventions, displaying their year's accomplishments in scrapbooks filled with documents known as R&R (Records and Recognition) Forms. R&R Forms are designed not only to provide a means of recognizing achievements but to train Jaycees in the organizational habits that might make them leaders. For every project a local chapter embarks on, the committee chairman fills out a Project Proposal Form, listing the Purpose and Benefits of the project, a Plan of Action ("This is an important administrative aid used by all good administrations"), a Budget, a Committee Organization Chart, a Committee Summary of Activities, and a Completed Project Report. With the help of these R&R Forms, Jaycees can gain leadership training from almost any activity; even organizing the District Three and Four Crab

Feed requires a systematic listing of what action is planned to gain the objective. In the scrapbooks that prize-winning chapters from each state brought to Phoenix, there were R&R Forms on typical Jaycee community projects—sponsoring a junior olympics, holding a children's Christmas party—and there were also forms presenting the benefits and plan of action and organization chart for such activities as attending a state convention, electing chapter officers, and holding regular meetings. Many scrapbooks included completed R&R Forms on the completion of R&R Forms. Jaycees can assign a benefit to any activity. A party improves relations among the members, and a bowling team helps public relations. Actually, almost any project can be seen as a public-relations benefit. "This project will benefit the city of Deer Park by having a flag in front of one of its buildings," the Deer Park, Texas, chapter wrote about a plan to buy a flag for a new civic center. "The chapter will benefit from the public relations for being civic-minded young men." Most of all, though, Jaycees find a local project—as well as a presidential campaign—beneficial in providing experience. The Minden, Louisiana, chapter wrote that its fund-raising candy sale would "help members develop the ability to sell themselves, the candy, and the Jaycees to the community." The Newton-Conover, North Carolina, Jaycees wrote that members would benefit from a peanut sale "by acquiring leadership training during their sale of peanuts to individuals." Leadership training, it says in *Young Men Can Change the World,* is the primary function of the United States Jaycees.

Other white-collar people, who lack the career orientation and autonomy of full professionals, are generally thought of as the lower-middle class. They are people for whom work is less than a central life interest. They have the dignity of clean work but not the financial rewards of blue-collar occupations such as plumber, truck driver, and electrician. Their work lacks intrinsic gratification and they may fail to find gratification elsewhere. They are caught in the countertrends of embourgeoisement and proletarianization,* and, according to C. Wright Mills, are in a state of panic.

In a quiz directed at higher executives, "status points" were given to the executive for such things as being visited regularly in the office by a bootblack and not having to hang up his own coat; "status points" were deducted, however, for using memo paper with the imprinted name of a supplier and for having artificial flowers in the office.†

A search for status may be even more intense among middle- and lower-middle-class individuals. Below the professionals and above the low-status white-collar workers are semiprofessionals, who may be thought of as the middle-middle class. Social workers, teachers, engineers, nurses, and pharmacists do not have the same degree of power, wealth, or prestige as physicians, lawyers, or higher executives. Semiprofessionals, more than any other group, are caught in a bind—upward emulation may mean higher status with unequal salary, while emulation of occupations below them may mean a loss of professional status but a gain of income.

White-collar workers beneath the semiprofessionals often are indistinguishable in status from blue-collar skilled workers. White-collar employees, however, are engaged in "clean" work. They may receive less pay than skilled blue-collar workers, and their only compensation may be that they view their occupation as having more status. It is difficult to predict whether white-collar employees will move toward protelarianization (becoming more working class) or embourgeoisement (becoming more middle class). At this point there is still the struggle for status, discussed in the following article by C. Wright Mills.

---

*See James W. Rinehart, "Affluence and Embourgeoisement of the Working Class: A Critical Look," paper presented before the annual meeting of the American Sociological Association, Washington, D.C., August, 1970. Embourgeoisement is the process of working-class individuals becoming more middle class; proletarianization is the middle class becoming more like the working class.

†George P. Nicholas, "Executive Status Quiz," *TWA Ambassador,* **3** (October, 1970), p. 20.

The Status Panic

C. WRIGHT MILLS

Prestige involves at least two persons: one to claim it and another to honor the claim. The bases on which various people raise prestige claims, and the reasons others honor these claims, include property and birth, occupation and education, income and power—in fact almost anything that may invidiously distinguish one person from another. In the status system of a society these claims are organized as rules and expectations which regulate who successfully claims prestige, from whom, in what ways, and on what basis. The level of self-esteem enjoyed by given individuals is more or less set by this status system.

The extent to which claims for prestige are honored, and by whom they are honored, may vary widely. Some of those from whom an individual claims prestige may honor his claims, others may not; some deferences that are given may express genuine feelings of esteem; others may be expedient strategies for ulterior ends. A society may, in fact, contain many hierarchies of prestige, each with its own typical bases and areas of bestowal, or one hierarchy in which everyone uniformly "knows his place" and is always in it. It is in the latter that prestige groups are most likely to be uniform and continuous.

Imagine a society in which everyone's

From C. Wright Mills, *White Collar: The American Middle Classes* (New York: Oxford University Press, 1956), pp. 239–358. Reprinted by permission; copyright 1951 by Oxford University Press, Inc.

prestige is absolutely set and unambivalent; every man's claims for prestige are balanced by the prestige he receives, and both his expression of claims and the ways these claims are honored by others are set forth in understood stereotypes. Moreover, the bases of the claims coincide with the reasons they are honored: those who claim prestige on the specific basis of property or birth are honored because of their property or birth. So the exact volume and types of deference expected between any two individuals are always known, expected, and given; and each individual's level and type of self-esteem are steady features of his inner life.

Now imagine the opposite society, in which prestige is highly unstable and ambivalent: the individual's claims are not usually honored by others. The way claims are expressed are not understood or acknowledged by those from whom deference is expected, and when others do bestow prestige, they do so unclearly. One man claims prestige on the basis of his income, but even if he is given prestige, it is not because of his income but rather, for example, his education or appearance. All the controlling devices by which the volume and type of deference might be directed are out of joint or simply do not exist. So the prestige system is no system, but a maze of misunderstanding, of sudden frustration and sudden indulgence, and the individual, as his self-esteem fluctuates, is under strain and full of anxiety.

American society in the middle of the twentieth century does not fit either of these projections absolutely, but it seems fairly clear that it is closer to the unstable and ambivalent model. This is not to say that there is no prestige system in the United States; given occupational levels, however caught in status ambivalence, do enjoy typical levels of prestige. It is to say, however, that the enjoyment of prestige is often disturbed and uneasy, that the bases of prestige, the expressions of prestige claims, and the ways these claims are honored, are now subject to great strain, a strain which often puts men and women in a virtual status panic.

White-Collar Prestige

The prestige position of white-collar employees has been one of the most arguable points about them as strata, the major point to be explained by those who would locate them in modern social structures. Although no one dimension of stratification can be adequate, the social esteem white-collar employees have successfully claimed is one of their important defining characteristics. In fact, their psychology can often be understood as the psychology of prestige striving. That it is often taken as their signal attribute probably reflects the effort, which we accept, to overcome the exclusively economic view of stratification; it also reflects the desire, which we reject, to encompass the entire group with a single slogan.

White-collar people's claims to prestige are expressed, as their label implies, by their style of appearance. Their occupations enable and require them to wear street clothes at work. Although they may be expected to dress somewhat somberly, still, their working attire is not a uniform, or distinct from clothing generally suitable for street wear. The standardization and mass production of fashionable clothing have wiped out

many distinctions that were important up to the twentieth century, but they have not eliminated the distinctions still typical between white-collar and wage-worker. The wage-worker may wear standardized street clothes off the job, but the white-collar worker wears them on the job as well. This difference is revealed by the clothing budgets of wage-workers and white-collar people, especially of girls and women. After later adolescence, women working as clerks, compared with wage-working women of similar income, spend a good deal more on clothes; and the same is true of men, although to a lesser extent.

The class position of employed people depends on their chances in the labor market; their status position depends on their chances in the commodity market. Claims for prestige are raised on the basis of consumption; but since consumption is limited by income, class position and status position intersect. At this intersection, clothing expenditure is, of course, merely an index, although a very important one, to the style of appearance and the life-ways displayed by the white-collar strata.

Claims for prestige, however expressed, must be honored by others, and, in the end, must rest upon more or less widely acknowledged bases, which distinguish the people of one social stratum from others. The prestige of any stratum, of course, is based upon its mutually recognized relations with other strata. The "middle position" of white-collar people between independent employers and wage-workers, "a negative characteristic—rather than definite technical functions," Emil Lederer wrote in 1912, "is the social mark of the salaried employees and establishes their social character in their own consciousness and in the estimation of the community."[1]

Salaried employees have been associated with entrepreneurs, and later with higher-ups in the managerial cadre, and they have borrowed prestige from both. In the latter nineteenth century, the foreman, the salesclerk, and the office man were widely viewed, and viewed themselves, as apprentices or assistants to old middle-class people. Drawing upon their future hopes to join these ranks, they were able to borrow the prestige of the people for whom they worked and with whom they were in close, often personal, contact. White-collar people intermarried with members of the old middle class and enjoyed common social activities; in many cases the salaried man represented the entrepreneur to the public and was recruited from the same social levels—mainly, the old rural middle class. All this—descent, association, and expectation—made it possible for earlier salaried employees to borrow status from the old middle class.

Today, in big city as well as small town, white-collar workers continue to borrow such prestige. It is true that in larger concerns personal contacts with old middle-class entrepreneurs have been superseded by impersonal contacts with the lower rungs of the new managerial cadre. Still, all white-collar people

do not lack personal contact with employers; not all of them are employed in the big layout, which, in many areas, is as yet the model of the future more than of present reality. The general images of the white-collar people, in terms of which they are often able to cash in claims for prestige, are drawn from present reality. Moreover, even in the big hierarchies, white-collar people often have more contact—and usually feel that they do—with higher-ups than do factory workers.

The prestige cleavage between "the shop" and "the front office" often seems to exist quite independently of the low income and routine character of many front-office jobs and the high pay and skills of jobs in the shop. For orders and pay checks come from the office and are associated with it; and those who are somehow of it are endowed with some of the prestige that attends its function in the life of the wage-worker. The tendency of white-collar people to borrow status from higher elements is so strong that it has carried over to all social contacts and features of the workplace.

Salespeople in department stores, as we have already seen, frequently attempt, although often unsuccessfully, to borrow prestige from their contact with customers, and to cash it in among work colleagues as well as friends off the job. In the big city the girl who works on 34th Street cannot successfully claim as much prestige as the one who works on Fifth Avenue or 57th Street. Writes one observer: "A salesgirl in Bonwit Teller's . . . will act and feel different from a salesgirl at Macy's. She will be more gracious, more helpful, more charming . . . but at the same time she will have an air of dignity and distance about her,

[1] According to a recent National Opinion Research rating, on a scale running from 90.8 for government officials and 80.6 for professionals and semi-professionals (both free and salaried) to 45.8 for non-farm laborers, the whole group of "clerical, sales, and kindred workers" stand at 68.2, about on a par with the "craftsmen, foremen, and kindred workers."

an air of distinction, that implies, 'I am more important than you because my customers come from Park Avenue.' "

It is usually possible to know the prestige of salespeople in department stores in terms of the commodities they handle, ranked according to the "expensiveness" of the people who typically buy them. Prestige may be borrowed directly from the commodities themselves, although this is not as likely as borrowing from the type of customer.

If white-collar relations with supervisors and higher-ups, with customers or clients, become so impersonal as seriously to limit borrowing prestige from them, prestige is then often borrowed from the firm or the company itself. The fetishism of the enterprise, and identification with the firm, are often as relevant for the white-collar hirelings as for the managers. This identification may be implemented by the fact that the work itself, as a set of activities, offers little chance for external prestige claims and internal self-esteem. So the work one does is buried in the name of the firm. The typist or the salesgirl does not think of herself in terms of what she does, but as being "with Saks" or "working at *Time.*" A $38-a-week clerk in a chrome and mahogany setting in Radio City will often successfully raise higher claims for prestige than a $50-a-week stenographer in a small, dingy office on Seventh Avenue. Help-Wanted ads ("Beautifully Furnished Office in Rockefeller Center," "Large Nation-wide Concern," "Offices located on 32nd floor of Empire State Building") reveal conscious appeal to the status striving of the office worker. Such positions are often easier to fill, not because of higher salary and more rapid promotion, but because of the prestige of the firm's name or location.

In identifying with a firm, the young executive can sometimes line up his career expectations with it, and so identify his own future with that of the firm's. But lower down the ranks, the identification has more to do with security and prestige than with expectations of success. In either case, of course, such feelings can be exploited in the interests of business loyalties.

In the impersonal white-collar hierarchies, employees often attempt to personalize their surroundings in order to identify with them more closely and draw prestige therefrom. In the personnel literature, there are many illustrations of an often pathetic striving for a sense of importance—for example, when a girl's chair is taken from her and she is given one thought more convenient for her work, her production drops. When questioned, she asks, "Why are you picking on me?" and explains that she had used the old chair for five years and it had her name plate on it. When the name plate is transferred to the new chair, it is explained, her attitude changes, and her production comes up to normal. Similar observations have been made in connection with the arrangement of desks in an office, in which, unknown to management, the old pattern had been in terms of seniority. Women are probably more alert to these prestige borrowings than men. The first consideration of one large group of women seeking employment had to do with "the office environment," the state of the equipment, the appearance of the place, the "class of people" working there. Periodical salary increases and initial salary were both ranked below such considerations. Of course, such prestige matters often involve the desire to be available on a market for more marriageable males, yet the material signs of the status environment are in themselves crucial to the white-collar sense of importance.

That white-collar work requires more mental capacity and less muscular effort than wage work has been a standard, historical basis for prestige claims. In the office, as we have seen, white-collar technology and social rationalization have definitely lessened technical differences between white-collar and factory work. Many white-collar people now operate light machinery at a pace and under conditions that are quite similar to those of light industrial operations, even if they do so while wearing street clothes rather than overalls. Still, the variety of operations and the degree of autonomous decision are taken as bases of white-collar prestige. And it is true that in thousands of offices and salesrooms, the receptionist, the sales-girl, the general secretary, and even the typist seems to perform a wide variety of different operations at her own pace and according to her own decisions.

The time required to learn white-collar skills and how they are learned has been an important basis of their prestige, even though as white-collar work is rationalized the time needed to acquire the necessary skills decreases. Some 80 percent of the people at work, it is frequently estimated, now perform work that can be learned in less than three months. Accompanying this rationalization of the work process, a stratum of highly skilled experts has arisen. Over the whole society, this stratum is popu-

larly, even if erroneously, associated with "white-collar" work, while the semi-skilled is associated with wage work. So those white-collar workers who are in fact quite unskilled and routinized still borrow from the prestige of the skills.

More crucial, perhaps, than type of skill is the fact that many white-collar skills are still acquired at school rather than on the job. The two ways of learning working skills that carry most prestige have been combined in many white-collar areas, whereas neither is now prevalent among wage-workers. Apprenticeships, involving close contact with entrepreneurs or managerial levels, continued in white-collar occupations after they had ceased to exist in wage work; then, formal education, in high school and "business college," became the typical white-collar way.

The shift from small independent property to dependent occupations greatly increases the weight of formal education in determining life conditions. For the new middle class, education has replaced property as the insurance of social position. The saving and sacrifice of the new middle class to insure a "good education" for the child replace the saving and sacrifice of the old middle class to insure that the child may inherit "the good property" with which to earn his livelihood. The inheritance of occupational ambition, and of the education that is its condition, replaces the inheritance of property.

To acquire some white-collar skills requires twenty years of formal and expensive education; others may be learned in one day, and are more efficiently performed by those with little education. For some white-collar jobs, people above the grammar-school level are not wanted, for fear boredom would lead to slowdown by frustration; for others, only the Ph.D. is allowed to go to work. But the educational center around which the white-collar worlds revolve is the high school.

In 1890, only 7 out of every 100 boys and girls between 14 and 17 were enrolled in high schools; by 1940, 73 out of every 100 were. During these fifty years, the number of children of this age increased some 82 percent, the number of high-school enrollments, 1,888 percent. The white-collar people, the great depository of the High School Culture implanted in U.S. youth, have completed an average of 12.4 years of school, compared with the free enterprisers' 8.4 and the wage-workers' 8.2 years.[2] On every occupational level, white-collar men and women are better educated, except for the single one of independent professionals, who, of course, lead educationally with 16.4 years of schooling. Many a clerk in a small office has a less educated, although more experienced, boss; many a salesclerk in a small store is supervised by a higher-up not so well educated as she. Of course, the higher educational level of the white-collar people in part reflects their youthfulness; being younger, they have had more opportunities for education. But they have availed themselves of it; for in the white-collar pyramids education has "paid off"; it has been a source of cash and a means of ascent. Here "knowl-

edge," although not power, has been a basis for prestige.[3]

Even today, white-collar occupations contain the highest general average of educated people; but twenty-five years ago this was much more strongly the case; in large part, white-collar people monopolized intermediate and higher education. Twenty-five years ahead it will not necessarily be the case; in fact, all trends point to the continued narrowing of the educational gap between white-collar and wage-worker.

Fifty years ago the general labor market was almost entirely composed of grade-school graduates; today of high-school graduates; by the early fifties, nine and a half million college-educated youth will be in the labor market. Most of them will reach for the white-collar job, and many of them will not find routinized white-collar jobs a challenge, for, as H. K. Tootle has estimated for an office-management association, "educated youth is being channeled into business faster than job satisfactions can be developed for it. . . . As there are not enough stimulating jobs for the hordes of college graduates we see descending upon us in the years to come like swarms of hungry locusts, they will have to take jobs that satisfy, or perhaps even now do not satisfy, the high-school graduate."

As the general educational level rises, the level of education required or advisable for many white-collar jobs falls. In

[2]The breakdown by detailed groups (median years of school completed, 1940): farmers, 7.6 years; businessmen, 9.9; free professionals, 16.4; managers, 10.8; salaried professionals, 14.9; salespeople, 12.1; office workers, 12.3; skilled workers, 8.5; semi-skilled, 8.4; unskilled, 8.2; rural workers, 7.3.

[3]No doubt some prestige accrues to white-collar people because of their youthfulness, first because if they are young they may, in the American ethos, still be hopefully seen as having more to win; and secondly, because youth itself often carries prestige, a prestige that is much advertised by displayed models and expected efficiency.

the early twenties, personnel men said: "I think it has become a principle with the majority of our progressive offices that they will not take into the office any person or candidate who has not had the benefit of at least a high-school education." But soon they began to say that too much education was not advisable for many white-collar jobs. In fact, the educated intelligence has become penalized in routinized work, where the search is for those who are less easily bored and hence more cheerfully efficient. "When you employ 2600 clerks," says one personnel supervisor, "you don't want all college people. I much prefer the young fellow who is fresh from high school, or graduated from normal school, and who is full of pep and ambition, and wants to get ahead. We could not use college men in many of our positions." Education, in short, comes to be viewed as a sort of frustrating trap.

The rationalization of office and store undermines the special skills based on experience and education. It makes the employee easy to replace by shortening the training he needs; it weakens not only his bargaining power but his prestige. It opens white-collar positions to people with less education, thus destroying the educational prestige of white-collar work, for there is no inherent prestige attached to the nature of any work; it is, Hans Speier remarks, the esteem the people doing it enjoy that often lends prestige to the work itself. Insofar as white-collar workers base their claims for external prestige and their own self-esteem upon educated skills, they open themselves to a precarious psychological life.

In the United States, white-collar people have been able to claim higher prestige than wage-workers because of racial, but to a greater extent and in a more direct way, national origin.

The number of Negroes in white-collar jobs is negligible, but especially since World War I, considerable numbers have worked in unskilled and semi-skilled factory jobs. The new middle class contains a greater proportion of white people than any other occupational stratum: in 1940, some 99.5 percent of the white-collar, compared with 90 percent of free enterprisers, 87 percent of urban wage-workers, and 74 percent of rural workers.

Nativity and immigration differences between white-collar and wage-work are probably more direct bases of white-collar prestige. When the "race peril" literature was popular, the textbook myth about the lowly character of newer immigrants was also widespread. Most of the major American historians of the period between 1875 and 1925 belligerently declared the superiority of "Anglo-Saxon" stock, concludes Edward Saveth. Being of old stock themselves, their "conception of the immigrant reflected, in some degree, their feeling that the newcomer somehow constituted a threat to what they held dear, ideologically and materially. . . ." Mass as well as academic publicity reflected and spread the fact of prestige distinctions between immigrant and native.

If the "American" stature of a group may be judged by the proportion of its native-born members, white-collar workers have been the most American of all occupational strata. In 1930, after mass immigration had been stopped, only 9 percent of the white population of the new middle class were foreign-born, compared to 16 percent of the free enterprisers and 21 percent of the wage-workers. But now there is no bulk immigration: soon, virtually all Americans will be American-born of American-born parents. Time will not automatically erase the prestige cleavages based on descent, but, for most white-collar and wage-workers, as they become more similar in origin, it probably will. In the meantime, nativity differences still underlie the prestige claims of white-collar groups.

Every basis on which the prestige claims of the bulk of the white-collar employees have historically rested has been declining in firmness and stability: the rationalization and down-grading of the work operations themselves and hence the lessening importance of education and experience in acquiring white-collar skills; the leveling down of white-collar and the raising of wage-worker incomes, so that the differences between them are decidedly less than they once were; the increased size of the white-collar labor market, as more people from lower ranks receive high-school educations, so that any monopoly of formal training adequate to these jobs is no longer possible; the decline in the proportion of people of immigrant origin and the consequent narrowing of nativity differences between white-collar and wage-worker; the increased participation of white-collar people, along with wage-workers, in unemployment; and the increased economic and public power of wage-workers because of their union strength, as compared with that of white-collar workers.

All these tendencies for white-collar occupations to sink in prestige rest upon the numerical enlargement of the white-collar strata and the increase in prestige which the wage-workers have enjoyed. If everybody belongs to the fraternity, nobody gets any prestige from belonging. As the white-collar strata have expanded they have included more offspring of wage-worker origin; moreover, insofar as their prestige has rested upon their sharing the authority of those in charge of the enterprise, that authority has itself lost much of its prestige, having been successfully challenged at many points by unionized wage-workers.

Although trends should not be confused with accomplished facts, it is clear that many trends point to a "status proletarianization" of white-collar strata.

THE SMALLER CITY

To understand the prestige of white-collar people we must examine the kinds of people among whom they successfully raise claims for prestige. For different groups do not honor white-collar claims to the same extent; in fact, their estimates often clash, and there is much ambivalence about white-collar prestige.

White-collar workers are city people; in the smaller cities, they live on the right side of the tracks and work "uptown"; in the larger cities they often live in suburbs and work "downtown." The city is their milieu and they are shaped by its mass ways. As the city has expanded, more and more of its inhabitants have been white-collar people. And it is in cities of differing size that they must raise their claims for prestige.

In the smaller cities, lower classes sometimes use the term "white collar" to refer to everyone above themselves. Sometimes their attitude is that white-collar people are "pencil pushers" who "sit around and don't work and figure out ways of keeping wages cheap"; and sometimes it is that "the clerks are very essential. They are the ones who keep the ball rolling for the other guy. We would be lost if we didn't have the clerks." The upper classes, on the other hand, never acknowledge white-collar people as of the upper levels and sometimes even place them with "the laborers." An upper-class man in a city of 60,000, for instance, says: "Next after retailers, I would put the policemen, firemen, the average factory worker and the white-collar clerks. . . . I've lived in this town all my life and come to the bank every day but Sunday and I can't name five clerks downtown I know."

This situation of white-collar prestige in the smaller city is in part due to the fact that white-collar occupations are divided into higher and lower, in terms of almost every basis on which prestige claims might be made: social origin, occupational history, income, education. Now, the images held of the white-collar people by upper-class groups seem to be derived, by and large, from the lower groups of these occupations, the "clerk" and the "salesperson." When upper-class individuals do focus upon higher-income salesmen, or professional and managerial employees, they think of them as part of "business" rather than as part of "white collar." Members of lower classes, on the other hand, tend to blend white collar, both higher and lower, into business and to make little distinction between them.

The ambiguous prestige of the smaller businessman in these smaller cities is

explained, in part, by the "power" ascribed to him by lower groups but denied to him by the upper. Insofar as power is concerned, the ambiguous status position of the white-collar worker rests less upon complications in his power position than upon his lack of any power. White-collar employees have no leaders active as their representatives in civic efforts; they are not represented as a stratum in the councils; they have no autonomous organizations through which to strive for political and civic ends; they are seldom, if ever, in the publicity spotlight. No articulate leaders appeal directly to them, or draw strength from their support. In the organized power of the middle-sized city, there is no autonomous white-collar unit.

The few organizations in which white-collar employees are sometimes predominant—the Business and Professional Women's Clubs, the Junior Chamber of Commerce, and the YWCA—are so tied in with business groups that they have little or no autonomy. Socially, the lower white-collar people are usually on "the Elk level," the higher in the No. 2 or 3 social club; in both they are part of a "middle-class mingling" pattern. They are "led," if at all, by higher-income salesmen and other "contact people," who are themselves identified with "business," and whose activities thus lend prestige to businessmen rather than to white-collar people.

Even in the smaller cities, then, there is no homogeneous social arena in which white-collar prestige is uniformly honored; in the big city this fact is the key to the character of white-collar prestige.

THE METROPOLIS

The rise of the big city has modified the prestige structure of modern society: it has greatly enlarged the social areas with reference to which prestige is claimed; it has split the individual from easily identifiable groups in which he might claim prestige and in which his claims might be acknowledged; it has given rise to many diverse, segregated areas in each of which the individual may advance claims; and it has made these areas impersonal. The prestige market of the big city is often a market of strangers, a milieu where contacts having relevance to prestige are often transitory and fleeting.

The neighbors of the small-town man know much of what is to be known about him. The metropolitan man is a temporary focus of heterogeneous circles of casual acquaintances, rather than a fixed center of a few well-known groups. So personal snoopiness is replaced by formal indifference; one has contacts, rather than relations, and these contacts are shorter-lived and more superficial. "The more people one knows the easier it becomes to replace them."

The metropolitan man's biography is often unknown, his past apparent only to very limited groups, so the basis of his status is often hidden and ambivalent, revealed only in the fast-changing appearances of his mobile, anonymous existence. Intimacy and the personal touch, no longer intrinsic to his way of life, are often contrived devices of impersonal manipulation. Rather than cohesion there is uniformity, rather than descent or tradition, interests. Physically close, but socially distant, human relations become at once intense and impersonal—and in every detail, pecuniary.

Apart from educational opportunities, the status of most middle- and working-class people becomes individualized, one generation cut off from the other. Among the propertyless, status must be won anew by each generation. The small businessman's sons or the farmer's might look forward to the inheritance of a more or less secure property as a basis for their status; the floorwalker's sons or the assistant manager's cannot expect to inherit such family position.

The more transparent lives of people in smaller cities permit status bases, such as social origin, to be more readily transferred to various occupational levels. The nature of the opaque contacts characteristic of big-city life make this difficult: members of one occupational level may see or even contact members of others, but usually in a stereotyped rather than in a personal manner. They meet on impersonal terms and then retire into their socially insulated personal lives. In smaller cities and smaller enterprises, the status lines between white-collar and wage-worker are, perhaps, drawn most clearly. In metropolitan areas white-collar people seldom contact wage-workers; the physical layout of the city, the segregation of routes of travel for different occupations often restrict people to separate circles of acquaintances.

The mass media, primarily movies and radio, have further enlarged the whole prestige area and the means of status expression. In the media the life styles of the top levels are displayed to the bottom in a way and to an extent not previously the case.

Some communication system is needed to cover any prestige area, and in modern times, with the enlargement of prestige areas, "being seen" in the formal media is taken as a basis of status claims as well as a cashing of them. When national prestige was focused in local society, local newspapers used to be the principal media involved in the prestige of local society matrons. But since the 1920's, radio and especially motion pictures and TV have supplemented newspapers and have created a national status market in which the movie star, a status type who suddenly acquires liquid assets and a lavish style of life, has replaced the local society matron. The deciders and originators in matters of the highest fashion and style of life have definitely passed from the old families of Boston, Philadelphia, Baltimore, and Newport to the stars of Hollywood and Radio City.

"In Newport, and on Fifth Avenue," Lloyd Morris has observed, "wealth had been a weapon indispensable to those who fought to win social power. In Hollywood, social prestige was an instrument essential to those determined to win wealth." The society reporters of all the eastern cities combined cannot compete with the several hundred journalists who cover Hollywood. Two dozen magazines are devoted to the film center; Louella Parsons reaches thirty million readers. Eighteen thousand movie houses are visited by ninety million people each week. The heterogeneous public appears avid for intimate details of the Hollywood elite. And the movies, which made them an elite, are set up to supply new images of them continuously. Not the society matron, but the movie star, becomes the model for the office girl.

The rich of previous eras could not so readily be known by the public, the way they lived being known only by hearsay and glimpses through curtained windows. But by the 1920's in America a democracy of status vision had come about; the area of prestige was truly national; now the bottom could see the top—at least that version of it that was put on display. It did not matter if this top was sometimes contrived and often a cloak. It did not matter if the real top was even more secluded and unseen than before. For those on the bottom, the top presented was real and it was dazzling.

The enlargement and animation, the anonymity and the transitoriness, the faster turnover and the increased visibility of the top, filling the individual's vision with a series of big close-ups—these changes have been paralleled by less noticed but equally intense changes in the prestige dynamics of the middle and lower strata.

THE STATUS PANIC

The historic bases of white-collar prestige are now infirm; the areas in which white-collar people must seek to have their claims honored are agitated. Both sides of the situation in which they are caught impel them to emphasize prestige and often to engage in a great striving for its symbols. In this, three mechanisms seem to be operating:

1. In the white-collar hierarchies, as we have seen, individuals are often segregated by minute gradations of rank, and, at the same time, subject to a fragmentation of skill. This bureaucratization often breaks up the occupational bases of their prestige. Since the individual may seize upon minute

distinctions as bases for status, these distinctions operate against any status solidarity among the mass of employees, often lead to status estrangement from work associates, and to increased status competition. The employees are thus further alienated from work, for, in striving for the next rank, they come to anticipate identification with it, so that now they are not *really* in their places. Like money, status that is exterior to one's present work does not lead to intrinsic work gratification. Only if present work leads to the anticipated goal by a progression of skills, and is thus given meaning, will status aspirations not alienate the worker. Status ascent within the hierarchy is a kind of illusionary success, for it does not necessarily increase income or the chance to learn superior skills. Above all, the hierarchy is often accompanied by a delirium for status merely because of its authoritarian shape: as Karl Mannheim has observed, people who are dependent for everything, including images of themselves, upon place in an authoritarian hierarchy, will all the more frantically cling to claims of status.

The sharp split of residence from work place, characteristic of urban life since the Industrial Revolution, is most clearly manifested in the big-city suburb, where work associates are formally segregated from neighbors. This means that the subordinate may compete in two status worlds, that of workplace in the big city and that of residence in the suburb.

At the workplace, it is difficult, even in large enterprises, to inflate real occupational status, although great status tensions are likely to be lodged there. But actual job position is not so well known to those whom one meets away from work. It may be that to the extent that status aspirations and claims are frustrated at work, there is a more intense striving to realize them off the job. If the status struggle within the job hierarchy is lost, the status struggle outside the job area shifts its ground: one hides his exact job, claims prestige from his title or firm, or makes up job, title, or firm. Among anonymous metropolitan throngs, one can make claims about one's job, as well as about other bases of prestige, which minimize or override actual occupational status.

The place of residence, which is a signal of income and style of life, limits this inflation of status; for neighbors, like job associates, will not readily cash in higher claims. But there are other areas. Anonymous and the just-known strangers, who cannot so readily "place" one, may cash in one's claims. Among them, the first, often the only, impression one makes may permit a brief success in status claiming, sometimes as a sort of mutual deal.

2. "Under modern conditions," Thorstein Veblen wrote, "the struggle for existence has, in a very appreciable degree, been transformed into a struggle to keep up appearance." Personal worth and integrity may count for something, but "one's reputation for excellence in this direction does not penetrate far enough into the very wide environment to which a person is exposed in modern society to satisfy even a very modest craving for respectability. To sustain one's dignity—and to sustain one's self-respect—under the eyes of people who are not socially one's immediate neighbors, it is necessary to display the token

of economic worth, which practically coincides . . . with economic success."

The leisure of many middle-class people is entirely taken up by attempts to gratify their status claims. Just as work is made empty by the processes of alienation, so leisure is made hollow by status snobbery and the demands of emulative consumption. It takes money to do something nice in one's off time—when there is an absence of inner resources and a status avoidance of cheaper or even costless forms of entertainment. With the urban breakdown of compact social groups in smaller communities, the prestige relations become impersonal; in the metropolis, when the job becomes an insecure basis or even a negative one, then the sphere of leisure and appearance become more crucial for status.

"One does not 'make much of a showing' in the eyes of the large majority of the people whom one meets with," Veblen continued, "except by unremitting demonstration of ability to pay. That is practically the only means which the average of us have of impressing our respectability on the many to whom we are personally unknown, but whose transient good opinion we would so gladly enjoy. So it comes about that the appearance of success is very much to be desired, and is even in many cases preferred to the substance . . . the modern industrial organization of society has practically narrowed the scope of emulation to this one line; and at the same time it has made the means of sustenance and comfort so much easier to obtain as very materially to widen the margin of human exertion that can be devoted to purposes of emulation."

Of an eighteenth-century nobility,

Dickens could say that "dress was the one unfailing talisman and charm used for keeping all things in their places," but in a mass society without a stable system of status, with quick, cheap imitations, dress is often no talisman. The clerk who sees beautifully gowned women in the movies and on the streets may wear imitations if she works hard and, skipping the spiced ham sandwich, has only cokes for lunch. Her imitations are easily found out, but that is not to say they do not please her. Self-respectability is not the same as self-respect. On the personality markets, emotions become ceremonial gestures by which status is claimed, alienated from the inner feelings they supposedly express. Self-estrangement is thus inherent in the fetishism of appearance.

3. The prestige enjoyed by individual white-collar workers is not continuously fixed by large forces, for their prestige is not continuously the same. Many are involved in status cycles, which, as Tom Harrison has observed, often occur in a sort of rhythmic pattern. These cycles allow people in a lower class and status level to act like persons on higher levels and temporarily to get away with it.

During weekdays the white-collar employee receives a given volume of deference from a given set of people, work associates, friends, family members, and from the transient glimpses of strangers on transport lines and street. But over the weekend, or perhaps a weekend once a month, one can by plan raise oneself to higher status: clothing changes, the restaurant or type of food eaten changes, the best theater seats are had. One cannot well change one's residence over the weekend, but in the big city one can get away from it, and in the small town one can travel to the near-by city. Expressed claims of status may be raised, and more importantly those among whom one claims status may vary—even if these others are other strangers in different locales. And every white-collar girl knows the value of a strict segregation of regular boyfriends, who might drop around the apartment any night of the week, from the special date for whom she always dresses and with whom she always goes out.

There may also be a more dramatic yearly status cycle, involving the vacation as its high point. Urban masses look forward to vacations not "just for the change," and not only for a "rest from work"—the meaning behind such phrases is often a lift in successful status claims. For on vacation, one can *buy* the feeling, even if only for a short time, of higher status. The expensive resort, where one is not known, the swank hotel, even if for three days and nights, the cruise first class—for a week. Much vacation apparatus is geared to these status cycles; the staffs as well as clientele play-act the whole set-up as if mutually consenting to be part of the successful illusion. For such experiences once a year, sacrifices are often made in long stretches of gray weekdays. The bright two weeks feed the dream life of the dull pull.

Psychologically, status cycles provide, for brief periods of time, a holiday image of self, which contrasts sharply with the self-image of everyday reality. They provide a temporary satisfaction of the person's prized image of self, thus permitting him to cling to a false consciousness of his status position. They

are among the forces that rationalize and make life more bearable, compensate for economic inferiority by allowing temporary satisfaction of the ambition to consume.

Socially, status cycles blur the realities of class and prestige differences by offering respite from them. Talk of the "status fluidity of American life" often refers merely to status cycles, even though socially these cycles of higher display and holiday gratification do not modify the long-run reality of more fixed positions.

Status cycles further the tendency of economic ambition to be fragmented, made trivial, and temporarily satisfied in terms of commodities and their ostentatious display. The whole ebb and flow of saving and spending, of working and consuming, may be geared to them. Like those natives who starve until whales are tossed upon the beach, and then gorge, white-collar workers may suffer long privation of status until the month-end or year-end, and then splurge in an orgy of prestige gratification and consumption.

Between the high points of the status cycle and the machinery of amusement there is a coincidence: the holiday image of self derives from both. In the movie the white-collar girl vicariously plays the roles she thinks she would like to play, cashes in her claims for esteem. At the peak of her status cycle she crudely play-acts the higher levels, as she believes she would like to always. The machinery of amusement and the status cycle sustain the illusionary world in which many white-collar people now live.

The same intensity that characterizes the middle-class quest for status characterizes its pursuit of leisure. Unlike the older Protestant Ethic that compelled the middle class to work hard, a new "work hard, play hard" ethic has blurred the distinction between work and play for the entire middle class. Greater availability of leisure time was followed by the development of leisure as a major industry. The middle class approaches leisure with such dedication and pursuit of achievement that objective standards of accomplishment often are applied. Lewis and Brissett, in the following essay, observe that although sex has been heralded as a form of recreation or "play" for the middle class, this does not mean that they are free to enjoy it. They feel compelled to be good at it—to be as technically competent as others. Thus, at least in the bedroom, upper-middle- and lower-middle-class persons share a similar life style.

Sex as Work: A Study of Avocational Counseling

LIONEL S. LEWIS
AND DENNIS BRISSETT

It is commonly accepted that America is a society of leisure. The society is said to have shifted from one of production to one of consumption.[1] The American of today spends little time working; he has a great deal of time to play.

With this surfeit of leisure, Americans have been called upon to engage in forms of consumption quite unknown to their inner-directed predecessors.

There exist extensive opportunities for play, but little knowledge of how to conduct oneself in this play. As Riesman has remarked, "To bring the individual into unfrightening contact with the new range of opportunities in consumption often requires some guides and signposts."[2] Knowing how to play has become problematic; it is something the individual must learn. He must, in a word, be socialized into the art of play.

Faced with this necessary socialization, the consuming American seeks out persons to teach him how to play. Very often this involves engaging the services of avocational counselors. The term avocational counseling ". . . describe[s] the activities undertaken by a number of relatively rapidly growing professions in the United States, including travel agents, hotel men, resort directors, sports teachers and coaches, teachers of the arts, including dancing teachers, and so on."[3] Each of the various counselors

From *Social Problems*, 15 (Summer, 1967), pp. 8–18. Reprinted by permission of the Society for the Study of Social Problems and the authors.

[1] Leo Lowenthal, "The Triumph of Mass Idols," in *Literature, Popular Culture, and Society* (Englewood Cliffs, N.J.: Prentice-Hall, 1961), pp. 109–140.

[2] David Riesman (with Nathan Glazer and Reuel Denney), *The Lonely Crowd* (Garden City, N.Y.: Doubleday Anchor Books, 1953), p. 341.
[3] Riesman, *loc. cit.*

supplies the American public with advice on play and leisure. The advice of one such group of counselors is the subject matter of this paper.

Quite recently, Nelson Foote has observed that sex, since it is becoming increasingly dissociated from procreation, is becoming more and more a kind of play activity. He states that "the view that sex is fun can . . . hardly be called the invention of immoralists; it is every man's discovery."[4] The arena of consumption is extended to include the realm of man's sexual activity, and the avocational counselor finds himself a place advising people on the vicissitudes of sex as play.

Concomitant with this increasing amount of leisure time, and the attendant problem of learning how to play, it has been observed that the play of most Americans has become a laborious kind of play. "Fun, in its rather unique American form, is grim resolve. . . . We are as determined about the pursuit of fun as a desert-wandering traveler is about the search for water. . . ."[5] Consumption, to most Americans, has become a job. Like work, play has become a duty to be performed. This interpretation is supported by the emergence of what Wolfenstein has labeled a "fun morality." Here "play tends to be measured by standards of achievement previously applicable only to work . . . at play, no less than at work, one asks: 'Am I doing as well as I should?' "[6] Consump-

tion very definitely has become production.

It is the purpose of this paper to examine the products of the avocational counselors of marital sex and to inquire as to their depiction of man's sexual behavior. If it is true that play is becoming work in the mass society, it might be necessary to amend Foote's notion of the character of sexual play. In focusing on how marital sex is handled by these avocational counselors, we will show how sex, an area of behavior usually not thought of as involving work, has been treated as such. We will emphasize how general work themes are presented as an essential part of sexual relations, and how the public is advised to prepare for sex just as they are advised to prepare for a job.

MARRIAGE MANUALS

The avocational counselors of sex with the widest audience are those who write what are frequently referred to as marriage manuals. These manuals are designed to explain all aspects of the sexual side of marriage. Their distribution is wide: many are in paperback and are readily available in drug stores; many can be found in multiple copies in public and university libraries; and some are distributed by facilities which offer services in sex, fertility, and contraception, such as Planned Parenthood clinics.

Fifteen manuals were selected from a listing of almost fifty for analysis in this study. They are listed at the end of this article. The first criterion for using a manual was wide circulation. This was determined by number of printings and number of copies sold. For example, one volume (15) in 1965 was in its forty-fifth

---

[4]Nelson Foote, "Sex as Play," in Eric Larrabee and Rolf Meyersohn (eds.), *Mass Leisure* (Glencoe, Ill.: Free Press, 1958), p. 335.

[5]Jules Henry, *Culture Against Man* (New York: Random House, 1963), p. 43.

[6]Martha Wolfenstein, "The Emergence of Fun Morality," in Eric Larrabee and Rolf Meyersohn, *op. cit.*, p. 93.

printing and had sold more than one-half million copies in the United States; a second (13) was in its forty-eighth printing and had sold almost six hundred thousand; a third (3) was in its thirtieth printing[7] and has "been read by" two million eight hundred thousand[8]; and a fourth (5) advertises on its cover "over a million and a half copies in print." Other criteria were that the book be still read and available. The fifteen volumes ranged from 14-page pamphlets to full-sized, indexed, hardbound books.

Each manual was read by both authors, and principal themes were recorded. Notes were taken, compared, and classified. Only material about whose meaning both authors agreed was utilized in drawing conclusions about the themes in a book.

WORKING AT SEX

Marital sex, as depicted by the marriage manuals, is an activity permeated with qualities of work. One need not even read these books, but need only look at the titles or the chapter headings to draw this conclusion. Thus, we have books titled *The Sex Technique in Marriage* (10), *Modern Sex Techniques* (14), *Ideal Marriage: Its Physiology and Technique* (15). There are also chapters titled "How to Manage the Sex Act" (3), "Principles and Techniques of Intercourse" (7), "The Fourth Key to Soundly Satisfying Sex: A Controlled Sexual Crescendo" (5).

[7]We were unable to obtain this most recent printing, and our copy was the twenty-ninth printing.
[8]These figures were published in *Newsweek*, October 18, 1965, p. 100.

From the outset, as we begin to read the books, we are warned not to treat sex frivolously, indeed not to play at sex:

> An ardent spur-of-the-moment tumble sounds very romantic. . . . However, ineptly arranged intercourse leaves the clothes you had no chance to shed in a shambles, your plans for the evening shot, your birth control program incomplete, and your future sex play under considerable better-be-careful-or-we'll-wind-up-in-bed-again restraint (5, pp. 34–35).

In other words, marital sex should not be an impromptu performance.

Moreover, sex should not be approached with a casual mien. Rather, we are counseled, sexual relations, at least good sexual relations, are a goal to be laboriously achieved. It is agreed that "satisfactory intercourse is the basis for happy marriage." However, it is added, "It does not occur automatically but must be striven for" (12, p. 39). In the plain talk of the avocational counselor, "Sexual relations are something to be worked at and developed" (7, p. 6).

This work and its development are portrayed as a taxing kind of endeavor; as behavior involving, indeed requiring, a good deal of effort. That sex involves effort is a pervasive theme in the fifteen manuals. From the start one is advised to direct his effort to satisfying his or her mate so that mutual climax is achieved, sexual activity is continual, and one's partner is not ignored after climax. Thus, we are told:

> Remember, couple *effort for* couple satisfaction! That's the key to well-paced, harmonious sex play (5, p. 62).

Certain positions of intercourse are also seen as particularly taxing, in fact so taxing that certain categories of people are advised not to use them. One author, in discussing a particularly laborious position, remarks that "This is no position for a couple of grandparents, no matter how healthy and vigorous they are for their age, for it takes both effort and determination" (4, p. 201). Quite obviously, certain kinds of marital sex are reserved only for those persons who are "in condition."

The female is particularly cautioned to work at sex, for being naturally sexual seems a trait ascribed only to the male. The affinity of sex to her other work activities is here made clear: "Sex is too important for any wife to give it less call upon her energy than cooking, laundry, and a dozen other activities" (5, p. 36). To the housewife's burden is added yet another chore.

Even the one manual that takes great pains to depict sex as sport injects the work theme. It is pointed out that

> *You certainly can [strive and strain at having a climax]—just as you can . . . help yourself to focus on a complex musical symphony. . . . Just as you strive to enjoy a party, when you begin by having a dull time at it. Sex is often something to be worked and strained at—as an artist works and strains at his painting or sculpture (6, p. 122).*

Sex, then, is considered a kind of work; moreover, a very essential form of labor. Regular sexual activity is said, for instance, to contribute to "physical and mental health" (7, p. 27) and to lead to *"spiritual unity"* (14, frontpiece). In the majestic functionalist tradition, "A happy, healthy sex life is vital to whole-some family life, which in turn is fundamental to the welfare of the community and of society" (1, xiii). Marital sex, most assuredly, is the cornerstone of humanity, but not any kind of marital sex—only that which leads to orgasm. "It is the orgasm that is so essential to the health and happiness of the couple . . ." (10, p. 80).

Indeed, it is the orgasm which may be said to be the *product* of marital sexual relations. It is the *raison d'être* for sexual contact, and this orgasm is no mean achievement. In fact,

> *Orgasm occasionally may be the movement of ecstasy when two people together soar along a Milky Way among stars all their own. This moment is the high mountaintop of love of which the poets sing, on which the two together become a full orchestra playing a fortissimo of a glorious symphony (4, pp. 182–183).*

In masculine, and somewhat more antiseptic terms, "ejaculation is the aim, the summit and the end of the sexual act" (15, p. 133). Woe be to the couple who fail to produce this state, as there are dire consequences for the unsuccessful, particularly for the woman.

> *When the wife does not secure an orgasm, she is left at a high peak of sexual tension. If this failure to release tension becomes a regular thing, she may develop an aversion to starting any sex play that might lead to such frustrations. . . . Repeated disappointments may lead to headaches, nervousness, sleeplessness, and other unhappy symptoms of maladjustment (1, p. 65).*

So important is it to reach orgasm, to have a product, that all the other sexual activities of marriage are seen as merely prosaic ingredients or decorative packaging of the product.

In fact, orgasm as a product is so essential that its occasion is not necessarily confined to the actual act of intercourse, at least for the women. Numerous counselors indicate that it may be necessary for the man to induce orgasm in the woman during afterplay. "A woman who has built up a head of passion which her husband was unable to requite deserves a further push to climax through intensive genital caress . . ." (5, p. 111). Particularly in the early years of marriage, before the husband has learned to pace his orgasm, he may have to rely on the knack of digital manipulation. In one author's imagery, "Sometimes it may be necessary for the husband to withdraw and continue the stimulation of his wife by a rhythmic fondling of clitoris and vulva until orgasm is attained" (1, p. 66).

The central importance of experiencing orgasm has led many of the authors to de-emphasize the traditional organs of intercourse. The male penis (member) is particularly belittled. It is considered "only one of the instruments creating sensation in the female, and its greatest value lies as a mental stimulant and organ of reproduction, not as a necessary medium of her sexual pleasure." The same author adds, ". . . the disillusioning fact remains that the forefinger is a most useful asset in man's contact with the opposite sex . . ." (14, p. 71). Furthermore, this useful phallic symbol should be directed primarily to the woman's seat of sensation, the clitoris. Only a man who is ignorant of his job directs his digital attention to the vulva, the female organ that permits conventional union.

One must often deny himself immediate pleasure when manufacturing the orgasm. One author, in referring to an efficient technique to attain orgasm, states that: "Unfortunately, some men do not care for this position. This, however, should be of little importance to an adequate lover, since his emotions are the less important of the two" (14, p. 122). Likewise, the woman may have to force herself in order to reach orgasm, even though she may not desire the activity which precedes it. It is specified that "If you conscientiously work at being available, you may ultimately find the feminine role quite satisfying even in the absence of ardor or desire" (5, p. 38). The work ethic of the sexual side of marriage, then, is one resting quite elaborately on what has been referred to as the "cult of the orgasm."

Still, one cannot easily perform one's job; its intricacies must first be mastered. After all, ". . . there is considerably more in the sexual relationship than . . . at first thought" (8, p. 136). "Remember that complete development of couple skills and adaptations takes literally years" (5, p. 206). There is a great deal to be learned. One author talks of eight steps "in order to facilitate sexual arousal and lead, finally, to satisfactory orgasm" and of seven "techniques which she and her mate may employ to help her attain full climax" (6, pp. 124–126).

All of this requires a good deal of mastery, a mastery that is necessary if the sex relationship is not to undergo "job turnover." Firstly, in the face of incompetence, the marriage partner may, at times, turn to auto-eroticism. One author stipulates that "There cannot be a shadow of a doubt that faulty technique, or a total lack of it on the man's part, drives thousands of wives to masturbation as their sole means of gratification" (3, p. 140). Moreover, if sexual skills are not acquired, the husband or wife may seek out new partners for sexual activity. The woman is admonished that adequate sexual relations will keep a man from "The Other Woman . . ." (4, pp. 264–265). The male also must be proficient in sexual encounters for "it is the male's habit of treating . . . [sexual relationships] as such [mechanically] which causes much dissatisfaction and may ultimately drive the wife to someone who takes it more seriously" (14, p. 77).

LEARNING SEX: PASSIVE AND ACTIVE

Marital sex is said to necessitate a good deal of preparation if it is to be efficiently performed. In one author's words: "This [complete satisfaction] cannot be achieved without study, practice, frank and open discussion . . ." (12, p. 45). This overall preparation seems to involve both a passive and an active phase. The passive phase seems most related to an acquisition of information previous to engaging in sexual, at least marital sexual, relations. The active phase best refers to the training, one might say on-the-job training, that the married couple receive in the sexual conduct of wedlock.

The matter of passive preparation receives a great deal of attention from the avocational counselors. Thirteen of the fifteen books call attention to the necessity of reading, studying, and discussing the various facets of sexual relationships. After listing a number of these activities, one author advises that "If the two of them have through reading acquired a

decent vocabulary and a general understanding of the fundamental facts listed above, they will in all likelihood be able to find their way to happiness" (1, p. 20). Another counselor cites the extreme importance of reciprocal communication by noting that ". . . the vital problem . . . must be solved through intelligent, practical, codified, and instructive discussion . . ." (14, p. 7). The general purpose of all this learning is, of course, to dispel ignorance, as ignorance is said to lead to "mistakes at work," and such cannot be tolerated. The learning of the other partner's physiology is particularly emphasized, most counselors devoting at least one chapter and a profusion of illustrations to relieve the ignorance of the marriage partners. One author, however, quite obviously feels that words and pictures are insufficient. Presenting a sketch of the woman's genitals, he asserts that "It should be studied; on the bridal night . . . the husband should compare the diagram with his wife's genital region . . ." (14, p. 18).

Together with learning physiology, the various manuals also stress the critical importance of learning the methodology of marital sex. Sexual compatibility seems not a matter of following one's natural proclivities, but rather "The technique of the sexual relation has to be learned in order to develop a satisfactory sex life" (13, p. 172). One must know one's job if one is to be successful at it. Not surprisingly, to like one's job also requires a learning experience, particularly for the woman. As one book scientifically asserts:

> There is a striking consensus of opinion among serious specialists (both men and women) that the average woman of our time and clime must learn to

develop specific sexual enjoyment, and only gradually attains to the orgasm in coitus. . . . They [women] have to learn how *to feel both voluptuous pleasure and actual orgasm (15, p. 262).*

In summary, then, passive learning involves the mastering of physiology and techniques. By the desexualized female of the marriage manuals, the fine art of emotional experience and expression is also acquired. And the naturally inept male must learn, for

If the husband understands in even a general way the sexual nature and equipment of his wife, he need not give the slightest offense to her through ignorant blundering (1, p. 20).

This learning process, according to most of the manuals, eventually becomes subject to the actual experience of matrimonial sex. The marriage bed here becomes a "training" and "proving" ground. Again, wives seems particularly disadvantaged: "Their husbands have to be their guides" (3, p. 108). However, generally the training experience is a mutual activity. As one author suggests in his discussion of the various positions for coitus,

In brief, the position to be used is not dictated by a code of behavior but should be selected as the one most acceptable to you and your mate. To find this you will examine your own tastes and physical conformations. By deliberate application of the trial and error method you will discover for yourselves which is most desirable for you both (11, p. 11).

In training, rigorous testing and practice is a must. In the words of one manual "experimentation will be required to learn the various responses within one's

own body as well as those to be expected from one's beloved . . ." (9, p. 7), and also, "After a variable time of practice, husband and wife may both reach climax, and may do so at the same time" (11, p. 10).

Both the husband and wife must engage in a kind of "muscular control" training if the sex act is to be efficiently performed. The woman's plight during intercourse is picturesquely portrayed with the following advice. "You can generally contract these muscles by trying to squeeze with the vagina itself . . . perhaps by pretending that you are trying to pick up marbles with it" (5, p. 97). Fortunately, the man is able to practice muscular control at times other than during intercourse. Indeed, the man, unlike the woman, is permitted to engage in activities not normally related to sexual behavior while he is training. It is advised that "You can snap the muscles [at the base of the penile shaft] a few times while you are driving your car or sitting in an office or any place you happen to think of it . . ." (5, p. 96). The practice field, at least for the male, is enlarged.

In general, then, careful learning and a studied training program are necessary conditions for the proper performance of marital sex. As seems abundantly true of all sectors of work, " 'Nature' is not enough. . . . Man must pay for a higher and more complex nervous system by study, training, and conscious effort . . ." (7, p. 34).

THE JOB SCHEDULE

As in most work activities, the activity of marital sex is a highly scheduled kind of performance. There is first of all a specification of phases or stages in the actual conduct of the sex act. Although there is disagreement here, some authors indicating four or five distinct phases (15, p. 1), the consensus of the counselors seems to be that "Sexual intercourse, when satisfactorily performed, consists of three stages, only one of which is the sex act proper" (11, p. 7).

The sexual act therefore is a scheduled act and the participants are instructed to follow this schedule. "All three stages have to be fitted into this time. None of them must be missed and none prolonged to the exclusion of others" (8, p. 155). Practice and study is said to insure the proper passage from one phase to another (12, p. 42). Moreover, to guarantee that none of the phases will be excluded, it is necessary to engage in relations only when the sexual partners have a sizeable amount of time during which they will not be distracted: ". . . husbands and wives should rarely presume to begin love-play that may lead to coitus unless they can have an hour free from interruptions" (1, p. 51). Even then, however, the couple must be careful, for there is an optimal time to spend on each particular phase. For instance, "Foreplay should never last less than fifteen minutes even though a woman may be sufficiently aroused in five" (14, p. 43). Likewise, the epilogue to orgasm should be of sufficient duration to permit the proper recession of passion.

Given this schedule of activity, the marriage manuals take great pains to describe the various activities required at each particular phase. It is cautioned, for instance, that "all contact with the female genital region . . . should be kept at an absolute minimum" (14, pp. 42–43) during foreplay. The man is warned fur-

thermore to "refrain from any excessive activity involving the penis" (14, p. 77) if he wishes to sustain foreplay. Regarding afterplay, the advice is the same; the partners must not permit themselves "any further genital stimulation" (15, p. 25).

The "job specification" is most explicit, however, when describing the actual act of intercourse. It is particularly during this stage that the sexual partners must strain to maintain control over their emotions. Innumerable lists of "necessary activities" are found in the various manuals. The adequate lovers should not permit themselves to deviate from these activities. Sometimes, in fact, the male is instructed to pause in mid-action, in order to ascertain his relative progress:

> *After the penis has been inserted to its full length into the vagina, it is usually best for the husband to rest a bit before allowing himself to make the instinctive in-and-out movements which usually follow. He needs first to make sure that his wife is comfortable, that the penis is not pushing too hard against the rear wall of the vagina, and that she is as ready as he to proceed with these movements (1, p. 61).*

Techniques

The "labor of love" espoused by the avocational counselors is one whose culmination is importantly based on the proper use of sexual technique. In fact, ". . . *miserable failure results from ignorance of technique*" (3, p. 49). Indeed, "no sex relationship will have permanent value unless technique is mastered . . ." (8, p. 177). Thirteen of the fifteen books devote considerable space to familiarizing the reader with the techniques of sexual activity. These discussions for the most part involve enumerating the various positions of intercourse, but also include techniques to induce, to prolong, to elevate, and to minimize passion. Many times the depiction of particular coital positions takes on a bizarre, almost geometric, aura. In one such position, "The woman lies on her back, lifts her legs at right angles to her body from the hips, and rests them on the man's shoulders; thus she is, so to speak, doubly cleft by the man who lies upon her and inserts his phallus; she enfolds both his genital member and his neck and head. At the same time the woman's spine in the lumbar region is flexed at a sharp angle . . ." (15, p. 218). Often, however, the mastery of sexual technique seems to involve little more than being able to keep one's legs untangled, ". . . when the woman straightens her right leg the man, leaving his right leg between both of hers, puts his left one outside her right, and rolls over onto his left side facing her" (1, p. 58).

At times, in order to make love adequately, it is required of the participants that they supplement their technique with special equipment. Some of this equipment, such as lubricating jellies, pillows, and birth control paraphernalia, is simple and commonplace. Others are as simple but not as common, such as chairs, foot-high stools, and beds with footboards or footrails. Some, like aphrodisiacs, hot cushions, medicated (carbonic acid) baths, and sitz baths, border on the exotic. Still others actually seem to detract from the pleasure of intercourse. In this vein would be the rings of sponge rubber which are slipped over the penis to control depth of pene-

tration and the various devices which make the male less sensitive, such as condoms and a local anesthetic applied to the glans.

This equipment that minimizes stimulation, while not particularly inviting, might be said to give greater pleasure than still other techniques that are suggested to add variety to the sex life. The latter, in fact, seem cruelly painful. For instance,

> . . . both partners tend to use their teeth, and in so doing there is naught abnormal, morbid or perverse. Can the same be said of the real love-bite that breaks the skin and draws blood? Up to a certain degree—yes (15, p. 157).

Indeed, a certain amount of aggression should be commonplace.

> . . . both of them can and do exult in a certain degree of male aggression and dominance. . . . Hence, the sharp gripping and pinching of the woman's arms and nates (15, p. 159).

At times, the authors seem to go so far as to indicate that the proper performance of the sex act almost requires the use of techniques that create discomfort. The element of irksomeness becomes an almost necessary ingredient of the conduct of marital sex.

Concluding Remarks

The kinds of impressions assembled here seem to support the notion that play, at least sexual play in marriage, has indeed been permeated with dimensions of a work ethic. The play of marital sex is presented by the counselors quite definitely as work.

This paradox, play as work, may be

said to be an almost logical outcome of the peculiar condition of American society. First of all, it seems that in America, most individuals are faced with the problems of justifying and dignifying their play. In times past, leisure was something earned, a prize that was achieved through work. In the present era, it might be said that leisure is something ascribed or assumed. Indeed, as Riesman and Bloomberg have noted, "leisure, which was once a residual compensation for the tribulations of work, may become what workers recover from at work."[9]

The American must justify his play. It is our thesis that he has done this by transforming his play into work. This is not to say that he has disguised his play as work; it is instead to propose that his play has become work.[10] To consume is, in most cases, to produce. Through this transformation of play, the dignity of consumption is seemingly established; it is now work, and work is felt to carry with it a certain inherent dignity. The individual now is morally free to consume, and moreover free to seek out persons to teach him how to consume, for learning how to play is simply learning how to do one's job in society.

This transformation of play into work has been attended by another phenomenon that is also quite unique to contemporary American society. Given the fact that work has always been valued in American society, a cult of efficiency has developed. As a consequence, the productive forces in America have become very efficient, and an abundance of consumer goods have been created. So that such goods will be consumed, Americans have been socialized into being extremely consumption-oriented. As Jules Henry[11] has noted, the impulse controls of most Americans have been destroyed. The achievement of a state of general satisfaction has become a societal goal. To experience pleasure is almost a societal dictum.

Thus there seem to be two antagonistic forces operating in American society. On the one hand, there is an emphasis on work and, on the other hand, there is an emphasis on attaining maximum pleasure. These two themes were recurrent in the fifteen manuals which we read, and as one writer put it:

> . . . it may well be that the whole level of sexual enjoyment for both partners can be stepped up and greatly enriched if the man is able to exercise a greater degree of deliberation and management (1, p. 33).

It was as if the avocational counselors were trying to solve a dilemma for their audience by reminding them to both "let themselves go" while cautioning them that they should "work at this." If sex be play, it most assuredly is a peculiar kind of play.

[11]Henry, *op. cit.*, pp. 20–21.

[9]David Riesman and Warner Bloomberg, Jr., "Work and Leisure: Tension or Polarity," in Sigmund Nosow and William H. Form (eds.), *Man, Work, and Society* (New York: Basic Books, 1962).
[10]Many investigators have observed the intertwining of work and play. We are here only interested in one aspect of admixture, the labor of play.

References

1. Oliver M. Butterfield, Ph.D., *Sexual Harmony in Marriage*. New York: Emerson Books, 1964 (sixth printing).
2. Mary Steichen Calderone, M.D., M.S.P.H., and Phyllis and Robert P.

Goldman, *Release from Sexual Tensions*. New York: Random House, 1960.

3. Eustace Chesser, M.D., *Love Without Fear*. New York: New American Library, 1947 (twenty-ninth printing).

4. Maxine Davis, *Sexual Responsibility in Marriage*. New York: Dial Press, 1963.

5. John E. Eichenlaub, M.D., *The Marriage Art*. New York: Dell, 1961 (fourteenth printing).

6. Albert Ellis, Ph.D., and Robert A. Harper, Ph.D., *The Marriage Bed*. New York: Tower Publications, 1961.

7. Bernard R. Greenblat, B.S., M.D., *A Doctor's Marital Guide for Patients*. Chicago: Budlong Press, 1964.

8. Edward F. Griffith, *A Sex Guide to Happy Marriage*. New York: Emerson Books, 1956.

9. Robert E. Hall, M.D., *Sex and Marriage*. New York: Planned Parenthood-World Population, 1965.

10. Isabel Emslie Hutton, M.D., *The Sex Technique in Marriage*. New York: Emerson Books, 1961 (revised, enlarged, and reset edition following thirty-fifth printing in 1959).

11. Lena Levine, M.D., *The Doctor Talks with the Bride and Groom*. New York: Planned Parenthood Federation, 1950 (reprinted, February 1964).

12. S. A. Lewin, M.D., and John Gilmore, Ph.D., *Sex Without Fear*. New York: Medical Research Press, 1957 (fifteenth printing).

13. Hannah M. Stone, M.D., and Abraham Stone, M.D., *A Marriage Manual*. New York: Simon and Schuster, 1953.

14. Robert Street, *Modern Sex Techniques*. New York: Lancer Books, 1959.

15. Th. H. Van de Velde, M.D., *Ideal Marriage: Its Physiology and Technique*. New York: Random House, 1961.

"LOWER-CLASS" LIFE STYLES

The term "lower class" generally is taken to refer to those at the lower end of the occupational scale—skilled, semiskilled, and unskilled workers —and those chronically unemployed and unemployable people outside the occupational structure. This large, inclusive category encompasses a variety of life styles. The life style of the stable working class, as typified by Kahl, is geared toward "getting by."* These are people who are likely to regard themselves as working class. A key question is: What does work mean to the working class? According to Fred Blum, who conducted a study of a Minnesota meat-packing plant, work is something that kills time and is different from life. Life begins after work ends.† Harvey Swados, in his analysis of the automobile assembly-line worker, said simply that the worker felt his job was "mindless, endless, stupefying, sweaty, filthy, noisy, exhausting, insecure in its prospects, and practically without hope of advancement. The plain truth is that factory work is degrading."‡

---

*Joseph Kahl, *The American Class Structure* (New York: Holt, 1957), p. 205.
†Fred H. Blum, *Toward a Democratic Work Process* (New York: Harper, 1953).
‡ Harvey Swados, "The Myth of the Happy Worker," *The Nation,* **185** (August 3, 1957), p. 67.

And Nathan Hurvitz has noted, "Although work and the work place are not central life interests, they are central life requirements."*

Life at home is also a source of strain. "Numerous studies have shown that divorce proneness is inversely related to husband's occupational rank."† Marital problems begin early in marriage for working-class people. Unlike middle-class couples, husbands and wives in the lower working class have fewer friends, belong to fewer voluntary associations, and are less likely to share common interests. Blue-collar husbands are likely to share interests with their male friends rather than with their wives, while wives are likely to have close relationships only with female relatives. When blue-collar wives want to learn about sex and child-bearing, they are more likely to consult their mothers than marriage manuals. Although women in the lower working class are the least satisfied of spouses in any stratum with their marriage, they do not seek reform through women's liberation or satisfaction outside their traditional sex role. Mirra Komarovsky studied 58 blue-collar couples in an eastern working-class community, which she called Glenton. The men generally are engaged in semiskilled occupations that offer little intrinsic interest to them. As Komarovsky found, there is no central life interest in maintaining a stable marital relationship.

*Nathan Hurvitz, "Marital Strain in the Blue-Collar Family," in Arthur B. Shostak and William Gomberg (eds.), *Blue-Collar World: Studies of the American Worker* (Englewood Cliffs, N.J.: Prentice-Hall, 1964), pp. 92–104.

† George Levinger, "Marital Cohesiveness and Dissolution: An Integrative Review," *Journal of Marriage and Family,* **27** (1965), pp. 19–28. See also William J. Goode, *After Divorce* (Glencoe, Ill.: Free Press, 1956); Thomas P. Monahan, "Divorce by Occupational Level," *Marriage and Family Living,* **17** (1955), pp. 323–324.

Learning Conjugal Roles

MIRRA KOMAROVSKY

Brides and bridegrooms in all social classes must reconcile their new marital relationships with former attachments to relatives and friends. Problems arise when a person finds it difficult to give up the rewards of the old ties. Parents (or more generally, any former "role partners") may contribute to the difficulty if they refuse to modify their claims despite the change in the status of the newly married person. Psychoanalysts and novelists have had much to tell us about "silver cords"—the strong ties to a parent that persist through life, impairing the capacity to love a mate.

It is not known whether the incidence of such excessive bonds to parents varies from class to class. We did find other conditions related to this problem that are likely to be class-linked. Within our sample of working-class families, the better-educated, as we shall see, emphasize the priority of marriage and demand a more complete transfer of loyalties to the mate, while the less-educated tolerate continuing ties to parents and friends.[1] All newly married persons must unlearn some old habits, but some

groups require more drastic changes than others.

Norms, or accepted rules of conduct, are not the only factors affecting ease of transition. The following pages show how the modes of life—residential, occupational, and leisure-time patterns—tend either to exacerbate the conflict between prior attachments and the demands of marriage or to minimize it. For example, the likelihood that the bride and the bridegroom will reside in the same community with their parents depends upon patterns of mobility characteristic of men and women in a given segment of the population.

MARRIAGE AS LIBERATION

The relative ease of rechanneling one's primary loyalty from parents to mate is obviously affected by the strength of the former ties. When a person is unhappy in the parental home, marriage may bring a welcome escape. This was brought out by the replies to the question: "How does marriage change a man's life?"[2] We had expected that, whatever else the husbands might say, they would feel that marriage put an end to the freedom and irresponsibility of bachelorhood. And, indeed, one-half of the men[3] did respond to this question with such replies as "He's got to settle down" and "A husband has more responsibility." Yet, 10 percent of the men emphasized the freedom they acquired with marriage. "Your wife can't boss you

From Mirra Komarovsky, *Blue Collar Marriage* (New York: Random House, 1962), pp. 23–44. Reprinted by permission of Random House, Inc.

[1]Similar findings about the strength of kinship ties are reported in a study of English working classes. See Michael Young and Peter Willmott, 1957.
[2]The author is indebted for this question to Gerald Gurin et al., 1960, p. 412.
[3]Twenty-five out of the 50 men who answered this question.

around the way your parents can," said a 32-year-old factory worker who married at age 23. A 25-year-old park employee (married three years) answered: "He's got his own place and he's boss. With my mother, I had to come home when she said or I wouldn't get anything to eat. Now I can come and go whenever I like." A 26-year-old bus driver, after three years of marriage, admitted that he married to escape an unhappy home. "I didn't get along with my stepfather, and Mother was always in the middle of it." It was only later that he recognized that marriage "wasn't just an out," that it was "something good in itself." The same thought was expressed by another respondent: "Your parents think they are cock of the walk. They don't let you do what you want to. When you have your own home, you can freewheel around."

Considering the responsibility that a man assumes with marriage, such a sense of liberation and escape is noteworthy. The working-class youth generally resides with his parents up to the time of his marriage. Aside from a complete break with the family, marriage is the usual means of release from oppressive parental control. An out-of-town college or an independent residence is available to middle-class youth, but for the young men in the present study military service generally constitutes the only period of separation from the parental home. Excluding those who married while in service, the one orphan, and four previously married men, 97 percent of the men had lived in the parental home until they married. Two-thirds of the men were over 20 years of age at the time of marriage to their present mates. That this may be

a fairly common pattern is suggested by the fact that an English study reports that it is rare for a working-class child to leave home before marriage unless he takes a non-manual job.[4]

Marriage provides the most acceptable escape from an unhappy home. Moreover, marriage in itself is less restrictive because the working-class bridegroom enjoys some privileges not granted the middle-class husband. Only a minority of Glenton's husbands, it is true, feel free to come and go as they please, but such a minority does exist.

The greater control which the family exercises over the adolescent daughter in comparison with the son no doubt largely explains the greater frequency with which women listed escape from home as one of the benefits of marriage. Almost three times as many women as men when asked "How does marriage change a woman's life?" spontaneously mentioned the escape from the parental home as a blessing.[5] "One reason I got married at sixteen," explained a 23-year-old wife, "was to get away from home." She told of constant squabbles, fights and "hollering" during childhood. Although her parents finally separated, she commented bitterly, "They would tell us kids that they stayed together for our sakes—that made us feel real good!" She said she dreaded the Sunday outings to the shore supposedly intended to give the children a good time; no sooner did they leave home than "the hollering would start." She never had a room of her own. Her bed was in the parlor, and she always had to wait till

---

[4]Peter Townsend, 1957, p. 79.
[5]Twenty-seven percent of the 43 who answered this question.

her brothers' friends would go home before she could go to sleep. She concluded: "I got married to get away from it all, but I got out of the frying pan into the fire."

The following remarks made by other women also stress escape as a motivation: "If my mother had been more free and easy I might not have married him." "It's regular to be married. It's a lot of headaches too, but I'd hate being in prison with my family. You get all cooped up and you don't know which way to bust out." "I got out from under" was the way still another wife described the advantages of marriage.

However, while the young people sometimes sought in marriage an escape from an unhappy home, lack of means for establishing a separate household frequently delayed their liberation. Thus, nearly 40 percent of the couples in this study began their married life in the home of parents of either the bridegroom or the bride.[6] The joint household with parents did not invariably cause marital strains, but it frequently did have unfavorable consequences. The accepted norm is the establishment of a separate household upon marriage. This is felt to be especially important precisely during the initial period of adjustment. Working-class couples share with the middle classes, then, the ideal of a separate establishment at marriage, but economic obstacles frequently render this ideal unattainable.

"SILVER CORDS"

For the husband, prior attachments occasionally creating strain in the first

year of marriage are to the mother and to a clique of buddies. For the wife, the competing relationships are those with her mother and, in two exceptional cases, those with father and sister. The following case illustrates such attachment to the mother:

"Our biggest problem when we were first married was my husband's fight to break me away from my mother. I can see now that he was right in trying to cut the apron strings, but I couldn't see it then. I used to take the bus home from work, and it stopped right in front of my mother's. I'd visit with her for a while before going home. But Jim got home an hour before I did and when I came in he'd say: 'I suppose you stopped at your mother's again today.' Then one time I got sick and I went to stay with my mother. That made him sore and he said: 'Next time you are sick, you stay home.' "

The attachment of the young wives to their mothers is reflected in the frequency of their contacts. The young wives see their mothers frequently. Ninety-two percent of wives married less than seven years whose mothers live in the community see their mothers several times a week or daily. But contacts decline with the duration of marriage. Only 59 percent of the wives married seven years and over see their mothers several times a week or daily. The corresponding figures for the husband's contacts with his mother are 60 percent for the husbands married under seven years, and 48 percent for the older men.

[6]In the country as a whole, about 20 percent of married couples in the early 1950's postponed setting up a separate home during the first year of marriage. Paul C. Glick, 1957, p. 60.

The men have fewer contacts with their mothers, but in a number of cases it is the husband's ties to his mother that caused marital conflict. A young wife bemoans such a relationship:

"He works for his dad, and the shop is right in front of their house, so he has lunch at his mother's every day. It's handy and saves money. And when he's mad at me he goes to his mother's and simply stuffs himself, the way he might have done when he was a little boy. . . . When we were first married he never wanted to do jobs around the house for me, but he did plenty when his mother sent for him to help at home. He was confused about being a loyal son and being a husband. . . . It burned me up and I raised Cain about it. . . . When he was living at home, his mother would sometimes bring his breakfast to him in bed. He knows now that when the alarm goes off I get up, and if he comes down late he has to eat his eggs cold. . . . He tells me he wishes I appreciated his mother more and could fit in better with his family."

A 19-year-old woman married her 21-year-old husband while he was in the army in the South. Back in Glenton, his home town, she became disturbed that they never went anywhere without his mother and his sister. But she did not know how to tell her husband that this upset her. She soon became pregnant and complained to her doctor about her depressions. The doctor told her that this was a natural reaction in pregnancy, and the young wife, using pregnancy as an excuse, asked her husband whether they could do a few things as a couple without his mother. "He didn't know at first how to say no to his family, how to accommodate both them and his wife," she explained.

. . . attachments to parents continue to play an important role in many older marriages. . . . The task of integrating the pre-marriage friends into a new social circle is another common problem of newly married couples. A most biting analysis of the loss of friends by marriage comes to us from another country and another century, in Charles Lamb's "A Bachelor Complaint on the Behavior of Married People."[7] But the mode of life characteristic of a given social class shapes this common problem in distinctive ways.

THE PULL OF THE MALE CLIQUE

Many Glenton families do not entertain friends at home and, in fact, the pattern of entertaining does not exist among these couples. Consequently, if the young husband wants to maintain association with old friends, he has to do so outside the home. It is thus more difficult for the working husband to continue old friendships than for the housekeeping wife. The women frequently see old girlfriends during the day. Although the husbands have evenings and weekends when they might have contacts with male friends, such leisure hours are to some extent claimed by the family. Meetings at lunch are feasible in rare situations, such as when an old friend is also a workmate.

A middle-class wife, if she dislikes her husband's friends, may subtly and gradually maneuver to alienate them. In the working class, however, there is no contact between the wife and the male clique. Any conflict over the husband's absence from home in order to be with

[7]See Willard Waller and Reuben Hill, 1951, pp. 264–266.

his friends is quickly forced into the open.

The conflict is not so sharp as a middle-class observer might expect because some social life for husbands with friends outside of the home is accepted in Glenton. In transitional families, however —those with both working and middle-class norms—inconsistencies arise that work to the disadvantage now of one sex, now of the other. For example, a 27-year-old husband confesses that he feels hampered by marriage. He would like to go out with the boys but "it just isn't done." The disapproval of the practice in this case may reflect the influence of the church (he is an active member) or the middle-class ideals of his wife. This couple, however, remains true to the working-class pattern in another respect. They do not entertain friends at home. This combination of patterns prevents the husband from maintaining any contact with male friends.

Fourteen percent of the total group reported having had conflicts over the husband's friends in the early years of marriage. Had we interviewed more couples soon after marriage, the percentage reported might have been higher.

The male clique retards the domestication or the marital socialization of the husband. The marriage of a member threatens the others with loneliness and the breakdown of their social world. They are quick to seize upon the concessions that a young husband has to make to his wife and are apt to taunt him for his "weakness." Fighting for its very existence, the clique rewards resistance to the new role, and it mocks capitulation to what the wife claims as her due.

Marriage at a young age was anticipated by clique members. The feeling of betrayal occasioned by the marriage of a buddy, mingled with his expectation of it, is revealed in the bitterness of a young husband: "They razzed me plenty, 'Now you are married, you have to go home.' That's how they are, and as soon as they get a girl, they'd drop you like a hot potato." One 19-year-old wife described how her husband's buddies used to call him up in the first year of her marriage and ". . . invite him to come along as if he had no wife. They would make wisecracks about his being henpecked." She decided to take things into her own hands and tell them that she and her husband had plans to go somewhere together. Marriage conflict was avoided mainly because the young husband shifted to night work and had less opportunity for evenings with his friends.

The pull of the male clique can exceed the accepted limits of tolerance in a variety of situations. Psychiatrists might suggest latent homosexual attachments as one explanation. But social conditions play their part. For one thing, the cliques often consist of men who had been friends as boys in school. Patterns of residential mobility will determine the chances for such persistence of school associations. In Glenton, the attraction of the clique was especially strong in those cases in which the circumstances of marriage were unfavorable. In two of the most extreme cases, a young husband had no regular employment, and a couple lived with parents. In such cases, acquisition of marriage roles was slow because marriage offered few rewards for severing old ties.

The circumstances involved in the tug-of-war between the clique and the wife are illustrated in the case of the 25-year-old wife of a truck driver, who married at the age of 17. She described a stormy first year of marriage. No sooner did they marry, the wife stated, than "he started going out with his four buddies almost every evening just as if he was still single. Sometimes if he drank too much he would go to his mother's house to sleep it off and not even come home at all." At one point she packed her husband's bag and told him that she was through with him. He moved back to his parents' home and started calling her up and courting her again. They became reconciled and, she says, "We get along good now."

The wife in this case is a Protestant who married a Catholic against her mother's wishes. We interviewed her mother and the opposition turned out to be less on grounds of religion than because of the young man's somewhat lower social status. The young couple did not have any furniture or any savings, and had to move in with the girl's parents. Both went to work.

In his own interview, the husband made it clear that *the conflict was not caused by any differences in normative expectations:*

> "I was a louse, it was all my fault. She is easy-going." But he tried to explain his side of the story. "I was broke and we moved in with her parents and had an audience whenever we had a fight. I was disgusted with my in-laws. There was a slump in the trucking business, and I'd ride around all day looking for work and getting very few jobs." His wife worked and saved her wages to buy the furniture. After some months, they moved into two furnished rooms in his friend's house but this didn't improve matters. "My wife got pregnant, I had no work and no money and was

> so disgusted with all this trouble that I'd say to hell with it and walk away from it all and go out with my buddies."

> He was then just 20 and the first of his four buddies to marry. So he would go out four or five nights a week, drink and gamble, "just like I was single."

> His mother used to say to him, "You got a wife now and you gotta treat her right." His father talked to him: "Are you going to stay with her or aren't you? Make up your mind." His married older brother (as we learned from the interview with the parents of this young husband) was "even wilder than he was." Our respondent explained that he himself was drinking and gambling and not running around with girls.

> The husband attributed the alleviation of this problem to job security and to parenthood. When asked to explain the improvement in his behavior, his answer was: "Steadier work. I began to earn good money. The baby was born. My wife stopped working. We moved into a better apartment. We moved back into my in-laws' house, but now we had a separate apartment on the top floor, we didn't have our meals with them and had more privacy." In another part of the interview he was asked: "How does marriage change a man's life?" Significantly his answer was: "I don't think it is marriage that does it. When I got married I worked, my wife worked. It was still like being single. But having children sure makes a difference; then you have responsibility."

> Eight years later, at the time of the interview, the major marriage problems have been "ironed out." The mother-in-law is resigned. "Half of the time," said the wife, "he is down with them [her parents] drinking coffee." The husband still has his Friday nights and Saturday afternoons playing pool or cards with the fellows. There still is some residue of conflict. "What is your

husband's idea of a good time?" his wife was asked. "To come and go as he pleases. . . . Over the weekend he stays home for an hour, and then goes out to see who he can find to talk to." But "We get along good" is the couple's own estimate of their present relationship.

The marital socialization of this young husband was hindered in several ways. His limited occupational skills and the lull in the trucking business made it difficult for him to assume the role of provider and establish a separate home. Frustrated in his efforts to enact the expected role, and finding few rewards in the new relationship, he was tempted to "walk away from it all." He credits parenthood with his domestication. The very unambiguous and inescapable nature of parental responsibility helped to control his behavior, whereas while his wife worked "it was still like being single." He had apparently internalized the sense of parental responsibility sufficiently to respond to its challenge. Paradoxically, then, the very magnitude of the responsibility of parenthood made it easier for him to accept it than the lesser demands of marriage as such.

The idea that the greater change in life comes not with marriage but with parenthood is likewise expressed by others. "There are two categories," remarked another husband, "marriage and family life. When married people don't have children they are still babies. The two of us worked before the children came. She worked for about four years and it was very different. It's having kids that makes for responsibility. You cannot go on doing what you like." Parenthood did not always have so beneficial an effect upon the marriage as in the case just cited. For some couples it

created new problems. In other studies of parenthood as a crisis it was noted that couples in which the husband was not a college graduate experienced greater strains of transition to parenthood.[8]

The male clique created difficulties for another young marriage described by the wife:

"We got married when I was sixteen and he was twenty. We moved in with his parents. They were nice to me—they even took my side against him—but it was awful living with them. Our bedroom was right next to theirs, you'd turn over in bed, they'd hear you. He didn't have any job; he'd work for a while and then quit. He used to go out every single night after supper, just as if he was single. His parents tried to shame him about leaving me to be with the fellows. I tried every trick in the pack. I cried and I cursed. I would have gone back home but by that time my parents were separated and there was no place to go. I don't think I would have split up, I would have gone home just to scare him, but I just had to stick it out."

When asked how her marriage improved, this wife explained that other fellows in the clique married too. In time the couple found an apartment of their own and he settled down to a steady job.

THE SEPARATE WORLDS OF THE SEXES

Men and women live in different psychological worlds, whatever their class position. Much of the zest and the exasperation of the early years of marriage results from each partner's introduction into the mental world of the opposite

[8]See, for example, Everett D. Dyer, 1963, and E. E. LeMasters, 1957.

sex. For many Glenton couples the confrontation brought more exasperation than delight.

The gulf between the sexes in interests and attitudes may be wider in the working classes than among the educated middle classes. A number of our couples found the gulf so wide that neither could serve as a satisfying audience to the other. They repeatedly missed the cues and, when they did understand the other's concerns, found them trivial and boring. "When I was first married, half of the time I didn't know what she was driving at, what it was all about," confessed a 23-year-old grade school graduate. "Sometimes I'd think I'd got her all figured out and then I don't make her out at all. The women in her bunch understood her pretty well though," he added. "They seemed to understand her better than I did sometimes. They'd tell their husbands about her and the fellows would tell me." His 22-year-old wife remarked, "Men are different. They don't feel the same as us."

This husband was not the only person who sought the help of his own sex to translate incomprehensible ways of the spouse. A young wife, for example, perplexed about her husband's refusal to explain his low spirits, turned to her mother-in-law for guidance. The latter in turn asked her husband and then passed along his suggestion to the young wife.

Several newly married men and women still exhibited watchful caution because they did not know, as one put it, "which way the other will jump."

> "You're supposed to tell your husband everything," said one young wife, "but you don't. Nobody can tell you what you ought to tell him. Sometimes you tell

> him just the little old nothings and it is just as wrong as it can be. And sometimes you tell him something you think will bring the roof down and he won't even bat an eyelash." . . .

THE SOCIALIZING ROLE OF THE "CROWD"

The male clique can survive only if it defends itself against the claims of the wives. But a "bunch" or a "crowd" composed of couples acquires a stake in enforcing marriage solidarity. Its social activities require that both husband and wife be present and that centrifugal interests be curbed. In our sample, however, only one-fifth of the young couples "go with a crowd," which usually consists of some three or four couples. A wife may see another woman by herself during the day, but the couples engage in many activities together.

The crowd serves as a *reference group enforcing common definitions of marriage roles.* A member of the group tests the legitimacy of his marital claims by asking the others or observing their behavior. In intimate matters the comparative evaluations are made tentatively, through trial and error. Thus, one bride troubled by a vulgar habit of her husband tested the reaction of a woman friend by attributing the habit to "a couple she heard about." When her friend remarked that the behavior is not unusual in husbands, the young wife divulged that she was describing her own experience.

The crowd enforces common definitions through direct pressure upon deviants. Thus in the case of one husband who was known for his excessive jealousy the crowd "teased him about it and kidded his wife along." Once they were dancing around in one of the houses, and all the fellows when dancing with this particular woman held her at a great distance and teased her husband. "He got sore about it at first, but then he got over it and we think he's better."

Another function of the crowd is to *drain off resentment against the mate for the common frustrations of marriage.* "I talked to the fellows and I found out that it is this way all around," remarked one husband. A wife said, "He needs sex a lot more than I do. I guess it's that way with everybody, at least that's what it seems like from what my girl friends tell me." The realization that the grievance or worry is a common one tends to take the sting out of it—to reassure and to promote resignation.

The line dividing permissible griping from the violation of marriage confidences is quite tightly drawn. When assembled, the sexes exchange accusations only about stereotyped short-comings of husbands and wives. *This ritualized criticism serves not so much to release irritation as to strengthen the self-image as a "wife" or a "husband."* In joking about the extravagance of women, husbands experience the fellowship of married men. Wives similarly exchange knowing looks about the awkwardness of men in the kitchen.

The crowd sometimes promotes marital communication. Under the guise of a joke and under the protective cover of the group, a person expresses a sentiment he had concealed from his spouse out of pride or caution. Perhaps a similar sentiment or criticism was expressed by another and he followed suit. The presence of others, he senses, will keep the expressed feeling from developing into a quarrel or will mute its deeper overtones (since the deeply troubling sentiments are supposedly reserved for private occasions).

As dissatisfied as the blue-collar worker is with his job or marital situation or both, his situation is still better than that of the true American underclass—the lower-lower class. This subgroup, alienated from the rest of society, lives on a poverty income, with no skills or hopes for the future and a feeling of defeat. Governmental financial-assistance programs do not even provide them with subsistence income. The life style that Lebeaux describes is not one of getting by but an attempt at survival.

Life on ADC: Budgets of Despair

CHARLES LEBEAUX

In September 1962 a grave crisis occurred in 6,000 needy families with children in Detroit. These families were recipients of Aid to Families with Dependent Children (AFDC), the aid program commonly known as ADC (Aid to Dependent Children) until its title was changed in 1962. In the early 1940's the Detroit welfare departments began supplementing AFDC grants out of general relief funds, because the Michigan state grant in AFDC was in many cases too small for the family to live on, and because it was often *less* than the same family would receive from general relief.[1] But due to Detroit's financial straits, about four years ago the city began cut-

From *New University Thought* (Winter, 1963). Reprinted by permission of New University Thought.

[1]AFDC is one of five categorical public assistance programs set up in the Social Security Act, in which the federal government shares costs with the states. These programs (AFDC, Old Age Assistance, Aid to the Blind, Aid to the Disabled, and Medical Aid to the Aged) are separate financially, and for the most part administratively, from general relief, which is run by the states and localities with no federal involvement. Detroit is in Wayne County where there are three relief offices: the Wayne County Bureau of Social Aid, which administers the categorical aid programs (including AFDC) for the entire county; the Detroit Department of Public Welfare, which handles general relief in Detroit; and the Wayne County Department of Social Welfare, which handles general relief in the rest of the county.

ting the amount of the supplement. In September 1962 the supplement was cut entirely. This last cut affected 6,000 of the city's 13,000 AFDC families—many more had been affected by earlier cuts. These many thousands of families are thus living below the minimum standards of health and decency, even as defined by this welfare program itself.

Few people in Michigan know about the plight of these families and even fewer seem to care. The AFDC mothers themselves, many without the clothes or carfare to go out of their homes, have almost no power to influence public policy or opinions. Although in the fall of 1962 members of the Detroit Chapter of the National Association of Social Workers (NASW) organized and supported efforts of some Negro organizations (primarily the Trade Union Leadership Council and the Federation of AFDC Mothers, a group of the mothers themselves), none of their appeals to rescind the cut, either to the mayor or the welfare department, were successful. When these efforts failed, the following survey of the families affected by the cut was made, in order to arouse the moribund consciences of the city and state.[2]

[2]After we were unable to obtain a list of the 6,000 from city, county, or state agencies, which made a full random sample impossible, the NASW decided that it had to proceed on its own, and quickly. A list of some hundred odd names was supplied by the Federation of AFDC Mothers, and a questionnaire was devised by faculty and students of the Wayne State University School of Social Work. Twenty-five members of NASW and twenty-five social work students volunteered to do the home interviewing, which was accomplished in April 1963. Ninety-three usable interviews were held, and are the basis of this report.

Because we could not obtain the list of 6,000 supplement-cut cases, we could not pick a statis-

THE PEOPLE ON AFDC

There are now about 7½ million people in the United States getting public assistance under all programs, special and general. Around four million of these are in AFDC families. There are about 33,000 AFDC families in Michigan; about 13,000 of these families, with some 40,000 children, live in Detroit. AFDC is the most controversial of the public assistance programs, not only because of its size and persistent growth, but because of the social characteristics of the recipients. When the program started in the late 1930's, death of the father was the common cause for being in need of aid. Today, more than 60 percent of AFDC cases are due to estrangement of parents—divorce, separation, desertion, or unmarried motherhood. The American public regards these as bad or unworthy reasons to be in need, and is less inclined to give help.

Over 40 percent of AFDC families are Negro (compared to about 10 percent of the general population). In northern industrial cities, the caseload is largely Negro (about 81 percent in Detroit), and in cities like Detroit, the proportion of illegitimate children is unusually high (although less than one-quarter of all illegitimate children in the country receive AFDC assistance).

The federal law says that to qualify under AFDC a child must be in "need,"

but the states define that status and determine the actual amount of money that each child and his family receive. The Michigan AFDC law says that they shall receive enough to permit them to live with "health and decency," at a level below which something suffers—health, church and school attendance, or self-respect. However, most states, including Michigan, interpret a health and decency standard to mean "minimum subsistence."

Dollar costs of a minimum subsistence budget are determined by home economists and other experts in the Federal Department of Agriculture, the State Department of Social Welfare, and home economics departments in universities by adding together minimum amounts for food, shelter, utilities, clothing, household supplies, and personal incidentals. For example, on the scale prepared by the Family Budget Council of the Detroit Visiting Nurses Association, $266.21 per month was the minimum income required in January 1960 by a family consisting of a mother age thirty-five, a boy age fourteen, and two girls, nine and four, with rent assumed to be $55 per month. For the identical family, paying identical rent, the Michigan State Department of Social Welfare in January 1961 has $223.05 as the monthly amount required to meet basic needs.

In practice, the welfare worker on the case adds up the amount needed to meet basic needs of the family according to state standards, subtracts any income there may be, and the unmet need should be the amount of the AFDC check. But in most cases in Detroit that is *not what the family gets*. The state sets ceilings on what each family can get, no

tically correct sample; but when a population is quite homogeneous with respect to the characteristic under investigation, just a few cases may represent all. So with the poverty aspect of our AFDC families. In fact, my guess is that our group is better off than the typical AFDC family, because women who participate in the Federation of AFDC Mothers also probably will be better managers than the average woman receiving AFDC.

matter what the budget figures show they need, according to the 1963 formula shown in Table 1.

ing in the home with no provision for his support.

Out of the ceiling grant rent and utili-

TABLE 1
THEORETICAL AND ACTUAL GRANTS

Family Size	Budget Requirements*	Maximum Grant	
Mother and 1 child	$151	$120	
Mother and 2 children	191	140	
Mother and 3 children	228	160	
Mother and 4 children	263	180	
Mother and 5 children	300	200	
Mother and 6 children	334	220	
Mother and 7 children	368	240	(absolute maximum)

*Includes food and incidentals allowance of $34 per person, $67 rent, and heat and utilities according to a standardized allowance based on family size.

How Are They Living?

Without important error, we can think of these families as living on the schedule of state ceiling grants. No income other than the relief grant was reported for seventy-nine families. This means that for 85 percent of the group, income is fixed by the state ceilings— $120 for a mother and one child, $140 for a mother and two children, and so on. Whenever income plus the ceiling grant exceeds the state subsistence standard for the family, the grant is reduced accordingly.

Court-ordered or voluntary support payments by the absent fathers of families on relief is the weakest of financial reeds. In many cases they are not actually forthcoming, and families dependent on them are chronically on the verge of utter destitution. Children over seventeen are excluded from the state-federal AFDC program, and since September 1962 are also eliminated from city welfare support. There are at least six families among our ninety-three with an unemployed child over seventeen liv-

ties must get paid, usually first. Table 2 shows the combined cost of rent and utilities to these families in the month of March 1963.

Fifty-two of the families live in city public housing projects, thirty-seven in private housing. Living in public housing projects is cheaper—the median rent and utility cost is $56, compared with $86 in private housing, but few public housing units are large enough for the biggest families, who naturally pay more for bigger private quarters.

What do these reasonable rent and utility costs mean to an AFDC family? Consider a mother with two children. Say that rent and utilities are $70 per month. Out of their $140 grant that leaves $70. But the state welfare department says that three people need $102 a month for food and incidentals. It is clear that for these families "something suffers."

One mother, three days after receipt of her check (and twelve days before the next one would come), had 56¢ left. She

TABLE 2
COMBINED COST OF RENT AND UTILITIES—MARCH 1963

Dollars	Public Housing	Private Housing	Type of Housing Not Ascertained
40-59	44	3	1
60-79	6	10	1
80-99	2	18	2
100-above	0	5	0
Total	52	36	4

had bought food and coal and paid the rent, but held off on the gas and electricity bills because there was no money to pay them. The gas and electricity may be cut off, she says, as they have been twice in the last two years. And what of school supplies, clothing, or carfare?

Sixteen mothers reported they were behind in rent. Half of these owed $50 or less, but one woman was $140 behind because her grant had stopped while the agency checked out a report that "a man was living with her." The lost income was never made up. Twenty-five families were behind in utilities; you need a roof overhead, at least in the winter, but you can exist without heat and light.

A surprising proportion of the mothers considered themselves not badly housed. In the words of the women:

(Private housing): *"It's good because the rent is fair and it's near school, relatives and shopping. But the house is too small and the neighborhood is unfriendly."* (High-rise public housing project): *"It's cold in winter, causing excess use of electricity. It's too far from the children outside, too small, and the elevators are a problem. But it is burglar- and fire-proof, and there's a good incinerator."* (Also high-rise): *"It's too*

crowded, noisy, and too high" (woman has hypertension). *"But it's warm, fire-proof, and the Neighborhood Service Organization has good programs for the kids."*

How Do AFDC Families Eat?

To get some detail on the quality of economic life on AFDC, we asked the mothers how much food they had on hand (meat, dairy products, and fresh or canned fruit). The information obtained was voluminous and interesting, but difficult to summarize and liable to misinterpretation. Just before check day, food stocks will naturally be low, and just after, there may be two weeks' supply of food newly purchased. Averages here would make no sense.

However, the trend of the information gathered indicated that hardly any mother had as much as a half-gallon of milk on hand, and very little meat. Often the meat listed was an inexpensive cut like neck bones, or a canned variety. There was a nearly universal report, "No fruit," "No fruit." And something we didn't inquire into was frequently volunteered: "No vegetables either." And in home economics courses in the schools they teach children about balanced diets!

Asked "Is your family adequately fed?" forty of the mothers answered "yes," six answered "sometimes," and forty-seven answered "no." "Never enough near the time the check is due. Hungry at other times too." "Before transfer to AFDC (from Detroit welfare) we ate well, but now food is inadequate." So the mothers respond who feel their families are inadequately fed. One mother had a doctor-prescribed high-protein diet (and TB too) that she has been unable to follow for two months.

Those that consider their families adequately fed have often given up something else. They say that they are getting behind in the rent, are without adequate clothing, and in one case without a phone, which was necessary because of a brain-damaged child with frequent convulsions. Those who feel they are adequately fed usually go without fruit, and eat little meat and vegetables.

FOOD STAMPS IN THE AFDC PROGRAM

For many years now the federal government has been disposing of some of the surplus foods accumulated under the farm subsidy program, by giving it to local relief agencies across the country who distribute it to poor people. In 1962 the food stamp program, which had been used before World War II, was started in a number of localities including Detroit to test whether it was a better way of distributing surplus foods. As a result, in Detroit surplus commodities are not now given directly to families, but food stamps are distributed by the City De-

partment of Public Welfare to all low-income people who wish to participate. The participant takes his cash to a stamp office and buys stamps which are worth more than the cash paid—for example, you may get $14 worth of stamps for $10. The amount one may purchase depends mostly on the size of the family, but most AFDC families qualify for less than a 50 percent bonus, e.g., for $30 cash, $43 in food stamps.

All AFDC families in Detroit are eligible to buy food stamps. Forty-seven out of our ninety-three families reported buying food stamps; forty-six did not. Most mothers who get the stamps say they are a great help. Those who do not get the stamps gave the following reasons (in order of frequency): not enough cash, restricts purchase selection, timing is off, and can't get to the stamp office.

Twenty-four families found the stamps restricted purchase selection. For example, the stamps don't buy soap, cleaning supplies, or toilet paper. They don't buy coffee or cocoa. These restrictions occur because the program, financed by the U.S. Department of Agriculture with farm subsidy funds, is designed to get rid of surplus food stores, not to help feed poor people. The resulting rules and procedures guard the interests of the farmers, who don't grow coffee or toilet paper, instead of the interests of the stamp users. Even a very careful home manager is penalized by the program's procedures; however, she still gains in dollars by using the stamps.

Not enough cash. This is the most important reason; and it causes all kinds of difficulties even for the families that buy food stamps. What happens is this: A family of mother and three children when receiving its semi-monthly AFDC check of $80 is certified to buy $30 worth of food stamps. But the rent of $55 is due and must be paid first; there is not enough left to get the food stamps. Suppose they pay only half the rent now (which many do); but some utility bills are due and a child must have a pair of shoes—again, not enough cash to buy the food stamps. They are not permitted to buy less than the amount they are certified for by the welfare department (this would be against the Department of Agriculture regulations). And they must buy regularly. Every time a family fails to buy the stamps at the appointed time, it is automatically decertified and must go through the application procedure again. If the family is very irregular in buying stamps, it becomes ineligible for the program for a while—a Department of Agriculture penalty to force regular participation. Thus those who most need the added food-buying power of the stamps are least able to get them.

Some find the "timing is off"—that the fixed time for buying stamps comes several days after (or before) the check comes. Meanwhile you have to eat, and there is then insufficient cash to buy stamps when the time comes. This problem is much less severe now than it was when the program was started because local relief officials, after fighting a long battle with Washington, have been able to get the check and stamp buying dates into approximate coincidence.

There are some cases where the mother wanted, and was able, to buy the stamps but couldn't get her relief worker to come out to certify her. Although occasionally workers are indifferent, the basic reason is that the Bureau of Social Aid is so understaffed

that planned contacts with ADFC families have been made only once in every six- to twelve-month period. This period has been reduced under the 1962 welfare amendments. Yet when no worker comes around, the family doesn't get food stamps.

WHAT DO THE CHILDREN WEAR?

As a further measure of the level of living on AFDC, information was obtained on the total wardrobe of the oldest school child in each family. As with the food data, the information obtained was voluminous and enlightening, but difficult to summarize and liable to misinterpretation. However, some startling facts emerged regarding what is one of the most critical problems in AFDC life, clothing for school children.

Only about half of the clothing is purchased, a good deal of it was bought before the supplement cut of September 1962, and a good deal of this purchased clothing is used. For the other half of their clothing the children depend on gifts from relatives and neighbors, and from school teachers. About eight out of ten boys have but one pair of shoes; about half the girls have only one pair of shoes, and half have two pairs. About half the children have no rubbers or boots of any kind, and about three-fourths have no raincoats of any description. There is obviously no room in a state ceiling grant for clothing.

WHAT ELSE DO THEY SPEND MONEY ON?

Although the grants hardly allow for it, the mothers are forced from time to time to spend money on things other than rent, utilities, and food. For the month prior to the interview they reported the following other expenditures—which, of course, are estimates from memory.

Sixty-nine had some expense for transportation, ranging in amount from under a dollar to $45 for a trip South to resettle a burned-out mother. Thirty spent one or two dollars, nineteen more spent three or four dollars. One woman said it cost $20 in carfare to make trips to the clinic for an asthmatic son. Twenty-four families apparently rode not at all.

A good deal of medical expense is reflected in the transportation figure, since the free clinic is their only medical provision. Many find Receiving Hospital care unsatisfactory because of long waits and responsibility for young children; thus we find thirty-one who had expenses for doctors, dentists, or medicines during the month. In twenty-four of these cases the amounts expended were less than $7, but one woman reported $48.68 for doctor and $4.25 for medicine, while another "pays what she can" on a $300 bill for braces for her son's teeth.

Eight families reported insurance premium payments of from $3 to $15 in the preceding month, and undoubtedly many more neglected to report such expenditures. Only ten families reported any expenditure for recreation, although all were specifically asked about this. Nine reported church expenses, from $1 to $6; nine had school expenses, from $1 to $10; eleven paid telephone bills; one paid $7.50 for house screens; one $2 for a horn mouthpiece for a child; one $3.09 for brooms and a mop; several had bought newspapers; one girl lost $10

from the sale of Girl Scout cookies and the mother had to make it good.

LIFE IN OUR "AFFLUENT SOCIETY"

The significance of these other expenditures is twofold. First, that they should exist at all, since there is usually no allowance at all for them in the grim budgets of these families; and second, even more important, that they should be so few and so small considering that we live in a money economy. What does it mean that families should spend nothing at all for transportation for a whole month in a city like Detroit? That most should spend nothing at all for recreation in families averaging over three children apiece? That with hundreds of school kids represented, only nine families reported expenses for school supplies?

As a refined measure of the economic situation of these families, they were asked the combined value of cash and food stamps on hand, and how many days until the next check came. AFDC checks are now issued twice monthly, rather than once, as formerly, to help families spread their income over the entire month, although this interferes with rent payment and purchase of food stamps. The essence of the financial situation of these people is contained in the fact that thirty-one families had between nothing and $4 on hand to last from three to fourteen days. Asked if they ever ran out of money, they all answered yes.

When asked what they did about running out of money, two-thirds said they borrowed, either from relatives and friends or storekeepers, and one-third said they just "stayed run out." "Stay run out" is the theme of their lives—and for those who borrow too, because the loan must be paid back, and each month they sink a little deeper. Besides borrowing and staying run out, some found other ways to cope with the continuing crisis: One "lets the bills go." (Where does this end?) One cashes in bottles and borrows food. One cried in shame: "The lady downstairs gives us food." One said, "If the children get sick, I call the police to take them to Receiving Hospital."

One has been "borrowing" secretly from the funds of a Ladies' Club of which she is treasurer. The club is her one meaningful adult social contact. There is soon to be an election for new club officers and she will be exposed. Her children ask: "Mama, why are you always so sad?" Half crazy with worry, she feels sick; at Receiving Hospital they have referred her to the psychiatrist.

One was in despair because a retarded son who delights in his monthly visit home from the County Training School was coming tomorrow, and there was little food and no money or food stamps in the house. One said bitterly: "A woman could always get $10 if she had to. I prefer not to resort to this."

Consider our affluent society: in an economy generating wealth sufficient to supply every family of four with nearly $10,000 per year income, we reduce a family to cashing in pop bottles to get food, we push a woman to thoughts of prostitution to feed her children, we force an honest woman into theft and then provide her with $25 an hour psychiatric treatment.

Impact of the Supplementation Cut

As noted above, only about two-thirds

of the ninety-three families received a supplement cut in September 1962. The families that had been cut were asked: Where did it hurt? What did you stop buying?

"No more clothes, fruit, milk. Clothes hurt most because mostly for school boy. Borrowed clothes to go to church." "Got behind in utilities—over $100." "Had to cut out food stamps. Hurt because came at time when children needed school supplies and clothing." "Shoes. Children have hard-to-fit feet so can't buy cheap shoes. Special treats cut out. We used to go as a family for small treats on holidays, but no more." "School clothing. They are ashamed of their ragged clothing. No spending money in school. This makes my children want to quit." "Boy dropped out of Boy Scouts. No shows, no getting away from the house."

No clothing, no school supplies, no gym shoes, no church, no Boy Scouts, no movies, no little treats, no ice cream cones—nothing like this if you want to keep the roof overhead. But after a while you lose interest even in that, and you quit school, quit church, quit Boy Scouts, begin to steal, or perhaps take money from a boyfriend. Every single family which had its supplement cut was seriously hurt by the income reduction—all gave stories like those above.

When the 6,000 AFDC cases were cut off supplemental relief in September 1962, it was expected at the welfare department that many would come to the department asking for reinstatement of supplementation. But few showed up. It was then suggested by some public assistance officials, "Maybe they are not so bad off as we thought. Maybe they don't really need it." As we have seen, they are wrong.

But how many went, what happened, and why didn't the rest go? Actually thirty-one of the sixty-five mothers who had received a budget cut *did* go to the city welfare to ask for help. None got it. Why didn't the other thirty-four mothers go? Perhaps they were wiser in anticipating refusal; they decided to save the time, the carfare, and the effort. Of course, in refusing aid the intake workers are simply carrying out departmental policy. So often in the position of having to deny aid to people who in their heart they know need help, the workers tend to develop what one former worker calls "the culture of intake"—methods of denying aid without fully examining the circumstances of the family.

SOCIAL POVERTY

These people are not starving or out on the street. But in our world lack of buying power, even when it is not so absolute as to lead to starvation or death, leads to a very real social starvation and social death.

Well-off people easily forget that almost all social relationships depend on the ability to spend some money. To go to school costs money—for books, notebooks, pencils, gym shoes, and ice cream with the other kids. Without these the child begins to be an outcast. To go to church costs money—for Sunday clothes, carfare to get there, and a little offering. Without these, one cannot go. To belong to the Boy Scouts costs money—for uniforms, occasional dues, shared costs of a picnic. Without these, no Scouts.

Poverty settles like an impenetrable prison cell over the lives of the very poor, shutting them off from every social contact, killing the spirit, and isolating them from the community of human life.

An important hypothesis is that a distinctive life style develops under such conditions as those described by Lebeaux. This life style has been called the "culture of poverty" and occurs in many societies. In this view, the poor in Mexico, Italy, and the United States are all very similar. Poverty becomes the overriding determinant of life style, superseding race, age, region, ethnicity, and any other variable generally affecting one's way of life. Oscar Lewis, an anthropologist who wrote extensively about the poor, characterizes the culture or life style of poverty in the following essay.

The Culture of Poverty

OSCAR LEWIS

Although a great deal has been written about poverty and the poor, the concept of a culture of poverty is relatively new. I first suggested it in 1959, in my book *Five Families: Mexican Case Studies in the Culture of Poverty.* The phrase is a catchy one and has become widely used and misued.[1] Michael Harrington used it extensively in his book *The Other America* (1961), which played an important role in sparking the national anti-poverty program in the United States. However, he used it in a somewhat broader and less technical sense than I had intended. I shall try to define it more precisely as a conceptual model, with special emphasis upon the distinction between poverty and the culture of poverty. The absence of intensive anthropological studies of poor families from a wide variety of national and cultural contexts, and especially from the socialist countries, is a serious handicap in formulating valid cross-cultural regu-

larities. The model presented here is therefore provisional and subject to modification as new studies become available.

Throughout recorded history, in literature, in proverbs, and in popular sayings, we find two opposite evaluations of the nature of the poor. Some characterize the poor as blessed, virtuous, upright, serene, independent, honest, kind, and happy. Others characterize them as evil, mean, violent, sordid, and criminal. These contradictory and confusing evaluations are also reflected in the in-fighting that is going on in the current war against poverty. Some stress the great potential of the poor for self-help, leadership, and community organization, while others point to the sometimes irreversible, destructive effect of poverty upon individual character, and therefore emphasize the need for guidance and control to remain in the hands of the middle class, which presumably has better mental health.

These opposing views reflect a political power struggle between competing groups. However, some of the confusion results from the failure to distinguish between poverty *per se* and the culture of poverty, and the tendency to focus upon the individual personality rather than upon the group—that is, the family and the slum community.

As an anthropologist I have tried to understand poverty and its associated traits as a culture or, more accurately, as a subculture[2] with its own structure and rationale, as a way of life which is passed down from generation to genera-

From Oscar Lewis, *La Vida* (New York: Random House, 1966). Reprinted by permission of Random House, Inc.; copyright 1966.

[1]There has been relatively little discussion of the culture of poverty concept in the professional journals, however. Two articles deal with the problem in some detail: Elizabeth Herzog, "Some Assumptions About the Poor," in *The Social Service Review,* December 1963, pp. 389–402; Lloyd Ohlin, "Inherited Poverty," Organization for Economic Cooperation and Development (no date), Paris.

[2]While the term "subculture of poverty" is technically more accurate, I have used "culture of poverty" as a shorter form.

tion along family lines. This view directs attention to the fact that the culture of poverty in modern nations is not only a matter of economic deprivation, of disorganization, or of the absence of something. It is also something positive and provides some rewards without which the poor could hardly carry on.

Elsewhere I have suggested that the culture of poverty transcends regional, rural-urban, and national differences and shows remarkable similarities in family structure, interpersonal relations, time orientation, value systems, and spending patterns. These cross-national similarities are examples of independent invention and convergence. They are common adaptations to common problems.

The culture of poverty can come into being in a variety of historical contexts. However, it tends to grow and flourish in societies with the following set of conditions: (1) a cash economy, wage labor, and production for profit; (2) a persistently high rate of unemployment and underemployment for unskilled labor; (3) low wages; (4) the failure to provide social, political, and economic organization, either on a voluntary basis or by government imposition, for the low-income population; (5) the existence of a bilateral kinship system rather than a unilateral one;[3] and finally, (6)

the existence of a set of values in the dominant class which stresses the accumulation of wealth and property, the possibility of upward mobility and thrift, and explains low economic status as the result of personal inadequacy or inferiority.

The way of life which develops among some of the poor under these conditions is the culture of poverty. It can best be studied in urban or rural slums and can be described in terms of some seventy interrelated social, economic, and psychological traits.[4] However, the number of traits and the relationships between them may vary from society to society and from family to family. For example, in a highly literate society, illiteracy

[3]In a unilineal kinship system, descent is reckoned either through males or through females. When traced exclusively through males it is called patrilineal or agnatic descent; when reckoned exclusively through females it is called matrilineal or uterine descent. In a bilateral or cognatic system, descent is traced through males and females without emphasis on either line.

In a unilineal system, the lineage consists of all the descendants of one ancestor. In a patrilineal

system, the lineage is composed of all the descendants through males of one male ancestor. A matrilineage consists of all the descendants through females of one female ancestor. The lineage may thus contain a very large number of generations. If bilateral descent is reckoned, however, the number of generations that can be included in a social unit is limited, since the number of ancestors doubles every generation.

Unilineal descent groups ("lineages" or "clans") are corporate groups in the sense that the lineage or clan may act as a collectivity: it can take blood vengeance against another descent group, it can hold property, etc. However, the bilateral kin group (the "kindred") can rarely act as a collectivity because it is not a "group" except from the point of view of a particular individual, and, furthermore, has no continuity over time.

In a unilineal system, an individual is assigned to a group by virtue of his birth. In contrast, a person born into a bilateral system usually has a choice of relatives whom he chooses to recognize as "kin" and with whom he wants to associate. This generally leads to a greater diffuseness and fragmentation of ties with relatives over time.

[4]The "culture of poverty," in John J. TePaske and S. N. Fischer (eds.), *Explosive Forces in Latin America* (Columbus: Ohio State Univ. Press, 1964), pp. 149–173.

may be more diagnostic of the culture of poverty than in a society where illiteracy is widespread and where even the well-to-do may be illiterate, as in some Mexican peasant villages before the revolution.

The culture of poverty is both an adaptation and a reaction of the poor to their marginal position in a class-stratified, highly individuated, capitalistic society. It represents an effort to cope with feelings of hopelessness and despair which develop from the realization of the improbability of achieving success in terms of the values and goals of the larger society. Indeed, many of the traits of the culture of poverty can be viewed as attempts at local solutions for problems not met by existing institutions and agencies because the people are not eligible for them, cannot afford them, or are ignorant or suspicious of them. For example, unable to obtain credit from banks, they are thrown upon their own resources and organize informal credit devices without interest.

The culture of poverty, however, is not only an adaptation to a set of objective conditions of the larger society. Once it comes into existence it tends to perpetuate itself from generation to generation because of its effect on the children. By the time slum children are age six or seven they have usually absorbed the basic values and attitudes of their subculture and are not psychologically geared to take full advantage of changing conditions or increased opportunities which may occur in their lifetime.

Most frequently the culture of poverty develops when a stratified social and economic system is breaking down or is being replaced by another, as in the case of the transition from feudalism to capitalism or during periods of rapid technological change. Often it results from imperial conquest in which the native social and economic structure is smashed and the natives are maintained in a servile colonial status, sometimes for many generations. It can also occur in the process of detribalization, such as that now going on in Africa.

The most likely candidates for the culture of poverty are the people who come from the lower strata of a rapidly changing society and are already partially alienated from it. Thus landless rural workers who migrate to the cities can be expected to develop a culture of poverty much more readily than migrants from stable peasant villages with a well-organized traditional culture. In this connection there is a striking contrast between Latin America, where the rural population long ago made the transition from a tribal to a peasant society, and Africa, which is still close to its tribal heritage. The more corporate nature of many of the African tribal societies, in contrast to Latin American rural communities, and the persistence of village ties tend to inhibit or delay the formation of a full-blown culture of poverty in many of the African towns and cities. The special conditions of apartheid in South Africa, where the migrants are segregated into separate "locations" and do not enjoy freedom of movement, create special problems. Here the institutionalization of repression and discrimination tend to develop a greater sense of identity and group consciousness.

The culture of poverty can be studied from various points of view: the relationship between the subculture and the larger society; the nature of the slum community; the nature of the family; and the attitudes, values, and character structure of the individual.

1. The lack of effective participation and integration of the poor in the major institutions of the larger society is one of the crucial characteristics of the culture of poverty. This is a complex matter and results from a variety of factors which may include lack of economic resources, segregation and discrimination, fear, suspicion or apathy, and the development of local solutions for problems. However, "participation" in some of the institutions of the larger society—for example, in the jails, the army, and the public relief system—does not *per se* eliminate the traits of the culture of poverty. In the case of a relief system which barely keeps people alive, both the basic poverty and the sense of hopelessness are perpetuated rather than eliminated.

Low wages, chronic unemployment, and underemployment lead to low income, lack of property ownership, absence of savings, absence of food reserves in the home, and a chronic shortage of cash. These conditions reduce the possibility of effective participation in the larger economic system. And as a response to these conditions we find in the culture of poverty a high incidence of pawning of personal goods, borrowing from local moneylenders at usurious rates of interest, spontaneous informal credit devices organized by neighbors, the use of second-hand clothing and furniture, and the pattern of frequent buying of small quantities of food many times a day as the need arises.

People with a culture of poverty produce very little wealth and receive very little in return. They have a low level of literacy and education, usually do not belong to labor unions, are not members of political parties, generally do not participate in the national welfare agencies, and make very little use of banks, hospitals, department stores, museums, or art galleries. They have a critical attitude toward some of the basic institutions of the dominant classes, hatred of the police, mistrust of government and those in high position, and a cynicism which extends even to the church. This gives the culture of poverty a high potential for protest and for being used in political movements aimed against the existing social order.

People with a culture of poverty are aware of middle-class values, talk about them and even claim some of them as their own, but on the whole they do not live by them. Thus it is important to distinguish between what they say and what they do. For example, many will tell you that marriage by law, by the church, or by both, is the ideal form of marriage, but few will marry. To men who have no steady jobs or other sources of income, who do not own property and have no wealth to pass on to their children, who are present-time oriented and who want to avoid the expense and legal difficulties involved in formal marriage and divorce, free unions or consensual marriage makes a lot of sense. Women will often turn down offers of marriage because they feel it ties them down to men who are immature, punishing, and generally unreliable. Women feel that consensual union gives them a better break; it gives them some of the freedom and flexibility that men have. By not giving the fathers of their children legal status as husbands, the women have a stronger claim on their children if they decide to leave their men. It also gives women exclusive rights to a house or any other property they may own.

2. When we look at the culture of poverty on the local community level, we find poor housing conditions, crowding, gregariousness, but above all a minimum of organization beyond the level of the nuclear and extended family. Occasionally there are informal, temporary groupings or voluntary associations within slums. The existence of neighborhood gangs which cut across slum settlements represents a considerable advance beyond the zero point of the continuum that I have in mind. Indeed, it is the low level of organization which gives the culture of poverty its marginal and anachronistic quality in our highly complex, specialized, organized society. Most primitive peoples have achieved a higher level of socio-cultural organization than our modern urban slum dwellers.

In spite of the generally low level of organization, there may be a sense of community and *esprit de corps* in urban slums and in slum neighborhoods. This can vary within a single city, or from region to region or country to country. The major factors influencing this variation are the size of the slum, its location and physical characteristics, length of residence, incidence of home and land ownership (versus squatter rights), rentals, ethnicity, kinship ties, and freedom or lack of freedom of movement. When slums are separated from the surrounding area by enclosing walls or other physical barriers, when rents are low and fixed and stability of residence is great (twenty or thirty years), when the population constitutes a distinct ethnic, racial, or language group, is bound by ties

of kinship or *compadrazgo,* and when there are some internal voluntary associations, then the sense of local community approaches that of a village community. In many cases this combination of favorable conditions does not exist. However, even where internal organization and *esprit de corps* is at a bare minimum and people move around a great deal, a sense of territoriality develops which sets off the slum neighborhoods from the rest of the city. In Mexico City and San Juan this sense of territoriality results from the unavailability of low-income housing outside the slum areas. In South Africa the sense of territoriality grows out of the segregation enforced by the government, which confines the rural migrants to specific locations.

3. On the family level, the major traits of the culture of poverty are the absence of childhood as a specially prolonged and protected stage in the life cycle, early initiation into sex, free unions or consensual marriages, a relatively high incidence of the abandonment of wives and children, a trend toward female- or mother-centered families and consequently a much greater knowledge of maternal relatives, a strong predisposition to authoritarianism, lack of privacy, verbal emphasis upon family solidarity which is only rarely achieved because of sibling rivalry, and competition for limited goods and maternal affection.

4. On the level of the individual, the major characteristics are a strong feeling of marginality, of helplessness, of dependence, and of inferiority. I found this to be true of slum dwellers in Mexico City and San Juan among families who do not constitute a distinct ethnic or racial

group and who do not suffer from racial discrimination. In the United States, of course, the culture of poverty of the Negroes has the additional disadvantage of racial discrimination, but as I have already suggested, this additional disadvantage contains a great potential for revolutionary protest and organization which seems to be absent in the slums of Mexico City or among the poor whites in the South.

Other traits include a high incidence of maternal deprivation, of orality, of weak ego structure, confusion of sexual identification, a lack of impulse control, a strong present-time orientation with relatively little ability to defer gratification and to plan for the future, a sense of resignation and fatalism, a widespread belief in male superiority, and a high tolerance for psychological pathology of all sorts.

People with a culture of poverty are provincial and locally oriented and have very little sense of history. They know only their own troubles, their own local conditions, their own neighborhood, their own way of life. Usually they do not have the knowledge, the vision, or the ideology to see the similarities between their problems and those of their counterparts elsewhere in the world. They are not class-conscious, although they are very sensitive indeed to status distinctions.

When the poor become class-conscious or active members of trade-union organizations, or when they adopt an internationalist outlook on the world, they are no longer part of the culture of poverty, although they may still be desperately poor. Any movement, be it religious, pacifist, or revolutionary, which organizes and gives hope to the poor and effectively promotes solidarity and a sense of identification with larger groups, destroys the psychological and social core of the culture of poverty. In this connection, I suspect that the civil rights movement among the Negroes in the United States has done more to improve their self-image and self-respect than have their economic advances, although, without doubt, the two are mutually reinforcing.

The distinction between poverty and the culture of poverty is basic to the model described here. There are degrees of poverty and many kinds of poor people. The culture of poverty refers to one way of life shared by poor people in given historical and social contexts. The economic traits which I have listed for the culture of poverty are necessary but not sufficient to define the phenomena I have in mind. There are a number of historical examples of very poor segments of the population which do not have a way of life that I would describe as a subculture of poverty. Here I should like to give four examples:

1. Many of the primitive or preliterate peoples studied by anthropologists suffer from dire poverty which is the result of poor technology and/or poor natural resources, or of both, but they do not have the traits of the subculture of poverty. Indeed, they do not constitute a subculture because their societies are not highly stratified. In spite of their poverty they have a relatively integrated, satisfying, and self-sufficient culture. Even the simplest food-gathering and hunting tribes have a considerable amount of organization, bands and band chiefs, tribal councils and local self-government—traits which are not found in the culture of poverty.

2. In India the lower castes (the Chamars, the leather workers, and the Bhangis, the sweepers) may be desperately poor, both in the villages and in the cities, but most of them are integrated into the larger society and have their own *panchayat*[5] organizations which cut across village lines and give them a considerable amount of power.[6] In addition to the caste system, which gives individuals a sense of identity and belonging, there is still another factor, the clan system. Wherever there are unilateral kinship systems or clans one would not expect to find the culture of poverty, because a clan system gives people a sense of belonging to a corporate body with a history and a life of its own, thereby providing a sense of continuity, a sense of a past and of a future.

3. The Jews of eastern Europe were very poor, but they did not have many of the traits of the culture of poverty because of their tradition of literacy, the great value placed upon learning, the organization of the community around the rabbi, the proliferation of local voluntary associations, and their religion which taught that they were the chosen people.

4. My fourth example is speculative and relates to socialism. On the basis of my limited experience in one socialist country—Cuba—and on the basis of my reading, I am inclined to believe that the culture of poverty does not exist in the socialist countries. I first went to Cuba in 1947 as a visiting professor for the State Department. At that time I began a study of a sugar plantation in Melena del Sur and of a slum in Havana. After the Castro Revolution I made my second trip to Cuba as a correspondent for a major magazine, and I revisited the same slum and some of the same families. The physical aspect of the slum had changed very little, except for a beautiful new nursery school. It was clear that the people were still desperately poor, but I found much less of the despair, apathy, and hopelessness which are so diagnostic of urban slums in the culture of poverty. They expressed great confidence in their leaders and hope for a better life in the future. The slum itself was now highly organized, with block committees, educational committees, party committees. The people had a new sense of power and importance. They were armed and were given a doctrine which glorified the lower class as the hope of humanity. (I was told by one Cuban official that they had practically eliminated delinquency by giving arms to the delinquents!)

It is my impression that the Castro regime—unlike Marx and Engels—did not write off the so-called lumpen proletariat as an inherently reactionary and anti-revolutionary force, but rather saw its revolutionary potential and tried to utilize it. In this connection, Frantz Fanon makes a similar evaluation of the role of the lumpen proletariat based upon his experience in the Algerian struggle for independence. In his recently published book[7] he wrote:

---

[5]A formal organization designed to provide caste leadership.

[6]It may be that in the slums of Calcutta and Bombay an incipient culture of poverty is developing. It would be highly desirable to do family studies there as a crucial test of the culture-of-poverty hypothesis.

[7]Frantz Fanon, *The Wretched of the Earth* (New York: Grove Press, 1965), p. 103.

It is within this mass of humanity, this people of the shanty towns, at the core of the lumpen proletariat, that the rebellion will find its urban spearhead. For the lumpen proletariat, that horde of starving men, uprooted from their tribe and from their clan, constitutes one of the most spontaneous and most radically revolutionary forces of a colonized people.

My own studies of the urban poor in the slums of San Juan do not support the generalizations of Fanon. I have found very little revolutionary spirit or radical ideology among low-income Puerto Ricans. On the contrary, most of the families I studied were quite conservative politically and about half of them were in favor of the Republican Statehood Party. It seems to me that the revolutionary potential of people with a culture of poverty will vary considerably according to the national context and the particular historical circumstances. In a country like Algeria which was fighting for its independence, the lumpen proletariat was drawn into the struggle and became a vital force. However, in countries like Puerto Rico, in which the movement for independence has very little mass support, and in countries like Mexico which achieved their independence a long time ago and are now in their postrevolutionary period, the lumpen proletariat is not a leading source of rebellion or of revolutionary spirit.

In effect, we find that in primitive societies and in caste societies, the culture of poverty does not develop. In socialist, fascist, and in highly developed capitalist societies with a welfare state, the culture of poverty tends to decline. I suspect that the culture of poverty flourishes in, and is generic to, the early free-enterprise stage of capitalism and that it is also endemic in colonialism.

It is important to distinguish between different profiles in the subculture of poverty depending upon the national context in which these subcultures are found. If we think of the culture of poverty primarily in terms of the factor of integration in the larger society and a sense of identification with the great tradition of that society, or with a new emerging revolutionary tradition, then we will not be surprised that some slum dwellers with a lower per capita income may have moved farther away from the core characteristics of the culture of poverty than others with a higher per capita income. For example, Puerto Rico has a much higher per capita income than Mexico, yet Mexicans have a deeper sense of identity.

I have listed fatalism and a low level of aspiration as one of the key traits for the subculture of poverty. Here too, however, the national context makes a big difference. Certainly the level of aspiration of even the poorest sector of the population in a country like the United States, with its traditional ideology of upward mobility and democracy is much higher than in more backward countries like Ecuador and Peru, where both the ideology and the actual possibilities of upward mobility are extremely limited and where authoritarian values still persist in both the urban and rural milieus.

Because of the advanced technology, high level of literacy, the development of mass media, and the relatively high aspiration level of all sectors of the population, especially when compared with underdeveloped nations, I believe that although there is still a great deal of poverty in the United States (estimates range from thirty to fifty million people), there is relatively little of what I would call the culture of poverty. My rough guess would be that only about 20 percent of the population below the poverty line (between six and ten million people) in the United States have characteristics which would justify classifying their way of life as that of a culture of poverty. Probably the largest sector within this group would consist of very low-income Negroes, Mexicans, Puerto Ricans, American Indians, and Southern poor whites. The relatively small number of people in the United States with a culture of poverty is a positive factor, because it is much more difficult to eliminate the culture of poverty than to eliminate poverty *per se.*

Middle-class people, and this would certainly include most social scientists, tend to concentrate on the negative aspects of the culture of poverty. They tend to associate negative valences to such traits as present-time orientation and concrete versus abstract orientation. I do not intend to idealize or romanticize the culture of poverty. As someone has said, "It is easier to praise poverty than to live in it"; yet some of the positive aspects which may flow from these traits must not be overlooked. Living in the present may develop a capacity for spontaneity and adventure, for the enjoyment of the sensual, the indulgence of impulse, which is often blunted in the middle-class, future-oriented man. Perhaps it is this reality of the moment which the existentialist writers are so desperately trying to recapture but which the culture of poverty experiences as natural, everyday phenomena. The frequent use of violence certainly provides a ready outlet for hostility, so that people in the culture of poverty suffer less from repression than does the middle class.

In the traditional view, anthropologists have said that culture provides human beings with a design for living, with a ready-made set of solutions for human problems so that individuals don't have to begin all over again each generation. That is, the core of culture is its positive adaptive function. I, too, have called attention to some of the adaptive mechanisms in the culture of poverty—for example, the low aspiration level helps to reduce frustration, the legitimization of short-range hedonism makes possible spontaneity and enjoyment. However, on the whole it seems to me that it is a relatively thin culture. There is a great deal of pathos, suffering, and emptiness among those who live in the culture of poverty. It does not provide much support or long-range satisfaction, and its encouragement of mistrust tends to magnify helplessness and isolation. Indeed, the poverty of culture is one of the crucial aspects of the culture of poverty.

The concept of the culture of poverty provides a high level of generalization which, hopefully, will unify and explain a number of phenomena viewed as distinctive characteristics of racial, national, or regional groups. For example, matrifocality, a high incidence of consensual unions, and a high percentage of households headed by women, which have been thought to be distinctive of Caribbean family organization or of Negro family life in the U.S.A., turn out to be traits of the culture of poverty and are found among diverse peoples in many parts of the world and among peoples who have had no history of slavery.

The concept of a cross-societal subculture of poverty enables us to see that many of the problems we think of as distinctively our own or distinctively Negro problems (or that of any other special racial or ethnic group) also exist in countries where there are no distinct ethnic minority groups. This suggests that the elimination of physical poverty *per se* may not be enough to eliminate the culture of poverty, which is a whole way of life.

What is the future of the culture of poverty? In considering this question, one must distinguish between those countries in which it represents a relatively small segment of the population and those in which it constitutes a very large one. Obviously the solutions will differ in these two situations. In the United States, the major solution proposed by planners and social workers in dealing with multiple-problem families and the so-called hard core of poverty has been to attempt slowly to raise their level of living and to incorporate them into the middle class. Wherever possible, there has been some reliance upon psychiatric treatment.

In the underdeveloped counties, however, where great masses of people live in the culture of poverty, a social-work solution does not seem feasible. Because of the magnitude of the problem, psychiatrists can hardly begin to cope with it. They have all they can do to care for their own growing middle class. In these countries, the people with a culture of poverty may seek a more revolutionary solution. By creating basic structural changes in society, by redistributing wealth, by organizing the poor and giving them a sense of belonging, of power, and of leadership, revolutions frequently succeed in abolishing some of the basic characteristics of the culture of poverty even when they do not succeed in abolishing poverty itself.

GEOGRAPHIC DIMENSIONS OF LIFE STYLES

Geographic dimensions include rural-urban differences, environmental variables such as proximity to large bodies of water, climate, and topography, and ecological factors such as the nature and extent of industrial development. Each region of the United States has a unique character by virtue of the manner in which these variables are combined as well as the characteristics of its population. The South, for example, is characterized by Mencken as the American stronghold of the "White Anglo-Saxon Protestant":

> He runs the whole South—and in the whole South, there are not as many first-rate men as in many a single city of the mongrel North. Wherever he is still firmly in the saddle, there Kukluxery flourishes and Fundamentalism, and lynching, and prohibition, and all the other stupid and anti-social crazes of inferior men.*

Historian J. G. Randall suggests that the uniqueness of the South is due to its white Anglo-Saxon settlers and the prevalence of a one-crop economy

---

*H. L. Mencken, *Prejudices: Fourth Series* (New York: Knopf, 1924), p. 28.

based on cotton.* *U. B. Phillips summed up the uniqueness of the South as "above all, . . . a resolve indomitably maintained—that it is and shall remain a white man's country."†*

Regional variation in the United States immediately suggests the importance of rural-urban differences, for one of the most notable differences among regions is the degree to which they are urbanized. The impact of this difference among regions is reflected in responses to public-opinion polls—for example, importance of religion, orientation toward pornography, and use of drugs. Traditional virtues associated with rural residence are most strongly endorsed in less-urbanized regions.‡ In general, the more urban the region, the more liberal the opinions regarding traditional values. Ruralism, as opposed to urbanness, represents a cherished life style that some people seek to preserve within small towns in all regions of the country. In the following article, Vidich and Bensman describe life style in a small town that represents, to its residents, a bastion of defense against the intrusion of urban industrialized society. The fact that Vidich and Bensman's study was conducted in highly urbanized New York State illustrates an important point: although regions of the United States differ, rural-urban differences are found throughout the nation.

*J. G. Randall, *The Civil War and Reconstruction* (Boston: Heath, 1937), pp. 2–26.

†U. B. Phillips, "The Central Theme in Southern History," *The American Historical Review,* **34** (October, 1928), p. 31.

‡In the urbanized East, for example, 38 percent of college students reported that organized religion was relevant to them; in the Midwest, 39 percent; in the West, 41 percent; and in the less-urbanized South, 50 percent. From *The Gallup Opinion Index: The Student Revolution,* Report No. 60 (Princeton, N.J.: The Gallup Organization, 1970), p. 18.

Springdale's Image of Itself

ARTHUR J. VIDICH
and JOSEPH BENSMAN

"Just Plain Folks"

When one becomes more intimately acquainted with the people of Springdale, and especially with the more verbal and more prominent inhabitants, one finds that they like to think of themselves as "just plain folks." The editor of the paper, in urging people to attend public meetings or in reporting a social event, says "all folks with an interest" should attend or "the folks who came certainly had a good time." Almost any chairman of a public gathering addresses his audience as folks—"all right, folks, the meeting will get underway"—and the interviewer in his work frequently encounters the same expressions—"the folks in this community," "the townfolk," "the country folk," "good folks," and "bad folks." Depending on context, the term carries with it a number of quite different connotations.

First and foremost, the term serves to distinguish Springdalers from urban dwellers, who are called "city people," an expression which by the tone in which it is used implies the less fortunate, those who are denied the wholesome virtues of rural life. City people are separated

From Arthur J. Vidich and Joseph Bensman, *Small Town in Mass Society: Class, Power and Religion* (Princeton, N.J.: Princeton University Press, 1958; Princeton Paperback, 1968), pp. 29–45. Reprinted by permission; copyright © 1958 by Princeton University Press.

from nature and soil, from field and stream, and are caught up in the inexorable web of impersonality and loneliness, of which the public statement in Springdale is: "How can people stand to live in cities?" In an understandable and ultimate extension of this valuation, one may occasionally hear references to the rural or country folk, in contrast to the villagers, the former being regarded by Springdalers as the "true folk."

The self-designation as "folk" includes everyone in the community; by its generality of reference it excludes neither the rich nor the poor, for everyone can share equally in the genuine qualities ascribed by the term. This is not to say that the community does not recognize scoundrels and wastrels in its own environment; quite the contrary, the scoundrel and allied types become all the more noticeable in the light of the dominant genuineness of rural life. It is rather to say that the standard of judgment by which character is assessed in Springdale includes no false or artificial values. To be one of the folks requires neither money, status, family background, learning, nor refined manners. It is, in short, a way of referring to the equalitarianism of rural life.

The term also includes a whole set of moral values: honesty, fair play, trustworthiness, good-neighborliness, helpfulness, sobriety, and clean-living. To the Springdaler it suggests a wholesome family life, a man whose spoken word is as good as a written contract, a community of religious-minded people, and a place where "everybody knows everybody" and "where you can say hello to anybody." The background image of urban society and city people gives force and meaning to the preferred rural way of life.

RURAL VIRTUES AND CITY LIFE

The sense of community-mindedness and identification has its roots in a belief in the inherent difference between Springdale and all other places, particularly the nearby towns and big cities. For the Springdaler surrounding towns all carry stigmata which are not found in Springdale: the county seat is the locus of vice and corruption, the Finnish settlement is "red," University Town is snobbish and aloof, and Industrial Town is inhuman, slummy, and foreign. In the big city the individual is anonymously lost in a hostile and dog-eat-dog environment. Being in the community gives one a distinct feeling of living in a protected and better place, so that in spite of occasional internal quarrels and the presence of some unwholesome characters, one frequently hears it said that "there's no place I'd rather live . . . there isn't a better place to raise a family . . . this is the best little town in the whole country." In the face of the outer world, Springdalers "stick up for their town."

The best example of community identification occurs when newspapers of neighboring towns choose to publicize negative aspects of Springdale life: making banner headlines over the dismissal of a school principal, publishing the names of youthful criminal offenders who come from good families. In such instances, irrespective of issue or factional position, anyone with an interest in the community comes to its defense: "We may have our troubles, but it's nothing we can't handle by ourselves— and quicker and better if they'd leave us alone." A challenge to the image of Springdale as a preferred place cuts deep and helps to re-create the sense of community when it is temporarily lost.

It is interesting that the belief in the superiority of local ways of living actually conditions the way of life. Springdalers *"make an effort* to be friendly" and *"go out of their way* to help newcomers." The newspaper always emphasizes the positive side of life; it never reports local arrests, shotgun weddings, mortgage foreclosures, lawsuits, bitter exchanges in public meetings, suicides, or any other unpleasant happening. By this constant focus on warm and human qualities in all public situations, the public character of the community takes on those qualities and, hence, it has a tone which is distinctly different from city life.

Relationships with nearby towns, in spite of the occasional voicing of hostility, also have a sympathetic and friendly competitive aspect. No one in Springdale would gloat over another town's misfortunes, such as a serious fire or the loss of an industry. Athletic rivalries have long histories and although there is a vocabulary of names and yells for "enemies," these simply stimulate competitiveness and arouse emotions for the night of the contest. No one takes victory or defeat seriously for more than a day or two, and only in a very rare instance is there a public incident when outsiders visit the town. "Nobody really wants trouble with other towns."

When one goes beyond neighboring communities, the Springdaler leaps from concrete images of people and places to a more generalized image of metropolitan life. His everyday experiences give him a feeling of remoteness from the major centers of industry, commerce, and politics. His images are apt to be as stereotyped as those that city people hold concerning the country. Any composite of these images would certanly include the following:

1. Cities breed corruption and have grown so big and impersonal that they are not able to solve the problems they create.

2. Cities are an unwholesome environment for children and families, and have had an unhealthy effect on family morals.

3. Urban politicians and labor leaders are corrupt and represent anti-democratic forces in American life.

4. Washington is a place overridden with bureaucrats and the sharp-deal, fast-buck operator, both of whom live like parasites off hard-working country folk.

5. Industrial workers are highly paid for doing little work. Their leaders foment trouble and work against the good of the country.

6. Cities are hotbeds of un-American sentiment, harbor the reds, and are incapable of educating their youth to Christian values.

7. Big universities and city churches are centers of atheism and secularism and in spite of occasional exceptions have lost touch with the spiritual lesson taught by rural life.

8. Most of the problems of country life have their origin in the effects which urban life has on rural ways.

What is central, however, is the feeling of the Springdaler that these things do not basically affect him. While he realizes that machinery and factory products are essential to his standard of life and that taxation and agricultural policy are important, he feels that he is independent of other features of industrial and urban life, or, better, that he can choose and select only the best

parts. The simple physical separation from the city and the open rural atmosphere make it possible to avoid the problems inherent in city life. Personal relations are face-to-face and social gatherings are intimate, churchgoing retains the quality of a family affair, the merchant is known as a person, and you can experience the "thrill of watching nature and the growth of your garden." Springdalers firmly believe in the virtues of rural living, strive to maintain them, and defend them against anyone who would criticize them.

"NEIGHBORS ARE FRIENDS"

Almost all of rural life receives its justification on the basis of the direct and personal and human feelings that guide people's relations with each other. No one, not even a stranger, is a stranger to the circumambience of the community. It is as if the people in a deeply felt communion bring themselves together for the purposes of mutual self-help and protection. To this end the community is organized for friendliness and neighborliness, so much so that the terms "friends" and "neighbors" almost stand as synonyms for "folk."

In its most typical form, neighborliness occurs in time of personal and family crisis—birth, death, illness, fire, catastrophe. On such occasions friends and neighbors mobilize to support those in distress: collections of money are taken, meals are prepared by others, cards of condolence are sent. A man whose house or barn has burned may unexpectedly find an organized "bee" aiding in reconstruction. Practically all organizations have "sunshine" committees whose sole purpose is to send greeting cards. These practices are so wide-spread and ultimately may include so many people that an individual, unable to acknowledge all this friendliness personally, will utilize the newspaper's "card of thanks" column to express his public appreciation.

Borrowing and "lending back and forth" is perhaps the most widespread act of neighborliness. Farmers say they like to feel that "in a pinch" there is always someone whom they can count upon for help—to borrow tools, get advice, ask for labor. In spite of the advent of mechanized and self-sufficient farming and consequently the reduction of the need for mutual aid, the high public value placed on mutual help is not diminished. Though a farmer may want to be independent and wish to avoid getting involved in other people's problems and, in fact, may privately resent lending his machinery, it is quite difficult for him to refuse to assist his neighbor if asked. Even where technological advance has made inroads on the need for the practice, to support the public creed remains a necessity.

For housewives in a community where "stores don't carry everything," domestic trading and borrowing is still a reality; they exchange children's clothing and *do* borrow salt and sugar. In Springdale they say "you never have to be without . . . if you need something bad enough you can always get it: of course, sometimes people overdo it and that makes it bad for everybody, but after a while you find out who they are." The process of selectively eliminating the bad practitioners makes it possible to keep the operation of the practice on a high plane.

Neighborliness has its institutional supports and so is given a firm foundation. Ministers and church groups make it a practice to visit the sick in hospitals and homes and to remember them with cards and letters, and all other organizations—the Legion, Masons, Community Club, book clubs—designate special committees to insure that remembrance is extended to the bereaved and ill. The Legion and Community Club "help our own" with baskets of food and clothing at Christmastime and organize fund drives to assist those who are "burned out." The ideology of neighborliness is reflected in and reinforced by the organized life of the community.

To a great extent these arrangements between friends and neighbors have a reciprocal character: a man who helps others may himself expect to be helped later on. In a way the whole system takes on the character of insurance. Of course some people are more conscious of their premium payments than others and keep a kind of mental bookkeeping on "what they owe and who owes them what," which is a perfectly permissible practice so long as one does not openly confront others with unbalanced accounts. In fact, the man who knows "exactly where he stands" with his friends and neighbors is better advised than the one who "forgets and can't keep track." The person who is unconsciously oblivious of what others do for him and distributes his own kindness and favor without thinking is apt to alienate both those whom he owes and doesn't owe. The etiquette for getting and giving in Springdale is an art that requires sensitive adjustments to the moods, needs, and expectations of others. This ability to respond appropriately in given situations is the sign of the good neighbor. That this sensitivity is possessed by large numbers of people is attested to by the fact that friendliness and neighborliness contribute substantially to the community's dominant tone of personalness and warmth.

Of course, everyone does not participate equally or at the same level in being a good friend and neighbor. Deviations and exceptions are numerous. Neighborliness is often confined to geographical areas and to socially compatible groups. The wife of the lawyer is on neighborly terms with others like herself rather than with the wife of a carpenter. Farmers necessarily have less to do with people in the village, and teachers are more apt to carry on friendly relations with each other. Those who are not willing to both give and take find themselves courteously eliminated from this aspect of local life. "People who are better off" simply by possessing sufficient resources do not find it necessary to call on friends and neighbors for help, though "everyone knows that if you went and asked them for something, they'd give it to you right away." Others have a more "independent turn of mind" and "will get by with what they have, no matter what, just to be free of mind"; the ideology of neighborliness is broad enough to include them "so long as they don't do anyone harm." The foreign elements, particularly the Poles, limit their everyday neighboring to their own group, but still by community definitions they are good neighbors because "you can always trust a Pole to deal square . . . if they owe you anything, they will always pay you back on time." Some folks are known as "just good people" who by choice "keep to themselves." By isolating themselves within the community, they neither add nor detract from the neighborly quality of the community life and so do not have an effect on the public character of the town.

The only group which does not fall within the purview of the conception of friend and neighbor is the 10 percent of the population that live "in shacks in the hills." The people who live in shacks "can't be trusted"; "they steal you blind"; "if you're friendly to them, they'll take advantage of you"; "if you lend them something you'll never see it again"; "they're bad . . . no-good people . . . live like animals." Hence by appropriately extending the social definition to give it a broader base than mutual aid, all groups in the community, except the shack people, fulfill the image of good friend and neighbor. The self-conception then reinforces itself, serves as a model for achievement, and adds to the essential appearance of community warmth.

GOOD FOLKS AND BAD FOLKS

"Of course, there are some people who just naturally have a dirty mouth. You'll find them anywhere you go, and I'd be lying if I said we didn't have a few here." The "dirty mouth" is a person who not only fabricates malicious gossip about his enemies but also wantonly and carelessly spreads his fabrications. He commits the double *faux pas* of being deliberately malicious and of not observing the etiquette of interpersonal relations, and he is perhaps the most despised person in the community.

There are a whole range of personal qualities which are almost unanimously disapproved in Springdale. These are identified in the person:

"who holds a grudge . . . who won't ever forget a wrong done to him."

"who can't get along with other people . . . who won't ever try to be friendly and sociable."

"who gives the town a bad name . . . always raising up a ruckus . . . always trying to stir up trouble."

"who trys to be something he isn't . . . the show-off . . . the braggart."

"who thinks he's better than everybody else . . . who thinks he's too good for the town . . . who thinks he's a cut above ordinary folks."

"who is bossy . . . thinks his ideas are always the best . . . tries to run everything . . . wants to be the center of attention all the time without working for it."

"who makes money by cheating people . . . who hasn't made his money honestly . . . you can't figure out where he got all that money."

"whom you can't trust . . . whose word is no good . . . who doesn't do what he says he was going to do . . . who doesn't carry through on anything."

In almost the exact reverse, the qualities of a good member of the community are found in the person who:

"forgives and forgets . . . lets bygones be bygones . . . never dredges up the past . . . lets you know that he isn't going to hold it against you."

"is always doing something for the good of the town . . . gives willingly of his time and money . . . supports community projects . . . never shirks when there's work to be done."

"gets along with everybody . . . always has a good word . . . goes out of his way to do a good turn . . . never tries

to hurt anybody . . . always has a smile for everybody."

"is just a natural person . . . even if you know he's better than you, he never lets you know it . . . never tries to impress anybody just because he has a little more money . . . acts like an ordinary person."

"always waits his turn . . . is modest . . . will work along with everybody else . . . isn't out for his own glory . . . takes a job and does it well without making a lot of noise."

"worked hard for what he's got . . . deserves every penny he has . . . doesn't come around to collect the first day of the month . . . you know he could be a lot richer."

"stands on his word . . . never has to have it in writing . . . does what he says . . . if he can't do it he says so, and if he can he does it . . . always does it on time."

Springdalers affirm that on the whole most people in the community have these qualities. They are the qualities of "average folk" and "we like to think of ourselves as just a little above the average." "Average people can get things done because nobody has any high-blown ideas and they can all work together to make the community a better place to live."

What is interesting about the usual definitions of good and bad people are the types that are excluded entirely. At this level those who go unrecognized, even in the negative statements, are the intellectuals, the bookish, and the introverts. In a community that places a high premium on being demonstrably average, friendly, and open, the person who appears in public and "doesn't say much" is a difficult character to understand: "He's a good fellow, but you never know what he's thinking." "Book reading and studying all the time," while they have a place, "shouldn't be carried too far . . . you have to keep your feet on the ground, be practical." The intellectual is respected for his education, is admired for his verbal facility and sometimes can provide the right idea, but nevertheless he is suspect and "shouldn't be allowed to get into positions of responsibility." It is apparent that where stereotyped public definitions do not easily fit, nonconformity is still tolerated so long as it does not seriously interfere with the workings of the town.

In the community setting, the test case of the toleration and sympathy for nonconformity lies in attitudes toward cranks, psychotics, and "odd" personalities: the ex-minister who writes poetry, the hermit who lives in the woods, the woman obsessed with the legal correctness of her husband's will, the spinster who screams at callers, the town moron and the clinical catatonic. Needless to say, these represent only a small percentage of the population. The point is that Springdale is able to absorb, protect, and care for them; when in the infrequent instance they intrude on the public scene, they are treated with the same sympathy and kindness accorded a child. So long as nonconformity does not interfere with the normal functioning of the town, no price is exacted from the nonconformist. At the worst, the nonconforming types are surrounded by humor. They become local "characters" who add color and interest to the everyday life of the community; because they are odd and different, they are always available as a standard conversational piece. In this way the community demonstrates its kindness and "lives and lets live."

"WE'RE ALL EQUAL"

With the exception of a few "old cranks" and "no-goods," it is unthinkable for anyone to pass a person on the street without exchanging greetings. Customarily one stops for a moment of conversation to discuss the weather and make inquiries about health; even the newcomer finds others stopping to greet him. The pattern of everyone talking to everyone is especially characteristic when people congregate in groups. Meetings and social gatherings do not begin until greetings have been exchanged all around. The person who feels he is above associating with everyone, as is the case with some newcomers from the city, runs the risk of being regarded a snob, for the taint of snobbishness is most easily acquired by failing to be friendly to everyone.

It is the policy of the Community Club to be open to "everyone, whether dues are paid or not," and hardly a meeting passes without a repetition of this statement. Those who are the leaders of the community take pride in this organization specifically because it excludes no one, and this fact is emphasized time and again in public situations. Wherever they can, community leaders encourage broad participation in all spheres of public life: everyone is urged and invited to attend public meetings and everyone is urged to "vote not as a duty, but as a privilege." The equality at the ballot box of all men, each according to his own conscience, in a community where you know all the candidates personally, where votes can't be bought, and where you know the poll-keepers, is the hallmark of equality that underpins all other equality. "Here no man counts more than any other"; this is stated in every affirmation of rural political equality—"if you don't like the rascals, use your vote to kick them out."

The social force of the idea finds its most positive expression in a negative way. The ladies of the book clubs, the most exclusive and limited membership groups in Springdale, find themselves in the ambiguous position of having to be apologetic for their exclusiveness. Because they are select in a community which devalues standoffishness, they are the only groups that are defensive in meeting the rest of the public. To the observer, they explain, "It's not that we want to be exclusive. It's just that sixteen is all you can manage in a book club. If anybody wants to be in a book club, she can start her own, like the Wednesday Group." By the same token they receive a large share of resentment; any number of vulgar expressions refer to this feminine section of the community.

The public ideology of equality has its economic correlates. One must not suppose that inequalities in income and wealth go unnoticed; rather, they are quite closely watched and known in Springdale. However, such differences, as in the image of the frontier community, are not publicly weighed and evaluated as the measure of the man.

In everyday social intercourse it is a social *faux pas* to act as if economic inequalities make a difference. The wealthiest people in town, though they have big homes, live quite simply without servants. The serviceman, the delivery boy, and the door-to-door canvasser knock at the front door and, though they may feel somewhat awkward on carpeted floors, are asked to enter even before stating their business. A man who flaunts his wealth, or demands deference because of it, is out of tune with a community whose "upper class" devalues conspicuous consumption and works at honest pursuits. "What makes the difference is not the wealth but the character behind it."

It is not a distortion to say that the good man is the working man and in the public estimation the fact of working transcends, indeed explains, economic differentials; work has its own social day of judgment, and the judgment conferred is self-respect and respectability. Work, in the first instance, is the great social equalizer, and the purest form of work which serves as a yardstick for all other work is farm work. By this mechanism the "hard-working poor man" is superior to the "lazy rich man." The quotation marks are advised and indicate the hypotheticalness of the case, because in common usage the two, work and wealth, go together. Where they don't it is because of misfortune, catastrophe, bad luck, or simply because the man is young and work has not yet had a chance to pay its dividends. But even wealth is the wrong word. Work is rather juxtaposed beside such terms as rich, solvent, well-off; wealth implies more economic differentiation than Springdalers like to think exists in their community. Thus, the measure of a man, for all public social purposes, is the diligence and perseverance with which he pursues his economic ends; the "steady worker," the "good worker," the "hard worker," in contrast to the "fly-by-night schemer," the "band-wagon jumper," and the "johnny-come-lately." For the Springdaler the test case is the vulgar social climber, the person who tries to "get in with the better people" by aping them in dress and possessions which only money can buy. In spite of the social and economic differences visible to the outside observer, the pervading appearance of the community is that of a social equality based on the humanness of rural life.

THE ETIQUETTE OF GOSSIP

Like other small rural communities, Springdale must face the classic problem of preserving individual privacy in the face of a public ideology which places a high valuation on positive expressions of equalitarianism and neighborliness. The impression of community warmheartedness which is given by the free exchange of public greetings and the easy way "everybody gets along with everybody else" has its counterpart in the absence of privacy implied by the factor of gossip. The observer who has been in the community for a length of time realizes that "everybody isn't really neighborly . . . that some people haven't talked to each other for years . . . that people whom you might think are friends hate each other . . . that there are some people who are just naturally troublemakers . . . that he'd skin his own grandmother for a buck." However, such statements are never made in public situations. The intimate, the negative, and the private are spoken in interpersonal situations involving only two or three people. Gossip exists as a separate and hidden layer of community life.

That is why it is at first difficult for the observer to believe the often-repeated statement that "everybody knows everything about everybody else in Springdale," or, as stated otherwise, "in a small town you live in a glass house." It develops that the statements are true only to a degree: while one learns intimate and verifiable details of people's private lives, these never become the subject of open, public discussion.

In the private sphere—at what is commonly regarded as the level of gossip, either malicious or harmless—Springdalers tend to emphasize the negative and competitive qualities of life. One learns about domestic discords, sexual aberrations, family skeletons, ill-gained wealth, feuds, spite fences, black sheep, criminal records, and alcoholism. The major preoccupation, however, is reserved for "what he's worth" in the strictly monetary and material meaning of the expression. The image of the sharp-trading farmer, the penny-wise homemaker, and the thrifty country folk is reflected in reverse in this concern with the state of other people's finances and possessions. All men, from the bartender to the clergyman, are capable of such concern, typically expressed as follows:

> "I'd say he's worth at least $30,000. Why the cows and buildings are worth that alone."
> "You'd think a man with his money would give more than $50 to the church."
> "The reason he's got so much is because he never spends any, hasn't taken a vacation for thirty years, never contributes a cent to anything."
> "There's a man who's got a fortune and you'd never guess it."
> "What I couldn't do with his dough."
> "The way they spend money, you'd

think it was like picking leaves off a tree."

"There's a guy making $2,800 and he's got a new Pontiac."

"Up to his neck in debt and he walks around like he had a million."

"Lend him a cent and you'll never see it again."

"He cleaned up during the war."

"There isn't anything he can't turn into a dollar."

"Figure it out. He's working, his wife's working, they haven't got any kids, and they're collecting rent on two houses besides."

"He could be doing well if he stopped drinking."

"He may be taking in more than me, but then he's killing himself doing it."

"If he'd loosen up and be human, this town would be a better place for everybody."

"But, then, I haven't done so bad myself. There's the car, only four years left on the house, and two kids through school."

These and similar statements, however, serve the function of enabling a person to calculate his relative financial standing. They are encountered almost everywhere in private gossip, but remain unspoken and hidden in ordinary public situations.

What is interesting about gossip is that in Springdale it seldom hurts anyone. Because it occurs in small temporarily closed circles and concerns those who are not present, the subject of the gossip need never be aware of it. Moreover, the *mores* demand, or better still one should say that it is an iron law of community life, that one not confront the subject of gossip with what is said about him. For this reason, though everyone engages in the practice, no one

has to learn what things are being said about him. In the rare instance where one hears about gossip about oneself, it comes as a distinct shock "to think that so-and-so could have said that about me."

In a way, then, it is true that everyone knows everything about everyone else but, because of the way the information is learned, it does not ordinarily affect the everyday interpersonal relations of people; in public view even enemies speak to each other. When the victim meets the gossiper, he does not see him as a gossip, and the gossiper does not let the privately gained information affect his public gestures; both greet each other in a friendly and neighborly manner and, perhaps, talk about someone else. Because the people of the community have this consideration for other people's feelings ("we like to think of ourselves as considerate and kind, not out to hurt anybody . . . that's one of the main reasons you live in a small town"), relationships between people always give the impression of personalness and warmth.

The etiquette of gossip which makes possible the public suppression of the negative and competitive aspects of life has its counterpart in the etiquette of public conversation, which always emphasizes the positive. There are thus two channels of communication that serve quite different purposes. In public conversation one hears comments only on the good things about people—"a man who has always done good things for the town"; "a swell guy"; "she's always doing good things for people"; "a person who never asks anything in return." More than this, the level of public conversation always focuses on the collective success of the community and the individual successes of its members. People comment on the success of a charitable drive, on the way a money-raising project "went over the top," on "what a good program it was," on the excellence of the actors' performance. These same themes become the subject of self-congratulatory newspaper articles. When failures occur, when the play "was a flop," as of course must happen from time to time, one senses what is almost a communal conspiracy against any further public mention of it. So too with the successes of individuals—the man who after many years of diligence finally gets a good job, the person who completes a correspondence course, the local girl who gets a college degree, the local boy who makes good in the city, the man who finally succeeds in establishing himself in business, the winner of a contest, the high scorer, the person who has his name in a city newspaper—all such successes are given recognition in conventional conversation and in the press. At the public level all types of success are given public recognition while failure is treated with silence. It is because of the double and separate set of communication channels that negative gossip seldom colors the friendly ethos and the successful mood of the public life of the community.

Political scientist James Q. Wilson has written:

> Let two Birchite loud-mouths pop off anywhere else in the country and we rush out to sociology texts to see whether it is alienation or the decline of the small entrepreneur that is the cause; let two of them say the same thing in Los Angeles, and we just smile knowingly and murmur, "It figures."*

Thus Wilson warns us of the danger of too readily accepting regional stereotypes. But regions of the United States do differ on superficial life style variables. Beer and Brat Houses abound in Wisconsin and Illinois, but are nowhere to be found in California. Grits are served with breakfast eggs in the South, while potatoes are served with eggs in the North. A "regular" coffee to an Easterner means with cream and sugar, while to a Westerner, it's black coffee. In Philadelphia, a sandwich with a variety of Italian meats is a "hoagie"; in other regions, a similar sandwich is known as a "grinder," "torpedo," "poor boy," "submarine," or some other name.† Even names for common objects differ throughout the nation. Thus a creek may be called a "kill" or "run" in the East, a "branch" or "stream" in the upper Midwest, a "crick" or "bayou" in parts of the South, and a "gully" or "wash" in the West.‡ Pronunciation also differs in the United States: orange *is pronounced "AWrange" in the West and "AREange"*

---

*James Q. Wilson, "A Guide to Reagan Country: The Political Culture of Southern California," *Commentary* (May, 1967), p. 371.

†Edwin Eames and Howard Robby, "The Socio-Cultural Context of an Italian-American Dietary Item," *Cornell Journal of Social Relations,* **2** (Fall, 1967), pp. 63–75.

‡George Lundberg, Clarence Schrag, Otto Larsen, and William R. Catton, Jr., *Sociology,* 4th ed. (New York: Harper & Row, 1968), p. 255.

in the East; wash *is pronounced "warsh" in parts of the Midwest; and we are all familiar with New York, Boston, or Southern accents. Thus there definitely are regional differences. What is still problematic is whether these superficial differences of food, vocabulary, and pronunciation can be taken as indications of significant life style differences.*

Robert Gover and Joan Didion, in the following two articles, present portraits that could be taken as typical of the Midwest and Southern California. Both Gover and Didion are journalists who, through description of specific events, attempt to portray the life style of a region.

"Culture" Comes to Indianapolis

ROBERT GOVER

On the plane from Los Angeles to Indianapolis to see Clowes (pronounced "clues") Memorial Hall for the performing arts and the Clowes family art collection, to contemplate the culture of Hoosierland, I marvel at what a squirming can of worms is that word, Culture.

And that other word, Art. What is an arts center? What is it for? Who is it for? Worthy questions, because greater and lesser Lincoln Center-type structures are mushrooming these days in America. Billions of dollars for art and culture.

As for art, I was carrying two books with me: *Home,* by LeRoi Jones, and *Symbol, Status and Personality,* by S. I. Hayakawa. To embark upon the cultural and artistic life of Indianapolis, I felt the need of navigational coordinates.

Jones says: "Thought is more important than art. Without thought, art

From *The New York Times* (December 24, 1967), pp. 6–7. Reprinted by permission; copyright © 1967 by the New York Times Co.

could certainly not exist . . . to revere art and have no understanding of the process that forces it into existence, is finally not even to understand what art is."

Hayakawa says: "Most people assume that language is the 'expression of thought.' Such a statement contains the unspoken implication that we have a 'thought' and then 'express' it by 'putting it into words.' [But] . . . we cannot speak without imposing upon the flux of experience an assumed structure implied by the formal or grammatical structure of the language we happen to speak."

The plane nears Indianapolis. I once lived near here and it left me with an abiding prejudice. I tend to refer to Hoosiers as Them, even as I admonish myself for such a baseless, nonexistent generality, for I developed an intense dislike for their rigid, conformist mores, their humorless provincialisms. And now, inside the airport, I am struck by the uniformity of clothing styles. Just in from L.A., this uniformity is startling. Trees bare, people bundled up in two general uniforms, his and hers. It's how they tell the boys from the girls here. In L.A., clothes are quite often expressive of one's inner self, one's desires or spiritual orientation. Here, it's as if each individual must assure all others that he thinks and feels just the same as they do. It gives me the creeps. I'm ready to hop the next plane out to either New York or L.A.

And as I wait for the luggage, I glance through a short biography of the man whose $2.3-million launched the building of the $3.5-million Clowes Hall, Dr. George Henry Alexander Clowes (1877–1958), coming upon this noteworthy indication of the sort of thinking that gets done here:

> *Biography and history attest to the fact that a culture can at most be established on a citywide basis—it cannot, unfortunately, be nationwide. The great cultures of the past—amongst them Athens, Byzantium, Florence, Venice, Edinburgh, and Vienna—have certainly not had any national scope. Neither can it be said that large 20th-century metropolitan areas have been able to produce distinctive cultures. The modern cities of Paris, London, Berlin, New York, Chicago, and Los Angeles have too much in quantity and too little in agreement upon objectives to produce more than a blur of a distinguished civilization. It is, therefore, the smaller cities of America which have the opportunity, afforded by singleness of purpose and selection, to form a civic personality which the babel of metropolitan centers makes impossible.*

On the way to the motel I drove through what seemed like a *blur* of insurance companies. I thought that by some strange mistake I'd landed in Hartford, Conn. And when I got to the motel, there was a convention happening—of insurance men.

Cul-ture 2: the raising, improvement or development of some plant, animal or product.

—Webster's New World Dictionary

In the lobby, an impossible babble. Just inside the door sits a baby-blue platinum doll in her bestest man-catchin' clothes, and bending over her, pushing a notepad and pen at her, is a hearty conventioneer full of good cheer and booze.

"Here, honey, right thar, write your address right thar."

"But sir . . ."

"Come on, come on, right thar, write it down."

"But sir, I just don't *give* my address out like this."

"I wanna send ya a *present*, honey. Write it down."

"Oh gee, thanks, sir, but . . . I just don't *give* my address *out*."

He knows as little about her Indiana as she knows of his, it seems. And how can she be certain he's not an undercover agent out to bust her, or a clickster out to "borrow" from her treasure trove of "presents"? Besides, judging by her accent, she's what the Hoosiers call "a Kentuckian"—of which more later.

I'd been invited to make it out to Clowes Hall, meet the general manager, Travis Selmier, and see this evening's offering of Culture from the big outside world: *Fiddler on the Roof.* And in the taxi I got to talking about "the hall" with the driver. Does he go there? "Oh, me and the missus makes it out there now and then. If something's happening in this town, it's in the hall. New Fords got unveiled there, and Bob Hope's been there. So has Johnny Carson."

Trav Selmier is friendly, quick-witted, hard-working, and would make many of his big-town counterparts look like hicks. He loaded me down with the information his job calls for him to load me down with. Like Clowes Hall housed the Metropolitan Opera National Company for nine weeks in 1965 as they prepared for their first tour, and they returned in 1966 because they found the hall just right for their purposes. And the American National Opera Company chose Clowes for its residency and world premiere, and the Harkness Ballet was here for five weeks prior to its New York season. Clowes is the home of the Indianapolis Symphony Orchestra and is used by Butler University music and drama students, and its biggest single money-maker has been—you guessed it—*Hello, Dolly!*

But the hall's architecture—I could hardly hear Mr. Selmier's pitch for the booming sight of the building itself. Cool, dignified, quietly dramatic. Well, I don't know what those imported operas and ballets have brought to the Hoosiers, but whoever created this building has brought them more than enough. I have never seen a theater better suited for theatergoers than Clowes Hall.

Mr. Selmier gave me the vital statistics: ". . . nine stories of Bedford limestone and bare concrete . . . 168 feet wide and 255 deep . . . unpainted concrete pylons, tapering as they rise, that show the building's basic structure and lend drama to the interior . . . the grand foyer across the entire front of the building. There are two passenger elevators . . . total floor space in the lobbies is 24,000 square feet, 12 square feet per person . . . seating for 2,200. The stage house is nine stories high and the stage can be extended or contracted to accommodate everything from grand opera to a single performer . . . it's 51 feet wide at the proscenium opening and 62 deep and 81 to the gridiron . . . the orchestra shell is an integral part of the stage and can

be electrically lowered for use in 15 minutes. Backstage facilities have accommodated four full opera companies at one time. . . ."

Credits: Lighting by Jean Rosenthal, Acoustics by Bolt, Beranek and Newman, Inc.; Seating and Sight-lines by Ben Schlanger. The acoustics are better than anything I've encountered in New York. So are the sight-lines. And from the stage, it looks like a much smaller theater than the 2,200-seater it is.

A remarkable architectural achievement—by any standards. From a distance, the building seems to speak to the Midwestern landscape in shapes and proportions that land understands and is impressed by. And inside, it's for people—not for a jam scene of paying customers, but people. I couldn't help thinking of that old saw, "Youth is wasted on the young." I mean, what's such a lovely thing as *this* doing *here?*

Well, at the moment, it's giving Sholem Aleichem a place to parade out his people, and Sholem Aleichem—even squeezed through the frantic needs of Broadway box office—is still Sholem Aleichem, clear and strong. And beautiful. When Tevye and the Villagers sing "Tradition—Everybody here knows who he is/And what God expects of him"—it gives my emotions a workout. I have relatives who migrated to Indiana from bad addresses in Kentucky, much the same way many people migrated to the United States of America from Europe and Russia. The trip for the Kentuckians wasn't so far in miles, but it wasn't so short either in folkways, social mores, and culture. The upstanding Hoosier citizen does not often look favorably upon those he calls "the Kentuckians." And tonight, as I watched the Sholem

Aleichem people deal with their situation in old Russia, I kept wondering what my people from the hinterland of Kentucky would think of this. What would they feel, what would they hear in these lines and see in these characters? Themselves, of course. Done up in different costumes, out of a different time and place, but themselves nonetheless.

On weekends, from the mill towns of Indiana go hundreds of carloads of Kentuckians on quick visits to the "old country." Some arrive just in time for the morning milking, or to help patch up an old house, and they floorboard it back to Indiana just in time to punch in at the factory Monday morning. They send money and clothes back to the old country, and many I've talked to plan to return, once they are set up financially, which of course they rarely manage. In the meantime they live as an ethnic minority among the Hoosiers, speaking a gentler, more melodic dialect than the harsh, guttural twang of their social "betters," who are much more all-American in the let's-bomb-Hanoi sense.

At intermission I found out there were "three busloads of Kentuckians" in the balcony. Children. So as the curtain went up on the second half, I slipped up there to watch them watch *Fiddler.* Naturally I had to fantasize that Sholem Aleichem's soul went with me for this, and that it made him very, very happy. If he can't tell his own people in a different time and place and costume, who can? And they sure were digging his other people. Most of the quick laughs came from the balcony. *Fiddler* has universal appeal, sure, but it also has certain lines that are strictly inside jokes, you know.

Cul-ti-vate: to promote the development or growth of; acquire and develop; as, he cultivated *a social conscience.*
—Webster's

Of all the countless dichotomies invented by scholars to account for the major differences in art styles and cycles, only one has been consistently unambiguous in its application to a variety of forms and cultures. However it may be verbalized, the basic distinction is this: Is the work war-oriented or not?
—From the December *Esquire* condensation of "Report from Iron Mountain on the Possibility and Desirability of Peace," which concludes that lasting peace is probably not in the best interests of our society.

Headline in *The Indianapolis News:*

"LBJ LASHES OUT AT PROTESTERS' 'BULLYING AND HOWLING' TACTICS"
Subhead: *"Bomb Halt Declared No Peace Aid."*

From the radio: an ad for Cornhuskers Hand Lotion for the he-man; a pop tune, "Bo Diddley Bach," who is sung of as the son of Johann Sebastian, and an ad for Polaroid sunglasses against the glare of the impending prairie snows.

On TV Sunday morning: Mahalia Jackson . . . Billy Graham . . . a hymn, *"Don't Tell Me God Is Dead, I Just Talked With Him This Morning."*

Cul-tu-ral shock: no definition of this in Webster's.

The creation of Clowes Hall is credited to an unusual architectural partnership—John Johansen of New Canaan,

Conn., and Evans Woollen 3d of Indianapolis. I go next to meet Mr. Woollen expecting to find him in an ultra-modern office building. But no. He is youthful, his office building isn't.

And how did such a partnership arrangement work? "On a fifty-fifty basis," he insists. "Most of the drawing was done here in Indianapolis, but John Johansen came out here often."

Which aspects of the hall are his and which are Johansen's, Woollen refuses to say. But it was Woollen who brought his former Yale teacher in on the project, I was to learn later, and as the Indianapolis half of the partnership it is he who has had to face the music since the hall came into existence.

"I was 32 years old then and just out of Yale. No one was ready to give me a project of that size, alone."

Things are different now. Soon he will be at work on a ten-million-dollar opera hall to be built fifty miles away on the campus of Indiana University. But let's defer that question—does the area need another opera hall?—and get to this: What did he and Johansen have in mind when they set about designing Clowes Hall?

"We worked on the idea that the audience becomes performers, too. You know, people dress up to go to the theater, and during intermissions they like to see others and be seen. They like to promenade."

And what was the public reaction to the hall when it first appeared? "Mixed, at first. A few city fathers wanted to tear up the seating and install a central aisle, and another group of conservatives wanted to paint the concrete exterior gold. It seemed pretty rough to them at first. But now they accept it. And

if it hadn't come to mean something to the public, it could not stay afloat financially. Really, the town's turned itself inside out for some of the performances the hall has had."

Then we speculated on a couple of matters: "The New Yorker's idea of the Midwesterner wasn't totally inaccurate, but the Midwesterner is changing much more rapidly than many New Yorkers seem ready to believe. Of course, there is still a certain schizophrenia here that makes the Midwesterner overrate things from the outside world. The home-grown talent usually has to go far away for opportunities."

Why Mr. Woollen did not have to go away for this opportunity I was to find out from a talk with the son of Dr. Clowes, Allen W. Clowes.

Cul-ti-va-ted: grown by cultivation; opposed to wild. Trained and developed; refined; cultured; as a cultivated person.
                                                                —Webster's

Although Dr. Clowes had arrived in Buffalo in 1901 (he was born in England), it appeared for a long time he was destined for the role of bachelor. This was not because he was averse to the fair sex; on the contrary, he seems to have had exactly the opposite reputation. At a minstrel show in the Buffalo Club, an end-man, who impersonated his English ways and accent, was asked by the interlocutor: 'Doctor, with how many girls in Buffalo are you in love?' And the reply was, 'How many girls are there in Buffalo?'

—From a short biography of Dr. Clowes

Dr. Clowes had been director of research for Eli Lilly & Co., the Indianapolis pharmaceutical company, and, according to his biographer, "was fortunate in his other financial ventures, fortunate in the many friends who could also bring the influence of wealth to bear upon the spread of cultural interests. . . ."

With the death of Mrs. Clowes earlier this year, Allen W. Clowes is the only heir in the Indianapolis area. He lives in the family home, a picturesque mansion in a section called Golden Hills. It houses the Clowes art collection, worth about three million dollars, now owned by the Clowes Foundation. It is open to the public from 4 P.M. to 6 P.M. daily.

"You're late, 10 minutes late," said Allen Clowes when I was ushered in to see him. "How do you expect to do two hours of interviewing in less than two hours?"

He sat me across from his famous self-portrait of Franz Hals, and I found I was being stared at by Titian's "Portrait of the Grand Chancellor of Venice, Andrea Del Francheschi, ca. 1550." I set up a tape recorder, for I'd heard that Mr. Clowes is a talker, not a listener.

"Well, the history of the hall goes back to 1937 when my father decided to raise enough money to make the Indianapolis Symphony first-rate. Then, as time went by, he started thinking about the possibility of a proper symphony hall, because the old Murat Theater downtown is really an old Shriner mosque, and was built by the Shuberts. It has a balcony overhanging the orchestra floor and terribly bad acoustics. . . . Anyway, old Mr. J. K. Lilly used to call Mother 'Sister Clowes,' and he used to tell her if it weren't for those awful taxes he'd *build* a symphony hall.

"Well, nothing occurred, and my father didn't feel that he could do the hall on his own. He left this art when he died—that was in 1958—and he left the rest of his estate to my mother, and we found by that time the Lilly stock had *grown,* and he had a bigger estate than he thought he had, so we decided to go ahead with what he'd always wanted.

"Anyway, I called up Evans Woollen the Third. Have you met him? He was a young architect in town, just out of Yale, mind you, and I asked him—rumor has it that one of his forefathers thought up the name Indianapolis—so I asked him, 'Are you interested?' and he said, 'Yes, I'll be out this Sunday in the afternoon to see you and your mother.' And when he got here he said, 'I phoned New Canaan, Conn.—John Johansen.' Well! Joe's a Harvard classmate of mine and Woollen had studied under him, so they made the association and became the designers of Clowes Hall, Woollen and Joe, as we call him.

"Now I'm very much wedded to the project and so far it's been going very well. It's primarily a *town* project and secondarily a *gown* project, and this is the thing that Butler University will *not* understand. Now mind you, I want to make certain it's called Clowes Hall *on* the campus of Butler and not *of*.

"Captain Kangaroo has been on stage, that's true, and one of your New York critics wasn't entirely pleased about this. So Mother wrote him, telling him we have something here for all types and Captain Kangaroo is for the children and we've had the conductor from the Met and done the Verdi *Requiem*. But this didn't impress dear Harold, so he finally showed up one night but he hated the audience. I was in Paris at the time and the Busoni Festival was on here and it wasn't well attended. I don't know what happened when this young man went back to New York with that. Busoni was a 19th-century not-very-good composer, but anyway Schonberg came out and heard this Busoni concert and also it was very near that dreadful Speedway thing, you know, and the town turns itself out for *that*."

I took the tour through the art collection, guided by the curator, Ian Frasier, who assured me the exhibition is well attended "except when the leaves all drop, then nobody comes because that's the weekend everybody has to rake. . . .

"Now this portrait here, which I suppose is the single most famous painting in the collection because it's the only certain self-portrait by Franz Hals; there are, in fact, 14 versions of this in the world and this is the only one that was disguised. It had been disguised as a woman, and it was in the collection of the King of Saxony. After the Depression, when the Silbermann brothers, art dealers, had to lend the king money, they got this as collateral, and then the king wasn't able to pay them back. So the Silbermanns brought it to this country and had it X-rayed and found it was not a Franz Hals portrait of a woman but a self-portrait that had been painted over. So they cleaned it off and, of course, it was obvious that all the others had been copies of this. Meanwhile, every museum that owned one of these, the other 13, was busy trying to prove that its was the original—until this one showed up. And then they just quietly put theirs in the basement. The Metropolitan in New York had one of the other versions. . . ."

I returned to my motel very tired and took another look at LeRoi Jones's essay, "Hunting Is Not Those Heads on the Wall." Then I skipped through some more Hayakawa and when, finally, I felt

the storm was over and I was back on course with my two main coordinates, I telephoned friends who now live in Evansville. I told them what I was seeing in Indianapolis and they told me they'd just seen Ionesco's *Rhinoceros* in Evansville.

They drove up and Saturday night we made the rounds of the town's other cultural attractions. Erroll Garner was playing at the Embers, a supper club on Meridian Street.

Cul-ture 8: the concepts, habits, skills, arts, instruments, institutions, etc., of a given people in a given period; civilization.

—Webster's

He was playing to buttoned-up crewcuts and their stiffly coifed wives. They talked loudly and a lot as he played, and now and then between conversational bouts they listened, snapping fingers and bobbing heads. "Love for Sale" . . . "Misty." . . .

We decided to leave, find out what else was happening in the Indianapolis civilization, and as we were on our way a loud, gruff, falsely deepened voice said, "Hey, what're you supposed t'be, huh? A student?"

I turned.

"Yeah, you with the hair. Naw, you're no student. What're ya takin' notes for, and what's with the long hair?"

His thatch was a small fraction of an inch long. I'd been tucked into my apartment working on a novel, then on a screenplay based on another of my novels, and I hadn't bothered going out to a barber. Just snipped some off when I felt the urge.

"Why should the length of my hair concern you?"

"Because I'm a *man!*" he bellowed,

thumping his chest like Tarzan.

"Because your hair is short?"

"Yeah, yeah, yeah!"

And he was very, very serious, too. So were the people he was with—one of them suggested we all go outside and he and I could fight about it. Which I'm happy he didn't feel inclined to do—I can't work up much adrenalin over anybody's hair length.

As we were going out the door, Erroll Garner was hamming, satirizing the classics, and this had the audience responding with howls of delight.

Down the street a short way, in the Carrousel, the audience was entirely different. Mixed, black and white, about half and half, and listening attentively, intensely, to the Buddy Parker Four doing a long, ingenious interpretation of "Ode to Billy Joe."

Cul-tur-ist: one who advocates, or is devoted to, general cultural advancement.

—Webster's

Nobody here was worried about the length of anybody's hair. They were busy absorbing, ingesting what this homegrown Indianapolis group was offering. Maybe news of our set-to at the Embers traveled with us, for soon the group was working out on lyrics about "long hair and shoes with holes" and what some people thought of that. And they did "Tobacco Road," "The Folks Who Live On the Hill" and "I'm a Lover."

It was sweet to be home. After those uptight crewcuts and stiff hairdos at the Embers, after all that brooding dark canvas out of ancient Europe, after the clean strength and beauty of Sholem Aleichem's people on stage at Clowes Hall. I have nothing against digging the arts from other cultures, other times and places—on the contrary, they have given and continue to give me perspective. On my own time and place. Because, indeed, hunting is not those heads on the wall. They may give you a sharper eye for the hunt, but your hunt is in your own culture, as it's always been. The King of Saxony knew this, and so did other art patrons of ancient Europe. And so perhaps did Allen Clowes when he commissioned Evans Woollen 3d to design Clowes Hall.

Now is about two decades too soon to say what impact Clowes Hall has had, is having, or will have on what can roughly be called civilization in Indianapolis. But some speculations are in order:

As time goes by, the hall will function less and less as a hick hippodrome and more and more as a true arts center. Because—to pick up from my other coordinate: ". . . we cannot speak without imposing upon the flux of experience an assumed structure. . . ." And by the fact of its existence, the hall is a clear and forceful statement of intentions, a determination to sharpen the minds, spirits, and tastes of the Indianapolis populace.

As one town critic, Henry Butler, has said, Clowes Hall kills "India-no-place." With such flexible accommodations for the performing arts from any time, any place, any culture, it's both an architectural triumph and a signal flag to the world that Indianapolis is ready, willing, and able to host the best.

Those children in the balcony watching *Fiddler on the Roof*: Sholem Aleichem blew their minds as sure as two apples plus two apples is four apples, and now they are open to other and more far-out things. Clowes Hall will play a part in their lives and by the time they are adults it's safe to assume they will have seen and heard much of the best produced by the gone European masters. Consequently, they will bring a keener ear to such as the Buddy Parker Four and/or their successors.

Trav Selmiers may use naked Fords and Captain Kangaroo to lure today's townfolk into the hall, but it's a fair bet that, having infiltrated their habits, he will expose them to some of the art treasures out of old Europe, called "culture." And that's no small feat. Like most Americans, most Indianapolitans have been pretty thoroughly bamboozled by the Mad Ave. marketeers who control the "hot" media which scream at us from waking to sleeping, trying to elbow everything else out of our minds.

Another difficulty: what gets called culture has got a bad reputation. To many in our society it seems bounded on the East by empty snobbery and on the West by boredom. So Mr. Selmier's task is something like trying to bring gold to Australian aborigines—the first thing they want to know is, what's it worth?

Finally, ever since I embarked on this project, I've been hearing the same questions from "cosmopolitan" people: "Does Indianapolis have a culture?" And now I have an answer: "Of course, but it's bound to get better."

How Can I Tell Them There's Nothing Left?

JOAN DIDION

This is a story about love and death in the golden land, and begins with the country. The San Bernardino Valley lies only an hour east of Los Angeles by the San Bernardino Freeway but is in certain ways an alien place: not the coastal California of the subtropical twilights and the soft westerlies off the Pacific but a harsher California, haunted by the Mojave just beyond the mountains, devastated by the hot dry Santa Ana wind

From Joan Didion, *Slouching Towards Bethlehem.* Reprinted by permission of Farrar, Straus & Giroux, Inc., copyright © 1966, 1968 by Joan Didion.

that comes down through the passes at 100 miles an hour and whines through the eucalyptus windbreaks and works on the nerves. October is the bad month for the wind, the month when breathing is difficult and the hills blaze up spontaneously. There has been no rain since April. Every voice seems a scream. It is the season of suicide and divorce and prickly dread, wherever the wind blows.

The Mormons settled this ominous country, and then they abandoned it, but by the time they left the first orange tree had been planted and for the next hundred years the San Bernardino Valley would draw a kind of people who imagined they might live among the talismanic fruit and prosper in the dry air, people who brought with them Midwestern ways of building and cooking and praying and who tried to graft those ways upon the land. The graft took in curious ways. This is the California where it is possible to live and die without ever eating an artichoke, without ever meeting a Catholic or a Jew. This is the California where it is easy to Dial-A-Devotion, but hard to buy a book. This is the country in which a belief in the literal interpretation of Genesis has slipped imperceptibly into a belief in the literal interpretation of *Double Indemnity,* the country of the teased hair and the Capris and the girls for whom all life's promise comes down to a waltz-length white wedding dress and the birth of a Kimberly or a Sherry or a Debbi and a Tijuana divorce and a return to hairdressers' school. "We were just crazy kids," they say without regret, and look to the future. The future always looks good in the golden land, because no one remembers the past. Here is where the hot wind blows and the old ways do not seem relevant, where the divorce rate is double the national average and where one person in every thirty-eight lives in a trailer. Here is the last stop for all those who come from somewhere else, for all those who drifted away from the cold and the past and the old ways. Here is where they are trying to find a new life style, trying to find it in the only places they know to look: the movies and the newspapers. The case of Lucille Marie Maxwell Miller is a tabloid monument to that new life style.

Imagine Banyan Street first, because Banyan is where it happened. The way to Banyan is to drive west from San Bernardino out Foothill Boulevard, Route 66: past the Santa Fe switching yards, the Forty Winks Motel. Past the motel that is nineteen stucco tepees: "SLEEP IN A WIGWAM—GET MORE FOR YOUR WAMPUM." Past Fontana Drag

City and the Fontana Church of the Nazarene and the Pit Stop A Go-Go; past Kaiser Steel, through Cucamonga, out to the Kapu Kai Restaurant-Bar and Coffee Shop, at the corner of Route 66 and Carnelian Avenue. Up Carnelian Avenue from the Kapu Kai, which means "Forbidden Seas," the subdivision flags whip in the harsh wind. "HALF-ACRE RANCHES! SNACK BARS! TRAVERTINE ENTRIES! $95 DOWN." It is the trail of an intention gone haywire, the flotsam of the New California. But after a while the signs thin out on Carnelian Avenue, and the houses are no longer the bright pastels of the Springtime Home owners but the faded bungalows of the people who grow a few grapes and keep a few chickens out here, and then the hill gets steeper and the road climbs and even the bungalows are few, and here—desolate, roughly surfaced, lined with eucalyptus and lemon groves—is Banyan Street.

Like so much of this country, Banyan suggests something curious and unnatural. The lemon groves are sunken, down a three- or four-foot retaining wall, so that one looks directly into their dense foliage, too lush, unsettlingly glossy, the greenery of nightmare; the fallen eucalyptus bark is too dusty, a place for snakes to breed. The stones look not like natural stones but like the rubble of some unmentioned upheaval. There are smudge pots, and a closed cistern. To one side of Banyan there is the flat valley, and to the other the San Bernardino Mountains, a dark mass looming too high, too fast, nine, ten, eleven thousand feet, right there above the lemon groves. At midnight on Banyan Street there is no light at all, and no sound except the wind in the eucalyptus and a muffled barking of dogs. There may be a kennel somewhere, or the dogs may be coyotes.

Banyan Street was the route Lucille Miller took home from the twenty-four-hour Mayfair Market on the night of October 7, 1964, a night when the moon was dark and the wind was blowing and she was out of milk, and Banyan Street was where, at about 12:30 A.M., her 1964 Volkswagen came to a sudden stop, caught fire, and began to burn. For an hour and fifteen minutes Lucille Miller ran up and down Banyan calling for help, but no cars passed and no help came. At three o'clock that morning, when the fire had been put out and the California Highway Patrol officers were completing their report, Lucille Miller was still sobbing and incoherent, for her husband had been asleep in the Volkswagen. "What will I tell the children, when there's nothing left, nothing left in the casket," she cried to the friend called to comfort her. "How can I tell them there's nothing left?"

In fact there was something left, and a week later it lay in the Draper Mortuary Chapel in a closed bronze coffin blanketed with pink carnations. Some 200 mourners heard Elder Robert E. Denton of the Seventh-Day Adventist Church of Ontario speak of "the temper of fury that has broken out among us." For Gordon Miller, he said, there would be "no more death, no more heartaches, no more misunderstandings." Elder Ansel Bristol mentioned the "peculiar" grief of the hour. Elder Fred Jensen asked "what shall it profit a man, if he shall gain the whole world, and lose his own soul?" A light rain fell, a blessing in a dry season, and a female vocalist sang "Safe in the Arms of Jesus." A tape recording of the service was made for

the widow, who was being held without bail in the San Bernardino County Jail on a charge of first-degree murder.

Of course she came from somewhere else, came off the prairie in search of something she had seen in a movie or heard on the radio, for this is a Southern California story. She was born on January 17, 1930, in Winnipeg, Manitoba, the only child of Gordon and Lily Maxwell, both schoolteachers and both dedicated to the Seventh-Day Adventist Church, whose members observe the Sabbath on Saturday, believe in an apocalyptic Second Coming, have a strong missionary tendency, and, if they are strict, do not smoke, drink, eat meat, use makeup, or wear jewelry, including wedding rings. By the time Lucille Maxwell enrolled at Walla Walla College in College Place, Washington, the Adventist school where her parents then taught, she was an eighteen-year-old possessed of unremarkable good looks and remarkable high spirits. "Lucille wanted to see the world," her father would say in retrospect, "and I guess she found out."

The high spirits did not seem to lend themselves to an extended course of study at Walla Walla College, and in the spring of 1949 Lucille Maxwell met and married Gordon ("Cork") Miller, a twenty-four-old graduate of Walla Walla and of the University of Oregon dental school, then stationed at Fort Lewis as a medical officer. "Maybe you could say it was love at first sight," Mr. Maxwell recalls. "Before they were ever formally introduced, he sent Lucille a dozen and a half roses with a card that said even if she didn't come out on a date with him, he hoped she'd find the roses pretty anyway." The Maxwells remember their daughter as a "radiant" bride.

Unhappy marriages so resemble one another that we do not need to know too much about the course of this one. There may or may not have been trouble on Guam, where Cork and Lucille Miller lived while he finished his Army duty. There may or may not have been problems in the small Oregon town where he first set up private practice. There appears to have been some disappointment about their move to California: Cork Miller had told friends that he wanted to become a doctor, that he was unhappy as a dentist and planned to enter the Seventh-Day Adventist College of Medical Evangelists at Loma Linda, a few miles south of San Bernardino. Instead he bought a dental practice in the west end of San Bernardino County, and the family settled there, in a modest house on the kind of street where there are always tricycles and revolving credit and dreams about bigger houses, better streets. That was 1957. By the summer of 1964 they had achieved the bigger house on the better street and the familiar accouterments of a family on its way up: the $30,000 a year, the three children for the Christmas card, the picture window, the family room, the newspaper photographs that showed "Mrs. Gordon Miller, Ontario Heart Fund Chairman. . . ." They were paying the familiar price for it. And they had reached the familiar season of divorce.

It might have been anyone's bad summer, anyone's siege of heat and nerves and migraine and money worries, but this one began particularly early and particularly badly. On April 24 an old friend, Elaine Hayton, died suddenly; Lucille Miller had seen her only the night before. During the month of May,

Cork Miller was hospitalized briefly with a bleeding ulcer, and his usual reserve deepened into depression. He told his accountant that he was "sick of looking at open mouths," and threatened suicide. By July 8, the conventional tensions of love and money had reached the conventional impasse in the new house on the acre lot at 8488 Bella Vista, and Lucille Miller filed for divorce. Within a month, however, the Millers seemed reconciled. They saw a marriage counselor. They talked about a fourth child. It seemed that the marriage had reached the traditional truce, the point at which so many resign themselves to cutting both their losses and their hopes.

But the Millers' season of trouble was not to end that easily. October 7 began as a commonplace enough day, one of those days that sets the teeth on edge with its tedium, its small frustrations. The temperature reached 102 degrees in San Bernardino that afternoon, and the Miller children were home from school because of Teachers' Institute. There was ironing to be dropped off. There was a trip to pick up a prescription for Nembutal, a trip to a self-service dry cleaner. In the early evening, an unpleasant accident with the Volkswagen: Cork Miller hit and killed a German shepherd, and afterward said that his head felt "like it had a Mack truck on it." It was something he often said. As of that evening Cork Miller was $63,479 in debt, including the $29,637 mortgage on the new house, a debt load which seemed oppressive to him. He was a man who wore his responsibilities uneasily, and complained of migraine headaches almost constantly.

He ate alone that night, from a TV tray in the living room. Later the Millers watched John Forsythe and Senta

Berger in *See How They Run,* and when the movie ended, about eleven, Cork Miller suggested that they go out for milk. He wanted some hot chocolate. He took a blanket and pillow from the couch and climbed into the passenger seat of the Volkswagen. Lucille Miller remembers reaching over to lock his door as she backed down the driveway. By the time she left the Mayfair Market, and long before they reached Banyan Street, Cork Miller appeared to be asleep.

There is some confusion in Lucille Miller's mind about what happened between 12:30 A.M., when the fire broke out, and 1:50 A.M., when it was reported. She says that she was driving east on Banyan Street at about 35 m.p.h. when she felt the Volkswagen pull sharply to the right. The next thing she knew the car was on the embankment, quite near the edge of the retaining wall, and flames were shooting up behind her. She does not remember jumping out. She does remember prying up a stone with which she broke the window next to her husband, and then scrambling down the retaining wall to try to find a stick. "I don't know how I was going to push him out," she says. "I just thought if I had a stick, I'd push him out." She could not, and after a while she ran to the intersection of Banyan and Carnelian Avenue. There are no houses at that corner, and almost no traffic. After one car had passed without stopping, Lucille Miller ran back down Banyan toward the burning Volkswagen. She did not stop, but she slowed down, and in the flames she could see her husband. He was, she said, "just black."

At the first house up Sapphire Avenue, half a mile from the Volkswagen,

Lucille Miller finally found help. There Mrs. Robert Swenson called the sheriff, and then, at Lucille Miller's request, she called Harold Lance, the Millers' lawyer and their close friend. When Harold Lance arrived he took Lucille Miller home to his wife, Joan. Twice Harold Lance and Lucille Miller returned to Banyan Street and talked to the Highway Patrol officers. A third time Harold Lance returned alone, and when he came back he said to Lucille Miller, "O.K. . . . you don't talk any more."

When Lucille Miller was arrested the next afternoon, Sandy Slagle was with her. Sandy Slagle was the intense, relentlessly loyal medical student who used to baby-sit for the Millers, and had been living as a member of the family since she graduated from high school in 1959. The Millers took her away from a difficult home situation, and she thinks of Lucille Miller not only as "more or less a mother or a sister" but as "the most wonderful character" she has ever known. On the night of the accident, Sandy Slagle was in her dormitory at Loma Linda University, but Lucille Miller called her early in the morning and asked her to come home. The doctor was there when Sandy Slagle arrived, giving Lucille Miller an injection of Nembutal. "She was crying as she was going under," Sandy Slagle recalls. "Over and over she'd say, 'Sandy, all the hours I spent trying to save him and now what are they trying to *do* to me?' "

At 1:30 that afternoon, Sergeant William Paterson and Detectives Charles Callahan and Joseph Karr of the Central Homicide Division arrived at 8488 Bella Vista. "One of them appeared at the bedroom door," Sandy Slagle remembers, "and said to Lucille, 'You've got ten minutes to get dressed or we'll take you as you are.' She was in her nightgown, you know, so I tried to get her dressed."

Sandy Slagle tells the story now as if by rote, and her eyes do not waver. "So I had her panties and bra on her and they opened the door again, so I got some Capris on her, you know, and a scarf." Her voice drops. "And then they just took her."

The arrest took place just twelve hours after the first report that there had been an accident on Banyan Street, a rapidity which would later prompt Luciller Miller's attorney to say that the entire case was an instance of trying to justify a reckless arrest. Actually what first caused the detectives who arrived on Banyan Street toward dawn that morning to give the accident more than routine attention were certain apparent physical inconsistencies. While Lucille Miller had said that she was driving about 35 m.p.h. when the car swerved to a stop, an examination of the cooling Volkswagen showed that it was in low gear, and that the parking rather than the driving lights were on. The front wheels, moreover, did not seem to be in exactly the position that Lucille Miller's description of the accident would suggest, and the right rear wheel was dug in deep, as if it had been spun in place. It seemed curious to the detectives, too, that a sudden stop from 35 m.p.h.—the same jolt which was presumed to have knocked over a gasoline can in the back seat and somehow started the fire—should have left two milk cartons upright on the back floorboard, and the remains of a Polaroid camera box lying apparently undisturbed on the back seat.

No one, however, could be expected to give a precise account of what did and did not happen in a moment of terror, and none of these inconsistencies seemed in themselves incontrovertible evidence of criminal intent. But they did interest the Sheriff's Office, as did Gordon Miller's apparent unconsciousness at the time of the accident, and the length of time it had taken Lucille Miller to get help. Something, moreover, struck the investigators as wrong about Harold Lance's attitude when he came back to Banyan Street the third time and found the investigation by no means over. "The way Lance was acting," the prosecuting attorney said later, "they thought maybe they'd hit a nerve."

And so it was that on the morning of October 8, even before the doctor had come to give Lucille Miller an injection to calm her, the San Bernardino County Sheriff's Office was trying to construct another version of what might have happened between 12:30 and 1:50 A.M. The hypothesis they would eventually present was based on the somewhat tortuous premise that Lucille Miller had undertaken a plan which failed: a plan to stop the car on the lonely road, spread gasoline over her presumably drugged husband, and, with a stick on the accelerator, gently "walk" the Volkswagen over the embankment, where it would tumble four feet down the retaining wall into the lemon grove and almost certainly explode. If this happened, Lucille Miller might then have somehow negotiated the two miles up Carnelian to Bella Vista in time to be home when the accident was discovered. This plan went awry, according to the Sheriff's Office hypothesis, when the car would not go over the rise of the embankment.

Lucille Miller might have panicked then—after she had killed the engine the third or fourth time, say, out there on the dark road with the gasoline already spread and the dogs baying and the wind blowing and the unspeakable apprehension that a pair of headlights would suddenly light up Banyan Street and expose her there—and set the fire herself.

Although this version accounted for some of the physical evidence—the car in low because it had been started from a dead stop, the parking lights on because she could not do what needed doing without some light, a rear wheel spun in repeated attempts to get the car over the embankment, the milk cartons upright because there had been no sudden stop—it did not seem on its own any more or less credible than Lucille Miller's own story. Moreover, some of the physical evidence did seem to support her story: a nail in a front tire, a nine-pound rock found in the car, presumably the one with which she had broken the window in an attempt to save her husband. Within a few days an autopsy had established that Gordon Miller was alive when he burned, which did not particularly help the State's case, and that he had enough Nembutal and Sandoptal in his blood to put the average person to sleep, which did: on the other hand Gordon Miller habitually took both Nembutal and Fiorinal (a common headache presciption which contains Sandoptal), and had been ill besides.

It was a spotty case, and to make it work at all the State was going to have to find a motive. There was talk of unhappiness, talk of another man. That kind of motive, during the next few weeks, was what they set out to estab-lish. They set out to find it in accountants' ledgers and double-indemnity clauses and motel registers, set out to determine what might move a woman who believed in all the promises of the middle class—a woman who had been chairman of the Heart Fund and who always knew a reasonable little dressmaker and who had come out of the bleak wild of prairie fundamentalism to find what she imagined to be the good life—what should drive such a woman to sit on a street called Bella Vista and look out her new picture window into the empty California sun and calculate how to burn her husband alive in a Volkswagen. They found the wedge they wanted closer at hand than they might have at first expected, for, as testimony would reveal later at the trial, it seemed that in December of 1963 Lucille Miller had begun an affair with the husband of one of her friends, a man whose daughter called her "Auntie Lucille," a man who might have seemed to have the gift for people and money and the good life that Cork Miller so noticeably lacked. The man was Arthwell Hayton, a well-known San Bernardino attorney and at one time a member of the district attorney's staff.

In some ways it was the conventional clandestine affair in a place like San Bernardino, a place where little is bright, or graceful, where it is routine to misplace the future and easy to start looking for it in bed. Over the seven weeks that it would take to try Lucille Miller for murder, Assistant District Attorney Don A. Turner and defense attorney Edward P. Foley would between them unfold a curiously predictable story. There were the falsified motel registrations. There were the lunch dates, the afternoon drives in Arthwell Hayton's red Cadillac convertible. There were the interminable discussions of the wronged partners. There were the confidantes ("I knew everything," Sandy Slagle would insist fiercely later; "I knew every time, places, everything") and there were the words remembered from bad magazine stories ("Don't kiss me, it will trigger things," Lucille Miller remembered telling Arthwell Hayton in the parking lot of Harold's Club in Fontana after lunch one day) and there were the notes, the sweet exchanges: "Hi Sweetie Pie! You are my cup of tea!! Happy Birthday—you don't look a day over 29!! Your baby, Arthwell."

And toward the end, there was the acrimony. It was April 24, 1964, when Arthwell Hayton's wife, Elaine, died suddenly, and nothing good happened after that. Arthwell Hayton had taken his cruiser, *Captain's Lady,* over to Catalina that weekend; he called home at nine o'clock Friday night, but did not talk to his wife because Lucille Miller answered the telephone and said that Elaine was showering. The next morning the Haytons' daughter found her mother in bed, dead. The newspapers reported the death as accidental, perhaps the result of an allergy to hair spray. When Arthwell Hayton flew home from Catalina that weekend, Lucille Miller met him at the airport, but the finish had already been written.

It was in the breakup that the affair ceased to be in the conventional mode and began to resemble instead the novels of James M. Cain, the movies of the late 1930's, all the dreams in which violence and threats and blackmail are made to seem commonplaces of middle-class life.

What was most startling about the case that the State of California was preparing against Lucille Miller was something that had nothing to do with law at all, something that never appeared in the eight-column afternoon headlines but was always there between them: the revelation that the dream was teaching the dreamers how to live. Here is Lucille Miller talking to her lover sometime in the early summer of 1964, after he had indicated that, on the advice of his minister, he did not intend to see her any more: "First, I'm going to go to that dear pastor of yours and tell him a few things. . . . When I do tell him that, you won't be in the Redlands Church any more. . . . Look, Sonny Boy, if you think your reputation is going to be ruined, your life won't be worth two cents." Here is Arthwell Hayton, to Lucille Miller: "I'll go to Sheriff Frank Bland and tell him some things that I know about you until you'll wish you'd never heard of Arthwell Hayton." For an affair between a Seventh-Day Adventist dentist's wife and a Seventh-Day Adventist personal-injury lawyer, it seems a curious kind of dialogue.

"Boy, I could get that little boy coming and going," Lucille Miller later confided to Erwin Sprengle, a Riverside contractor who was a business partner of Arthwell Hayton's and a friend to both the lovers. (Friend or no, on this occasion he happened to have an induction coil attached to his telephone in order to tape Lucille Miller's call.) "And he hasn't got one thing on me that he can prove. I mean, I've got concrete—he has nothing concrete." In the same taped conversation with Erwin Sprengle, Lucille Miller mentioned a tape that she herself had surreptitiously made, months before, in Arthwell Hayton's car.

"I said to him, I said 'Arthwell, I just feel like I'm being used.' . . . He started sucking his thumb and he said 'I love you. . . . This isn't something that happened yesterday. I'd marry you tomorrow if I could. I don't love Elaine.' He'd love to hear that played back, wouldn't he?"

"Yeah," drawled Sprengle's voice on the tape. "That would be just a little incriminating, wouldn't it?"

"Just a *little* incriminating," Lucille Miller agreed. "It really *is.*"

Later on the tape, Sprengle asked where Cork Miller was.

"He took the children down to the church."

"You didn't go?"

"No."

"You're naughty."

It was all, moreover, in the name of "love"; everyone involved placed a magical faith in the efficacy of the very word. There was the significance that Lucille Miller saw in Arthwell's saying that he "loved" her, that he did not "love" Elaine. There was Arthwell insisting, later, at the trial, that he had never said it, that he may have "whispered sweet nothings in her ear" (as her defense hinted that he had whispered in many ears), but he did not remember bestowing upon her the special seal, saying the word, declaring "love." There was the summer evening when Lucille Miller and Sandy Slagle followed Arthwell Hayton down to his new boat in its mooring at Newport Beach and untied the lines with Arthwell aboard, Arthwell and a girl with whom he later testified he was drinking hot chocolate and watching television. "I did that on purpose," Lucille Miller told Erwin

Sprengle later, "to save myself from letting my heart do something crazy."

January 11, 1965, was a bright warm day in Southern California, the kind of day when Catalina floats on the Pacific horizon and the air smells of orange blossoms and it is a long way from the bleak and difficult East, a long way from the cold, a long way from the past. A woman in Hollywood staged an all-night sit-in on the hood of her car to prevent repossession by a finance company. A seventy-year-old pensioner drove his station wagon at five miles an hour past three Gardena poker parlors and emptied three pistols and a twelve-gauge shotgun through their windows, wounding twenty-nine people. "Many young women become prostitutes just to have enough money to play cards," he explained in a note. Mrs. Nick Adams said that she was "not surprised" to hear her husband announce his divorce plans on the Les Crane Show, and farther north, a sixteen-year-old jumped off the Golden Gate Bridge and lived.

And, in the San Bernardino County Courthouse, the Miller trial opened. The crowds were so bad that the glass courtroom doors were shattered in the crush, and from then on identification disks were issued to the first forty-three spectators in line. The line began forming at 6 A.M., and college girls camped at the courthouse all night, with stores of graham crackers and No-Cal.

All they were doing was picking a jury, those first few days, but the sensational nature of the case had already suggested itself. Early in December there had been an abortive first trial, a trial at which no evidence was ever presented because on the day the jury was seated the San

Bernardino *Sun-Telegram* ran an "inside" story quoting Assistant District Attorney Don Turner, the prosecutor, as saying, "We are looking into the circumstances of Mrs. Hayton's death. In view of the current trial concerning the death of Dr. Miller, I do not feel I should comment on Mrs. Hayton's death." It seemed that there had been barbiturates in Elaine Hayton's blood, and there had seemed some irregularity about the way she was dressed on that morning when she was found under the covers, dead. Any doubts about the death at the time, however, had never gotten as far as the Sheriff's Office. "I guess somebody didn't want to rock the boat," Turner said later. "These were prominent people."

Although all of that had not been in the *Sun-Telegram's* story, an immediate mistrial had been declared. Almost as immediately, there had been another development: Arthwell Hayton had asked newspapermen to an 11 A.M. Sunday morning press conference in his office. There had been television cameras, and flash-bulbs popping. "As you gentlemen may know," Hayton had said, striking a note of stiff bonhomie, "there are very often women who become amorous toward their doctor or lawyer. This does not mean on the physician's or lawyer's part that there is any romance toward the patient or client."

"Would you deny that you were having an affair with Mrs. Miller?" a reporter had asked.

"I would deny that there was any romance on my part whatsoever."

It was a distinction he would maintain through all the wearing weeks to come.

So they had come to see Arthwell, these crowds who now milled beneath the dusty palms outside the courthouse, and they had also come to see Lucille, who appeared as a slight, intermittently pretty woman, already pale from lack of sun, a woman who would turn thirty-five before the trial was over and whose tendency toward haggardness was beginning to show, a meticulous woman who insisted, against her lawyer's advice, on coming to court with her hair piled high and lacquered. "I would've been happy if she'd come in with it hanging loose, but Lucille wouldn't do that," her lawyer said. He was Edward P. Foley, a small, emotional Irish Catholic who several times wept in the courtroom. "She has a great honesty, this woman," he added, "but this honesty about her appearance always worked against her."

By the time the trial opened, Lucille Miller's appearance included maternity clothes, for an official examination on December 18 had revealed that she was then three and a half months pregnant, a fact which made picking a jury even more difficult than usual, for Turner was asking the death penalty. "It's unfortunate but there it is," he would say of the pregnancy to each juror in turn, and finally twelve were seated, seven of them women, the youngest forty-one, an assembly of the very peers—housewives, a machinist, a truck driver, a grocery-store manager, a filing clerk—above whom Lucille Miller had wanted so badly to rise.

That was the sin, more than the adultery, which tended to reinforce the one for which she was being tried. It was implicit in both the defense and the prosecution that Lucille Miller was an erring woman, a woman who perhaps wanted too much. But to the prosecution she was not merely a woman who would want a new house and want to go to parties and run up high telephone bills ($1,152 in ten months), but a woman who would go so far as to murder her husband for his $80,000 in insurance, making it appear an accident in order to collect another $40,000 in double indemnity and straight accident policies. To Turner she was a woman who did not want simply her freedom and a reasonable alimony (she could have had that, the defense contended, by going through with her divorce suit), but wanted everything, a woman motivated by "love and greed." She was a "manipulator." She was a "user of people."

To Edward Foley, on the other hand, she was an impulsive woman who "couldn't control her foolish little heart." Where Turner skirted the pregnancy, Foley dwelt upon it, even calling the dead man's mother down from Washington to testify that her son had told her they were going to have another baby because Lucille felt that it would "do much to weld our home again in the pleasant relations that we used to have." Where the prosecution saw a "calculator," the defense saw a "blabbermouth," and in fact Lucille Miller did emerge as an ingenuous conversationalist. Just as, before her husband's death, she had confided in her friends about her love affair, so she chatted about it after his death, with the arresting sergeant. "Of course Cork lived with it for years, you know," her voice was heard to tell Sergeant Paterson on a tape made the morning after her arrest. "After Elaine died, he pushed the panic button one night and just asked me right out, and that, I think, was when he really—the first time he really faced it." When the sergeant asked why she had agreed to talk to him, against the specific instructions of her lawyers, Lucille Miller said airily, "Oh, I've always been basically quite an honest person. . . . I mean I can put a hat in the cupboard and say it cost ten dollars less, but basically I've always kind of just lived my life the way I wanted to, and if you don't like it you can take off."

The prosecution hinted at men other than Arthwell, and even, over Foley's objections, managed to name one. The defense called Miller suicidal. The prosecution produced experts who said that the Volkswagen fire could not have been accidental. Foley produced witnesses who said that it could have been. Lucille's father, now a junior-high-school teacher in Oregon, quoted Isaiah to reporters: *"Every tongue that shall rise against thee in judgment thou shalt condemn."* "Lucille did wrong, her affair," her mother said judiciously. "With her it was love. But with some I guess it's just passion." There was Debbie, the Millers' fourteen-year-old, testifying in a steady voice about how she and her mother had gone to a supermarket to buy the gasoline can the week before the accident. There was Sandy Slagle, in the courtroom every day, declaring that on at least one occasion Lucille Miller had prevented her husband not only from committing suicide but from committing suicide in such a way that it would appear an accident and ensure the double-indemnity payment. There was Wenche Berg, the pretty twenty-seven-year-old Norwegian governess to Arthwell Hayton's children, testifying that Arthwell had instructed her not to allow Lucille Miller to see or talk to the children.

Two months dragged by, and the headlines never stopped. Southern California's crime reporters were headquartered in San Bernardino for the duration: Howard Hertel from the *Times,* Jim Bennett and Eddy Jo Bernal from the *Herald-Examiner.* Two months in which the Miller trial was pushed off the *Examiner's* front page only by the Academy Award nominations and Stan Laurel's death. And finally, on March 2, after Turner had reiterated that it was a case of "love and greed," and Foley had protested that his client was being tried for adultery, the case went to the jury.

They brought in the verdict, guilty of murder in the first degree, at 4:50 P.M. on March 5. "She didn't do it," Debbie Miller cried, jumping up from the spectators' section. "She didn't *do* it." Sandy Slagle collapsed in her seat and began to scream. "Sandy, for God's sake please *don't,*" Lucille Miller said in a voice that carried across the courtroom, and Sandy Slagle was momentarily subdued. But as the jurors left the courtroom she screamed again: "You're murderers. . . . Every last one of you is a *murderer.*" Sheriff's deputies moved in then, each wearing a string tie that read "1965 SHERIFF'S RODEO," and Lucille Miller's father, that sad-faced junior-high-school teacher who believed in the word of Christ and the dangers of wanting to see the world, blew her a kiss off his fingertips.

The California Institution for Women at Frontera, where Lucille Miller is now, lies down where Euclid Avenue turns into country road, not too many miles from where she once lived and shopped and organized the Heart Fund Ball. Cattle graze across the road, and Rainbirds sprinkle the alfalfa. Frontera has

a softball field and tennis courts, and looks as if it might be a California junior college, except that the trees are not yet high enough to conceal the concertina wire around the top of the Cyclone fence. On visitors' day there are big cars in the parking area, big Buicks and Pontiacs that belong to grandparents and sisters and fathers (not many of them belong to husbands), and some of them have bumper stickers that say "SUPPORT YOUR LOCAL POLICE."

A lot of California murderesses live here, a lot of girls who somehow misunderstood the promise. Don Turner put Sandra Garner here (and her husband in the gas chamber at San Quentin) after the 1959 desert killings known to crime reporters as "the soda-pop murders." Carole Tregoff is here, and has been ever since she was convicted of conspiring to murder Dr. Finch's wife in West Covina, which is not too far from San Bernardino. Carole Tregoff is in fact a nurse's aide in the prison hospital, and might have attended Lucille Miller had her baby been born at Frontera; Lucille Miller chose instead to have it outside, and paid for the guard who stood outside the delivery room in St. Bernardine's Hospital. Debbie Miller came to take the baby home from the hospital, in a white dress with pink ribbons, and Debbie was allowed to choose a name. She named the baby Kimi Kai. The children live with Harold and Joan Lance now, because Lucille Miller will probably spend ten years at Frontera. Don Turner waived his original request for the death penalty (it was generally agreed that he had demanded it only, in Edward Foley's words, "to get anybody with the slightest trace of human kindness in their veins off the jury"), and settled for life imprisonment with the possibility of parole. Lucille Miller does not like it at Frontera, and has had trouble adjusting. "She's going to have to learn humility," Turner says. "She's going to have to use her ability to charm, to manipulate."

The new house is empty now, the house on the street with the sign that says

PRIVATE ROAD
BELLA VISTA
DEAD END

The Millers never did get it landscaped, and weeds grow up around the fieldstone siding. The television aerial has toppled on the roof, and a trash can is stuffed with the debris of family life: a cheap suitcase, a child's game called "Lie Detector." There is a sign on what would have been the lawn, and the sign reads "ESTATE SALE." Edward Foley is trying to get Lucille Miller's case appealed, but there have been delays. "A trial always comes down to a matter of sympathy," Foley says wearily now. "I couldn't create sympathy for her." Everyone is a little weary now, weary and resigned, everyone except Sandy Slagle, whose bitterness is still raw. She lives in an apartment near the medical school in Loma Linda, and studies reports of the case in *True Police Cases* and *Official Detective Stories*. "I'd much rather we not talk about the Hayton business too much," she tells visitors, and she keeps a tape recorder running. "I'd rather talk about Lucille and what a wonderful per-son she is and how her rights were violated." Harold Lance does not talk to visitors at all. "We don't want to give away what we can sell," he explains pleasantly; an attempt was made to sell Lucille Miller's personal story to *Life,* but *Life* did not want to buy it. In the district attorney's offices they are prosecuting other murders now, and do not see why the Miller trial attracted so much attention. "It wasn't a very interesting murder as murders go," Don Turner says laconically. Elaine Hayton's death is no longer under investigation. "We know everything we want to know," Turner says.

Arthwell Hayton's office is directly below Edward Foley's. Some people around San Bernardino say that Arthwell Hayton suffered; others say that he did not suffer at all. Perhaps he did not, for time past is not believed to have any bearing upon time present or future, out in the golden land where every day the world is born anew. In any case, on October 17, 1965, Arthwell Hayton married again, married his children's pretty governess, Wenche Berg, at a service in the Chapel of the Roses at a retirement village near Riverside. Later the newly-weds were feted at a reception for seventy-five in the dining room of Rose Garden Village. The bridegroom was in black tie, with a white carnation in his buttonhole. The bride wore a long white *peau de soie* dress and carried a shower bouquet of sweetheart roses with steph-anotis streamers. A coronet of seed pearls held her illusion veil.

SEX ROLES AND LIFE STYLES

There She Is . . . Miss America

JUDITH MARTIN

"Anybody here over 35?" shouted Bert Parks.

"Yaaay" came back the answer from the crowd gathered in Atlantic City's Convention Hall last weekend to watch the Miss America Pageant.

They had come to cheer their idea of what youth should be like and 50 girls had tried all week to personify that idea. Miss America girls do not smoke, drink,

From *The Washington Post* (September 14, 1969). Reprinted by permission of the Washington Post.

date, discuss controversial topics or go around unchaperoned during the pageant—the winner agrees to behave that way for a year—and they are very polite to their elders.

They support their government, condemn dissent, and set their goals on spending a year or two in traditional female occupations—modeling or elementary school teaching—until the right man comes along.

Miss America of 1970, Pamela Anne Eldred of Detroit, gave a press conference in which she said she was a spokesman for her generation and she made a statement about the Establishment:

"I feel that the people who were voted into office must have the intelligence to know what to do and that everybody should have faith in them."

She said she did not object when pageant officials refused to let her speak on certain subjects. "I feel that they are older and wiser than I am and I can always learn something, especially from someone who is older. If I am told I can't do something, I am told for a reason and I don't challenge it."

"God love you," said a state pageant official from Michigan.

Other pageant officials, the audience, and the judges all talked about how comforting it was to see this girl and the others like her. They called them "true representatives of American youth."

For a few magic days the drug scene, the sexual revolution, and the civil rights, antiwar, female liberation, and student protest movements seemed to them to have been just bad dreams populated by "a tiny minority of kooks."

Miss America told her admirers that the war was right because otherwise the government never would have gotten into it. Miss Minnesota, Judith Claire Mendenhall, a runner-up to the title, told them that women shouldn't try to run things "because they are more emotional and men can overcome their emotions with logic."

Miss Virginia, Sydney Lee Lewis, won a talent award for a speech in which she condemned student reform movements but lauded her generation for things like "conceiving the Rally for Decency."

The theme of this year's pageant was "the sound of youth." There was much talk in it about the new sound and then one talent winner sang "Get Happy" and another played "Bumble Boogie" on the piano.

"Each generation has its own translation of young, and this generation's is a search for the golden rainbow of peace and understanding," said Parks to introduce Miss America 1969, Judi Ford, who wore a Ginger Rogers white pleated chiffon dress and danced the kind of number which used to be the finale of motion picture musical comedies of the '40s.

The pastel chiffon dresses with sequined tops, which the girls wore with 18-button length white cotton gloves in the evening dress competition, had to be specially made. So did the one-piece, solid-color, no-cutouts bathing suits, which are no longer stocked commercially. Spiked-heeled, pointed-toes shoes dyed to match were worn with the bathing suits.

Evening culottes were permitted during the talent competition, but most girls favored the sequined, drum majorette type of costume. Several chose mid-knee cocktail dresses just a shade longer than the new habits of a group of nuns who attended the preliminary competition one night.

Make-up was used in the shows to create the kewpie doll look of decades ago—bright red lipstick, blue eye shadow, and hair teased into beehives with wiglets of curls added.

Offstage, however, the girls were more contemporary, with shoulder-length hairstyles and little wool dresses which gave them the look of 50 Tricia Nixons.

The judges said they were gratified at what they saw and had a hard time picking a winner.

"It renews my faith in youth," said Hollywood make-up man Bud Westmore, a judge, whose wife was Miss California of 1952.

"We have a complete misconception of what is going on when we see the New York hippies who don't wash," said Leon

Leonidoff, another judge, who has been staging Radio City Music Hall spectaculars since 1932. "This country is wholesome and healthy." His wife is a former Miss New Jersey, and he had been going around all week offering contracts to his favorite contestants.

"We really haven't got a thing to worry about," said judge Jane Pickens Langley, who describes herself as "singer, artist, and philanthropist."

"These aren't the girls you hear about, because there is never any scandal attached to them," said judge Zelma George, executive director of the Cleveland Job Corps Center for Women. "Someone should do a master's thesis on them."

"You don't hear about them later because basically they are not ambitious," said writer John Crosby, a judge. "They want to be good wives and mothers."

No one seemed to know, however, why most of the past Miss Americas have been divorced at least once.

The pageant officials expressed their delight with the way Miss America 1970 handled reporters' questions.

Topics on which she smiled and said "I really couldn't voice an opinion—I don't know enough about that" included drugs, nudity in the theater, unisex fashions, student unrest, what the priorities of America should be, and whether 18-year-olds should have the vote. She also said that she was happy about the moon shot "which proves that the United States is a great country" and that her goal in life is "to be a nice person."

Her mother, Mrs. William B. Eldred, who broke in once just after the crowning to tell Miss America, "You are no expert," said that she and her daughter feel alike on all topics. "There is no generation gap," said Mrs. Eldred.

Miss America's one moment of confusion was when she was asked where her father works. He is an employe of Chrysler, and loyalty to the pageant's sponsors, one of which is Oldsmobile, is an important quality of Miss America. Miss America 1969 said that, during her year, love of Toni hair products, Pepsi-Cola, and Oldsmobile became a spontaneous part of her.

The past and present Miss Americas looked very much alike—both with blond bouffant hairdos, green eyes, pale skin, and wide smiles. They are both, said Bert Parks, "composites of positive wonders. All Miss Americas are," he said.

The Miss America Pageant can be described as a commercialized celebration of the ideal life style of the young unmarried woman. According to the stereotype, she is a young Doris Day with a modicum of talent, an overabundance of wholesomeness, and great love for parents and country. But above all, she is a sincere believer that fulfillment lies in a future of raising children, encouraging her husband, and serving her community. In this viewpoint, the central life interest for all women should be home and family. In the past, acceptance of this life style could generally be assumed, although there were always a few rebels in male-dominated professions. In the 1920s there was a minor flourish of feminist activism;

however, after women attained minor goals, such as establishment of women's colleges, interest declined. *

Temporarily, during the 1940s, women assumed a more active role in the occupational structure; but when the men returned from war, women returned to their traditional life style. The 1950s and 1960s brought about increasing numbers of college-educated women, many of whom were not content to be educated housewives. Educated women in the occupational structure tended to be underpaid or overqualified for their jobs. Influenced by the success of other minority groups in attaining their rights, women began to organize a protest.

Irma Kurtz, a British journalist writing for the London Times, *presents her view of the Women's Liberation Movement in the United States. Women's Lib is not a single organization; nor is there agreement among women who endorse social change as to the kind and extent of changes required in order to change the status of women. More conservative liberationists ask for a better chance to develop their potential and still remain women, while the more radical women demand that sex differences be abolished. Obviously, biological differences cannot be abolished; they argue, however, that social rather than biological constraints account for the subordination of women.*

* Jessie Bernard, *Academic Women* (University Park, Pa.: Pennsylvania State Univ. Press, 1964), pp. 36–37.

Make Love Not War

IRMA KURTZ

When they manage to stop laughing, American men are in for a shock; they are going to find themselves forehead to forehead with their women. But this time it won't be just another ambitious wife, a domineering mother, a virgin

From *The Sunday Times Magazine* (London) (September 14, 1969), pp. 22–28. Reprinted by permission of A. D. Peters and Co.

flirt; this time it will be women, organized, angry and militant.

American women are striking for what they call their human rights: they want an end to what they see as centuries of oppression, they want an end to condescension, an end to drudgery, some of them want an end to marriage, sex roles and motherhood, others of them simply want equal job opportunities, most of them want repeal of the brutal abortion laws, all of them are willing to fight for something they want, from the super-logical to the absurd.

Late this year, when a national meeting of radical women is called in Boston, all the cells and small groups that compose the nationwide liberation movement will stand still for their first head-count. It seems likely that the membership will total thousands of American women with clear, high-pitched voices: a chorus that will be hard to laugh down. Oppression, they feel, has been their lot as long as it has been the lot of the American black, and longer; the male, they say, is the oppressor of the female, and for his frantic, face-saving tactics, for his struggle to support himself and his family, for his ulcers and early heart attacks, the women have no sympathy; for their own subjugated position, they will take no responsibility. They are innocent, they say, of contributing to the climate of neurosis and violence in their country, a climate in which oppression can be born and flourish. According to the truly radical feminist, it is the men who must change; women, they imply, are nearly perfect creatures in a nation which men have, all on their own and without any pressure from their so-called victims—their wives, sisters, and mothers—made unbearable.

When its members are counted, the female liberation movement in America will probably split neatly down the middle; on one side the radicals, on the other side the conservatives, sharing some complaints such as inequality of pay, imposition of stereotyped sex-roles, discrepancies in education, but miles of thought and theory apart on their basic aims. "We deny any difference between the sexes except one, and that is unimportant," say the radicals. "Female is beautiful." "We respect the differences between the sexes," say the conservatives, "but we want a fair chance to be fully-developed human beings in what we admit looks like a man's world."

N O W

Among the conservative groups, the most powerful is the perfectly acceptable National Organization of Women; NOW has no wild dreams, just a raging hunger for women "to get their share of the pie." Betty Friedan, founder of NOW, is not a fanatic but an enthusiast. Recently divorced, she lives with her three children in a large flat, its living room watched over by a bust of Lincoln, The Great Emancipator. "The world is a man's world, built by men. It is essential for women to be in all mainstream organizations with a real voice, so we can have our say and surface to positions of real power. As long as this is a capitalistic society, women will be dependent on men if they haven't equal opportunities to earn. Yes, we are a political organization, but don't talk to me about any revolution unless my revolution is included."

Ironically, NOW was the result of cynical gallantry on the part of a reactionary Southern senator who tried to make a farce out of the equal employment Title VII of the 1964 Civil Rights Bill by moving that the word "sex" be added every time "race" was mentioned. The day the bill passed went down as "Ladies' Day" in the House, and the esteemed gentlemen were too blinded by mirth to notice the ranks of angry petticoats closing in around them. Forty percent of the complaints that followed Title VII were based on sex discrimination; white women's earning power is higher only than that of the black women they employ as domestics.

By 1966, Miss Friedan saw the need for NOW; hastily assembled, its name invented in a restaurant and inscribed on the back of a napkin, the organization has become a genuine political force with chapters and membership all over America. The 1968 NOW newsletter for the New York area points out definite action and progress: a boycott of Colgate-Palmolive in protest at job discrimination; and a successful picketing of the *New York Times,* which forced them to de-sex-segregate their want ads. The resemblance of NOW to the classic suffragettes was never more dramatic than when Miss Friedan led her group on a furious besiegal of a bar in the Plaza Hotel where women are allowed only during certain hours and as guaranteed sex-objects on grey flannel arms. A meeting of the NOW executive board is cool and businesslike; members devote themselves to supporting a woman as president of the City Council or any of the other projects NOW pursues within the establishment.

Betty Friedan's social analysis *The Feminine Mystique* is the doctrine of NOW. Simone de Beauvoir's immensely wise *The Second Sex* transcends the differences between conservative and radical feminists to become a document admired by both of them, as indeed it should be. At the source of the radical movement, however, is a third book: *The S.C.U.M.* [Society for Cutting Up Men] *Manifesto* by Valerie Solanas, a homicidal feminist whose aim was not so steady as her intention. "Life in this society being, at best, an utter bore and no aspect of society being at all relevant to women," wrote Solanas, not long before she sighted her father-figure Andy Warhol down the barrel of a gun, "there remains to civic-minded, responsible, thrill-seeking females only to overthrow the government, eliminate the money

system, institute complex automation, and destroy the male sex."

In all but the last point, the extreme and murderous manifesto of Solanas has found friends among radical women who admit, almost affectionately, that it is overstatement, but at its core there is a great truth: men have done women nothing but harm since the beginning of procreation. Solanas simply carried to its conclusion a disgust with the male sex implicit in much of the radical feminist literature in America.

THE FEMINISTS

An obscurity and a mystique slip into the theories of those radical women who see their liberation not as a social struggle, but as a kind of crusade. They are obsessed with defining and detesting the enemy: men, all men, whose powers when under feminist attack seem almost supernatural. One celebrated guru within this radical segment is Ti-Grace Atkinson, erstwhile officer in NOW, who found her position in a conservative group was untenable. One of the leaders of The Feminists: a Political Organization to Annihilate Sex Roles, Ti-Grace, who is working towards her doctorate in philosophy, is an articulate Southerner with cool, white hands. Over her desk is a framed picture of herself in her wedding dress; the glass was smashed perhaps in some frenzy that preceded her divorce, and it has never been repaired.

"Originally, there was mankind," said Ti-Grace in her neutral, bookish accent, "then one class moved on top of another and women were expelled from mankind. I call the process that took place 'metaphysical cannibalism'; that is, to eat one's own kind, especially that aspect considered most potent to the victim when alive, and to destroy the evidence that the aggressor and the victim are the same. Any man will say, 'It's not my fault; I'm just doing it,' but he is the agent of oppression and the female's role is not to think but to be an extension of his body, guided by his mind." According to Ti-Grace's new feminist mythology, the victimization of one sex by the other began when the mystery of paternity was solved and women were revealed as envelopes of the reproductive system and a container for heirs and tyrants. Ti-Grace says that the original rape was political rape. "And the most common female escape," she writes in one of her treatises, "is the psychopathological condition of love. . . . 'Love' is the natural response of the victim to the rapist." Ti-Grace is a member of the board of a corporation called Human Rights for Women, a body which will be sponsoring research projects in the area of feminism, financed by unclaimed legacies of the original suffragettes as well as contributions from "anonymous males."

A number of Ti-Grace's followers among The Feminists risk her outspoken scorn by getting married, an act which probably reveals confusion rather than hypocrisy since in open discussions, or more private ones with their husbands, The Feminists are marked by phenomenal intolerance. "It is not easy being married to a Feminist," said Renos Mandlis, the Greek husband of novelist Lila Karp. "And I would not advise it to men who haven't much character. Do I resent being called an oppressor? Well, the tone of the complaint often makes real analysis impossible, because it throws you into a classification and takes away any chance of talking together. Women don't seem to realize that there is no gratification for us in male supremacy."

"In 1969," says Lila, "if a woman is being exploited it is by a male society. God in 1969 to most women is a man; that is her training."

The Feminists, a closed, small group, meet twice a week. They see themselves, eventually, as a propaganda machine to organize a nationwide sisterhood of anguish. One of the most provocative leaflets thus far was written by Anne Koedt, a long-legged blonde of about 30; her work, which provoked a roar of approval throughout the movement, was called *The Myth of the Vaginal Orgasm.* In about 4000 words, Miss Koedt dispenses with men as a source of sexual pleasure; the vaginal orgasm, according to her paper, is a male lie designed to enslave women to the family unit and force them to endure the abuses of a male society. The only real orgasm for a woman, says Miss Koedt, is a clitoral orgasm, which can be enjoyed by lesbians or by a fantasist alone. Add to Miss Koedt's statement the fact that Americans are more sanguine about the development of test-tube babies than are nationalities less addicted to technology, and a lot of women are squinting down the barrel of that gun with Valerie Solanas.

The Feminist Repertory Theatre is a group of actresses and a few rueful actors who dramatize in coffee-bars and small theatres the points that the Feminists explore in group discussions. Some of the skits bring sympathy from any woman, such as the one that shows two thirsty girls trying to get drinks at a New York bar, where unescorted women cannot be served but escorted prostitutes can drink their fill; other skits however are as pompous as political theatre often turns out to be.

"Have you made my body an incubator of your artificial passion?" cried the actress.

"As good as Albee," whispered a lady in the audience.

Anselma Del'Ollio, director of the group, is a classic beauty who trembles with revolutionary glee as she stands at a piano singing, to the tune of *The Battle Hymn of the Republic:*

> *There'll be men upon their knees to us*
> *And begging for their life.*
> *And some we'll spare,*
>   *and some we'll not,*
> *For justice is our knife.*
> *There'll be judo and karate*
> *And a rifle for each wife*
> *For it's liberation time . . .*

Freudian symbolism aside, and every member of the liberation agrees that the night Freud was conceived was a very black one for womankind, silly extremism does the cause no good. As Betty Friedan points out in her book, twenty minutes of American television is more enraging for any intelligent female than hours of amateurish dramatics. Every other TV commercial is telling women either that they are full-time man-traps, or that the laundry is a creative, intellectual challenge worth a lifetime's devotion. "You've come a long way, baby," says the hopeful man's voice-over; "now you have your own cigarette."

The Radical Women

The New York Radical Women form an umbrella group to shelter many small cells which are in turn composed of refugees from left-wing and civil-rights organizations where, say the girls, they can no longer endure the cool tolerance of radical men. Left-wing radical men are generally considered the worst male chauvinists of the lot since they own no banks, no Cadillacs, no big desks, no symbols at all, but only the real thing: "their damned virility." A decade or so younger than the NOW membership or many of The Feminists, the voluble radical women have put aside most political issues in order to analyze the state of their own oppression: often synonymous with the mysteries of their own emerging psyches.

Ellen Willis, one of the leaders among the Radical Women, looks so much like a serious child that it is hard to ascribe to her either her broken marriage or her pop column in *The New Yorker* magazine. "Women have to develop their own consciousness before they can work for the Left. We seem apolitical now because politics have never ever had anything to do with our problems. Usually marriage, for example, is not seen as political; we think it is. The more a woman realizes that the most she can do in life is to be a house nigger, the more she wants to free herself."

Every Sunday evening, the New York Radical Women and related groups hold consciousness-raising meetings to orient new members and to keep old members at a constant peak of awareness.

"I used to blame my mother for being domineering," said one young radical, "but I see more since women's liberation, I see now how she was oppressed by my father."

"The main thing I've been learning," said another, "is how much my mother didn't tell me."

"Why didn't mother tell me about the clitoris!" someone cried out.

"My father never said four words to any of us, but he was always there: quiet, strong, . . ."

"And insidious," Ellen Willis finished the confession.

"I made no contact with my mother until I joined the women's liberation, and then the two of us ganged up on my father for a change."

"My mother taught me to survive with male chauvinists, and that is not freedom!"

"I go all out for female liberation, and I go and fight big political causes," said one plump 20-year-old, "and then what happens? I go home and fall in love with a man just like my father."

Red Stockings

Red Stockings is a radical women's group which emerged from the anti-inaugural demonstration in Washington; a dispirited demonstration of how to lean against the door of an empty barn. Shulamith Firestone, painter, art student, and job hunter, described the scene in Washington when one of her colleagues was hissed and heckled by the audience of her feminist speech. "When it was my turn to speak, the audience shouted obscenities and pulled the microphone away from me. My statement was Black Power in feminist terms: 'We've had it! No more patronizing, boys!' Our own women in the Left wouldn't believe the men were so bad. Do you know, not one radical paper mentioned the scene in Washington, so it was difficult to persuade other Radical Women what

had happened. That's when we decided to form a new action group. Not really a split from Radical Women, but a radical group within the movement." Red Stockings, with a core of about twenty young women, refuses to cooperate with any left-wing organization which does not recognize women as a force.

"Someday, maybe we'll need violence," said Shuli. "Theoretically, I'm in favor of it, but women are conditioned against it. Anyway, when we reconsider things about femininity, non-aggression may be something we want to keep. If we can find out why half the race has not developed aggressiveness, maybe we can pass the secret on to men." Shuli the job-hunter has quaintly feminist ideas: "If men are going to set up the system, then to hell with it. Why should I be a stenographer? Why should I get 90 dollars a week for a job that a man would get more money for just because he's a man? Why should I get paid less for holding on to my virtue when I can make 50 dollars in three hours as a topless go-go dancer?"

The angriest females appear to be the job-hunting girls who have emerged from sheltered women's colleges to find unspoken quotas of women in most fields and outspoken discrimination against them in ranks above typists. "I went to Barnard College for Women," read the placard of one protesting graduate, "and I get a typing test. He went to Columbia College for Men and he gets an executive training course."

WITCH

Women's International Terrorist Corps from Hell, WITCH, once the most active of the liberation groups, is moving underground, chased there by a mob of reporters and photographers. Last year, in its heyday, WITCH made scintillating copy with street corner "guerilla theatre," the casting of public hexes on Wall Street's bastions, and their hilarious participation in the burning of bras, girdles, and women's magazines on the beach at Atlantic City during the Miss America contest. Their organization, now in a moment of transition, is composed of three groups with about 30 members in each. In an alarmist community like New York, it is hard to say where caution ends and paranoia begins, but WITCH women are reluctant to be photographed or to publicize their surnames. They maintain that some of their proposed actions will bring down the hammers of the CIA or New York's little-publicized TPF: Tactical Police Force, a body of armed men with special responsibilities towards liberation.

"In order to continue this struggle," says Judith, whose prudence slows her diction, "we must recognize that the institution of money is very basic to the oppression of women. Private property, capitalism, and money have to go; but at the same time, a psychological revolution has to happen among women. Women are more human than men. Men must learn to share in the humanity they've been denied, and women must have a share of achievement. Of course, I can't discount the possibility that men are genetically flawed; but we need much more time to be sure." Judith, who is separated from her husband, tells the story of a woman who refused to divorce her male chauvinist mate because she said that she knew how to handle him, while some less liberated woman would be oppressed by him.

Like most of the groups, WITCH is devoted to educating masses of women to the facts of male oppression. Rather than doing this job with pamphlets, speeches, or magazines, they are developing a system of infiltration into factories, offices, and suburban communities where they can approach less knowledgeable women and talk them into the sorority. Judith, for example, has a personal project of persuading a rural acquaintance of hers that it is criminal for any adult human being to be locked up in the company of three infants all day long while her husband leaves their car in his company's car park.

FEMALE LIBERATION MOVEMENT

Manhattan is a hectic place where Buddhist "monks" fresh from the California surf chant their word for peace under a canopy of polluted air; it is not the city from which the steely lines of a revolution will emerge. Although New York ladies are the most articulate, the seeds of their movement are scattered all over the country, and in Boston they fell on very ripe ground. The Boston-based Female Liberation Movement is serene in its revolutionary convictions, although it has been stung by every salaried wasp in media. The Boston girls scorn all men except Mao, Che, and Vernon Grizzard, an obliging left-wing youth who does a great deal of their typing for them. Their Lysistrata is another Southerner named Roxanne Dunbar. "Of course a lot of women who have come into contact with our movement have left their husbands," said Roxanne, a college teacher of Afro-American history, "but the lives of women who leave husbands are tough, although I think they are invariably better off than in a marriage situation. Our movement is an end in itself, a historical necessity; we aren't saying that men and women have separate but equal rights, we're saying that the biological differences between men and women mean nothing. We are deepening revolutions all over the world, undercutting them, until it will be possible for a real, basic revolution to take place that will end inequities between people."

Most of the nine or ten members of the Boston nucleus group are either divorced or separated from their husbands; yet as they sit around the kitchen table of their meeting house, they look like a group of small-town housewives regretting thickening waistlines and helping themselves to ice-lollies from the freezer. Roxanne, who is bright-eyed and nervous, dominates the discussion, and it is to her that most comments are addressed or to the other sophisticated member of the group, Abbey Rockefeller. Sired by the Chase Manhattan Bank, with a relative who has brushed the Presidential chair, Abbey speaks with filial ardor when she deplores capitalism and the ownership of private property. The Boston girls have some contempt for the psychoanalytical methods of the New York radical feminists; their own terms are strictly political even when they treat the stuff of madness and poetry. "Love between a man and a woman," said Abbey in the tended accent of the American upper-crust, "is debilitating and counter-revolutionary. Love affairs are exclusive and non-functional. It is not possible to develop a revolutionary sensibility when you are in the process of being in love."

"Love," said Roxanne, "can be controlled only by a strong political sense and not by any personal therapy. We're tired of talking about sex; the subject of orgasm doesn't come up at our meetings. Sex is just a commodity, a programmed activity, it is not a basic need." At least until after the revolution, the Boston group advises women to look to their comrades for an affection which does not depend upon fantasy and false eyelashes. "And if, despite all this, genital tensions persist," they advise in an article called *On Celibacy,* "you can still masturbate."

The Bostonians for the moment are concerned with leading classes in revolution among women at universities, where the turn-out for their lectures is a high percentage of the student body. Much of their instruction deals with how to talk to men who are not eager to liberate their women.

In about a year, when their teaching machine is perfected, the Boston women plan to go further afield: out of the universities where women's liberation has its strongest hold, and into the wider world. Female Liberation, say the Bostonians, is not just a part of the bigger revolution but its very trigger; and when the time comes, the liberated blacks and liberated white males will join the liberated women and squash the rotten system flat.

The idiosyncrasies of the Boston movement, such as the eschewal of cosmetics and the exchange of patronymics for extravagances like Betsy Warrior and Jane Challenge, has won it the title of 'lunatic fringe' even among the New York sisterhood. Led by the chic press, establishment figures prefer to overlook the Bostonians' genuine revolutionary nature in order to laugh easily at the fact that the girls are learning karate and have two green belts in their membership. The reasons for learning karate, say the Bostonians, are to create a prop for the corroded female ego, to provide protection against rude males, and finally to release men from despicable, condescending gallantry and make women able to protect themselves and each other.

"But I don't need a wildest dream," said Abbey, "to see karate being used by women aggressively."

According to Ti-Grace Atkinson in New York, "Karate is a good equalizer, but a pistol would be better. If you dislike a man enough to do that to him, you certainly don't want to touch him."

POINTS OF AGREEMENT

Although there is a good deal of the in-fighting which mars any minority movement, on three points all American female liberationists are agreed: each woman's body is her own and therefore abortion must be a matter for her conscience alone; the institution of marriage is, to say the least, imperfect and must be redesigned to allow those women who want it freedom from the home and the constant company of children; and finally, the morale and spirit of female liberation is bound to that of black liberation. Since most of the white feminist leaders spring full-armed from the privileged classes, their sympathy for black women is tinged with condescension; black women, in any case, are clearly able to fight their own battle, which most of them see as a battle to free their race. There are some black women, however, who are sounding the trumpet for feminism within the great dark army.

"The poor black woman," writes Patricia Robinson in a leaflet called *Poor Black Women,* "still occupies the position of domestic in this society . . . when the frustrated male deserts her and the children." Miss Robinson, who is a psychotherapist in a slum community, disagrees with those black male chauvinists who have called the Pill and abortion new forms of genocide being practiced upon their race by the white one.

"The poor black woman," she writes, "realizes that her children will be used as all poor children have been used through history: as poorly paid mercenaries fighting to keep or put an elite group in power"; thus, says Miss Robinson, the black woman must question aggressive male domination even within her own race.

Rose Mary Byrd, her face like well-carved onyx, is an active Black Panther; her ideas, although they are often as smooth as rehearsed directives from above, have obviously been thought through. "The oppressors," she said, "sit around and they pay people billions of dollars a year to think up how to drive Americans crazy. They build institutions and they put you in them and make you pay for your madness. I see the gripe of the white women now as something the power structure has put down on the people to alienate women from men. The power structure's whole thing has always been divide and conquer; now they're doing it with men and women.

"If the women in their movement want to call themselves revolutionary, they're going to have to stop relating to personal things, like I'm not getting enough respect from a man; they've really got to do something to demand respect; they've got to stand up and say 'I'm a freedom fighter and I intend to liberate masses of oppressed people by any means necessary, so judge me by what I'm doing, not by my sex!' While we're trying to defend ourselves against the wrath of the whole power structure, those white chicks are talking about individual hang-ups like getting jobs. Man, when the mess hits the fan there ain't going to be any jobs to have! If you start hating someone because he's a man, without knowing what that particular man has done, then you're on a way-out trip. When they talk about myths of orgasms, their minds are on the Moon. If you get mad people together with a mad leader, you'll get nothing but madness. I hope these women will open up their eyes, open up their minds, and see where the real problem is coming from: the main thing they can't put up with is themselves."

Feminism is no modern phenomenon; it has existed in America for more than a century and has always demanded more than just the vote.

"Do not put such unlimited power into the hands of the husbands," Abigail Adams wrote to her own husband, the second President of the United States. "Remember, all men would be tyrants if they could. If particular care is not paid to the ladies, we are determined to foment a rebellion . . ." That ladies' rebellion is well under way now, composed of thousands of unhappy sisters each with her private self, her mass of memories, her unique complaints. The motives for female liberation are as complex and varied as the liberationists, who are certainly not all lesbians, nymphomaniacs, or frigid harridans. Their common failings are a confusion of sex roles with sexuality, and a refusal to admit that the victim is ultimately the oppressor and thus that freedom must be the aim of men and women against their common condition.

The female liberation movement cannot be dismissed lightly, however, for at its heart is a great anguish which is by no means peculiarly American: the agonizing truth that neurotic love is the only yield of a neurotic society.

Some women's liberationists want to eliminate sex-specific styles of life. In the occupational world this would be accomplished by doing away with sex-based specialization—for example, by admitting more women into engineering and more men into nursing. In the family, mother and father roles would be replaced by the parent role. Some women's liberationists want only to minimize sex-based life style differences. As one professional woman stated, "I'd still like men to open doors for me, but not at the expense of $3,000 income differential." Thus, if confronted with the choice, many women will opt for desexualization of life styles rather than subjugation.

Charles Winick feels that the United States is undergoing desexualization—not through the efforts of militant women, but through the influence of creators and manipulators of popular culture. Unisex fashions and hair styles result in a similarity of physical appearance, paralleling the trend in mass processing of food that brings about a uniformity of taste. Even sexual behavior per se is becoming desexualized, in Winick's view; for example, oral sex, in which there is no specific male or female role, is increasing. Names given to children and behavior expected of them are more often the same for both sexes, helping to create a "new people," desexualized and indistinguishable in appearance and behavior.

Childhood, a Journey with New Maps

CHARLES WINICK

Father Calls me William,
Mother calls me Will,
Sister calls me Willie,
But the fellers call me Bill.[1]

The confusion of sex roles that pervades our environment would be meeting more opposition if our young people had not previously been prepared for the change. The culture which reflects our social system, which is part and parcel of personality itself, demands that childhood reflect our new values.

The authors of the nursery rhyme ("Natural History") could once have easily answered questions like "What are little boys made of?" and "What are little girls made of?" Such positive responses cannot be given lightly today. A number of milestones on the once

familiar road of child development have been knocked down, including traditional name preferences, dolls, children's involvement in fairy tales, and established identities and roles of children. Each of these changes seriously affects how a child assimilates traditional ideals of masculinity and femininity. The nursery and playroom provide ample evidence.

FROM DICK AND JANE TO LESLIE AND TANE

As Jack Paar once admitted, he had answered his daughter's puzzlement as to why she was named Randy with a counter-question: "Why don't you ask your mother George?"[2] A few years before his quip, Americans were discussing two prominent women called Pat and Jackie. Our new enthusiasm for given names that are not necessarily associated with either sex is important, because personality may be shaped, reinforced, and reflected in a name. The individuality of a given name can be seen in the great painters whose signatures consisted only of their first names. Vincent Van Gogh, Rembrandt Harmenszoon van Rijn, and Michelangelo Buonarroti underscored their given

From Charles Winick, *The New People: Desexualization in American Life* (New York: Pegasus, 1968), pp. 197–206, 217–221.
[1]Eugene Field, "Jest 'Fore Christmas," in *The Writings in Prose and Verse of Eugene Field,* Vol. 4, *Poems of Childhood.* New York: Scribner's, 1894.

[2]March 6, 1964, on the Jack Paar program.

names' uniqueness, even if others shared the family name.

The associations of names, often half-conscious, came from such wildly diverse sources as novels, historical figures, movie stars, comic strip heroes, religious leaders, friends and relatives, even places and pleasures.[3] They identify a person's family, reinforce his status, link him with a culture hero, provide a tie between tradition and the individual, and help to position him in society. A person's name carries his spirit and clothes him, just as the "soul is forme and doth the body wear," in Spenser's lovely phrase.

A given name is the only thing of value in our society which may be taken from anywhere, without asking. Everyone must have a given name, perhaps the one aspect of popular culture that touches us all. In several religions, to be dead is to have no name. Although a name does not necessarily influence self-identity, its ability to identify a person makes it easier for his attitudes toward a name to become closely related to feelings about himself.

As a child becomes aware of his name, between the ages of one and two, the fantasies forming around it tend to become deeply involved in the development of his idea of self. The given name is recognized as part of one's self long before the family name. Many children assume fantasy names because of concern about whether they have the "right" name. Children constantly test the effects of a name, and their ability

to do so determines the extent to which they can accept it and its connotations.

Some rather striking effects of names on their owners are suggested by a finding that Harvard students with unusual names are significantly represented among students with superior personality, neurotics, and flunk-outs.[4] Another study concludes that boys with peculiar first names are more disturbed than those with ordinary names.[5] Such findings could, of course, result less from any intrinsic properties of a name than the attitudes toward a child that originally led the parents to select a particular name.

It is not unreasonable, then, to suspect that names given to children will reflect our culture's neuterization and what is becoming the game of sexual identity. One way of measuring this is to note birth announcements and to compare the names of the children with their parents'. In a large sample of birth announcements between 1948 and 1963, over one-fifth (21.3%) of the children's names were not found among the parents', and three kinds of names accounted for practically all of the difference: surnames used as given names, names linked with both sexes, and those having no established connotations.[6]

[3] Daniel Adelson, "Attitudes Toward First Names," *International Journal of Social Psychiatry,* Special Edition I, Section A, 1964, pp. 81–86; William F. Murphy, "A Note on the Significance of Names," *Psychoanalytic Quarterly,* **26,** 1957, pp. 91–106.

[4] B. M. Savage and F. L. Wells, "A Note on Singularity in Given Names," *Journal of Social Psychology,* **27,** 1948, pp. 271–272.

[5] Albert Ellis and R. M. Beechley, "Emotional Disturbance in Children with Peculiar Given Names," *Journal of Genetic Psychology,* **85,** 1954, pp. 337–339.

[6] It was hypothesized that the names given to children would reflect our culture's tendency toward depolarization of sex. Birth announcements between the current and preceding generations appearing in *The New York Times* over a fifteen-year period (1948–1963) were analyzed, in terms of a

The surname as given name was originally a device to give a mother's maiden name to her son. The practice was once popular in the South, where a given name like Page, Saunders, Mallory, Logan, or Pierce was not uncommon even for a girl. Its previously established surname use tends to give such names a genderless quality.

The largest category of new names consisted of those given to both sexes. Some names have historically been given to either sex, e.g., Maria in Latin countries. England has had generals and admirals named Vivian, Jocelyn, and Joyce. But such established historical trends in other countries are quite different from our recent increase in ambisexual names.

One reason for the increase could be a more liberal interpretation of how names may be derived from religious sources. American Catholics still relate a child's baptismal name to a saint, who is a prestigious and protective model and

guiding figure for the child. But today, a saint's name may appear on the baptismal certificate (e.g., Anastasia) and a related but secular name on the birth certificate (e.g., Stacey). Another approach is to add a saint's name to a secular one, so that Dana on a birth certificate might become Dana Anne at baptism. Jewish parents interpret the requirement to relate a name's initial letter to a deceased ancestor in an increasingly free manner. An ancient Hebrew name like Rachel may appear on family records but metamorphose into Robin on a birth certificate.

Another sanction for names that could be used by either sex is the growing number of prominent persons with such names: Alexis (Smith, Johnson), Babe (Didrickson, Ruth), Connie (Francis, Mack), Dale (Evans, Robertson), Dana (Wynter, Andrews), Gene (Tierney, Tunney), Jan (Sterling, Murray), Jean (Seberg, Shepherd), Jeff (Donnell, Chandler), Jo (Stafford, Davidson), Joey

comparison between names of the children and their parents.

A listing was made of every third one of the 43,337 children whose births were announced during this period. The frequency of occurrence of each name found among the 14,446 newborn, along with the incidence of the names of their parents, was tabulated. There were 816 different given names in the 14,446 that were sampled.

It was possible to prepare a table consisting of five columns, with the first containing the name, the second the number of fathers with the name, and the third column the number of mothers who had the name. The fourth column represented the number of boy children who had the name, and the fifth the number of girl children with the same name.

With a frequency count in each of the five columns it was possible to use a chi-square test in order to compare the distribution of parents' versus

children's names to see whether they were significantly different, with the 5% level representing significance of difference. All differences cited in the text were significant at the 5% level or better. The chi-square test was used because it is nonparametric and makes no assumptions about the existence of a normal or Gaussian distribution pattern in the universe of names published in the newspaper.

The same kind of analysis was conducted to measure the extent to which the names were sex-linked. It was assumed that the expected distribution for a name is to have it ascribed only to persons of one sex, with no persons of the opposite sex possessing it. This would be true if names had a unimodal distribution by sex. To the extent that the statistical analysis indicated significant differences from such a distribution, such differences would suggest that the names are being assigned to boys and girls on a basis other than the 100–0% ratio.

(Heatherton, Adams), Joyce (Brothers, Cary), Kay (Kendall, Kyser), Lee (Remick, Tracy), Leslie (Caron, Howard), Loren (MacIver, Eisely), Lynn (Fontanne, Riggs), Michael (Strange, Wilding), Noel (Adam, Coward), Pat (Carroll, Boone), Ray (Dooley, Milland), Ruby (Keeler, Goldstein), Shelley (Winters, Berman), Shirley (MacLaine, Povich), and Vivian (Blaine, Fuchs).[7]

There is a busy traffic in names from one sex to the other. Kipling's Kim was a man, but in America three famous actresses bear the name (Hunter, Novak, Stanley). Miss Novak has indicated the confusion caused by her name: "I like Kim. . . . I see a little boy or girl with a shining face looking you straight in the eye."[8] Dana and Robin, once used for boys, have become very popular for girls. A number of names (Shirley, Leslie, Michael, Sidney) that are still masculine in England are used for both sexes in this country. Many other previously masculine names are now shared with women, but fewer feminine names have been taken by men (e.g., Winifred).

Children born in the last twenty years are more likely than their parents to have similarly pronounced names, differentiated only by spelling, e.g., Barrie-Barry, Claire-Clair, Jessie-Jesse, Rae-Ray, Sydney-Sidney. The popularity of such names has further contributed to blurring of sex differences. Some formerly sex-linked names have become homophonic, with Jessica, for example, becoming Jessie.

Unfortunately, ambiguous names continue to plague draft boards—women constantly receive notices to report for military duty. Such names have also led some steamship lines—inadvertently—to pair a man and woman in the same cabin. Another side of the problem is illustrated by a young man originally named Leslie Towne Hope, who has become better known as Bob Hope. After falling hopelessly in love with a young kindergarten classmate called Leslie, he renamed himself Lester in order to assert his maleness. Names' ability to convey problems in sexual identity is suggested in two films released during the war year of 1943. Both had heroines called Charlie and a third heroine was called Chris.[9] The films were released when men were away from home and women assumed many previously male tasks. Such sexual confusion has become routine in today's movies, with Irving an attractive blonde in *Breakfast at Tiffany's,* and Charlie the heroine of *Goodbye, Charlie.*

Still a third category of children's names that differed significantly from parents' consisted of those that were freshly minted and lacked established connotations, e.g., Tane, Abar. The increase in names without antecedents among the New People may well support Ortega y Gasset's observation on the tendency of the masses to avoid history, since not using names from the past represents an excellent way of losing identification with it. After all, a name connected with nothing in particular involves loss of a ready-made identity.

The parents who made Washington the most popular post-Revolutionary

---

[7]Jo Hubbard Chamberlin, "I'm Tender About Gender," *Coronet,* February 1960, pp. 55–57; the woman's name, of course, precedes the man's.

[8]Ezra Goodman, *The Fifty-Year Decline and Fall of Hollywood.* New York: Simon and Schuster, 1961, p. 281.

[9]James Agee, *Agee on Film.* New York: McDowell Obolensky, 1958, p. 29.

boys' name were expressing admiration for the first President and a belief in contagious magic. The unfortunate child saddled with a name which has historical connotations may identify with or rebel against them. But even more importantly, beliefs about the sort of personality associated with a name may strongly influence otherwise latent traits.[10]

In the 1948–1963 sample and in earlier large-scale studies, unusual names were twice as frequent among girls as boys. Fathers have more to say about sons' than daughters' names and naturally seem to prefer more ordinary first names. Women carry and enjoy less common names.[11] Their favoring relatively unusual names is contrary to the stereotype about women being less adventurous and more comforming than men.[12] Some mothers may select masculinized or ambisexual names for daughters as an expression of identification, rivalry, or ambivalence.

All three name types found in children—surnames, ambisexual, and those without connotations—have neuter qualities. Such names may have a variety of effects on their innocent young bearers. Latent anti-masculine tendencies of a boy or anti-feminine tendencies of a girl may be reinforced. Other persons may look for sexual ambivalence

in a person with such a homogenized name, and the name can cause its owner to react against such tendencies.

Even the sounds of names are significant. Many neuter names have more sibilants and liquids than guttural consonants. They tend to be shorter than the parents' and many have become thinner: Mark becomes Marc and John's son is Jon.

An attempt is sometimes made to distinguish sex by pronunciation. A boy Cecil may have the first vowel short but a girl often has it long. A male Leslie can be identified by a sibilant *s* while a female might have the *s* pronounced like a *z*. For most ambisexual names, however, such distinctive pronunciation for either sex is not possible.

Other related trends reinforce the new generation's neuter names. There is a growing penchant for initials that do not stand for anything, like Harry S Truman's middle initial. Many young people have added such initials in recent years. Among the prominent men who prefer to be identified by their initials are former presidents Kaufman Thuma Keller of Chrysler Corporation, Cyrus Rowlett Smith of American Airlines, and toymaker Alfred Carlton Gilbert. Actress K. T. Stevens is known by her initials, presumably inspired by great admiration for Katie Hepburn.

The homogenization of names can be seen in the LBJ brand. The name of each member of the First Family has similar syllabication and initials. Although the similarity among the Johnson names may inspire some names with identical syllabication and initials on the banks of the Pedernales, it has not become a national consensus and it is unlikely that many children have been named

[10]G. Jahoda, "A Note on Ashanti Names and Their Relationship to Personality," *British Journal of Psychology,* **45,** 1954, pp. 192–195.

[11]H. L. Mencken, *The American Language:* Supplement II. New York: Knopf, 1956, p. 472; L. Allen, V. Brown, L. Dickinson, and K. C. Pratt, "The Relation of First Name Preferences to Their Frequency in the Culture," *Journal of Social Psychology,* **14,** 1941, pp. 279–293.

[12]Alfred I. Kolatch, *These Are the Names.* New York: Jonathan David Co., 1948.

after the President and First Lady. There was not one Lyndon or Lady Bird in a large sample of children born in New York City in 1964, although a substantial number in previous years had been named after Presidents or their wives.[13] The very homogenization of the First Family names could make it more difficult for parents to be emotionally involved with any one Johnson and to reflect such identification in naming a child than was possible with White House occupants who had more singular names.

Homogenization of names is also encouraged by the growing popularity of neutral diminutives and nicknames: Jerry, Bobbie, Jo, Willie, Mickey, Rusty, Bunny, Jackie, and Billie can identify either gender. Governor Nelson Rockefeller is called Rocky and his wife is known as Happy, but many a happy woman is nicknamed Rocky, e.g., Gary Cooper's widow. Happy is also a popular name for men, e.g., sportscaster Happy Felton.

Even famous athletes compound the confusion through neuter nicknames or diminutives. Consider a baseball team which included Ruby Gomez, Nellie Fox, Elly Howard, Sal Maglie, Babe Ruth, Lena Styles, Birdie Tebbets, Vickie Power, Gussie Triandos, and Gene Woodling.[14] Such neutering of sports figures' names is relatively unexpected, because athletes often have complex and non-euphonious names. Typical are Zoilo Versalles of the Minnesota Twins, Felipe Alou of the Atlanta Braves, Yelberton A. Tittle of the New York Giants, Erich (pronounced Eerish, not Eric) Barnes of the Cleveland Browns, Vada Pinson of the Cincinnati Reds, and jockeys Angel, Ishmael, and Mario Valenzuela and Braulio Baeza.

The same name may even belong to two people of different sex and in different fields of endeavor: Terry Moore, a brilliant center fielder for the St. Louis Cardinals, and also a prominent actress. Such ambiguity may increase the difficulty of a boy or girl Terry in finding an appropriate resonance for his or her name.

But how are ambiguous names regarded by others? The connotations of six first names were investigated by personal interviews. Two were unequivocally masculine (William and John), two were clearly feminine (Mary and Elizabeth), and two of the recently popular ambiguous names were rotated from a roster of six (Dale, Dana, Leslie, Lynn, Robin, Tracy) that had not differentiated sex in our study of birth announcements. The majority of both younger (17-30) and older (31-50) adults who were interviewed failed to associate the ambiguous names with either one sex or the other, although neither group had any such difficulty with the traditional names. The younger persons were better able to relate a range of personality characteristics to the ambiguous names, but tended to ascribe non-sex-linked qualities to them.[15]

---

[13]Bureau of Records and Statistics, New York City Health Department, Report on Preferred Names for 1928, 1948, and 1964, dated April 28, 1965.

[14]John G. Fuller, "Trade Winds," *Saturday Review,* October 19, 1963, p. 8.

[15]It proved possible to conduct interviews with a probability sample of adults between the ages of 17 and 50 about the connotations of these names. The sample, interviewed in connection with a larger study, consisted of 983 women and 957 men in the

The new American propensity for neuter names is not found in England, which does favor names that are connected with movie stars but clearly communicate the sex of their owners. A study of names given to workers and their children in London found sharp differences between generations. Older parents tended to name their children after themselves, with most (58%) husbands and many (38%) wives passing on their own names. Few (20%) of the youngest husbands and none of the wives conveyed their names to children. The inherited names tend to be simple (John, George, James, Mary, Alice, Ada), but Hollywood's influence here can be seen in the post-World War II children (Glenn, Gary, Maureen, Lana, and Linda).[16]

Although the incidence and neuter qualities of recent American names were unequivocal, the names of parents who submitted birth announcements might themselves have differed from their own parents'. When files of the same newspaper were studied and similar comparisons made for 1923–1938, some 19.4% of the names of children born during the earlier period differed from their

metropolitan New York area. In order to avoid any influence of the positioning of the ambiguous names in the total list, their sequence in the list was systematically rotated. The subject was handed a card on which the name had been typed and asked, "Could you please describe the kind of person that someone with this first name is likely to be?" He was encouraged to respond until he commented on both the sex as well as the personality characteristics of the name. He was then shown the next card in the series, until he had responded to all six cards.

[16]Michael Young and Peter Willmott, *Family and Kinship in East London.* London: Routledge and Kegan Paul, 1957, p. 10.

parents'—but only 3.1% were surnames, sexually ambiguous, or lacking in connotations. Then and now, the great majority of parents seem loyal to established names, but perhaps one-fifth are responsive to other possibilities.

Yet, it is possible that people who arrange newspaper birth announcements may not be representative of the general population. There is no complete directory of the children born during the period studied, but spot checks with hospital birth records and school records substantially confirmed the incidence of neuter names. Why are they in the air at this time? Because like all names, they express attitudes toward the self, one's own sex, the opposite sex, and toward sexuality itself.[17] To a parent, such names may seem to be one way of being different, although, sadly, they provide still more evidence of conformity. They may also represent, along with spelling changes like Edythe for Edith, a desire to provide a classier name and identity for the New People who can expect to enjoy the age of affluence.[18]

•   •   •

[17]Manuel Prenner, "Ora Jones Married Ora Jones," *American Speech,* **17**, 1942, pp. 84–88. It is possible that such attitudes are especially important in large cities and may be less significant in rural areas. Dr. Earle H. MacCannell of Portland State College was able to identify the sex of 99% of the children born in Chelan County in 1954 (a rural area in the state of Washington) by their given names (personal communication).

[18]Intersexual first names represent the most obvious use of names to express crisscrossing of sex roles. A subtler approach is found in retention of a clearly sex-linked name like John or Mary, but selecting it from an ancestor related to the opposite sex. A study of middle-class Chicago families in the 1950's concluded that their sons were more apt

PLAYING AND WEARING ROLES

At a government conference on recruiting women scientists, a major toy manufacturer stressed that "we need to develop new lines of toys which have no 'sex,' which would appeal equally to girls as well as boys. Giant magnifiers, our lens comparer, incubators, stethoscopes, flexible mirrors, etc., are precisely such items. . . . Let us start recruiting women scientists . . . during the years from two to seven."[19] Science-oriented, neuter toys are receiving more attention as playthings specifically designed for each sex decline in popularity.

Play preferences of boys and girls now overlap at a relatively early age, in addition to traditional shared sports like hiking and roller-skating. Girls are learning to play with model cars, Erector sets, baseball equipment, and guns, and are "pretend" space travelers or western heroes. High-riser bicycles, with handlebars resembling the horns of a longhorn steer, are rapidly eliminating the need for boys and girls to own different bicycles. Pangloss's buttockless people would have been delighted with the very high thin seat that tops the high risers' small

frames and wheels. The crossbar connecting the seat of a boy's model with the steering apparatus is low enough not to injure a girl while she is mounting or dismounting. As a result, many girls are now using their brothers' high-riser bicycles, and sales of girls' models have declined.

Just as the profile of boy and girl cycling on their high risers is indistinguishable at a distance, the profile of school studies for both sexes shows much overlap. A number of schools offer boys sewing in the fifth and sixth grades. Many eighth-grade boys learn cooking, while girls study tool and die work, plumbing repairs, metalcrafts, and lathe work. Both sexes are taught to type in high school.

Once upon a time, young people used to have masculine or feminine fountain pens. Boys' pens were long and stubby while girls' tended to be thin and short, but the use of standardized ball-point pens has largely erased these differences. Sex differences in handwriting were easily communicated by nib pens, but are now relatively difficult to identify because ball points make strokes of uniform width.

Young people of each sex are more likely than ever before to have read books formerly associated with the other sex. Girls who never owned a *Nancy Drew* story may have read *Treasure Island* or *Huckleberry Finn*. Many boys who are oblivious to the appeal of the *Hardy Boys* enjoy *Heidi* or *Peter Pan*. Some very successful recent books have a girl hero but seem of equal interest to both sexes, like *Island of the Blue Dolphins* and *The Moon Spinners*. Except for boys' interest in sports, both sexes are now almost equally interested

---

to be named for maternal grandparents and maternal collateral kin and less likely to be named for paternal relatives than in the 1920s. Girls were more likely to be named for paternal grandparents and paternal collateral kin and less apt to derive names from maternal grandparents and aunts than in the 1920s. Such a tendency, like the popularity of neutral names, could become even more conspicuous as our culture sidesteps toward depolarization. See Alice S. Rossi, "Naming Children in Middle-Class Families," *American Sociological Review*, **30**, 1965, pp. 499–513.

[19]*Help Them to Grow Every Day,* Catalog of Creative Playthings, 1964, p. 27.

in all categories of books, although there were distinct reading preferences even twenty-five years ago.

Television programs watched by children also seem to be devoid of qualities that appeal to one sex or the other. The most extensive study of television and children found little support for the view that girls are more squeamish than boys in connection with violence. Other studies concluded that middle-class adolescent girls took greater responsibility than boys for aggressive action toward a frustrating authority.[20] The girls will probably be even more forceful in the era of the mannequin doll.

In the past, parents tended to punish boys more often than girls with beatings and other physical measures. Recently the frequency with which such punishment is administered to boys and girls has become less distinguishable. Many a mother who never was physically disciplined as a girl has spanked her daughter, perhaps reluctantly at first, as she has learned to make few distinctions between measures applied to sons and daughters. Twenty-five years ago, when little girls were perhaps still believed to be made of "sugar and spice and all things nice," Talcott Parsons could accurately observe that "there is really no feminine equivalent of the expression 'bad boy.' "[21] But today we do not hesitate to speak of and punish a "naughty" or even "bad" girl. Contemporary parents are more willing than the previous generation to recognize that their daughters can behave unpleasantly and even destructively.

The formerly considerable gap that once separated the allowances given to girls from those received by boys has been dwindling steadily as girls have been getting more money from parents. Eleven-year-old girls in one study received 76¢ a week, while boys of the same age averaged 97¢ a week.[22] Girls of thirteen tend to get and spend more money than boys, and many fourteen-year-old girls expect allowances to be large enough to cover their wardrobe expenses. Barbie owners are especially likely to press for money for clothes.

Many other lines of evidence support the view that a wide range of forces is helping to cast boys and girls in the same mold. Even before a name is selected, the blurring of sex differences may begin. Parents once bought pink for a girl and blue for a boy. The pink-clad girl was "darling" and "beautiful" and the boy in blue was "handsome" or "strong." Although pink is still restricted to girls, blue is now worn by infants of either sex. But an even more important change is the popularity of maize, aqua, pale green, gray, and other neutral colors for both boys and girls. The near-disappearance of clothing differences should prepare the toddler for later blurring of visible signs of masculinity and femininity.

[20]Hilde T. Himmelweits, A. N. Oppenheim, and Pamela Vince, *Television and the Child.* New York: Oxford University Press, 1958; Leonard M. Lansky, Vaughn T. Crandall, and Jerome Kagan, "Sex Differences in Aggression and Its Correlates in Middle-Class Adolescents," *Child Development,* **32**, 1961, pp. 45–58. Eleanor E. Maccoby et al., *The Development of Sex Differences* (Stanford: Stanford University Press, 1966) provides the most thorough coverage of this subject.
[21]Talcott Parsons, "Age and Sex in the Social Structure," *American Sociological Review,* **7**, 1942, pp. 604–616.
[22]Judith Kranes, "What About Children's Allowances?," *Understanding the Child,* **26,** 1957, pp. 13–17.

The signs are even disappearing from diapers. A diaper folded in front conveyed masculinity and one folded in the back connoted femininity, because of differences in the direction of the child's urination. In the last fifteen years, this difference has almost vanished, as a result of the disposable diaper and the "ready fold" with a rectangular panel along its center, both front and rear.

Diapers are only the beginning, and children soon learn to wear other desexualized clothing. Identical coats and jackets are favored by both boys and girls.[23] Colors like sage seem to have been created because children of either sex wear similar clothing. As designer John Stephen summed it up: ". . . the hottest story in young fashion: boy/girl, his/hers, either/or clothes and haircuts."[24]

Even in the first years of school, girls wear trousers so often that some school systems have required them to wear dresses. Young boys' footwear is almost indistinguishable from their sisters'. Boys' sneakers were formerly ankle-high, but today are often cut as low as girls'. Many a boy strolls down the street in sneakers and bobby sox interchangeable with his sister's. Little boys and their sisters wear shoes of similar colors. Brown boys' shoes have gone the way of the black or white that formerly accounted for most little girls' footwear. Ten years ago, the Mary Jane that once was available only in black patent leather or white kid blossomed forth in a variety of colors and fabrics on young feet.

Boys are letting their hair grow longer. Now that girls are cutting their hair shorter, they are relatively unlikely to have the pigtails that boys of an earlier generation used to enjoy pulling. The ambisexual Oliver haircut, which represented one mark of a well-dressed young person, led logically to the Beatle non-haircut. The many other similarities in the appearance of boys and girls provide a bridge to adult clothing and help to explain why leading designers of women's clothes, like Courrèges and Gernreich, have been so successful in creating children's wear. Parents in our psychoanalytically sophisticated times are so tolerant of neutering that they permit crisscrossing of sex roles in children's appearance that would have been considered pathological just one generation ago.

The word "sissy," which derives from "sister," was once a terrible fate for a young man. With so many boys resembling and adapting clothes from their sisters, perhaps "sissy" should be retired. The phrases used to describe boys' wear sound as if they had been taken directly from women's fashion magazines ("the ultimate in wash 'n' wear," "the elegance of simplicity").

By 1963, young girls began saying goodbye to ruffles and bows and adopted the little-boy look. Now that a typical girl's costume consists of a shirt with a bib front and suspenders, worn with a boy's cap, there would seem to be considerable understatement in a report that identified twelve as the age at which a girl begins to raid her brother's wardrobe.[25] Girls' clothing is sold in quantities commensurate with the proportion

[23]"Report on Children's Wear," *New York Times,* August 11, 1963, Section 6, Part 2.

[24]Dick Schaap, "Tomorrow the World," *New York Herald Tribune,* August 6, 1965.

[25]*New York Times,* August 11, 1963, *op. cit.*

of girls in the population. Boys' costumes are, however, sold in much greater quantity than the proportion of boys, suggesting that girls are far more likely than boys to dress in the others' costumes.

Over a generation ago, when writing anonymously, three times as many girls as boys wished to be of the opposite sex.[26] The many traditional boys' attributes that have been taken over by girls make it likely that fewer girls would express such a wish today, and in a more recent investigation, only 40 percent more girls than boys wanted to be of the opposite sex.[27] If current trends toward role reversal continue, and literary critics continue to raise questions about Huck Finn's masculinity, more boys than girls will soon be expressing a desire to change gender.

[26]Theodore Reik, *Psychology of Sex Relations*. New York: Rinehart, 1945, p. 117.

[27]Study conducted by the author in the metropolitan New York area in 1956 with 1,203 high school students. The questions were put to young people who were being interviewed as part of a larger study. See Charles Winick, "Tendency Systems and the Effects of a Movie Dealing with a Social Problem," *Journal of General Psychology,* **68,** 1963, pp. 289–305.

SOCIAL CHANGE: TEMPORAL DIMENSIONS OF LIFE STYLES

Political and economic forces that give a distinct character to an era also shape life styles. Fads in popular culture make their mark on life style—for example, the eras of the Charleston, the bobby-soxers, the silent generation of the 1950s, and the turned-on generation of the 1970s. U.S. involvement in foreign wars, repression of dissent, awakening of minority groups, and other factors are related to cultural changes that have been called "the life-style revolution." At any point in time, new values replace old ones and standards of acceptable behavior change, as do motivations for behavior. But the rate of change varies; life-style changes are not always revolutionary. Lacking a precise measure of the rate at which life style changes, we can contrast popular culture at different points in time. Argot or slang of an era may be an indication of its values. In the 1970s popular argot deals with drugs, revolution, and sex, while that of the more innocent 1950s dealt with alcohol, cars, and clothes.

As They Used to Say in the 1950s . . .

HOWARD JUNKER

When the time comes, it may not be easy, despite the rebirth of Richard Nixon and Elvis Presley, to muster nostalgia for the Fifties. (Davy Crockett and Roy Cohn, Grace Kelly and the Playboy Bunny, *My Fair Lady* and adult Westerns, filter tips and instant coffee, Zen and the art of the Roller Derby, Ban the Bomb and togetherness, Harry Belafonte, Jack Kerouac, Dr. Kinsey, and The Golden Age of Television.)

But some of the words we used to use already have the power to charm, so great is the distance between then and now.

Jargonwise, the Fifties spoke a finalized version of advertisingese. Euphemists offered: the Police Action, peaceful coexistence, nuclear blackmail, freedom fighter, creeping Momism, desegregation, payola, cleavage, recession, pinko. Korea did little to enrich the language (brainwashing, gook). But from Russia came Sputnik, hence beatnik, jetnik. . . .

One kind of nostalgia for the Eisenhower Era looks back to an age of innocence. But this apparent innocence was protected at a cost. Irony, ambiguity, complexity were academic passwords that sophomores enacted as apathy. The common language was designed to not

From *Esquire*, 72 (August, 1969), pp. 70–71, 141. Reprinted by permission; copyright © 1969 by Esquire, Inc.

say what was meant: Would you like to have a cup of coffee/come up for a drink? (In the Sixties, *pace* Lenny Bruce: Let's ball.) Sarcasm (Wanna lose ten ugly pounds? Cut off your head) and innuendo (I have here the names) were basic modes of conversation. Much literary imagination went toward developing acceptable variations on Mailer's (1948) fuggin, as in effing, frigging. Sick jokes finally mentioned other unmentionables, and with *Lady Chatterley's Lover* (1959) the unprintable became available in drugstores and at your local supermarket.

Beneath much of the (dirty) white buck, saccharine, other-directed innocence of the Fifties lurked a smug obliviousness. You could still say colored. (Ixnay, ofay.) Niggerlipping didn't seem such a terrible way to describe wetting the end of a cigarette. A riot was really funny. A soul kiss involved the tongue. The ghetto was where the Jews had escaped from. Race as in arms, rat, and drag. A pill was like a dope. A bust was a pair of knockers, as in M.M., B.B., and Diana Dors. A joint was maybe a bar.

Getting stoned meant hitting the hard stuff (not horse, booze). A quick brew: quaff a foamy. Whales' tails, Thumper. Here's to the Cardinal once. Chug-a-lug. Getting blotto, stinko, loaded, smashed, plowed, bombed out of your ever-loving mind. Then: heaving, tossing, blowing your lunch (cookies). Upchuck, barf, puke. The problem of youth was getting served. Do you have proof (an I.D.)? Churchkey.

In short, in the Fifties, culture still enjoyed a literary base. Words (the novel) still mattered. Awareness was limited, not electronically total. And regionalisms, celebrated during the Thirties when the middle class stayed home, were not yet erased by television, which went coast to coast in 1951, and commercial jets, which crossed the Atlantic in 1958. Have gun, will travel.

In the Fifties, it was dangerous to take anyone at face value. (Are you for real?) In conformist times, you worried about Image (status), doubly anxious because words functioned as costume: are you hip?

Now you're talking (speaking my language). Certain key terms, dig, became juvenile gestures: L7 equaled square (cube or octagon meant supersquare). The three-ring sign indicated cool; screwy was the finger twirled at the temple, then flung at the nut.

Status was divvied up into geographical dualisms: in, out; with it, from squaresville. Hepcat. Beat/Jazz contributed: daddy-o, pad, bread, gig, slip me some skin. And all that, like, well, you know, man, incoherence. (Holden Caulfield, Marty, Brando and the Method, action painting, the silent generation, Nichols and May, taking the fifth.)

Don't hand me any of that jazz. Take five.

Alienation was the absurd egghead bit. (Did Adlai sell out?) Psychology was Krazy, man, like, I nearly flipped. The best minds. The orgone box. Or, as the get-well card said: I'm glad you're sick, but I'm sorry you're ill. You only got hung up when somebody flaked out on you. If you psyched a test, you had it made. What, me worry?

Yes, above all, anti-frantic. Stay cool. Hang loose. No sweat (negative perspiration). Under control. Made in the shade. Big deal.

Duhhhh!

The antithesis of cool was the slow burn, indicated by touching the index finger to the tongue, extending it toward the unfortunate victim, and announcing "Psss" as if touching a hot stove. A variation: same gesture: Chalk one up for me! Tuftittie. The way the cookie crumbles. The Royal Screw, hence The Royal Shaft, hence The King's Elevator. Up the creek without a paddle.

Cruising for a bruising. Don't give me any grief. You want a knuckle sandwich. Get Bent. Your ass is grass. Blast off. Suck gas. Wise up. Don't bug me. Drop dead. DDT. Finally gonna shut you down. Dump all over you. How's that grab you? Forty lashes with a wet noodle.

Who cut the cheese? The true clue: he who smelt it dealt it. Silent but deadly.

Hardeeharhar.

Antlers in the Treetop or Who Goosed the Moose.

That went over like a pregnant pole vaulter with a broken stick.

What a fake out.

Almost everything was a drag (negative attitude), although some guys did get a charge (some kicks). Have a blast. Really hairy. Going ape. Bad, Mean, Wicked, Evil. Bitchin. I eat her up. She sends me. Gone, man, gone. Into the air, junior birdmen.

If you weren't grounded, you could take off. And hack, screw, mess around. Goof off.

Where did you go? (Take me to your leader.) I donno, waddya wanna do? Catch some rays. (Shades.) Play charades, spin-the-bottle, Frisbee, pogo stick, Hula-Hoop, bowling, knock-knock, why did the moron?

Precisely at age thirteen, you became a teen-ager. And there were pajama parties and sock hops with a thumbful of 45's. Only bird dogs cut in on a slow dance. Every party has a pooper, that's why we invited you. They tried to tell us we're too young. Grow up.

Certain college studs stuffed phone booths, smashed pianos and, from automobiles, displayed their naked asses to passersby, an act variously called dropping trou, mooning, handing out the b.a. gotcha. Slipping them some pressed ham involved pressing one's bare butt against the window. In the city, you could nerf a cab, i.e., bump it gently at a light. On the highway: chicken.

M*I*C*K*E*Y*M*O*U*S*E

The J.D.'s emerged. The hood. The Rock. (Don't knock the Rock.) Baddass. Tough as nails. Switchblade and zip gun for stomping, mixing it up, rumbles. (Squeezing a beer can.) Pegged pants and a greasy D.A.

Or: butch, crew cut, flat top. Charcoal-grey flannel, belt-in-the-back, paisley, Shetland, Madras, bermudas. Our fine-quality pink button-down. Tweedy and preppy.

The common ground: blue jeans, as in the one and only Levi's. (I'm wise to the rise in your Levi's.) As in shrink 'em in the bathtub. As in James Dean lives. As in engineer boots. Classy.

With a digression to honor circle pins, knee socks, saddle shoes, fruit boots, straight skirts, ponytails. On the one hand. On the other: beards, sandals, and leotards—not yet called tights. Who wears short shorts? If you wore green on Thursday. . . .

As for sex, there was going steady (I.D. bracelet, ring-on-the-necklace, letter or sweater or jacket). And breaking up. But mostly the eternal search for a little action, etc. Bedroom eyes. Hot lips.

The first thing a make-out artist asked: Is she fast? (Nice or good.) Does she put out? Lay it on the line? Do the deed?

He, of course, was always horny. When really hard up, he would even overlook her b.o., cooties, flat chest. (Scuzzy, grungy.) Her zits.

It was suspected that sometimes she, too, was climbing up the wall. Hot to trot.

In that case, if he didn't get shot down (stood up), he might suggest catching a flick. The passion pit. Parking. Let's go watch the submarines race.

For openers, a snow job. Coming on like Gang Busters. Are you trying to feed me a line?

She might come across if he were a big wheel, a B.M.O.C. On the ball, divine, clean-cut, casual, snazzy, a really good (great) guy, the living end. Cute. Neat. Smooth. Peachy keen. A hunk. Hey, bobo. She would certainly be turned off if he were grubby, a phony, a sex fiend, bad news, out to lunch, a banana, weenie, yo-yo, turkey, spastic, nebbish. Gross. A fink. With a bad case of the uglies. A dumb cluck. A loser, creep, simp. A nothing. Of course, if he were a straight arrow, there'd be no danger of his trying to go too far. (Goodnight kiss. Heavy petting.) Meanwhile, awaiting his chance to go all the way, a circular bulge etched itself into his wallet.

Back with the guys, he would be asked, especially if he had a rep as a hot ticket: Get much?

And at school next day, where the brains were grinds and usually brown-nosers, her friends noticed the hickey on her neck.

Which brings us to that ultimate, fabulous Fifties' experience: wheels.
Bombing around
In a '49 Ford.
A '55 Chevy.
A Merc.
T-Bird.
Vette.
Coming and going in a Studey.
(Edsel.)
Stick shift, as in grind me a pound.
Hang a left.
Fins and tails and two-tone and one year there was a three-tone.

Raked and flamed, decked and lowered, chopped and channeled.
Dual
Glass
Fuelie   ail.
I don't   long
as I've g
A No.
Driver
I got to cut   r.
Take it easy.
Anyway I can get it.
See you later, alligator.

After a significant Supreme Court decision in 1954, Brown vs. the Board of Education, a decade of token integration followed before the revolution in black life style. The sit-ins of the early 1960s gave way to the ghetto riots of the late 1960s and the cultural revolution that followed. The life style of the Negro was imposed, and therefore not an expression of values or free choice. Contemporary Afro style may not be authentically African, but it is an expression of ethnic pride.

Black periodicals such as Ebony *reflect black life style in America.* Ebony *presents to its readers models of behavior, achievement, and life style to which they may aspire. Although the ideal life style pervades its feature articles, its advertising may more directly portray the actual life style of its readers. In the following article, Irwin Rinder reports on the black life style as reflected in the products sold through advertisements in the black periodical. This essay can be taken as an important documentation of a revolution in the life style of black Americans, indicated by the sale of such products as skin lighteners and other cosmetics that minimize blackness. In contrast, a recent* Ebony *featured ads for soft drinks against a background of soul food.*

A Sociological Look into the Negro Pictorial

IRWIN D. RINDER

A great many persons have probably picked up and read a "Negro Pictorial" at one time or another in recent years. We propose to do something of the sort in this essay, but rather than idle curiosity ours shall be directed inquiry, and rather than some specific issue we shall look over some imagined composite constructed out of numerous typical features of the Negro pictorials currently vended.[1] Such a perusal may reveal something about the life of Americans who happen also to be Negroes—their dreams, their fears, their particular problems.

Perhaps the first point worthy of attention is the very existence of a literature for and about Negroes. The phenomenal success of contemporary Negro journalism becomes even more noteworthy against the historical background of failure which so long dogged most efforts in this direction. While many nationality groups in the United States, far smaller in size, were supporting foreign-language publications, the

Negro press going into the twentieth century had suffered a mortality rate estimated at sixty percent.[2] This century's two major wars, the sharp reduction in immigration, and the subsequent movement of many Negroes out of the rural South and into the industrial urban North and Midwest brought about an improvement in both the socioeconomic status and the educational level of this tenth of the nation. Literacy and the ability to pay, both *sine qua non* for the survival of mass publications, had to await this combination of circumstances. Two other developments, consequences of those just mentioned, also contributed greatly to the newfound vitality of Negro publishing. First, Negroes have come increasingly to reside in the cities, their denser population concentrations providing a greater potential readership base within a compact area. Second, the doctrine of white racial supremacy has helped evoke a counter-ideology, that of Negro "race pride." This has generated among many Negroes a passionate group identification which did not exist previously. The support of their own publications by Negroes is a manifestation of this new sense of belonging as well as a means of satisfying the appetite for information and confirmation of this newfound self.

At the center of this new development is the Negro pictorial, the most spectacular growth occurring in one house, the Johnson Publishing Company. The publisher, thirty-eight-year-old John H.

From *Phylon,* **20** (Summer, 1959), pp. 169–177. The postscript was added for this book.
[1]Although all the excerpts and citations which follow were taken from *Ebony* for the sake of economy in footnoting, the claim of typicality is made in the same sense that *Life* might be taken as the norm of all pictorials.

[2]F. J. Brown and J. S. Roucek, *One America* (New York, 1952). See especially Chap. 13, "The Foreign-Language Press and Radio," by J.S. Roucek, and Chap. 14, "The Negro Press," by C. R. Jones.

Johnson, selected by the Junior Chamber of Commerce as one of the ten outstanding young men of 1951, puts out *Hue, Jet, Tan,* and *Ebony* with circulations ranging from two hundred thousand to half a million. The impressive success of this genre testifies that the pictorials are striking responsive chords and meeting certain needs of their readers. From such magazines we should be able to learn something about the attitudes and opinions, the sources of conflict and modes of adjustment, and the changing status of the Negro in American Society.

Social scientists have developed careful and revealing techniques for analyzing the contents of spoken, written, or visual media of communication. This technique, called content analysis, involves the discernment, classification, and measurement of the themes or messages being communicated. This essay is an impressionistic content analysis which attempts only to detect certain themes and indicate their significance. Although we cannot prove anything conclusively in this manner, we may inform and sensitize the reader's future perceptions of this material.

As we leaf through our typical composite issue of a Negro pictorial, one of the first features that comes to our attention is the department, "Letters to the Editor." Even with allowance for editorial selection, the range of attitudes we find here and the varying intensity with which they are expressed is a useful antidote for those who stereotypically think that there is a Negro "mind" or virtual uniformity of opinion in the Negro community. Sociologists know that minority group members will probably show greater consensus on issues

which affect them than will another and more secure group which by contrast is less self-conscious about its status and less mobilized ideologically. What is often overlooked is that this does not mean that minority group members show no differences of opinion—the spectrum of attitudes and feelings here is as far-ranging as elsewhere—but it does mean that the distribution along this spectrum will show somewhat greater concentration or bunching. Those who emphasize the bunching and neglect the range of distribution, thereby conceiving of Negro opinion as endorsing some one homogeneous point of view, would be surprised at the mixed reception accorded stories and editorials advancing any given point of view. In fact, where "race" is involved, the point of view need not even be advanced, only implicit—or imagined—for some readers to take pen in hand. An article about a Negro woman taking in and caring for motherless white children drew the following, among other responses (September, 1956):

> I must commend you on your article, "The Power of Love" in the July issue of Ebony. I think Mrs. Amelia Brown is truly a wonderful person to have the love and courage enough to forget the color of skin and take in four homeless children. The world needs more people like her. . . .

> . . . For the life of me I can't understand why the Negro people, with all of their love and sympathy, wealth and education, can always see where all other races outside of their own always need help while the orphaned Negro children go unwanted, unloved, and otherwise deserted. For example, the wealthy Negroes who got together and sent thou-

sands of miles abroad to bring over the brown babies to America while the black babies of America are so in need. . . .

An article in an issue two years earlier was followed by four letters pro and four con, of which we shall sample one of each kind (November, 1954):

I get your magazine monthly, and never enjoyed such an amusing, refreshing article as Mr. Louis Armstrong's "Why I Like Dark Women." It is good for the black gal's morale to know that some-one in the 'chips' prefers us in marriage to the usual pastel shades.

. . . Usually the material is educational, entertaining, and inspiring; but your August edition carried the lousiest piece of writing I have ever read, entitled "Why I Like Dark Women" by Louis Armstrong.

I read the story—or article—out of curiosity, wondering what might one write so wonderful about dark women, or light women, so far as that is con-cerned. If a man likes a dark woman, a light woman, a white woman, or a green woman, what difference does it make, as long as she has those basic qualities so necessary in each of us for wholesome, lovable living and compan-ionship?

After reading the story, I still could not find why Armstrong likes dark women. Did he forget to state the reason why or was it erroneously omitted from the article? He states that none of the four women he married were light-colored; this is proof that he is as biased in his thinking as white men from Mississippi about this color business—though Armstrong's case is in the reverse.

Let us read more about the man as the great artist he is in music and stop there. Otherwise I can only see that we

are perpetuating this crazy nonsense and evil concerning the color of a per-son's skin—which has no importance at all!

Whenever the issue of interracial in-timacy is discussed, alluded to, or pho-tographed, be it anything from friend-ship to marriage, there soon after appear letters which support positions ranging from the assimilationist to the separatist and all points between. There are those who thank the editor for "showing how some human beings can rise above the petty hatreds of our society on the strength of a love which is color-blind." Others write, "I was sickened by your article and pictures showing Negroes married to whites. People who have to look outside their own group should be ashamed of themselves. Stop glorifying these Negro-haters."

Articles on segregation, discrim-ination, and jim crow inspire letters which laud the efforts to expose injustice and the good fight for perfect equality. But there are also letters urging gradual-ism, the cleaning up of one's own house first, and so forth. Among Negroes, as among any other group, there exist dif-ferences of opinion, as these letters amply testify. While this is not to say that there is an up-the-middle split in opinion, neither is there any party line of Negro thought.

The subject under discussion here is receiving the largest amount of space given to any topic because of its impor-tance. Increasing opportunity for a peo-ple permits their increasing differentia-tion in terms of innate differences, training, and others. We may therefore expect that the already visible evidence of differences in intelligence, education, sophistication, socioeconomic status, religiosity, and other questions of values points to a continuing and increasing trend.

An article which appeared some five years ago about one of the religious sects, predominantly Negro in membership, brought these contributions to the Letters column (April, 1952):

> *. . . Daddy Grace has proven himself to the whole world. His work is outstanding both spiritually and naturally. So the least you can do, is to quote what he says and publish what's right, otherwise we will take further steps.*

> *I recently read your article. "America's Richest Negro Minister." I think that Daddy Grace is the biggest farce to hit this country since someone said you could grow hair by putting your feet in onion juice! . . . I cannot see why people follow this self-centered, egotistical faker. And I only hope that more people are not persuaded to join his following.*

William Faulkner accepted an invitation to write a piece for *Ebony*, and as one might easily have expected, his personal essay stimulated considerable response. Again it is the variety which may surprise one who does not read the Negro press.

> *I would also like to congratulate you upon the Faulkner article, "If I Were A Negro"—that is, on your foresight in procuring such a controversial literary giant. This makes many of your readers feel that now more than ever,* Ebony *gives us outstanding provocative reading. Whether we agree with Faulkner's views is not the important point here— but that his ideas are presented here expressly for* Ebony *readers is quite significant. (December, 1956)*

> *. . . If you were a Negro, Mr. Faulkner, you would be the same man you are now, only unable to be free in Mississippi. You would have the same brains you have now, and desire the same education that you have had. The brain that is educated and allowed to think and act accordingly is most likely to succeed. Would you continue to have patience your only active weapon, year after year, until finally your hope becomes your children's hope, generation after generation? This is all right for a person with exceptional value of patience, given to him by God. An entire race of people are not so. (November, 1956)*

> *I want to commend you, Mr. William Faulkner, on your recent effort on how to maintain segregation, oh, pardon me, sir, I meant on your written article in the September issue of* Ebony *magazine, "If I Were An Uncle Tom"—there I go again! Please bear with me, oh yes, "If I Were A Negro"—there! I was so moved by it I would follow in your footsteps today, that is, if they would end tomorrow. You get the message, I got yours. From a Negro who is a Negro. (November, 1956)*

The editorial page may not show all of the steps on the scale as do the letters, but it nevertheless has progressed from an earlier—and undoubtedly less secure—period. The editorials often select and develop themes which are diversified and subtle; develop them through either exposition or fantasy; with treatment ranging from the tolerant to the acid. They attack the bastions of prejudice and dissect the nuances. And most significantly, they shift back and forth from the injustice and hypocrisy of the larger society to self-scrutiny and self-criticism. The editorial for January,

1957, "Stop Misbehavin'," said:

> . . . *Today, the Negro stands on the threshold of integration. Behavior is his last big barrier. Just as "inferior mentality" once prevented him from obtaining skilled jobs, so are "criminal tendencies" and "bad conduct" barring him from living in the house next door and his children being welcome at the school across the street. Happily he has overcome the mental block by proving that members of his race can and do excel in every field of endeavor. To obtain full equality, he must now prove his moral fitness to live and associate with other men.*

This last editorial excerpt, from March, 1957, entitled "Full-Time Negro," should convey to the reader the feeling that the editorial talents involved represent more than literary grace but testify to maturity of conviction and acceptance of responsibility.

"I get so tired of all this talk about race," sighed a Negro engineer, "that I am glad that I can bury myself in work and escape for a few hours, the eternal 'problems.'" Then the engineer launched into a long discussion about his favorite topic—race.

This paragraph introduces a double-column, full-page editorial with section headings, "Obsessed With Race"; "Mulatto In Mind"; "Mental Passing"; and a concluding section, "Full Emancipation," as follows:

> *Being a part-time Negro does not mean the denial of racial heritage. It does not mean the rejection of racial traits or the loss of valued traditions. It does mean, however, that he who demands first-class citizenship must be prepared to put citizenship first, race second. He will not be expected to ease*

> *up on his campaign to stop the persecution of Negroes by segregationists in Mississippi, but will double his efforts to include aid to Whites being persecuted by the Communists in Europe. He must continue his fight for the reinforcement of civil rights in America, but he must also be concerned with the human rights of yellow, brown, red, and white men throughout the world.*

> *It will not be easy for the Negro to raise his sights to the needs of others while justice for his Southern brothers is still being denied. Just as he cannot afford to jeopardize his soul by remaining outside the church because some members of the congregation misbehave, the part-time Negro, one fully emancipated from his obsession of race, must join other citizens with his voice and his vote in making America a democracy for all of its people.*

No simplistic recourse, here, to the too-easy formulas of passive resignation and accommodation (Uncle Tom or Old Handkerchief Head) on the one hand, nor on the other to the contemporary, hence even easier, reaction in the form of a parochial race chauvinism (Race Man). Here is a position which is embedded in a comprehensive rather than narrow outlook; which balances rather than resolves the ambiguities of Negro status; which bespeaks the whole and the sane man.

Of the feature stories which appear in the pictorial, inspection suggests that they may be usefully grouped into the following categories: (a) stories which are excuses for pin-up pictures, e.g., "A Day in the Life of a Chorus Cutie" (although close to one, I hope I have not appropriated a real title); (b) stories with a racial theme, e.g., Negroes who have crossed and/or recrossed the color line, the bombing or terrorization of a civil rights leader in the South, the riots accompanying the settlement of a Negro family in a public housing project in the North, etc.; (c) stories about Negro personalities, e.g., professional athletes, entertainers, government employees, domestic servants of famous white persons, etc.; (d) a last category, "Negroes who made good," which overlaps somewhat with the preceding one, the distinguishing feature being whether the emphasis is upon the individual personality or upon the role being played. Negroes who have accumulated wealth, entered new fields, accomplished new feats, and the like are written up in these latter-day Horatio Alger stories. In fact, the Negro pictorial is probably the foremost contemporary exponent of the Alger myth. While it is undeniable that these stories do document new and significant developments of Negro life in America, the actual modesty of many of the accomplishments which are a source of pride is a sad commentary on the status to which the Negro has hitherto been restricted. Not to be overlooked is the function of these stories, in addition to the vicarious satisfaction they afford, in building up a fund of success. If a group is to aspire and achieve at ever higher levels, it needs the supporting base of a tradition of success as much as it does the spur of motivation to impel it.

The advertisements take up appreciable room here, as they do in any slick-paper pictorial magazine. In their own way, these advertisements tell us as much about the changing status of the Negro as do the editorial columns. While there continues to be a large amount of advertising beamed specifically at the

Negro consumer as a Negro (more about this later), the important change has been the growth of his role as a consumer. There has taken place a considerable increase in the advertising dollars invested in this medium by nationally known brand name products like foods, toilet goods, electrical appliances, and so on, as well as the omnipresent advertisements for gum, whiskey, and cigarettes. Sellers seem not only aware of the increased purchasing power of the Negro community, but the need to meet it on its own terms. For example, Johnson's company claims a penetration of this vast new market at a rate fourteen to fifteen times greater than that of the top white publications.

While the use of well-known Negro celebrities, primarily from the fields of sports and entertainment, as endorsers of various products is a routine and easily anticipated development, another interesting trend in advertising technique may also be discerned. This is the use of Negro models portraying ordinary folks in the conventional boy-meets-girl and typical-wholesome-family scenes. Whereas advertisers formerly used the same advertising plates designed for the general mass media, they seem to be shifting increasingly, despite the additional expense, to the creation of special ones for the Negro pictorial. This again illustrates the democratizing influence of the market, and the willingness of seller to meet buyer on his own terms. In the January, 1957, issue the following were some of the products whose advertisements featured Negro models: Libby's Vienna Sausages, Manischewitz Wine, Ami Juke Box, Sal Hepatica, Bufferin, Remington Rand Safe-File, Champale, Chateau Martin, the city of

Miami (tourist information), Old Gold, Carnation Milk, etc.

We have already referred to the advertisements beamed specifically at the Negro consumer as Negro. Some of these involve unique products while others involve ordinary products which are being uniquely marketed. Preeminent among the unique products are those cosmetics designed to bleach dark skin lighter and straighten kinky hair. These have long been staples of Negro American cosmetic treatment and the backbone of advertising support in Negro publishing. The popularity of these products shows no signs of diminishing. In one issue this year, two full-page advertisements for hair straighteners on two consecutive pages contained these statements:

Soft Beautiful Hair That Won't Go Back . . . Even in Wet Weather. No Hot Combs, No Irons, No Redness . . . Guaranteed Safe.

Extra Soft Natural-Looking Straight Hair!
. . . perfectly prepares your hair for straightening . . . conditions it for the very finest results with America's favorite cream hair straightener. Quick, simple . . . you remove all the undesirable kink and too-tight curls from your hair. Hair becomes softly, smoothly straight . . . just as you've always wanted it to be.

This apparent acceptance of the aesthetic standards of beauty as defined by whites remains one of the exceptions to a trend toward increased "race pride" on the part of the Negro. If this exception seems paradoxical in the light of the Negro press's continuous editorial exhortation of the Negro to be himself,

to accept and have pride in what he is, has been, and can be, imagine the psychic embarrassment such inconsistencies must have caused Marcus Garvey, one of the most outspoken advocates of race pride and Negro "nationalism" of this century. Garvey had to accept revenue from skin bleach and hair straightener advertisements in order to keep solvent the very publication within whose pages he argued that life among whites was so intolerable that Negroes should emigrate and form their own nation.

An amusing contrast has sometimes been made between Negro attitude toward hair texture and skin color and the seemingly reverse enthusiasm of white persons for curling their straight hair and sun-tanning their pale skin. These phenomena are not psychologically equivalent, however, for the cosmetic "correction" is almost always a matter of greater moment for the Negro than for the white and the motivation for Negroes, again almost always, seems to be one of self-hatred, the desire to look less Negro. Whereas white males rarely wave their hair, Negro males (in large numbers) go in for treatments which "condition" their hair. Similarly, the large number of Negro men cultivating mustaches may be understood as demonstrating their share of the Caucasoid trait of facial hairiness.

Turning from the subject of unique products to that of the unique marketing of standard products, we must note as significant the number of advertisements found in the Negro pictorial for the mail ordering of clothing. In addition to ordering of his own clothes, the reader is offered numerous inducements to become a door-to-door canvasser for men's and women's suits, dresses, shoes, socks, hats, etc. This type of advertising and the behavior pattern it suggests are not difficult to explain. In many parts of the South the Negro is not permitted to try on articles of clothing in the store but must estimate by size and hope that the fit will prove to be satisfactory. In other places the Negro customer may be permitted to try on an article, but having worn it, has no alternative but to pay for it, regardless of the nature of the fit. Although these conditions do not exist in the North, the dislike or feeling of anxiety about shopping for clothing—something whites take for granted or look forward to as a pleasurable excursion—apparently persists widely among Negroes.

One interesting phenomenon to which we shall call attention but offer no explanation is the prominence of advertisements for men's shoes. Some are sold by mail order and others are to be found in stores. There are shoes featuring a large variety of exotic leathers and *avant-garde* design; some pioneering years ahead of men's fashions for the general public; and some just out of this world. It would be most interesting to see an analysis in depth by an anthropologist, a sociologist, and a psychologist on the importance and meanings of shoes to the Negro male.

Not very prominent because it is hidden among the other small advertisements is a most revealing and saddening facet of Negro life in these contemporary United States. It is the offer for sale at a dollar or two of a particular type of touring guide variously called "travel guide," "green book," "guide to pleasant motoring," or the like. These promise "Vacation and Recreation Without Humiliation: A Directory of Accommodations," and "Travel Without Fear Anywhere in the United States, Canada, Alaska, and Mexico." In other words, the Negro who travels for business or recreation has nothing so trivial to worry about as whether the food will be good at the place up ahead, or whether there will be vacancies for the night's lodging. Rather, he must consider, even though vacancies exist, whether he will be given a room, and whether he will be served, told to go around to the kitchen entrance, or coldly ignored. The advertisements for these latter-day versions of the underground railroad are poignant reminders that we are still somewhat short of putting into practice all of our professed values concerning the equality and dignity of man.

The Negro pictorial does for life in general what the travel guides do for touring in particular, i.e., it provides the individual with a pictorial tour of life in the United States without humiliation. So long as the status of the Negro remains to any degree a disadvantaged one, this tour is likely to continue a popular one despite, or perhaps because of, its emphasis on the struggles for acceptance on the one hand and the evidences of success on the other.

POSTCRIPT: ELEVEN YEARS LATER

Going through a pile of current *Ebony* with the 1959 article in mind, I was impressed with the continuity between past and present. Feature articles still heavily stress personalities, and these personalities still come from segregated institutions of education and religion, or from the alternative opportunity structures of athletics and entertainment. While the editors remain willing to publish divergent views in the Letters column, one gets the feeling they are throwing raw meat (or is it catnip?) to the tigers. Integrationists and gradualists take a tougher beating as time goes by: there is diversity, but militancy is increasingly difficult to oppose. To even dare to do so is to be labeled "accommodationist" (read "Negro"). The canons of loyalty in thought and vocabulary become more stringent. There may eventually be a danger that Black people will have gotten themselves so well together they will find themselves tyrannized. Similarly, editorials include much less self-criticism, this having become unacceptable for these times.

Viewing the advertisements as a reflection of both the marketplace and the collective imagery diffused by the mass media, I note increasing attention from the sellers of the larger economy. *Ebony* is very prosperous in its volume of ads. There are still unique products for the black consumer but I think they have declined both in absolute number and relative to the volume of mass market items being advertised. Nevertheless, the shoes and hats with advanced styling are still here, fewer in number and with less visual salience. There is now much less appeal to direct mail ordering of clothing, testimony perhaps to the opening up of downtown retail trade outlets to black customers, or less reticence about store shopping, at least for those who read *Ebony*.

With regard to esthetics and self-conceptions as these are revealed through the still considerable advertising for cosmetic and grooming products, there can be seen the expected rise in Afro and natural looks. This is accompanied by a decline but far from disappearance of skin treatments and of hair relaxers, conditioners and straighteners. These are now proffered under the aegis of "doing your own thing."

There remains an innocence about *Ebony*. With no embarrassment and apparently not even a flush of self-consciousness, it can run a several-page story on the preparation and marketing of "Julia dolls"—brown Barbies for the children of the Black Bourgeoisie. The magazine remains so completely absorbed in the black experience in America it seems almost therapeutically insulated from other pressing concerns like Vietnam and pollution. In many respects *Ebony* is so establishment it makes white pictorials seem radical in their range and criticalness of concerns.

Finally, in the several issues I went through carefully, I nowhere found the items I concluded the original essay by noting, i.e., "underground" guide books to travel in the United States without embarrassment. I hope this means that the Civil Rights Acts have succeeded in democratizing facilities involved in interstate commerce and travel.

Irwin D. Rinder

One of the most publicized arenas of life-style change is the college campus. Martin Trow and Burton Clark have suggested that there are four distinct undergraduate subcultures on the college campus.* One is the collegiate subculture, which lives the stereotyped collegiate life of panty raids, beer parties, football games, and the Gentleman's C. Not interested in ideas, this subculture does maintain a strong identity with its institutions. Members of this subculture may not know their academic subjects, but they do know the words to the "fight song." Although other subcultures † existed in the 1950s, in general it was the era of the collegiate subculture. Willie Morris grew up in Yazoo City, Mississippi, attended the University of Texas, and later became the editor-in-chief of Harper's Magazine. *His description of the collegiate subculture of the fifties could almost be read by today's college students as an ethnographic study of a foreign life style, bearing little relationship to college life today.*

*Burton R. Clark, *Educating the Expert Society* (San Francisco: Chandler, 1962), pp. 202–243.
†The authors note the existence of a *vocational* subculture that sees college as a place to learn a trade, an *academic* subculture that considers college a place of learning and ideas, and a *nonconformist* subculture that, although interested in ideas, has little interest in or identity with the traditional rigors of the academic life.

University of Texas: 1953

WILLIE MORRIS

What strikes me most in reading books like Alfred Kazin's haunting poetic reminiscences of boyhood in an immigrant Jewish neighborhood in the East, is the vast gulf which separates that kind of growing up and the childhood and adolescence of those of us who came out of the towns of the American South and

From Willie Morris, *North Toward Home* (Boston: Houghton Mifflin, 1967), pp. 149–162. Reprinted by permission of Houghton Mifflin Co.; copyright 1967 by Willie Morris.

Southwest a generation later. With the Eastern Jewish intellectuals who play such a substantial part in American cultural life, perhaps in the late 1960s a dominant part, the struggle as they grew up in the 1930s was for one set of ideas over others, for a fierce acceptance or rejection of one man's theories or another man's poetry—and with all this a driving determination to master the language which had not been their parents' and to find a place in a culture not quite theirs. For other Eastern intellectuals and writers whom I later was to know, going to the Ivy League schools involved, if not a finishing, then a deepening of perceptions, or of learning, or culture.

But for so many of us who converged on Austin, Texas, in the early 1950s, from places like Karnes City or Big

Spring or Abilene or Rockdale or Yazoo City, the awakening we were to experience, or to have jolted into us, or to undergo by some more subtle chemistry, did not mean a mere finishing or deepening, and most emphatically did not imply the victory of one set of ideologies over another, one way of viewing literature or politics over another, but something more basic and simple. This was the acceptance of ideas themselves as something worth living by. It was a matter, at the age of eighteen or nineteen, not of discovering *certain* books, but the simple *presence* of books, not the nuances of idea and feeling, but idea and feeling on their own terms. It is this late coming to this kind of awareness that still gives the intellectuals from the small towns of our region a hungry naive quality, as opposed to the sharp-elbowed over-intellectuality of some Easterners, as if those from down there who made it were lucky, or chosen, out of all the disastrous alternatives of their isolated lower- or middle-class upbringings, to enjoy and benefit from the fruits of simply being educated and liberal-minded.

What we brought to the University of Texas in the 1950s, to an enormous, only partially formed state university, was a great awe before the splendid quotations on its buildings and the walls of its libraries, along with an absolutely prodigious insensitivity as to what they implied beyond decoration. Minds awakened slowly, painfully, and with pretentious and damaging inner searches. Where an Alfred Kazin at the age of nineteen might become aroused in the subway by reading a review by John Chamberlain in the *New York Times* and rush to his office to complain, we at eighteen or nineteen were only barely

beginning to learn that there *were* ideas, much less ideas to arouse one from one's self. If places like City College or Columbia galvanized the young New York intellectuals already drenched in literature and polemics, the University of Texas had, in its halting, unsure, and often frivolous way, to teach those of us with good minds and small-town high school diplomas that we were intelligent human beings, with minds and hearts of our own that we might learn to call our own, that there were some things, many things—ideas, values, choices of action—worth committing one's self to and fighting for, that a man in some instances might become morally committed to honoring every manifestation of individual conscience and courage. Yet the hardest task at the University of Texas, as many of us were to learn, was to separate all the extraneous and empty things that can drown a young person there, as all big universities can drown its young people, from the few simple things that are worth living a life by. Without wishing to sound histrionic, I believe I am thinking of something approaching the Western cultural tradition; yet if someone had suggested that to me that September night in 1952, as I stepped off the bus in Austin to be greeted by three fraternity men anxious to look me over, I would have thought him either a fool or a con man.

I emerged from that bus frightened and tired, after having come 500 miles non-stop over the red hills of Louisiana and the pine forests of East Texas. The three men who met me—appalled, I was told later, by my green trousers and the National Honor Society medal on my gold-plated watch chain—were the kind that I briefly liked and admired, for their facility at small talk, their clothes, their manner, but whom I soon grew to deplore and finally to be bored by. They were the kind who made fraternities tick, the favorites of the Dean of Men at the time, respectable B or C-plus students, tolerable athletes, good with the Thetas or the Pi Phis; but one would find later, lurking there inside of them despite—or maybe because of—their good fun and jollity, the ideals of the insurance salesman and an aggressive distrust of anything approaching thought. One of them later told me, with the seriousness of an early disciple, that my table manners had become a source of acute embarrassment to all of them. That night they drove me around the campus, and they were impressed that I knew from my map-reading where the University library was, for two of them were not sure.

It was early fall, with that crispness in the air that awakened one's senses and seemed to make everything wondrously alive. My first days there I wandered about that enormous campus, mingling silently with its thousands of nameless students. I walked past the fraternity and sorority houses, which were like palaces to me with their broad porches and columns and patios, and down "The Drag" with its bookstores and restaurants, a perfectly contained little city of its own. On a slight rise dominating the place was a thirty-story skyscraper called the "Tower," topped with an edifice that was a mock Greek temple; the words carved on the white sandstone said, *"Ye Shall Know the Truth and the Truth Shall Make You Free,"* causing me to catch my breath in wonder and bafflement. That first morning I took the elevator to the top,

and looked out on those majestic purple hills to the west, changing to lighter shades of blue or a deeper purple as wisps of autumn clouds drifted around the sun; this, they would tell me, was the Great Balcones Divide, where the South ended and the West began, with its stark, severe landscape so different from any I had known before. I saw the state capitol, only a few blocks to the south, set on its sloping green acres, its pink granite catching the morning light, and away to the east the baseball field dug into the native rock, and the football stadium, the largest and most awesome I had ever seen. Then down again to the campus, where all the furious construction and demolition was going on, and where the swarms of students back for another year greeted each other with such shouts and screams of delight, war-whoops, and hoohaws and wild embracing, and twangy "hello there's" with the "r's" exploited as nowhere else in the South, that I suddenly felt unbearably displaced and alone. Everything around me was brisk, burgeoning, *metropolitan.* It was bigger than Memphis when I was twelve.

I was a desperately homesick Mississippi boy of seventeen, and the life I saw about me was richer and more flamboyant than anything I had known before. There was a kind of liberality of spirit there, an *expansiveness* which, as I was one day to learn, is one of the most distinctive qualities of Texans, even though it can be directed toward things that do not deserve being expansive about. There was something frenetic, almost driven, about the organized pursuits of these Texas students; even by the gregarious standards of my own high school there was not enough loneliness in them, not enough disaffection; they moved about in packs, and they would organize a committee—a service committee, a social committee, a committee on committees—on the merest excuse. Today this characteristic, which reaches far into adult life, seems most curious in a state which in most established quarters glorifies, perhaps more than any other region of America, some mystical individualism, with sources more contemporaneous with Goldwater and Buckley than Rousseau.

Yet I myself shared that compulsion to join, and join I did, everything from the Freshman Council to student government to the ROTC Band. This, I thought, was the mark of success, something one assumed without dispute. Versatility, gregariousness, the social graces, these were the important things, just as they had been in Yazoo; these were what the University of Texas could provide, only bigger and better. Yet as time passed I would grow progressively more lonely, more contemptuous of this organized anarchy, more despairing of the ritualized childishness and grasping narcissism of the fraternity life.

This taste of fraternities had a curious effect. The experience of seeing grown men twisting paper-maché into flowers for a float, or of social lions advising how best to impress the sorority girls, at least gave one some early insight into priorities. And in that day this fraternity was the best one there; the further one got down the scale, the more insufferable were the practices. The new members who had not been initiated were called out at all hours, for "exercise rallies," "walks," or "serenades," the latter custom consisting of group singing at midnight to some sorority; while the idiotic

fraternity songs were sung, the girls on their balconies or porches would giggle or squeal their approval, with proper gradations of intensity depending on how close to the top those doing the serenading came on the social register. Some fraternities beat their new members with paddles and other instruments, or gave elaborate "pig" parties, in which each member was expected to bring the ugliest girl he could manage to get for the evening. Around the campus one got to know of the "perennial" fraternity boys; one in particular was over thirty years old, registered each semester for the minimum of courses and seldom if ever went to class, his purpose being to indulge as freely as possible in all aspects of the Greek Life. He escorted girls twelve years his junior, and gave bright little lectures on how to handle yourself in the best social circumstances. Once he turned on me for some minor trespass and said, "I wonder when you're going to grow up." Another "perennial" came to school each fall semester on what amounted to an athletic scholarship; he ran a service station in San Antonio, and because he was adept at throwing a football, his group paid his tuition so he could play on the intramural touch football team. Then he would drop out of school after the season and just before examinations.

I was unhappy and insecure with the fraternity men. I and another young country boy from a small South Texas town walked the six blocks from Brackenridge Hall for dinner with the brothers each evening, dreading what organized torments they might have in store for us next. Our talk was bitter, but mainly frightened. He had the courage of his fear to get out, but I did not, for it would have implied some failure in me, and I would not admit failure even when I felt it. I simply went less and less and became more unhappy, until late in my junior year when I was beginning to campaign for the editorship of the student newspaper; with cynicism in my heart and the tally of the fraternity and sorority vote in my secret ledger, I sought their support. The difference was that in my first year I would not have had the self-awareness to be cynical, because I did not know that cynicism existed.

Some excellent men were involved in this debilitating preoccupation. Their names were Mohr, Little, Penn, Nagle, Jacoby, Higgins, Eastland, Eckert, Williams, Dahlin, Finch, Bailey, Ogden, Schmucker, Voekel, and a dozen others, most with appropriately vivid and wildly Texan nicknames—they were better by far as individuals than the organization to which they gave allegiance. For the organization itself, within the broader social framework of the fraternity and sorority system on a big state university campus, was pernicious and destructive—too encouraging of petty provincial snobbism, simple human waste, and downright prejudice, too demanding on its immature young people of social appurtenances and the trappings of respectability. At its worst this system could be cruel and despicably smug; at its best it was merely an easy substitute for more intelligent and mature forms of energy.

Early in that year I was taken on my first "walk" by a campus "service organization." It was late on a Saturday night in the fall; the members blindfolded me and put me in their car. We drove for miles, until the concrete gave out, and down some interminable gravel

road until we stopped. They took all my clothes, including my shoes, and tied me to a tree. After I heard the car drive away, I worked the rope loose and started down the road, walking in the middle of it to avoid the beer cans, broken whiskey bottles, and other debris that always clutter the sides of Texas roads. It was the last indignity: homesick, cold, alone, naked, and lost, off on some meaningless adolescent charade.

That afternoon I had escorted to the football game a gat-toothed brunette they had picked out for me, from a "wealthy family in Dallas" the thirty-two-year-old perennial had said, and she had spent the whole time making fun of the way I drawled! Finally, at the top of a lonely hill, I got my bearings. Looking down from the hill I caught sight of Austin in the cold night air: the Tower, lit orange because of the day's football victory, and the state capitol, and the curved boulevards faintly outlined in the pale blue artificial moonlight from the old street lamps. There it all was, miles away, and I was bruised and tired, but that skyline almost struck me over with its strange open beauty, the clear open beauty of the Southwest plains. Then, all of a sudden, I got mad, probably the maddest I had ever been in my whole life—at homesickness, at blond majorettes, at gat-toothed Dallas girls, at fraternities, at twangy accents, at my own helpless condition. *"I'm better than this sorry place,"* I said to myself, several times, and be damned if I didn't believe it. Then I started walking again, having made a kind of toga of a greasy piece of canvas I had found by the side of the road. Two hours later I reached the concrete and flagged down the third car that came past, and got back to my dormitory just as the sun began to appear.

After an appropriate time for this kind of activity, there was a fraternity institution known as "hell week," a four-day ordeal of petty torture and sadism which preceded "initiation" as a full-fledged brother. As victims of this institution, we were made to go sleepless for most of the four days, and were forced to wear burlap under our usual clothes when we went to class during the daytime, causing a most agonizing itch that would have made any lecture intolerable. At night the established brothers amused themselves with a great variety of entertainment. One night we were herded into a large room, and for an hour or more our seniors, who had chosen as usual not to be in libraries or at lectures, poured molasses, castor oil, chicken feed, and sand on us. Then several hundred eggs were brought in, in large cardboard boxes, and from the far side of the room the brothers used us as moving targets. I was chosen as the special object for this diversion; a relentless stream of eggs smashed against me, and I was covered with the oozing yellow yolk, which stuck against the molasses and chicken feed and castor oil in a great soggy mess. Finally the brothers, having sated themselves, began drifting out of the room to watch television. The last to leave was an ex-Marine who chose to spend as much of his leisure time as possible on such scholarly pursuits. He was about to depart on what was colloquially known as a "fuck-date," and hence he was dressed immaculately in a navy-blue suit and bow tie. As we were being herded out of another door, I sighted an unbroken egg on the floor near me. I picked it up, took aim on the

ex-Marine just as he was departing, let the egg fly, dashed through the back door, and heard the words: "*Hot*—damned!" The egg had smashed against the back of his neck, and the yolk had oozed under his shirt. This accomplishment proved to be the noblest of my first semester.

On the last night of "hell week" I was again blindfolded and taken on a drive by three of the senior members. Again we went up a gravel road, and I was led from the car and up a grassy, rolling hill. "Kneel right here," one of them said, in the tones of a Baptist preacher announcing a hymn. "Don't take the blindfold off for three minutes, and then when you see where you are, meditate for a while. Meditate *seriously*. This is your last responsibility as a pledge. Tomorrow you become one of us." I followed his instructions: when I heard the car leave I took off the blindfold. I was in the middle of a cemetery, kneeling on a grave; the gravestone identified the occupant as one of the founding members of the fraternity. "Well, hot shit," I said to myself, and went home to sleep for the first time in four days.

The next day the initiation was a traditional ceremony handed down by the generations. It was full of such garbled mumbo-jumboes and high-flown adolescent sputterings, all thrown together in some uneasy overlay of illiteracy, that I was reminded of the way Huck Finn and Tom Sawyer had negotiated their own private blood-oaths as pirates. It was so juvenile that the Ku Klux Klan, in contrast, might have resembled the American Association of University Professors. But when the new brothers were lined up and presented with fraternity pins, I noticed that several of my fellow novitiates were crying, apparently from the impressiveness of it all. I could not avoid admitting to myself that, even though I was fresh out of a small town in the Mississippi delta, I was either smarter than everyone else in the room or a damned sight less emotionally involved.

It was two things, and the bare suggestion of a third, that made my lonely and superficially gregarious freshman year tolerable, and helped shape my knowledge of that campus.

One was the mad, rudimentary life of the dormitory. Old Brackenridge Hall, a yellow-brick affair with Spanish stucco roofs, stood right at the edge of the long intramural field, only a quarter of a mile from the capitol, and just across a narrow street from a line of dingy shops and greasy cafés. We called it "The Slum Area," not only for its general dinginess but for its violence, both organized and sporadic, which erupted inevitably on the weekend nights after the beer houses across the street closed down. Brackenridge Hall was where life was, stripped of its pretenses, where one saw every day the lonely, the pathetic, the hopeless young men—often poor though sometimes not, often ignorant but not always, but never anything if not various. Here a fairly sensitive boy could not avoid a confrontation with his basic and bare-boned self, and see a big state university in its true dimensions. My first roommate, who flunked out soon enough with five F's and a D-plus, was an alcoholic from Dallas who saw giant roaches in the middle of the night, though the roaches may have been for my benefit. He would throw his slide rule against the wall, or piss in the

trashcan from a range of six feet. As I sat in front of my typewriter composing my pieces for the *Daily Texan,* he and his friends played poker and drank rotgut bourbon on the other side of the table, interrupting themselves occasionally to make fun of my literary output which, when they read it, to their eternal honor, they did not appreciate.

I lived on the fourth floor, with a room overlooking the intramural field and the entire Slum Area, and down on the third floor lived the baseball players. I became a sort of poet laureate of that group, the resident egghead, it may have been, because I at least tried to study my books, and I actually did try to write for the student paper, which they called "The Daily Wipe."

Their floor was unquestionably the filthiest establishment I have ever seen, and from it emanated the most savage and grotesque, though until now unrecorded, happenings at the University of Texas in the 1950s. It was the decade of McCarthy, of Eisenhower and Dulles, the decade of students that David Riesman would characterize for posterity as outer-directed, the silent generation, I think it was called. These were promising labels, but they missed the closer truth, for real life at the University of Texas in the 1950s was like a circle with many rings—the smallest ring in the middle consisting of those students who were conscious of the labels and what they meant, the other inner circles progressively less aware. At the outside of that ring, the farthest out of all, was the third floor of Brackenridge Hall. They came from small ranch towns and middle-sized cities on the plains, and it was their decade right along with Ike's. Old newspapers covered the floors, and two of their number slept on cots in the hall so that one room could be a combination TV room, bar, and pornography library. Every so often they had rummage sales there, and for bargain prices tried to get rid of old water-wings, empty bottles, stale socks, and waterlogged baseballs. Dust and dirt covered the newspapers and the walls. Held most in contempt there were leaders of student government, fraternities, and deans, and they could smell out a stuffed shirt fifty yards away.

They wandered around at night in the pipes under the campus, breaking into office buildings through the sewage system in search of examination papers. Somewhere under there they found the mechanism which controlled the big clock on top of the Tower, and whenever the chimes struck eighteen, twenty, or twenty-four, I knew they were down there again. One afternoon I went up to the top of the Tower with one of them and his girl; when we were on the observation deck he suddenly climbed over the barrier, balanced himself on a rainpipe, looked toward the ground thirty stories below, and shouted: *"Hee-haw: Sani-Flush!"* They would spend hours on cheat notes, for they felt that an elaborate and successful set of cheat notes was a work of art, and in itself a kind of intellectual achievement. These were cunningly indexed with rubber bands for manual maneuvering, so that for a quick look at the Causes of the American Revolution one had only to flick the rubber band to C—and there, sure enough, were all seven causes, and in the right order. On a history identification test, one of them, his cheat notes not working, identified Daniel

Webster as a colored Senator from Arkansas.

Once they caught several cadets from Texas A&M, the rival school out in the boondocks, marauding around the campus at night, and summoned aid from the whole dormitory; they shaved the Aggies' heads, painted them in orange and white enamel, paraded them at close drill around the intramural field, and in an unexpected burst of Christian charity sent them home in time for reveille. For fifty cents they would take anyone to see the cadavers in the Biology Building. They had a public address system which they would occasionally place in the window of the third floor and turn on at full blast. Once I was standing at rigid attention in the ranks of the ROTC on the intramural field while in total silence the troops were being reviewed by a general from San Antonio. Suddenly I heard a booming voice down the field, loud enough to be heard all the way to the capitol building: "Private Morris, Private Willie Morris, Company D, Squad C, take charge of your troops and dismiss them!" At another ROTC drill I noticed them up in the window again, fiddling with the loudspeaker, and I feared the worst, but the voice merely said: "The War is over, boys! General Lee just gave his sword to ol' Grant! Go home to your families and your crops!"

They spied on parked cars behind the baseball field, sneaking right up to the windows and looking inside, then startling the passionate couples by setting off firecrackers under the cars and shouting and circling around like Apache Indians. Some two dozen of them, myself included, hiding in the grass under the bleachers at the baseball field late one night, watched while the starting pitcher for next day's game performed the act of love on a waitress on the pitcher's mound. The only times I saw them attentive, or ruminative, was during "Dragnet," or "The Ed Sullivan Show," or when they were listening to telephone conversations with an elaborate device that tapped the dormitory switchboard. All this was far more representative of the American state university generation in the 1950s than deans would likely have admitted. Nihilism was more articulate than silence, and more colorful than respectability. In the souls of all of us is anarchy, and it can erupt on a whim—especially in the young. That is why college administrators, like politicians, would have us believe they have had a glimpse of the higher truth. They need every defense they can get.

The concept of social change deals not only with how today is different from yesterday, but how tomorrow will differ from today. Evan Stark, a radical community organizer, feels that today's youth culture is no better than that of the 1950s unless it assumes a revolutionary perspective. Youth life style of the 1950s for the most part had little impact on social institutions and did little to change them. Youth culture of the 1970s, in Stark's view, will have as little impact unless it becomes actively involved in social change.

Up from Underground: Notes on Youth Culture

EVAN STARK

Like kids waiting for flu shots, millions of young Americans watched three short-haired guys eat pills for a week, get bored with each other, and finally land on the moon. The astronauts were

This article was prepared especially for this volume.

robots. Man-on-the-moon was a *drag.*

A decade earlier President Kennedy had told Congress, "Vast areas of the unknown have been explored for military, medical, technical, and other reasons." The "do it" generation is growing up for "other reasons."

The moon trip was the final blast of an era during which most young Americans asked what they could do for (not *to*) their country, and accepted conventional morals and politics as *faits accomplis* for which they were obliged to find uses. A few "radicals" tried to stop American "business as usual." But many more used the American Revolution as an excuse for insisting that a liberation, once complete, needn't be repeated. LBJ habitually referred to White House guests as his "fellow revolutionaries." The fact that America was less than perfect was used to justify cruelty, stupidity, and duplicity. The U.S.A. was "free and equal" by definition; only "aliens" could insist otherwise.

CBS claimed air pollution endangered the health of persons lingering at outdoor lunch counters. The White House damned the moral pollution of our schools. Work was increasingly characterized by the absence of human labor; while war, once an emergency to fend off bullies, became the normal business of slaughtering underdogs. So were chronic low-grade crises fed to a generation filled from birth with anxiety about the bomb.

As weapons were stockpiled, white suburbanites talked of a "population explosion" to make themselves forget about the real explosion, which is atomic. Parents told kids to "try and forget it." Hannah Arendt shows that German Jews didn't believe the Nazis meant to exterminate them. "Nobody could be *that* crazy," they thought. The era which began with war casualties cited like stock quotations on TV ended with the reading of domestic casualties from protest demonstrations.

Today, youth and rebel are synonymous. Despite the media's attempts to transform youthful anger and anguish into harmless entertainment, government surveys show that the majority of kids hold radical views. The heir of a respected Shaker Heights family defends disruption, rebellion, and dope as vehemently as the low-income waif en route to Frisco. Even small children packed in station wagons communicate by flashing peace signs. As quickly as "adults" escape to suburbia's human bargain basements, kids return to cities to get into the middle of things.

The massive youth gatherings on campuses and in cities are historically unique. Unlike Caesar's mobs, today's young people debate fine points of academic metaphysics (e.g., "Should we take the Dean or the Armory?"). But they are as ready as the Romans were to fight. The young have discovered the power of their numbers—as has big business—and they mean to make something of it. The question is, what?

The future of youth revolt is unclear because, unlike the workers who believed in electoral reform as a means for extending democracy to industry, the young reject both electoral politics and reform. In addition, their notion of the "good life" directly contradicts the traditional aspirations and habits of most Americans.

While in principle a democracy may repudiate its policies at election time, youth sees that changing elected leaders has little effect on war or economic injustice. The seriousness of many problems, they feel, demands change more rapid and widespread than electoral petition allows.

Certainly youth has immediate problems. Youth unemployment is over 30 percent; budget cuts hurt all students; juveniles have few rights; miseducation remains compulsory; and police treat long-hairs the way the French treated female collaborators. Yet, even where protest has occasionally developed around these issues, its militancy discourages "responsible" reform. As one Berkeley leaflet put it, "The issue is not the issue."

Initially kids disobeyed rules when authority seemed morally wrong. But early civil disobedience is quite different from the present rejection of authority's overall legitimacy. Now the young seek to establish their own legitimacy and the hegemony of their culture. But youth has yet to convince mainline America to abandon its status quo.

The "good life" in America has traditionally meant jobs, stable families, and enough income to own property, keep up with fads, and provide education for one's children. These aspirations presuppose that hard work combined with "know-how" (technology) will eventually meet all needs. A distinct psychology sustains this premise against the facts of poverty and unhappiness. At its root is the democratization of guilt, so that failure appears to result only from personal inadequacy. Ads remind us that we're worried, nervous, and smelly, and then make millions promising that relief of our "bad" feelings is just "minutes away." Where people feel guilty about everything from being late to school to not achieving orgasm, they cannot muster the individual confidence required for bold action. Impulses to deal with reality-as-it-is are repressed by Puritan warnings to "think before you act."

Though remaining a pipe dream for most, the "good life" has provided justification for virtually all reform. Yet youth holds that the "dream" is nightmare. Granted that its rejection is marred by cooptation and subtle forms of repression, and that some schools of authoritarian rebellion rebel against authority with much dogmatic dissidence. No matter. Youth demands that basic needs be met without toil, that the patriarchal family be abandoned as au-

thoritarian, that "junk" production stop, that private property be abolished, and that formal education be either revised or dumped. Youth opposes the entire way of thinking that has served as a vehicle for scientific and technical achievement in the West. The young refuse to weigh experience against fixed values. They want to "do it" and take their chances.

The new social psychology combats guilt inhibitions. Instead of courting popularity by repressing guilt and anger, the kids seek intense emotional relief, reward frankness and spontaneity, criticize conventions openly, "struggle" with hostility, and are unashamed of sloppiness. Moreover, they seek outlet in play, not work. Adults find them rude, egotistical, immoral, dirty, disloyal, unproductive, ungrateful, and tasteless.

The search for self-definition is expressed symbolically in youth music and attitudes toward drugs, sex, work, and politics. The embryonic youth philosophy dichotomizes experiences into those that are *cool, groovy, far out, right on,* or *together,* and those that are a *drag.* Kids are either *somewhere* or *nowhere. Somewhereness* is expressed by signs, like the raised fist, which indicate prior understanding and say "I dig it, man" and "there's no need to elaborate." This need to know the score without having it spelled out reveals that youth culture is, in part, a response to the complexity of modern life.

The future of youth rebellion depends on the revolutionary quality of youth culture and on the validity of its premise that cultural revolution can and must precede political revolution.

Seeking to avoid the deadening choice

between an elitist culture and an idiot culture of popular commerce, kids create a music of their own. Riding to school and work, at lunch, at evening gatherings, in dormitory rooms, and on the streets, teen-agers not only listen to sounds, they use them, controlling the volume to suit their needs. The noises "inside" their heads—police sirens, headlines, TV images, job worries—create "bad vibes" which kids try to counter by turning up their music. The poorer the neighborhood, the more time people have to "listen" to events, the louder the music. As crises intensify, so does cultural amplification. The black kid hears Brahms at Lincoln Center and becomes fidgety. He doesn't lack "appreciation," but violins cannot soothe what he hears inside. Woodstocks become commonplace. Millions face loudspeakers blasting indistinguishable sounds into their heads, deadening human ganglia and paralyzing the apparatus of stimuli in terribly calculated ways.

Even in the communal settings required for its performance, the new music conveys more than its message. It takes its form from modern technology—its overwhelming noise, its dependence on capital, and its effect on the mind and body.

Mechanical reproduction shifts control over music from performers and composers to listeners and promoters. The record is the "original" which "live" artists must mimic, and its acoustics can be freely adjusted to fill ballroom or bedroom. It is "effect," not performance, place of performance, or composition that counts. The willingness of mass audiences to use the medium as vicarious outlet for their worries is decisive.

Rock music is inconceivable without expensive electronic amplification, and thus depends on promotional capital and the technology of recording studios. This capital outlay necessitates the presentation of rock to huge crowds at high prices; makes rock, unlike the jazz or protest music of the 50s, a mass art; and subjects it (and the kids) to commercial manipulation. The multi-million-dollar record and instrument businesses; the rock festivals; the competitive exploitation of rock groups; the star system; and the use of lyrics to promote such salable items as motorcycles—all reveal how simply the kids' feeling of *nowhereness* is seduced when props give the appearance of *somewhereness*. Thus Woodstock, in a parody of People's Park, symbolized the depoliticization of youth struggles by commercializing the need to liberate (not momentarily occupy) urban (not rural) territory permanently (not occasionally), to live (not listen) freely (not "for free"). Anxiety cannot be worked out at such "festivals," too far removed from the sources of anger to serve youth better than TV and sports events serve their parents.

The fascination with Hindu surrender patterns, Japanese Zen exercises, and "blues," the prevalent notion that "freedom is in the mind," and the imitation of disfranchised peoples—all reveal that rock serves pacification as well as liberation. The juxtaposition of slave ideology with illusions of inner freedom demonstrates that outwardly slaves and free men and women are alike. Both seem happy and carefree, reckless and irresponsible. Marx's ideal picture of Communist Man, the "Sambo" stereotype, and the "flower child" are portraits which might easily be confused. By turning sorrow into a spiritual commodity and encouraging communal tension release, rock music not only portrays the world's crimes but helps compensate for them.

Only the visual side of rock remains unchallenged by salesmen of authority. The Beatles and their followers created images of rebellion that delegitimized older voices and, by talking to youth in its own idiom about their feelings, fears, and hopes, set the stage for youth's taking itself seriously and organizing a culture around its own aspirations for community. Through their demands for free music and dope, songs dealing with real life, order maintained by themselves, and a share of profits, youth increasingly forces the culture industry to produce a "fire insurance" like the fire it seeks to put out. So youth makes *Do It* a best-seller, one notch behind *The Making of the President.*

Sexual revolution opposes patriarchal authority and the double standard it maintains. In patriarchal families, through direct coercion and indirect socialization, boys learn to be aggressive, to direct anger at other men and at women and to seek sex without "falling" in love (thereby risking family investments). Girls learn to internalize hostility and then to define the consequent pent-up misery as their "natural emotionality." They must feel deeply, or simulate such feeling, without growing openly angry at confinement. They may cry, but must accept love without compromising their "value" ("selling themselves cheap"), and must say, when asked, "I want to but I can't" (or shouldn't). Meanwhile, boys think "I can't want to, but I must." The ambigu-

ity of the phrase "making her" reveals that force is used to support male supremacy and to ensure that power based on sex rank will cross caste and class lines.

Since not loving (or even liking) your husband has never been sufficient cause to leave him, in America, it is not shocking that kids practice sex without commitment or switch mates like TV channels. Studies showing increases in divorce, venereal disease, and "illegitimate" births tell more about recording methods than about promiscuity. At any rate, statistics say little about the quality of sexual life. The problem is further complicated by those who define "satisfaction" solely in terms of sexual performance.

The competition of ever-increasing numbers of women in marriage markets causes traditional attitudes toward sex-without-love patterns to be drastically modified. The result is severe mother-daughter misunderstanding and hostility, and the development of a "sex education" outside the home which stresses that sex is "only natural."

Youth heroes remain "all man." Tough anti-heroes like James Dean and Marlon Brando resist phoniness in everything but their sexual relations. Here, from Presley through the Beatles, rebels sow wild oats while a harem competes for their attention. The man roams wild. The female is his property, his steady girl and later his "housewife." He can explode, but her problems are only solved "when we get married." Rock women are "dolls," "queens," and "babes" praised for physical attributes and cajoled into hugging, squeezing, kissing, dancing, loving, and coming back. Rock stars are followed by "groupies" who collect sexual experiences instead of autographs. The cease-fire in the battle of the sexes helps boys enlist girls in the fight to replace Dad as head of the tribe.

Massive heterosexual gatherings where kids dance, fight, listen, and just be allow them to submerge competitive sex roles in collective play. Here boys and girls make love or punch, sit quietly or "freak out," drink or smoke dope, dress up or undress, without negative sanction. The emotional pluralism of these endeavors, their deliberate lack of direction, partially responds to the inhuman precision of market plans and quotas. But the "love" of the "love-in" is too abstract to enhance autonomy or to sustain feelings of intimacy. Such collectives only momentarily offset workaday loneliness. Anger is not repressed, but it is diffused. The result is "beatitude," a feeling that nothing counts and that everything is the same.

The intimacy of automobile back seats in the '50s, after spreading to dormitory bedrooms and urban flats, has matured in the early '70s in formal encounter groups and self-criticism sessions of youth collectives. These originate in intellectual seduction scenes—two persons of opposite sex try to communicate "everything" "honestly," to expose and "work out" insecurities. Boys pressured to "get something" must "break her down" when she says "No." The resulting "dialogues" have been formalized and expanded into "encounters" which replace rather than culminate in coitus. At today's "encounters," people pay to come together simply to stop being lonely by telling others how they feel and by acting out in concert what relations in a genuine community might be like.

Colleges now hold "encounter classes."

The success of such encounter groups is limited by the social origin of many problems that cannot be resolved outside the political arena. Talk cannot make a boring job interesting and, when attempts to deal interpersonally with public malaise fail, participants often become cynical about contacts of any sort. Since the most sensitive coed cannot meet the therapeutic burdens of handling political problems personally, sex is often resorted to as reflex despair. Encounters break down "defenses"; but the return of exposed persons to workaday life without the group is frustrating, even dangerous. Encounters intensify emotional contact but provide no mechanism for its resolution.

Youth collectives form in response to youth unemployment and attitudes toward "straight" work and living. Where normal pairing is absent, a harem situation emerges. Women sit around the house, care for children, cook, clean, do arts and crafts, roll dope, and provide sex on demand. There is little "group sex," and homosexuality is usually absent, if not scorned. All in all, the hip commune is what it calls itself, a "family" extending patriarchy in a community of equals.

Americans prefer "gossip" (treating sexual facts as titillating) to a "philosophy of sex." Kids trying to integrate sex with other aspects of their lives have yet to cure the pathology of the American family. Sex is more available to the kids, but love seems no more accessible.

Marijuana is the major social connection in youth culture, the peace pipe ritually passed on all occasions. It is the democratizing agent of the youth culture and symbolizes the fact that "drug culture" tries to minimize dependence on the status quo while infinitely extending the range of bodily sensation. The eccentricities of drugs and the varied experiences of users constitute the folklore of the youth underground. Novices learn to roll and smoke pot, to cut hash, to cope with psychedelic surprise and "bad trips," and to survive on a diet of amphetamine. Drugs unite kids across race, class, and sex lines in the experience and vocabulary of the high. Kids from poor families smoke pot as equals before the law with the rich. Unlike good brandy, good dope is shared, not hoarded. The universality of the drug culture highlights the historically unique potential of an opposition politics which is generational in scope.

But, by making the mundane exciting, drugs help make it acceptable. Precisely because they offer "freedom" amidst scarcity, drugs discourage workaday politics. To paraphrase, "pot can be the opium of the people," making social inequality seem inconsequential compared with the common high. As millions of mothers take amphetamines to "wake up" and fathers drink to "forget," so too millions of kids who greatly need a loving community smoke pot to believe they already live in one. They end by identifying with the most superficial aspects of youth culture, those created by the commercial media, and by playing the role of the drop-out while remaining, more than ever, tied to a lonely status quo. Drug culture gives life to the philosophy of *somewhereness,* but somewhere may be anywhere, in a community or at home, in front of the TV.

Set within youth culture, however, drugs have profound significance. Rock music generally deadens sensitivity to both "problems" and commercial propaganda. Drugs re-sensitize specific feelings, awakening repressed energies and imaginings, and act as a kind of mental massage or filter helping users dig the sounds, ideas, and experiences of youth culture while shutting out the rest. To the observer, users seem to "escape" reality and to experience only "what the world might be like if . . ." But for kids who are high, the trip is "real," a coming back as well as a going away, an end as well as a means. Drugs force a confrontation between "reality as it is" and the "far-out" reality the user experiences. While social pressure and obsolete forms of authority motivate rebellion, and music provides its "background," drugs connect kids in deeply committed ways to the new culture and, by so doing, make the utopian politics of youth culture emotionally intelligible.

Sensing that community is available, the kids set out to make it accessible. The drop-out utopianism of youth culture begins in the cultural underground, the perpetual home of "good" community against its materialist counterpart. Here, in the subterranean world of the hobo, the bohemian, the street prophet, and the political fanatic, men hold their ground against barbarization or, like the beats and the hippies, take to "the road" to extend human experience. The underground is the exception that proves the materialist rule. Against its vision, glittering models of success are displayed.

The underground mimics the poor in dress, language, and life style. The hippie leaves his class of origin (though he lives off it) and refuses to identify with any group. The radical identifies with any group "on the move," and so is viewed as a "traitor" by his own class. Alone, both embrace a "freedom is in the mind" ethos, the philosophy of impatient slaves. Youth subculture is nothing new.

What *is* new is the adaptation of the underground vision by a generation revolting against American lifeways. American conscience surfaces and, as youth culture, seeks not only purity but popularity. The kids seek to shatter the double-bind of the damned—they want to sin and be free. The success of the "do it" ethic depends on its expression in the communal culture of youth revolt. Yet, this culture compromises the vision in fundamental ways.

If youth revolt is to remain a way of living rather than a life style, an alternative set of means and ends rather than an exciting means to the increasingly dangerous ends of American materialism, kids must face their music. They have made clear what they want to become. Youth culture reveals where they're at. The mind plays funny tricks and can be convinced it is where it wants to be, that there is no need to change, to open, to act out or do it. The kids' communal vision began in their minds. It would be sad if, despite long hair and beards, pot, sex, rock, and "love," that is where it stays.

ETHNIC
LIFE STYLES

*"An ethnic group consists of those who conceive of themselves as being
alike by virtue of their common ancestry, real or fictitious, and who are
so regarded by others."* Thus the American upper class, as discussed
by MacNamara in Part 3 of this book, is an ethnic group, as are Jews,
Italians, Negroes, and Indians. The only way to gain membership in an
ethnic group is to be born into it. It does not matter how devout a convert
one is, or how well one has mastered the group's life style, full membership
in an ethnic group can occur only through the process of ascription. By
definition, then, an ethnic life style is genetically influenced—a life style
to which one is predisposed at birth and which is perpetuated by intra-
marriage. Thus sanctions for failing to engage in the ethnic life style cannot
be meted to converts or non-ethnics; but sanctions may be conferred upon
an ethnic who does not choose to engage in the ethnic life style.*

*There is thus a dilemma: Is the accepted American life style symbolized
by being a member of one of the many groups that make up the ethnic
mix in America and maintaining an ethnic life style? Or is the accepted
American style that of conforming to the middle-majority life style? We
can distinguish between cultural pluralism (the process of preserving
separate ethnic life styles) or Anglo-conformity (the process by which ethnic*

*Tomatsu Shibutani and Kian M. Kwan, *Ethnic Stratification* (New York: Macmillan, 1965).

groups disappear by conforming to the white Anglo-Saxon standard). *
    *Herbert Gans describes the process of perpetuating ethnicity in a mid-
dle-class suburb. Half-hearted commitment to Jewish identity became for
some of his respondents a life style. Mothers who wanted their children
indoctrinated in some Jewish traditions also wanted middle-majority life
style. As a consequence, balancing their ambivalence became an almost
full-time role.*

* See Milton Gordon, *Assimilation in American Life* (New York: Oxford Univ. Press, 1964),
pp. 88–114.

Park Forest: Birth of a Jewish Community

HERBERT J. GANS

In November 1949, the author of this article completed a study of the Jews of Park Forest, Illinois. The study had one especially intriguing aspect: under its very eyes—in the midst of answering questionnaires, as it were—Park Forest's Jews gave birth to a young, awkward, but unmistakable Jewish community. It was an entirely natural birth, and the witnessing of it was an illuminating introduction to some of the whys and wherefores of Jewish life and of present-day Judaism in America.

Obviously, Park Forest is not Flatbush or Scarsdale or Detroit—so undoubtedly there are limitations in what it has to teach us. On the other hand, when we think of the present composi-

From *Commentary,* 2 (April, 1951), pp. 16–30. Reprinted by permission; copyright © by the Society for the Psychological Study of Social Issues.

tion of American Jewry—which is by and large second generation, mostly business and professional in occupation, and overwhelmingly middle class—perhaps Park Forest is not so atypical after all. What we can see happening there may be chiefly different from what is occurring in other locales only in being more visible and accessible to the student. Park Forest may thus turn out to be a by-no-means unrepresentative Jewish neighborhood in today's rapidly changing American scene. Here, in any case, is what happened, and how.

Park Forest is a garden-apartment housing project located thirty miles south of Chicago. The project, privately developed, was started in 1947, when the Chicago housing shortage was at its height. The first tenants moved in on August 30, 1948, and for two years they continued to come in as new sections of the village were completed. By November 1949, there were 2,000 families—nearly 8,000 people—renting garden apartments at $75 to $100 per month. One hundred and forty-one of these families were Jewish. Of these, about thirty had not been in the village long enough to have relations with the other Jewish families; another fifteen were "mixed marriages," with both husband and wife having rejected any identification as Jews; and the remainder, approximately one hundred families (including a few mixed marriages), 5 percent of the project, formed a fledgling "Jewish community."

In Park Forest the accent is on youth; the project naturally attracted the people most sorely pressed for housing: veterans with children. The men average thirty to thirty-five years of age, the women somewhat less (anyone over forty is generally considered old). Most of the men are at the beginning of their careers, in professional, sales, administrative, and other business fields. (Only four of the men interviewed owned their own businesses.) Although not long removed from the GI Bill of Rights, they were in 1949 already earning from $4,000 to $10,000 a year—most of them perhaps around $5,000. Few of the men, and few of the wives even, are without some college experience, and educationally the Jews as a whole stand even higher than the rest of the Park Forest community. Ninety percent of the Jewish men interviewed have college training, 60 percent hold degrees, and no less than 36 percent have graduate degrees.

The Jews of Park Forest dress as do the other Park Foresters, enjoy similar leisure-time activities, read the same newspapers, look at the same movies, hear the same radio programs—in short they participate with other Park Foresters in American middle-class culture. They observe few traditional Jewish religious practices; the village's isolation from synagogues and kosher food shops has probably discouraged observant Jews from becoming tenants, and brought problems to those few who did.

Not only do Park Forest Jews live like other Park Foresters, they live with them. Whereas most American cities have "neighborhoods" dominated by one ethnic group or another—in atmosphere and institutions if not in numbers—this is not true of Park Forest. Most Park Foresters live in what are called "courts"—*culs de sac* surrounded in circular fashion by twenty to forty two-story garden apartments. Each "apartment" is actually a house, built together with five or seven others into a single unit. Privacy is at a minimum, and each court is almost an independent social unit. Many of the Park Foresters find all their friends in their own court—but this is not the case with the Jews. The Jewish families are scattered all over the village, and only rarely are two Jewish families to be found in adjacent apartments. Yet in just one year, a Jewish community consisting of informal groups of friends, a B'nai B'rith lodge, a National Council of Jewish Women's chapter, a Sunday school, and even a Board of Jewish Education had emerged.

How did this happen?

From the very beginning it seemed to be important to Jewish Park Foresters to "recognize" whether or not any of their neighbors were Jewish. And the widespread labeling, in America and Europe, of certain Mediterranean-Armenoid facial features as "Jewish," plus the monopolization of certain surnames by Jews, has resulted in a stereotypical formula of recognition, used by Jews and non-Jews, which is accurate more often than not.

One early resident related: "I saw Mrs. F. in the court a couple of times. . . .

I thought she looked Jewish. With me, there's no mistaking it. Then someone told me her name, and I went up to talk to her. Finally we talked about something Jewish, and that was it."

"Jewish mannerisms" were also used to establish, or at least guess at, the other person's Jewishness. "The woman across the street, her actions were typical New York, so we recognized them as Jewish immediately. . . ." People very skillfully explored each other through conversations, attempting to discover whether the other person was Jewish or not, and offering clues to their own Jewishness. "She's been told I'm Jewish, and I know she's Jewish, we haven't discussed it, but she uses Jewish expressions she wouldn't use in front of other people." Others turned the conversation to favorite foods: "It was a slow process, we told them what kind of food we like, corned beef, lox. . . ." Sometimes there are no symbols or formulas which can be applied, and people find out by accident: "I asked before Passover if they wanted macaroons, and we found out."

Many Jewish Park Foresters had known each other previously, had mutual friends or acquaintances elsewhere, or bore introductions from mutual friends to "go look up so-and-so when you get to Park Forest." The people with such previous contacts, however loose these may have been, quickly established friendships and often became "charter members" of social circles which then attracted strangers. In this respect, the Jews differ sharply from other Park Foresters, most of whom knew no one and had no "introduction" to anyone when they arrived in the village. (Even in cities as large as New York and Chicago, a surprisingly large number of Jews know or know of each other, because there are relatively few groups which they join, few temples which they can belong to, and few neighborhoods in which they choose to live.)

Barely had this informal network of friendships and acquaintances sprung up among the first Jews moving into Park Forest (it did not, of course, preclude friendships with non-Jewish neighbors—though these, as we shall see later, were rather different in quality from the friendships with Jews), when two formal Jewish organizations were set up—a chapter of the B'nai B'rith and a chapter of the National Council of Jewish Women. Both enrolled only about forty members—those who, for various motives and reasons, were "organization-minded," and those, especially women, who had no Jewish neighbors and wanted to meet Jews from other parts of the village.

Both almost immediately found a purpose: "doing something" about the Jewish children of the growing Park Forest community. And through them steps were soon taken to establish the single most important Jewish institution in Park Forest: the Sunday school.

By June 1949, less than a year after the first resident moved in, the chapters of the B'nai B'rith and National Council of Jewish Women were already fairly well established. Eighty-six Jewish families were now living in the rapidly growing project. Passover had come and gone; the handful of Jewish people who observed it in the traditional way had banded together to order *matzos* and all the trimmings from Chicago. The men who had organized the B'nai B'rith lodge and now formed its ruling clique had begun to talk of a congregation. Some of them were "Jewish professionals," men who make their careers within the American Jewish community; others were men who had been active in big-city Jewish affairs and whose social life had been oriented around a congregation and its activities. But it was generally agreed that Park Forest's prime problem was a Sunday school for the forty-odd eligible children then in the village, and for the others who were to come.

The B'nai B'rith leadership met one evening and sketched out the organization of a Sunday school as part of a congregation—Reform or Conservative, it was not yet clear—to be established in the village. At a meeting with a delegation of women from the Council, however, the latter refused to help organize a congregation, insisting that what Park Forest needed was a Sunday school now, and a congregation later, perhaps. One man said of the women: "They don't care for Jewish values, but they recognize that they are Jewish and they need a Sunday school because the kids ask for it. . . . They want a nonsectarian school." The women, on the other hand, accused the men of trying to take over the community for their own political ambitions, of wanting a "Jewish Community Incorporated."

Eventually a steering committee of four men and four women was formed to proceed with the organization of a Sunday school. While the administrative organization and the budget were being prepared, largely by the men, the school's curriculum was left to a young

Chicago rabbi who had become interested in Park Forest. Quite unexpectedly to some, he supported the women in their rejection of a congregation, and formulated instead a Sunday school that would involve the parents in their children's Jewish education: "As we train the children," he told the parents, "you will have to train yourselves. . . . You'll have to move toward a community center and a synagogue eventually. . . ." The parents' major contribution would be to prevent such inconsistencies as would be apt to arise from not practicing at home the content of the Sunday school curriculum.

At a meeting of parents there was a sharp reaction to the rabbi's plans. A large number of those present objected to the curriculum proposed; they wanted a "secular" Sunday school, one which would teach the child *about* Jewish traditions, but which would not put pressure on the parents to *observe* these traditions in the home. For the reasons that they did not want a congregation, they did not want a school that would involve them either. The committee resigned and a new committee was formed.

But exactly what type of "Jewish content" should be brought into the school, and how? The new committee did not have sufficient Jewish background to set up any kind of Jewish curriculum, secular or otherwise, and called for aid from a Jewish professional family that lived in Park Forest, the husband a group worker and his wife a trained Sunday school principal. The group worker was finally successful in devising a formula that reconciled the two sides, and the basis of the reconciliation is revealing: "The children will not be taught that parents have to light candles; the children will be informed of the background of candles. . . . We're teaching the child not that he must do these things, we just teach him the customs. . . . Why, we even teach them the customs of the Negro Jews . . . and that the customs have been observed for many years, and are being modified."

In "Yankee City's" Jewish community,[1] the conflict over the synagogue was between generations, the foreign-born and the first-generation American. In Park Forest, where almost everyone is native-born, the conflict over the Sunday school was of a different nature: it was between those who wanted what may be called an *adult-oriented* community and those who wanted a *child-oriented* one.

The adult-oriented community is the traditional (but not necessarily Orthodox) one whose activities are focused around its congregation of adults, and in which the role of the children is to become Jewish adults and assume an adult role. The men who wanted a congregation, with its Sunday school, were thinking of such an adult Jewish community, training its children for eventual membership in the organized Jewish group. In a child-oriented community, the community's energy is focused almost exclusively around the children, around their problems and needs as Jewish children—but, of course, as the adults see these needs. Thus, the women wanted a school for the children and,

[1] W. Lloyd Warner and Leo Srole, *The Social Systems of American Ethnic Groups* (Yale University Press, 1945).

as became clear, not one that would involve the adults in Jewish community life.

The focus of Park Forest's problem—and conflicts—lies in the family. The Sunday school, much as other Jewish institutions, is recognizably an ethnic rather than a religious institution—more correctly, an American reaction to an ethnic situation—which transmits ethnic behavior and identity; the Jewish home, however, is run by American middle-class behavior patterns. The women feared that the contradictions between the traditional Jewish home, whose features are now incorporated in the Sunday school curriculum, and the American home, which embodies their primary present-day values, would lead to family tensions. So, although they wanted their children to learn about traditional Jewish life, they did not want it brought home.

The situation in Park Forest, then, is that many parents reject involvement in the cultural-religious aspects of the Jewish tradition for themselves as adults, while they demand that their children involve themselves to the extent of learning about this tradition, without, however, getting so involved as to wish to practice it. The fruit of this might well be a Judaism that ends rather than begins with Bar Mitzvah.

Why, however, did the parents want the children to go to Sunday school at all?

First, and quite important, was the fact that the children, in contrast to the parents of Park Forest, having found their friends within the court without concern for ethnic origin, would see their non-Jewish friends leave for school on Sunday mornings. As one mother explained: "Our kids want to get dressed up and go to church too. The Sunday school [the Jewish one] will give them something to do." A few children were actually sent to the Protestant Sunday school a couple of times, but the overwhelming majority of the parents found this intolerable, so the pressure from the children was translated into parental demand for a Jewish Sunday school.

Second, and this is perhaps the more important reason, the parents wanted to send their children to Sunday school because they wanted to make them aware of their ethnic identity, to acquaint them with Jewishness through Jewish history and customs. (Quite frequently, this explanation was complemented by the qualification, ". . . so that later he can choose what he wants to be." The notion that the Jewish child would have a choice between being Jewish or not Jewish, a decision he would make in adolescence or early adulthood, was voiced even by parents who admitted their own continuing confusion as to how to act, and as to the identity they had and wanted to have.)

But why become aware of ethnic identity and of "Jewish customs"? Because parents want their Jewish identity explained to their children, often as a *defense* against hardships they might run into because they are Jews. Representative of this rather widespread sentiment was the comment: "A Jewish child, he's something different, he's never one of the boys in a Gentile group, even if he's the best guy, he's one of the outsiders, the first to get abused, and if he doesn't know why, it's going to be a shock. It's part of his training, the Sunday school, he needs it."

A number of parents of six-and seven-year-olds were particularly clear in their hopeful expectation that Sunday school would supply the children with answers about their identity. It seems to be at that age that questions first develop in the children's play groups as to what they are, in terms of religion or nationality. Sometimes the children are stimulated by a remark made in school or kindergarten, sometimes by something overheard in parents' conversation. One child may thus discover that he is Protestant, and that there are also Catholics and Jews. He brings this information to the group, which then tries to apply these newly discovered categories to its members. Soon the children come home and ask their parents what they are, and are they Jewish, and perhaps even "Papa, why do I have to be Jewish?" Here the Sunday school is asked to come to the rescue. One father reported of his son now in Sunday school: "He can probably tell me more than I can tell him."

It is not only the Sunday school that is child-oriented. The entire community shows itself child-oriented: during the first fourteen months of existence, the largest part of its organized adult activities was for the children. B'nai B'rith nearly collapsed because its leadership was drawn off into the task of establishing the Sunday school; and after the school had been set up, the lodge immediately went to work on a Chanukah party which it hoped to make an annual event. Even among those who wished to found a congregation, a goodly portion explained they wanted it exclusively for the sake of the children: "I don't believe in praying . . . in God . . . I want it for my son and daughter. I want them to know what it's like. I have had the background . . . I remember I enjoyed it at the time."

The Jewish holidays have become perhaps the chief mechanism of teaching and reinforcing Jewish identity. All the "happy" holidays—Pesach, Purim, Sukkoth, and Chanukah, especially the last—are emphasized and made into children's festivals. At Chanukah time 1948, when the Park Forest Jewish community consisted of less than twenty families, the problem of Chanukah versus Christmas first presented itself to Jewish parents. A year later, the problem loomed so large in everyone's mind that people discussed it wherever they gathered. The women's Council devoted its November meeting to "Techniques of Chanukah Celebration," that is, techniques of competing with Christmas.

By late November, the non-Jewish friends of the Jewish children are eagerly awaiting Christmas and Santa Claus. Naturally, the Jewish children are inclined to join in these expectations, and ask their parents for Christmas trees. In 1948 and 1949, the parents acted quickly. One mother explained: "The F.'s had a big menorah in their window, that was very fine, maybe I'll do the same next year. . . . I could put my little menorah up there, I could wire it, is that O.K., we could have different color lights—no, that's too much like Christmas." Another parent said: "My child wanted a Christmas tree and we talked her out of it. . . . I make a fuss about Chanukah to combat Christmas, I build up Chanu-

kah and she appreciates it just as much."

Other parents told how they decorated the menorah, and even the entire house, and used electric candles instead of wax ones. They tried hard to emphasize and advertise Chanukah to the child, and at the same time to exclude the Christmas tree and its related symbols from his environment. Parents were very bitter about the Jewish families who displayed Christmas trees. "In our house we do certain things, and in other Jewish houses they don't, and the children ask questions. . . . It's very confusing. . . ."

In the process of making a children's holiday in December (or sometimes in November) just as good as the Christian one, the parents' adult participation in the holiday is forgotten, and Chanukah, more than any other holiday, becomes completely child-oriented. In this, ironically, the fate of Chanukah closely resembles that of the American Christmas, which has tended to be transformed from a solemn religious festival to a day of delights for children.

Meanwhile, the adults were not nearly so lavish in providing for their own needs as Jews.

Park Forest has a number of families, either Reform or mildly Conservative, whose social life before moving to Park Forest took place largely in or near the congregation of their choice. Some of these people did not hesitate long before joining a wealthy congregation in Chicago Heights—especially those whose own income and social position were more or less equal to that of the Heights community. In addition there are a number of families, probably less than ten, who have maintained enough of the traditional system of religious attitudes and ritual practices to be called Orthodox or Conservative. They favor the establishment of a congregation, preferably Orthodox or Conservative, in the village.

But for the remainder, the large majority of the Jews, religious institutions and practices play no role. Of forty-odd families interviewed, more than half reported that they observed no customs or holidays, and had not attended synagogues or temples "for years." Ten reported attending High Holiday services only; seven attended on High Holidays, some other holidays, and a few Friday evenings during the year.

For the majority of Park Foresters, the problems of traditional observance (such as the kosher home) or of attending religious services simply do not exist. They spend Friday nights as others do in Park Forest, entertaining, or going out occasionally when Saturday is not a workday for the man of the house, or staying at home if it is. Saturdays are reserved for work around the house, shopping, visiting, and taking care of the little things suburbanites have no time for during the week.

There are, however, two religious patterns which are still being observed, not universally but by many. First, as has been indicated, there are those holidays and traditions that concern the children. Second are those aspects of death and birth that relate the Jew to his parents. Several of the men remarked matter-of-factly that they were not interested in religious observances, but added just as matter-of-factly, "except of course *Yortzeit*" (anniversary of the death of a parent). Another said: "The only thing we did—at my son's birth we had a rabbi at the circumcision, mostly for my wife's

parents, they would have felt bad." (Circumcision is probably all but universal. As for Bar Mitzvah, as yet there are almost no children as old as thirteen.)

Some people celebrate the Jewish holidays by spending them with parents or in-laws, not as religious holidays but as family get-togethers. One woman explained, jokingly: "I believe Rosh Hashanah should be two days, Passover too, for practical purposes. One day we go to his family, the other to mine."

There have been some attempts to establish the beginnings of a religious institutional system in Park Forest. In January 1949, when the Jewish population did not exceed twenty-five families, the group already had a rabbi-substitute, a gregarious "Jewish professional" who roamed through the Jewish community and from his Conservative background ministered to occasional religious needs. "Someone needed Hebrew writing on a tombstone, they were told to call me, someone else wanted *Yizkor* [prayer for the dead] or *Yortzeit* services, they called me. . . ."

Before Rosh Hashanah 1949, two men, one an early comer, the other just arrived, tried independently to set up a *minyan* (minimal group of ten) for the High Holidays. Since communication between Jewish tenants in the older courts and the newer ones had not yet been established, these men never knew of each other's attempts. Both were unsuccessful. Various groups have talked sporadically about setting up a regular congregation.[2] Most interesting in this demand for a congregation is the reason given by many supporters: "They'll have

[2] In November 1950, after the completion of this study, a congregation was finally organized.

more respect for us, to show that we have arrived, that we're not merely a bunch of individuals."

The "they" referred, of course, to the non-Jewish neighbors. This congregation movement was thus born not entirely of a religious impulse, but of one which attempted to demonstrate the solidarity and respectability of the Jewish community to the rest of Park Forest. Significantly enough, the area of Park Forest in which this congregation movement sprang up was populated by a large number of small-towners and Southerners who from the first indicated that they did not think favorably of Jews.

Uninterested as Park Foresters may be in "the Jewish heritage," they are nevertheless very much Jews. Clearly and unmistakably, that is, they remain, both matter-of-factly and by conscious design, members of identifiably Jewish groups. This Jewish group may be another Jewish couple with whom they spend much of their time; it may be a regular and more or less stable group which gathers, in full or in part, almost every weekend and on special occasions. These groups make up the informal Jewish community, the "spontaneous" community that did not require professionals and organizers to be created.

For the most part, this informal community exists at night. In the daytime, when only housewives and the children inhabit Park Forest, the Jewish housewife participates in the general court social life. She interrupts her household duties to chat with a neighbor, while "visiting" over a morning cup of coffee or while watching the children in the afternoon. In most cases, there is no distinction here between the Jewish and

the non-Jewish housewife; they belong together to the bridge and sewing clubs that have been established in many courts. There are a few courts in which religious or ethnic cliques of women have formed, and where "visiting" is restricted to such groups. In most courts, however, there are few ethnic distinctions in daytime social life. This applies even more to the men when they participate with other men in court life on weekends (and occasional evenings) through athletic teams and poker clubs. As one of the women observed: "The boys are real friendly. I imagine they don't think about it [ethnic distinctions], but the women have different feelings. Women have little to do; they talk about it in the afternoons."

At night, however, in the social relations among "couples," the Jewish husband and wife turn to other Jews for friendship and recreational partnership. As one person summarized it: "My real close friends, my after-dark friends, are mostly Jewish; my daytime friends are Gentile." Of thirty Jewish residents who listed the names of Park Foresters they see regularly, ten named only Jews; ten named mostly Jews, and one or two non-Jews; ten named a majority of non-Jews or only non-Jews. And many of the people who named both Jews and non-Jews pointed out, like the person quoted above, that their most intimate friends were Jewish.

There are, of course, all types of friendship circles in this informal Jewish community. One of the largest groups is made up predominantly of older, well-to-do Park Foresters, many of them previously active in big-city Jewish congregations and groups. Most of these men are employed by business or industry, or in the non-academic professions (medicine, dentistry, law, engineering). A second group consists largely of young academic intellectuals (research scientists, teachers, writers) and their wives. A third is made up of people who have only recently emerged from lower-middle-class Jewish neighborhoods, and are just exploring, with occasional distaste, the life of the middle- or upper-middle-class American Jew. And there are many others.

It is easy to explain the tendency to find friends in one's own group, even when this takes one from one's own front door, as it does in Park Forest. As the Park Foresters say, "It's easier being with Jews"—it is psychologically more accommodating, and there is less strain in achieving an informal, relaxed relationship with other Jews: "You can give vent to your feelings. If you talk to a Christian and say you don't believe in this, you are doing it as a Jew; with Jewish friends you can tell them point-blank what you feel."

The in-group attitude, and the anti-out-group feeling that often goes with it, are expressed most frequently at the informal parties and gatherings where the intimate atmosphere and the absence of non-Jews create a suitable environment. Often these feelings are verbalized through the Jewish joke—which generally expresses aspects of the Jew's attitude toward himself, his group, and the out-group—or through remarks about the *goyim*. At parties that are predominantly Jewish, it is of course necessary to find out if everyone is Jewish before such attitudes can become overt.

One man, who had been converted to Judaism in his twenties, when he was married to a Jewish girl, became disturbed, at an informal party, over a discussion of how to inculcate Judaism into the children "and to keep them away from the *goyim*," and felt it time to announce that he had been until a number of years ago a member of a Christian denomination. The declaration broke up the party, and upset many people. After that he felt: "From now on, they'll be on their guard with me, they've lost their liberty of expression, they don't express themselves without restriction now. At a party, if anybody says something, everybody looks to see if I've been offended and people are taken into a corner and told about me." This man has adopted the Jewish religion, is bringing up his children as Jews, and has been more active than the average person in Jewish community life. Yet he is no longer a member of the Jewish in-group, although he remains a member both of the Jewish community and his smaller Jewish group. In his presence, the group sheds the informality and intimacy of the in-group, and is "on guard."

There are many Jewish Park Foresters who reject these in-group attitudes as "chauvinistic," and when asked about their friends, are quick to reply that they do not distinguish between Jews and non-Jews in choosing friends. Yet as one said: "The funny thing is, most of our friends are Jewish, even though we say we don't care." And to quote another: "I think we should try to have friends that aren't Jewish. I don't like the fact that all my friends are Jewish."

But these Jewish Park Foresters, too, feel that they differ from the majority of the non-Jewish Park Foresters—and not only because their friends are Jews. The focus of these feelings of difference was summarized by one person: "I have a friend who is not Jewish who told me how fortunate I was in being born Jewish. Otherwise I might be one of the sixteen to eighteen out of twenty Gentiles without a social conscience and liberal tendencies; he is cruel and apathetic. . . . Being Jewish, most of the Jews, nine out of ten, are sympathetic with other problems, they sympathize, have more culture and a better education; strictly from the social and cultural standpoint a man is lucky to be born a Jew."

These feelings have a basis in Park Forest reality. The Jews are distinguished by a feeling of "social consciousness," by concern over political and social problems, by a tendency toward a humanistic agnosticism, and by an interest in more "highbrow" leisure activities: foreign films, classical music, the fine arts, and in general the liberal intellectual-aesthetic leisure culture of America, and perhaps the Western world. There seem to be proportionately more Jews than non-Jews in Park Forest who participate in this culture. Jews who seek other people with whom they can share these attitudes and interests tend to find other Jews. This culture—which includes an important proportion of Park Forest's Jews—itself is largely devoid of Jewish content, and the Jews who come together in it would seem to do so not primarily because they are Jews but because they share a culture. When Jewish problems are discussed by these people (and they are discussed), they are seen from a generalized world view, rather than from an in-group perspective.

Just as Jews form a large proportion of those interested in "culture," they form a large proportion of those interested in the self-government of Park Forest, and in other local activities. Although in November 1949 the Jews made up only 9 percent of Park Forest's population, eleven of thirty-seven candidates in the first two village elections were Jewish. All but one member of the first Board of Education, and half of the original six-man Board of Trustees that runs the village, are Jewish. The community newspaper was started by a group of women many of whom are Jewish, the American Veterans Committee and the local affiliate of the Democratic party were organized with the help of a number of Jewish men.

If for a moment we take a broader view and consider non-Jewish Park Forest, we discover that the Jewish community is only one of three quite similar organized ethnic-religious groups. Both the large Catholic group (close to 25 percent of the village population is Catholic) and the smaller Lutheran one also consist of a religious body, men's and women's social organizations, and a more or less extensive informal community. The two Christian groups, unlike the Jewish one, are organized primarily for adult activities, but also emphasize the Sunday school. Both communities developed much more quickly than the Jewish one—largely because there was much less internal disagreement as to what to do and how to proceed—and both were in 1949 already engaged in building programs. The Catholic and Lutheran groups are primarily religious bodies (although they are in part ethnic groups), and have fewer members who reject the group culture. Those who do reject it can quite easily "resign" and become part of the large amorphous body of Americans not strongly identified by religious or ethnic group, something that is much more difficult for the Jew.

In its first year, the Jewish community was very sensitive to the problem of anti-Semitism. Just as every newly arrived tenant would try to recognize other Jews, he would also try to discover the attitudes of non-Jewish neighbors toward Jews. This led quickly to the sprouting of a grapevine which transmitted actual cases, suspicions, and imagined occurrences of anti-Semitism throughout the Jewish community, and sometimes dominated conversation among Jews. A number of people complained strongly that there was a great deal too much talk about anti-Semitism.

Actually, there has probably been very little anti-Semitism in Park Forest. In the interviewing, which covered thirty-five of the fifty-five courts occupied by November 1949, only seven people from seven different courts mentioned incidents they considered to be anti-Semitic. For the most part, these were the cases of exclusion, Jewish women (and sometimes children) being left out of some formal and informal activities of the Christian members of the court. There are a number of courts where Jewish and non-Jewish women have split off into separate cliques. It would perhaps be surprising to expect these rather traditional forms of segregation to be absent, especially since Park Forest harbors so many people from different parts of the country, including small-town people from regions generally not friendly to Jews. And one must always ask how much this segregation results from the tendency, described above, of Jews to seek each other out as friends. And it seems certainly true that if anti-Semitism played any role in the formation of the community, it was the fear and expectation of anti-Semitism rather than actual experience of anti-Semitism in Park Forest, on the part of either children or parents.

On the other hand, there are many "liberals" in Park Forest, so that friendly and unquestioned social mixing of Jews and non-Jews is perhaps more common here than elsewhere. This spirit is perhaps typified by an incident that occurred early in the life of the village. A door-to-door salesman asked a non-Jewish resident to point out the Jews in the court because he did not want to sell to Jews. The next day the company was requested not to send any more salesmen to the village.

Park Forest is a new and growing community; it has changed since this study was made, and will continue to change in the future as its present tenants are replaced by others or decide to stay and settle down. Nevertheless, the Jewish community has already become oriented around a number of elements which are not likely to change.

Whereas their parents were not only socially "clannish" but culturally different from their non-Jewish neighbors, the adult Jews of Park Forest are "clannish" but culturally not very different. (Or, rather, their cultural distinctiveness, when it exists, is not along Jewish lines.) Their adjustment to American society and their present status can be described as one of cultural assimilation and continued social distinctiveness. Thus, the Jews of Park Forest remain an ethnic group, albeit different from the parental one.

It is this feeling of Jewish togetherness, to sum up, which provides the impetus for child-orientation, for the parents' insistence on a Sunday school, their transformation and use of the Chanukah holiday, and the unending attempt to indoctrinate the child with a sense of Jewishness.

It is noteworthy that whereas in most cultures the transmission of the group's *esprit de corps* is carried out unconsciously through the children's imitation of, and partial participation in, adult activities, in Park Forest this transmission has become conscious, has become indoctrination—without the parents accepting for themselves the things they are passing on. This no doubt affects the very process of transmission, the thing transmitted, as well as the way the child receives it. Nevertheless, the transmission does take place. Child-orientation is the mechanism that would seem to guarantee the existence of the ethnic group for another generation, even when the adult carriers of the group's culture are ambivalent about it, or have rejected it. So long as Judaism is the curriculum for teaching and transmitting Jewishness, the traditional behavior patterns will be studied, discussed, and taught. However, the high cultural assimilation of the group makes improbable the incorporation of traditional Jewish elements into the rules of daily life.

A major force in the development of the Park Forest Jewish community has been the "Jewish professional," who so far has been the spearhead, "the catalyt-

ic agent," as one called himself, in the process of community formation. It was Jewish professionals who helped bring the Jews together, ministered to their early religious needs, started the men's social organization, tried to organize a congregation, helped in forming the Sunday school, resolved the crisis that resulted, and have since supervised Jewish education in the village.

The Jewish professional is a new man on the Jewish scene. He is not a rabbi, but a leader of adults, a youth worker, a teacher, a fund-raiser, a social worker, a contact man, a community relations director, etc. The Jewish professional may not have special training in how to start a Jewish community, but he is expert at being Jewish, something other Park Forest Jews are not. Sometimes this expert Jewishness is a part of his background, and his reason for becoming a professional; sometimes it is the result of a desire to work in the Jewish community, among Jews rather than non-Jews. Sometimes the expert's Jewishness may be only a career, and the professional's activities in these organizations are for him a means of advancing in his career. Whatever his motives, however, the Jewish professional, rather than the rabbi, would seem to have taken over the initiatory role and the largest part of the work of creating the formal Jewish community. In the informal community, his influence is much smaller.

A final factor for an understanding of the Park Forest Jewish community is the sexual division of social labor that takes place within it. The Jewish informal community is based on the Jewish woman. It is she who generally inaugurates and stimulates acquaintances and friendships, who founds the social circles and sets their pattern and content. She has in addition the opportunity of establishing all-female groups which reinforce the groups of couples. Most of the men seem to lay less emphasis on ethnic association, and although there are some all-Jewish male groups, male activities are more likely to take place in groups which more or less ignore ethnic distinctions. Perhaps that is why the B'nai B'rith lodge has been less successful than the women's group in uniting its membership into an active and developing organization. The larger concern of the women with Jewish education, and their more intense interest in the Sunday school, obviously arise from the fact that the women generally have the major role in bringing up the child. In general, the women live a greater part of their life within the Jewish group, and are more concerned with it and about it than the men. In Park Forest, and presumably in communities like it, they seem to be the most influential element in determining the nature of "Jewish" activities. At a somewhat later stage these activities may be handed over to the men.

As to how representative the events and processes that took place in this one Jewish community are, the writer would not be able to hazard a guess, and certainly his study, being of a single community and not comparative, would throw little light on this question. But his impression is that it is very unlikely that they are unique to Park Forest. Perhaps in other American Jewish communities these developments are masked by the fact that the group is not so distinctively limited to young married couples with one or two children as it is in Park Forest. In all of them, however, it would seem reasonable to suppose that developments such as have been described must play an increasingly important role in the future Jewish community life in America. Certainly it would not be claiming too much to suggest that the Park Forest Jewish community offers much illustrative and prophetic material as to the next major stage in the process of Jewish adjustment to American society: the stage in which it is the relations between the second and third generations, both American-born, not the relations between a foreign-born first and a native-born second generation, that are the crucial ones.

Ethnic culture affects many aspects of an individual's life—the food he eats, his friendship patterns, his aspirations. The following article by Mark Zborowski demonstrates the far-ranging impact of ethnic culture—it even extends to the way people react to the physiological process of pain. Zborowski studied Italian Americans, Jewish Americans, and old Americans, noting how they reacted to pain in public and in private, both in the hospital and in the family setting. The three ethnic groups studied attached different meanings to pain, and thus experienced the physiological process differently.

Cultural Components in Responses to Pain

MARK ZBOROWSKI

Some Basic Distinctions

In human societies, biological processes vital for man's survival acquire social and cultural significance. Intake of food, sexual intercourse, or elimination—physiological phenomena which are universal for the entire living world—become institutions regulated by cultural and social norms, thus fulfilling not only biological functions but social and cultural ones as well. Metabolic and endocrinal changes in the human organism may provoke hunger and sexual desire, but culture and society dictate to man the kind of food he may eat, the social setting for eating, or the adequate partner for mating.

Moreover, the role of cultural and social patterns in human physiological activities is so great that they may in specific situations act against the direct biological needs of the individual, even to the point of endangering his survival. Only a human being may prefer starvation to the breaking of a religious dietary law or may abstain from sexual intercourse because of specific incest regulations. Voluntary fasting and celibacy exist only where food and sex fulfill more than strictly physiological functions.

Thus, the understanding of the significance and role of social and cultural patterns in human physiology is necessary to clarify those aspects of human experience which remain puzzling if studied only within the physiological frame of reference.

Pain is basically a physiological phenomenon and as such has been studied by physiologists and neurologists such as Harold Wolff, James Hardy, Helen Goodell, C. S. Lewis, W. K. Livingston, and others. By using the most ingenious methods of investigation they have succeeded in clarifying complex problems of the physiology of pain. Many aspects of perception and reaction to pain were studied in experimental situations involving most careful preparation and complicated equipment. These investigators have come to the conclusion that "from the physiological point of view pain qualifies as a sensation of importance to the self-preservation of the individual."[2] The biological function of pain is to provoke special reactive patterns directed toward avoidance of the noxious stimulus which presents a threat to the individual. In this respect the function of pain is basically the same for man as for the rest of the animal world.

However, the physiology of pain and the understanding of the biological function of pain do not explain other aspects of what Wolff, Hardy, and Goodell call the *pain experience*, which

From *Journal of Social Issues,* **8** (1951), pp. 16–30. Reprinted by permission; copyright © by the Society for the Psychological Study of Social Issues. This paper is based upon material collected as part of the study "Cultural Components in Attitudes toward Pain," under a grant of the U.S. Public Health Service.

[2]James D. Hardy, Harold G. Wolff, and Helen Goodell, *Pain Sensations and Reactions* (Baltimore: Williams and Wilkins, 1952), p. 23.

includes not only the pain sensation and certain automatic reactive responses but also certain "associated feeling states."[3] It would not explain, for example, the acceptance of intense pain in torture which is part of the initiation rites of many primitive societies, nor will it explain the strong emotional reactions of certain individuals to the slight sting of the hypodermic needle.

In human society, pain, like so many other physiological phenomena, acquires specific social and cultural significance, and accordingly, certain reactions to pain can be understood in the light of this significance. As Drs. Hardy, Wolff, and Goodell state in their recent book, ". . . the culture in which a man finds himself becomes the conditioning influence in the formation of the individual reaction patterns to pain. . . . A knowledge of group attitudes toward pain is extremely important to an understanding of the individual reaction."[4]

In analyzing pain it is useful to distinguish between self-inflicted, other-inflicted, and spontaneous pain. Self-inflicted pain is defined as deliberately self-inflicted. It is experienced as a result of injuries performed voluntarily upon oneself, e.g., self-mutilation. Usually these injuries have a culturally defined purpose, such as achieving a special status in the society. It can be observed not only in primitive cultures but also in contemporary societies on a higher level of civilization. In Germany, for instance, members of certain student or military organizations would cut their faces with a razor in order to acquire scars which would identify them as

members of a distinctive social group. By other-inflicted pain is meant pain inflicted upon the individual in the process of culturally accepted and expected activities (regardless of whether approved or disapproved), such as sports, fights, war, etc. To this category belongs also pain inflicted by the physician in the process of medical treatment. Spontaneous pain usually denotes the pain sensation which results from disease or injury. This term also covers pains of psychogenic nature.

Members of different cultures may assume differing attitudes towards these various types of pain. Two of these attitudes may be described as pain expectancy and pain acceptance. Pain expectancy is anticipation of pain as being unavoidable in a given situation, for instance, in childbirth, in sports activities, or in battle. Pain acceptance is characterized by a willingness to experience pain. This attitude is manifested mostly as an inevitable component of culturally accepted experiences, for instance, as part of initiation rites or part of medical treatment. The following example will help to clarify the differences between pain expectancy and pain acceptance: Labor pain is expected as part of childbirth, but while in one culture, such as in the United States, it is not accepted and therefore various means are used to alleviate it, in some other cultures, for instance in Poland, it is not only expected but also accepted, and consequently nothing or little is done to relieve it. Similarly, cultures which emphasize military achievements expect and accept battle wounds, while cultures which emphasize pacifistic values may expect them but will not accept them.

[3]*Ibid.*, p. 204.
[4]*Ibid.*, p. 262.

In the process of investigating cultural attitudes toward pain, it is also important to distinguish between pain apprehension and pain anxiety. Pain apprehension reflects the tendency to avoid the pain sensation as such, regardless of whether the pain is spontaneous or inflected, whether it is accepted or not. Pain anxiety, on the other hand, is a state of anxiety provoked by the pain experience, focused upon various aspects of the causes of pain, the meaning of pain, or its significance for the welfare of the individual.

Moreover, members of various cultures may react differently in terms of their manifest behavior toward various pain experiences, and this behavior is often dictated by the culture, which provides specific norms according to the age, sex, and social position of the individual.

The fact that other elements as well as cultural factors are involved in the response to a spontaneous pain should be taken into consideration. These other factors are the pathological aspect of pain, the specific physiological characteristics of the pain experience, such as the intensity, the duration, and the quality of the pain sensation, and, finally, the personality of the individual. Nevertheless, it was felt that in the process of a careful investigation it would be possible to detect the role of the cultural components in the pain experience.

THE RESEARCH SETTING

In setting up the research we were interested not only in the purely theoretical aspects of the findings in terms of possible contribution to the understanding of the pain experience in general; we also had in mind the practical goal of a contribution to the field of medicine. In the relationship between the doctor and his patient the respective attitudes toward pain may play a crucial role, especially when the doctor feels that the patient exaggerates his pain while the patient feels that the doctor minimizes his suffering. The same may be true, for instance, in a hospital, where the members of the medical and nursing staff may have attitudes toward pain different from those held by the patient, or when they expect a certain pattern of behavior according to their cultural background while the patient may manifest a behavior pattern which is acceptable in his culture. These differences may play an important part in the evaluation of the individual pain experience, in dealing with pain at home and in the hospital, in administration of analgesics, etc. Moreover, we expected that this study of pain would offer opportunities to gain insight into related attitudes toward health, disease, medication, hospitalization, medicine in general, etc.

With these aims in mind, the project was set up at the Kingsbridge Veterans Hospital, Bronx, New York,[5] where four ethno-cultural groups were selected for an intensive study. These groups included patients of Jewish, Italian, Irish, and "Old American" stock. Three groups—Jews, Italians, and Irish—were

[5] I should like to take the opportunity to express my appreciation to Dr. Harold G. Wolff, Professor of Neurology, Cornell University Medical College; Dr. Hiland Flowers, Chief of Neuropsychiatric Service; Dr. Robert Morrow, Chief of Clinical Psychology Section; Dr. Louis Berlin, Chief of Neurology Section; and the management of the hospital for their cooperation in the setting up of the research at the Kingsbridge Veterans Hospital.

selected because they were described by medical people as manifesting striking differences in their reaction to pain. Italians and Jews were described as tending to "exaggerate" their pain, while the Irish were often depicted as stoical individuals who are able to take a great deal of pain. The fourth group, the "Old Americans," were chosen because the values and attitudes of this group dominate in the country and are held by many members of the medical profession and by many descendants of the immigrants who, in the process of Americanization, tend to adopt American patterns of behavior. The members of this group can be defined as white, native-born individuals, usually Protestant, whose grandparents, at least, were born in the United States and who do not identify themselves with any foreign group, either nationally, socially, or culturally.

The Kingsbridge Veterans Hospital was chosen because its population represents roughly the ethnic composition of New York City, thus offering access to a fair sample of the four selected groups, and also because various age groups were represented among the hospitalized veterans of World War I, World War II, and the Korean War. In one major respect this hospital was not adequate, namely, in not offering the opportunity to investigate sex differences in attitude toward pain. This aspect of research will be carried out in a hospital with a large female population.

In setting up this project we were mainly interested in discovering certain regularities in reactions and attitudes toward pain characteristic of the four groups. Therefore, the study has a qualitative character, and the efforts of the

researchers were not directed toward a collection of material suitable for quantitative analysis. The main techniques used in the collection of the material were interviews with patients of the selected groups, observation of their behavior when in pain, and discussion of the individual cases with doctors, nurses, and other people directly or indirectly involved in the pain experience of the individual. In addition to the interviews with patients, "healthy" members of the respective groups were interviewed on their attitudes toward pain, because in terms of the original hypothesis those attitudes and reactions which are displayed by the patients of the given cultural groups are held by all members of the group regardless of whether or not they are in pain, although in pain these attitudes may come more sharply into focus. In certain cases the researchers have interviewed a member of the patient's immediate family in order to check the report of the patient on his pain experience and in order to find out what are the attitudes and reactions of the family toward the patient's experience.

These interviews, based on a series of open-ended questions, were focused upon the past and present pain experiences of the interviewee. However, many other areas were considered important for the understanding of this experience. For instance, it was felt that complaints of pain may play an important role in manipulating relationships in the family and the larger social environment. It was also felt that in order to understand the specific reactive patterns in controlling pain, it is important to know certain aspects of child-rearing in the culture, relationships between parents and children, the role of infliction of pain in punishment, the attitudes of various members of the family toward specific expected, accepted pain experiences, and so on. The interviews were recorded on wire and transcribed verbatim for an ultimate detailed analysis. The interviews usually lasted for approximately two hours, the time being limited by the condition of the interviewee and by the amount and quality of his answers. When it was considered necessary, an interview was repeated. In most of the cases the study of the interviewee was followed by informal conversations and by observation of his behavior in the hospital.

The information gathered from the interviews was discussed with members of the medical staff, especially in the areas related to the medical aspects of the problem, in order to get their evaluation of the pain experience of the patient. Information as to the personality of the patient was checked against results of psychological testing by members of the psychological staff of the hospital when these were available.

The discussion of the material presented in this paper is based on interviews with 103 respondents, including 87 hospital patients in pain and 16 healthy subjects. According to their ethnocultural background the respondents are distributed as follows: "Old Americans," 26; Italians, 24; Jews, 31; Irish, 11; and others, 11.[6] In addition, there were

[6]Italian respondents are mainly of South Italian origin; the Jewish respondents, with one exception, are all of East European origin. Whenever the Jews are mentioned they are spoken of in terms of the culture they represent and not in terms of their religion.

the collateral interviews and conversations noted above with the family members, doctors, nurses, and other members of the hospital staff.

With regard to the pathological causes of pain, the majority of the interviewees fall into the group of patients suffering from neurological diseases, mainly herniated discs and spinal lesions. The focusing upon a group of patients suffering from a similar pathology offered the opportunity to investigate reactions and attitudes toward spontaneous pain which is symptomatic of one group of diseases. Nevertheless, a number of patients suffering from other diseases were also interviewed.

This paper is based upon the material collected during the first stage of study. The generalizations are to a great extent tentative formulations on a descriptive level. There has been no attempt as yet to integrate the results with the value system and the cultural pattern of the group, though here and there there will be indications to the effect that they are part of the culture pattern. The discussions will be limited to main regularities within three groups, namely, the Italians, the Jews, and the "Old Americans." Factors related to variations within each group will be discussed after the main prevailing patterns have been presented.

PAIN AMONG PATIENTS OF JEWISH AND ITALIAN ORIGIN

As already mentioned, the Jews and Italians were selected mainly because interviews with medical experts suggested that they display similar reactions to pain. The investigation of this similarity provided the opportunity to check a rather popular assumption that similar reactions reflect similar attitudes. The differences between the Italian and Jewish culture are great enough to suggest that if the attitudes are related to cultural pattern they will also be different, despite the apparent similarity in manifest behavior.

Members of both groups were described as being very emotional in their responses to pain. They were described as tending to exaggerate their pain experience and being very sensitive to pain. Some of the doctors stated that in their opinion Jews and Italians have a lower threshold of pain than members of other ethnic groups, especially members of the so-called Nordic group. This statement seems to indicate a certain confusion as to the concept of the threshold of pain. According to people who have studied the problem of the threshold of pain, for instance Harold Wolff and his associates, the threshold of pain is more or less the same for all human beings regardless of nationality, sex, or age.

In the course of the investigation, the general impressions of doctors were confirmed to a great extent by the interview material and by the observation of the patients' behavior. However, even a superficial study of the interviews has revealed that though reactions to pain appear to be similar, the underlying attitudes toward pain are different in the two groups. While the Italian patients seemed to be mainly concerned with the immediacy of the pain experience and were disturbed by the actual pain sensation which they experienced in a given situation, the concern of patients of Jewish origin was focused mainly upon the symptomatic meaning of pain and

upon the significance of pain in relation to their health, welfare, and, eventually, for the welfare of the families. The Italian patient expressed in his behavior and in his complaints the discomfort caused by pain as such, and he manifested his emotions with regard to the effects of this pain experience upon his immediate situation in terms of occupation, economic situation, and so on; the Jewish patient expressed primarily his worries and anxieties as to the extent to which the pain indicated a threat to his health. In this connection it is worth mentioning that one of the Jewish words to describe strong pain is *yessurim,* a word which is also used to describe worries and anxieties.

Attitudes of Italian and Jewish patients toward pain-relieving drugs can serve as an indication of their attitude toward pain. When in pain the Italian calls for pain relief and is mainly concerned with the analgesic effects of the drugs which are administered to him. Once the pain is relieved the Italian patient easily forgets his sufferings and manifests a happy and joyful disposition. The Jewish patient, however, often is reluctant to accept the drug, and he explains this reluctance in terms of concern about the effects of the drug upon his health in general. He is apprehensive about the habit-forming aspects of the analgesic. Moreover, he feels that the drug relieves his pain only temporarily and does not cure him of the disease which may cause the pain. Nurses and doctors have reported cases in which patients would hide the pill which was given to them to relieve their pain and would prefer to suffer. These reports were confirmed in the interviews with the patients. It was also observed that many Jewish patients, after being relieved from pain, often continued to display the same depressed and worried behavior, because they felt that though the pain was currently absent it might recur as long as the disease was not cured completely. From these observations it appears that when one deals with a Jewish and an Italian patient in pain, in the first case it is more important to relieve the anxieties with regard to the sources of pain, while in the second it is more important to relieve the actual pain.

Another indication as to the significance of pain for Jewish and Italian patients is their respective attitudes toward the doctor. The Italian patient seems to display a most confident attitude toward the doctor, which is usually reinforced after the doctor has succeeded in relieving pain; whereas the Jewish patient manifests a skeptical attitude, feeling that the fact that the doctor has relieved his pain by some drug does not mean at all that he is skillful enough to take care of the basic illness. Consequently, even when the pain is relieved, he tends to check the diagnosis and the treatment of one doctor against the opinions of other specialists in the field. Summarizing the difference between the Italian and Jewish attitudes, one can say that the Italian attitude is characterized by a present-oriented apprehension with regard to the actual sensation of pain, and the Jew tends to manifest a future-oriented anxiety as to the symptomatic and general meaning of the pain experience.

It has been stated that the Italians and Jews tend to manifest similar behavior in terms of their reactions to pain. As both cultures allow for free expression of feelings and emotions by words, sounds, and gestures, both the Italians and Jews feel free to talk about their pain, complain about it and manifest their sufferings by groaning, moaning, crying, etc. They are not ashamed of this expression. They admit willingly that when they are in pain they do complain a great deal, call for help, and expect sympathy and assistance from other members of their immediate social environment, especially from members of their family. When in pain they are reluctant to be alone and prefer the presence and attention of other people. This behavior, which is expected, accepted, and approved by the Italian and Jewish cultures, often conflicts with the patterns of behavior expected from a patient by American or Americanized medical people. Thus they tend to describe the behavior of the Italian and Jewish patient as exaggerated and over-emotional. The material suggests that they do tend to minimize the actual pain experiences of the Italian and Jewish patient, regardless of whether they have the objective criteria for evaluating the actual amount of pain which the patient experiences. It seems that the uninhibited display of reaction to pain as manifested by the Jewish and Italian patient provokes distrust in American culture instead of provoking sympathy.

Despite the close similarity between the manifest reactions among Jews and Italians, there seem to be differences in emphasis, especially with regard to what the patient achieves by these reactions and as to the specific manifestations of these reactions in the various social settings. For instance, they differ in their behavior at home and in the hospital. The Italian husband, who is aware of his role as an adult male, tends to avoid verbal complaining at home, leaving this type of behavior to the women. In the hospital, where he is less concerned with his role as a male, he tends to be more verbal and more emotional. The Jewish patient, on the contrary, seems to be more calm in the hospital than at home. Traditionally the Jewish male does not emphasize his masculinity through such traits as stoicism, and he does not equate verbal complaints with weakness. Moreover, the Jewish culture allows the patient to be demanding and complaining. Therefore, he tends more to use his pain in order to control interpersonal relationships within the family. Though similar use of pain to manipulate the relationships between members of the family may be present also in some other cultures, it seems that in the Jewish culture this is not disapproved, while in others it is.

In the hospital one can also distinguish variations in the reactive patterns among Jews and Italians. Upon his admission to the hospital and in the presence of the doctor the Jewish patient tends to complain, ask for help, be emotional even to the point of crying. However, as soon as he feels that adequate care is given to him he becomes more restrained. This suggests that the display of pain reaction serves less as an indication of the amount of pain experienced than as a means to create an atmosphere and setting in which the pathological causes of pain will be best taken care of. The Italian patient, on the other hand, seems to be less concerned with setting up a favorable situation for treatment. He takes for granted that adequate care will be given to him, and in the presence of the doctor he

seems to be somewhat calmer than the Jewish patient. The mere presence of the doctor reassures the Italian patient, while the skepticism of the Jewish patient limits the reassuring role of the physician.

To summarize the description of the reactive patterns of the Jewish and Italian patients, the material suggests that on a semi-conscious level the Jewish patient tends to provoke worry and concern in his social environment as to the state of his health and the symptomatic character of his pain, while the Italian tends to provoke sympathy toward his suffering. In one case the function of the pain reaction will be the mobilization of the efforts of the family and the doctors toward a complete cure, while in the second case the function of the reaction will be focused upon the mobilization of effort toward relieving the pain sensation.

On the basis of the discussion of the Jewish and Italian material, two generalizations can be made:

1. Similar reactions to pain manifested by members of different ethno-cultural groups do not necessarily reflect similar attitudes to pain.

2. Reactive patterns similar in terms of their manifestations may have different functions and serve different purposes in various cultures.

Pain Among Patients of "Old American" Origin

There is little emphasis on emotional complaining about pain among "Old American" patients. Their complaints about pain can best be described as reporting on pain. In describing his pain, the "Old American" patient tries to find the most appropriate ways of defining the quality of pain, its localization, duration, etc. When examined by the doctor he gives the impression of trying to assume the detached role of an unemotional observer who gives the most efficient description of his state for a correct diagnosis and treatment. The interviewees repeatedly state that there is no point in complaining and groaning and moaning, etc., because "it won't help anybody." However, they readily admit that when pain is unbearable they may react strongly, even to the point of crying, but they tend to do it when they are alone. Withdrawal from society seems to be a frequent reaction to strong pain.

There seem to be different patterns in reacting to pain depending on the situation. One pattern, manifested in the presence of members of the family, friends, etc., consists of attempts to minimize pain, to avoid complaining and provoking pity; when pain becomes too strong there is a tendency to withdraw and express freely such reactions as groaning, moaning, etc. A different pattern is manifested in the presence of people who, on account of their profession, should know the character of the pain experience because they are expected to make the appropriate diagnosis, advise the proper cure, and give the adequate help. The tendency to avoid deviation from certain expected patterns of behavior plays an important role in the reaction to pain. This is also controlled by the desire to seek approval on the part of the social environment, especially in the hospital, where the "Old American" patient tries to avoid being

a "nuisance" on the ward. He seems to be, more than any other patient, aware of an ideal pattern of behavior which is identified as "American," and he tends to conform to it. This was characteristically expressed by a patient who answered the question how he reacts to pain by saying, "I react like a good American."

An important element in controlling the pain reaction is the wish of the patient to cooperate with those who are expected to take care of him. The situation is often viewed as a team composed of the patient, the doctor, the nurse, the attendant, etc., and in this team everybody has a function and is supposed to do his share in order to achieve the most successful result. Emotionality is seen as a purposeless and hindering factor in a situation which calls for knowledge, skill, training, and efficiency. It is important to note that this behavior is also expected by American or Americanized members of the medical or nursing staff, and the patients who do not fall into this pattern are viewed as deviants, hypochondriacs, and neurotics.

As in the case of the Jewish patients, the American attitude toward pain can be best defined as a future-oriented anxiety. The "Old American" patient is also concerned with the symptomatic significance of pain, which is correlated with a pronounced health-consciousness. It seems that the "Old American" is conscious of various threats to his health which are present in his environment and therefore feels vulnerable and is prone to interpret his pain sensation as a warning signal indicating that something is wrong with his health and therefore must be reported to the physician. With some exceptions, pain is considered bad and unnecessary and therefore must be immediately taken care of. In those situations were pain is expected and accepted, such as in the process of medical treatment or as a result of sports activities, there is less concern with the pain sensation. In, general, however, there is a feeling that suffering pain is unnecessary when there are means of relieving it.

Though the attitudes of the Jewish and "Old American" patients can be defined as pain anxiety, they differ greatly. The future-oriented anxiety of the Jewish interviewee is characterized by pessimism or, at best, by skepticism, while the "Old American" patient is rather optimistic in his future-orientation. This attitude is fostered by the mechanistic approach to the body and its functions and by the confidence in the skill of the expert which are so frequent in the American culture. The body is often viewed as a machine which has to be well taken care of, be periodically checked for disfunctioning, and eventually, when out of order, be taken to an expert who will "fix" the defect. In the case of pain the expert is the medical man who has the "know-how" because of his training and experience and therefore is entitled to full confidence. An important element in the optimistic outlook is faith in the progress of science. Patients with intractable pain often stated that though at the present moment the doctors do not have the "drug" they will eventually discover it, and they give the examples of sulpha, penicillin, etc.

The anxieties of a pain-experiencing "Old American" patient are greatly relieved when he feels that something is being done about it in terms of specific activities involved in the treatment. It seems that his security and confidence increase in direct proportion to the number of tests, x-rays, examinations, injections, etc., that are given to him. Accordingly, "Old American" patients seem to have a positive attitude toward hospitalization, because the hospital is the adequate institution which is equipped for the necessary treatment. While a Jewish and an Italian patient seem to be disturbed by the impersonal character of the hospital and by the necessity of being treated there instead of at home, the "Old American" patient, on the contrary, prefers the hospital treatment to the home treatment, and neither he nor his family seems to be disturbed by hospitalization.

To summarize the attitude of the "Old American" toward pain, he is disturbed by the symptomatic aspect of pain and is concerned with its incapacitating aspects, but he tends to view the future in rather optimistic colors, having confidence in the science and skill of the professional people who treat his condition.

SOME SOURCES OF INTRA-GROUP VARIATION

In the description of the reactive patterns and attitudes toward pain among patients of Jewish and "Old American" origin, certain regularities have been observed for each particular group regardless of individual differences and variations. This does not mean that each individual in each group manifests the same reactions and attitudes. Individual variations are often due to specific aspects of pain experience, to the character of the disease which causes the pain, or to elements in the personality of the patient. However, there are also other factors that are instrumental in provoking these differences and which can still be traced back to the cultural backgrounds of the individual patients. Such variables as the degree of Americanization of the patient, his socio-economic background, education, and religiosity may play an important role in shaping individual variations in the reactive patterns. For instance, it was found that the patterns described are manifested most consistently among immigrants, while their descendants tend to differ in terms of adopting American forms of behavior and American attitudes toward the role of the medical expert, medical institutions, and equipment in controlling pain.

It is safe to say that the further the individual from the immigrant generation, the more American is his behavior. This is less true for the attitudes toward pain, which seem to persist to a great extent even among members of the third generation and even though the reactive patterns are radically changed. A Jewish or Italian patient born in this country of American-born parents tends to *behave* like an "Old American," but often expresses *attitudes* similar to those which are expressed by the Jewish or Italian people. They try to appear unemotional and efficient in situations where the immigrant would be excited and disturbed. However, in the process of the interview, if a patient is of Jewish origin he is likely to express attitudes of anxiety as to the meaning of his pain, and if he is an Italian he is likely to be rather unconcerned about the significance of his pain for his future.

The occupational factor plays an important role when pain affects a specific area of the body. For instance, manual workers with herniated discs are more disturbed by their pain than are professional or business people with a similar disease, because of the immediate significance of this particular pain for their respective abilities to earn a living. It was also observed that headaches cause more concern among intellectuals than among manual workers.

The educational background of the patient also plays an important role in his attitude with regard to the symptomatic meaning of a pain sensation. The more educated patients are more health-conscious and more aware of pain as a possible symptom of a dangerous disease. However, this factor plays a less important role than might be expected. The less educated "Old American" or Jewish patient is still more health-conscious than the more educated Italian. On the other hand, the less educated Jew is as much worried about the significance of pain as the more educated one. The education of the patient seems to be an important factor in fostering specific reactive patterns. The more educated patient, who may have more anxiety with regard to illness, may be more reserved in specific reactions to pain than an unsophisticated individual, who feels free to express his feelings and emotions.

THE TRANSMISSION OF CULTURAL ATTITUDES TOWARD PAIN

In interpreting the differences which may be attributed to different socio-economic and educational backgrounds, there is enough evidence to conclude that these differences appear mainly on the manifest and behavioral level, whereas attitudinal patterns toward pain tend to be more uniform and to be common to most of the members of the group regardless of their specific backgrounds.

These attitudes toward pain and the expected reactive patterns are acquired by the individual members of the society from earliest childhood, along with other cultural attitudes and values which are learned from the parents, parent-substitutes, siblings, peer groups, etc. Each culture offers to its members an ideal pattern of attitudes and reactions, which may differ for various subcultures in a given society, and each individual is expected to conform to this ideal pattern. Here, the role of the family seems to be of primary importance. Directly and indirectly the family environment affects the individual's ultimate response to pain. In each culture the parents teach the child how to react to pain, and by approval or disapproval they promote specific forms of behavior. This conclusion is amply supported by the interviews. Thus, the Jewish and Italian respondents are unanimous in relating how their parents, especially mothers, manifested overprotective and overconcerned attitudes toward the child's health, participation in sports, games, fights, etc. In these families the child is constantly reminded of the advisability of avoiding colds, injuries, fights and other threatening situations. Crying in complaint is responded to by the parents with sympathy, concern, and help. By their overprotective and worried attitude they foster complaining and tears. The child learns to pay attention to each painful experience and to look for help and sympathy which are readily given to him.

In Jewish families, where not only a slight sensation of pain but also each deviation from the child's normal behavior is looked upon as a sign of illness, the child is prone to acquire anxieties with regard to the meaning and significance of these manifestations. The Italian parents do not seem to be concerned with the symptomatic meaning of the child's pains and aches, but instead there is a great deal of verbal expression of emotions and feelings of sympathy toward the "poor child" who happens to be in discomfort because of illness or because of an injury in play. In these families a child is praised when he avoids physical injuries and is scolded when he does not pay enough attention to bad weather or drafts, or when he takes part in rough games and fights. The injury and pain are often interpreted to the child as punishment for the wrong behavior, and physical punishment is the usual consequence of misbehavior.

In the "Old American" family the parental attitude is quite different. The child is told not to "run to mother with every little thing." He is told to take pain "like a man," not to be a "sissy," not to cry. The child's participation in physical sports and games is not only approved but is also strongly stimulated. Moreover, the child is taught to expect to be hurt in sports and games and is taught to fight back if he happens to be attacked by other boys. However, it seems that the American parents are conscious of the threats to the child's health, and they teach the child to take immediate care of any injury. When hurt, the right thing to do is not to cry and get emotional but to avoid unnecessary pain and prevent unpleasant consequences by applying the proper first aid medicine and by calling a doctor.

Often attitudes and behavior fostered in a family conflict with those patterns which are accepted by the larger social environment. This is especially true in the case of children of immigrants. The Italian or Jewish immigrant parents promote patterns which they consider correct, while the peer groups in the street and in the school criticize this behavior and foster a different one. In consequence, the child may acquire the attitudes which are part of his home-life but may also adopt behavior patterns which conform to those of his friends.

The direct promotion of certain behavior described as part of the child-rearing explains only in part the influence of the general family environment and the specific role of the parents in shaping responses to pain. They are also formed indirectly by observing the behavior of other members of the family and by imitating their responses to pain. Moreover, attitudes toward pain are also influenced by various aspects of parent-child relationship in a culture. The material suggests that differences in attitudes toward pain in Jewish, Italian, and "Old American" families are closely related to the role and image of the father in the respective cultures in terms of his authority and masculinity. Often the father and mother assume different roles in promoting specific patterns of behavior and specific attitudes. For example, it seems that in the "Old American" family it is chiefly the mother who stimulates the child's ability to resist pain, thus emphasizing his masculinity. In the Italian family it seems that the mother is the one who inspires the child's emotionality, while in the Jewish family both parents express attitudes of worry

and concern which are transmitted to the children.

Specific deviations from expected reactive and attitudinal patterns can often be understood in terms of a particular structure of the family. This became especially clear from the interviews of two Italian patients and one Jewish patient. All three subjects revealed reactions and attitudes diametrically opposite to those which the investigator would expect on the basis of his experience. In the process of the interview, however, it appeared that one of the Italian patients was adopted into an Italian family, found out about his adoption at the age of fourteen, created a phantasy of being of Anglo-Saxon origin because of his physical appearance, and accordingly began to eradicate everything "Italian" in his personality and behavior. For instance, he denied knowledge of the Italian language despite the fact that he always spoke Italian in the family, and even learned to abstain from smiling, because he felt that being happy and joyful is an indication of Italian origin. The other Italian patient lost his family at a very early age because of family disorganization and was brought up in an Irish foster home. The Jewish patient consciously adopted a "non-Jewish" pattern of behavior and attitude because of strong sibling rivalry. According to the respondent, his brother, a favored son in the immigrant Jewish family, always manifested "typical" Jewish reactions toward disease, and the patient, who strongly disliked the brother and was jealous of him, decided to be "completely different."

This analysis of cultural factors in responses to pain is tentative and incomplete. It is based upon only one year of research, which has been devoted exclusively to collection of raw material and formulation of working hypotheses. A detailed analysis of the interviews may call for revisions and reformulations of certain observations described in this paper. Nevertheless, the first objectives of our research have been attained in establishing the importance of the role of cultural factors in an area relatively little explored by the social sciences. We hope that in the course of further research we shall be able to expand our investigation into other areas of the pain problem, such as sex differences in attitudes toward pain, the role of age differences and the role of religious beliefs in the pain experience. We hope also that the final findings of the study will contribute to the growing field of collaboration between the social sciences and medicine for the better understanding of human problems.

Until recently, it was assumed that black Americans were members of a racial rather than an ethnic group. They lacked self-definition as a people with common ancestry, for they came from many different tribes and could not trace their ancestry. Blacks, however, have developed a distinct life style, including food, music, dance, language, and interaction patterns. What is now called soul food is a mark of ethnic pride. Foods such as pig intestines, cheap greens, and cornmeal were once eaten by blacks because that was all they could obtain; now blacks eat these foods not only because they enjoy them, but also as a symbol of ethnic pride.

The distinctive version of the English language used by blacks in the ghetto is an example of an argot or in-group language that is understood by insiders but not by those outside of the group. Thus it is a private language that may be used to display exclusiveness or deliberately to exclude outsiders. According to Kochman's analysis in the following essay, the language used in the black ghetto also reflects and is an integral part of a particular life style.

"Rapping" in the Black Ghetto

THOMAS KOCHMAN

"Rapping," "shucking," "jiving," "running it down," "gripping," "copping a plea," "signifying," and "sounding" are all part of the black ghetto idiom and describe different kinds of talking. Each has its own distinguishing features of form, style, and function; each is influenced by, and influences, the speaker, setting, and audience; and each sheds light on the black perspective and the black condition—on those orienting values and attitudes that will cause a speaker to speak or perform in his own way within the social context of the black community.

I was first introduced to black idiom in New York City, and, as a professional linguist interested in dialects, I began to compile a lexicon of such expressions. My real involvement, however, came in Chicago, while preparing a course on black idiom at the Center for Inner City Studies, the southside branch of Northeastern Illinois State College.

Here I began to explore the full cultural significance of this kind of verbal behavior. My students and informants within black Chicago, through their knowledge of these terms, and their ability to recognize and categorize the techniques, and to give examples, gave me much reliable data. When I turned

From *Trans-action*, **6** (February, 1969), pp. 26–34. Reprinted by permission; copyright by Trans-action Magazine, New Brunswick, N.J.

for other or better examples to the literature—such as the writings of Malcolm X, Robert Conot, and Iceberg Slim—my students and informants were able to recognize and confirm their authenticity.

RAPPING

While often used to mean ordinary conversation, *rapping* is distinctively a fluent and a lively way of talking, always characterized by a high degree of personal style. To one's own group, rapping may be descriptive of an interesting narration, a colorful rundown of some past event. An example of this kind of rap is the answer from a Chicago gang member to a youth worker who asked how his group became organized:

"Now I'm goin' tell you how the jive really started. I'm goin' to tell you how the club got this big. 'Bout 1956 there used to be a time when the Jackson Park show was open and the Stony show was open. Sixty-six Street, Jeff, Gene, all of 'em, little bitty dudes, little bitty . . . Gene wasn't with 'em then. Gene was cribbin' (living) over here. Jeff, all of 'em, real little bitty dudes, you dig? All of us were little.

"Sixty-six (the gang on Sixty-Sixth Street), they wouldn't allow us in the Jackson Park show. That was when the parky (?) was headin' it. Everybody say, If we want to go to the show, we go! One day, who was it?—Carl Robinson. He went up to the show . . . and Jeff fired on him. He came back and all this was swelled up 'bout yay big, you know. He come back over to the hood (neighborhood). He told (name unclear) and them dudes went up there. That was when mostly all the main Sixty-six boys was over here, like Bett Riley. All of

'em was over here. People that quit gang-bangin' (fighting, especially as a group), Marvell Gates, people like that.

"They went on up there, John, Roy, and Skeeter went in there. And they start humbuggin' (fighting) in there. That's how it all started. Sixty-six found out they couldn't beat us, at that time. They couldn't whup seven-o. Am I right, Leroy? You was cribbin' over here then. Am I right? We were dynamite! Used to be a time, you ain't have a passport, man, you couldn't walk through here. And if didn't nobody know you it was worse than that. . . ."

Rapping to a woman is a colorful way of "asking for some pussy." "One needs to throw a lively rap when he is 'putting the make' on a broad." (John Horton, "Time and Cool People," *Trans-action,* April, 1967)

According to one informant, the woman is usually someone he has just seen or met, looks good, and might be willing to have sexual intercourse with him. My informant says the term would not be descriptive of talk between a couple "who have had a relationship over any length of time." Rapping, then, is used at the beginning of a relationship to create a favorable impression and be persuasive at the same time. The man who has the reputation for excelling at this is the pimp, or "mack man." Both terms describe a person of considerable status in the street hierarchy, who, by his lively and persuasive rapping ("macking" is also used in this context) has acquired a stable of girls to hustle for him and give him money. For most street men and many teen-agers he is the model whom they try to emulate. Thus, within the community you have a pimp walk, pimp-style boots and clothes—and perhaps most of all "pimp

talk," a colorful literary example of a telephone rap. One of my informants regards it as extreme, but agrees that it illustrates the language, style, and technique of rapping. "Blood" is rapping to an ex-whore named Christine in an effort to trap her into his stable:

"Now try to control yourself, baby. I'm the tall stud with the dreamy bedroom eyes across the hall in Four-twenty. I'm the guy with the pretty towel wrapped around his sexy hips. I got the same hips on now that you x-rayed. Remember that hump of sugar your peepers feasted on?"

She said, "Maybe, but you shouldn't call me. I don't want an incident. What do you want? A lady doesn't accept phone calls from strangers."

I said, "A million dollars and a trip to the moon with a bored, trapped, beautiful bitch, you dig? I'm no stranger. I've been popping the elastic on your panties ever since you saw me in the hall. . . ."

Rapping between men and women often is competitive and leads to a lively repartee, with the women becoming as adept as the men. An example follows:

A man coming from the bathroom forgot to zip his pants. An unescorted party of women kept watching him and laughing among themselves. The man's friends "hip" (inform) him to what's going on. He approaches one woman—"Hey, baby, did you see that big black Cadillac with the full tires? Ready to roll in action just for you." She answers—"No, motherfucker, but I saw a little gray Volkswagen with two flat tires." Everybody laughs. His rap was "capped" (excelled, topped).

When "whupping the game" on a "trick" or "lame" (trying to get goods or services from someone who looks like he can be swindled), rapping is often descriptive of the highly stylized verbal part of the maneuver. In well-established "con games" the rap is carefully prepared and used with great skill in directing the course of the transaction. An excellent illustration came from an adept hustler who was playing the "murphy game" on a white trick. The murphy game is designed to get the trick to give his money to the hustler, who in this instance poses as a "steerer" (one who directs or steers customers to a brothel), to keep the whore from stealing it. The hustler then skips with the money.

> *"Look, Buddy, I know a fabulous house not more than two blocks away. Brother, you ain't never seen more beautiful, freakier broads than are in that house. One of them, the prettiest one, can do more with a swipe than a monkey can with a banana. She's like a rubber doll; she can take a hundred positions."*
>
> *At this point the sucker is wild to get to this place of pure joy. He entreats the con player to take him there, not just direct him to it.*
>
> *The "murphy" player will prat him (pretend rejection) to enhance his desire. He will say, "Man, don't be offended, but Aunt Kate, that runs the house, don't have nothing but high-class white men coming to her place. . . . You know, doctors, lawyers, big-shot politicians. You look like a clean-cut white man, but you ain't in that league, are you?"* (Iceberg Slim, *Pimp: The Story of My Life*)

After a few more exchanges of the "murphy" dialogue, "the mark is separated from his scratch."

An analysis of rapping indicates a number of things:

1. For instance, it is revealing that one raps *to* rather than *with* a person, supporting the impression that rapping is to be regarded more as a performance than verbal exchange. As with other performances, rapping projects the personality, physical appearance, and style of the performer. In each of the examples given, the intrusive "I" of the speaker was instrumental in contributing to the total impression of the rap.
2. The combination of personality and style is usually best when "asking for some pussy." It is less when "whupping the game" on someone or "running something down."

In "asking for some pussy," for example, where personality and style might be projected through nonverbal means—stance, clothing, walking, looking—one can speak of a "silent rap." The woman is won here without the use of words, or rather, with words being implied that would generally accompany the nonverbal components.

3. As a lively way of "running it down," the verbal element consists of personality and style plus information. To someone *reading* my example of the gang member's narration, the impression might be that the information would be more influential in directing the listener's response. The youth worker might be expected to say "So that's how the gang got so big," instead of "Man, that gang member is *bad* (strong, brave)," in which instance he would be responding to the personality and style of the rapper. However, if the reader would *listen* to the gang member on tape or could have been present when the gang member spoke, he more likely

would have reacted more to personality and style, as my informants did.

Remember that in attendance with the youth worker were members of the gang who *already knew* how the gang got started (e.g. "Am I right, Leroy? You was cribbin' over here then") and for whom the information itself would have little interest. Their attention was held by the *way* the information was presented.

4. The verbal element in "whupping the game" on someone, in the preceding example, was an integral part of an overall deception in which information and personality/style were skillfully manipulated for the purpose of controlling the trick's response. But again, greater weight must be given to personality/style. In the murphy game, for example, it was this element which got the trick to trust the hustler and leave his money with him for "safekeeping."

The function of rapping in each of these forms is *expressive*. By this I mean that the speaker raps to project his personality onto the scene or to evoke a generally favorable response. When rapping is used to "ask for some pussy" or to "whup the game" on someone, its function is *directive*. By this I mean that rapping becomes an instrument to manipulate and control people to get them to give up or to do something. The difference between rapping to a "fox" (pretty girl) for the purpose of "getting inside her pants" and rapping to a "lame" to get something from him is operational rather than functional. The latter rap contains a concealed motivation, where the former does not.

SHUCKING

"Shucking," "shucking it," "shucking and jiving," "S-ing and J-ing" or just "jiving," are terms that refer to language behavior practiced by the black when confronting "the Man" (the white man, the establishment, or *any* authority figure), and to another form of language behavior practiced by blacks with each other on the peer group level.

In the South, and later in the North, the black man learned that American society had assigned to him a restrictive role and status. Among whites his behavior had to conform to this imposed station and he was constantly reminded to "keep his place." He learned that it was not acceptable in the presence of white people to show feelings of indignation, frustration, discontent, pride, ambition, or desire; that real feelings had to be concealed behind a mask of innocence, ignorance, childishness, obedience, humility, and deference. The terms used by the black to describe the role he played before white folks in the South was "tomming" or "jeffing." Failure to accommodate the white Southerner in this respect was almost certain to invite psychological and often physical brutality. A description related by a black psychiatrist, Alvin F. Poussaint, is typical and revealing:

> *Once last year as I was leaving my office in Jackson, Miss., with my Negro secretary, a white policeman yelled, "Hey, boy! Come here!" Somewhat bothered, I retorted: "I'm no boy!" He then rushed at me, inflamed, and stood towering over me, snorting "What d'ja say, boy?" Quickly he frisked me, and demanded, "What's your name, boy?" Frightened, I replied, "Dr. Poussaint. I'm a physician." He angrily chuckled and hissed, "What's your first name, boy?" When I hesitated he assumed a threatening stance and clenched his*

fists. As my heart palpitated, I muttered in profound humiliation, "Alvin."

He continued his psychological brutality, bellowing, "Alvin, the next time I call you, you come right away, you hear? You hear?" I hesitated. "You hear me, boy?" My voice trembling with help-lessness, but following my instincts of self-preservation, *I murmured, "Yes, sir."* Now fully satisfied that I had performed and acquiesced to my "boy" status, *he dismissed me with, "Now, boy, go on and get out of here or next time we'll take you for a little ride down to the station house!"* (Alvin F. Pous-saint, "A Negro Psychiatrist Explains the Negro Psyche," *The New York Times Magazine,* August 20, 1967) (emphasis mine)

In the Northern cities the black encountered authority figures equivalent to Southern "crackers": policemen, judges, probation officers, truant officers, teachers, and "Mr. Charlies" (bosses), and soon learned that the way to get by and avoid difficulty was to shuck. Thus, he learned to accommodate "the Man," to use the total orchestration of speech, intonation, gesture, and facial expression for the purpose of producing whatever appearance would be acceptable. It was a technique and ability that was developed from fear, a respect for power, and a will to survive. This type of accommodation is exemplified by the Uncle Tom with his "Yes sir, Mr. Charlie," or "Anything you say, Mr. Charlie."

Through accommodation, many blacks became adept at concealing and controlling their emotions and at assuming a variety of postures. They became competent actors. Many developed a keen perception of what affected, motivated, appeased, or satisfied the au-

thority figures with whom they came into contact. Shucking became an effective way for many blacks to stay out of trouble, and for others a useful artifice for avoiding arrest or getting out of trouble when apprehended. Shucking it with a judge, for example, would be to feign repentance in the hope of receiving a lighter or suspended sentence. Robert Conot reports an example of shucking in his book, *Rivers of Blood, Years of Darkness:* Joe was found guilty of possession of narcotics. But he did an excellent job of shucking it with the probation officer.

The probation officer interceded for Joe with the judge: "His own attitude toward the present offense appears to be serious and responsible and it is believed that the defendant is an excellent subject for probation."

Some field illustrations of shucking to get out of trouble came from some seventh-grade children from an inner-city school in Chicago. The children were asked to talk their way out of a troublesome situation.

You are cursing at this old man and your mother comes walking down the stairs. She hears you.

To talk your way out of this:

"I'd tell her that I was studying a scene in school for a play."

What if you were in a store stealing something and the manager caught you?

"I would start stuttering. Then I would say, 'Oh, oh, I forgot. Here the money is.'"

A literary example of shucking comes from Iceberg Slim's autobiography. Iceberg, a pimp, shucks before "two red-faced Swede rollers (detectives)" who catch him in a motel room with his whore. My italics identify which elements of the passage constitute the shuck.

> *I put my shaking hands into the pajama pockets* ... I hoped I was keeping the fear out of my face. I gave them a wide toothy smile. *They came in and stood in the middle of the room. Their eyes were racing about the room. Stacy was open-mouthed in the bed.*
>
> *I said,* "Yes, gentlemen, what can I do for you?"
>
> *Lanky said, "We wanta see your I.D."*
>
> *I went to the closet and got the phony John Cato Fredrickson I.D. I put it in his palm. I felt cold sweat running down my back. They looked at it, then looked at each other.*
>
> *Lanky said, "You are in violation of the law. You signed the motel register improperly. Why didn't you sign your full name? What are you trying to hide? What are you doing here in town? It says here you're a dancer. We don't have a club in town that books entertainers."*
>
> *I said,* "Officers, my professional name is Johnny Cato. I've got nothing to hide. My full name had always been too long for the marquees. I've fallen into the habit of using the shorter version.
>
> "My legs went out last year. I don't dance any more. My wife and I decided to go into business. We are making a tour of this part of the country. We think that in your town we've found the ideal site for a Southern fried chicken shack. My wife has a secret recipe that should make us rich up here." (Iceberg Slim, *Pimp: The Story of My Life*)

Another example of shucking was related to me by a colleague. A black gang member was coming down the stairway from the club room with seven guns on him and encountered some policemen and detectives coming up the same stairs. If they stopped and frisked him, he and others would have been arrested. A paraphrase of his shuck follows: "Man, I gotta get away from up there. There's gonna be some trouble and I don't want no part of it." This shuck worked on the minds of the policemen. It anticipated their questions as to why he was leaving the club room, and why he would be in a hurry. He also gave *them* a reason for wanting to get up to the room fast.

It ought to be mentioned at this point that there was not uniform agreement among my informants in characterizing the above examples as shucking. One informant used shucking only in the sense in which it is used among peers, e.g., bull-shitting, and characterized the above examples as "jiving" or "whupping game." Others, however, identified the above examples as shucking, and reserved jiving and whupping game for more offensive maneuvers. In fact, one of the apparent features of shucking is that the posture of the black when acting with members of the establishment be a *defensive* one.

Frederick Douglass, in telling of how he taught himself to read, would challenge a white boy with whom he was playing by saying that he could write as well as he. Whereupon he would write down all the letters he knew. The white boy would then write down more letters than Douglass did. In this way, Douglass eventually learned all the letters of the alphabet. Some of my informants regarded the example as whupping game. Others regarded it as shucking. The former were perhaps focusing on the manuever rather than the language used. The latter may have felt that any maneuvers designed to learn to read were justifiably defensive. One of my informants said Douglass was "shucking *in order to* whump the game." This latter response seems to be the most revealing. Just as one can rap to whup the game on someone, so one can shuck or jive for the same purpose; that is, assume a guise or posture or perform some action in a certain way that is designed to work on someone's mind to get him to give up something.

"Whupping Game" to Con Whitey

The following examples from Malcolm X illustrate the shucking and jiving in this context, though *jive* is the term used. Today, *"whupping game"* might also be the term used to described the operation. Whites who came at night got a better reception; the several Harlem nightclubs they patronized were geared to entertain and jive (flatter, cajole) the night white crowd to get their money. (Malcolm X, *The Autobiography of Malcolm X)*

The maneuvers involved here are clearly designed to obtain some benefit or advantage.

> *Freddie got on the stand and went to work on his own shoes. Brush, liquid polish, brush, paste wax, shine rag, lacquer sole dressing . . . step by step, Freddie showed me what to do.*
>
> *"But you got to get a whole lot faster. You can't waste time!" Freddie showed me how fast on my own shoes. Then, because business was tapering off, he had time to give me a demonstration of how to make the shine rag pop like a firecracker. "Dig the action?" he asked. He did it in slow motion. I got down and tried it on his shoes. I had the principle of it. "Just got to do it*

*faster," Freddie said. "It's a jive noise, that's all. Cats tip better, they figure you're knocking yourself out." (Malcolm X, *The Autobiography of Malcolm X)*

An eight-year-old boy whupped the game on me one day this way:

> *"My colleague and I were sitting in a room listening to a tape. The door to the room was open and outside was a soda machine. Two boys came up in the elevator, stopped at the soda machine, and then came into the room.*
>
> *"Do you have a dime for two nickels?" Presumably the soda machine would not accept nickels. I took out the change in my pocket, found a dime, and gave it to the boy for two nickels.*
>
> *After accepting the dime, he looked at the change in my hand and asked, "Can I have two cents? I need carfare to get home." I gave him the two cents.*

At first I assumed the verbal component of the maneuver was the rather weak, transparently false reason for wanting the two cents. Actually, as was pointed out to me later, the maneuver began with the first question, which was designed to get me to show my money. He could then ask me for something that he knew I had, making my refusal more difficult. He apparently felt that the reason need not be more than plausible because the amount he wanted was small. Were the amount larger, he would no doubt have elaborated on the verbal element of the game. The form of the verbal element could be in the direction of rapping or shucking and jiving. If he were to rap, the eight-year-old might say, "Man, you know a cat needs to have a little bread to keep the girls in line." Were he to shuck and jive, he might make the reason for needing the money more compelling, look hungry, etc.

The function of shucking and jiving as it refers to blacks and "the Man" is designed to work on the mind and emotions of the authority figure for the purpose of getting him to feel a certain way or give up something that will be to the other's advantage. Iceberg showed a "toothy smile" which said to the detective, "I'm glad to see you" and "Would I be glad to see you if I had something to hide?" When the maneuvers seem to be *defensive,* most of my informants regarded the language behavior as shucking. When the maneuvers were *offensive,* my informants tended to regard the behavior as "whupping the game."

Also significant is that the first form of shucking described, which developed out of accommodation, is becoming less frequently used today by many blacks, because of a newfound self-assertiveness and pride, challenging the system. The willingness on the part of many blacks to accept the psychological and physical brutality and general social consequences of not "keeping one's place" is indicative of the changing self-concept of the black man. Ironically, the shocked reaction of some whites to the present militancy of the black is partly due to the fact that the black was so successful at "putting Whitey on" via shucking in the past. This new attitude can be seen from a conversation I recently had with a shoeshine attendant at O'Hare Airport in Chicago.

I was having my shoes shined, and the black attendant was using a polishing machine instead of the rag that was generally used in the past. I asked whether the machine made his work any easier. He did not answer me until about ten seconds had passed and then responded in a loud voice that he "never had a job that was easy," that he would give me "one hundred dollars for any *easy* job" I could offer him, that the machine made his job "faster" but not "easier." I was startled at the response because it was so unexpected, and I realized that here was a new "breed of cat" who was not going to shuck for a big tip or ingratiate himself with "Whitey" any more. A few years ago his response probably would have been different.

The contrast between this "shoeshine" scene and the one illustrated earlier from Malcolm X's autobiography, when "shucking Whitey" was the common practice, is striking.

Shucking, jiving, shucking and jiving, or S-ing and J-ing, when referring to language behavior practiced by blacks, is descriptive of the talk and gestures that are appropriate to "putting someone on" by creating a false impression. The terms seem to cover a range from simply telling a lie, to bullshitting, to subtly playing with someone's mind. An important difference between this form of shucking and that described earlier is that the same talk and gestures that are deceptive to the "the Man" are often transparent to those members of one's own group who are able practitioners at shucking, themselves. As Robert Conot has pointed out, "The Negro who often fools the white officer by 'shucking it' is much less likely to be successful with another Negro. . . ." Also, S-ing and J-ing within the group often has play overtones in which the person being "put on" is aware of the attempts being made and goes along with it for enjoyment or in appreciation of the style.

Running It Down

"Running it down" is the term used by speakers in the ghetto when it is their intention to give information, either by explanation, narrative, or giving advice. In the following literary example, Sweet Mac is "running this Edith broad down" to his friends:

> Edith is the "saved" broad who can't marry out of her religion . . . or do anything else out of her religion, for that matter, especially what I wanted her to do. A bogue religion, man! So dig, for the last couple weeks I been quoting the Good Book and all that stuff to her; telling her I am now saved myself, you dig. (Woodie King, Jr., "The Game," *Liberator*, August, 1965)

The following citation from Claude Brown uses the term with the additional sense of giving advice:

> If I saw him (Claude's brother) hanging out with cats I knew were weak, who might be using drugs sooner or later, I'd run it down to him.

It seems clear that *running it down* has simply an informative function, that of telling somebody something that he doesn't already know.

Reactions to Fear

"Gripping" is of fairly recent vintage, used by black high school students in Chicago to refer to the talk and facial expression that accompanies a *partial* loss of face or self-possession, or showing of fear. Its appearance alongside "copping a plea," which refers to a total loss of face, in which one begs one's adversary for mercy, is a significant new perception. In linking it with the street code which acclaims the ability to "look

tough and inviolate, fearless, secure, 'cool,' " it suggests that even the slightest weakening of this posture will be held up to ridicule and contempt. There are always contemptuous overtones attached to the use of the term when applied to the others' behavior. One is tempted to link it with the violence and toughness required to survive on the street. The intensity of both seems to be increasing. As one of my informants noted, "Today, you're *lucky* if you end up in the hospital"—that is, are not killed.

Both *gripping* and *copping a plea* refer to behavior produced from fear and a respect for superior power. An example of gripping comes from the record *Street and Gangland Rhythms* (Band 4, "Dumb Boy"). Lennie meets Calvin and asks him what happened to his lip. Calvin says that a boy named Pierre hit him for copying off him in school. Lennie, pretending to be Calvin's brother, goes to confront Pierre. Their dialogue follows:

> Lennie: "Hey you! What you hit my little brother for?"
> Pierre: "Did he tell you what happen, man?"
> Lennie: "Yeah, he told me what happened."
> Pierre: "But you . . . but you . . . but you should tell your people to teach him to go to school, man." (Pause) "I, I know, I know I didn't have a right to hit him."

Pierre, anticipating a fight with Lennie if he continued to justify his hitting of Calvin, tried to avoid it by "gripping" with the last line.

"Copping a plea" originally meant "to plead guilty to a lesser charge to save the state the cost of a trial" (with the hope of receiving a lesser or suspended sentence), but is now generally used to mean "to beg," "plead for mercy," as in the example "Please, cop, don't hit me. I give." *(Street and Gangland Rhythms,* Band 1, "Gang Fight") This change of meaning can be seen from its use by Piri Thomas in *Down These Mean Streets.*

> *The night before my hearing, I decided to make a prayer. It had to be on my knees, 'cause if I was gonna cop a plea to God, I couldn't play it cheap.*

The function of gripping and copping a plea is obviously to induce pity or to acknowledge the presence of superior strength. In so doing, one evinces noticeable feelings of fear and insecurity which also result in a loss of status among one's peers.

SIGNIFYING

"Signifying" is the term used to describe the language behavior that, as Abrahams has defined it, attempts to "imply, goad, beg, boast by indirect verbal or gestural means." (Roger D. Abrahams, *Deep Down in the Jungle)* In Chicago it is also used as a synonym to describe language behavior more generally known as "sounding" elsewhere.

Some excellent examples of signifying as well as of other forms of language behavior come from the well-known "toast" (narrative form), "The Signifying Monkey and the Lion," which was collected by Abrahams from Negro street-corner bards in Philadelphia. In the above toast the monkey is trying to get the lion involved in a fight with the elephant:

> *Now the lion came through the jungle one peaceful day,*
> *When the signifying monkey stopped him, and that is what he started to say:*
> *He said, "Mr. Lion," he said, "A bad-assed motherfucker down your way,"*
> *He said, "Yeah! The way he talks about your folks is a certain shame.*
> *"I even heard him curse when he mentioned your grandmother's name."*
> *The lion's tail shot back like a forty-four*
> *When he went down that jungle in all uproar.*

Thus the monkey has goaded the lion into a fight with the elephant by "signifying," that, is indicating that the elephant has been "sounding on" (insulting) the lion. When the lion comes back, thoroughly beaten up, the monkey again "signifies" by making fun of the lion:

> *. . . lion came back through the jungle more dead than alive,*
> *When the monkey started some more of that signifying jive.*
> *He said, "Damn, Mr. Lion, you went through here yesterday, the jungle rung.*
> *Now you come back today, damn near hung."*

The monkey, of course, is delivering this taunt from a safe distance away, on the limb of a tree, when his foot slips and he falls to the ground, at which point,

> *Like a bolt of lighting, a stripe of white heat,*
> *The lion was on the monkey with all four feet.*

In desperation the monkey quickly resorts to "copping a plea":

> *The monkey looked up with a tear in*
> *his eyes,*
> *He said, "Please, Mr. Lion, I apolo-*
> *gize."*

His "plea," however, fails to move the lion to show any mercy, so the monkey tries another verbal ruse, "shucking":

> *He said, "You lemme get my head out*
> *of the sand, ass out of the*
> *grass, I'll fight you like a*
> *natural man."*

In this he is more successful as

> *The lion jumped back and squared for*
> *a fight.*
> *The motherfucking monkey jumped*
> *clear out of sight.*

A safe distance away again, the monkey returns to "signifying":

> *He said, "Yeah, you had me down, you*
> *had me at last,*
> *But you left me free, now you can still*
> *kiss my ass."*

This example illustrates the methods of provocation, goading, and taunting artfully practiced by a signifier.

Interestingly, when the *function* of signifying is *directive,* the *tactic* employed is *indirection,* i.e., the signifier reports or repeats what someone else has said about the listener; the "report" is couched in plausible language designed to compel belief and arouse feelings of anger and hostility. There is also the implication that if the listener fails to do anything about it—what has to be "done" is usually quite clear—his status will be seriously compromised. Thus the lion is compelled to vindicate the honor of his family by fighting or else leave the impression that he is afraid, and that he is not "king" of the jungle. When used for the purpose of directing action, "sig-

nifying" is like "shucking" in also being deceptive and subtle in approach and depending for success on the naïveté or gullibility of the person being "put on."

When the function of signifying is to arouse feelings of embarrassment, shame, frustration, or futility, to diminish someone's status, the tactic employed is direct in the form of a taunt, as in the example where the monkey is making fun of the lion.

"Sounding" to Relieve Tensions

"Sounding" is the term which is today most widely known for the game of verbal insult known in the past as "playing the dozens," "the dirty dozens," or just "the dozens." Other current names for the game have regional distribution: signifying or "sigging" (Chicago), joning (Washington, D.C.), screaming (Harrisburg), etc. In Chicago, the term "sounding" would be descriptive of the initial remarks which are designed to sound out the other person to see whether he will play the game. The verbal insult is also subdivided, the term "signifying" applying to insults which are hurled directly at the person and "the dozens" applying to insults hurled at your opponent's family, especially the mother.

Sounding is often catalyzed by signifying remarks referred to earlier, such as "Are you going to let him say that about your mama?" to spur an exchange between members of the group. It is begun on a relatively low key and built up by verbal exchanges. The game goes like this:

> *One insults a member of another's*
> *family; others in the group make disap-*
> *proving sounds to spur on the coming*
> *exchange. The one who has been in-*

sulted feels at this point that he must reply with a slur on the protagonist's family which is clever enough to defend his honor (and therefore that of his family). This, of course, leads the other (once again, more due to pressure from the crowd than actual insult) to make further jabs. This can proceed until everyone is bored with the whole affair, until one hits the other (fairly rare), or until some other subject comes up that interrupts the proceedings (the usual state of affairs). (Roger D. Abrahams, "Playing the Dozens," *Journal of American Folklore*, July-September, 1962)

Mack McCormick describes the dozens as a verbal contest

in which the players strive to bury one another with vituperation. In the play, the opponent's mother is especially slandered. . . . Then, in turn, fathers are identified as queer and syphilitic; sisters are whores, brothers are defective, cousins are "funny," and the opponent is himself diseased. (Mack McCormick, "The Dirty Dozens," book jacket in the record album *The Unexpurgated Folksongs of Men*, Arhoolie Records)

An example of the "game" collected by one of my students goes:

Frank looked up and saw Leroy enter the Outpost. Leroy walked past the room where Quinton, "Nap," "Pretty Black," "Cunny," Richard, Haywood, "Bull," and Reese sat playing cards. As Leroy neared the T.V. room, Frank shouted to him.
Frank: "Hey Leroy, your mama—calling you, man."
Leroy turned and walked toward the room where the sound came from. He stood in the door and looked at Frank.
Leroy: "Look, motherfuckers, I don't play that shit."

Frank (signifying): "Man, I told you cats 'bout that mama jive" (as if he were concerned about how Leroy felt).
Leroy: "That's all right, Frank; you don't have to tell these funky motherfuckers nothing; I'll fuck me up somebody yet."
Frank's face lit up as if he were ready to burst his side laughing. Cunny became pissed at Leroy.
Cunny: "Leroy, you stupid bastard, you let Frank make a fool of you. He said that 'bout your mama."
Pretty Black: "Aw, fat-ass-head Cunny, shut up."
Cunny: "Ain't that some shit. This black slick-head motor-flicker got nerve 'nough to call somebody 'fat-head.' Boy, you so black, you sweat Permalube Oil."

This eased the tension of the group as they burst into loud laughter.

Pretty Black: "What 'chu laughing 'bout, Nap, with your funky mouth smelling like dog-shit."
Even Leroy laughed at this.
Nap: "Your mama motherfucker."
Pretty Black: "Your funky mama, too."
Nap (strongly): "It takes twelve barrels of water to make a steamboat run; it takes an elephant's dick to make your Grandmammy come; she been elephant fucked, camel fucked, and hit side the head with your Grandpappy's nuts."
Reese: "Godorr-damn; go on and rap, motherfucker."

Reese began slapping each boy in his hand, giving his positive approval of Nap's comment. Pretty Black, in an effort not to be outdone, but directing his verbal play elsewhere, stated:

Pretty Black: "Reese, what you laughing 'bout? You so square, you shit bricked shit."

Frank: "Whooowee!"

Reese (sounded back): "Square, huh, what about your nappy ass hair before it was stewed; that shit was so bad till, when you went to bed at night, it would leave your head and go on the corner and meddle."

The boys slapped each other in the hand and cracked up.

Pretty Black: "On the streets meddling, bet Dinky didn't offer me no pussy and I turned it down."

Frank: "Reese scared of pussy."

Pretty Black: "Hell yeah; the greasy mother rather fuck old ugly, funky cock Sue Willie than get a piece of ass from a decent broad."

Frank: "Godorr-damn! Not Sue Willie."

Pretty Black: "Yeah, ol' meat-beating Reese rather screw that cross-eyed, clapsy bitch, who when she cry, tears rip down her ass."

Haywood: "Don't be so mean, Black."

Reese: "Aw shut up, you half-white bastard."

Frank: "Wait, man, Haywood ain't gonna hear much more of that half-white shit; he's a brother too."

Reese: "Brother, my black ass; that white-ass landlord gotta be this motherfucker's paw."

Cunny: "Man, you better stop foolin' with Haywood; he's turning red."

Haywood: "Fuck y'all" (as he withdrew from the "sig" game).

Frank: "Yeah, fuck y'all; let's go to the stick hall."

The group left enroute to the billiard hall. (James Maryland, "Signifying at the Outpost," unpublished term paper for the course *Idiom of the Negro Ghettos,* January 1967)

The above example of sounding is an excellent illustration of the "game," as played by 15-to 17-year-old Negro boys,

some of whom have already acquired the verbal skill which for them is often the basis for having a high "rep." Ability with words is apparently as highly valued as physical strength. In the sense that the status of one of the participants in the game is diminished if he has to resort to fighting to answer a verbal attack, verbal ability may be even more highly regarded than physical ability.

The relatively high value placed on verbal ability must be clear to most black boys at an early age. Most boys begin their activity in sounding by compiling a repertoire of "one-liners." When the game is played, the one who has the greatest number of such remarks wins. Here are some examples of "one-liners" collected from fifth- and sixth-grade black boys in Chicago:

Yo' mama is so bowlegged, she looks like she bit out of a donut.

Yo' mama sent her picture to the lonely hearts club, and they sent it back and said "We ain't that lonely!"

Your family is so poor the rats and roaches eat lunch out.

Your house is so small the roaches walk single file.

I walked in your house and your family was running around the table. I said, "Why you doin' that?" Your mama say, "First one drops, we eat."

Real proficiency in the game comes to only a small percentage of those who play it. These players have the special skill in being able to turn around what their opponents have said and attack them with it. Thus, when someone indifferently said "fuck you" to Concho, his retort was immediate and devastating: "Man, you haven't even kissed me yet."

The "best talkers" from this group

often become the successful street-corner, barber-shop, and pool-hall story-tellers who deliver the long, rhymed, witty, narrative stories called "toasts." They are, as Roger D. Abrahams has described, the traditional "men of words" and have become on occasion entertainers such as Dick Gregory and Redd Fox, who are virtuosos at repartee, and preachers, whose verbal power has been traditionally esteemed.

The function of "the dozens" or "sounding" is to borrow status from an opponent through an exercise of verbal power. The opponent feels compelled to regain his status by "sounding" back on the speaker or other group member whom he regards as more vulnerable.

The presence of a group seems to be especially important in controlling the game. First of all, one does not "play" with just anyone, since the subject matter is concerned with things that in reality one is quite sensitive about. It is precisely *because* Pretty Black has a "black slick head" that makes him vulnerable to Cunny's barb, especially now when the Afro-American "natural" hair style is in vogue. Without the control of the group, sounding will frequently lead to a fight. This was illustrated by a tragic epilogue concerning Haywood: when Haywood was being sounded on in the presence of two girls by his best friend (other members of the group were absent), he refused to tolerate it. He went home, got a rifle, came back and shot and killed his friend. In the classroom from about the fourth grade on, fights among black boys invariably are caused by someone sounding on the other person's mother.

Significantly, the subject matter of sounding is changing with the changing self-concept of the black with regard to those physical characteristics that are characteristically "Negro" and which in the past were vulnerable points in the black psyche: blackness and "nappy" hair. It ought to be said that, for many blacks, blackness was always highly esteemed, and it might be more accurate to regard the present sentiment of the black community toward skin color as reflecting a shifted attitude for only a *portion* of the black community. This suggests that sounding on someone's light skin color is not new. Nevertheless, one can regard the previously favorable attitude toward light skin color and "good hair" as the prevailing one. "Other things being equal, the more closely a woman approached her white counterpart, the more attractive she was considered to be, by both men and women alike. 'Good hair' (hair that is long and soft) and light skin were the chief criteria." (Elliot Liebow, *Tally's Corner*)

"The dozens" has been linked to the over-all psycho-social growth of the black male. McCormick has stated that a "single round of a dozen or so exchanges frees more pent-up aggressions than will a dose of sodium pentothal." The fact that one permits a kind of abuse within the rules of the game and within the confines of the group which would otherwise not be tolerated, is filled with psychological import. It seems also important, however, to view its function from the perspective of the non-participating members of the group. Its function for them may be to incite and prod individual members of the group to combat for the purpose of energizing the elements, of simply relieving the boredom of just "hanging around" and the malaise of living in a static and restrictive environment.

SUMMARY OF LANGUAGE BEHAVIOR

A summary analysis of the different forms of language behavior which have been discussed above permit the following generalizations:

The prestige norms which influence black speech behavior are those which have been successful in manipulating and controlling people and situations. The function of all of the forms of language behavior discussed above, with the exception of "running it down," was to project personality, assert oneself, or arouse emotion, frequently with the additional purpose of getting the person to give up or do something which will be of some benefit to the speaker. Only "running it down" has as its primary function to communicate information and often here, too, the personality and style of the speaker in the form of rapping is projected along with the information.

The purpose for which language is used suggests that the speaker views the social situations into which he moves as consisting of a series of transactions which require that he be continually ready to take advantage of a person or situation or defend himself against being victimized. He has absorbed what Horton has called "street rationality." As one of Horton's respondents put it: "The good hustler . . . conditions his mind and must never put his guard too far down, to relax, or he'll be taken."

I have carefully avoided limiting the group within the black community of whom this language behavior and perspective of their environment is characteristic. While I have no doubt that it is true of those who are generally called "street people," I am uncertain of the extent to which it is true of a much larger portion of the black community, especially the male segment. My informants consisted of street people, high school students, and blacks who, by their occupation as community and youth workers, possess what has been described as a "sharp sense of the streets." Yet it is difficult to find a black male in the community who has *not* witnessed or participated in the dozens or heard of signifying, or rapping, or shucking and jiving, at some time during his growing up. It would be equally difficult to imagine a high school student in a Chicago inner-city school not being touched by what is generally regarded as "street culture."

In conclusion: by blending style and verbal power, through rapping, sounding, and running it down, the black in the ghetto establishes his personality; through shucking, gripping, and copping a plea, he shows his respect for power; through jiving and signifying, he stirs up excitement. With all of the above, he hopes to manipulate and control people and situations to give himself a winning edge.

Many black Americans are still trapped by poverty. Unlike the experience of other ethnic groups in American history, the black experience has been subjected to both legal restrictions, such as segregated schooling and public *accommodations, and an American tradition of white racism.**

The following article by Horton discusses the life style of poor black Americans. Their life style combines coping strategies in response to their poverty and powerlessness with an emerging pattern of ethnic awareness and pride. Although Horton studied the Los Angeles black community, the life style that he discovered could be found in the ghetto of any American city.

*See especially Otto Kerner (chmn), *Report of the National Advisory Commission on Civil Disorders* (New York: Bantam, 1968).

Time and Cool People

JOHN HORTON

Street culture exists in every low-income ghetto. It is shared by the hustling elements of the poor, whatever their nationality or color. In Los Angeles, members of such street groups sometimes call themselves "street people," "cool people," or simply "regulars." Whatever the label, they are known the world over by outsiders as hoods or hoodlums, persons who live on and off the street. They are recognizable by their own fashions in dress, hair, gestures, and speech. The particular fashion varies with time, place, and nationality. For example, in 1963 a really sharp Los Angeles street Negro would be "conked to the bone" (have processed hair) and "togged-out" in "continentals." Today "natural" hair and variations of mod clothes are coming in style.

From *Trans-action,* 4 (April, 1967), pp. 5–12. Reprinted by permission; copyright © by Trans-action Magazine, New Brunswick, N.J.

Street people are known also by their activities—"duking" (fighting or at least looking tough), "hustling" (any way of making money outside the "legitimate" world of work), "gigging" (partying)—and by their apparent nonactivity, "hanging" on the corner. Their individual roles are defined concretely by their success or failure in these activities. One either knows "what's happening" on the street, or he is a "lame," "out of it," "not ready" (lacks his diploma in street knowledge), a "square."

There are, of course, many variations. Negroes, in particular, have contributed much to the street tongue which has diffused into both the more hip areas of the middle class and the broader society. Such expressions as "a lame," "taking care of righteous business," "getting down to the nitty-gritty," and "soul" can be retraced to Negro street life.

The more or less organized center of street life is the "set"—meaning both the peer group and the places where it hangs out. It is the stage and central marketplace for activity, where to find out what's happening. My set of Negro street types contained a revolving and sometimes disappearing (when the "heat," or police pressure, was on) population of about 45 members ranging in age from 18 to 25. These were the local "dudes," their term meaning not the fancy city slickers but simply "the boys," "fellas," the "cool people." They represented the hard core of street culture, the role models for younger teenagers. The dudes could be found when they were "laying dead"—hanging on the corner, or shooting pool and "jiving" ("goofing" or kidding around) in a local community project. Isolated from "the man" (in this context the man in power—the police, and by extension, the white man); they lived in a small section of Venice outside the central Los Angeles ghetto and were surrounded by a predominantly Mexican and Anglo population. They called their black "turf" "Ghost-town"—home of the "Ghost-men," their former gang. Whatever the origin of the word, Ghost-town was certainly the home of socially "invisible" men.

THE STREET SET

In 1965 and 1966 I had intensive interviews with 25 set members. My methods emerged in day-to-day observations. Identified as white, a lame, and square, I had to build up an image of being at least "legit" (not working for police). Without actually living in the area, this would have been impossible without the aid of a key fieldworker, in this case an outsider who could be accepted inside. This field worker, Cowboy, was a white dude of 25. He had run with "Paddy" (white), "Chicano" (Mexican), and "Blood" (Negro) sets since the age of 12 and was highly respected for having been president of a tough gang. He knew

the street, how to duke, move with style, and speak the tongue. He made my entry possible. I was the underprivileged child who had to be taught slowly and sympathetically the common-sense features of street life.

Cowboy had the respect and I the toleration of several set leaders. After that, we simply waited for the opportunity to "rap." Although sometimes used synonymously with street conversation, "rap" is really a special way of talking—repartee. Street repartee at its best is a lively way of "running it down," or of "jiving" (attempting to put someone on), of trying "to blow another person's mind," forcing him "to lose his cool," to give in or give up something. For example, one needs to throw a lively rap when he is "putting the make on a broad."

Sometimes we taped individuals, sometimes "soul sessions." We asked for life histories, especially their stories about school, job, and family. We watched and asked about the details of daily surviving and attempted to construct street time schedules. We probed beyond the past and present into the future in two directions—individual plans for tomorrow and a lifetime, and individual dreams of a more decent world for whites and Negroes.

The set can be described by the social and attitudinal characteristics of its members. To the observer, these are expressed in certain realities of day-to-day living: not enough skill for good jobs, and the inevitable trouble brought by the problem of surviving. Of the 25 interviewed, only four had graduated from high school. Except for a younger set member who was still in school, all were dropouts, or perhaps more accurately kicked-outs. None was really able to use or write formal language. However, many were highly verbal, both facile and effective in their use of the street tongue. Perhaps the art of conversation is most highly developed here where there is much time to talk, perhaps too much—an advantage of the *lumpen*-leisure class.

Their incomes were difficult to estimate, as "bread" or "coins" (money) came in on a very irregular basis. Of the 17 for whom I have figures, half reported that they made less than $1,400 in the last year, and the rest claimed income from $2,000 to $4,000 annually. Two-thirds were living with and partially dependent on their parents, often a mother. The financial strain was intensified by the fact that although 15 of 17 were single, eight had one or more children living in the area. (Having children, legitimate or not, was not a stigma but proof of masculinity.)

At the time of the interview, two-thirds of them had some full- or part-time employment—unskilled and low-paid jobs. The overall pattern was one of sporadic and—from their viewpoint—often unsatisfactory work, followed by a period of unemployment compensation, and petty hustling whenever possible and whenever necessary.

When I asked the question, "When a dude needs bread, how does he get it?" the universal response was "the hustle." Hustling is, of course, illegitimate from society's viewpoint. Street people know it is illegal, but they view it in no way as immoral or wrong. It is justified by the necessity of surviving. As might be expected, the unemployed admitted that they hustled and went so far as to say that a dude could make it better on the street than on the job: "There is a lot of money on the street, and there are many ways of getting it," or simply, "This has always been my way of life." On the other hand, the employed, the part-time hustlers, usually said, "A dude could make it better on the job than on the street." Their reasons for disapproving of hustling were not moral. Hustling meant trouble. "I don't hustle because there's no security. You eventually get busted." Others said there was not enough money on the street or that it was too difficult to "run a game" on people.

Nevertheless, hustling is the central street activity. It is the economic foundation for everyday life. Hustling and the fruit of hustling set the rhythm of social activities.

What are the major forms of hustling in Ghost-town? The best hustles were conning, stealing, gambling, and selling dope. By gambling, these street people meant dice; by dope, peddling "pills" and "pot." Pills are "reds" and "whites"—barbiturates and benzedrine or dexedrine. Pot is, of course, marijuana—"grass" or "weed." To "con" means to put "the bump" on a "cat," to "run a game" on somebody, to work on his mind for goods and services.

The "woman game" was common. As one dude put it, "If I have a good lady and she's on County, there's always some money to get." In fact, there is a local expression for getting county money. When the checks come in for child support, it's "mother's day." So the hustler "burns" people for money, but he also "rips off" goods for money; he thieves, and petty thieving is always a familiar hustle. Pimping is often the hustler's dream of the good life, but it was almost unknown here among the small-time hustlers. That was the game of the real professional and required a higher level of organization and wealth.

Hustling means bread and security but also trouble, and trouble is a major theme in street life. The dudes had a "world of trouble" (a popular song about a hustler is "I'm in a World of Trouble")—with school, jobs, women, and the police. The intensity of street life could be gauged in part by the intensity of the "heat" (police trouble). The hotter the street, the fewer the people visible on the street. On some days the set was empty. One would soon learn that there had been a "bust" (an arrest): Freddy had run amok and thrown rocks at a police car. There had been a leadership struggle: "Big Moe" had been cut up, and the "fuzz" had descended. Life was a succession of being picked up on suspicion of assault, theft, possession, "suspicion of suspicion" (an expression used by a respondent in describing his life). This was an ordinary experience for the street dude and often did lead to serious trouble. Over half of those interviewed claimed they had felony convictions.

THE STRUCTURE OF STREET TIME

Keeping cool and out of trouble, hustling bread, and looking for something interesting and exciting to do created the structure of time on the street. The rhythm of time is expressed in the high and low points in the day and week of an unemployed dude. I stress the pattern of the unemployed and full-time hustler because he is on the street all day and night and is the prototype in my interviews. The sometimes-employed will also know the pattern, and he will

be able to hit the street whenever released from the bondage of jail, work, and the clock. Here I describe a typical time schedule gleaned through interviews and field observation.

Characteristically the street person gets up late, hits the street in the late morning or early afternoon, and works his way to the set. This is a place for relaxed social activity. Hanging on the set with the boys is the major way of passing time and waiting until some necessary or desirable action occurs. Nevertheless, things do happen on the set. The dudes "rap" and "jive" (talk), gamble, and drink their "pluck" (usually a cheap, sweet wine). They find out what happened yesterday, what is happening today, and what will hopefully happen on the weekend—the perpetual search for the "gig," the party. Here peer socialization and reinforcement also take place. The younger dude feels a sense of pride when he can be on the set and throw a rap to an older dude. He is learning how to handle himself, show respect, take care of business, and establish his own "rep."

On the set, yesterday merges into today, and tomorrow is an emptiness to be filled in through the pursuit of bread and excitement. Bread makes possible the excitement—the high (getting loaded with wine, pills, or pot), the sharp clothes, the "broad," the fight, and all those good things which show that one knows what's happening and has "something going" for himself. The rhythm of time—of the day and of the week—is patterned by the flow of money and people.

Time is "dead" when money is tight, when people are occupied elsewhere— working or in school. Time is dead when one is in jail. One is "doing dead time" when nothing is happening, and he's got nothing going for himself.

Time is alive when and where there is action. It picks up in the evening when everyone moves on the street. During the regular school year it may pick up for an hour in the afternoon when the "broads" leave school and meet with the set at a corner taco joint. Time may pick up when a familiar car cruises by and a few dudes drive down to Johnny's for a "process" (hair straightening and styling). Time is low on Monday (as described in the popular song, "Stormy Monday"), Tuesday, Wednesday, when money is tight. Time is high on Friday nights when the "eagle flies" and the "gig" begins. On the street, time has a personal meaning only when something is happening, and something is most likely to happen at night—especially on Friday and Saturday nights. Then people are together, and there may be bread—bread to take and bread to use.

Human behavior is rational if it helps the individual to get what he wants, whether it is success in school or happiness in the street. Street people sometimes get what they want. They act rationally in those situations where they are able to plan and choose because they have control, knowledge, and concern, irrationally where there are barriers to their wants and desires.

When the street dude lacks knowledge and power to manipulate time, he is indeed irrational. For the most part, he lacks the skills and power to plan a move up and out of the ghetto. He is "a lame" in the middle-class world of school and work; he is not ready to operate effectively in unfamiliar organizations where his street strengths are his visible weak-

nesses. Though irrational in moving up and out of the street, he can be rational in day-to-day survival in the street. No one survives there unless he knows what's happening (that is, unless he knows what is available, where to get what he can without being burned or busted). More euphemistically, this is "taking advantage of opportunities," exactly what the rational member of the middle class does in his own setting.

To know what's happening is to know the goods and the bads, the securities, the opportunities, and the dangers of the street. Survival requires that a hustling dude know who is cool and uncool (who can be trusted); who is in power (the people who control narcotics, fences, etc.); who is the "duker" or the fighter (someone to be avoided or someone who can provide protection). When one knows what's happening he can operate in many scenes, providing that he can "hold his mud," keep cool, and out of trouble.

With his diploma in street knowledge, a dude can use time efficiently and with cunning in the pursuit of goods and services—in hustling to eat and yet have enough bread left over for the pleasures of pot, the chicks, and the gig. As one respondent put it, "The good hustler has the know-how, the ambition to better himself. He conditions his mind and must never put his guard too far down, to relax, or he'll be taken." This is street rationality. The problem is not a deficient sense of time but deficient knowledge and control to make a fantasy future and a really better life possible.

The petty hustler more fully realizes the middle-class ideal of individualistic rationality than does the middle class itself. When rationality operates in hustling, it is often on an individual basis. In a world of complex organization, the hustler defines himself as an entrepreneur; and indeed, he is the last of the competitive entrepreneurs.

The degree of organization in hustling depends frequently on the kind of hustling. Regular pimping and pushing require many trusted contacts and organization. Regular stealing requires regular fences for hot goods. But in Ghost-town when the hustler moved, he usually moved alone and on a small scale. His success was on him. He could not depend on the support of some benevolent organization. Alone, without a sure way of running the same game twice, he must continually recalculate conditions and people and find new ways of taking or be taken himself. The phrase "free enterprise for the poor and socialism for the rich" applies only too well in the streets. The political conservative should applaud all that individual initiative.

Clock Time vs. Personal Time

Negro street time is built around the irrelevance of clock time, white man's time, and the relevance of street values and activities. Like anyone else, a street dude is on time by the standard clock whenever he wants to be, not on time when he does not want to be and does not have to be.

When the women in school hit the street at the lunch hour and he wants to throw them a rap, he will be there then and not one hour after they have left. But he may be kicked out of high school for truancy or lose his job for being late and unreliable. He learned at an early age that school and job were neither interesting nor salient to his way of life. A regular on the set will readily admit being crippled by a lack of formal education. Yet school was a "bum kick." It was not *his* school. The teachers put him down for his dress, hair, and manners. As a human being he has feelings of pride and autonomy, the very things most threatened in those institutional situations where he was or is the underdeveloped, unrespected, illiterate, and undeserving outsider. Thus whatever "respectable" society says will help him, he knows oppresses him, and he retreats to the streets for security and a larger degree of personal freedom. Here his control reaches a maximum, and he has the kind of autonomy which many middle-class males might envy.

In the street, watches have a special and specific meaning. Watches are for pawning and not for telling time. When they are worn, they are decorations and ornaments of status. The street clock is informal, personal, and relaxed. It is not standardized nor easily synchronized to other clocks. In fact, a street dude may have almost infinite toleration for individual time schedules. To be on time is often meaningless, to be late an unconsciously accepted way of life. "I'll catch you later," or simply "later," are the street phrases that mean business will be taken care of, but not necessarily now.

Large areas of street life run on late time. For example, parties are not cut off by some built-in alarm clock of appointments and schedules. At least for the unemployed, standard time neither precedes nor follows the gig. Consequently, the action can take its course. It can last as long as interest is sustained and die by exhaustion or by the intrusion of some more interesting event. A gig may endure all night and well into another day. One of the reasons for the party assuming such time dimensions is purely economic. There are not enough cars and enough money for individual dates, so everyone converges in one place and takes care of as much business as possible there, that is, doing whatever is important at the time—sex, presentation of self, hustling.

COLORED PEOPLE'S TIME

Events starting late and lasting indefinitely are clearly street and class phenomena, not some special trait of Afro-Americans. Middle-class Negroes who must deal with the organization and coordination of activities in church and elsewhere will jokingly and critically refer to a lack of standard time sense when they say that Mr. Jones arrived "CPT" (colored people's time). They have a word for it, because being late is a problem for people caught between two worlds and confronted with the task of meshing standard and street time. In contrast, the street dudes had no self-consciousness about being late; with few exceptions they had not heard the expression CPT. (When I questioned members of a middle-class Negro fraternity, a sample matched by age to the street set, only three of the 25 interviewed could not define CPT. Some argued vehemently that CPT was the problem to be overcome.)

Personal time as expressed in parties and other street activities is not simply deficient knowledge and use of standard time. It is a positive adaptation to generations of living whenever and wherever possible outside of the sound and control of the white man's clock. The personal clock is an adaptation to the chance and accidental character of events on the street and to the very positive value placed on emotion and feeling. (For a discussion of CPT which is close to some of the ideas presented here, see Jules Henry, "White People's Time, Colored People's Time," *Trans-action,* March-April 1965.)

Chance reinforces personal time. A dude must be ready on short notice to move "where the action is." His internal clock may not be running at all when he is hanging on the corner and waiting for something to do. It may suddenly speed up by chance: Someone cruises by in a car and brings a nice "stash" of "weed," a gig is organized and he looks forward to being well togged-out and throwing a rap to some "boss chick," or a lame appears and opens himself to a quick "con." Chance as a determinant of personal time can be called more accurately *uncertain predictability.* Street life is an aggregate of relatively independent events. A dude may not know exactly what or when something will happen, but from past experience he can predict a range of possibilities, and he will be ready, in position, and waiting.

In white middle-class stereotypes and fears—and in reality—street action is highly expressive. A forthright yet stylized expression of emotion is positively evaluated and most useful. Street control and communication are based on personal power and the direct impingement of one individual on another. Where there is little property, status in the set is determined by personal qualities of mind and brawn.

The importance of emotion and expression appears again and again in street tongue and ideology. When asked, "How does a dude make a rep on the set?" over half of the sample mentioned "style," and all could discuss the concept. Style is difficult to define, as it has so many referents. It means to carry one's self well, dress well, to show class. In the ideology of the street, it may be a way of behaving. One has style if he is able to dig people as they are. He doesn't put them down for what they do. He shows toleration. But a person with style must also show respect. That means respect for a person as he is, and since there is power in the street, respect for another's superior power. Yet one must show respect in such a way that he is able to look tough and inviolate, fearless, secure, "cool."

Style may also refer to the use of gestures in conversation or in dance. It may be expressed in the loose walk, the jivey or dancing walk, the slow cool walk, the way one "chops" or "makes it" down the street. It may be the loose, relaxed hand rap or hand slap, the swinger's greeting which is used also in the hip middle-class teen sets. There are many refined variations of the hand rap. As a greeting, one may simply extend his hand, palm up. Another slaps it loosely with his finger. Or, one person may be standing with his hand behind and palm up. Another taps the hand in passing, and also pays his respect verbally with the conventional greeting "What's happening, Brother." Or, in conversation, the hand may be slapped when an individual has "scored," has been "digging," has made a point, has got through to the person.

Style is a comparatively neutral value compared to "soul." Soul can be many

things—a type of food (good food is "soul food," a "bowl of soul"), music, a quality of mind, a total way of acting (in eating, drinking, dancing, walking, talking, relating to others, etc.). The person who acts with soul acts directly and honestly from his heart. He feels it and tells it "like it is." One respondent identified soul with ambition and drive. He said the person with soul, once he makes up his mind, doesn't wait and worry about messing up a little. Another said soul was getting down to the nitty-gritty, that is, moving directly to what is basic without guise and disguise. Thus soul is the opposite of hypocrisy, deceit, and phoniness, the opposite of "affective neutrality" and "instrumentality." Soul is simply whatever is considered beautiful, honest, and virtuous in men.

Most definitions tied soul directly to Negro experience. As one hustler put it, "It is the ability to survive. We've made it with so much less. Soul is the Negro who has the spirit to sing in slavery to overcome the monotony." With very few exceptions, the men interviewed argued that soul was what Negroes had and whites did not. Negroes were "soul brothers," warm and emotional—whites cold as ice. Like other oppressed minorities, these street Negroes believed they had nothing except their soul and their humanity, and that this made them better than their oppressors.

THE PERSONAL DREAM

Soul is anchored in a past and present of exploitation and deprivation, but are there any street values and activities which relate to the future? The regular in the street set has no providential mission; he lives personally and instrumentally in the present, yet he dreams about the day when he will get himself together and move ahead to the rewards of a good job, money, and a family. Moreover, the personal dream coexists with a nascent political nationalism, the belief that Negroes can and will make it as Negroes. His present/future time is a combination of contradictions and developing possibilities. Here I will be content to document without weighing two aspects of his orientation: *fantasy personal future* and *fantasy collective future*. I use the word *fantasy* because street people have not yet the knowledge and means and perhaps the will to fulfill their dreams. It is hard enough to survive by the day.

When the members of the set were asked, "What do you really want out of life?" their responses were conventional, concrete, seemingly realistic, and—given their skills—rather hopeless. Two-thirds of the sample mentioned material aspirations—the finer things in life, a home, security, a family. For example, one said, in honest street language, "I want to get things for my kids and to make sure they have a father." Another said, jokingly, "A good future, a home, two or three girls living with me." Only one person didn't know, and the others deviated a little from the material response. They said such things as "for everyone to be on friendly terms—a better world . . . then I could get all I wish," "to be free," "to help people."

But if most of the set wanted money and security, they wanted it on their own terms. As one put it, "I don't want to be in a middle-class bag, but I would like a nice car, home, and food in the icebox." He wanted the things and

the comforts of middle-class life, but not the hypocrisy, the venality, the coldness, the being forced to do what one does not want to do. All that was in the middle-class bag. Thus the home and the money may be ends in themselves, but also fronts, security for carrying on the usual street values. Street people believed that they already had something that was valuable and looked down upon the person who made it and moved away into the middle-class world. For the observer, the myths are difficult to separate from the truths—here where the truths are so bitter. One can only say safely that street people dream of a high status, and they really do not know how to get it.

THE COLLECTIVE FUTURE

The Negro dudes are political outsiders by the usual poll questions. They do not vote. They do not seek out civil rights demonstrations. They have very rudimentary knowledge of political organization. However, about the age of 18, when fighting and being tough are less important than before, street people begin to discuss their position in society. Verbally they care very much about the politics of race and the future of the Negro. The topic is always a ready catalyst for a soul session.

The political consciousness of the street can be summarized by noting those interview questions which attracted at least a 75 percent rate of agreement. The typical respondent was angry. He approves of the Watts incident, although from his isolated corner of the city he did not actively participate. He knows something about the history of discrimination and believes that if something isn't done soon

America can expect violence: "What this country needs is a revolutionary change." He is more likely to praise the leadership of Malcolm X than Lyndon Johnson, and he is definitely opposed to the Vietnam war. The reason for his opposition is clear: Why fight for a country which is not mine, when the fight is here?

Thus his racial consciousness looks to the future and a world where he will not have to stand in the shadow of the white man.

But his consciousness has neither clear plan nor political commitment. He has listened to the Muslims, and he is not a black nationalist. True, the Negro generally has more soul than the white. He thinks differently, his women may be different, yet integration is preferable to separatism. Or, more accurately, he doesn't quite understand what all these terms mean. His nationalism is real as a folk nationalism based on experience with other Negroes and isolation from whites.

The significance of a racial future in the day-to-day consciousness of street people cannot be assessed. It is a developing possibility dependent on unforeseen conditions beyond the scope of their skill and imagination. But bring up the topic of race and tomorrow, and the dreams come rushing in—dreams of superiority, dreams of destruction, dreams of human equality. These dreams of the future are salient. They are not the imagination of authoritarian personalities, except from the viewpoint of those who see spite lurking behind every demand for social change. They are certainly not the fantasies of the hipster living philosophically in the present without hope and ambition. One hustler summarized the Negro street concept of ambition and future time when he said:

The Negro has more ambition than the whites. He's got farther to go. "The man" is already there. But we're on your trail, daddy. You still have smoke in our eyes, but we're catching up.

The American Indian's life style has been stereotyped for years in novels, movies, and television shows. It has become a commercialized attraction; in Indian settlements from Cherokee, North Carolina, to Pueblo, Colorado, and beyond, tourists purchase symbols of Indian life style in the form of orlon Indian blankets and plastic Japanese-made tepees. The life style of Indians, either on isolated reservations or urban ghettos, is still poorly understood. In the following article, Donald Jewell shows that the Indian way of life is so alien, even to "experts," that it may be taken as a sign of mental illness.

A Case of a "Psychotic" Navaho Indian Male

DONALD P. JEWELL

Increased psychological and ethnological rapproachement has resulted in a greater understanding of American subgroups and the processes of acculturation. Examples of this integrated approach are to be seen in Barnouw's study of Chippewa Indian acculturation[1] and, on the individual level, Devereux's psychotherapy of an alcoholic Sioux.[2]

Sometimes identified as the "culture-personality" orientation, this approach has reached a degree of clarification which justifies consistent designation. It is suggested here that it be defined as ethnopsychological. It is an approach which, as Kluckhohn has shown, has about a century of development.[3] Ethnopsychology has generally concerned itself with a definition of general normal personality characteristics of other cultures, only occasionally with the neu-

From *Human Organization,* 11 (Spring, 1952), pp. 32–36. Reprinted by permission of the Society for Applied Anthropology.

[1]Barnouw, V., "Acculturation and Personality Among the Wisconsin Chippewa," *American Anthropologist,* Memoir Number 72, Vol. 52, 1950.
[2]Devereux, G., *Reality and Dream* (International Universities Press, 1950).
[3]Kluckhohn, C., "The Influence of Psychiatry on Anthropology in America During the Past One Hundred Years," in J. K. Hall, G. Zilboorg, and E.A. Bunker (eds.), *One Hundred Years of American Psychiatry* (Columbia University Press, 1947), pp. 589–617.

rotic individual, and rarely with the psychotic.

PURPOSE OF THIS STUDY

The writer had the opportunity recently to make a rather extensive observation of a Navaho Indian institutionalized as a psychotic in a California state mental hospital. By drawing from the literature of Navaho ethnopsychology and the writer's own experience among the Navaho people, it was hoped that the dynamics of the patient's maladjustment would be revealed. It was also anticipated that some sort of psychotherapy would evolve.

This report is a summary of those endeavors to understand and assist the Navaho patient. Cultural and linguistic obstacles prohibited an ideal approach, but enough was accomplished to permit considerable insight into the patient's behavior. There were features about the patient's personality which would not fit harmoniously with concepts of psychiatric symptomatology derived from European culture, those concepts dealing particularly with the dynamics of the diagnosis of catatonic schizophrenia. The unique characteristics of this individual's personality leads, in fact, to the question as to what extent he should be considered psychotic, and whether that consideration should be viewed from Navaho or Anglo perspective.

During his many interviews with the patient, some of them with the aid of a Navaho interpreter, the writer developed an increasing awareness that to call the patient psychotic was an arbitrary matter. When this Navaho is referred to as psychotic, then, it is merely because he carried such a diagnosis during his 18 months of hospitalization as a mental patient.

ORIENTATION

Considerable literary attention has been given to the general psychological characteristics of Navaho Indians.[4] These have related psychological findings to ethnological contexts, and so offer a background against which the atypical Navaho individual may be examined.

On the behavioral level, the Navahos are in many ways unique, not only with respect to white people but other Indian tribes as well. One of their most characteristic traits may be seen in crisis situations. Kluckhohn and Leighton describe it as a passive resistance, the individual masking his fear by quiet unmovingness, an appearance of stoicism. If forced into action, the response is a mechanical, apparently uncomprehending behavior.[5]

Another form of withdrawal is often expressed in periods of depression, apparently a morbid preoccupation with health.[6]

These being salient aspects of the typical Navaho personality, the question now arises as to how those traits would be characterized on the psychotic level. Under prolonged psychological stress, what would develop from the stoicism and moods of morbid preoccupation?

In an endeavor to answer this question

a survey was made of those mental hospitals which would most likely be caring for Navaho patients. The Bureau of Indian Affairs' policy is not to concentrate Indian patients, but to subsidize their care in whatever hospital they may have been committed. It is thus possible that a few Navahos may be hospitalized some distance from their reservation area of New Mexico, Utah, and Arizona, and have not been located in this survey. It is felt, however, that a survey of those mental hospitals in the Southwest only would be adequate to show general trends. The findings are summarized in Table 1.

Elimination of the organic psychoses leaves one manic, one depressive, and 10 schizophrenics. Of the schizophrenics, seven are catatonic. This is an unusually high incidence of catatonic schizophrenia, and seems to indicate that Navahos are predisposed toward that particular psychosis. This immediately suggests that the above-described stoicism has been carried to pathological extremes, and possibly that the stoicism is actually a transient form of catatonia. It was with this problem in mind that the Navaho patient discussed in this report was studied.

THE PATIENT

The patient was a 26-year-old Navaho male. For purposes of anonymity he will be referred to as Bill. He came to the writer's attention through a survey of Indian patients at the hospital. He was the only Navaho of 13 Indian patients scattered throughout the various wards and cottages, and of the 4,000 general-patient population.

The outlook for examination and

[4]Henry, W., "The Thematic Apperception Technique in the Study of Culture-Personality Relations," *Genetic Psychology Monographs,* Vol. 35, 1947, pp. 3–135; Kluckhohn, C., and Leighton, D., *Children of the People* (Harvard University Press, 1948).
[5]Kluckhohn and Leighton, *ibid.,* p. 108.
[6]*Ibid.,* p. 110.

TABLE 1

SUMMARY OF SURVEY OF NAVAHO INDIAN MENTAL PATIENTS HOSPITALIZED IN
SOUTHWESTERN UNITED STATES, EXCLUDING MENTAL DEFECTIVES*

Diagnosis	Number	Sex and Age
Psychosis with syphilis of the C.N.C.	2	1f: 47; 1m: 31
Psychosis with cerebral arteriosclerosis	1	1f: 62
Psychosis due to trauma (organic)	1	1m: 47
Epilepsy	8	6 m: 20, 24, 29, 33 37, 39; 2f: 20, 32
Schizophrenia, Simple Type	1	1m: 25
Schizophrenia, Mixed Type	1	1f: 26
Schizophrenia, Hebephrenic Type	1	1f: 30
Schizophrenia, Catatonic Type	7	4m: 26, 28, 28, 36; 3f: 20, 30, 38
Depressed State	1	1f: 37
Manic-Depressive Psychosis, Manic Type	1	1m: 42

*Acknowledgement of the hospitals cooperating in this survey must be regretfully omitted, due to the need to protect the identity of the patients.

therapy seemed at first quite discouraging. The patient was in a cottage ordinarily reserved for the most regressed patients. Unlike most of the others in this cottage, however, he was not there because of repeated failure of such routine therapies as shock treatment, occupational therapy, etc. It was unusual for a patient in his condition, who had been at the hospital for eight months, not to have received at least electric shock treatment.

A preliminary period was spent at the cottage, observing Bill's behavior. He was very withdrawn. Most of his day was spent in inactive sitting or sleeping. He would rouse himself only for eating or attending to other personal needs. He would assist with floor waxing, dish washing, or other activities the attendants might require of him, but in a perfunctory and apathetic manner. His behavior was not patently catatonic, but certainly suggestive of it.

Most of the attendants reported never having heard Bill speak. A few, however,

indicated that Bill would occasionally approach them and, in almost unintelligible English, ask if he could go home.

Shortly thereafter Bill was brought to the writer's office where he was greeted in Navaho. Bill responded in that language, glancing briefly at the writer before returning his gaze to the floor.

This closer inspection of Bill revealed occipital flattening, resulting from the cradle board as a child, and the pierced ear lobes of a conservative Navaho. During this first interview he complained about the close haircuts he received at the hospital, further evidence that he belonged to the old-fashioned, "long-hair" conservatives of the reservation.

The interview proceeded very slowly, but gradually a system of communication began to evolve. By utilizing mutually understood Navaho and English words, by means of pantomine, and with the aid of penciled sketches, the system became increasingly refined during the following interviews.

Bill was seen three hours a week for three months. The writer then took an eight-month leave of absence from the hospital, during which time he spent several months in Bill's home area near Shiprock, New Mexico.

While in the Shiprock area, the writer endeavored to locate Bill's family to advise them of the patient's circumstances. Bill had previously drawn a map indicating the approximate location of his family's *hogans* (dwellings), but it proved impossible to find them. The *hogans* were located about five miles from the nearest road, and even if a horse and interpreter had been available, the chances of locating the specific *hogans* were slight. The situation was complicated by the fact that the family did not have American names and the writer did not know their Navaho names. Missionaries and Bureau of Indian Affairs personnel were consequently given the problem of finding the family, but several months elapsed before they were equipped with sufficient information to do so.

Although he could not communicate with Bill's family, the writer succeeded in talking with several Navahos who had known Bill, and in obtaining ecological and further case-history material.

Shortly after the writer's return to the hospital a Navaho interpreter was brought in from the Sherman Institute, a large Indian school not far from the hospital. Interviews with the patient through the interpreter corroborated the case history material obtained, and further satisfied the writer in his clinical evaluation of the patient. Both of these areas are separately discussed in the following text.

CASE HISTORY

The gathering of Bill's history extended over a period of 11 months, and was obtained piecemeal from a variety of sources. In summarizing, however, this material will be integrated for greater coherency.

Bill was born in a part of the reservation noted for being both very conservative and poverty-stricken. Only 50 miles away is the markedly contrasting community of Shiprock, considered to be one of the most acculturated Navaho communities. It is also prospering from recently developed uranium operations in the region.

During his early years Bill saw very little of Shiprock, and was reared in the traditional Navaho way. He was born during an eclipse (it is not known whether of the sun or moon), and was thus destined to take part in a periodic ceremony identified to the writer as the "Breath of Life" sing. The first of this series of ceremonies was held while he was still an infant, the second about six years ago. During the ceremony he inhales the breath of a great deity, and is thus assured of continued good health in the respiratory and vocal organs.

Bill lived with his immediate family until he was six years of age. He had only one younger sister at that time, although the family was later to include seven living siblings. He did not become well acquainted with his family, however, as he was given to his grandfather when he was six years old. The grandfather, a widower, lived several miles deeper into the reservation and required Bill's assistance as a sheep herder.

Bill worked for his grandfather as a sheep herder until he was 17, except for one interruption when, at the age of 15, he spent 50 days in the Shiprock hospital with a back ailment. Bill reports that the old man never talked to him.

At his grandfather's death Bill went to work for the railroad in Colorado. This was cut short by an illness which confined him to the Navaho Medical Center in Fort Defiance, Arizona. The illness was diagnosed as tuberculosis, pulmonary, moderately advanced. He was in the hospital for eight months and was discharged in the summer of 1944.

Bill returned to railroad employment, and worked in Utah, Oregon, and Nebraska. He was always part of Navaho crews and thus never exposed to acculturative influences. His father and a younger brother were also part of these crews.

Bill returned home for a brief visit in 1949, accompanied by his brother and father. He had saved $1,022. Subsequently, he went to Phoenix, Arizona, to pick cotton, a job that had been found for him by the employment agency at Shiprock. This was his first trip from home without a family member.

The employment at Phoenix did not last long and in December, 1949, on the advice of an Indian friend he went to Barstow, California, seeking railroad employment. At the section camp there his attempt to find work was unsuccessful, and after three days he started by bus back to Phoenix.

On this return trip he stopped for dinner at Colton. A white man he met there promised to obtain railroad employment for him. The stranger said that he required funds for this effort and in some way relieved Bill of his savings, which had now dwindled to $725.

Bill returned home penniless, pawned some jewelry, borrowed some money, and returned to Colton to try to find the man who had taken his savings. He also looked for Navahos who might have information about employment. The many hours of waiting around the bus station searching for his man apparently caused suspicion, for he was arrested for vagrancy.

In jail he met some Navahos with whom he went to Barstow after his release. But in Barstow he was still unable to find employment, and after six days he was completely out of funds. He started walking toward Phoenix, and was picked up by a man driving a truck. This man gave Bill one day's employment, which allowed funds for a return to Barstow and another attempt to find work.

He managed to raise a little money doing odd jobs about the section camp near Barstow, and then returned to San Bernardino on the first lap of his return to Phoenix and home. It occurred to him that if he could get to a hospital, the officials there would send him to a reservation hospital, from whence he would be sent home. This was logical thinking: on the reservations, the hospitals, schools, and trading posts are the major source of assistance in all sorts of troubles.

As this idea occurred to Bill, he noticed a woman dressed in white whom he took to be a nurse. He approached her and endeavored to explain that he was sick, but his endeavors were misinterpreted and he was taken to jail.

At the county jail Bill was apparently mistaken for a Mexican, since a Mexican interpreter had tried to interview him. When the interview failed he was transferred to the psychopathic ward. Interviewed by the medical examiner there, he reportedly demonstrated an anguished appearance and repeated, "Me sick." He was diagnosed as Schizophrenia, Catatonic Type, and delivered to the state mental hospital.

Upon admission to the hospital, Bill was first taken to be a Filipino. The psychiatric admission note indicated that he was ". . . confused, dull, and preoccupied. He has a look of anguish and appears to be hallucinating. . . . He repeats "I don't know.'" He was diagnosed as Dementia Praecox, which was later specified as Hebephrenic Type.

Several months later the psychiatrist on Bill's cottage tested him for *cerea flexibilitas* (waxy flexibility) and, finding it to be present, altered the diagnosis to Catatonic Type.

Eight months after his admittance he was discovered by the writer.

Psychological Aspects

Concomitant with gathering the case history material presented above, endeavors were made to evaluate the patient's intelligence and personality. The lack of culturally-biased examining techniques made this extremely difficult.

Bill's performance on the various tests that were administered led to a conclusion that his probable I.Q. was in the vicinity of 80. This had to take into consideration the patient's slowness. At best, a Navaho refuses to be put under pressure of time, and to what extent Bill's slowness was cultural rather than psychotically pathological was a question of primary concern.

Bill's apathetic and withdrawn behavior has already been described. For diagnostic purposes, however, this syndrome is confused by cultural factors. It is common for Navahos, with their morbid fear of hospitals, to demonstrate just such a withdrawal patterning.[7] It is not known whether or not this would reach a stage of *cerea flexibilitas* or how long this behavior will persist. Accordingly it was concluded that Bill's apparent catatonia should not be accepted as a symptom of schizophrenia until underlying signs of schizophrenic processes could be detected.

During the first interview Bill was given the Draw A Person Test. The figure he drew was indistinct and without facial features and clearly reflected his withdrawal.

On the seventh interview the test was again given. Compared with the earlier attempt, the second drawing clearly reflected an improvement. It probably indicated the therapeutic benefits derived from the extensive individual treatment the patient was receiving.

The second drawing filled the paper, the facial features were portrayed, the arms were extended, and the drawing generally implied those signs which are held to indicate good contact with reality.

Although Bill's second drawing seems to infer considerable personality change, no changes could be observed in his behavior. He continued to appear apathetic and withdrawn. On several occasions he indicated his reluctance to talk because "me no good this place," pointing to his chest. This suggested the characteristic organ cathexes of schizophrenia. However, the patient's thinking behind this statement was

[7] *Ibid.*, pp. 108–109.

made clear during the later interviews through an interpreter.

Bill was concerned about the fact that he had not completed the second series of the "Breath of Life" ceremony. This matter had gone too long unattended, and he assumed that he must conserve his vocal energies until they could be supplemented by the breath of the deity. He expressed a great need to return home to pursue the ceremony.

In continued endeavor to detect schizophrenic underlay of his apparent catatonia, Bill was given a series of tests, none of which revealed responses normally associated with schizophrenia.

During the early course of the interviews with Bill, although not satisfied that the patient was not psychotic, the writer recommended that the best therapeutic environment for him would be his own home. This recommendation was not acted upon, partly because no one knew where his home was, or how he could be supervised there, but chiefly because he continued to appear catatonic.

Later, as the writer became convinced that the catatonia—if such it could be termed—was not symptomatic of underlying schizophrenia, efforts were renewed to release the patient. The outcome of these endeavors is summarized in the following section.

OUTCOME

As mentioned earlier, the final interviews with Bill were carried on with the aid of a Navaho interpreter. Bill conversed quite freely with the other Navahos and expressed gratitude at being able to talk to someone in his own language. The conversations did not add much to the history and understanding previously gained, but did offer an opportunity to inquire for the presence of hallucinations, delusions, and more subtle clues of schizophrenic thinking. Unless Bill's anxiety regarding the uncompleted "Breath of Life" ceremony could be considered bizarre, nothing of significance was elicited.

The interpreter's reaction to the interviews represented their most significant outcome. He was a professional interpreter, with vast experience in interviewing Navaho youths in strange environments. He expressed a strong conviction that Bill's behavior and attitudes were not unusual under the circumstances.

The interpreter communicated his feelings to the superintendent of the Sherman Institute, who took an immediate and active interest in the case. After several interviews with Bill, satisfied that he could observe nothing about Bill's behavior which could be considered atypical under the circumstances, the superintendent offered to accept him into the flexible program of the Sherman Institute.

Bill was accordingly released under custody of the superintendent and careful plans were made to assure his adjustment at the school. At first, he was quartered in the school hospital, but allowed to participate in the school's social and recreational activities. He was employed with the animal husbandry and gardening program.

The writer's last visit to the Sherman Institute disclosed that Bill's adjustment had been quite rapid. He had put on weight and after about two weeks announced that he "felt right at home, now."

It had been difficult at first, because

in spite of all precautions the students had learned something of Bill's past hospitalization. To the Navahos the hospital symbolizes death, and death is particularly abhorrent to them as they have no clearly structured concepts of an after-life. The students consequently shied away from Bill a little when he arrived, but he has since found acceptance.

He will go back to the reservation in the spring, at the close of the school year, and attend to the unfinished business of the "Breath of Life" ceremony.

Concluding Discussion

In the course of this Navaho's commitment and 18 months of hospitalization, he was routinely examined by several psychiatrists, all of whom concurred with the diagnosis of schizophrenia. Without verbal communication with the patient, diagnosis was necessarily derived from observation of his overt behavior. Diagnosis was apparently confident as the patient was not referred to staff clinic or for psychological testing, the normal procedure with questionable cases.

Most of the psychiatrists' diagnostic observations were based on information received from the attendants of Bill's cottage, who reported the patient's withdrawn and apathetic behavior. Upon closer examination the patient would demonstrate *cerea flexibilitas.* Because of these factors the patient was assumed to be catatonic and hence schizophrenic.

Actually, many of the classic symptoms of catatonia were not present in this patient. He was not markedly stuporous or mute; he was clean in his personal habits and would eat willingly; he tended to doze as he sat rather than stare fixedly into space as does the typical catatonic. The writer, too, examined Bill for *cerea flexibilitas,* but learned later that the patient held grotesque positions because he thought it was expected of him.

With the assumption, however, that the patient's overt behavior could be interpreted as symptomatic of catatonic schizophrenia, it remains to be explained why testing and closer observation did not reveal the underlying ego disintegration which should be expected.

General personality traits of the Navaho people, as briefly reviewed earlier in this paper, could possibly infer a potential for schizophrenic disintegration. Navahos do not have the imaginative activity and the inner control which is so important to adjustment in the Anglo world. The scales are balanced, however, by a defense of rigidity and construction. In a threatening situation they strive to maintain ego structure by psychic withdrawal.

The few tests that were applicable in examining Bill did not permit a very intensive examination of the dynamics of his withdrawal, but all indications were that he continued to maintain ego strength. He could account for his acts rationally, he performed very well with conceptualization, he maintained orientation for time and place, and could hold in mind simultaneously various aspects of situations or problems. His visuo-motor performance exhibited no signs of distorted perspective. Many of his expressions could be considered naive, but hardly bizarre.

The apparent incongruity between the patient's overt behavior and underlying personality dynamics, although not fully understood psychologically, should not be considered as psychotic manifestation. Culturally derived, it can probably be explained as a defense mechanism characterized by an extreme and sustained withdrawal.

To what extent Bill's case may be typical of other Navaho patients diagnosed as catatonic schizophrenia cannot, of course, be proposed. It would be necessary to know if those patients were similarly diagnosed on the basis of overt behavior alone.

It is also unknown to what degree Bill may personify on-reservation Navaho youth. Superficially at least, his history appears quite typical. His lack of school, his years as a sheep herder for his grandfather, his attack of tuberculosis, and his railroad employment, are circumstances and events common to many Navahos. His grandfather's apparent lack of affection implies an almost feral existence for the growing boy, but even this situation is not unusual. It is, in fact, difficult to discern some way in which this patient could be atypical as evaluated against his cultural background. Except for his possible low intelligence, he appears to represent a typical Navaho youth, a fact heavy with implication when his 18 months of hospitalization as a mental patient is considered.

The previously cited survey of hospitalized Navaho mental patients shows an amazingly small percentage of the total Navaho population (which is about 65,000). This is probably because few Navahos are currently coming in very close contact with Anglo structure.

Of the catatonic schizophrenics, it would be of value to know more about the details of their admission. If they were referred from the reservation it probably meant that they were considered psychotic within the Navaho milieu; if, on the other hand, they were referred by agencies off the reservation (as was Bill), it would imply an evaluation derived from Anglo perspective. This will become a more poignant problem with increasing off-reservation movement of the Navaho people.

In addition to what this study may infer with respect to the Navaho Indians, it is hoped also that it may illustrate the need to consider the influence of cultural environment in any study of individual personality. The psychiatric approach usually concerns itself with the abnormal personality, and evaluates the individual according to concepts of what constitutes the normal personality. Too often these concepts are preconceived and stereotyped, giving very little consideration to the individual's cultural frame of reference. This factor naturally varies in proportion to the degree of the individual's acculturation.

The cultural factor seems to be particularly important in reconciling overt behavior with covert personality dynamics. This is often a difficult reconciliation even with patients of the general American cultural patterning, and becomes increasingly more difficult the farther removed the individual is from acculturation.

The need to consider emotional maladjustment with respect to cultural factors has long been recognized. It has, however, been somewhat of an academic acknowledgment which demands greater practical application on the clinical level.

DEVIANT
LIFE STYLES

Deviant life styles may be thought of as those that are discredited and stigmatized by the middle majority. The labels "wino," "whore," "faggot," and "bum" are used to designate and degrade those whose life styles are regarded as deviant. Given their power, the middle majority enacts laws against deviants, while they use other laws, such as loitering, as a means of repression and control.[†]*

Secrecy is frequently an important aspect of deviant life styles. Some individuals may secretly utilize the services of deviant groups—for example, the suburbanites who attend a strip show or the conventioneers who pick up prostitutes. Other individuals are secret members of subcultures,[‡] appearing to be part of the straight world while maintaining membership in a deviant group. Leznoff and Westley[§] studied the homosexual community of a large Canadian city and found that secret homosexuals were more likely to be in the professions, management, or sales positions than

*Erving Goffman, *Stigma: Notes on the Management of Spoiled Identity* (Englewood Cliffs, N.J.: Prentice-Hall, 1963), pp. 1–40.

[†]Richard Quinney, *The Social Reality of Crime* (Boston: Little, Brown, 1970), pp. 3–25.

[‡]Howard S. Becker, *Outsiders* (New York: Free Press, 1963), pp. 19–39.

[§] Maurice Leznoff and William Westley, "The Homosexual Community," *Social Problems*, **3** (April, 1956), pp. 257–263.

overt homosexuals. The covert homosexuals maintained their secrecy for fear of job dismissal or ridicule, or to protect their families. Overt homosexuals were more likely to come from lower-status occupations or those that have traditionally accepted homosexual behavior, such as the fine arts or hairdressing.

Merle Miller, a novelist and script writer, made public the fact that for years he had been a homosexual, while masquerading as part of the "straight" community. The following letter in the San Francisco Chronicle *in response to Miller, vividly describes the life style dilemmas of secret deviants.*

Just Hiding

To the Editor—*Merle Miller is very lucky that he no longer has to masquerade as a heterosexual. Many of us have to live a masquerade for at least eight hours a day just to earn a living. And living in the web of lies and pretense of this masquerade is not easy.*

I am a college-educated, under-30 homosexual worming my way up in a large corporation. I do not expect to get too far, though. My career will probably stop at the lower end of middle management. To go any farther I would have to be married, to a woman.

I have been married for the past three years, but to a man. The company considers me single. I certainly would not tell them I am married. Yet marriage is a very significant fact of my life. And it is my biggest problem. Marriage between men is very hard in this world that requires people to seem heterosexual.

For eight hours a day I must pretend that I am single; straight and single. Our kind of marriage does not exist at work. Any upsets, any financial problems, any crises of our marriage do not exist either. I must be very careful not to say anything that would make my roommate and me sound "too" close.

When I was transferred from another city some time ago, I had to hide the fact that my roommate came along; and then weave a fabric of lies to explain why he was here when I accidentally mentioned him. And we are married! If he had been a woman, the company would have given me extra money to bring him here.

How often people tell me I act like a married man. Most of them find out I am single later on. Then the fun begins. The young women at work think I am a good prospect ("with a bright future"). They expect me to be interested in them—but I am married!

I must join in "stag" talk with the fellows. It is a big bore, but I had better not show it. To satisfy my boss' curiosity about my life

I must intimate that a good friend of mine, who happens to be female, is having an affair with me.

I am trapped in a cage of pretending. I do not look at all different. How is anyone to know I am a homosexual? A respectable, married, aggressive, "bright future" homosexual? I do not look one bit different from other respectable, aggressive, married young men.

ANONYMOUS

Thus there is a public and a private deviant community. The public deviant community consists of those who are known deviants, while the larger deviant community consists of those who are public deviants, secret deviants, and consumers of deviance. The private deviant community may consist of those who are deviant in behavior but not in public identity. A distinct life style develops around public membership in the deviant community—the deviant role becomes a central life interest.

In response to repression launched against them, deviant groups become organized into close-knit communities with their own language, set of values, and behavior patterns. These shared linguistic, value, and behavior patterns create a feeling of solidarity to insulate the deviant in-group from the pressures bombarding it from the outside world.

A critical pattern of behavior is symbolic behavior, notably the way deviants label and hence view themselves. The public may call them "bums,"* "queers," or "whores," but they call themselves "tramps," "gay people," or "exotic dancers."

In the three essays that follow, the life styles of tramps, homosexuals, and strippers are described. Deviance is explored from the perspective of three academic fields: James Spradley, an anthropologist; Martin Hoffman, a psychiatrist; and James Skipper and Charles McCaghy, sociologists.

According to a recent study, skid-row areas are gradually disappearing within the United States. For example, the winter population of the Bowery, in New York City, was estimated at about 7,000 people in 1963. By 1971 this figure is expected to drop to about 3,000.† Reasons for the decline include greater economic prosperity and changing welfare policies that "induce men to live elsewhere."‡

---

*Spradley notes that for those who call themselves *tramps,* there is a popular identity of *bums,* a sociological identity of *homeless men,* a medical identity of *alcoholics,* and a legal identity of *drunks* or *vagrants.* James P. Spradley, *You Owe Yourself a Drunk* (Boston: Little, Brown, 1970), pp. 65–68.

† Howard M. Bahr, "The Gradual Disappearance of Skid Row," *Social Problems,* **15** (1967), pp. 41–45.

‡ Bahr, *ibid.,* p. 43.

James Spradley and others* have noted that, although inhabitants of skid row are homeless, 'they are not without a sense of community. Like other deviant groups, they have an argot and unique values, most of which center around the central life interest of obtaining and consuming alcohol or its equivalents.† Earl Rubington has noted the tacit set of norms centering around group alcohol consumption on skid row. Norms specify the number of "swigs" each person takes before passing the bottle, what people say to each other while drinking, and rules for disposing of the empty.‡ James Spradley, in the following essay, notes that a crucial aspect of skid-row life style focuses on obtaining alcohol. This life style shows a sense of resourcefulness and a higher degree of social organization than would be expected from the popular stereotype of tramps.

* Spradley, *op. cit.*; Samuel Wallace, *Skid Row as a Way of Life* (Ottawa: Bedminster Press, 1965); Earl Rubington, "Variations in Bottle-Gang Controls," in Earl Rubington and Martin Weinberg (eds.), *Deviance: The Interactionist Perspective* (New York: Macmillan, 1968), pp. 308–316.

† Samuel Wallace has noted, "To be fully integrated and acculturated on Skid Row is to be a drunk. . . ." Samuel Wallace, "The Road to Skid Row," *Social Problems,* **16** (1968), pp. 92–105.

‡ Rubington, *op. cit.,* p. 311. Rubington studied an Eastern city of about 165,000. He also notes that "bottle-gang" norms on the East Coast differ from those in other regions.

Down and Out on Skid Road

JAMES P. SPRADLEY

He moves slowly down the street, and everything about him announces to the world that he is down and out. Ill-fitting clothes cover a hollow chest and sagging muscles. The lines in his face, half hidden beneath the shadow of a faded hat, suggest that he is old before his time. His shoes are cracked with age and exposure to the weather. An overcoat, pocket bulging from a half-empty bottle,

This article was prepared especially for this book.

covers a sports jacket which long ago found its way to the secondhand clothing store. His course is unsteady, his face unshaven, and those who pass him by are assaulted by the odor of cheap wine. An outstretched hand with a few coins is thrust toward the affluent who have entered his world that morning from a distant suburb. Who is this man? A bum to be pitied? A vagrant to be jailed? A homeless man to be rehabilitated? An alcoholic in need of medical treatment? He must be down on his luck and out of resources—one who can no longer organize his behavior or achieve goals. He is adrift at the bottom of society, cut off from a life style ordered by cultural rules. In the minds of many he is even beneath the tribal savage whose way of life may be different, but not derelict. But let us look more closely at this man and the thousands like him who live in every large American city.

Anthropologists have long emphasized the importance of discovering the native point of view for their descriptions of non-Western cultures. This simple but difficult perspective is even more important in the study of urban subcultures. Recent developments in anthropology, known as ethnoscience, have proved especially useful for discovering the way insiders conceptualize their own life style. The goal of ethnoscience is to discover the characteristic ways in which members of a subculture categorize, code, and define their experiences. In every society "reality" is socially constructed, and this definition of the situation is used by individuals to organize their behavior. Those who live by other cultures do not identify their religion as "pagan superstition," their parents' brothers as "uncles," nor do they divide the rainbow into seven distinct colors. In a similar manner we shall misconstrue the culture of Skid Road men unless we enter their world and see life from their point of view. An understanding of those with different life styles must begin with a description of the cognitive maps they employ in everyday life.

In order to tap the cognitive and symbolic world of the down-and-outers, it was necessary to study their language. Although language does not exhaust the system of symbols for a particular culture, it certainly involves a central portion of it. In the study of a non-western society, the researcher is forced to learn their language before he can make headway in his studies. At first this did not appear to be the case with the population on Skid Road. The informants I

encountered spoke a dialect of English which was similar to my own in both sound and grammar. After several months of participant observation and listening, however, I discovered that the semantic aspect of their language was very different. The questions which were relevant to informants had not been anticipated. The terms which they used to categorize and identify the objects in their environment would not have been included on a pretested survey questionnaire. It soon became clear that these men could only be considered "down and out" by those who did not understand their perspective. Their behavior became comprehensible in terms of the meaning systems which they had learned and were using to order their daily activities. After a brief description of the major features in this culture, we shall examine one set of strategies used to achieve the goals which these men consider appropriate.

THE CULTURE OF TRAMPS

There are five major scenes where these men carry out their activities: buckets (jails), farms (treatment centers), jungles (encampments), skids (Skid Roads), and freights (railroad cars). The most important identity which a man has in all of these scenes is referred to as "tramp." There were more than fifteen different kinds of tramps recognized by informants. For example, a "box-car tramp" is an independent person who is arrested often and travels by means of freight trains. A "bindle stiff" is a tramp who travels on freight cars but always carries a bed-roll and a few personal belongings. A "mission stiff" travels from mission to mission, drawing upon their resources for his needs. A semantic analysis of the terms for various tramps led to the discovery that the criteria for distinguishing among tramps were mobility-related. This reflects the importance of the nomadic style of life which tramps follow. This category system constitutes only one of the social-identity domains in this subculture.

When a man is arrested and placed in jail, usually on the charge of public intoxication, he assumes the identity of inmate. There are five major kinds of inmates which a man may become, the most important of which is *trusty*. In the particular jail studied there were over sixty different kinds of trusties. In this capacity nearly 150 men provided janitorial services for the city hall, outlying police precincts, and the jail. They assisted in the preparation of food, maintained the firing range, cared for police vehicles, and did numerous other tasks. Many tramps felt they were arrested and charged with public drunkenness, not because they were inebriated, but in order to provide cheap labor for the police department.

In each of the major scenes in this subculture there are specialized modes of action for solving common problems. For example, when a man is in jail, he discovers that his freedom is restricted and he often lacks food, cigarettes, and clothing. One solution to these problems is to engage in actions which tramps refer to as "hustling." This is a cover term for a large number of specific actions or plans which tramps group into the following equivalence classes: "conning," "peddling," "kissing ass," "making a run," "taking a rake-off,"

"playing cards," "bumming," "running a game," "making a pay-off," "beating," and "making a phone call." A knowledge of the different ways to "hustle" can mean the difference between doing "hard time" and "easy time." One younger tramp who was a college graduate gave the following description of hustling:

Speaking of survival in jail, there are various ways, of course. If you come in with some money, of course you have commissary twice a week. That way you can get eight packages of cigarettes and eight candy bars, toothbrush, toothpaste, that's about the limit of what you can buy, and of course postage stamps. If you do not have commissary you have to find other means if you wish to have more than two packs of Bull Durham a week. In any case you are shaking for the first few days from nothing more than malnutrition, and so one asks the doctors who come around twice a day, you might ask him for some librium or some phenobarbital to quiet you, or whatever you might be able to get from him, cold pills even (conning), but the wise drunk who has no money at all will just go through the whole thing cold turkey, suffer though he will, he'll save his pills and trade two quarter-grain phenobarbital for a package of Bull Durham or 1.25 mg. librium for a pack of Bull Durham (peddling). Some of them will even do push-ups or something like that before the doctor comes, just to be shaking and sweating (conning). But in general, within a very short time, 4–5 days, you're shut off completely from any of that. So then you have to find another way. By that time you've eaten enough so you're in pretty good balance and then you can make sandwiches. Sometimes you get a tray at night, which is your big meal, and you can barely make a sandwich out of it using the whole tray. But in any case you can trade them for a package of Bull Durham if that's what you need. Of course the ideal thing, if you are going to be sentenced, is to become a trusty if possible.

It might be necessary to "make a pay-off" in order to become a trusty, but once in this position a man has many more opportunities to hustle.

When a tramp is out of jail, he usually refers to goals in a specific manner, and the techniques used to attain the goal will be classified as "ways of making it." In contrast to the view that these men are "down and out," they have numerous resources in the form of survival strategies which are compatible with a life style of mobility. These "ways of making it" are employed in the pursuit of many objectives, including the following: "I'm trying to make a flop," "I need something to eat," "I pled guilty in order not to do dead time," and "Let's make the mission for some clothes."

An important activity for most tramps is the drinking of alcoholic beverages. In part, this drinking has great social significance and binds together men with spoiled identities. Many men spend months at a time in jail, and when released they feel they owe themselves a drunk. Others drink to solve personal problems, and many admit they do not know why they drink. Whatever the reason, one of the recurring goals in this culture is the acquisition of some alcoholic beverage, conceptualized by tramps as "making a jug." In the remainder of this paper, we shall examine the cultural techniques used by men who are "down and out" to achieve this goal.

WAYS TO MAKE A JUG

Every language functions to identify objects, events, and actions which are part of experience. Linguistic labels allow man to treat his experience symbolically. This involves continuous categorization, cognitive acts whereby different things are treated as equivalent. Thus, a group of individuals on a college campus, all of whom are unique, are treated as equivalent and labeled "students." A student engages in different activities which are identified as "studying." A knowledge of different "ways to study" is of great value to the student for organizing his behavior and achieving certain academic objectives. Whether one is a student or a tramp, the use of categories and linguistic labels is necessary if we are to simplify and organize our experience.

It may not seem very significant to have discovered that tramps identify their actions for obtaining alcoholic beverages as "ways to make a jug." But many other questions could be asked which would not lead to the exhaustive mapping of the cognitive world of informants. For example, it would have been possible—indeed, numerous researchers have done so—to ask these men about their income, type of employment, and where they live. On the basis of what was *significant to informants* the following question was used: "Are there different ways to make a jug?" The various techniques elicited by this question make up the following taxonomy of ways to make a jug.

Ways to Make a Jug

1. Making the blood bank
2. Bumming

   a. Panhandling (stemming)
   b. Making a 'Frisco Circle
   c. Bumming
3. Stealing
   a. Boosting
   b. Rolling
      (1) Rolling
      (2) Jackrolling
   c. Beating
   d. Clipping
4. Peddling
5. Taking a rake-off
6. Pooling
7. Cutting in on a jug
8. Borrowing
9. Buying
10. Making your own
    a. Making pruno
    b. Making raisin jack
    c. Making sweet lucy
    d. Squeezing heat
    e. Squeezing shoe polish
    f. Making home brew
    g. Straining shellac
    h. Mixing bay rum
    i. Mixing solax
    j. Mixing shaving lotion
    k. Mixing ruby-dub
    l. Mixing gasoline
11. Meeting a live one
12. Hustling a queer
13. Hustling a broad
14. Making a run
15. Spot jobbing
16. Making the mission
17. Making the V.A.
18. Junking

These ways to get an alcoholic beverage provide an exhaustive mapping of the strategies which tramps learn in their culture for meeting this particular need. Let us consider several ways to make a jug in more detail, for they clearly demonstrate the skill and resourcefulness which are present in this culture.

"Making the blood bank" is a common way to make a jug. In response to this behavior, there are blood banks in the Skid Road districts of many cities. One informant described this strategy:

Well, in my case I have too much blood and I'm a regular blood donor, but on the average a guy will make the blood bank for money to buy a bottle. Fifty percent of the guys that sells blood does it for a bottle. They give you about $5 a time. Whole blood you can only sell once every eight weeks unless you know how to lie and get by. Plasma you can sell from two to three times a week. I'll be drinking with a group and some guy will say, "You gonna make the blood bank today?" Or, "When's your day at the blood bank?" They're open from 7 til 5, but you got to be in there by three in the afternoon or you're out. See, if you went into the blood bank in the morning or any time during the day and you didn't have an appointment, you have to wait. You could go in there at seven in the morning and wait two or three hours. I come in and go right up there because I have an appointment. It only takes fifteen minutes or a half hour at the most to give whole blood, it all depends on the person. For plasma it will take from an hour to two hours, and if you're in a hurry or got something to do, you want to give whole blood. A lot of guys might not be able to give plasma when they could give whole blood, because if you lay on the table for an your or two hours, you might fall asleep or pass out where you're not supposed to.

Actually, they ain't supposed to take your blood if you're too sick or drinking, but at some places where you walk into *and your blood pressure is high or low or your temperature isn't right, maybe you haven't slept good, or maybe you ain't eating right, or maybe you've climbed a hill too fast on the way there, there are different reasons why your pressure may be up—anyway, if you take a shot of wine it will make you normal, it calms your nerves. The doctors tell you it isn't so, but I know it works. That's why a lot of tramps will take one or two shots of wine before going to give blood. If you've been drinking for a time and have the shakes, the girls at the blood bank will see you're shaking and nervous and so you can't give blood. But if they know you and see you got the shakes and need a drink, they'll sometimes say, "Well, here's 75¢, go down and get yourself a bottle and drink it and then come back." They get to know you after a while, and if they give you money to get a drink first, they just take it out of the $5 you get from your blood later. That's a good way to make a jug.*

Another strategy frequently employed by tramps is "bumming." There are many specific acts involved in bumming, but tramps classify them as panhandling, making a 'Frisco Circle, and bumming. Some tramps become very skilled in these activities, and may even become "professional panhandlers," a kind of tramp known to some as a "ding." One informant reported:

Bob and I went stemming in Chinatown yesterday. While he was stemming the street corners, I would be bumming the bars. You are stemming strictly for money. Panhandling is the same as stemming. You are always on the streets, and the best place is where there are a lot of tourists. Now you can be bumming anyplace, you can go to a

grocery store or a business place or some church, or on the street or even a bar, you could be anyplace. You could be bumming for clothes, or groceries, or money, or drinks; but if you're panhandling, you're doing it strictly for money. Before you start bumming you have to have a drink to get your courage up, some guys cannot stem unless they do have a drink, they just haven't got the nerve.

Another informant reported the strategies which he used to induce a man on the street to give him some money to buy something to drink.

Most generally you hit for the right tourists, you start bummin' where there's a lot of tourists, or you get downtown where the business person is. If I want a bottle, if I'm bummin' for a drink, I'll tell a man I'm sick and need a drink, or I'm short on a bottle, and nine times out of ten I'll get it. But if I tell a person I'm hungry and want something to eat, or wanted a place to sleep, nine times out of ten he'd turn me down, he wouldn't give it to me. You gotta use psychology, now like a good professional panhandler will go around in ragged clothes, some of them are misers and some of them bum all the time. Now an ordinary panhandler, just an ordinary guy bummin', he's just gonna get his drink and go get drunk. He might get more than he needs right at that one time, but he won't keep on. The other guy will keep on. I don't mind askin' others, a working man or something, I try to pick somebody who looks like he has a little something and can afford to share a little bit.

"Making a 'Frisco Circle" is a unique kind of bumming where one tramp stands in a bar or on the street and with a piece of chalk draws a circle on the ground or on the floor. He then asks others to toss into the 'Frisco Circle, or to "help out the circle." When there is sufficient money, those who contributed will share a drink together.

Since begging is against the law in many states, there is some degree of risk involved in bumming. One man reported his strategy for circumventing this risk or reducing it.

> *It's getting to where it's generally two that prefers to panhandle. I'm walking down the street, I'm gonna stop those people and bum, and I got another guy on the other side of the street, or behind me a ways, and if he sees a cop or the fuzz, plain-clothes ragpicker, why he's gonna high-sign me and let me know— because I got my mind on you and the public, and I'm not exactly watching for the law.*

The risk of arrest is not always as easily avoided. Consider the experience of another tramp:

> *A ragpicker would see you with change and ask you, "Are you short?" and I'd say, "Yeah, fifteen cents, can you spare it?" and he would say, "Yes," give you fifteen cents and then show you his badge and get you for bumming, or stemming.*

There are a variety of laws which a tramp can violate and end up in jail. Bumming and stealing are only two of them. In addition, a man may be arrested for being drunk in public, drinking in public, urinating in public, and for purchasing liquor during days or hours when its sale is illegal. This latter case sometimes involves the ragpickers, as one man pointed out:

> *You know, one sorry deal is those rag-pickers. That's a sorry-ass goddam deal, those ragpickers picking these tramps up. They'll come down there dressed like a tramp and come up and say, "Hey, you know where I can get a bottle?" and you show him where he can get a bottle, maybe the guy's trying to make him some money or something. I don't give a damn, if I want a drink and I have to pay out a little more I'll pay it, but they'll come down and get you to do something and know that it's wrong and turn around and arrest your ass. He gives you the loot to buy the bottle and you buy the bottle and he'll throw your ass in jail.*

Tramps survive in part by "stealing." In their culture this involves a variety of acts which are classified into different categories. "Rolling" almost always involves theft from an individual who has passed out from too much alcohol or who must be overcome by the use of force. "Beating" involves stealing from a person or institution. A man in jail will beat another man for his money. For example, a drunk in the drunk tank will ask a trusty to bring him a package of cigarettes and give him $5, expecting change. The trusty may take the money and never return, thus beating the drunk for his money, which he will use to purchase a bottle upon release. "Clipping" is stealing by stealth. In a bar when one has placed money on the table, a tramp might clip him for it without his awareness.

"Boosting" almost always involves stealing articles which can then be sold or "peddled" from stores or other business establishments. One informant reported:

Boosting out of a parked car or boosting out of a store, a lot of them call the store "shoplifting" instead of "boosting," but both would be the same thing. Like Sears and Roebucks, that's one of their main places where guys shoplift and boost. I got a buddy, and the only thing he would boost is measuring tapes. He would get a pocket full of them, they're three- or four-dollar tapes, and come down and get his wine and come back. Some of them tramps go in for tools or most anything you can put in your pocket or shirt. Like a good booster, he can steal T.V.'s or radios or anything else, he'll walk into a store, most generally there's two guys or a guy and a woman; one will be buying something and keep the clerk busy, and the other will pick up something and walk off with it.

Tramps find little difficulty in peddling on the street those things which they have boosted. In fact, tools, transistor radios, shirts and other clothing are all items which can be sold fast on the street. One informant reported:

The main thing is getting what you know you can sell and get rid of fast, and if you're selling them fast on a streetcorner, like clothes or tools, why then most generally there's two of you and one keeps their eye out for the fuzz, while the other one is talking, or if you go into a bar, it's the same thing. Wrist watches and pocket watches is another thing that you boost because they are easy to sell, particularly in a bar or on a streetcorner. You will get more money selling them in a bar or on the street than you will if you take it into a hock shop, and there ain't as much risk.

The risk involved in peddling makes some men shy away from it. Even when there is no evidence that the item was stolen, it is possible to get arrested. One man reported:

On April 3rd, 1968, I was in a hock shop on First and Pike trying to pawn my radio. When I came out I met a cop and he said I stole the radio but he could not prove it. So he booked me as drunk in the city jail.

Some tramps are future-oriented and when they do have money from working in the harvest, or at a spot job, they will purchase items which can be peddled at some later date. One man summarized this practice:

Well, most generally, like a fruit tramp, when they get paid they will buy a pile of expensive stuff, knowing that sooner or later they will go broke and they will always have something that they can take and hock, or peddle to get ready cash for it. They'll go in for expensive rings or wrist watches to do this.

The strategies which a tramp uses are not the impulses of a derelict. Indeed, each way to make a jug requires the processing of a great deal of information. The man who is bumming must learn effective approaches, evaluate people that he would beg from, and be on the alert for the police. The individual who makes the blood bank must keep track of when he was there last and how well those in the blood bank know him. He must be aware of his own physical condition in case he has to use subterfuge in order to sell his blood. Stealing of one sort or another involves careful calculations regarding other people and the chances of selling the item boosted. As a man begins a day in pursuit of a jug of wine, this map is especially useful for achieving his goal.

Many of the strategies for making a jug involve cooperation with other tramps. One of the myths that has grown up about Skid Road men, "the down-and-outers," is that they are friendless, isolated and alone. This study revealed that many of the ways to make a jug involve cooperative action with other men. Panhandling will often be done in pairs, as well as stealing and peddling, in order to reduce the risk of arrest. Both "pooling" and "cutting in on a jug" involve a group of men who are usually willing to share with other men who are looking for some alcohol. In fact, the question is raised as to whether drinking is the prime need one feels when he pools or cuts in on a jug. It may well be that one is seeking human companionship among other men, who, like himself, have been stigmatized by the larger society.

"Meeting a live one" also involves other people and shows the bonds that exist between tramps as well as the generosity of this culture. A live one is defined by these men as anyone who will purchase a drink for you or give you a larger amount of money than the usual person on the street. A tramp walking down the street may have someone come up to him and say, "I'll buy you a drink." This is usually someone who just seeks to talk. Tramps often become "live ones" to other tramps, and when they have money they share it. One man reported the following experience:

> *He came out of Firland's (T.B. sanitarium) and he came down there drunk. Well, he pieced me off and he pieced Charlie off. He had four hundred bucks, he had three one-hundred-dollar bills. He took us up to the Morrison Hotel*

> *and paid for our dinner and all that and he bought us a jug. Then he went out and got racked up and you know, he wakes up in the morning and he's got twenty dollars in his property box in the jail.*

Another man who had returned from the harvest related his experience of being a live one:

> *I was over picking apples in the apple harvest and I stayed over after the harvest was done and worked on and they gave me a bonus. And I came to Seattle and had $299. I bought a bus ticket for $5 and came to Seattle. When I got to Seattle everyone was getting off the bus and there was a big crowd and they were headed in to get their luggage and I wanted a drink pretty bad, so I didn't even pick up my suitcase. I had gotten some new clothes and I headed right downtown to the Pike Street area where there's a liquor store that closes kind of early. I got myself a room and paid for two nights, got a bottle of Jim Beam and got a chaser and was headed back to my room when I met a fellow, an Indian boy, who I had known. We'd been in the same little shack where we lived, and he and I talked and he'd lost all his money, spent it and lost it in some way. So I gave him some money and bought him a room and we got something to eat. And I'd had a couple drinks by then but I wasn't blacking out or even staggering or anything like that, I knew what I was doing. I got picked up by the police coming out of the restaurant.*

Many tramps have learned to make their own in one way or another. This may be done in order to have a large supply, or because they do not have money or resources to get a bottle that has been made commercially. One man reported:

I know guys who drink nothing but beer, but if you've been on a drunk it's just like pop or water. Some drink nothing but apple wine. That generally makes me sick, and before I'd take apple wine, I'd rather make my own jug—sterno, bay rum, ruby-dub, or something else. If you get the sterno or canned heat in a red can it's o.k., but the one in the gray wrapper is poison. You squeeze the canned heat through a handkerchief, sock, or even an old rag to get out the alcohol. One big can of sterno makes a fifth of a pretty good drink after you cut it with water or coke. You can also mix bay rum and water, rubbing alcohol and orange juice, shaving lotion and water, or solax and coke. There are tramps who will go to the filling station after it closes and get the drips of gasoline which are left in the hose and mix it with sweet milk to make a jug. Others will strain shellac or shoe polish through a loaf of bread to get the impurities out and mix what's left with something for a drink.

It takes a good deal of knowledge and care to mix your own, and just as much to make pruno, raisin jack, or sweet lucy. One man described his recipe as follows:

For raisin jack you take two pounds of raisins, seven pounds of sugar, one cake of yeast, and put it in a large plastic bucket. You can use a glass bottle, but a can or a pan is liable to give you ptomaine poisoning. You put warm water in with all the stuff and let it sit for 72 hours. When it's done you get about nine gallons of raisin jack that's 14-20% alcohol. A guy on the road usually won't make pruno, but take a couple guys who are staying in town or living in a jungle,

they can make out pretty well making their own that way.

Conclusion

In this paper we have discussed life styles of men on Skid Road—but it is important to point out that this description is not based on observation. Instead, using the techniques of ethnoscience, I attempted to elicit their perception of their own behavior. Every culture provides its members with cognitive maps which they use to organize their behavior—plans which are carried out in the achievement of goals. Individuals who are socialized into the culture of the tramps not only learn new identities, but also new patterns of behavior. One of these is to "make a jug," an activity learned as the value and importance of alcohol becomes significant in the lives of these men. They then learn systematic ways to achieve this goal along with the others that are important in this culture. They may appear "down and out on Skid Road" from the perspective of outsiders. In the experience of tramps there are many resources available—strategies which are especially appropriate to a nomadic style of life where drinking has enormous personal and social value.

Notes

The research for this paper was carried out from July 1967 to August 1968 in Seattle, Washington. This study was partially supported by the Departments of Psychiatry and Anthropology, University of Washington; U.S. Public Health Service Undergraduate Training in Human Behavior Grant, No. 5-T2-

MH-7871-06 from the Institute of Mental Health; and the State of Washington Initiative 171 Funds for Research in Biology and Medicine.

The term "Skid Road" is used here in preference to "Skid Row" which appears in much literature. Skid Road is a term which originated in Seattle to describe the road down which logs were skidded to the sawmill and where bars, flophouses, and gambling houses were prevalent. The name often became Skid Row as it was adopted throughout the country, but in Seattle it remains Skid Road.

A more complete discussion of the methods used in this research as well as an analysis of other aspects of this culture appears in *You Owe Yourself a Drunk: An Ethnography of Urban Nomads* by the author (Little, Brown, and Company, Boston, 1970).

In a questionnaire given to college students, the question was raised: What is a deviant? The category of deviance most frequently named was homosexuality.* In consequence of being identified publicly as homosexual, one is disbarred from many social positions and deprived of social rewards. Within the homosexual subculture there are places of meeting and patterns of interaction that form the basis of a deviant life style. Gay bars, restrooms, and steam baths are identified by Martin Hoffman, in the following article, as centers of homosexual interaction. These gathering places are used to establish sexual contacts. Much interaction among homosexuals, however, is not sexual in nature; rather it is concerned with community activities such as disseminating news and discussing a shared problem—the stigma that attaches to being homosexual.†

Homosexuals are the only deviant group to have organized a liberation movement that seeks public acceptance of their deviant behavior. A premise of homosexuals who seek to remove their stigma of deviance is that they could then participate in the straight community rather than in a deviant subcommunity. Thus an implicit assumption of the Gay Liberation Movement is that the life style of homosexuals is imposed by the public's labeling them as deviant.

*J. L. Simmons, "Public Stereotypes of Deviants," *Social Problems,* **13** (Fall, 1965), pp. 223–232. Forty-nine percent of respondents labeled homosexuality as deviant. This exceeded all other forms of deviance, including murder and drug addiction.
†For a discussion of deviant communities, including homosexuals, see Alfred Lindesmith and Anselm Strauss, *Social Psychology,* 2nd ed. (New York: Holt, 1968), pp. 410–435.

The Public Places of Gay Life

MARTIN HOFFMAN

When a young man begins to define himself as homosexual, he is faced with the problem of where to find sexual partners. He will soon discover that there are various public places in which homosexual partners can be found. They are, principally, gay bars, particular steam baths, rest rooms, and certain areas of streets and parks which are known to the homosexual community. To a very large extent, the active homosexual's life revolves around these public places, since he typically finds himself in a constant search for new partners.

As we shall see, one of the most striking features of the homosexual world is the great degree of sexual promiscuity to be found in it. Since the sexual relationships in gay life tend to be transitory, the sexually active homosexual constantly needs new partners in order to obtain a reasonable amount of sexual satisfaction. In response to the need for homosexual meeting places, public places for sexual encounters tend to develop. I don't wish to deny that there do exist some fairly stable homosexual relationships, sometimes called "gay marriages," which last over a period of years; nevertheless, my own experience agrees with Kinsey's findings that: "Long term relationships between two

From Martin Hoffman, *The Gay World* (New York: Basic Books, 1968), pp. 44–63. Reprinted by permission of Basic Books, Inc.

males are notably few." This question of the stability of paired relationships is one which is debated constantly among homosexuals and is especially a point of disagreement between the homosexual organizations which have sprung up within the last ten years and those authorities in the scientific community who maintain that homosexuality and promiscuity go hand in hand. It should be pointed out that Kinsey was not at all unsympathetic to homosexuals and that he had the benefit of studying a large sample of the general population, so that his statement is the best scientific evidence we now have on this disputed issue.

At this point, I think we should introduce a distinction which is not often made in the literature, namely, between sexual promiscuity (or at any rate, a propensity for sexual promiscuity among males) and an inability to develop close and lasting sexual-interpersonal relationships. Kinsey's statement does not mean that homosexuals are promiscuous, although this is true. What it really means is that they do not form lasting, paired, sexual relationships with each other in the way in which heterosexual couples characteristically do. The reasons for this we will postpone discussing until somewhat later. Nevertheless, it should be made quite clear that sexual promiscuity is one of the most striking, distinguishing features of gay life in America.

STREETS, PARKS, AND REST ROOMS

A competent social ethnographer could write a very detailed description of the activity which goes on in streets, parks, and rest rooms, on the part of male homosexuals. It is not really my intention to do so here, since it is not necessary to write a complete ethnography in order to outline the points which I wish to make. John Rechy's second novel, *Numbers,* contains much detailed ethnographic description of homosexual contacts made in rest rooms and especially in parks. As the reader might well imagine, contacts which are made in such places are characterized by their brevity and their casualness more than by anything else. Homosexuals who meet sexual partners in the street do not have sex with them on the street, but usually adjourn to one of their apartments. In the parks and in the rest rooms, sex right then and there may or may not occur, depending upon the propensities of the two individuals involved. Sometimes a sexual act takes place in the park or in the rest room, and sometimes partners will adjourn to an apartment, although this is more likely the case for park contacts than for rest-room contacts. All these places are under a good deal of surveillance by the police, and the individuals who engage in sexual solicitation and sexual activity there take great risks. For some, this factor of risk unquestionably adds to the excitement of the sexual encounter. Needless to say, the chances of meeting someone with whom one can have a prolonged, satisfactory, personal relationship are not very great, although occasionally such relationships do develop from such brief and casual meetings.

A prominent attorney told how he met the man with whom he has been living for six years by cruising a street in the bohemian section of town. He surveyed all the people walking along the thoroughfare and loitered around some of the store windows, as if he were window-shopping, in order that a possible partner might get the idea that he was interested in making a sexual contact. When he finally attracted the attention of a suitable prospect, the two of them engaged in what one might perhaps regard as a little ceremonial dance, in which they exchanged searching glances and then moved on a little bit to the next store window. Finally, the attorney became somewhat tired of this and walked in the direction of his apartment, which was nearby. He was not sure whether the other man was going to follow him—but he did. The attorney went into his apartment and the other man followed him inside and proceeded immediately to take off his clothes. A sexual encounter followed. No words were spoken until after the sexual experience was over. They were surprised to find that they both had some extra-sexual interests in common, and a friendship gradually developed between them. As is so typically the case, the beginning of the relationship was characterized by a sexual affair, but the sexual activity has been terminated, and they now seek sexual partners outside the home.

One of the most curious aspects of the homosexual community—insofar as it may be called a community—is that news travels very fast, and information as to the location of those particular streets, those sections of the public parks, and those particular rest rooms where homosexual contacts may be found becomes rapidly circulated among the active members of the community. When police activity interferes with the sexual meetings in these locales, the places of activity will often switch to another location. Police interference, however, does not always stop homosexuals from cruising in a particular spot. Sometimes it is obvious even to these homosexual men themselves that they find the danger of arrest an inducement to seek sexual excitation in such places.

It is not true that the majority of homosexuals are recognizable on sight by the uninitiated. It is often true, however, that they can recognize each other. This is not because of any distinguishing physical characteristics, but, rather, because when cruising, they engage in behavioral gestures which immediately identify themselves to each other. A large part of cruising is done with the eyes, by means of searching looks of a prolonged nature and through the surveying of the other man's entire body. It is also done by lingering in the presence of the other person, and by glancing backward. After a few minutes of cruising, the prospective partner will readily get the message that someone is interested in him. In rest rooms, protocol for making contacts is based on giving signals to the individual in the next booth, usually done by a tapping of the foot or sometimes by passing notes underneath the partition or by standing at the urinal for rather long periods of time, fondling one's own penis, then looking at and finally touching the penis of the man at the adjacent spot. Vice-squad officers are, of course, aware of these techniques and make considerable use of them in procuring arrests.

Sometimes homosexuals—when, for example, cruising a park—will make a more direct approach by engaging in direct physical contact with the prospective partner, often by touching his genitals. This approach has at least three serious disadvantages, one being that the other person might not be homosexual and thus be very offended and perhaps stunned by this direct approach, and may resort to physical violence. The second danger is that a police officer could be nearby and view the scene, and an arrest might ensue. Third, even if the other person is a homosexual who is cruising the park, he might not care for such an overt approach and might leave the scene, even though he may have found the person who groped him physically attractive.

The homosexual's expectation in these three public places is for direct sexual contact with a minimum of conversation or social preliminaries, and the implied contract is for immediate sex, either in the public place itself or, directly following, in a private locale. Whether one wants to describe an encounter such as this as a "one-night stand" is a matter of definition. It is certainly no more than that.

THE BATHS

In certain of the larger cities in America there are steam baths which cater exclusively to male homosexuals. Whether or not these baths are viable commercial institutions depends upon police attitudes, since there is no question that a market for them exists among the male homosexual population. The attitude of police toward such institutions varies widely, from toleration to suppression, just as police attitudes toward gay bars differ from city to city. Some police feel they want no homosexual gathering places in their domain, while other law enforcement agencies feel that homosexuals should be allowed to segregate in their own public, but enclosed, places in order to prevent them from becoming a nuisance in the more open areas which we have described above. It is said that proprietors of establishments such as baths and gay bars pay off police for the privilege of running their businesses; I have no direct evidence on this question. In any case, it would seem that even if such payoffs do occur, they only occur within the framework of an already established police policy of toleration. To my knowledge, there exists nothing even approaching a satisfactory study of how attitudes are developed on the part of police agencies toward homosexuals and the relation between these attitudes and actual police practice. One thing is clear, and that is that cities vary widely in the reception which they afford to homosexual activity. Consequently, homosexuals frequently move from more repressive cities and towns into areas where there is less repression.

Physically, the baths are divided into two parts. One is a public area which may be a steam room or simply a very large enclosed chamber, sometimes referred to by the clientele as an "orgy room." In these public rooms sexual contact can be made or group sexual activity may occur. The second main area of the baths is the individual room, which is assigned to the client as he enters the establishment. Its main features are a bed and a door with a lock on it. These private rooms exist primarily for the purpose of sexual activity, although clients often sleep there between sexual escapades. One way in which the individual homosexual can make sexual contact is by leaving the door of his room slightly ajar. His preference for a particular type of sexual activity may be indicated by the position in which he lies on the bed while the door remains ajar. If he lies on his back, it may indicate he prefers to be fellated; if he lies on his side or sits on the bed, then it is not clear what his preference is; if he lies on his stomach, the chances are high that he wishes to take the receptor role in anal intercourse.

As in the streets and parks, the encounters in the baths tend to be completely focused on sexual activity without much attempt at socialization, although this does occasionally occur. One of the remarkable features of the baths is the really very great amount of sexual contact that a man can have during a single visit to the bath. In fact, many customers are disappointed if they go to the baths and have only one sexual experience, even though they may feel it is satisfactory. I once interviewed a young man who preferred to take the receptor role in anal intercourse and had 48 sexual contacts in one evening, simply by going into his room, leaving the door open, lying down on his belly and letting 48 men in succession sodomize him. Just as a matter of note, it should be remarked that this young man had been married and was the father of two children.

In the baths one will see customers roaming around the halls, looking into rooms, and observing those that they meet in the halls. Like the gay bar, the bath is a sexual marketplace and one is judged by one's physical attributes. The baths as a social system are only possible because of the strong tendency to sexual promiscuity among male homosexuals, and it is simply not conceivable that lesbians, for example, would ever be able to develop such an institution. Just why there is this marked discrepancy in the promiscuity rate between male and female homosexuals is a fascinating subject which we shall defer to a later part of the discussion.

Jack is a 32-year-old insurance broker who is a frequent customer of the baths. He is married and has three children and lives in many ways a completely conventional suburban life. He tells his wife that he likes to go out on Friday nights with the boys, and she has no real reason to question this, since there has never been any question of adultery during the six years that they have been married. He checks into the baths around 10:30 and stays there until about 3:00 A.M., during which time he has numerous sexual encounters. He goes there purely for the sex and has no interest in having any social contact with any of the people in the baths other than the most casual of conversations. He does not reveal his identity in any way. He signs the enrollment book with a false name and address.

One of the advantages of the baths, of course, is the almost complete anonymity which they offer. The client is not dressed nor does he have to take his sexual partner back to his own hotel or apartment and, in fact, does not really have to engage him in much conversation. Such a setup is a perfect one for a respectable married man, such as Jack, who wishes to have some homosexual satisfaction without becoming involved in the social and interpersonal aspects of the homosexual community. He will usually get his room assignment and then walk around the halls a bit to see if he can find anyone he likes. He

then goes to the "orgy room," where he engages in a certain amount of reciprocal oral-genital activity. There is actually very little anal activity in the "orgy room"; fellatio is the main kind of sexual practice there. After he tires of this he will cruise the halls until he sees a room in which there is somebody to whom he is sexually attracted. He goes in and has sex. This may happen once or twice. When he feels sexually gratified, he will leave the baths and go home.

In most other aspects of his life, Jack seems to be quite the normal husband and father, and says that he has a reasonably satisfactory sexual relationship with his wife. He finds homosexual sex, however, more exciting, but does not feel that it in any way detracts from the meaningfulness of his marital relationship. When he is asked if he is worried whether he will run into anyone he knows from the baths, he says that sometimes this bothers him a little bit, but then he realizes that if they are there, then they are homosexuals too, and he has really nothing to fear. In the city in which he lives the baths are considered quite safe and there have not been any police raids, although this is not true of a number of major cities in the country.

If one were called upon to justify the existence of the homosexual baths, this would not be too difficult a task, since they are basically only known to those who are already homosexually oriented, and provide no nuisance to the public. If anything, they keep homosexuals out of those public places where they most frequently run into trouble with the police. The almost exclusive focus there on genital activity in preference to any other kind of relationship that might take place between two persons is, of course, not one which can evoke much enthusiasm from anyone who feels that sexual activity should be integrated into a meaningful human relationship. Nevertheless, it is difficult to see how the baths do any harm, since their clientele have already reached the stage which perhaps could be best described as a concentration upon sexual activity for its own sake.

THE GAY BAR

The gay bar has almost become a social institution in America. It is the central public place around which gay life revolves and is to be found in all large and medium-sized cities across the country. We would like to describe here the "typical gay bar," although, of course, there is no such thing, any more than there is a "typical straight bar." Perhaps, narrowing our focus a bit, what we want to describe is what I call the "middle-class" gay bar, by which I mean not that all its members are necessarily middle-class socioeconomically, but rather that middle-class proprieties are observed and that there is nothing unique or specialized about the bar. We will not, for example, be concerned with the leather-jacket motorcycle bars, nor with the hustler bars so beautifully described by Rechy, nor with those bars which provide entertainment such as drag shows and male go-go dancers.

Perhaps the most important fact about a gay bar is that it is a sexual marketplace. That is, men go there for the purpose of seeking sexual partners, and if this function were not served by the bar there would be no gay bars, for, although homosexuals also go there

to drink and socialize, the search for sexual experience is in some sense the core of the interaction in the bar. It should, however, be obvious that there must be more going on in the bar than simply people meeting and leaving; otherwise the bar could not exist as a commercial enterprise. People have to come there for a time long enough to drink, in order to make it profitable to the management to run these bars. And gay bars are very profitable and have sprung up in large numbers. It is estimated that there are about 60 gay bars in Los Angeles and about 40 in San Francisco. A number of heterosexuals have converted their own taverns into gay bars simply because they have found it more profitable to run a gay bar, even though they are sometimes not particularly delighted with the clientele. The gay bar plays a central role in the life of very many homosexuals—one which is much more important than the role played by straight bars in the life of all but a few heterosexuals. This is connected intimately with the use of the gay bar as a sexual marketplace and, of course, with the fact that homosexuals, as homosexuals, have really no place else where they can congregate without disclosing to the straight world that they are homosexual.

What does a gay bar look like? In the first place, unlike most middle-class straight bars, it is almost exclusively populated by males. Sometimes non-homosexuals accidentally walk into a gay bar and it is usually this lack of women that makes them aware that they may have inadvertently walked into a homosexual setting. There are a few bars in which lesbians congregate along with male homosexuals, especially in cities which are not large enough to support a lesbian bar. But even in the larger cities, lesbian bars are not very common. They are never as large as the large metropolitan male gay bars. This is because female homosexuals are much less promiscuous than male homosexuals and really not able to support a sexual marketplace on the scale that males do.

Occasionally, "fruit flies," i.e., women who like to associate with male homosexuals, are found in gay bars, although they are not a very prominent part of any gay bar scene. Why a woman who is not a lesbian would like to associate with male homosexuals is a question which cannot be altogether answered in general, except to say that some of these women obviously find homosexual men a lot less threatening than heterosexual men, since the former are not interested in them sexually. Since these women are not potential sexual partners for the males, they are not potential sources of rejection for them either, and thereby they find themselves the subject of much attention by the male clientele. Consequently, they are the beneficiaries of a great deal of sociability without being objects of seduction. Some women find this a very appealing position.

In the gay world there is a tremendous accent on youth, and this is reflected in the composition of the bar clientele. Youth is very much at a premium, and young men will go to the bars as soon as they have passed the legal age limit. This varies from state to state; it is 18 in New York and 21 in California. Along with the younger men, there are somewhat older men who are trying to look young. They attempt to accomplish this primarily by dress. The typical bar cos-

tume is the same style of dress that an average college undergraduate might wear. It would consist of a sport shirt, Levis, and loafers or sneakers. In this "typical" middle-class gay bar which I am attempting to describe, extremely effeminate dress and mannerisms are not well tolerated. Nevertheless, it would not be correct to say that the scene in a gay bar looks like a fraternity stag party. There is a tendency toward effeminacy in the overall impression one gets from observing the bar, although this may not necessarily be anything striking or flagrant. There is a certain softness or absence of stereotypical masculine aggression present in the conversations and behavior of the bar patrons. Also, in spite of the fact that the modal bar costume is very much like that one would see on a college campus, there is a good deal of special attention paid by the bar patrons to their dress, so that they seem almost extraordinarily well groomed.

There is thus a feeling of fastidiousness about the appearance of the young men in the bar which, along with their muted demeanor, rather clearly differentiates the overall *Gestalt* of the gay bar from that which would be experienced upon entering a gathering of young male heterosexuals. There are usually a few clearly identifiable homosexuals, although the majority of individuals in the bar are not identifiable and would not be thought homosexual in another setting. It seems to be the general consensus of gay bar observers that fights are less likely to break out in a gay than in a straight bar. This is, I think, probably attributable to the psychological characteristics of the clientele rather than to anything about the structure of the bar itself. Male homosexuals would certainly rather make love than war.

One of the clearest differences between the gay and the straight bar is that in the gay bar the attention of the patrons is focused directly on each other. In a gay bar, for example, the patrons who are sitting at the bar itself usually face away from the bar and look toward the other people in the room and toward the door. When a new patron walks in, he receives a good deal of scrutiny, and people engaged in conversation with each other just naturally assume that their interlocutors will turn away from them to watch each new entering patron. All this is, of course, part of the pervasive looking and cruising which goes on in the bar.

There is a great deal of milling about in the bar and individuals tend to engage in short, superficial conversations with each other. They try to make the circuit around the bar to see everyone in it, perhaps stopping to chat with their friends but usually not for very long. In a way, the shortness and superficiality of the conversations in the bar mirror that same brevity and shallowness of interpersonal relations which characterize gay life as a whole.

Heterosexual observers and even homosexuals who are not habitués of the bar scene often express great perplexity about the bars—they cannot quite understand what's going on there. They seem to be bewildered by the sight of all these young men standing around and communicating so little with one another. The patrons stand along the walls, it seems, for hours, without speaking. They move around the room and talk at length with almost no one.

One heterosexual observer said that he felt as if everyone in the room were standing around waiting for some important figure to come in, but of course he never comes. He likened the scene to a reception for a foreign ambassador, where everyone stands around simply marking time until the dignitary arrives. In a sense, this observer was correct, for the young men *are* waiting for some important person to arrive, one who will never arrive—but it is not a foreign ambassador. Each is waiting for a handsome young prince to come and carry him off in his arms. They're waiting for the ideal sexual object, and if they don't find him they may very well go home alone, in spite of the fact that there are sometimes hundreds of other attractive young men right there in the bar.

The gay bar, then, in a sense may be thought of as a stage on which is played out a fantasy in which the hero never arrives. The reason why heterosexuals and even some homosexuals cannot understand what is going on is because they are not a party to this fantasy. They imagine that if you are going to a place to seek a sexual partner, you go in, look around a little bit, walk up to somebody that you like, engage in a conversation, and then go out together. And sometimes this is precisely what does occur in the gay bar. Very often, in fact. But the bewildering problem which confronts the uninitiated observer is why this does not happen more often; why, in fact, all these good-looking and well-dressed young men are standing around uncommunicative.

Sherri Cavan has made the suggestion that in the homosexual pickup bar it may happen that encounters are never begun because each party is waiting for the other to offer first words of greeting. This is presumably due to the fact that when the situation involves two males, it is not clear who is expected to make the initial overture. One cannot deny the saliency of this observation. Nevertheless, I do not think it alone accounts fully for the strange situation in the gay bar, since one would expect the reverse to occur just as well, i.e., since both parties can make the initial overture, one would think that at least one of the members of the hypothetical pair could overcome his shyness. I think the sociological explanation fails to take into account the psychological factors involved. As many observers have noted, homosexuals are very much afraid of rejection, and hence have an inordinate hesitancy about making an approach. I think this is due to the following reason: the only aspect of their self which male homosexuals are able to adequately present in a bar situation is their physical appearance. If they are rejected in making a conversational opening, this is interpreted (probably correctly) to mean a rejection of that crucial part of themselves, namely, their desirability as a sexual partner. Hence, their self-esteem is very much at stake and they have a great deal to lose by being rejected.

It must be remembered that in the gay world the only real criterion of value is physical attractiveness; consequently, a rejection by a desired partner is a rejection of the only valued part of one's identity in that world. When we understand this, I think we understand why the fear of rejection is so prevalent among homosexual men.

The gay bar is, then, a lot less licentious than people who are not aware of what is going on there might be inclined to think. When heterosexual men enter a gay bar for the first time for the purpose of simply visiting it, they often seem afraid that somehow they will be rapidly approached, or perhaps even attacked, by the sexual deviants present inside the bar. This, of course, is about as far from reality as it is possible to imagine. It would not be unusual if none of the patrons would engage them in conversation during the entire course of the evening. If they are not young and handsome, they may well have great difficulty in communicating with anyone after even a great deal of effort on their part.

A word should be said, I suppose, about the function of the gay bar as a source of group solidarity and as a place where one can meet one's friends and exchange gossip. I think, however, that this function is obvious and that it need not be elaborated upon. Many homosexuals frequent gay bars for reasons other than seeking sexual partners. If sex eventuates from the bar interaction, this is fine, but it is not the reason they went there in the first place. They went there for sociability. And yet this too must be qualified, for in the back of their minds is usually the thought that perhaps that special person will walk through the door tonight and they will meet him and go home with him.

The "cosmetic" quality of the gay bar is a result, in large part, of the need for anonymity which pervades all the public places of the gay world. If one can only present the visible and non-identifying aspect of one's identity, one's physical appearance will be the central aspect that can be displayed to others. If homosexuals could meet *as homosexuals* in the kinds of social settings in which heterosexuals can (e.g., at school, at work), where the emphasis on finding sexual partners is not the controlling force behind all the social interaction which transpires, a great deal of the anonymous promiscuity which now characterizes homosexual encounters would be replaced by a more "normal" kind of meeting between two persons. Perhaps, then, the sexual relationships which develop would become more stable. Maybe the gay bar itself would not change—this can only be a matter for conjecture—but, at any rate, it would not be so central to gay life.

Choosing a Locale for Sexual Liaisons

I shall conclude this chapter on public places with a few comments about the comparative merits of the various homosexual public places as regards their value as sexual marketplaces. I think in this regard the great divide would be between the bar, on the one hand, and the baths, street, parks, and rest rooms, on the other. The latter places are much more suitable for those homosexuals whose immediate interest is focused upon genital contact and who will not go to the bars because they don't wish to stand around for several hours in the hope that they might possibly meet a sexual partner. They know that if they go to the baths, for example, they will almost certainly find one, if not many. However, the streets, parks, and rest rooms have two clear advantages over the baths for such an individual. First, there is not much immediate competition for the sexual partner. Homosexuals who go there generally run into the

other person alone and thus, in the eyes of the cruiser, the desired sexual partner will probably have to take him unless he wants to wait an undetermined amount of time for another person to come along. Second, there is an admission charge, in the range of three to six dollars (depending upon time of day and day of the week), to the baths, whereas the parks, streets, and rest rooms are free (providing, of course, one does not get arrested, in which case the evening's diversion may be very expensive indeed). Furthermore, in none of the places except the bar are there the distractions of conversation, alcohol, music, and sometimes even dancing or entertainment. Excluding the bars, public places are used almost exclusively by homosexuals for explicit sexual purposes. The advantage of the bar, of course, is that it provides a chance for a conversation with a potential partner before the sexual contract is made. Thus, individuals who are concerned about the psychological characteristics of their partners have a chance to find out something about them. Also, of course, this lends a great aura of respectability to the whole affair, whereas simply meeting for a sexual enounter in a rest room is, in our society, quite clearly defined as disreputable.

It is interesting that the specification of the sexual act(s) to occur is not part of a contract for a sexual encounter, that is, individuals who meet in a bar or in a park and then adjourn to one of their apartments do not usually discuss what kind of sexual behavior is going to take place. I think this can be accounted for by the fact that male homosexuals are quite able to vary their sexual performance so as to find some satisfactory *modus operandi* in bed. While they might not find a partner who likes to do what they find most enjoyable sexually, the chances are very high that they will be able to find some kind of sexual behavior which is mutually satisfactory, at least to some extent. Occasionally, of course, this does not happen and one hears, every so often, stories told in the form of gossip about the time the individual met someone, went home with him, and they both found out that they wished to take precisely the identical role and that they were looking for someone to take a reciprocal role and this could not be done. This is, however, not a very common happening. One thing is clear, and that is that it is not very predictable from the physical appearance and mannerisms of the potential partner just what he will or will not do in bed. In extreme cases of effeminacy one can usually predict that the individual will take a receptor role with regard to his partner's penis, but aside from this, predictability is poor. The only other exception is the hustler, who classically only takes the insertor role, feeling that this is consistent with his image (either to himself and/or to his partner) of his "real" heterosexuality.

This might be an appropriate place to introduce the term "fetishization." Marx spoke of the fetishism of commodities, meaning that in industrial society individuals were bemused by the plethora of material goods and so they sacrificed a rich, non-alienated existence to perform alienated work, in order to be able to obtain material goods. Happiness is to be achieved by the acquisition of automobiles, clothes, homes, televisions, etc. Psychiatrists, on the other hand, speak of fetishism in connection with a particular kind of sexual perversion in which the individual is sexually excited only by either a part of his sexual partner's body—for example, the foot—or by a non-human object which has some connection with sexuality, such as a shoe or other piece of clothing.

Both the Marxian and the psychiatric notions of fetishization have in common the idea of a narrowing down of one's range of action from a rich or a full existential encounter, to a narrow, segmented area of experience. The purpose of this narrowing is that it enables the individual to gain some control and sense of efficacy in the interaction. In the case of commodity fetishism, this is the only meaningful activity in which industrial man can engage, since his work is alienated. The acquisition of commodities, then, becomes something which is to him the source of meaning in life. In sex fetishism, the individual, because of psychological problems, is unable to relate to the sexual partner as a total human being and relates only to a part of the body or to a piece of clothing.

As has been pointed out by the Russian philosopher Vladimir Soloviev, if a man relates to a woman only as a sexual object, e.g., only as a vagina, this is a form of fetishization. I think, then, it will be very clear to the reader that the public places of gay life are based on and, at the same time, encourage sex fetishization of a most dehumanizing kind. The focus in some of the public places is on a very brief sexual encounter, measured in terms of minutes, which occurs often under the most degrading circumstances. The gay bar tends to encourage the "one-night stand." This is sex without obligation or commitment, without significant personal encounter, sex for the sake of sex alone. It cannot be denied that long-term relationships do result from encounters in bars and even, to a minor extent, in the other public places, but these are more the exception than the rule, and these more significant relationships can certainly not be expected as a result of a visit to one of these places—or, for that matter, by repeated visits to such places. The individual who frequents the public places soon learns not to expect any more than a brief sexual experience. He looks to the public places for sex and must look elsewhere for the remaining meaning around which he can center his life. It is not difficult, I think, to see that such fragmentation of sex from the rest of one's human world is not conducive to personal happiness or good social adjustment.

The occupation of a stripper, although not illegal, is stigmatized. To be stigmatized means that the stripper is isolated from participation in the straight community from which her paying audience is drawn, and may be forced into more deviant roles such as prostitution or lesbianism. Social pressures imposed on strippers and other deviants severely restrict their choices among life-style alternatives. Unlike the poor, who lack the resources, strippers may accumulate the money to improve their style of life. Typically, they do not. As Skipper and McCaghy indicate in the following essay, the occupation of stripper (except for a few who become "headliners") is not a route to success, but one to isolation, public degradation, and deviance.

Stripping: Anatomy of a Deviant Life Style

CHARLES H. MCCAGHY
JAMES K. SKIPPER, JR.

The subjects of this paper are a group of women who undress on stage for their living. They are in an unusual occupation; there are only an estimated 7,000 strippers in the entire United States

This article was prepared especially for this volume.

(Jones, 1967). But our subjects are even more unusual because they are anomalies, if not anachronisms, in the world of strippers: they are on the burlesque theater tour. Most girls who could be called strippers or "exotics" will be found performing in night clubs. It is estimated that more girls are employed in clubs today than all the burlesque theaters could have hired in their heyday.[1] Thus the girls performing in the few remaining theaters are a definite minority. The performances of touring strippers, when compared with club performances, more

[1] This information comes from a private communication from Mr. Morgan James of the American Guild of Variety Artists.

closely approximate those of the original striptease and, on rare occasions, one who could be considered an "authentic" stripteaser will appear as a star attraction. Furthermore, the touring strippers are surrounded by vestiges of the past: many of the theaters were formerly great burlesque houses; in many cases the theater managers and backstage personnel have roots in early burlesque or show business; and the tour includes comics who were once mainstays of burlesque in its better days. Thus, unlike their sisters in most clubs, touring strippers can feel an affinity with "show business," however tenuous that relationship may be.[2]

In this paper, we will examine a slice of the life style of strippers on the theater tour. Specifically, we will consider their reactions toward various aspects of their occupation. The discussion is based on observations and interviews by male researchers with 35 strippers on tour during the spring and summer of 1968 on the "eastern wheel," a burlesque theater circuit of ten cities east of the Mississippi River. The research site was one theater on the circuit where the authors and a clinical psychologist had access to the backstage area. Here the

[2]The theaters of touring strippers are not to be confused with some which have relatively permanent casts of strippers. In this latter type, the music for stripping is usually provided by records rather than being live, from a small group of musicians. Both types of theaters are likely to alternate a movie with the stripping acts. The theaters with touring acts will have the smaller audiences for the movies, whereas in the theaters with resident talent, a sizable proportion of the audience leaves after the movie. In our experience the audience reaction is justified: the "scratch house" with non-touring performers provides the nadir in strip shows.

researchers were introduced by the stage manager to each touring group of four or five girls, which changed weekly. After the introduction the researchers spent about two hours in conversation with the girls concerning general aspects of their occupation. During these conversations one or two girls were asked to participate in an interview over dinner or drinks. Potential respondents were selected on the basis of perceived ability to communicate well and willingness to discuss their experiences in the occupation. Overall, an attempt was made to obtain a representative range of ages, length of time in the occupation, and salary levels. The interviews usually took place at a secluded table in nearby bars and restaurants, and consisted of inquiries into the subject's background and perceptions of her life in the business.

Because our sample of strippers was not randomly selected, it is impossible to say to what extent the characteristics of the sample mirror those of the population of touring strippers. It should be noted, however, that there was surprising diversity of backgrounds within the sample: families of orientation spanned the entire range of social classes and religions; places of birth included five foreign countries and all sections of the United States except the deep South; and range of formal education was from 7 to 16 years, most having completed high school.

GETTING STARTED

We found that among the great majority of our sample, stripping is not a job which girls "plan" to enter in the sense that there is a lengthy consideration of alternatives and consequences, and a period of time spent in preparation.[3] Instead, nearly all of the subjects decided to strip under somewhat spontaneous circumstances, and few had even considered it as a possibility until shortly before their initial performance. They were either employed in relatively low-paying occupations or faced with a shortage of jobs they would normally undertake when they learned that stripping would provide a relatively high financial return in a short period of time. Most knew little about what stripping entailed except that they would remove their clothes in public, would be well paid, and could start work almost immediately. Furthermore, they were usually encouraged by friends, employers, agents, or acquaintances who assured them of their qualifications for reasonable, if not great, success.

Once the decision to strip was made, all that was left was: to obtain an agent, if they did not already have one; to select a stage name; and to purchase a costume.

The agent's role is essentially one of an employment reference for his clients: he refers them to potential employers, makes them aware of different job openings, and arranges the job contracts. For these services he receives at least five percent of the client's salary. Most of our subjects were referred to their agents by friends or employers; in some cases in which the subject was already in some aspect of show business, her agent simply began to contract her as a stripper instead of a dancer or singer.

A stage name is selected on the basis that it has a "ring" to it, will fit on a marquee, and will be an appropriate trademark which will hopefully attract a stream of steady customers in the near future. Although some names selected by strippers have obvious sexual connotations (such as Helen Bedd, Starke Naked, and Terry and Her Privates), most are either neutral (Sally Lane, Mickey Jones) or have a contemporary motif (Saki Tu-Me, Barbe Doll).[4] Five of our subjects used their given name, or some variation of it, as their stage name. Seven of the remaining 30 subjects selected their own pseudonym; most of the others had their names chosen by their agents.

One of the few tools of the stripping trade, aside from the most obvious one, is the costume. When purchasing her first costume, the novice discovers the occupation is not all profit. Stripping costumes must be especially designed, since a means of effortless egress has to be built in; being custom-made, they are expensive. Among strippers it is felt that quality costumes contribute a great deal to the impact of an act, hence a minimum of $300 for a basic outfit is a necessity. We were assured that costumes are subject to more wear-and-tear than might be imagined, and replacement was frequent. Furthermore, the number and cost of costumes rise with the success of the stripper. As one headliner told us: "I would not be caught dead in the same costume in the same city in the same year." Although some make their own outfits, costumes constitute strippers' major occupational expense.[5]

[3] For a detailed description of touring strippers' background characteristics and the process by which they entered the occupation, see Skipper and McCaghy (1970).

[4] None of the subjects interviewed in our research are named here.

[5] Most strippers appear more concerned with their

With an agent, a name, and a costume, modern strippers have all the basics they need to begin. There are trivial matters such as union initiation fee and dues to the American Guild of Variety Artists (AGVA), plus some rehearsals, but essentially they are ready to go on stage. They have little training in the fundamentals of stripping prior to their first act. What they learn about the elements of a successful performance they must pick up through their own experience.

Most strippers' first job is in a club, and most of these will never perform in any other setting. For those who do eventually go on tour, the club provides the opportunity to formulate and perfect their acts. It is also in the clubs that strippers first face some of the realities of their chosen occupation and begin forming their attitudes toward that occupation.

ATTITUDES

The Setting

Nearly all of our subjects performed their first strip act in a club; all had performed in clubs sometime during their career. There were mixed opinions among the girls as to the desirability of clubs as a place to work. Three of the subjects whose backgrounds and inclinations involved a "show business" orientation were divided as to which setting, the club or the theater, allowed them more artistic integrity: two of them complained that the club act requires even less finesse than expected of a tour-

costumes than with their own bodies. Only 11 of the 35 we interviewed did anything more than diet in order to maintain the most essential feature of their acts.

ing act. Furthermore, they felt the club bands were likely to be less capable than those in burlesque houses, and the artistic quality of the acts could not help being jeopardized by a lack of props and by boisterous drunks in club audiences.

But most opinions about the relative merits of clubs and theaters did not concern workmanship on stage. More important to our subjects is the fact that in most clubs they find that the stripper's job is not limited to a stage performance: she is expected to "mix," that is, interact with customers for the purpose of encouraging them to buy drinks. Several expressed a distinct distaste for mixing because they were forced to sit with persons in whom they had no interest and who, in many cases, were repulsive to them because of their heavy drinking and sexual importuning. When we asked our subjects about the places in which they liked to perform, 18 of the 35 based their preference on not having to mix: 11 preferred theaters for that reason, five preferred clubs where mixing was not permitted or necessary, and two claimed it made no difference where they performed as long as they did not have to mix. Two of these subjects expressed concern over the ethics of mixing. As one put it:

> I think it is not right to put a guy on, promising him all kinds of things to make him buy drinks. Then when he's spent all his money you leave him flat and go on to somebody else.

For strippers who find mixing disagreeable, touring burlesque theaters allows them to perform without becoming involved with their audiences. As D'Andre (1965) found in her study of strippers:

What seemed to be most critical in their relatively positive attitudes toward burlesque houses is that the performer is always on a stage, separated by a physical barrier between herself and the patrons. When she is on stage, she is aloof from the customers and in slight danger from them. When she walks off stage, she is entirely on her own.

Our sample was not unanimous in dislike for clubs, however. Some would happily perform anywhere so long as the pay was attractive; others preferred clubs because such employment meant a relatively permanent residence could be maintained. Two subjects liked club work because it provided easier opportunity for prostitution. There was general agreement in the sample that for the girl seeking to supplement her income through prostitution, the club setting was ideal: it provides a constant aggregate of potential "johns" and allows some degree of discrimination in the selection of customers. Our subjects estimated that from 75 to 90 percent of the strippers performing in clubs were engaged in systematic prostitution. On the other hand, they estimated that less than half the strippers on tour ever engaged in prostitution, either because they did not wish to or because of the greater difficulty of making contacts in the working situation.

The Audience

One of the more striking findings of our study concerns the feelings of ambivalence which touring strippers hold toward their audiences. Nearly all of our sample expressed a belief that the majority consists of businessmen, college students, and couples on the town; all of these were considered "respectable."

But paramount in many strippers' minds is a minority in the audience whom they label as "degenerates." The girls did not anticipate these when they entered the occupation, but are now daily reminded of their existence. We are speaking of the gentlemen one will find in the first rows of almost any burlesque theater, particularly during the afternoon performances. They are steady customers and frequently are equipped with binoculars or folded newspapers in their laps, the latter being used to conceal masturbation activity.

These customers probably attract a disproportionate share of the girls' attention for two reasons: first, because of lighting conditions in many theaters they are the only segment of the audience clearly visible from the stage; second, because of their proximity they are the logical persons to communicate with during the course of the act.

The "degenerates" continue to be a source of sarcasm, if not dismay, to many strippers regardless of their number of years in the occupation. Eleven of our subjects claimed that "degenerates" were highest on the list of things they disliked about the occupation. Such claims often seemed paradoxical, however. For example, one stripper, upon leaving the stage after an act of prolonged sexual spasms which included spreading her vagina, complained that someone in the first row had been exposing himself.

The Performance

Complicating strippers' relationships with their audience and views of their occupation is the increasing pressure put on them by club and theater managers to "work strong," that is, to put more overt sex into their acts. This means more lewd gesticulation and more "flashing" (exposing the pubic area) where local authorities permit it.[6] As discussed in the introduction, pressures for "stronger" acts are probably the result of competition from other sources of vicarious sex. The majority of the subjects stated, however, that they did not care to flash and did so only because they had no other choice.[7] A quarter of the sample were very vehement on this point: they cited flashing or working strong as aspects of the job they disliked most.

Two general reasons were given for reluctance to flash. Some girls felt it was an unnecessary practice insofar as most of the audience was concerned, while it appealed mainly to the distasteful segment of the audience, the "degenerates." One said:

> I don't know why we have to do it. It really makes the whole thing seem so dirty. Most people can appreciate the act without it, but some guys just sit there waiting for it so they can get their jollies.

Others felt that strong acts were making it more difficult for stripping to maintain a semblance of artistry. This group expressed concern that flashing and "dirty work" were effectively killing stripping as an art, because many of the better strippers refuse to flash and thus are not likely to be hired. Their places were being taken by younger girls of lesser talent and experience who have no compunction about what they do on stage.

While there was unhappiness among our subjects over the amount of sexuality expected in their performances, there were no delusions about sexuality being a stripper's principal product. Consistent with what one would expect of stage performers, many strippers usually have a particular image or mood they are trying to project. Although the girls occasionally described their acts in terms of satire ("comic routine") or conventional entertainment ("I am a good dancer"), the predominant theme was some variation on sex, the most frequent being "sophisticated" sex. Two subjects apparently avoid such subtleties in their acts; one claimed, "I show off my big breasts," and the other said, "I just take my clothes off."[8]

The "Stars"

As mentioned before, the strippers in our sample moved in an atmosphere of show business history. But the museum

---

[6]The degree of exposure allowed varies greatly across the United States. In some areas there is little question that as much female anatomy will be seen on beaches as in a strip act. At the other extreme, the city in which this research took place permits strong acts. Technically, *something* must be worn by the performer at all times; in practice, this means that toward the conclusion of performances the G-string is worn around the kneecap or ankle nearly as much as in its customary location.

[7]In the theater which was the site of this research, all strippers were to flash, although the strongest performance in the touring group was the prerogative of the headliner. We encountered one instance in which the headliner's refusal to flash caused a dispute between her and the manager. She told us that it meant she would not be hired by him again, but it was a matter of "principle" with her.

[8]Contrast the styles of today's strippers with the advice of Tessie the Tassel Twirler to Gypsy Rose Lee: "In burlesque, you've got to leave 'em hungry for more. You don't just dump the whole roast on the platter." (*Time:* 1970:89)

surroundings of the tour appeared to have little effect on them. None felt any particular humility or debt to the relics. While many realized that performing in burlesque theaters is as near to involvement in show business as they are likely to come, they are neither in awe of the "stars" of their profession nor admit to patterning their lives or acts after any other stripper. Except for some of the older subjects, few knew anything about the great burlesque personalities aside from incidental information picked up from the comics.

When we asked our subjects whether there was anyone in the occupation they particularly admired or whom they might use as a model, only three of the 35 mentioned someone. Most felt either that they themselves were individualistic, following their own unique career pattern, or that no one in the occupation was worth emulating.

This lack of role models reflects a general sense of cynicism among strippers concerning the stars of their occupation. The overwhelming majority of the sample agreed that money (in our sample, a minimum of $200 per week) is the primary reason why they or anyone else strips, but there was little agreement as to what is necessary to become a success in the business. Given that stripping is essentially an unskilled job, yet one capable of bringing moderate fame and fortune, it is perhaps not surprising that strippers find it difficult to agree on the elements of success, and that the less fortunate view their more fortunate colleagues with some puzzlement and suspicion.

According to seven of our subjects, none of whom were "headliners" or feature attractions of the tour, the road to success simply requires the "right connections" or "sleeping with the right people." Another six, a mixture of headliners and "line girls," claimed that physical attributes were most important: youth, beauty, and/or large breasts. Still another six felt that there were certain crucial indefinables contributing to the successful stripping act: personality, rapport with audiences, and "showmanship." Four others said a strong act is the prime requisite. The remainder were unsure, although they suggested "luck" and "effort" might be important. Only one, a headliner, mentioned talent.

Anyone who views many strip acts will agree that "talent," as used in the conventional sense, is notably lacking. Furthermore, little or no training is necessary to enter the occupation. In our sample, no one had any formal training in their stripping acts, although some subjects had experience or training in some aspect of show business such as chorus dancing or singing, and some had received brief informal instruction or advice from established performers.[9] Within our sample there was little evidence that such a modicum of experience or training contributed substantially to the girls' success as measured by salary level.

While the ingredients necessary for success and headliner status in the business are in question, the evidence from our sample allows us to make one generalization. That is, if a girl is ever to reach headliner status she will do so in the first few months of her career. Among

[9]Although "schools" for strippers do exist in cities on both coasts, we did not meet any of their graduates.

the headliners we spoke to, all had attained that position within a year of their first appearance on stage. Although we were able to make this generalization early in our research, we also found that strippers do not have a similar perception. Among line girls with two to five years in the occupation, there were some who still had hopes of becoming a "star." But there is nothing in our research findings to encourage such aspirations.

The Tour

In the planning stages of this study we spoke with several persons who had knowledge of and contacts with strippers. During these conversations we were impressed by a recurring blend of affection for and sympathy toward the girls. "The loneliest people in the world" and "an unhappy, mixed-up bunch of kids" are representative of the remarks we encountered. Our informants led us to believe that loneliness and disillusionment were constant companions of strippers, and that these were due less to the characteristics of the girls than to the occupation.

The loneliness of the tour, while an important consideration to some strippers, is seen as being relatively easy to remedy; it is simply a temporary situation resulting from working conditions which are themselves temporary. There is, however, another kind of isolation more keenly felt by nearly all strippers: whether they like their occupation or not, they are conscious of a social isolation due to invidious opinions and low esteem from conventional society. Our subjects pointed out that negative reactions to them come from all quarters. Some rejections came from unexpected sources, as one explained:

I once went to a church and the next day the minister came around and told me I wasn't welcome.

Another stated:

Even a psychiatrist told me that stripping is immoral and not normal, but I think I got him straightened out, but it took a long time.

A third subject was firmly convinced she was denied admission to a college because of her occupation.

In short, our subjects discovered that one's identity as a stripper connotes to the public characteristics which were not presumed when the individual was a waitress, dancer, or housewife. A clue to the public image of strippers is suggested by two studies. The first, conducted by the authors, was a survey of 75 college students who were asked, "What type of women do you think make their living by stripping?" Representative replies were: "hard women," "dumb," "uneducated," "can't do anything else for a living," "oversexed," "immoral," and "prostitutes." The second study, a survey of 155 university students (none of them art students) and 122 of their parents, indicated that strippers were assigned a lower occupational ranking than other low-status occupations such as janitors, artist models, and professional gamblers (Jessor and Donovan, 1969).

In an earlier study of club strippers, D'Andre (1965) wrote:

". . . They (strippers) are widely believed to be engaged in a host of peculiar, atypical, aberrant, offbeat forms of activity. In the laymen's view, the stripper is an underworld figure who inhabits the dark places of the urban community. She is thought to consort with various

hoodlums, hustlers, drug addicts, pimps, prostitutes, and other disreputable characters who populate the "tenderloin" area of the large city.

The existence of a disparaging public image was admitted by all but three of our subjects, and resented by most. Five felt that this image was the major drawback of the occupation. A consequent reaction of many is a reluctance to identify themselves as strippers outside the occupational context; they prefer to use such terms as dancers or entertainers.

Another common complaint was that the occupational image served to attract an assortment of persons bent on exploitation: those males who would treat the stripper strictly as a sexual object, those seeking to satisfy unusual sexual proclivities, and those who would become financially dependent on the stripper. With experience, strippers view the attention of males with varying degrees of caution and skepticism. Even the attention of other females is likely to be suspected as an attempt to establish a homosexual liaison and regarded as an exploitive maneuver. This wariness of social interaction, regardless of how justified it may be, serves as another element to be added to the working conditions of the tour and the reactions from conventional society, all of which contribute to strippers' isolation.

Perhaps one of the best indicators of strippers' isolation is the lack of persons whom they regarded as "close friends." Forty-three percent of our sample could name no one. they considered to be a close friend; 14 percent could name only a relative who would function in that capacity.[10] While the feelings of isolation

and mistrust among strippers can be attributed in some part to the consequences of being in the occupation, there is also evidence that one or possibly more other factors may be involved. For example, we found that of the 24 subjects in our sample who had ever been married, 20 had at least one divorce. Since nearly half the divorces occurred prior to entering the occupation, it may be conjectured that strippers or, more precisely, girls who become strippers, have difficulty in sustaining affective social relationships whether in or out of the occupation. This inability may be more important in explaining why the girls lack close friends than is their occupation. However, there is little doubt that the occupation is at least a reinforcing if not a contributing factor to these difficulties.

A BALANCED VIEW

The reader may be wondering at this point how any occupation apparently plagued with so many perceived difficulties manages either to recruit or to retain its members. But complaints about the occupation should not be overemphasized. There were subjects who found little to fault about their job: these were ambitious young strippers who were intoxicated by their real or potential rise to high salary levels and popularity. They felt assured of great success in the business and were exuberant over their careers.

[10]Although the comparison is scarcely a valid one, it is interesting to note that in Davis and Kahl's survey in Cambridge, Mass., the highest proportion of "isolates" (those without close friends) was among unskilled workers: 30 percent. (Kahl, 1957:137–138)

The most bitter expressions of disillusionment and cynicism with the occupation were expressed by those who appeared to be at the opposite extreme from the young enthusiasts. These were older women who found themselves in a steep decline after a relatively long career of stripping, with few savings or much else to show for it.

Between these extremes are the majority of strippers. Most of these may be characterized as having begun recently but, because of their older age or lack of commitment, having few illusions about their futures in the occupation. They feel they will continue to strip until something better comes along, either marriage or another career, but they do not aspire to becoming big names in the business. The remainder of this majority are those performers with relatively long careers behind them who, whether they have reached headliner status or not, will continue with the anticipation of retiring in adequate, if not comfortable, circumstances within the next few years.

It is this majority who present the most balanced view of the occupation. For them, stripping unquestionably has some important shortcomings, but it also provides them with a life style they enjoy for the most part and which would probably be unobtainable for them in other occupations. In the last analysis, they felt the occupation's virtues overshadowed its faults.

The question remains, what contributes to strippers' dissatisfactions with aspects of the job which we have discussed? For those strippers who have recently entered the occupation, their dissatisfaction appears to be aggravated by their initial ignorance of what the occupation would entail and by their failure to consider the consequences of identifying themselves with the occupation.[11] As we indicated earlier, most girls entered the occupation with little training or planning. They knew they would undress on stage and would receive a good salary, if not public acclaim. What they did not anticipate were the ignoble aspects of the life: the pressures to mix in the clubs, the degenerates, the lack of clear-cut means to success, and the social repudiation which results from being identified with a pariah occupation.

Another factor contributing to strippers' dissatisfactions concerns the evolution of the occupation toward stronger performances. This is particularly aggravating to those strippers who feel an affinity with show business. They believe that there is still a place for art on the burlesque stage, but this ideal is contradicted by the increased emphasis on flashing and particularly by the ascendancy of young headliners willing to vigorously pantomime an enormous range of sexual activity. All indications are that this trend will continue. Indeed, it must if burlesque is to survive in a society where sex is increasingly graphically portrayed. But, for some strippers, it means they must eventually face the realization that stripping is more a "sex form" than an "art form."

A final factor contributing to the dissatisfactions of strippers concerns the loneliness so many claim to feel. Becker

[11]This is probably not a unique phenomenon. Any occupation without adequate role models and anticipatory socialization is likely to produce the same type of disillusionment, especially if there is an initial high expectation of success.

(1963), in his study of jazz musicians, found that this group, which is relatively isolated from the larger society, maintains an *esprit de corps* which is justified and reinforced by feelings of societal rejection. A similar situation is found among homosexual groups (Leznoff and Westley, 1956). No such cohesion appears to exist among strippers. Few claim other strippers as close friends, and our observations verified a general lack of interaction among the girls on tour. Cohesiveness among the girls, which could neutralize the impact of societal rejection, is minimal or nonexistent. As a result, strippers' loneliness is accentuated by their isolation not only from conventional society but from their peers as well.

Stripping as "Show Business"

While it is tempting to generalize that strippers are in the occupation only for the "buck," this would be an unfair and inaccurate inference. If money were the sole consideration, most could enter prostitution on a full-time basis for even greater financial return.[12] There are more perceived assets to stripping than money. One of the most important of these is the fact that stripping is, in their opinion, "show business." While strippers recognize that their occupation ranks low as a form of show business, they feel it is simply a matter of degree: stripping is a base from which they can move into other types of show business with the right breaks or when openings develop.[13]

Moreover, stripping as show business is valued for itself. Nearly all of the most pleasant recollections our subjects had of the occupation involved a particularly satisfying performance before a large enthusiastic audience. Stripping performances are generally drab, routine affairs before hushed audiences, but strippers value their occasional "great" performances as would any entertainer. It is intangibles such as these which strippers regard as positive attributes in their work; there is glamour and excitement that only life on the stage can provide.

References

Becker, Howard S., *Outsiders: Studies in the Sociology of Deviance.* London: Collier-Macmillan, 1963.

D'Andre, Ann Terry, "An Occupational Study of the Strip-Dancer Career." Paper read at the Pacific Sociological Association meetings, Salt Lake City, Utah, 1965.

Dempsey, David, "The Mead and Her Message: Some Field Notes on an Anthropological Phenomenon." *New York Times Magazine,* May 3, 1970.

---

[12]This is not to say that opportunities for prostitution do not enter into the financial picture, however. Eighteen of our 35 subjects admitted they had engaged in prostitution at some time since they had begun stripping, usually when performing in clubs. The subjects estimated that as many as 75 percent of strippers had prostituted. Prostitution on a systematic basis while touring is difficult: only six (17 percent) of the sample claimed to be turning tricks regularly. Two of these said that prostitution was the major source of their income.

[13]Ann Corio reportedly once said, "I always wanted to be a legitimate actress, but nobody would listen to my lines. They just wanted to see them." (Dempsey, 1970:74)

Jessor, Clinton J., and Louis P. Donovan, "Nudity in the Art Training Process: An Essay with Reference to a Pilot Study." *Sociological Quarterly,* **10** (Summer 1969):355–371.

Jones, Libby, *Striptease.* New York: Simon and Schuster, 1967.

Kahl, Joseph A., *The American Class Structure.* New York: Holt, Rinehart and Winston, 1957.

Leznoff, Maurice, and William A. Westley, "The Homosexual Community." *Social Problems,* **3** (April 1956):257–263.

McCaghy, Charles H., and James K. Skipper, Jr., "Lesbian Behavior as an Adaptation to the Occupation of Stripping." *Social Problems,* **17** (Fall 1969):262–270.

Skipper, James K., Jr., and Charles H. McCaghy, "Stripteasers: The Anatomy and Career Contingencies of a Deviant Occupation." *Social Problems,* **17** (Winter 1970):391–405.

Time, **95** (May 11, 1970):89.

Erving Goffman* has suggested that a common human trait is a desire for action. Adults can find their action fairly easily at the race track, Las Vegas, or some other legal enterprise that capitalizes on this desire for action. Most of these enterprises are closed to those under a certain age, but younger people too have a desire for action. One avenue left open to them is the commission of delinquent acts. Matza and Sykes question the divergence of values between delinquents and the public at large. Delinquent behavior may be an expression of an action orientation, and the values that delinquents hold and express may, in essence, be the values of society.

*Erving Goffman, *Interaction Ritual* (Garden City, N.Y.: Doubleday Anchor, 1967), pp. 144–270.

Juvenile Delinquency and Subterranean Values

DAVID MATZA
GRESHAM M. SYKES

Current explanations of juvenile delinquency can be divided roughly into two major types. On the one hand, juvenile delinquency is seen as a product of personality disturbances or emotional conflicts within the individual; on the other hand, delinquency is viewed as a result of relatively normal personalities exposed to a "disturbed" social environment—particularly in the form of a deviant sub-culture in which the individual learns to be delinquent as others learn to conform to the law. The theoretical conflict between these two positions has been intensified, unfortunately, by the fact that professional pride sometimes leads psychologists and sociologists to define the issue as a conflict between disciplines and to rally behind their respective academic banners.

Despite many disagreements between these two points of view, one assumption is apt to elicit common support. The delinquent, it is asserted, is deviant; not only does his behavior run counter to the law but his underlying norms, attitudes, and values also stand opposed to those of the dominant social order. And the dominant social order, more often

than not, turns out to be the world of the middle class.

We have suggested in a previous article that this image of delinquents and the larger society as antagonists can be misleading.[1] Many delinquents, we argued, are essentially in agreement with the larger society, at least with regard to the evaluation of delinquent behavior as "wrong." Rather than standing in opposition to conventional ideas of good conduct, the delinquent is likely to adhere to the dominant norms in belief but render them ineffective in practice by holding various attitudes and perceptions which serve to neutralize the norms as checks on behavior. "Techniques of neutralization," such as the denial of responsibility or the definition of injury as rightful revenge, free the individual from a large measure of social control.

This approach to delinquency centers its attention on how an impetus to engage in delinquent behavior is translated into action. But it leaves unanswered a serious question: What makes delinquency attractive in the first place? Even if it is granted that techniques of neutralization or some similar evasions of social controls pave the way for overt delinquency, there remains the problem of the values or ends underlying delinquency and the relationship of these values to those of the larger society. Briefly stated, this paper argues that (a) the values behind much juvenile delinquency are far less deviant than they are commonly portrayed; and (b) the faulty picture is due to a gross over-

From *American Sociological Review* (October, 1961), pp. 712–719. Reprinted by permission of the American Sociological Association and the authors.

[1]Gresham M. Sykes and David Matza, "Techniques of Neutralization," *American Sociological Review,* **22** (December, 1957), pp. 664–670.

simplification of the middle-class value system.

THE VALUES OF DELINQUENCY

There are many perceptive accounts describing the behavior of juvenile delinquents and their underlying values, using methods ranging from participant observation to projective tests.[2] Although there are some important differences of opinion in the interpretation of this material, there exists a striking consensus on actual substance. Many divisions and sub-divisions are possible, of course, in classifying these behavior patterns and the values on which they are based, but three major themes emerge with marked regularity.

First, many observers have noted that delinquents are deeply immersed in a restless search for excitement, "thrills," or "kicks." The approved style of life, for many delinquents, is an adventurous one. Activities pervaded by displays of daring and charged with danger are highly valued in comparison with more mundane and routine patterns of behavior. This search for excitement is not easily satisfied in legitimate outlets such as organized recreation, as Tappan has indicated. The fact that an activity involves breaking the law is precisely the fact that often infuses it with an air of excitement.[3] In fact, excitement or "kicks" may come to be defined with clear awareness as "any act tabooed by 'squares' that heightens and intensifies the present moment of experience and differentiates it as much as possible from the humdrum routines of daily life."[4] But in any event, the delinquent way of life is frequently a way of life shot through with adventurous exploits that are valued for the stimulation they provide.

It should be noted that in courting physical danger, experimenting with the forbidden, provoking the authorities, and so on, the delinquent is not simply enduring hazards; he is also creating hazards in a deliberate attempt to manufacture excitement. As Miller has noted, for example, in his study of Rox-

[2]Frederick M. Thrasher, *The Gang* (Chicago: University of Chicago Press, 1936); Clifford R. Shaw and Maurice E. Moore, *The Natural History of a Delinquent Career* (Chicago: University of Chicago Press, 1931); Albert K. Cohen, *Delinquent Boys: The Culture of the Gang* (Glencoe, Ill.: The Free Press, 1955); Albert K. Cohen and James F. Short, "Research in Delinquent Subcultures," *Journal of Social Issues,* **14** (1958), pp. 20–37; Walter B. Miller, "Lower Class Culture as a Generating Milieu of Gang Delinquents," *Journal of Social Issues,* **14** (1958), pp. 5–19; Harold Finestone, "Cats, Kicks, and Color," *Social Problems,* **5** (July, 1957), pp. 3–13; Solomon Kobrin, "The Conflict of Values in Delinquent Areas," *American Sociological Review,* **16** (October, 1951), pp. 653–661; Richard Cloward and Lloyd Ohlin, "New Perspectives on Juvenile Delinquency" (unpub-

lished manuscript); Dale Kramer and Madeline Karr, *Teen-Age Gangs* (New York: Henry Holt, 1953); Stacey V. Jones, "The Cougars—Life with a Delinquent Gang," *Harper Magazine* (November, 1954); Harrison E. Salisbury, *The Shook-Up Generation* (New York: Harper and Brothers, 1958); William C. Kvaraceus and Walter B. Miller (eds.), *Delinquent Behavior: Culture and the Individual,* National Education Association of the United States, 1959; Herbert A. Bloch and Arthur Neiderhoffer, *The Gang* (New York: Philosophical Library, 1958); Beatrice Griffith, *American Me* (Boston: Houghton Mifflin, 1948); Sheldon Glueck and Eleanor Glueck, *Unraveling Juvenile Delinquency* (New York: Commonwealth Fund, 1950).
[3]Paul Tappan, *Juvenile Delinquency* (New York: McGraw-Hill, 1949), pp. 148–154.
[4]Finestone, *op. cit.*

bury, for many delinquents "the rhythm of life fluctuates between periods of relatively routine and repetitive activities and sought situations of greater emotional stimulation."[5] The excitement, then, that flows from gang rumbles, games of "chicken" played with cars, or the use of drugs is not merely an incidental by-product but may instead serve as a major motivating force.

Second, juvenile delinquents commonly exhibit a disdain for "getting on" in the realm of work. Occupational goals involving a steady job or careful advancement are apt to be lacking, and in their place we find a sort of aimless drifting or grandiose dreams of quick success. Now it takes a very deep faith in the maxims of Benjamin Franklin—or a certain naiveté, perhaps—to believe that hard work at the lower ranges of the occupational hierarchy is a sure path to worldly achievement. The delinquent is typically described as choosing another course, rationally or irrationally. Chicanery or manipulation, which may take the form of borrowing from social workers or more elaborate modes of "hustling"; an emphasis on "pull," frequently with reference to obtaining a soft job which is assumed to be available only to those with influential connections: all are seen as methods of exploiting the social environment without drudgery, and are accorded a high value. Simple expropriation should be included, of course, in the form of theft, robbery, and the rest; but it is only one of a variety of ways of "scoring" and does not necessarily carry great prestige in the eyes of the delinquent. In fact, there is some evidence that, among certain

delinquents, theft and robbery may actually be looked down upon as pointing to a lack of wit or skill. A life of ease based on pimping or the numbers game may be held out as a far more admirable goal.[6] In any event, the delinquent is frequently convinced that only suckers work and he avoids, if he can, the regimen of the factory, store, and office.

Some writers have coupled the delinquent's disdain of work with a disdain of money. Much delinquent activity, it is said, is non-utilitarian in character and the delinquent disavows the material aspirations of the larger society, thus protecting himself against inevitable frustration. Now it is true that the delinquent's attacks against property are often a form of play, as Cohen has pointed out, rather than a means to a material end.[7] It is also true that the delinquent often shows little liking for the slow accumulation of financial resources. Yet rather than saying that the delinquent disdains money, it would seem more accurate to say that the delinquent is deeply and constantly concerned with the problem of money in his own way. The delinquent wants money, probably no less than the law-abiding, but not for the purposes of a careful series of expenditures or some long-range objective. Rather, money is frequently desired as something to be squandered in gestures of largesse, in patterns of conspicuous consumption. The sudden acquisition of large sums of money is his goal—the "big score"—and he will employ legal means if possible and illegal means if necessary. Since legal means are likely to be thought of

---

[5]Miller, *op. cit.*

[6]Finestone, *op. cit.*
[7]Cohen, *op. cit.*

as ineffective, it is far from accidental that "smartness" is such an important feature of the delinquent's view of life: "Smartness involves the capacity to outsmart, outfox, outwit, dupe . . ."[8]

A third theme running through accounts of juvenile delinquency centers on aggression. This theme is most likely to be selected as pointing to the delinquent's alienation from the larger society. Verbal and physical assaults are a commonplace, and frequent reference is made to the delinquent's basic hostility, his hatred, and his urge to injure and destroy.

The delinquent's readiness for aggression is particularly emphasized in the analysis of juvenile gangs found in the slum areas of large cities. In such gangs we find the struggles for "turf," the beatings, and the violent feuds which form such distinctive elements in the portrayal of delinquency. As Cloward and Ohlin have pointed out, we can be led into error by viewing these gang delinquents as typical of all delinquents.[9] And Bloch and Niederhoffer have indicated that many current notions of the delinquent gang are quite worn out and require reappraisal.[10] Yet the gang delinquent's use of violence for the maintenance of "rep," the proof of "heart," and so on, seems to express in extreme form the idea that aggression is a demonstration of toughness and thus of masculinity. This idea runs through much delinquent activity. The concept of *machismo,* of the path to manhood through the ability to take it and hand it out, is foreign to the average delinquent only in name.

[8]Miller, *op. cit.*
[9]Cloward and Ohlin, *op. cit.*
[10]Bloch and Niederhoffer, *op. cit.*

In short, juvenile delinquency appears to be permeated by a cluster of values that can be characterized as the search for kicks, the disdain of work and a desire for the big score, and the acceptance of aggressive toughness as proof of masculinity. Whether these values are seen as pathological expressions of a distorted personality or as the traits of a delinquent sub-culture, they are taken as indicative of the delinquent's deviation from the dominant society. The delinquent, it is said, stands apart from the dominant society not only in terms of his illegal behavior but in terms of his basic values as well.

DELINQUENCY AND LEISURE

The deviant nature of the delinquent's values might pass unquestioned at first glance. Yet when we examine these values a bit more closely, we must be struck by their similarity to the components of the code of the "gentleman of leisure" depicted by Thorstein Veblen. The emphasis on daring and adventure; the rejection of the prosaic discipline of work; the taste for luxury and conspicuous consumption; and the respect paid to manhood demonstrated through force—all find a prototype in that sardonic picture of a leisured elite. What is *not* familiar is the mode of expression of these values, namely, delinquency. The quality of the values is obscured by their context. When "daring" turns out to be acts of daring by adolescents directed against adult figures of accepted authority, for example, we are apt to see only the flaunting of authority and not the courage that may be involved. We suspect that if juvenile delinquency were highly valued by the dominant society—as is the case, let us say, in the deviance of prisoners of war or resistance fighters rebelling against the rules of their oppressors—the interpretation of the nature of delinquency and the delinquent might be far different.[11]

In any event, the values of a leisure class seem to lie behind much delinquent activity, however brutalized or perverted their expression may be accounted by the dominant social order. Interestingly enough, Veblen himself saw a similarity between the pecuniary man, the embodiment of the leisure class, and the delinquent. "The ideal pecuniary man is like the ideal delinquent," said Veblen, "in his unscrupulous conversion of goods and services to his own ends, and in a callous disregard for the feelings and wishes of others and of the remoter effects of his actions."[12] For Veblen this comparison was probably no more than an aside, a part of polemical attack on the irresponsibility and pretensions of an industrial society's rulers. And it is far from clear what Veblen meant by delinquency. Nonetheless, his barbed comparison points to an important idea. We have too easily assumed that the delinquent is deviant in his values, op-

posed to the larger society. This is due, in part, to the fact that we have taken an overly simple view of the value system of the supposedly law-abiding. In our haste to create a standard from which deviance can be measured, we have reduced the value system of the whole society to that of the middle class. We have ignored both the fact that society is not composed exclusively of the middle class and that the middle class itself is far from homogeneous.[13]

In reality, of course, the value system of any society is exceedingly complex and we cannot solve our problems in the analysis of deviance by taking as a baseline a simplicity which does not exist in fact. Not only do different social classes differ in their values, but there are also significant variations within a class based on ethnic origins, upward and downward mobility, region, age, etc. Perhaps even more important, however, is the existence of subterranean values—values, that is to say, which are in conflict or in competition with other deeply held values but which are still

---

[11]Merton's comments on in-group virtues and out-group vices are particularly germane. The moral alchemy cited by Merton might be paraphrased to read:

> I am daring
> You are reckless
> He is delinquent

Cf. Robert K. Merton, *Social Theory and Social Structure* (Glencoe, Ill.: The Free Press, 1957), pp. 426–430.

[12]Thorstein Veblen, *The Theory of the Leisure Class* (Modern Library, 1934), pp. 237–238.

[13]Much of the current sociological analysis of the value systems of the different social classes would seem to be based on a model which is closely akin to an outmoded portrayal of race. Just as racial groups were once viewed as a clustering of physical traits with no overlapping of traits from one group to the next (e.g., Caucasians are straight-haired, light-skinned, etc., whereas Negroes are kinky-haired, dark-skinned, etc.), so now are the value systems of social classes apt to be seen as a distinct grouping of specific values which are unique to the social class in which they are found. The model of the value systems of the different social classes we are using in this paper is more closely allied to the treatment of race presently used in anthropology, i.e., a distribution of frequencies. Most values, we argue, appear in most social classes; the social classes differ, however, in the frequency with which the values appear.

recognized and accepted by many.[14] It is crucial to note that these contradictions in values are not necessarily the opposing viewpoints of two different groups. They may also exist within a single individual and give rise to profound feelings of ambivalence in many areas of life. In this sense, subterranean values are akin to private as opposed to public morality. They are values that the individual holds to and believes in but that are also recognized as being not quite *comme il faut*. The easier task of analysis is to call such values deviant and to charge the individual with hypocrisy when he acts on them. Social reality, however, is somewhat more intricate than that and we cannot take the black and white world of McGuffey's Readers as an accurate model of the values by which men live.

Now the value of adventure certainly does not provide the major organizing principle of the dominant social order in modern, industrial society. This is especially true in the workaday world where so much activity is founded on bureaucratization and all that it implies with regard to routinization, standardization, and so on. But this is not to say that the element of adventure is completely rejected by the society at large or never appears in the motivational structure of the law-abiding. Instead, it would appear that adventure, i.e., displays of daring and the search for excitement, are acceptable and desirable but only when confined to certain circumstances such as sports, recreation, and holidays. The last has been frequently noted in the observation that

conventions are often viewed as social events in which conventional canons of conduct are interpreted rather loosely. In fact, most societies seem to provide room for Saturnalias in one form or another, a sort of periodic anomie in which thrill-seeking is allowed to emerge.

In other words, the middle class citizen may seem like a far cry from the delinquent on the prowl for "thrills," but they both recognize and share the idea that "thrills" are worth pursuing and often with the same connotation of throwing over the traces, of opposing "fun" to the routine. As members of the middle class—and other classes—seek their "kicks" in gambling, night-clubbing, the big night on the town, etc., we can neither ignore their use of leisure nor claim that it is based on a markedly deviant value. Leisure-class values have come increasingly to color the activities of many individuals in the dominant society, although they may limit their expression more sharply than does the delinquent. The search for adventure, excitement, and thrills, then, is a subterranean value that now often exists side by side with the values of security, routinization, and the rest. It is not a deviant value, in any full sense, but it must be held in abeyance until the proper moment and circumstances for its expression arrive. It is obvious that something more than the delinquent's sense of appropriateness is involved, but it is also clear that in many cases the delinquent suffers from bad timing.

Similarly, to characterize the dominant society as being fully and unquestioningly attached to the virtue of hard work and careful saving is to distort reality. Notions of "pull" and the soft

[14]Robert S. Lynd, *Knowledge for What?* (Princeton: Princeton University Press, 1948).

job are far from uncommon and the individual who entertains such notions cannot be thrust beyond the pale merely because some sociologists have found it convenient to erect a simplified conception of *the* work values of society. As Chinoy and Bell, and a host of other writers, have pointed out, the conditions of work in modern society have broken down earlier conceptions of work as a calling and there are strong pressures to define the job as a place where one earns money as quickly and painlessly as possible.[15] If the delinquent carries this idea further than many of society's members might be willing to do, he has not necessarily moved into a new realm of values. In the same vein it can be argued that the delinquent's attachment to conspicuous consumption hardly makes him a stranger to the dominant society. Just as Riesman's "inside dopester," Whyte's "organization man," and Mills' "fixer" have a more authentic ring than an obsolete Weberian image in many instances, the picture of the delinquent as a spender seems more valid than a picture of him as an adolescent who has renounced material aspirations. The delinquent, we suggest, is much more in step with his times. Perhaps it is too extreme to say with Lowenthal[16] that "the idols of work have been replaced by the idols of leisure," but it appears unquestionable that we are witnessing a compromise between the Protestant Ethic and a Leisure Ethic. The delinquent conforms to society, rather than deviates from it, when he incorporates "big money" into his value system.[17]

Finally, we would do well to question prevalent views about society's attitudes toward violence and aggression. It could be argued, for one thing, that the dominant society exhibits a widespread taste for violence, since fantasies of violence in books, magazines, movies, and television are everywhere at hand. The delinquent simply translates into behavior those values that the majority are usually too timid to express. Furthermore, disclaimers of violence are suspect not simply because fantasies of violence are widely consumed, but also because of the actual use of aggression and violence in war, race riots, industrial conflicts, and the treatment of delinquents themselves by police. There are numerous examples of the acceptance of aggression and violence on the part of the dominant social order.

Perhaps it is more important, however, to recognize that the crucial idea of aggression as a proof of toughness and masculinity is widely accepted at many points in the social system. The ability to take it and hand it out, to defend one's rights and one's reputation with force, to prove one's manhood by hardness and physical courage—all are widespread in American culture. They cannot be dismissed by noting the equally valid observation that many people will declare that "nice children do not fight." The use of aggression to demonstrate

[15]Daniel Bell, *Work and Its Discontents* (Boston: Beacon Press, 1956); Ely Chinoy, *Automobile Workers and the American Dream* (Garden City, N.Y.: Doubleday and Company, 1955).

[16]Leo Lowenthal, "Historical Perspectives of Popular Culture," in Bernard Rosenberg and David M. White (eds.), *Mass Culture: The Popular Arts in America* (Glencoe, Ill.: The Free Press, 1957).

[17]Arthur K. Davis, "Veblen on the Decline of the Protestant Ethic," *Social Forces,* 22 (March, 1944), pp. 282–286.

masculinity is, of course, restricted by numerous prohibitions against instigating violence, "dirty" fighting, bullying, blustering, and so on. Yet even if the show of violence is carefully hedged in by both children and adults throughout our society, there is a persistent support for aggression which manifests itself in the derogatory connotations of labels such as "sissy" or "fag."[18]

In short, we are arguing that the delinquent may not stand as an alien in the body of society but may represent instead a disturbing reflection or a caricature. His vocabulary is different, to be sure, but kicks, big-time spending, and rep have immediate counterparts in the value system of the law-abiding. The delinquent has picked up and emphasized one part of the dominant value system, namely, the subterranean values that coexist with other, publicly proclaimed values possessing a more respectable air. These subterranean values, similar in many ways to the values Veblen ascribed to a leisure class, bind the delinquent to the society whose laws he violates. And we suspect that this sharing of values, this bond with the larger social order, facilitates the frequently observed "reformation" of delinquents with the coming of adult status.[19] To the objection that much juvenile behavior other than simply delinquent behavior would then be analyzed as an extension of the adult world rather than as a product of a distinct

adolescent subculture we can only answer that this is precisely our thesis.

DELINQUENCY AND SOCIAL CLASS

The persistence of the assumption that the juvenile delinquent must deviate from the law-abiding in his values as well as in his behavior can be traced in part, we suspect, to the large number of studies that have indicated that delinquents are disproportionately represented in the lower classes. In earlier years it was not too difficult to believe that the lower classes were set off from their social superiors in most attributes, including "immorality," and that this taint produced delinquent behavior. Writers of more recent vintage have avoided this reassuring error, but, still holding to the belief that delinquency is predominantly a lower-class phenomenon, have continued to look for features peculiar to certain segments of the lower class that would create values at variance with those of the rest of society and which would foster delinquency.

Some criminologists, however, have long expressed doubts about the validity of the statistics on delinquency and have suggested that if all the facts were at hand the delinquency rate of the lower classes and the classes above them would be found to be far less divergent than they now appear.[20] Preferential treatment by the police and the courts and better and more varied means for handling the offender may have led us to underestimate seriously the extent to which juvenile delinquency crops up in

[18]Albert Bandura and Richard Haig Walters, *Adolescent Aggression* (New York: Ronald Press, 1959), ch. 3.

[19]See, for example, William McCord, Joan McCord, and Irving K. Zola, *Origins of Crime* (New York: Columbia University Press, 1959), p. 21.

[20]Milton L. Barron, *The Juvenile in Delinquent Society* (New York: Alfred A. Knopf, 1954).

382   *David Matza and Gresham M. Sykes*

what are euphemistically termed "relatively privileged homes."

Given the present state of data in this field, it is probably impossible to come to any firm conclusion on this issue. One thing, however, seems fairly clear: juvenile delinquency does occur frequently in the middle and upper classes, and recent studies show more delinquency in these groups than have studies in the past. We might interpret this as showing that our research methods have improved or that "white-collar" delinquency is increasing—or possibly both. But in any event, the existence of juvenile delinquency in the middle and upper classes poses a serious problem for theories which depend on status deprivation, social disorganization, and similar explanatory variables. One solution has been to change horses in the middle of the stratification system, as it were, shifting from social environment to personality disturbances as the causative factor as one moves up the social ladder. Future research may prove that this shift is necessary. Since juvenile delinquency does not appear to be a unitary phenomenon, we might expect that no one theoretical approach will be adequate. To speak of juvenile delinquency in general, as we have done in this paper, should not obscure the fact that there are different types of delinquency and the differences among them cannot be ignored. Yet it seems worthwhile to pursue the idea that some forms of juvenile delinquency—and possibly the most frequent—have a common sociological basis, regardless of the class level at which they appear.

One such basis is offered, we believe, by our argument that the values lying behind much delinquent behavior are the values of a leisure class. All adolescents at all class levels are to some extent members of a leisure class, for they move in a limbo between earlier parental domination and future integration with the social structure through the bonds of work and marriage.[21] Theirs is an anticipatory leisure, it is true, a period of freedom from the demands for self-support which allows room for the schooling enabling them to enter the world of work. They thus enjoy a temporary leisure by sufferance rather than by virtue of a permanent aristocratic right. Yet the leisure status of adolescents, modified though it may be by the discipline of school and the lack of wealth, places them in relationship to the social structure in a manner similar to that of an elite which consumes without producing. In this situation, disdain of work, an emphasis on personal qualities rather than technical skills, and a stress on the manner and extent of consumption all can flourish. Insofar, then, as these values do lie behind delinquency, we could expect delinquent behavior to be prevalent among all adolescents rather than confined to the lower class.

CONCLUSION

This theory concerning the role of leisure in juvenile delinquency leaves unsolved, of course, a number of problems. First, there is the question why some adolescents convert subterranean

[21] Reuel Denney, *The Astonished Muse* (Chicago: University of Chicago Press, 1957). See also Barbara Wooton, *Social Science and Social Pathology* (New York: Macmillan, 1959); Arthur L. Porterfield, *Youth in Trouble* (Austin, Tex.: Leo Potishman Foundation, 1946).

values into seriously deviant behavior while others do not. Even if it is granted that many adolescents are far more deviant in their behavior than official records would indicate, it is clear that there are degrees of delinquency and types of delinquency. This variation cannot be explained simply on the basis of exposure to leisure. It is possible that leisure values are typically converted into delinquent behavior when such values are coupled with frustrations and resentments. (This is more than a matter of being deprived in socioeconomic terms.) If this is so, if the delinquent is a sort of soured sportsman, neither leisure nor deprivation will be sufficient by itself as an explanatory variable. This would appear to be in accordance with the present empirical observations in the field. Second, we need to know a good deal more about the distribution of leisure among adolescents and its impact on their value systems. We have assumed that adolescents are in general leisured, i.e., free from the demands for self-support, but school drop-outs, the conversion of school into a tightly disciplined and time-consuming preparation for a career, the facilities for leisure as opposed to mere idleness will all probably have their effect. We suspect that two variables are of vital importance in this area: (a) the extent of identification with adult symbols of work, such as the father; and (b) the extent to which the school is seen as providing roles to enhance the ego, both now and in the future, rather than as an oppressive and dreary marking of time.

We conclude that the explanation of juvenile delinquency may be clarified by exploring the delinquent's similarity to the society that produced him rather than his dissimilarity. If his values are the subterranean values of a society that is placing increasing emphasis on leisure, we may throw new light on Taft's comment that the basic values in our culture are accepted by both the delinquent and the larger society of which he is a part.[22]

[22]Donald R. Taft, *Criminology* (New York: Macmillan, 1950).